THE ASHGATE RESEARCH COMPANION TO INTERNATIONAL TRADE POLICY

This book's emphasis on the importance of trade is extremely timely in view of pressures for trade protectionism following the 2007–9 global financial crisis. Unlike most edited works on trade, the book provides an integrated and comprehensive approach to the most significant aspects of international trade relations. The highly readable chapters by both acknowledged experts and upcoming academics and practitioners will be very useful for students, faculty, those involved with governments, international organizations and NGOs, and others interested in trade and trade-related issues.

Theodore Cohn,
Simon Fraser University, Canada

... an indispensable guide to the current state of world trade policy and the arguments surrounding it. The various contributions are carefully selected not merely to cover the various aspects and areas of trade policy but to lucidly present a full picture of a fascinating subject. It raises the question as to how we now find ourselves facing the failure of the Doha Development Round with the consequential damage to the system that the World Trade Organisation embodies. I found it truly excellent.

Peter D Sutherland KCMG,
former Director-General of GATT & the WTO

This book is as timely as it is thoughtful. Turmoil in today's global economic environment is adding to the pressure from well-established special interests to turn away from trade liberalization in favor of new and old forms of protectionism. The authors point to the fallacy of such a backward looking approach and make a strong case in favor of open markets. At the same time they correctly emphasize that trade liberalization alone is insufficient to ensure widespread and inclusive growth. By highlighting explicitly the essential role of complementary policies, from active labor market to social protection measures, the authors illustrate how the potential created by more open markets can be turned into reality for workers and for firms, both in developing and developed economies. This is what really matters in all economic activity, human progress; and this is what we very much need today.

Angel Gurría,
Secretary-General of the Organisation for Economic
Cooperation and Development (OECD)

ASHGATE
RESEARCH
COMPANION

The *Ashgate Research Companions* are designed to offer scholars and graduate students a comprehensive and authoritative state-of-the-art review of current research in a particular area. The companions' editors bring together a team of respected and experienced experts to write chapters on the key issues in their speciality, providing a comprehensive reference to the field.

The Ashgate Research Companion to International Trade Policy

Edited by

KENNETH HEYDON
London School of Economics, UK

STEPHEN WOOLCOCK
London School of Economics, UK

ASHGATE

Published by
Ashgate Publishing Limited
Wey Court East
Union Road
Farnham
Surrey GU9 7PT
England

Ashgate Publishing Company
Suite 420
101 Cherry Street
Burlington,
VT 05401-4405
USA

www.ashgate.com

British Library Cataloguing in Publication Data
The Ashgate research companion to international trade
  policy.
  1. International trade. 2. Commercial treaties.
  3. International economic relations.
  I. Research companion to international trade policy
  II. Heydon, Kenneth. III. Woolcock, Stephen.
  382.3-dc23

Library of Congress Cataloging-in-Publication Data
The Ashgate research companion to international trade policy / edited by
Kenneth Heydon and Stephen Woolcock.
    p. cm.
  Includes bibliographical references and index.
  ISBN 978-1-4094-0835-2 (hbk) -- ISBN 978-1-4094-0836-9 (ebook)
  1. International trade. 2. Commercial treaties. 3.
International economic relations. I. Heydon, Kenneth. II. Woolcock,
Stephen.
  HF1379.A84 2011
  382'.3--dc23
                                                                    2011046426

ISBN 9781409408352 (hbk)
ISBN 9781409408369 (ebk)

Printed and bound in Great Britain by
MPG Books Group, UK

Contents

List of Figures

List of Tables

Acronyms

AB	Appellate Body (WTO)
AC	Andean Community
ACP	African Caribbean and Pacific States
ACTA	Anti-Counterfeit Trade Agreement
AD	Anti-dumping
ADB	Asian Development Bank
AERC	African Economic Research Consortium
AFL-CIO	American Federation of Labour – Congress of Industrial Organizations
AGOA	African Growth and Opportunity Act
ALBA	Bolivarian Alliance for the Peoples of Our America
AMS	Aggregate Measure of Support (agriculture)
APEC	Asia-Pacific Economic Cooperation
ASEAN	Association of South East Asian Nations
ASG	Agreement on Safeguards
ASP	American Selling Price
BIT	Bilateral Investment Treaty
BoP	Balance of Payments
BSE	Bovine Spongiform Encephalopathy
CAA	Clean Air Act
CACM	Central American Common Market
CAFTA	Central American Free Trade Agreement or China Asean Free Trade Agreement
CAP	Common Agricultural Policy
CARIFORUM	Caribbean Forum
CBI	Caribbean Basin Initiative
CCP	Common Commercial Policy (EU)
CEFACT	Centre for Trade Facilitation and Electronic Business (UN)
CEPR	Centre for Economic Policy Research
CET	Common External Tariff
CGE	Computable General Equilibrium (model)
CIF	Cost, Insurance and Freight
CITES	Convention on Trade in Endangered Species
COMESA	Common Market for Eastern and Southern Africa
COREPER	Committee of Permanent Representaives (EU)

CPs	Contracting Parties
CPA	Cotonou Partnership Agreement
CSO	Civil Society Organization
CTD	Committee on Trade and Development
CTE	Committee on Trade and Environment
CUTS	Consumer Unity and Trust Society
CVD	Countervailing Duty
DCs	Developing Countries
DDA	Doha Development Agenda
DFAT	Department of Foreign Affairs and Trade (Australia)
DFQF	Duty-Free Quota-Free
DNA	Deoxyribonucleic Acid
DR	Diversion Removal
DR-CAFTA	Dominican Republic-Central American Free Trade Agreement
DRAM	Dynamic Random Access Memory
DSB	Dispute Settlement Body
DSS	Dispute Settlement System
DSU	Dispute Settlement Understanding
EABC	East African Business Council
EAC	East African Community
EALA	East African Legislative Assembly
EBA	Everything but Arms
EC	European Community
ECDPM	European Centre for Development Policy Management
ECIPE	European Centre for International Political Economy
ECLAC	Economic Commission for Latin America (UN)
EEC	European Economic Community
EFTA	European Free Trade Association
EHP	Early Harvest Programme (China)
EIF	Enhanced Integration Framework
EPA	Economic Partnership Agreements
EPRC	Economic Policy Research Centre (Uganda)
ERP	Effective Rate of Protection
ESRF	Economic and Social Research Foundation (Tanzania)
EU	European Union
FANs	Friends of Antidumping Negotiations
FAO	Food and Agricultural Organisation
FDI	Foreign Direct Investment
FRI	Fujitsu Research Institute
FTA	Free Trade Agreement
FTAA	Free Trade Area of the Americas
GATS	General Agreement on Trade in Services
GATT	General Agreement on Tariffs and Trade
GCC	Gulf Cooperation Council
GDP	Gross Domestic Product

GI	Geographic Indication
GM	Genetically Modified
GMO	Genetically Modified Organism
GPA	Government Procurement Agreement
GSM	Global Systems Mobile Communications
GSP	Generalized System of Preferences
GTAP	Global Trade Analysis Project
HS	Harmonised System (of tariffs)
IBRD	International Bank for Reconstruction and Development (World Bank)
ICC	International Chamber of Commerce
ICFTU	International Confederation of Free Trade Unions
ICN	International Competition Network
ICT	Information Communication Technology
IEA	Institute of Economic Affairs (Kenya)
IIP	Index of Industrial Production
IITC	Inter-Institutional Trade Council (Uganda)
ILO	International Labour Organization
IMF	International Monetary Fund
IMO	International Maritime Organization
INTA	International Trade Committee (European Parliament)
IP	Intellectual Property
IPAR	Institute of Public Analysis and Research (Rwanda)
IPCC	Intergovernmental Panel on Climate Change
IPPC	Integrated Pollution Prevention and Control
IPR	Intellectual Property Rights
ISI	Import Substitution Industrialization
ISO	International Organization for Standardization
IT	Information Technology
ITA	Information Technology Products Agreement
ITC	International Trade Centre
ITO	International Trade Organization
ITPM	Inclusive Trade Policy Making Index
KIPPRA	Kenya Institute for Public Policy Research and Analysis
LAC	Latin America and the Caribbean
LAFTA	Latin American Free Trade Association
LAIA	Latin American Integration Association
LAPBI	Latin American Pacific Basin Initiative
LDC	Least Developed Country
MAST	Multi-Agency Support Team
MA-TTRI	Market Access-Trade Tariff Restrictiveness Index
MCAT	Multilateral Assistance Treaty
MEA	Multilateral Environment Agreement
MEP	Member of the European Parliament
MERCOSUR	Common Market of the South

MFA	Multi-Fibre Arrangement or Ministry of Foreign Affairs (China)
MFN	Most Favoured Nation
MIIT	Ministry of Industry and Information Technology (China)
MLAT	Mutual Legal Assistance Treaty
MMPA	Marine Mammal Protection Act
MNE	Multinational Enterprise
MOA	Ministry of Agriculture (China)
MOFCOM	Ministry of Commerce (China)
MOFTEC	Ministry of Foreign Trade and Cooperation (China)
MOT	Ministry of Trade (Kenya)
MPU	Micro Processing Units
MRA	Mutual Recognition Agreement
MTI	Ministry of Trade and Industry (Rwanda)
MTIM	Ministry of Trade, Industry and Marketing (Tanzania)
MTTI	Ministry of Trade, Tourism and Industry (Uganda)
NAALC	North American Agreement on Labour Cooperation
NAFTA	North American Free Trade Agreement
NAMA	Non-Agricultural Market Access
NBER	National Bureau of Economic Research (US)
NDRC	National Development and Reform Commission (China)
NFIDC	Net Food-Importing Developing Countries
NGO	Non-Governmental Organization
NICs	Newly Industrializing Countries
NPC	Nominal Protection Coefficient (in agricultural trade) or National People's Congress (China)
NRA	Nominal Rate of Assistance (in agricultural trade)
NT	National Treatment
NTB	Non-tariff Barrier
NTM	Non-tariff Measure
OECD	Organisation for Economic Cooperation and Development
OIE	Organization for International Epizootics
OLP	Ordinary Legislative Procedure (EU)
OS	Operating Systems
PAFTAD	Pacific Trade and Development Forum
PCT	Patent Cooperation Treaty
PECC	Pacific Economic Cooperation Council
PPA	Protocol of Provisional Application
PPM	Process and Production Methods
PRC	People's Republic of China
PSE	Producer Support Estimate
PTA	Preferential Trade Agreement
QMV	Qualified Majority Voting
R&D	Research and Development
REACH	Regulatory Evaluation Authorisation and Restriction of Chemicals
RMB	Renminbi

RoO	Rules of Origin
RTAA	Reciprocal Trade Agreements Act
SADC	Southern African Development Community
SCM	Agreement on Subsidies and Countervailing Measures
SDOC	Suppliers' Declaration of Conformity
SDR	Special Drawing Rights (IMF)
SDT	Special and Differential Treatment
SME	Small and Medium Sized Enterprises
SOE	State-Owned Enterprise
SPS	Sanitary and Phytosanitary
SSG	Special Safeguard
SSM	Special Safeguard Mechanism
STDF	Standards and Trade Development Facility
SVE	Small and Vulnerable Economy
TAA	Trade Adjustment Assistance (US)
TBT	Technical Barriers to Trade
TCP/IP	Transmission Control Profile/Internet Protocol
TDCA	Trade Development and Cooperation Agreement (EU and South Africa)
TEC	Treaty Establishing the European Community
TED	Turtle Excluder Device
TFEU	Treaty on the Functioning of the European Union (Lisbon Treaty)
TNC	Trade Negotiations Committee
TPA	Trade Promotion Authority (US)
TPC	Trade Policy Committee (EU)
TPP	Trans-Pacific Partnership
TPRM	Trade Policy Review Mechanism
TQ	Tariff Quota
TRAINS	Trade Analysis and Information System (UNCTAD)
TRAPCA	Trade Policy Training Centre in Africa
TRIMs	Trade-Related Investment Measures
TRIPS	Trade-Related Intellectual Property Rights
TRTA	Trade-Related Technical Assistance
TSMC	Taiwan Semi Conductor Manufacturing Company
UDS	Understanding on Dispute Settlement
UN	United Nations
UNASUR	Union of South American Nations
UNCED	United Nations Conference on Environment and Development
UNCTAD	United Nations Conference on Trade and Development
UNECA	United Nations Economic Commission for Africa
UNECE	United Nations Economic Commission for Europe
UNEP	United Nations Environment Programme
UNESCAP	United Nations Economic and Social Commission for Asia and the Pacific
UNESCO	United Nations Educational, Scientific and Cultural Organisation

UNFCCC	United Nations Framework Convention on Climate Change
UNIDO	United Nations Industrial Development Organization
UPOV	International Convention for the Protection of New Varieties of Plants
UR	Uruguay Round
URAA	Uruguay Round Agreement on Agriculture
USDOC	United States Department of Commerce
USDOJ	United States Department of Justice
USITC	United States International Trade Commission
USTR	United States Trade Representative
VAT	Value Added Tax
VER	Voluntary Export Restraint
VRA	Voluntary Restraint Agreement
WCO	World Customs Organisation
WHO	World Health Organization
WIPO	World Intellectual Property Organization
WTO	World Trade Organization
WWF	World Wide Fund for Nature

Notes on Contributors

Steve Charnovitz teaches international law at George Washington University in Washington, DC. Before joining the faculty, he worked in the US government on trade and competitiveness policy. In the early 1980s, he was a US trade negotiator for the Caribbean Basin Initiative specializing on the labour conditionality provisions and, in the early 1990s, he was policy director of the US Competitiveness Policy Council. He was also the first director of the Global Environment & Trade Study at Yale University.

Caiphas Chekwoti is the Trade Policy Expert at the Trade Policy Training Centre in Africa (trapca) in Arusha, Tanzania. Prior to this, he was a lecturer at the Department of Economic Theory and Analysis, Makerere University. He holds a PhD in economics from Dar es Salaam University. He has been involved in various research activities and consultancies on trade policy and development issues.

Kamala Dawar is a Policy Analyst and Lecturer in international trade law and development policy. Following studies at the LSE and the University of Amsterdam, she has published on government procurement, competition, consumer policy, preferential trading arrangements and the EC's Generalized System of Preferences. She conducts training on trade and development issues and is pursuing doctoral research in competition regimes at the Graduate Institute, University of Geneva.

Nora Dihel is Senior Trade Economist in the Africa Region of the World Bank. The main focus of her current work is on trade in services and regional integration. Prior to joining the World Bank in 2008, she has worked in the Chief Economist Unit of the Directorate General for Trade of the European Commission and the OECD Trade Directorate. She has published work on the economic impact of services trade policies, regional integration and South–South linkages. She has a doctorate degree in economics from the Helmut Schmidt University, Germany.

Robert Falkner (PhD) is Senior Lecturer in International Relations at the London School of Economics and Political Science (LSE). He is an associate of the LSE Grantham Research Institute on Climate Change and the Environment and of the Energy, Environment and Development Programme at Chatham House. He is the author of *Business Power and Conflict in International Environmental Politics* (Palgrave, 2008).

Ana Margarida Fernandes is currently a Senior Economist in the Trade and International Integration Unit of the Development Research Group at the World Bank. Her work has focused on the consequences of openness for firm-level productivity, technological innovation, and quality upgrading in manufacturing and services sectors. Recently she has been examining the impact of trade assistance projects.

Michael J. Ferrantino is Lead International Economist at the US International Trade Commission, where he has served since 1994, providing trade-related economic analysis to the executive branch and Congress. He has taught at Southern Methodist, Youngstown State, Georgetown, American, and George Washington Universities, and has published widely on international trade topics, including non-tariff measures and trade facilitation, US–China trade, and the relationship of trade to the environment, innovation and technology.

Andrew Grainger (PhD) is an academic and trade facilitation practitioner. He is currently based at Nottingham University Business School and conducts consultancy work for governments, companies and international organizations around the world. In previous roles he worked as Deputy Director at SITPRO, the former UK trade facilitation agency, and Secretary for EUROPRO, the umbrella body for European trade facilitation organizations.

Göte Hansson was Professor of International Economics at Lund University and one of the founders of, and the Academic Director at, the Trade Policy Training Centre in Africa (trapca). For many years he worked in the Dean's office at the Faculty of Social Sciences, Lund University. His PhD thesis was on social clauses and international trade and he continued with research on trade and development with a focus on Africa and the Horn of Africa.

Sebastian Herreros (BA, MSc) is Regional Expert, Trade and Integration Division, UN Economic Commission for Latin America and the Caribbean. Previously he worked on trade policy issues at the Chilean Ministry of Foreign Affairs (1996–2009), including a term as Counsellor at the Chilean Mission to the WTO (2002–2007). He has lectured and written several articles and book chapters on Chilean trade policy, Latin American integration and the multilateral trading system.

Kenneth Heydon is a Visiting Fellow at the LSE. From 1999 to 2006 he was Deputy Director of the OECD Trade Directorate. In the Australian civil service (1962–1999), he was Deputy Director-General of the Office of National Assessments (1990–1999) after serving as economic policy adviser in the Departments of Foreign Affairs and Trade and Prime Minister and Cabinet and as Principal Private Secretary to the Prime Minister (1976–1979).

Peter Holmes teaches the economics of trade and integration at the University of Sussex and is a visitor at the College of Europe, Warsaw. He has written extensively on regulatory aspects of trade policy including standards, intellectual property rights and in particular trade and competition. He has undertaken studies and participated in workshops for UNCTAD, the World Bank and DFID.

Gary Clyde Hufbauer is the Reginald Jones Senior Fellow at the Peterson Institute for International Economics. Previously he was Marcus Wallenberg Professor of International Financial Diplomacy at Georgetown University. He has written extensively on globalization, international trade, international taxation and economic sanctions.

John H. Jackson is Professor of Law and Director of the Institute of International Economic Law at Georgetown University. He has served on the board of editors for the *American Journal of International Law*, is the Editor-in-Chief and a founding editor of the *Journal of International Economic Law* (JIEL) and was a member of the Consultative Board to WTO D-G Supachai Panitchpadki. Among his more recent books is *The Jurisprudence of the GATT and the WTO: Insights on Treaty Law and Economic Relations* (Cambridge University Press, 2000).

Alejandro Jara is Deputy Director General of the WTO. Following law studies (Universidad de Chile, University of California at Berkeley), he served in the Chilean Foreign Service (1976–2005) as GATT Delegation Director for Trade Negotiations, Director General for International Economic Relations, Senior Official to APEC and chief negotiatior of FTAs with Canada, Mexico and Central America. In 2000 he was appointed Ambassador of Chile to the WTO and chaired the Committee on Trade and Environment (2001) and the Services negotiations of the Doha Round (2002–2005).

Nico Jaspers is a Post-doctoral Researcher at the Free University of Berlin. He studied economics at Columbia University, New York, international political economy at the Institut d'Etudes Politiques (Sciences Po) and received a doctorate in international relations from the LSE in 2011. He has published widely on nanotechnology policy and in 2009 co-authored an EU commissioned report on transatlantic cooperation in nanotechnology regulation.

Yang Jiang is Associate Professor in the Political Economy of China and East Asia at the Asia Research Center, Copenhagen Business School. She has published in, amongst other journals, the *Review of International Political Economy*, *The Pacific Review*, the *International Journal of Emerging Markets* and the *Journal of Contemporary China*.

Peter Kiuluku (MPhil) is currently the Executive Director of the Trade Policy Training Centre in Africa (trapca) in Arusha, Tanzania. He is an International Business Management expert and previously worked as a Management Consultant with Price Waterhouse, Nairobi. He has served as Director of the Leadership and

Management Sustainability Programme and Manager Marketing and Business at the Eastern and Southern African Management Institute (ESAMI).

Przemyslaw Kowalski is an Economist at the Organisation for Economic Co-operation and Development. He has published on international trade theory and policy, applied trade analysis, international finance, development and emerging economies. He has taught at the Institut d'Etudes Politiques (Sciences Po), University of Sussex and University of Warsaw. He obtained his MSc in Economics from the University of Warsaw and his DPhil in Economics from the University of Sussex.

Peter Lunenborg is a Researcher at the South Centre and provides trade-related capacity building to developing countries mainly in the context of WTO and FTA negotiations. He has been a manager in maritime shipping. His areas of interest include non-tariff measures, CGE modelling, aid for trade, trade facilitation, regional integration and monitoring and evaluation.

Mark S. Manger (PhD) is a Lecturer in International Political Economy at the London School of Economics. He previously taught at McGill and was a Research Fellow in the Harvard US-Japan programme. His research focuses on North–South trade relations, with a particular interest in the Asia-Pacific region.

Aaditya Mattoo (PhD, MPhil) is Research Manager, Trade and Integration, at the World Bank. He specializes in trade policy analysis and the operation of the WTO, and provides policy advice to governments. Prior to joining the Bank in 1999, he was Economic Counsellor at the World Trade Organization. Between 1988 and 1991, he taught economics at the University of Sussex and Churchill College, Cambridge University. He has published widely in academic and other journals on trade, trade in services, development and the WTO.

Patrick Messerlin is Professor of Economics and Director, Groupe d'Economie Mondiale at Sciences Po. He specializes in international trade policy and regulatory reforms. He was special advisor to Mike Moore, WTO Director General (2001–2002) and co-chair, with Ernesto Zedillo, of the UN Millennium Development Goals Task Force (2003–2005). He is co-chair of the joint World Bank and UK Department for International Development Task Force on *Global Finance and Trade Architecture* and Chair of the Global Trade Council of the World Economic Forum.

Matthias Meyer is a lawyer and economist now heading a consultancy on aid for trade and trade policy. He was a negotiator in the Doha Round of multilateral trade negotiations after spending 30 years in international development. He has served on the Board and in the Staff of the World Bank, directed economic cooperation in the Swiss Government and led a Division at the Inter-American Development Bank.

Sébastien Miroudot is a Trade Policy Analyst at the OECD Trade and Agriculture Directorate where he is in charge of the work on global value chains and investment. He holds a PhD in International Economics from Sciences Po, Paris. Before joining the OECD, he worked for several years at the Groupe d'Economie Mondiale as research assistant and lecturer.

Risaburo Nezu is a Senior Executive Fellow at the Fujitsu Research Institute. He is responsible for a range of activities in the fields of ICT, science & technology, industry and various corporate management issues. He was formerly a government official at the Ministry of Economy, Trade and Industry (METI) and is currently the chairman of the OECD Steel Committee.

Arvind Panagariya is a Professor of Economics and Jagdish Bhagwati Professor of Indian Political Economy at Columbia University. In the past, he has been the Chief Economist of the Asian Development Bank. The *Economist* magazine listed his recent book, *India: The Emerging Giant*, as a top pick of 2008.

Meir Perez Pugatch (MSc, PhD) is Senior Lecturer at the University of Haifa in Israel, where he is also the Chair of the Division of Health Systems Administration at the School of Public Health. He specializes on innovation, intellectual property policy, management and exploitation of knowledge assets, technology transfer, entrepreneurship, health technology assessment and the political economy of public health systems. He is also Director of Research of the Stockholm Network.

Joakim Reiter is Ambassador of Sweden to the WTO. Until recently, he represented Sweden in the Trade Policy Committee of the European Union, which he chaired during the Swedish Presidency in 2009. He has also worked as trade negotiator for the European Commission and at the Swedish Ministry for Foreign Affairs, including as advisor to the Minister for Industry.

Christopher Roberts is a former career British civil servant, and the UK Director-General for Trade Policy from 1987 to 1997. In that capacity he was the principal UK trade negotiator during the Uruguay Round. From 1998 to 2011 he was Senior Trade Adviser to the international law firm Covington and Burling LLP. From 2001 to 2008 he chaired the policy committee of the European Services Forum, representing to the Commission and the governments of EU member states the views of European service industries on trade issues.

David Robertson (PhD) is a former Professor of International Economics at Melbourne University and a Commissioner at the Productivity Commission. He has interspersed university teaching and research in Australia, Britain and the United States, with periods in national government and international agencies. He has published widely on international economics, development and environmental policy. His latest book is *International Economics and Confusing Politics* (Edward Elgar, 2006).

Razeen Sally (PhD) is Visiting Associate Professor at the Lee Kuan Yew School of Public Policy, National University of Singapore and Director of ECIPE, which he co-founded in 2006. He is on the faculty of the LSE and has held adjunct teaching, research and advisory positions at universities and think tanks in the United States, Europe, Africa and Asia. His research focuses on global trade policy, Asia in the world economy, FTAs, and the history of economic ideas. He has consulted for governments, international organizations and businesses in Europe and Asia.

Christopher Stevens (PhD) currently a Senior Research Fellow at the Overseas Development Institute (ODI), London has undertaken research and policy advice for over 30 years on EU trade policy, on the international dimension of food security and on the other policies affecting developing countries and has advised a wide range of governments and agencies.

Kati Suominen is Resident Fellow in Economics at the German Marshall Fund in Washington, DC and American Assembly's Next Generation Fellow. She served as Trade Economist at the Inter-American Development Bank in 2003–2010. She has published eight books and numerous articles on global trade and economics, most recently *Peerless and Periled: The Paradox of America's World Economic Order* (Stanford University Press, 2011).

Stefan Tangermann was until end-2008 Director for Trade and Agriculture at the Organisation for Economic Cooperation and Development (OECD), Paris. He is now professor emeritus at the Department of Agricultural Economics and Rural Development at the University of Göttingen, Germany, and a member of the Academy of Science at Göttingen.

Stephen Woolcock (PhD) is a Lecturer in the International Relations Department of the LSE. He is head of the LSE's international Trade Policy Unit. Before joining the LSE he was a Senior Research Fellow at the Royal Institute of International Affairs, London, 1979–1983 and 1989–1993; Paul-Henri Spaak Fellow at Harvard University 1984–1985; and Deputy Director for International Affairs with the Confederation of British Industry 1986–1989.

Preface and Acknowledgements

Trade policy issues have been kept at centre stage by the debate about globalization and its impact on jobs, the environment and public health, by the proliferation of bilateral deals in trade, and by the difficulty of advancing a multilateral agenda involving a wider range of topics and an ever increasing number of players. The objective of this volume is to provide a state-of-the-art review of current thinking on these issues, addressing the economic, political and strategic dimensions of international trade policy. The volume contains a systematic examination of specific trade policy instruments, sectoral concerns, trade linkages to other policy areas and systemic considerations – what role for the WTO?

The volume seeks to add value to, and be differentiated from, existing trade literature in that it is neither a collection of conference papers nor the editing authors' characterization of the views of others but rather an integrated set of original and comprehensive perspectives from a diverse group of experts, linked by a common organizational thread.

The contributing authors are a mix of internationally recognized authorities on trade, together with younger specialists making their mark in trade policy analysis; academics as well as trade policy practitioners; and representatives of both big and small trading nations.

The primary intended readership is the teaching and student clients of academic libraries. But the volume is written in a way that also makes it accessible to the informed public and useful to government officials in trade and other ministries, to international organizations concerned with trade-related issues, and to the NGO community.

Though the book is meant to be read as a whole, individual chapters can also be taken on their own. Each chapter is intended therefore to be self-contained, at the cost of some repetition.

In producing this book, we have incurred many debts and take this opportunity to express our thanks.

Our first debt of gratitude is to our contributing authors – for their insights, and their patience. A special tribute goes to Göte Hansson. With his death we have lost a highly regarded colleague and friend. We take this opportunity to acknowledge, in particular, his invaluable contribution to the work of the Trade Policy Training Centre in Africa.

We also owe a substantial intellectual debt to colleagues, former colleagues and associates from government departments, the OECD, the WTO, the World Bank and the LSE, with whom we have had the benefit of discussion over the years and whose work we have been able to draw on.

Finally, we would like to thank all those involved with bringing this book into its published state. We are particularly appreciative of the work of two LSE graduate students, Emily Partington and Jeanette Rodrigues, who helped with the editing of this volume. We thank our anonymous referees for their helpful comments. And last but not least, we are indebted to Kirstin Howgate and her colleagues at Ashgate without whom this book would not have been possible.

Introduction

Kenneth Heydon

The Scope of the Book

The organizing theme of this volume is that open markets for trade and investment yield large potential gains in human welfare as long as trade policy is conducted as an integral part of broader domestic economic management and regulatory reform, and as long as the particular challenges facing developing countries are effectively addressed. This argument is presented on the basis of analysis of first principles and of empirical experience among key trading nations.

This book thus has a strong and deliberate normative perspective on the benefits of free trade. This does not mean that those who may have questioned this perspective are ignored. Refinements to the free trade case are acknowledged where they contribute to a better understanding of the issue – such as the writings of Joseph Stiglitz on the particular challenges facing developing countries or the work of Paul Krugman on strategic trade policy. It is also acknowledged that the *strength* of the linkage between trade and growth is open to question. But arguments invoking the need for 'policy space' to allow developing countries to forsake open markets in the pursuit of selective industrial policies and infant industry support are strongly rebutted. Similarly, the advocacy of trade sanctions to seek to force compliance with non-trade objectives, such as those related to the environment or labour standards, is also opposed.

In addressing the underlying issues in trade policy, the volume seeks to avoid an undue focus on transient factors, such as the twists and turns in negotiating the Doha Development Agenda (DDA) or the impact of purely cyclical forces that are likely to be reversed. This said, the DDA cannot be ignored. Similarly, the financial crisis and global recession of 2008–2009 will be seen, in different chapters of this book, to offer important lessons about the impact on trade policy of external shocks, the linkages between trade policy and macro-economic imbalances, the importance of the regulatory environment, the role of global supply chains in lessening protectionist forces and the differing resilience to downturns of the services and manufacturing sectors.

The approach taken in this book is essentially state-centric. There has of course been some blurring of the role of the state – some would say, even a diminution in that role – as a result of a number of factors: the onset of the global supply chain, as manufacturing and services activity of transnational corporations has come to transcend national borders; the inevitable dilution of national sovereignty that comes with membership of international rule-making bodies; the challenge to state authority arising from the vocal engagement of non-governmental organizations; and the pursuit of regulatory reform, often with a lighter hand from the state, if falling short of outright laissez-faire. But the fact remains that, at the heart of the trading system, the WTO is a member-driven body. It is national governments who define, negotiate and implement trade policy and trade agreements, whether multilaterally or increasingly on a bilateral basis, and who are accountable for decisions taken. In doing so, governments are likely to be influenced by national strategic objectives as well as by purely 'trade' considerations. And it is states that set the policy framework that attracts, or discourages, the foreign direct investment that drives the global supply chain.

The focus therefore will be on the role of the state as the principal agent of trade policy, although many chapters of this book will address, and attest to the importance of, the role of non-state actors.

Some of the Puzzles of Trade

We start with a paradox. Trade and trade policies are being conducted in a world characterized by both heightened interdependence and by the growing fragmentation of global production – by linkages that are both stronger and yet more dispersed. And within this framework, the conduct of trade policy itself is seen to be full of contradictions and tensions that this book will address and seek to explain.

- *Accountability and efficiency.* As the multilateral agency responsible for trade policy, the WTO is itself the scene of internal tensions as calls for increased accountability, through greater transparency and more inclusive participation in decision-making, are said to complicate the search for increased efficiency in reaching and implementing decisions (see for example Chapter 21).
- *Entry and exit.* Though trade liberalization brings overall gains at the national level, each trading nation will have both winners and losers from market opening, and successful policies of trade-related structural adjustment will of necessity involve both the entry and the exit of firms and regulatory conditions that facilitate both the creation and, more controversially, the destruction of business entities (Chapter 2).
- *Ends and means.* Where a particular trade instrument serves multiple ends, policy change may have mixed, and potentially conflicting, results. Tariffs for example serve both to protect and to raise revenue. A tariff reduction

therefore can bring both efficiency gains through reduced protection but also budget strains via reduced customs revenue. This will be a particularly acute tension for developing countries dependent on tariffs for income (Chapter 4).

- *Present and future.* Trade policy instruments may also have a time dimension with sometimes contradictory effects. The protection of intellectual property rights for example involves the 'paradox of patents' – limiting access to knowledge now in order to foster greater knowledge in the future (Chapter 16).

- *Complements and substitutes.* The relationship between flows of goods and services and other factor flows can be as complements or as substitutes. For example, foreign direct investment (FDI) can be a substitute for trade in the presence of high trade barriers, when it is easier to invest in a market than to export to it, or a complement when the investment is efficiency- or resource-seeking and hence a facilitator of exports from the market in which the investment is made (Chapters 6, 10, 11 and 22).

- *Cooperation and sovereignty.* Policies of trade liberalization, and associated adjustment, involve finding a balance between, on the one hand, the pursuit of gains from international cooperation and, on the other, the preservation of national sovereignty that such cooperation may well diminish. This is particularly the case in agriculture or when trade policy impinges on behind-the-border measures that go to the heart of domestic regulation (Chapters 8 and 9).

- *Unilateral and multilateral.* This cooperation–sovereignty tension may go some way to explaining the fact that many countries have seemingly been prepared to engage in unilateral liberalization, reducing their own domestic barriers to trade, while remaining reluctant to commit fully to multilateral market opening on a reciprocal basis – as one author puts it, to be open at home and assertive abroad (Chapters 3 and 24).

- *Preferential and non-discriminatory.* The exercise of sovereignty in hand-picking one's partners, and hence the scope of liberalization, may also be a factor in explaining the widespread resort to bilateral and regional preferential trade agreements despite the fact that, because of inherent trade diversion at the expense of third parties, such agreements are 'second best' to multilateral approaches which involve no such trade diversion (Chapter 22).

- *Market success and market failure.* Policies of trade liberalization tend to acknowledge the advantages of market-friendly policies and yet, at the same time, the notion of market failure is frequently invoked in support of government intervention, often under the principle of 'precaution' when there may be uncertainty about the outcome that the market will produce (Chapters 1, 14 and 17).

- *Good and bad for the environment.* It is thus widely, and correctly, observed that trade, market opening and associated growth have both positive and negative effects on the environment, with a consequential temptation, albeit misguided, to use trade restrictions as a stick to enforce non-trade objectives (Chapters 2 and 13).

These tensions and contradictions – both apparent and real – are what make trade policy analysis such an intriguing topic and trade policy implementation such a challenge. Responding to that challenge means resolving the problem, identified in behavioural economics, of 'bounded rationality' or the tendency to avoid policies that are rational but counterintuitive. It is not immediately obvious that exposing domestic producers to more intense competition will yield overall benefits to the economy. But this indeed is the case.

Structure of the Book

In Part I of this book, these and other issues are examined within the political and economic context of trade policy, tracing the intellectual history of the free trade–protectionist debate, the underlying political economy of trade, and the evolution of the trading system. This is essentially a section of first principles and historical context.

Part II focuses on the key policy areas – the instruments of trade policy: tariffs, non-tariff measures (NTMs), rules and trade facilitation. It will be seen that though NTMs have come to assume greater importance as impediments to trade, tariffs still matter, not least because of tariff peaks and tariff escalation. This section is concerned with the tools of liberalization, or, on the other side of the coin, the tools of protection.

Part III of the book looks at the principles and instruments of trade policy from the perspective of the three major sectors of productive activity: agriculture, services and manufacturing. In each case, in order to bring out the immediacy and relevance of the issues at hand, a particular focus will apply: in agriculture, the dominant and distorting role of developed country policies of domestic support; in services, the difficulties inherent in establishing multilateral disciplines in this area of trade; and in manufacturing, the challenges and opportunities of the global supply chain as highlighted by the mixed fortunes of producers from one advanced industrial country.

Part IV addresses some of the most complex dimensions of trade analysis in examining the links between trade policy and policies concerned with investment, competition, the environment, risk assessment, labour standards and intellectual property rights. Promotion of these linkages, though not without controversy in allegedly diverting attention from the core business of trade policy while in some cases running the risk of protectionist capture, will be seen to foster important synergies and potential complementarities.

Because of the contribution of trade to growth, elaborated in Part I, trade inevitably has a development dimension that pervades all the issues addressed in this book. In Part V, however, attention is devoted to some particular aspects of the link between trade and development: the benefits of a shift from policies of import-substitution towards greater outward orientation; the evolution of special and differential treatment (SDT) and aid-for-trade for developing countries; the nature and impact of trade preferences for developing countries; and the catalytic role of the service economy in fostering growth and development in developing countries.

Part VI looks at the institutional dimension of issues addressed in previous sections by examining the structure and function of the World Trade Organization (WTO) and the evolving relationship between preferential trade agreements and the multilateral trading system. It is in this section that the interplay between international cooperation and the exercise of national sovereignty comes to the fore.

Part VII serves as a reality check for elements of all the preceding chapters by examining the development, main characteristics and impact of trade policy-making in the United States, the European Union, Latin America, Africa and China. This section thus offers tangible case studies and empirical support for the earlier analysis while also identifying practical issues that will shape the evolution of trade policy in the years ahead.

And the concluding chapter identifies the key themes emerging from this book, the future challenges that the trading system will face and the policies necessary to deal with them.

PART I
The Political and Economic Context of Trade Policy

Free Trade versus Protection:
An Intellectual History

Razeen Sally

*The doctrine of free trade, however widely rejected in the world of policy,
holds its own in the sphere of the intellect.*

Frank Taussig

All theory is grey, my friend, but green is life's glad golden tree.

Goethe, *Faust*, Part Two

Introduction

The two quotes above signal the polar extremes in the debates for and against free
trade. Since Adam Smith, classical and neoclassical economists have proclaimed the
superiority of free trade in theory. The American economist Frank Graham called it
'a ubiquitous and timeless principle'. To Stanley Jevons it was 'a fundamental axiom
of political economy'. At the other end of the spectrum, implacable opponents of
free trade, from counter-Enlightenment Romantics such as Carlyle and Ruskin to
today's anti-globalization postmodernists, reject it on anti-economic grounds. It is
a product of the 'dismal science' and the 'quackery' of economists, as Carlyle put it.
It is a bloodless laboratory experiment, they say; a utopia grafted onto the human
skin, with damaging social consequences.

The free trade-versus-protection debate is not as Manichean as the views above
suggest. The reality, of course, has shades of grey in between. This chapter tries
to get a sense of where thinking on the issue stands today. It does so via a potted
history of ideas. The controversies swirling around free trade and protection are
first traced back to their roots in Classical Antiquity and brought forward to the
Middle Ages. Then follows a section on mercantilism pre-Adam Smith. After that
comes the emergence and establishment of free trade doctrine in classical political
economy, especially in the writings of Adam Smith and David Hume. Then follow
nineteenth- and twentieth-century developments.

The purpose of this roundabout method is to avoid a shallow repetition of current – and mostly ahistorical – arguments pro and contra free trade. Intellectual history, hopefully, will give us a wider, but also less superficial, panorama of this central debate in early twenty-first century globalization.

From Classical Antiquity to the Middle Ages[1]

Political, philosophical, ethical and legal arguments for and against free trade have existed since ancient Greek and Roman times. But these are all non- or meta-economic arguments. Economic analysis – the systematic observation and interpretation of how economic phenomena interact – came much, much later in the mercantilist tradition.

The leading and oldest non-economic argument in favour of free trade – namely that it leads to international peace – probably originated in an early Christian 'universal economy' tradition. It had a cosmopolitan outlook and welcomed unfettered trade across the seas as a means of bringing about better contact, understanding and friendship among peoples, eventually leading to the universal brotherhood of man. This was seen as a sign of beneficent divine intervention. In the Middle Ages, natural-law theorists, from Vittoria and Suarez to Grotius and Pufendorf, regarded free trade as part of the *jus gentium*, the law of nations. The eighteenth- and nineteenth-century classical liberals, along with Immanuel Kant, made an explicit connection between free trade and international peace. Richard Cobden was perhaps the most powerful advocate of free trade as the central means of ensuring peaceful international relations. That idea was carried forward in the thinking of Woodrow Wilson and Cordell Hull. The latter, arguably, was the spiritual father of the post-1945 multilateral trading system. As he declared, 'unhampered trade dovetails with peace; high tariffs, trade barriers and unfair economic competition with war … I will never falter in my belief that enduring peace and the welfare of nations are indissolubly connected with friendliness, fairness, equality and the maximum practicable degree of freedom in international trade' (Hull 1948: 81).

Protectionist arguments – again overwhelmingly non-economic – were probably more influential down the ages. Plato and Aristotle embodied a Greek political-philosophical tradition that denigrated economic activity as something for social inferiors, especially women and slaves. Politics was the superior, virtuous activity, the preserve of male citizens in the *polis*. The latter was supposed to be politically self-contained, for which it had to be economically self-sufficient, save for trading in necessities. That meant minimal contact with foreigners.

Finally, much Christian thought over the centuries had an anti-economic streak, with a bias against foreign trade. The latter supposedly inflames the vices

---

[1]   This section draws on Jacob Viner's brilliant Wabash lectures. These wonderful miniatures are found in Viner (1991: 39–81). Also see Irwin (1996: chapter 1).

of worldliness and avarice. It pulls people away from the religious life, which is intimately bound up with ascetic virtues.

Mercantilism[2]

Mercantilist thinking dominated in the two centuries before Adam Smith's publication, in 1776, of *The Wealth of Nations*, in Britain, France and elsewhere in Europe. Economic analysis emerged slowly and imperceptibly during this period, though Schumpeter says that mercantilism was essentially 'pre-analytic': its proponents were mostly pamphleteers full of assertions, opinions and axes to grind, not dispassionate analysts.

Mercantilism's political context was the ascendancy of the Westphalian system of nation-states. Kings and princes were in the business of nation-building. They projected their power within by centralizing control over domestic societies and economies; and projected their power externally in warlike international relations, not least to grab or defend overseas territory. In the economic sphere, the self-interested, profit-seeking merchant, and wealth creation more generally, were increasingly welcomed – a radical departure from antecedent attitudes. But it was considered folly to leave merchants to their own devices. Rather the state had to ensure that self-interested behaviour was guided, deliberately and forcefully, so that it served national interests. It was incumbent on the state to make trade flow in the 'right' channels while avoiding the 'wrong' channels. Hence, notwithstanding a ragbag of diverse and often conflicting views within the mercantilist canon, its organizing principle was *raison d'état*.

Mercantilism had at least five main planks: the accumulation of specie; a favourable balance of trade; promotion of infant industries; the belief in an international zero-sum game; and the preservation of domestic stability.

Firstly, some mercantilist writers sought to accumulate specie (gold in particular) in the national exchequer through maximizing exports and minimizing imports. They considered a hoard of specie to be a leading indicator of national wealth. It was also 'the sinews of war', a repository of funds to pay mercenaries and fight wars. The accumulation-of-specie argument is now considered outdated, even by modern-day mercantilists.

Secondly, many (perhaps most) mercantilists advocated a healthy trade surplus by means of export promotion and import protection – mercantilism's 'two great engines', according to Adam Smith. Many considered this to be the leading indicator of national wealth. As Thomas Mun, a leading English mercantilist, put it:

---

² This section draws on Irwin (1996: chapter 2), Viner (1991: 262–76) and Schumpeter (1950: 335–78).

> The ordinary means therefore to encrease our wealth and treasure is by Forraign Trade, wherein wee must ever observe this rule; to sell more to strangers yearly than wee consume of theirs in value.[3]

Thus intervention in foreign trade, through customs duties, bounties, quotas, foreign exchange controls and outright bans, was to complement a panoply of internal controls on production and consumption.

Thirdly, from Elizabethan times onwards, mercantilists favoured the promotion and protection of infant industries to kickstart industrialization. Manufacturing was considered a superior wealth generator to agriculture and other forms of economic activity.

Fourthly, mercantilists generally believed in Hobbesian international politics and economics. One nation could only gain at the expense of other nations, since international wealth was finite.

Fifthly, domestic social stability was a mercantilist imperative. Foreign trade had to be controlled precisely because, if left uncontrolled, it would disrupt the domestic social balance.

'Mainstream' economists, from David Hume and Adam Smith to Eli Heckscher (1935) and Jacob Viner, have gone out of their way to dismiss mercantilism's central planks as economic nonsense. A trade surplus (or deficit), in isolation, does not tell us anything; and it is certainly not a good indicator of national wealth. Manufacturing is not intrinsically superior to other forms of economic activity. And international trade, if governed by market forces, is a positive-sum game that delivers all-round gains. Hence Paul Krugman's dismissal of mercantilist shibboleths as 'pop internationalism'. To David Henderson (1986), this is 'do-it-yourself economics'. Nevertheless, the main tenets of pre-Adam Smith mercantilism endured into the nineteenth and twentieth centuries, and are alive and well today. They retain powerful ideological appeal.

The Emergence of Free Trade Doctrine[4]

The *economic* defence of free trade, as opposed to its defence from non-economic standpoints, only got going in the eighteenth century. In the interstices of mercantilism, several writers had insightful flashes of the benefits of an unrestricted international division of labour, with, at its core, the interdependence of self-adjusting imports and exports, and of trade and payments. Some came close to saying that free trade, not protection, delivers a superior gain in terms of national wealth creation. Charles Davenant expressed this position pithily:

---

[3] Quoted in Robbins (1998: 52).

[4] This section draws on Irwin (1996: chapters 3, 4).

> Trade is in its nature free, finds its own channel, and best directs its own course: and all laws to give it rules and direction, and to limit and circumscribe it, may serve the particular ends of private men, but are seldom advantageous to the public.[5]

This turned the mercantilist presumption – that the state should direct trade into 'good' and not 'bad' channels – on its head. It set up the principle of non-intervention in trade, akin to the French Physiocrats' governing principle of laissez-faire.

Now it is time for Adam Smith to enter the scene. His genius was not originality; rather it was to draw on a range of thought before him, seasoned with acute observation of history and the world around him, to come up with a sweeping *synthesis* of the economic system and its interrelated parts. The result was his *Inquiry into the Nature and Causes of the Wealth of Nations*. He drew particularly on preceding economic analysis (from the Physiocrats, for example) and his own Scottish–English tradition of moral philosophy.

The governing principle of the Smithian economic system is 'natural liberty' (or non-intervention), which allows 'every man to pursue his own interest his own way, upon the liberal plan of equality, liberty and justice'. And as Smith went on to say, 'All systems of preference or restraint, therefore, being thus completely taken away, the obvious and simple system of natural liberty establishes itself of its own accord' (Smith 1976 (1776), Book 4, chapter 9: 208). Thus self-interest (broadly conceived), if left to its own devices, conduces to the public good, particularly by maximizing the wealth of the nation. The crucial qualification is that this is not a vision of anarcho-capitalism or unadulterated laissez-faire. Rather, it depends fundamentally on an appropriate framework of rules ('justice' in Smith's terminology), which the state is charged with instituting, updating and enforcing.

Smith extended this economic system animated by natural liberty from the domestic to the international sphere, from intranational to international trade. Book 4 of *The Wealth of Nations* laid out a comprehensive system of international trade, with a many-sided defence of free trade that remains unsurpassed. Smith's contemporary and close friend David Hume wrote some brilliant sketches on international trade,[6] but it was Smith who furnished the overarching system.

Free Trade in Smith and Hume: An Elaboration[7]

By the end of the eighteenth century, free trade had become the established presumption in Scottish–English political economy. British policy at the time,

---

[5] Quoted in Irwin (1996: 54).

[6] See Hume (1970).

[7] This section draws especially on Sally (1998: chapter 3). Also see Irwin (1996: chapter 5), Robbins (1998: lectures 11–16), Schumpeter (1950: 181–94) and Viner (1991: chapters 2, 10).

however, was still largely protectionist; and the political economy consensus outside Britain still favoured protection over free trade. Let us now probe deeper into the classical-liberal system of free trade in Hume and Smith.

Both Hume and Smith made a full-frontal attack on mercantilism as their point of departure. Hume's attack was directed at the accumulation-of-specie argument, which he considered self-defeating given automatically adjusting movements of trade and payments. Smith attacked 'real-economy' distortions caused by import protection and export promotion in the pursuit of a trade surplus. Both Scotsmen reserved some of their most vivid language to excoriate mercantilism's dog-eat-dog, zero-sum view of international trade. Here is a sampling from Hume:

> Nothing is more unusual, among states which have made some advances in commerce, than to look on the progress of their neighbours with a suspicious eye, to consider all trading states as their rivals, and to suppose that it is impossible for any of them to flourish, but at their expense. In opposition to this narrow and malignant opinion, I will venture to assert, that the increase of riches and commerce in any one nation, instead of hurting, commonly promotes the riches and commerce of all its neighbours.[8]

And here is Smith in a similar vein:

> By such maxims as these, however, nations have been taught that their interest consisted in beggaring all their neighbours. Each nation has been made to look with an invidious eye upon the prosperity of all the other nations with which it trades, and to consider their gain as its own loss. Commerce, which ought naturally to be, among nations, as among individuals, a bond of union and friendship, has become the most fertile source of discord and animosity.[9]

Hume and Smith: Economic Analysis

Smith grasped the insight that moving from protection to free (or freer) trade generates a one-shot efficiency gain: imports replace costlier domestic production, thereby releasing domestic resources for more productive uses, including exports. He then dismissed various protectionist arguments as a wasteful diversion of resources. His analysis was based on absolute cost advantages. What he failed to grasp was the essential insight of comparative advantage, later established by Torrens and Ricardo.

That said, Hume and Smith were much more concerned with a dynamic, rather than a static, view of international trade. To them, the dynamic gains from trade are critical to the long-run progress of commercial society, far more important than short-term resource-allocation effects.

---

[8]   Quoted in Hume (1970: 78, 82).
[9]   Quoted in Smith (1976 (1776), Book 4, chapter 3: 519).

Hume's main observation on the dynamic gains from trade relates to what we now call 'technology transfer'. He viewed unfettered international trade as a conveyor belt for the transmission of ideas and technology across borders. This allows individuals and enterprises within nations to spot and then imitate better practice abroad, leading to improvements in their own performance, and, in the aggregate, to overall economic growth. To Hume, this is a process of mutually beneficial competitive emulation among nations, akin to competition in economic markets. As Hume said, 'A noble emulation is the source of every excellence'.

Smith's major insight was that international trade widens the geographical extent of the market. This allows a deepening of the division of labour (that is, more specialization), which enables enterprises to reap economies of scale and increase productivity. This in turn feeds into economic growth. Today this is known as the 'increasing returns' argument.

Both Hume and Smith – Smith in particular – stressed the role of institutions in linking openness to the world economy and economic growth. The gradual improvement of domestic institutions is the linchpin of the system. Opening to the world economy creates new incentives to firm up 'hard' and 'soft' infrastructure (to use modern terms). For example, traders link farmers and other small-scale producers in the hinterland to coastal ports, whence their goods are exported. Then come roads, railways, the telegraph and other forms of transport and communications. Competition from abroad and awareness of international trading possibilities create the demand to improve property rights, contract enforcement, and other forms of regulation and (what we now call) governance. Such institutions help to maximize the gains from trade and associated foreign investment. Over time, this interaction between institutions and external openness leads to capital accumulation, investment, entrepreneurship and the diversification of a growing economy. Such was Smith's vision of development. His was a model of an open-ended, dynamic, institution-rich economy. Its assumptions were realistic – a far cry from the perfect-competition, general-equilibrium, institution-free comparative-advantage models that have held sway in the nineteenth and twentieth centuries.[10]

Hume and Smith: Political Economy

Hume and Smith – again, Smith in particular – fortified their economic defence of free trade with explicitly political arguments that highlighted the dangers of protectionism in practice. Three arguments stand out.

Firstly, there is what we now call the 'rent-seeking' or 'government-failure' argument. To Smith, protectionism issues directly from the struggle of organized interests within the state. Producers organize for collective action; they lobby and capture government in order to protect their supernormal profits from being competed away by more efficient domestic and foreign rivals. In excoriating

---

[10] See Hla Myint's brilliant essays on Adam Smith's theory of external trade and its link to development. Especially Myint (1958) and Myint (1977).

language, Smith referred to 'the clamorous importunity of partial interests', which, 'like an overgrown standing army … have become formidable to the government, and upon many occasions intimidate the legislature'. And further: 'Thus are the sneaking arts of underling tradesmen erected into the political maxims for the conduct of a great empire' (Smith 1976 (1776), Book 4, chapter 2: 494 and chapter 3: 518).

Hence, to Smith, protectionism is neither a passing, cyclical phenomenon, nor primarily the result of zero-sum interstate competition. Rather it is a structural feature of domestic politics that spills over into international economic and political conflict.

Secondly, Smith saw free trade in *constitutional*, not just superficially political, terms. Apart from being an economic-efficiency device, it is an instrument of domestic constitutional refurbishment. Protectionism is inherently arbitrary and opaque: it is all about backroom deals between producer interests, politicians and bureaucrats – at the expense of the public good. Free trade, by limiting such activity, brings an element of fairness and transparency to politics and government. Above all, free trade is non-discriminatory in the procedural sense. Protectionism fixes the results of the competitive game, thereby discriminating between persons. In contrast, under free trade outcomes emerge from the competitive game itself, buttressed by the equal (that is non-discriminatory) treatment of persons before the law. This is central to Smith's notions of the rule of law and justice.

Thirdly, Smith pondered the pros and cons of unilateralism versus reciprocity. Should governments liberalize trade unilaterally, that is independently of the trade policies of other governments? Or should they liberalize reciprocally, that is only if others do likewise? On balance, Smith came down in favour of unilateral free trade, more on practical political grounds than through hard economic reasoning. Reciprocity involves incessant haggling between governments; it is governed by the vagaries of 'that insidious and crafty animal otherwise known as a statesman or legislator'; it can be taken hostage by interest groups; and could easily degenerate into tit-for-tat protectionist retaliation. All this can be short-circuited by unilateral trade liberalization ('Just Do It', in Nike brand terminology), to the benefit of consumers and efficient producers alike. According to Lord Robbins, 'From Adam Smith onwards, the classical tradition in regard to retaliation had been quite definitely that it was seldom worth the candle; and while the matter had not been talked about at great length, the general tone of the literature certainly favoured a unilateral progress to free trade' (Robbins 1958: 255).

Hume and Smith: International Relations

In terms of international relations, Hume and Smith were economic liberals but political realists. They advocated free trade, but took as given a state of international political anarchy, that is a system of sovereign nation-states without overarching international government. This stands in contrast to other economic liberals such as Kant, Cobden, and later Robbins and Hayek, who looked forward to the day when national governments would be limited and restrained by 'international authorities' and 'world government'.[11]

Hume and Smith, though living in a different time and context, were sober realists who believed that people's patriotic attachment would not extend beyond the nation-state, and that 'global governance' (as we would now call it) is too artificial and unrealistic. Hence Adam Smith's reference to the wealth of *nations*, and his advocacy of free markets and free trade in terms of *national* interest. As he saw it, governments unilaterally liberalize trade in the national interest, and others would (or might) follow unilaterally, in their own interests, when they saw the benefits of such a policy. Both Hume and Smith envisioned international economic integration through markets ('globalization' in today's terms), but alongside an enduring international political system of nation-states. Governance, rather than going global, would continue to reside primarily at the national level.

Free Trade versus Protection: Nineteenth-Century Developments[12]

The second half of the nineteenth century was free trade's golden age. In the 1840s Britain switched to unilateral free trade, whose anchor and emblem was the repeal of the Corn Laws. Then followed waves of liberalization and deregulation that took Britain to almost complete free trade, and kept it there right until the First World War. A phalanx of interests – manufacturers, the City of London, the newly enfranchised and unionized working classes – and an impregnable intellectual and political consensus underpinned British free trade in practice.

It was very different outside Britain. Protectionism, not free trade, was the norm on the European continent (except for a brief interlude in the 1860s and 1870s), in the United States, and even in the British self-governing colonies of Canada and Australia. This was reflected in the world of ideas. While mercantilist thought was marginalized in Britain, it endured and held sway in Europe and the United States. Alexander Hamilton and Friedrich List powerfully advocated infant industry protection to jumpstart industrialization in the United States and Germany. The German Historical School saw protectionism, and mercantilism more generally, in the frame of nation- and state-building – *raison d'état*, in other words.

Such arguments were political and economic in flavour, but, like pre-Adam Smith mercantilism, they were mostly devoid of solid economic analysis. However, even within mainstream English classical economics, there was, according to Jacob Viner, 'a protectionist skeleton in the free-trade closet'. Robert Torrens developed the terms-of-trade argument in favour of protection, or at least reciprocity in trade

---

[11]   See Robbins (1936) and Hayek (1944: 163–76).

[12]   This section draws on Irwin (1996: chapters 6–8), Robbins (1998: lectures 17–25), Schumpeter (1950: Part 3, chapters 2–5) and Viner (1937). Also see Howe (1997).

policy. This was later refined into the theory of the 'optimum tariff'. John Stuart Mill and Alfred Marshall conceded the case for temporary protection of infant industries in emerging, industrializing countries.

Nevertheless, while most English classical economists accepted limited *theoretical* departures from the free trade presumption, they strongly opposed protectionism *in practice*. It was bound to be hijacked by producer interests, and invite tit-for-tat retaliation. To J.S. Mill, protection is 'an organised system of pillage of the many by the few'. And to F.Y. Edgeworth, 'direct use of theory is likely to be small. But it is to be feared that its abuse will be considerable … Let us admire the skill of the analyst, but label the subject of his investigation POISON'.[13]

Now turn back to the free trade side of the ledger. English classical economists took the baton from Scottish moral philosophers. From Ricardo onwards, they overhauled and refined economic analysis on trade, payments, prices, wages, production and distribution. On international trade, they paid less attention than Smith and Hume to dynamic and institutional factors, and adopted highly simplified assumptions, moving away from a rough-and-ready but realistic model of the economy to one based on perfect competition.

Ricardo and Torrens laid out the theory of comparative advantage, which was further refined by John Stuart Mill (Torrens 1815; Ricardo 1817; Mill 1848). This holds that the gains from trade spring from comparative costs (comparing costs of producing a good *within* one country as opposed to comparing absolute costs *between* countries): imports can replace domestic production even if they are more expensive to produce in absolute terms. Comparative advantage, the foundation of international trade theory from Ricardo onwards, points to wider and deeper specialization, and all-round gains from trade, while absolute advantage points to more partial specialization and partial gains from trade.

Despite these shifts in relatively narrow and technical economic analysis, there was continuity in broad political economy: the nineteenth-century English economists and their fellow travellers generally shared the classical-liberal 'framework assumptions' of their Scots forbears.

Firstly, they had a cosmopolitan outlook. Free trade, they thought, conduces to international peace. Many stretched this belief to the point of naivety. Notably, Richard Cobden believed that free trade could substitute for military force and other means of power to preserve the global *Pax*. Hume and Smith were not so credulous.

Secondly, the English classical economists vigorously defended free trade in the round, on economic *and* political grounds. Their strong preference was for unilateral free trade, not reciprocity. And free trade was coupled strongly with laissez-faire at home, a limited, 'knaveproof' state (that is, one protected from rent-seeking interests), sacrosanct property rights (including those of foreigners), Gladstonian public finance (low taxation, low expenditure and budget balance), and the gold standard. The package formed a mid-Victorian social contract of sorts. As Schumpeter said, 'free trade (in 19th century Britain) is but an element

---

[13] Quoted in Irwin (1996: 114).

of a comprehensive system of economic policy and should never be discussed in isolation' (Schumpeter 1950: 398). It was a moral and political attitude, an integral part of a wider system of economic liberalism.

Free Trade versus Protection: Twentieth-Century Developments[14]

Between 1914 and 1945, the nineteenth-century economic system was ripped apart and shredded. It was replaced by rampant protectionism, competing currency blocs, exchange controls, and generally spiralling government intervention. The Soviet Union and then Nazi Germany were turned into hermetically sealed centrally planned economies.

Post-1945, the United States led the attempt to establish a new liberal international economic order. This was an exercise in partial restoration. The objective was to return to a world of open trade and stable payments, but with sizeable exceptions and 'safety valves'. There was no intention to return to full-blown free trade and a rigid gold standard. That was because 'Smith abroad', that is freer trade, had to be reconciled with 'Keynes at home', the label for greater government intervention in the domestic economy. Lastly, new international organizations such as the International Monetary Fund (IMF), World Bank and General Agreement on Tariffs and Trade (GATT) were created to manage this compromise between international openness and domestic intervention.

Turning to theory, comparative advantage was overhauled by Eli Heckscher (1950) and Bertil Ohlin (1957). Ricardian analysis depended on the real costs of production based on one factor, labour. Hecksher and Ohlin's neoclassical theory focused on different factor endowments (land, labour and capital) and their opportunity costs between countries. Wolfgang Stolper and Paul Samuelson (1941) refined Hecksher–Ohlin by demonstrating how factor proportions drive international trade. Free trade increases the real return to the abundant factor while decreasing the real return to the scarce factor. This points to the in-country distribution of the gains from free trade, creating domestic winners and losers (see Chapter 2).

Mainstream economic thinking on international trade also reflected the real-world transformations mentioned above. The post-1945 theory of commercial policy decoupled free trade from laissez-faire. James Meade (1955) Harry Johnson (1965), Max Corden (1997), Jagdish Bhagwati and others argued that free trade is compatible with a series of targeted 'first-best' interventions to correct domestic market failures. For example, trade protection to promote infant industries is inefficient and costly. Far better to stick to free trade, but use targeted subsidies or

---

[14] This section draws on Irwin (1996: chapters 12–15), Bhagwati (2002) and Lal (2006: chapters 1–3).

other domestic instruments to rectify market failures such as undeveloped financial markets or deficient skill levels in the labour market. But the main point is that free trade was no longer considered part of the bigger classical-liberal package of small government and free markets: it became compatible with bigger government and the mixed economy.

Arguments for protection were virulent in the first half of the twentieth century, and continued to have force thereafter. After 1945, mercantilist thinking was especially potent in newly decolonized 'underdeveloped' countries. High levels of protection, in the context of escalating government intervention, were justified to promote infant industries, preserve domestic stability, protect national security and secure better positions in the international political pecking order. Soviet central planning, not the Western market economy, was the preferred model. Like mercantilism in previous eras, this was an exercise in nation-state-building. Milder mercantilism prevailed in the West and in the emerging Tiger economies of east Asia. There international trade and capital flows were progressively liberalized, but mercantilism found an outlet in policies to promote 'strategic' industries.

The climate of ideas shifted in favour of freer markets alongside the breakdown of the Keynesian consensus in the West, and in reaction to the failure of import-substitution and other dirigiste policies in the developing world. The collapse of Soviet-type economies delivered the *coup de grâce* to command-and-control economics. Developing countries and countries in transition witnessed widespread and radical liberalization of trade and capital flows, following what had already been done in the West.

Nevertheless, protectionism, albeit in muted form, remained popular in the West and in the Rest. Many protectionist ideas – accumulating trade surpluses, protecting infant industries, securing national positions in zero-sum international competition – harked back to traditional mercantilism. They were products of pre-analytic, pop-internationalist, do-it-yourself economics, bereft of sound economic analysis and supporting real-world evidence. That did not make them less popular or politically influential.

That still left arguments for protection that emerged from within mainstream economics. Several cropped up over the course of the twentieth century. All justified departures from free trade due to the incidence of international or domestic market failures. These ranged from increasing returns to scale, wage differentials and unemployment to, more recently, strategic interaction among firms in oligopolistic industries. In some cases, protectionism remains the wrong answer, even in theory. For example, it is better to tackle unemployment through labour-market policies or an exchange rate devaluation than by slapping on a tariff. In other cases, theoretical assumptions can be narrow and unrealistic when applied to real-world conditions. Not least, they demand high levels of information, intelligence and competence from government. This is true of 'strategic trade policy' (Krugman 1987, 1992).

Does government have the knowledge and capability to target strategic sectors and administer the right doses of protection to achieve desired results? Can it be insulated from interest-group capture? Will other governments retaliate, possibly threatening national welfare gains from protection? The free trader's answer would echo Jacob Viner, who concluded that 'these conditions are sufficiently restrictive in combination to guarantee, I am convinced, that the scope for nationally profitable long-run protection is, in practice, very narrowly limited' (Viner 1937: 298). John Maynard Keynes summed it up thus: '(Protectionism) is a treacherous instrument for the attainment of its ostensible objective since private interest, administrative incompetence and the intrinsic difficulty of the task may divert it into producing results directly opposed to those intended.[15]

Free Trade versus Protection: Early Twenty-First Century Developments

The quarter-century up to the recent global economic crisis saw the fastest increase in economic growth, globalization and prosperity in history. But the financial crisis that exploded in September 2008 brought about a sharp contraction of global growth. This was reinforced by even sharper contractions in trade, foreign investment, financial flows and other channels of globalization. The world suffered its worst 'deglobalization' since the Second World War. This was followed by a halting global recovery. The West, with some exceptions, remains anaemic, weighed down by wrecked public finances. But Asian and other emerging markets, with reasonably healthy banks and balance sheets, have roared ahead. Thus the crisis has induced markedly diverging economic performance between the West and emerging markets; but this has accelerated the long-run convergence of emerging markets with the West.

Even before the crisis, pro-market reforms had slowed down around the world, and there was rising scepticism of the liberalization-and-globalization policies associated with the Washington Consensus. On the whole reforms were not reversed, but their forward momentum stalled. The crisis, however, triggered a big shift in ideas and policies against free markets and in favour of government interventionism. So far, government interventions have been most evident in domestic economic policy – huge bailouts and subsidies, especially to banks in the West, fiscal stimulus packages and loose monetary policies. But upfront trade protectionism hardly increased, affecting barely 1 per cent of international trade. More worrying, however, is the increase in domestic regulatory measures – many of them 'crisis interventions' – that threaten to spill over the border and restrict foreign competition (Erixon and Sally 2010).

The shift in the climate of ideas since the heyday of the Washington Consensus in the late 1990s is subtle rather than dramatic. There is, now as before, an extreme anti-globalization critique. But this is street theatre on the fringe. Of greater political importance is a more mainstream critique that accepts the reality of the

---

[15] Quoted in Irwin (1996: 199).

market economy and more-or-less open borders, but rejects the comprehensive liberalization associated (perhaps unfairly) with the Washington Consensus.

Critics point to supposedly tenuous links between liberalization, openness, growth and poverty reduction; wider inequalities within and between countries that result from globalization; the damaging effects of large and sudden trade liberalization in developing countries; the renewed emphasis on aid to poorer developing countries, without which trade liberalization will not work; the need for developed country liberalization while retaining developing country protectionism; and the need for 'policy space' – more flexible international rules – to allow developing country governments to pursue selective industrial policies, especially to promote infant industries (Rodrik 1998 and 2001; Chang 2002; Oxfam 2002; Stiglitz 2002; Sachs 2005).

To address just three of these critiques: firstly, comparative indepth country studies by the OECD (Little et al. 1970), NBER (Bhagwati 1978; Krueger 1978) and World Bank (Michaely et al. 1991) suggest strongly that countries with more liberal trade policies have more open economies and grow faster than those with more protectionist policies. These are much more reliable than superficial cross-country regression analyses (Lal and Myint 1996; Bhagwati and Srinivasan 1999). That said, even most of the latter point to large gains from trade liberalization (Sachs and Warner 1995; Winters 2004a and 2004b). 'New globalizers' – developing countries that have liberalized and globalized significantly in recent decades – have seen big increases in growth, and dramatic reductions in poverty and improvements in human welfare indicators (World Bank 2002; Maddison 2003).

Secondly, NGOs and developing country governments have been clamouring for one-sided liberalization in the Doha round. They want developed countries to liberalize, but developing countries should not have to reciprocate with their own liberalization. What Oxfam and others fail to say is that developing countries' own protectionist policies harm them even more than developed country barriers. For example, the World Bank estimates that 80 per cent of the developing country gain from worldwide agricultural liberalization would come from developing countries' liberalization of their highly protected agricultural markets (Ingco and Nash 2004).

Thirdly, the historical record is not kind to 'hard' industrial policies of the infant-industry variety. Infant-industry success in the nineteenth-century United States and Germany is contested. In east Asia, its record is mixed at best in Japan, South Korea and Taiwan (see Chapter 17); nonexistent in free trade Hong Kong and Singapore; and failed in southeast Asia (for example national car policies in Malaysia and Indonesia). In northeast Asia, there is scant evidence to show that protection of infants actually led to higher social rates of return and higher overall productivity growth (World Bank 1993; Little 1999). Finally, infant-industry protection in Latin America, south Asia and Africa has been a disaster not dissimilar to industrial planning in ex-command economies. Protected infants sooner or later ran into severe problems; and governments continued to subsidize and protect perpetual children. Such incestuous government–business links provided a fertile breeding ground for corruption. Besides, most developing country markets are too small to support infant-industry promotion; and their states are too weak, incompetent and corrupt to efficiently administer the complex instruments required (Wolf 2004: 202–3; Panagariya 2011).

Early twenty-first century advocates of infant-industry protection have three blind spots. They seem ignorant of mainstream trade theory, which rejects trade protection as a first-best intervention for domestic market failures. They associate examples of hard industrial policy, including selective trade protection, with aggregate economic success – without empirically demonstrating the link between the two. Lastly, the twenty-first century world economy has highly fragmented production, complex global supply chains and ever-intensifying competition, especially for manufactured goods but spreading to parts of services and agriculture. In these conditions, 'smart' industrial policy, including infant-industry protection, requires governments to have even greater information, intelligence and capacity to intervene successfully.

Despite these flaws in modern arguments for protection, one cannot help feeling that the standard economic case for free trade, based on neoclassical welfare economics, is too narrow and mechanical, and maybe a little unreal. Firstly, free trade theory has highly simplified assumptions such as no cross-border factor mobility and zero transport costs. But distance and geography still make a difference to international trade; international capital mobility, and, to a lesser extent international labour mobility, are engines of global economic integration. Secondly, standard theory emphasizes the static gains from trade, but says little or nothing about the dynamic gains from trade and their institutional foundations. Thirdly, post-1945 trade theory also assumes a neat division between what is 'international' (the *dominium* of free trade) and what is 'domestic' (the *imperium* of government intervention). But modern globalization is thinning and blurring these international–domestic boundaries.

Recent theoretical developments have attempted to fill some of these gaps. The 'trade-and-geography' literature takes account of distance, clustering effects and increasing returns to scale (Krugman 1991). The 'trade-in-tasks' literature models how comparative advantage applies in a world of vertically fragmented international production, intra-industry trade and integrated global supply chains (Grossman and Rossi-Hansberg 2008). This is also a world in which trade, foreign direct investment (FDI) and labour mobility can be combined in complementary ways (see Chapter 11).

Conclusion

The theoretical case for free trade is strong and compelling. On the economic front, free trade delivers short-term (static) gains through specialization according to comparative advantage; and longer-term (dynamic) gains through economies of scale and technology transfer, among other factors. On the political front, it contributes to peaceful international relations. Both economic and political arguments for free trade repose on the foundation of individual freedom – the freedom of people to transact within and across borders. Thus Adam Smith's 'natural liberty' is free trade's bedrock. Individual choice is the engine of free trade, and of progressive commercial society more generally. It sparks what Hume called a 'spirit of industry'; it results in much better life-chances, not just for the select few but for individuals in the broad mass of society who are able to lead more varied and interesting lives.

To sum up: free trade is of course associated with standard economic efficiency arguments. But the classical-liberal case for free trade is more rounded, taking in the moral imperative of individual freedom and linking it to prosperity. Finally, free trade contributes to, though it does not guarantee, peaceful international relations. Freedom, prosperity, security: this trinity lies at the heart of the case for free trade.

Most protectionist arguments are mercantilist old wine in new bottles: they are economic nonsense. But there are more solid theoretical arguments for protection where significant domestic or international market failures can be identified. However, even these arguments, such as for an optimum tariff or strategic trade policy, fail the reality test almost all the time. Their assumptions are very restrictive and politically naive. They presume too much government intelligence and capability, and overlook the probability of interest-group capture.

Since 1945, the case for free trade has been made in the context of what I would call 'Mixed-Systems Thinking' and 'Liberalism From Above'. The Bretton Woods and GATT settlements combined a partial restoration of nineteenth-century free trade with expanding government intervention at home. Post-war trade theory reinforced this Mixed-Systems Thinking by decoupling free trade from laissez-faire. Liberalism From Above has also prevailed: trade liberalization has relied on international organizations and intergovernmental negotiations.

Both Mixed-Systems Thinking and Liberalism From Above were politically expedient after the Second World War; but, over time, they have entrenched misguided conventional wisdoms. The first is that Big Government interventionism at home will not flood across borders and overly damage international commerce. The second is that international institutions deliver trade liberalization 'from outside', and only through 'concessions' to foreigners in a game of haggling. On both counts, anti-globalization critics and even supposedly globalization-friendly social democrats believe that governments have the knowledge, capacity and honesty to remedy domestic and international market failures. They persistently underestimate government failure, both at home and abroad.

Mixed-Systems Thinking forgets that free trade is part and parcel of free markets; it is but an element of a constitutional whole that includes limited government and laissez-faire at home. And Liberalism From Above forgets that the liberalization impulse comes less from international institutions and more from national governments acting unilaterally (or autonomously), and spreads internationally by example (or competitive emulation). Unilateral free trade makes economic sense, since welfare gains come quicker from a country's own, unconditional import liberalization than they do from protracted international negotiations. It makes political sense too. Governments have the flexibility to initiate policies and emulate better practice abroad in experimental, trial-and-error fashion, tailored to specific local conditions. The WTO and bilateral/regional trade agreements can be helpful auxiliaries in advancing a liberalization agenda, but they are poor substitutes to unilateral, bottom-up liberalization.

In light of such reservations, there are strong grounds to return to eighteenth- and nineteenth-century roots, and to put the general case for free trade back in a *classical-liberal* frame. Free trade should be recoupled with laissez-faire: it should be part and parcel of the wider case for free markets, limited government and economic freedom. Its dynamic, institutional features should be emphasized. The links between free trade and market-oriented domestic policies should also be emphasized. Finally, free trade should be seen bottom-up, more in terms of unilateral national action and competitive emulation, and less as a top-down product of international organizations and reciprocal bargaining (Lindsey 2002; Lal 2006: chapter 3).

References

Bhagwati, J. 1978. *Foreign Trade Regimes and Economic Development: Anatomy and Consequences of Exchange Control Regimes*. Cambridge, MA: Ballinger.

Bhagwati, J. 2002. *Free Trade Today*. Princeton: Princeton University Press.

Bhagwati, J. and Srinivasan, T.N. 1999. Outward-orientation and development: are revisionists right? *Yale University Economic Growth Centre Discussion Paper*, No. 806.

Chang, H.J. 2002. *Kicking Away the Ladder: Development Strategy in Historical Perspective*. London: Anthem Press.

Corden, W.M. 1997. *Trade Policy and Economic Welfare*. Oxford: Oxford University Press.

Erixon, F. and Sally, R. 2010. Trade, globalisation and emerging protectionism since the crisis. *ECIPE Working Paper no. 2* [Online]. Available at: www.ecipe.org/publications/ecipe–working–papers/trade–globalisation–and–emerging–protectionism–since–the–crisis/PDF [accessed: 15 March 2011].

Grossman, G. and Rossi-Hansberg, E. 2008. Trading tasks: a simple theory of offshoring. *American Economic Review* 98(5), 1978–97.

Hayek, F.A. 1944. *The Road to Serfdom*. London: Routledge.

Heckscher, E. 1935. *Mercantilism*. London: George Allen and Unwin.

Heckscher, E. 1950. The effect of foreign trade on the distribution of income, in *Readings in the Theory of International Trade*, edited by H.S. Ellis and L.A. Metzler. Homewood: Irwin, 272–300.

Henderson, D. 1986. *Innocence and Design: The Influence of Ideas on Economic Policy*. London: Blackwell.

Howe, A. 1997. *Free Trade and Liberal England, 1846–1946*. Oxford: Clarendon.

Hull, C. 1948. The true nature of trade, in *The Memoirs of Cordell Hull*. New York: Macmillan.

Hume, D. 1970. Of the jealousy of trade, in *Writings on Economics (1758)*, edited by E. Rotwein. Madison: University of Wisconsin Press, 330–31.

Ingco, M.D. and Nash, J.D. (eds) 2004. *Agriculture and the WTO: Creating a Trading System for Development*. Washington, DC: World Bank.

Irwin, D.A. 1996. *Against the Tide: An Intellectual History of Free Trade*. Princeton: Princeton University Press.

Johnson, H.G. 1965. Optimal intervention in the presence of domestic distortions, in *Trade, Growth and the Balance of Payments: Essays in Honour of Gottfried Haberler*, edited by R.E. Caves, P.B. Kenen and H.G. Johnson. Amsterdam: North-Holland, 3–34.

Krueger, A.O. 1978. *Foreign Trade Regimes and Economic Development: Liberalisation Attempts and Consequences*. Cambridge, MA: Ballinger.

Krugman, P. 1987. Is free trade passé? *Journal of Economic Perspectives* 1(Fall), 131–41.

Krugman, P. 1991. *Geography and Trade*. Cambridge, MA: MIT Press.

Krugman, P. 1992. Does the new trade theory require a new trade policy? *The World Economy* 15(July), 423–41.

Lal, D. 2006. *Reviving the Invisible Hand: The Case for Classical Liberalism in the Twenty-First Century*. Princeton: Princeton University Press.

Lal, D. and Myint, H. 1996. *The Political Economy of Poverty, Equity and Growth: A Comparative Study*. Oxford: Clarendon Press.

Lindsey, B. 2002. *Against the Dead Hand: The Uncertain Struggle for Global Capitalism*. Washington, DC: John Wiley.

Little, I.M.D. 1999. Trade and industrialisation revisited, in *Collection and Recollections*, edited by I.M.D. Little. Oxford: Clarendon, Part III.

Little, I.M.D., Scitovsky, T. and Scott, M.F.G. 1970. *Industry and Trade in Some Developing Countries*. Oxford: Oxford University Press.

Maddison, A. 2003. *The World Economy: Historical Statistics*. Paris: OECD.

Meade, J. 1955. *Trade and Welfare*. Oxford: Oxford University Press.

Michaely, M., Papageorgiou, D. and Choksi, A. (eds) 1991. *Liberalising Foreign Trade: Lessons of Experience in the Developing World*. Cambridge, MA: Blackwell.

Mill, J.S. 1848 [1909]. *Principles of Political Economy*. London: Longmans, Green.

Myint, H. 1958. The 'classical theory' of international trade and the underdeveloped countries. *Economic Journal* LXVIII(270), 317–37.

Myint, H. 1977. Adam Smith's theory of international trade in the perspective of economic development. *Economica* 44, 231–48.

Ohlin, B. 1957. *Interregional and International Trade*. Cambridge, MA: Harvard University Press.

Oxfam. 2002. *Rigged Rules and Double Standards: Trade, Globalisation and the Fight Against Poverty*. Oxford: Oxfam International.

Panagariya, A. 2011. A reexamination of the infant industry argument for protection. *The Journal of Applied Economic Research* 5(1), 7–30.

Ricardo, D. 1817 [1884]. *Principles of Political Economy and Taxation*. London: Everyman.

Robbins, L. 1936. *Economic Planning and International Order*. London: Macmillan.

Robbins, L. 1958. *Robert Torrens and the Evolution of Classical Economics*. London: Macmillan.

Robbins, L. 1998. *A History of Economics Thought: The LSE Lectures*, edited by S. Medema and W. Samuels. Princeton: Princeton University Press.

Rodrik, D. 1998. *The New Global Economy and Developing Countries: Making Openness Work*. Washington, DC: Overseas Development Council.

Rodrik, D. 2001. Trading in illusions. *Foreign Policy* [Online], March/April.

Sachs, J. 2005. *The End of Poverty: How We Can Make it Happen in our Lifetime*. London: Penguin.

Sachs, J. and Warner, A. 1995. Economic reform and the process of global integration. *Brookings Papers on Economic Activity* No. 1.

Sally, R. 1998. *Classical Liberalism and International Economic Order: Studies in Theory and Intellectual History*. London: Routledge.

Schumpeter, J.A. 1950. *History of Economic Analysis*. London: Routledge.

Smith, A. 1976. *An Inquiry into the Nature and Causes of the Wealth of Nations (1776)*, edited by E. Cannan. Chicago: University of Chicago Press.

Stiglitz, J. 2002. *Globalisation and its Discontents*. London: Allen Lane.

Stolper, W. and Samuelson, P.A. 1941. Protection and real wages. *Review of Economic Studies* 9(November), 58–73.

Torrens, R. 1815. *Essay on the External Corn Trade*. London: J. Hatchard.

Viner, J. 1937. *Studies in the Theory of International Trade*. London: George Allen and Unwin.

Viner, J. 1991. *Jacob Viner: Essays on the Intellectual History of Economics*, edited by D.A. Irwin. Princeton: Princeton University Press.

Winters, A.L. 2004a. Trade liberalisation and economic performance: an overview. *Economic Journal* 114(February), F4–F21.

Winters, A.L. 2004b. Trade liberalisation and poverty. *Journal of Economic Literature* 42(1), 72–105.

Wolf, M. 2004. *Why Globalisation Works*. New Haven: Yale University Press.

World Bank. 1993. *The East Asian Miracle*. Washington, DC: World Bank.

World Bank. 2002. *Globalisation, Growth and Poverty: Building an Inclusive World Economy*. Washington, DC: World Bank, 34.

The Political Economy of International Trade

Kenneth Heydon

Introduction

Through successive General Agreement on Tariffs and Trade (GATT) rounds, extensive unilateral liberalization and the liberalizing effects of global supply chains, international trade has become more open. But much remains to be done and the job is getting harder. This chapter examines why. The first section looks at the recent record of market opening, before an examination, in the second section, of the political economy of trade liberalization's concentrated costs and dispersed gains. The third section addresses some new challenges facing trade policy – multi-polarity and bilateralism, increased complexity, and the role of non-state players – and suggests that their importance stems from their linkage to the 'old' issue of the political economy of trade. The chapter concludes with some suggested ways forward – most importantly the need to place trade policy firmly within the overall framework of sound domestic economic management.

The Job gets Harder: Resistance to Liberalization

Economic analysis has long established free trade as a beneficial economic policy. Douglas Irwin has even claimed that free trade has achieved an intellectual status unrivalled by any other doctrine in the field of economics (Irwin 1996).

Moreover, there is clear evidence of past movement towards freer trade. A series of multilateral negotiations under the GATT saw industrialized countries' average tariff on manufactures come down from close to 40 per cent in 1947 to under 5 per cent at the close of the Uruguay Round in 1994. Many countries, particularly developing countries of south-east Asia and South America, have engaged in unilateral trade liberalization (Sally 2008). And the two major financial crises of recent times have failed to trigger the protectionist responses that many feared.

Recovery from the Asian Financial Crisis of 1997–8 was facilitated by export-driven growth as markets stayed open. And in the global financial crisis of 2008–9, the share of the value of trade covered by new direct trade policy instruments amounted to only 1 per cent of world imports (WTO 2009). Commitments to stay open to foreign products and services and concerns to keep global supply chains open – effectively lowering the optimal tariff (see Chapter 11) – together with the disciplines stemming from the WTO's rules-based system, helped countries to resist protectionist pressures (OECD 2010).

Yet, notwithstanding the support for the principle of free trade and evidence of progress towards its realization, the job remains incomplete and appears to be getting harder. Trade in agriculture and in sensitive areas of manufacturing is subject to tariff peaks and tariff escalation, as border impediments rise with higher degrees of processing. Where countries have unilaterally reduced their tariffs, this has often been accompanied, as in the case of India (Panagariya 2008), by increased resort to non-tariff barriers, such as antidumping action. Behind-the-border distortions such as domestic subsidies and local preference in government procurement abound. And a plethora of domestic regulations serve to impede international trade in services.

We thus see that during the global financial crisis, the share of imports affected by direct trade policy instruments was very high in selected sectors, reaching 36 per cent and 29 per cent respectively in the agricultural sector and the base metal industries. In the course of the crisis, a significant number of non-tariff measures (NTMs) were activated to restrict trade, such as the tightening of licensing requirements, safeguard measures and antidumping investigations, with developing countries accounting for 80 per cent of all antidumping initiations in the period October 2008–October 2009. And the crisis triggered widespread resort to behind-the-border trade-related measures. One-third of Organisation for Economic Cooperation and Development (OECD) countries offered some form of financial support to their motor vehicle industry and a number of countries incorporated preferential treatment in public procurement as part of their macroeconomic stimulus packages (OECD 2010).

While it may be argued that periods of acute crisis are not the norm, the trade policy response to the crisis of 2008–9 serves to highlight the vulnerability of open markets when political sensitivities are at their sharpest. Moreover, during a much longer period, there has been a marked failure to advance the Doha Development Agenda (DDA). Experience with the DDA serves to demonstrate the pervasive reluctance to further liberalize trade.

In July 2007, major players declined to commit to disciplines that were less onerous than the status quo, whether in agriculture, where the United States refused a domestic support cap of $13 billion though current outlays were only $11 billion, or in non-agricultural market access (NAMA), where Brazil refused tariff bindings that would have required no change in levels of protection. The situation was ripe for a continued standoff.

The standoffs came in many forms. Most critically, some parties (including the agricultural protectionists) showed reluctance to move further on agriculture until others moved on services and NAMA, while other parties (including some developing countries) baulked on services and NAMA until they saw progress in agriculture. Japan resisted agricultural liberalization without assurances that there would be matching action in the rules area, notably that antidumping disciplines would be strengthened. There were also standoffs within sectors, as in services for example, where developing country expectations on mode 4 (the 'presence of natural persons', or the short-term movement of service providers) were pitted against developed country expectations on mode 3 (the supply of a service by one Member 'through commercial presence in the territory of any other Member') (see Chapter 9). Nor were standoffs an exclusively North–South affair. In agriculture, US demands that the EU do more on market access were matched by EU demands that the United States introduce more discipline on its domestic support.

The WTO ministerial meeting of 21–30 July 2008 moved some way in turning standoffs (I will do nothing on agriculture until you do something on NAMA) into trade-offs. However, the trade-offs tended to be negative (I will let you exclude X from liberalization if you let me exclude Y) rather than positive (I will liberalize X if you liberalize Y). The result of the mutual lowering of ambition was that in the end the potential deal was not worth fighting for. For example, allowing the special safeguard mechanism in agriculture to be triggered by an import surge of only 10 per cent, as sought by a group of developing countries, would mean that 82 per cent of China's food imports and 64 per cent of India's would be subject to a tariff as high as 30 percentage points above pre-Doha bound rates.

Why is progress so difficult?

The Political Economy of International Trade: Understanding and Responding to an Old Problem

The underlying failure in recent years to advance multilateral trade liberalization stems from insufficient political will to confront the vested interests benefiting from the rents of protection.

The Political Impediments to Open Markets

Trade liberalization yields overall benefits to the liberalizing country. But because it causes domestic prices to converge on those applying in the international market, the resulting change in relative prices within the domestic economy affects the returns to different factors of production – whether wages in different sectors, wages at different skill levels, or returns to capital. There are winners and losers. The politics of trade is then highly dependent on two key factors: the relative size of the stakes of winners and losers and the respective ability of winners and losers to organize and defend their interests.

Political influence tends to be greater for those seeking government assistance or protection because those who stand to gain have more at stake than those who stand to lose. In the words of Vilfredo Pareto, 'a protectionist measure provides large benefits to a small number of people, and causes a very great number of consumers a slight loss' (Pareto 1971: 379). The validity of this observation is amply demonstrated by recent experience with the Common Agricultural Policy (CAP) of the European Union. In 2009, 1,212 individual recipients received at least one million euro in CAP support (farmsubsidy.org cited in Bridges 2010). The number of beneficiaries is impressive, but it is dwarfed by the number of consumers living in the EU27 – close to 500 million.

Relatively concentrated groups, whether geographically, by number of enterprises or by subsector (the top CAP beneficiaries are predominantly sugar producers), are also better placed to meet the costs of collective action by monitoring political contributions or excluding free riders (Olsen 1965). This observation helps to explain the urban–rural tensions in many developing countries, not least in Africa, where a well organized and politically active manufacturing sector benefits from protection and overvalued exchange rates, at the expense of the politically disorganized agricultural sector, despite the comparative advantage in agricultural goods (Bates 1981).

It is these two elements of the political economy of international trade – the concentrated benefits of protection and the organizational strength of well-focused groups – that helps explain the enduring feature of protection: once protective policies are in place they are very difficult to change (Irwin 2002). Hence the unwillingness of trade negotiators, from both developed and developing countries, in the course of the Doha negotiations to move away from the status quo. It is these elements that also explain why, in very broad terms, resistance to reform and market opening is particularly acute for developed countries in the area of agriculture and for developing countries in the areas of manufacturing and services.

In recognition of the political impediments to free trade, and consistent with the writings of the Political Capture theorists, attempts have been made to shelter the process of trade policymaking from the influence of sectional interests and to prevent financially powerful groups from prejudicing the interests of the majority (Alt et al. 1996; Cohen et al. 2003; Destler 2005; Krasner 1976; Rogowski 1989; Stigler 1971, 1974). Hence in the United States, the Trade Act of 1974 introduced a 'fast-track' procedure whereby Congress would vote expeditiously on trade legislation without the possibility of amendment. According to Access Point theory, such delegation to the president makes it harder for interest groups to lobby policymakers (Ehrlich 2008). And in the EU, the Treaty of Rome delegated to the European Commission the implementation of trade remedies and the conduct of negotiations.

As the country chapters in this volume show, these attempts have had only mixed success. The question then arises: what might be done to address the challenge arising from the political economy of trade? Attention here will focus on three requirements: communicating the benefits of open markets, helping those who lose, and putting trade policy in a broader context.

Communicating the Gains from Trade

Communicating more effectively the gains from market opening means resolving the problem, identified in behavioural economics, of 'bounded rationality' or the tendency to avoid policies that are rational but counterintuitive (Brennan 2007: 137). It is not immediately obvious that exposing domestic producers to more intense competition will yield overall benefits to the economy. But this indeed is the case.

If we think of a continuum – trade, innovation, growth – then, while the link between innovation and growth is fairly well understood, the link from trade to innovation (and hence to growth) is less so. There are four channels through which trade stimulates innovation, involving a mixture of market opening and the strengthening of trade rules (OECD 2007a).

- Increased competition: a number of studies find that trade openness makes markets more competitive, reducing prices and raising incentives to innovate (Licandro and Navas 2007) while also raising productivity (Melitz and Ottaviano 2005). Bigsten et al. (2004) have shown that trade can also improve productivity through efficiency gains from learning by exporting. There is recent evidence that stronger competition has particularly powerful effects on productivity in countries far away from the technological frontier, reflecting stronger incentives to adopt new technologies (OECD 2007b). Underpinning these observations is the work of Robert Solow pointing out that there are two components to productivity growth (Ten Raa and Mohnen 2008): a Schumpeterian technical change element centred on the more efficient use of *capital* (Schumpeter 1954), and a neoclassical efficiency change element centred on the more efficient use of *labour*.

- Technology transfer: trade, particularly when accompanied by foreign direct investment (FDI), is likely to promote the transfer of skills and innovation. Beyond this direct transfer of technology embodied in trade, or as spillovers from trade (Nordas et al. 2006), there is also an indirect contribution as trade serves to lower prices and hence the cost of accessing such embodied technologies. In short, trade allows firms to access technologies that are essential for improving their productivity and competitiveness.

- Economies of scale: companies producing for both the domestic and foreign markets are better able to recoup research and development (R&D) investments over a larger quantity of sales than if selling only for the domestic market.

- Globalization of value chains: trade and trade reform can help foster the global fragmentation of production processes. They do so in a number of ways: by promoting harmonization around international technical standards to which firms in fragmented value chains must conform; by addressing the danger that restrictive rules of origin (designed to ensure that only imports from partners in bilateral or regional Preferential Trade Agreements (PTAs) have preferential access) will disadvantage low-cost suppliers within the chain; and by encouraging trade facilitation, enabling suppliers to respond quickly to developments further down the value chain.

In summary, despite differences of opinion on the strength and the direction of causality, there is strong analytical support for the view that openness to trade, backed by stronger trade rules, generally leads to welfare gains (Dollar and Kraay 2002; Winters 2004). Putting numbers on this is difficult, but there is evidence that an increase in the share of trade in gross domestic product (GDP) of 1 percentage point raises the income level by between 0.9 per cent and 3 per cent (Nordas et al. 2006). Economies with more open trade policies tend to perform better than those with more restrictive trade policies, as evidenced by the experience of South Korea and Taiwan, which began to liberalize their trade policies in the 1960s, Chile, in the 1970s, and China, India, Mexico and Vietnam, which undertook measures of market opening in the 1980s and 1990s.

But there is a fourth element in the continuum: trade, innovation, growth and *poverty reduction*. Economic theory tells us that trade should contribute directly to reduced poverty in developing countries through the process whereby trade increases the returns to the most abundant factor of production, which in developing countries tends to be low-skilled labour. The fact that income inequality has risen in most countries over the past two decades is due more to technological progress increasing the wages of skilled relative to unskilled workers, than to trade (Billmeier and Nannicini 2007; Cling 2006). As we have seen, some technological innovation will of course be undertaken in response to the intensified competition arising from trade. But this is nevertheless likely to represent a relatively small – though still significant – proportion of overall technological change. It has thus been estimated (Bloom et al. 2011) that between 2000 and 2007, 15 per cent of technology upgrading in Europe can be explained as a response to competition from China.

Recent events have underlined the importance of the trade link to productivity improvement. The unprecedented fiscal expansion in response to the 2008–9 global financial crisis and associated debt only add to the existing long-term imperatives for increased productivity growth needed to address demographic ageing and greenhouse gas abatement and other costs. Productivity growth can help service the debt now accumulating from fiscal deficits, as well as offset the effects on future income of withdrawal of governments' stimuli from consumer spending (OECD 2010; Productivity Commission 2009).

The other side of the gains-from-trade coin is the cost of protection. Following the work of Max Corden, this cost is now commonly addressed in terms of the effective rate of protection (ERP) (Corden 1966). The ERP calculates the effect on the returns to labour and capital in an industry of the use of tariffs and other forms of assistance by measuring the entire structure of protection, taking into account the effect of tariffs and NTMs on inputs (raw materials and intermediate products) as well as on outputs. The higher the tariffs and NTMs on imported inputs, the lower the ERP will be for the goods that use those inputs (Hoekman and Kostecki 2009). When allowance is made for the effect of restrictions on the import of services – and hence on services as an input – the results are striking. It has been found that when account is taken of barriers to services imports, the ERP for motor vehicle production in Brazil actually becomes negative: the protection of both services and non-services inputs results in the effective taxation of this industry (Dihel and Dee 2006).

It is analysis such as this that underpins the broader, and no less striking, proposition that a tax on imports is a tax on exports, both directly, as the cost of inputs increases, and indirectly, as the reduced incentive for import-competing industries to contain costs spreads to the economy at large. But exporters are generally unable to pass on any cost increases. They will either lose export sales or become less profitable. Either way, jobs will be lost.

There is thus a weighty body of analysis in favour of open markets. The challenge is to communicate effectively this analysis, through all channels available: through government agencies, such as the Productivity Commission in Australia; through communications of the international agencies, such as the Trade Fact Sheets prepared by the OECD (OECD 2009); and through dissemination of the academic literature. What these channels share in common is that they engage organizations that are concerned with improving the welfare of the community at large, rather than of sectional interests within it (Olsen 1982).

Helping Those Who Lose

Public acceptance of the case for open markets requires more than simply demonstrating the gains from liberalization. It also calls for acknowledgement that there are losers as well as winners from market opening and that support will be given to those who lose – support that will be less costly than the protectionist alternative (Bhagwati 1988).

In principle, such support should rely on economy-wide action, in order to treat individuals in similar circumstances equally, to provide assistance to those in genuine need and to avoid compounding distortions in the economy (OECD 2005; WTO 2008). In practice, however, experience suggests that successful episodes of trade-related structural adjustment have almost always involved some measure of sector-specific assistance. Recalling the Pareto principle of concentrated gains from protection and hence concentrated costs of liberalization, targeted assistance may be called for particularly where structural decline in a particular sector causes geographically concentrated job loss beyond what existing labour market programmes can cope with.

The United States Trade Adjustment Assistance (TAA) legislation, appears to have been the source of innovative practices related to the provision of earnings-replacement benefits, such as the wage insurance programme introduced in 2003 (Kletzer and Rosen 2004). But the economic rationale of TAA has been controversial because it is not evident that trade-displaced workers should receive more adjustment assistance than other job losers. A similar scheme in Australia was abandoned for the same reason (OECD 2005).

Should governments consider it necessary to target assistance in particular cases, experience suggests that problems of both equity and efficiency will be minimized to the extent that such assistance is: time-bound, with a clear exit strategy; decoupled from production with incentives to adjust and innovate; aimed at re-employing displaced workers; compatible with general safety net arrangements;

and transparent and accountable (OECD 2005. See also Evans-Klock et al. 1998; Kaivanto 2007; Leigh 1990; Winter-Ebmer 2003).

Putting Trade Policy in a Broader Context

As well as communicating the gains from market opening and helping to compensate for the losses, an effective response to the challenge of the political economy of trade will also require that trade policy be seen in a broader context. Advancing *multilateral* trade liberalization – whether in the present round of negotiations or within the continuing work programme of the WTO – will, somewhat paradoxically, necessitate placing trade liberalization more firmly within the framework of *domestic* economic management.

This idea was well articulated some 25 years ago by former Australian Prime Minister Robert Hawke who, while calling for the launch of a new GATT round, spoke of the need:

> for trade policy to be seen more as an integral part of broad domestic economic management and less exclusively as the subject of international negotiations. (Speech to the Centre for European Policy Studies in Brussels, 4 February 1985, cited in Snape et al. 1998: 415)

The idea was later elaborated by the OECD, in observing that:

> The benefits of a liberal trade regime will only be fully realised in an economy with appropriate macroeconomic policies, efficient labour markets and a regulatory environment which facilitate mobility of workers and the entry and exit of firms, and an education system which enables skills to match evolving needs. (OECD 2005: 16; see also Sally 2008: 91)

In short, market opening works best – and maybe only works at all – in a coherent, holistic policy environment that facilitates the movement of labour and capital from declining to expanding areas of activity. While trade liberalization is positively linked to growth, it is associated with a lower standard of living in economies that heavily regulate new entry or impose high costs on exiting or downsizing (Bartelsman et al. 2004; Bolaky and Freund 2004; Hoekman and Javorcik 2004).

Placing trade policy in its broader setting is another way of saying that *trade cannot do it all*. And here we are reminded of the crucial point identified by Jan Tinbergen that for policy to work there must be as many independent effective instruments as there are feasible targets (Tinbergen 1956). This highlights the challenge faced by the poorest countries where the entry of new firms calls for 'effective instruments' in the provision of human capital and bank finance – each of which, as Joseph Stiglitz has pointed out, may be in serious short supply (Stiglitz 2002: 59). But this is an argument for policy action in those areas of deficiency, backed by necessary development assistance, not for forgoing the benefits of more open markets. Similarly, when developing countries' trade-related adjustment is complicated because they are dependent on tariffs for revenue, the answer is not to forgo the benefits of their own liberalization but to broaden the tax base, as many developing countries have managed to do (OECD 2005).

Through this wider lens, trade reform can be promoted as one of a number of tools of growth and development rather than as a concession paid to others. Something of this spirit prevailed in Australia in the 1980s, when each of the three policy elements discussed here was evident (see Box 2.1).

Box 2.1   The political economy of Australian trade liberalization

During the 1980s, Australia, on a largely unilateral basis, began successfully dismantling protection of highly sheltered sectors, such as automobiles, dairy, shipbuilding and textiles and clothing. Market opening – and consequential improvements in productivity and growth – was facilitated by action in the three key areas identified in this chapter.

Communicating the gains was effected by:

- the Industries Assistance Commission (later the Productivity Commission) playing the role of Mancur Olsen's 'encompassing organization' by fostering a culture of evaluation (Messerlin 2006), demonstrating the economy-wide benefits of reduced domestic protection;
- the public advocacy of a strongly reformist Prime Minister, Robert Hawke, and Treasurer, Paul Keating, and their close personal advisors, working hand-in-glove with the permanent bureaucracy, thus effectively combining the top-down and bottom-up drive for reform; and by
- the public support given to liberalization by those emerging sectors – notably in services – which stood to gain and which served to weaken the lobbying power of traditional protectionist forces in the Country Party.

Helping losers and encouraging structural adjustment saw transitional budget support given to textiles and clothing producers to help them compete in a low-tariff environment; time-bound and decoupled assistance (see Chapter 8) to dairy farmers to compensate for adjustment-related falls in the value of farm assets; and more rigorous eligibility criteria for shipbuilding bounties, designed to focus assistance on those enterprises most likely to succeed in the future.

Putting trade in a broader policy framework saw complementarities developed with *macroeconomic policy*, via the floating of the Australian dollar in 1983 and the real depreciation needed to cushion adjustments in the traded sector following reductions in protection. Supportive *labour market policies* were introduced, which, via the Accord with the trades unions, preserved the real depreciation and associated competitive benefits by discounting wages from full indexation. Fiscal policy saw a *broadening of the tax base*, including through the taxation of capital gains. *Regulatory reform* of inefficient government monopolies began the process of upgrading vital transport,

---

communications and energy infrastructure. *Competition culture* was strengthened through the identification and correction of anticompetitive arrangements. And reforms were undertaken of the *education system*, including through changes to the basis of university funding.

Underpinning these domestic factors was an international environment conducive to reform, characterized by relatively strong growth, the implosion of the Soviet system, developing country abandonment of policies of import-substitution and the widespread embrace of the market economy.

Source: Edwards 1996; OECD 2005; Snape et al. 1998; Productivity Commission 2001.

A Changed Context: Understanding and Responding to Some New Challenges

Three new factors are often invoked as helping to explain why trade liberalization has become more difficult: the onset of multi-polarity and the growth of bilateralism; the increased complexity of issues; and the rise of non-state actors, accentuating concerns about a perceived race-to-the-bottom in trade-related areas. Each of these new factors will be considered briefly in turn, together with their links to the not-so-new underlying political economy of trade.

Multi-Polarity and the Rise of Bilateralism

The replacement of Cold War certainties with a more multi-polar world has had one decisive effect on the international trading system. Multi-polarity, by limiting the ability of the United States to control the agenda, has prompted a moderated US commitment to multilateral approaches to economic diplomacy and, correspondingly, to reduced US leadership of such approaches. Moderated US engagement has been compounded by ongoing American concerns about 'free riding' in the multilateral trading system, through application of the Most Favoured Nation (MFN) principle, and periodic US disenchantment with the dispute settlement system.[1]

A moderated US commitment to multilateralism has also been fuelled by the need to keep things simple given the transparency of US domestic politics and the requirement for the administration to engage and be accountable to Congress and to work within the constraints imposed by US domestic interests (Bayne and

---

[1]   See Chapter 3 for more detail on the evolution of the trading system from a US-led to a multi-polar system.

Woolcock 2011). The role of Congress and the need to be accountable to it have greatly contributed to the pursuit of bilateral deals, in the interests of simplicity.

The United States has not been alone of course in the pursuit of bilateralism. Preferential agreements have become the principal arm of trade diplomacy. Though political and strategic factors are often an important driver, PTAs are also widely seen as a way of dealing with the political economy of trade liberalization's concentrated costs and dispersed gains: by focusing on a narrow range of selected partners and thus making it possible to exclude politically sensitive sectors; by avoiding MFN commitments and alleged free riding; by securing reciprocity from partners; and by addressing perceived unfair competition linked to noncompliance with labour or environmental standards.

As well as diverting scarce negotiating skills away from multilateral efforts, bilateral arrangements can frustrate multilateral efforts in other ways: by creating vested interests against multilateral liberalization on the part of those benefiting from preferences; by weakening the incentive to negotiate multilaterally on the part of countries for whom excluded issues, like investment and competition, are particularly important and which can be addressed in bilateral agreements; by spoiling the atmospherics of multilateral negotiations by bringing controversial issues like core labour standards into the trade debate; and by complicating the agenda with a proliferation of rules.

But the dangers arising from reduced US leadership and the rise of bilateralism should not be exaggerated. The United States is still engaged. And bilateral deals through their ambition, particularly in the area of rules, 'can complement the multilateral system – but only if that system is itself robust – strengthening trade rules and bringing down MFN barriers so that the distorting effects of PTAs are held in check' (Heydon and Woolcock 2009: 260).

Increased Complexity: More Players and More Issues

It is frequently asserted that the multilateral liberalization of trade has become more difficult because of the greater number of participants and topics involved, and because of associated shifts in negotiating power and the emergence of new coalitions (Baldwin 2006; Gallagher 2008; Hurell and Narlikar 2006; Krugman 1997; Odell 2007). But it is not the increased numbers of players and issues per se that creates the challenge but rather the way in which the wider scope of the liberalization debate has changed the conception of gains and losses in the political economy of trade.

The WTO, which now (spring 2012) has 157 Members, is a more complicated place in which to do business than was the GATT in its early days. But the number of present Members is not greatly different to the 128 at the end of the Uruguay Round. Moreover, the new Members, who are essentially developing countries, have brought with them a record of, albeit qualified, unilateral liberalization. The challenge comes rather from the fact that the new Members, concerned about the development dimensions of trade and a need to redress perceived injustice, have come to place greater emphasis on the *relative*, as opposed to the *absolute*, gains from liberalization. The failure to advance in NAMA is due in no small measure to the concern of many developing countries to maximize their share of the gains from market opening even if it means forgoing greater absolute gains that would come from deeper own-liberalization – an outcome that is distributionally attractive but suboptimal in terms of efficiency.

The range of issues under active discussion has also become more complex. While the Uruguay Round introduced valuable frameworks for freer trade in agriculture and services, much of the actual job of liberalizing and of strengthening rules was left undone (Irwin 2002). At the same time, the debate has become much broader, with increased recognition of the importance of the conditions relating to FDI and competition policy for the conduct of trade.

But again, it is not the number of issues per se that creates the problem. The 2003 WTO ministerial meeting in Cancun is a case in point. Notwithstanding suggestions to the contrary (see for example Maswood 2007), the failure at Cancun was not the result of North–South conflict over an overloaded agenda. As the Cancun negotiations drew towards a close, it is true that the Africa Group was still demanding withdrawal from the negotiating agenda of all four Singapore Issues (investment, competition, government procurement and trade facilitation). However, with the agreement of the EU, the main *demandeur*, to remove all but trade facilitation, the Singapore Issues were no longer a deal breaker. The cause of breakdown lay rather in a well-established issue involving long-standing players. Luis Ernesto Derbez, the Mexican minister chairing the negotiations, brought the ministerial to a premature close not because of the new issues, but because he believed, from talks with representatives of the US Department of Agriculture, that there was no way that agreement could be reached between the United States and EU on agriculture, and therefore no prospect of movement in other areas, including NAMA and services. In short, failure at Cancun was the result of insufficient political will to tackle core business – the 'old' issue of the political economy of trade.[2]

Experience at the 2008 WTO ministerial meeting serves also to refute the too-many-issues argument. The chances of success at that meeting would have been enhanced, not weakened, by bringing in the opportunities from services liberalization and making more of potential cross-issue trade-offs (Diego-Fernandez 2008; Fergusson 2008).

The challenge of issue-complexity comes rather from the fact that the scope of the debate has changed. The pursuit of deeper integration has focussed attention on domestic issues such as sanitary and phytosanitary standards (SPS), technical barriers to trade (TBT) and intellectual property protection (Sally 2008; Wolf 2005). The notion of market access – including in the key areas of agriculture, manufacturing or services – has thus come to embrace behind-the-border policies and regulations, adding a new dimension to the notion of the costs of liberalization and intensifying concerns about national sovereignty and the political economy of trade.

---

[2]   Based on discussions in Cancun with officials engaged in the negotiations.

The Complicating Role of Non-State Actors

Non-state actors, principally in the form of non-governmental organizations (NGOs), have in recent years become much more significant players in economic diplomacy (Bhagwati 2007; Robertson 2006). On occasion, NGO activity has been for the better, as when Oxfam drew attention to the damaging effects of US cotton subsidies on producers in sub-Saharan Africa (Alston et al. 2007) or when various medical NGOs urged changes to the Trade-Related Aspects of Intellectual Property Rights (TRIPS) agreement to facilitate developing countries' access to medicines. Some commentators even speak of NGOs as embodying disinterested objectivity, so raising both efficiency and legitimacy in the conduct of trade policy (Albin 1999; Pigman 1999; Scholte 1999).

Such views are misplaced. NGOs are themselves largely unaccountable. They are no substitute for the ballot box (Anderson and Rieff 2005; Henderson 1999). In Member-driven bodies, like the WTO, IMF or World Bank, it is the job of democratically elected governments to formulate and implement policy, and to take responsibility for it. 'The bedrock of the trading system is enforceable agreements *among states*, most of them embodied in domestic law' (Wolf 2005: 209 [emphasis added]).

On balance, NGOs have made it harder for governments to deal with the political economy of trade, by exaggerating the costs of market opening and questioning the gains. The campaign of disinformation about the supposed risks to national health, culture and education (Sinclair 2000) that would come from the liberalization of trade in services has been both unhelpful and wrong. The General Agreement on Trade in Services (GATS) enshrines the right to regulate and countries are totally free not to liberalize any sectors of their choice (OECD 2002). And NGO-urging that developing countries seek the removal of investment, competition and government procurement from the multilateral trade agenda was a pyrrhic victory. Conditions of investment and competition are now a vital dimension of market access and it is developing countries that suffer most from the often arbitrary and opaque allocation of government contracts.

In addressing the costs of market opening, NGOs have been particularly active in stressing the trade-related dimension of liberalization and the perceived dangers of a race-to-the-bottom as countries supposedly disregard environmental and labour standards in order to gain a competitive advantage. In fact there is no evidence of such a race-to-the-bottom and, rather to the contrary, strong analytical and empirical indications that trade and trade liberalization have served to improve compliance with both environmental objectives (World Bank 2000) and core labour standards (OECD 2000). But this, perhaps counterintuitive, view is not easy to convey. NGOs, by claiming the higher moral ground have, in the words of Jagdish Bhagwati, 'put the proponents of free trade into a battle that is harder than ever to wage' (Bhagwati 2002: 48).

The role of NGOs should not be exaggerated. It is the exercise of government will, or lack of it, that ultimately determines the success, or failure, of policy. But neither should the role be unquestioningly welcomed, particularly at a time when the pro-trade voice of business seems particularly mute. As multilateral negotiating cycles get progressively longer and product cycles get shorter it is not surprising that business is attracted to the promise – not always realized – of PTAs. The result is a mixture of fear and complacency – fear on the part of a public, ever more attentive to the critics of liberalization, and complacency on the part of a business community, ever more supportive of bilateral deals (Heydon 2006).

Concern about the challenges raised by these new issues has led to suggestions as to how they might be dealt with. These often amount to a policy of capitulation: bilateral PTAs would be embraced as an alternative to multilateral negotiation; growing complexity would be met by narrowing the scope of the agenda, lowering ambition or seeking agreements among subsets of the willing; and the increased presence of NGOs would be met by giving them a more formal role in the process of policy formulation.

The conclusions reached here are rather different. Just as an understanding of the political economy of trade helps us judge the significance of the new issues so it provides guidance on ways to deal with them:

- *Articulating more effectively the case for broad-based multilateral liberalization* would increase the chances that a strengthened multilateral system would foster complementarity with bilateral PTAs and that cross-linkage of trade topics would reduce the dangers inherent in a mutual lowering of ambition to the point where a multilateral deal is not worth fighting for (Sutherland 2010).
- *Helping those who lose* from market opening would allay many of the concerns expressed by non-state actors and obviate the need to give them a formal role in policy formulation.
- *And placing trade liberalization in its broader domestic policy context* would address the complexity of issues while ensuring that distinct objectives, such as those linked to the environment or social standards, were addressed directly by dedicated policies and not by misguided attempts to enforce compliance through restrictions on trade.

References

Albin, C. 1999. Can NGOs enhance the effectiveness of international negotiations? *International Negotiation* 4(3): 371–87.

Alston, J.M., Sumner, D.A. and Brunke, H. 2007. *Impact of Reductions in US Cotton Subsidies on West African Cotton Producers*. Oxfam America.

Alt, J., Frieden, J., Gilligan, M.J., Rodrik, D. and Rogowski, R. 1996. The political economy of international trade: enduring puzzles and an agenda for inquiry. *Comparative Political Studies* 29(6): 689–717.

Anderson, K. and Rieff, D. 2005. Global civil society: a sceptical view. In *Global Civil Society*, edited by M. Anheier, M. Glasius and M. Kaldor. Baltimore: Johns Hopkins University Press, 26–39.

Baldwin, R. 2006. Failure of the WTO Ministerial Conference at Cancun: reasons and remedies. *World Economy* 29(6): 677.

Bartelsman, E., Haltiwanger, J. and Scarpetta, S. 2004. Microeconomic evidence of creative destruction in industrial and developing countries. *IZA Discussion Paper No. 1374*. Bonn: IZA Institute for the Study of Labour.

Bates, R. 1981. *Markets and State in Tropical Africa*. London: University of California Press.

Bayne, N. and Woolcock, S. 2011. *The New Economic Diplomacy: Decision-Making and Negotiations in International Economic Relations*. 3rd Edition. Aldershot: Ashgate.

Bhagwati, J. 1988. *Protectionism*. Cambridge, MA: MIT Press.

Bhagwati, J. 2002. *Free Trade Today*. Princeton: Princeton University Press.

Bhagwati, J. 2007. *In Defense of Globalization*. New York: Oxford University Press.

Bigsten, A., Gebreeyesus, M. and Soderbom, M. 2004. Do African manufacturing firms learn from exporting? *Journal of Development Studies* 40(3): 115–41.

Billmeier, A. and Nannicini, T. 2007. Trade openness and growth: pursuing empirical glasnost. *IMF Working Paper WP/07/156*. Washington, DC: International Monetary Fund.

Bloom, N., Draca, M. and Van Reenan, J. 2011. Trade induced technical change? The impact of Chinese imports on innovation, IT and productivity. *CEPR Discussion Paper 8236* (February). London: Centre for Economic Policy Research.

Bolaky, B. and Freund, C. 2004. Trade, regulations and growth. *World Bank Policy Research Working Paper*. Washington, DC: World Bank.

Brennan, G. 2007. Behavioural economics and public policy, in Australian Productivity Commission, *Roundtable Proceedings: Behavioural Economics and Public Policy*, Melbourne, 8 –9 August. Melbourne: Productivity Commission.

Bridges 2010. Weekly Trade News Digest. Available at: http://ictsd.org/news/bridgesweekly/ [accessed 2 March 2011].

Cling, J.P. 2006. Commerce, croissance, pauvrété et inégalités dans les PED: une revue de littérature. *Document de Travail DIAL*. Paris: Développement, Institutions et Analyses de Long Terme.

Cohen, S.D., Blecker, R.A. and Whitney, P.D. 2003. *Fundamentals of US Foreign Trade Policy: Economics, Politics, Laws and Issues*. Oxford: Westview Press.

Corden, W.M. 1966. The structure of a tariff system and the effective protective rate. *The Journal of Political Economy* 74(3): 221–37.

Destler, I.M. 2005. *American Trade Policy*. Washington, DC: Institute for International Economics.

Diego-Fernandez, M. 2008. Trade negotiations make strange bedfellows. *World Trade Review* 7(2): 423–53.

Dihel, N. and Dee, P. 2006. Services as outputs and intermediate inputs: the impact of liberalization, in *Trading Up: Economic Perspectives on Development Issues in the Multilateral Trading System*. Paris: Organisation for Economic Cooperation and Development, 163–91.

Dollar, D. and Kraay, A. 2002. Spreading the wealth. *Foreign Affairs* 81(1): 120–33.

Edwards, J. 1996. *Keating: The Inside Story*. Ringwood, Victoria: Penguin Books Australia.

Ehrlich, S.D. 2008. The tariff and the lobbyist: political institutions, interest group politics, and US trade policy. *International Studies Quarterly* 52: 427–45.

Evans-Klock, C., Kelly, P., Richards, P. and Vargha, C. 1998. Worker displacement: public policy and labour management initiatives in selected OECD countries. *ILO Employment and Training Papers*. Geneva: International Labour Organisation.

Fergusson, I.F. 2008. World Trade Organization negotiations: the Doha Development Agenda and prospects for the WTO. *CRS Report for Congress*. Washington, DC: Congressional Research Service.

Gallagher, K.P. 2008. Understanding developing country resistance to the Doha Round. *Review of International Political Economy* 15(1): 62–85.

Henderson, D. 1999. *The MAI Affair: A Story and its Lessons*. London: Royal Institute of International Affairs.

Heydon, K. 2006. Advancing the Doha Development Agenda. *Agenda* 13(2): 161–74.

Heydon, K. and Woolcock, S. 2009. *The Rise of Bilateralism: Comparing American, European and Asian Approaches to Preferential Trade Agreements*. Tokyo: United Nations University Press.

Hoekman, B. and Javorcik, B.S. 2004. Policies facilitating firm adjustment to globalization. *CEPR Discussion Paper No. 4692*. London: Centre for Economic Policy Research.

Hoekman, B. and Kostecki, M. 2009. *The Political Economy of the World Trading System*. 3rd Edition. Oxford: Oxford University Press.

Hurrell, A. and Narlikar, A. 2006. A new politics of confrontation? Brazil and India in multilateral trade negotiations. *Global Society* 20(4): 415–33.

Irwin, D.A. 1996. *Against the Tide*. Princeton: Princeton University Press.

Irwin, D.A. 2002. *Free Trade Under Fire*. Princeton: Princeton University Press.

Kaivanto, K. 2007. Trade-related job loss, wage insurance and externalities: an ex ante efficiency rationale for wage insurance. *The World Economy* 30(6): 962–71.

Kletzer, L. and Rosen, H. 2004. Honoring the commitment: assisting US workers hurt by globalization. Paper presented at the conference: Job Loss, Causes, Consequences and Policy Responses. Chicago Reserve Bank, Chicago 18 –19 November.

Krasner, S.D. 1976. State power and the structure of foreign trade. *World Politics* 28: 317–47.

Krugman, P. 1997. What should trade negotiators negotiate about? A review essay. *Journal of Economic Literature* 35: 113–20.

Leigh, D. 1990. *Does Training Work for Displaced Workers? A Survey of Existing Evidence*. Kalamazoo: W.E. Upjohn Institute for Employment Research.

Licandro, O. and Navas, A. 2007. Trade liberalization, competition and growth. *CEPR Discussion Paper No. DP6500*. London: Centre for Economic Policy Research.

Maswood, J. 2007. Developing countries and the G20 in the Doha Round, in *Developing Countries and Global Trade Negotiations*, edited by L. Crump and J. Maswood. Oxford: Routledge, 41–61.

Melitz, M.J. and Ottaviano, G. 2005. Market size, trade and productivity. *NBER Working Paper No. 11393*. Massachusetts: National Bureau of Economic Research.

Messerlin, P. 2006. *Europe After the 'No' Votes: Mapping a New Economic Path*. London: Institute of Economic Affairs.

Nordas, H., Miroudot, S. and Kowalski, P. 2006. Dynamic gains from trade. *OECD Trade Policy Working Paper No. 43*. Paris: OECD.

Odell, J.S. 2007. Growing power meets frustration in the Doha Round's first four years, in *Developing Countries and Global Trade Negotiations*, edited by L. Crump and S. Javed Maswood. Oxford: Routledge.

OECD. 2000. *International Trade and Core Labour Standards*. Paris: OECD.

OECD. 2002. *GATS: The Case for Open Services Markets*. Paris: OECD.

OECD. 2005. *Trade and Structural Adjustment: Embracing Globalisation*. Paris: OECD.

OECD. 2007a. Global Forum on Trade: Trade, Innovation and Growth, Paris, France, 15–16 October [Online]. Available at: www.oecd.org/tad/tradeglobalforum2007 [accessed 2 March 2011].

OECD. 2007b. *Economic Policy Reforms: Going for Growth 2007*. Paris: OECD.

OECD. 2009. *Trade Fact Sheets* [Online]. Available at: www.oecd.org/document/26/ 0,3746,en_2649_37431_43544221_1_1_1_37431,00.html [accessed 2 March 2011].

OECD. 2010. Responding to the Economic Crisis: Implications for Trade Policy. *TAD/TC/WP(2010)11*. Paris: OECD.

Olsen, M. 1965. *The Logic of Collective Action*. Cambridge, MA: Harvard University Press.

Olsen, M. 1982. *The Rise and Decline of Nations: Economic Growth, Stagflation and Social Rigidities*. New Haven: Yale University Press.

Panagariya, A. 2008. *India: The Emerging Giant*. New York: Oxford University Press.

Pareto, V. 1971. *Manual of Political Economy*. Translated by Ann S. Schwier. New York: Augustus M. Kelley.

Pigman, G.A. 1999. States, sovereignty and trade, in *Trade Politics*, edited by B. Hocking and S. McGuire. London: Routledge, 309–11.

Productivity Commission. 2001. *Structural Adjustment: Key Policy Issues*. Canberra: Productivity Commission.

Productivity Commission. 2009. Australia's Productivity Performance. *Submission to the House of Representatives Standing Committee on Economics*, September. Canberra: Productivity Commission.

Robertson, D. 2006. *International Economics and Confusing Politics*. Cheltenham: Edward Elgar.

Rogowski, R. 1989. *Commerce and Coalitions*. Princeton: Princeton University Press.

Sally, R. 2008. *Trade Policy New Century: The WTO, FTAs and Asia Rising*. London: The Institute of Economic Affairs.

Scholte, J.A. 1999. The World Trade Organization and civil society, in *Trade Politics*, edited by B. Hocking and S. McGuire. London: Routledge, 162–78.

Schumpeter, J. 1954. *History of Economic Analysis*. Published posthumously, edited by Elizabeth Boody Schumpeter. Oxford: Oxford University Press.

Sinclair, S. 2000. *How the World Trade Organisation's New 'Services' Negotiations Threaten Democracy*. Ottawa: Canadian Centre for Policy Alternatives.

Snape, R., Gropp, L. and Luttrell, T. 1998. *Australian Trade Policy 1965–1997: A Documentary History*. St. Leonards: Allen & Unwin.

Stigler, G.J. 1971. The theory of economic regulation. *Bell Journal of Economics and Management Science* 2: 3–21.

Stigler, G.J. 1974. Free riders and collective action: an appendix to theories of economic regulation. *Bell Journal of Economics and Management Science* 5: 359–65.

Stiglitz, J.E. 2002. *Globalization and its Discontents*. London: Penguin Books.

Sutherland, P. 2010. ECIPE Jan Tumlir Lecture. Brussels: ECIPE.

Ten Raa, T. and Mohnen, P. 2008. Competition and performance: the different roles of capital and labor. *Journal of Economic Behavior and Organization* 65: 573–84.

Tinbergen, J. 1956. *Economic Policy: Principles and Design*. Amsterdam: North Holland.

Winter-Ebmer, R. 2003. Coping with a structural crisis: evaluating an innovative redundancy-retraining project. *IZA Discussion Paper No.277*. Bonn: IZA Institute for the Study of Labour.

Winters, L.A. 2004. Trade liberalization and economic performance: an overview. *The Economic Journal* 114: 4–21.

Wolf, M. 2005. *Why Globalization Works*. New Haven: Yale University Press.

World Bank. 2000. Is globalization causing a race to the bottom in environmental standards? Part 4 of *Assessing Globalization*, PREM Economic Policy Group and Development Economics Group. Washington, DC: The World Bank.

WTO. 2008. *World Trade Report 2008: Trade in a Globalizing World*. Geneva: World Trade Organisation.

WTO. 2009. *Report to the TPRB from the Director General on the Financial and Economic Crisis and Trade-related Developments*. Geneva: WTO.

The Evolution of the
International Trading System

Stephen Woolcock

Introduction

Among the various issues in the current debate on the future of the international trading system, three stand out: can the World Trade Organization (WTO) function in a progressively more multi-polar trading system; has the WTO reached the limits of what it can sensibly cover; and is the multilateral system being undermined by the rise of – predominantly bilateral – preferential trade and investment agreements?[1] Various chapters in this volume address these issues, but in seeking an understanding of such current trends it helps to know how the system has evolved. This chapter therefore considers the period from the establishment of the General Agreement on Tariffs and Trade (GATT) in 1947 to the Doha Development Agenda (DDA) negotiations of the WTO. It shows how the trading system has evolved from a US-led system, through one shaped by a club of developed Organization for Economic Cooperation and Development (OECD) countries, to one with a much more heterogeneous power structure. In other words, the trading system has had to accommodate shifts in relative economic power before. The scope of agreements has also expanded, largely in line with the contemporary preferences of major players concerning what constituted trade issues rather than any objective criteria. Trade policy, like other fields, has also been shaped by precedent or path dependency. The positions of countries and interest groups today have evolved from those ten or 30 years ago, but trade preferences may be the result of capture and often change slowly, so that the past can form the basis of current preferences. Finally, the chapter shows that 'multilateralism' needs some qualification. What existed before the rise of bilateralism after the mid-1990s, was based on multilateral

---

[1]   For a discussion of the challenges facing the WTO and various proposals for how it should be reformed see Sutherland Report (2007), Warwick Commission (2007) and Jones (2010).

principles, but shaped by a more complex combination of plurilateral, regional and bilateral influences on negotiations.[2]

The Founding of the Post-1947 International Trading System

The post-war trading system was shaped by the experience of protection, economic nationalism and trade discrimination in the 1920s and 1930s that contributed to the collapse of the international economy and the political conflict of the interwar period. The United States emerged from the Second World War as the dominant economic power and it was the United States that provided leadership in the establishment of the GATT. This policy was based on the US domestic consensus and on the position of the US Congress, which favoured reciprocal trade liberalization. This principle was codified in the 1933 US Reciprocal Trade Agreements Act, which reversed the protectionist Smoot–Hawley Tariff of 1930. The US-led system therefore differed from the unilateral trade policy pursued by Britain before 1914.

The original intention had been to establish an International Trade Organization (ITO) alongside the Bretton Woods institutions of the International Monetary Fund (IMF) and the World Bank (IBRD). Indeed, negotiations on trade began before those on international monetary relations, but broke down because of an American determination to put an end to preferential trade agreements (PTAs) and the British reluctance to dismantle the Imperial Preferences established at the Ottawa Conference of 1933. The Havana Charter was negotiated in 1948, but was never presented to the US Congress for ratification. The demise of the ITO has been explained by opposition from protectionists, who saw the liberal intent as a threat, and perfectionists who saw too much scope for government intervention (Diebold 1952). Foreign policy also played a role in the sense that the Truman Administration preferred, at the onset of the Cold War, to expend its political capital getting legislation on the Marshall Plan and NATO through the Congress rather than the ITO. The GATT, which had been negotiated in 1947 as part of the ITO process, also offered much of what the United States wanted and a contractual agreement between states required no congressional approval.

The GATT, as the name implies, was an agreement rather than an international organization, and a negotiating forum in which initiatives for new trade liberalization or rulemaking came from the Contracting Parties (CPs) and not from the staff of a large secretariat. In actual fact, staff and the offices of the old League of Nations were initially used as the secretariat. The GATT consisted of a framework of basic principles and rules as well as a series of tariff reductions; the first of a series of multilateral tariff reductions that were to follow in the next 70 years.

[2] For general readings covering the evolution of and current status of the world trading system see Jackson (2000), Trebilcock and Howse (1995) and Hoekman and Kostecki (2001).

Principles of the GATT

The GATT 1947 was based on non-discrimination in international trade. The codification of this took two forms, the most favoured nation (MFN) principle (Article I, GATT) and national treatment (NT) (Article III, GATT). The MFN provision obliged all CPs not to discriminate between countries. Any favourable treatment, such as a reduced tariff, provided to another – most favoured – nation had to be extended to all CPs. National treatment required that all products imported into a customs territory be treated the same as nationally made like products. MFN therefore allowed for no PTAs and thus discrimination. National treatment precluded discrimination against foreign products, but left national governments scope to regulate (Jackson 2000).

The GATT 1947 was also based on some de facto norms, notably reciprocity and flexibility. The understanding was that tariff liberalization would be achieved through mutual tariff concessions that ensured 'global' or across-the-board reciprocity. Global reciprocity meant a broad balance of benefits for CPs and differed from the more protectionist idea of reciprocity within narrow sectors. Tariff negotiations were conducted bilaterally between an importer and the 'principal suppliers' of a product, but then multilateralized through the MFN obligation. Provided there was global reciprocity, CPs could therefore decide how fast they wished to liberalize. Multilateral rounds of negotiations offered a means of ensuring 'concessions' in areas of 'defensive' interests could be traded against lower tariffs in sectors of 'offensive' interests.

The GATT 1947 was flexible in that it did not require national governments to deregulate or adopt any specific standards, but merely not to use regulation to discriminate or as a disguised form of protection. There was also flexibility in that governments could decide how they wished to liberalize, but free riding aside, limited concessions meant limited satisfaction of offensive interests. The GATT also provided – and continues to provide – flexibility in the form of various exceptions to the rules. Article VI (GATT 1947) provides for the application of antidumping duties on imports that cause or threaten 'injury' to a national industry and are sold, 'unfairly' or at a price below the cost of production (see Chapter 6). Relatively loose wording in the GATT rules and the fact that such duties could be applied selectively against certain exports meant that this provision found, and continues to find, wide application as a means of easing import competition. Article XVIII allows restrictions on imports when a CP is suffering balance of payments (BoP) difficulties. This provision found application among developing countries in particular and was, for example, used by India on a regular basis well into the 1990s. Article XIX provides for non-selective safeguard measures, for example tariffs or quotas, when there is substantial injury to an industry due to an unforeseen surge in imports. A country applying safeguards is, however, required to compensate the exporting countries affected by reducing tariffs on other products.

Article XX provides a general exemption from GATT rules for measures taken to protect human, animal and plant life. Such measures have to be proportionate. This article found use during the 1980s with increased awareness of environmental concerns (see Chapter 13). Finally, Article XXIV offers an exemption from MFN for customs unions and free trade areas. The motives behind the inclusion of Article XXIV in 1947 are not fully clear, but it was not drafted with major preferential agreements like the European Union in mind and was probably intended to provide for smaller customs unions that existed when the GATT 1947 was drafted. Subsequently Article XXIV has found very wide application as a legal basis for free trade agreements (FTAs) (see Chapter 22). Rather than a charter for free trade, the GATT could therefore be best described as a system of managed trade liberalization.

The Kennedy Round 1963–7: The First Major Multilateral

Following the original tariff reductions of 1947 further but limited liberalization was agreed in a number of early multilateral trade rounds between 1949 and 1961. These rounds brought in the Federal Republic of Germany in 1950 and Japan in 1955. In early November 1961 the United States proposed a new comprehensive round of trade negotiations that was to become the Kennedy Round. The principal US motivation was to limit the effects of the common external tariff (CET) of the European Economic Community (EEC) and to establish GATT discipline over the EEC's Common Agricultural Policy (CAP). The CET replaced the bound MFN tariffs of the individual EEC members so the US wanted to ensure the CET bindings were as low or lower than the bound tariffs of the individual EEC member states it replaced in order to minimize trade diversion.[3] There was no discipline of agricultural trade following the 1953 waiver of GATT rules for US agricultural support programmes. The CAP was based on a price support scheme which implied export subsidies to dispose of any surpluses when world prices were lower than the prices guaranteed under the CAP. Such subsidies were seen as 'unfair' competition for US agricultural exports on third markets.[4] The Kennedy Round was also motivated by a strategic interest in strengthening the western capitalist system in the face of Soviet competition at what was the height of the Cold War following the Cuban missile crisis (Evans 1971).

The enhanced market power of the EEC, thanks to the CET, facilitated significant mutual, linear tariff reductions averaging 30 per cent in manufactures. This necessitated concessions from the US Congress, which viewed tariff reductions of more than 20 per cent as going beyond the 'peril point' at which US industries would be injured. The Trade Expansion Act of 1962 in fact provided for up

---

[3]   Trade diversion is the reduction of more competitive imports from a third country as a result of a tariff preference established between members of a customs union or free trade area. Less competitive products are imported from within the preferential area because of the lower tariff. Generally speaking, trade diversion always accompanies the trade creation resulting from a preference.

[4]   For agricultural trade in general see Chapter 8.

to 50 per cent reductions.[5] In terms of non-tariff rules, there was agreement on antidumping measures that sought to codify practice in this field, but neither this nor the abolition of the American Selling Price (ASP) tariff system for chemicals was implemented by the US Congress. Such selective approval of agreements by the US Congress led ultimately to the introduction of the so-called 'fast-track' procedure in 1974 that would provide only for approval or rejection of a trade agreement, and not of selected parts. EEC opposition blocked the reintroduction of GATT discipline over agriculture but in May 1967 the foreign policy considerations of the State Department prevailed in the face of opposition from the US Department of Agriculture and the US Executive opted for an agreement without agriculture rather than no agreement.

The Kennedy Round was more transatlantic than multilateral. Other developed economies, such as Australia, had ambiguous positions on liberalization and although the 1960s saw many developing countries (DCs) join the GATT on independence, these were accommodated by the introduction of Part IV of the GATT (see also Chapter 18). Part IV facilitated the exemption of DCs from the obligation of making reciprocal liberalization commitments, whilst guaranteeing them MFN treatment under Article I. Developing countries favoured this because it allowed them to follow the development paradigm of the time which was the promotion of infant industry policies as a means of ensuring economic as well as political independence (see Chapter 2). For the developed countries Part IV simplified negotiations by removing many smaller economies from the equation, but the adoption of Part IV in 1964 and the subsequent enabling clause effectively created a two-tier trading system.

The Tokyo Round 1973–9: Containing New Protectionism

Launched with the Tokyo Declaration in September 1973, this GATT round was the product of US pressure for stronger GATT discipline of what it saw as the 'unfair' policies of its main trading partners. Agreement to negotiate had formed part of the Smithsonian Agreement of December 1971 that sought to ease tensions following the end of dollar convertibility with gold and the 1971 imposition by the United States of a 10 per cent tariff to pressurize the Federal Republic of Germany and Japan to revalue their currencies. Faced with a rising trade deficit, the United States argued that its competitors needed to revalue their exchanges rates and stop intervening to support national champions by means of subsidies, preferential use of public contracts and technical barriers to trade. For the United States therefore

---

[5]   The timetable of trade negotiations up to and including the Uruguay Round has been in effect determined by US trade legislation. For example, it was no accident that the Kennedy Round negotiations finished one day before the expiry of trade authority under the 1962 Trade Expansion Act. The timetable of other rounds has been similarly influenced by the existence and duration of negotiating authority granted by the US Congress.

the trade agenda had to be extended by including such non-tariff or behind-the-border issues and by strengthening the dispute settlement provisions of the GATT to improve enforcement of the rules. There was also a concern, shared by the European Community, about increased competition from Japan, the Newly Industrializing Countries (NICs) and DCs in low value added sectors such as textiles and clothing. In other words, the trade agenda was already being extended and responding to a shift in the balance of market power.

The negotiations were therefore framed by the United States and driven by domestic interests to include tariffs, agriculture and non-tariff issues on the agenda.[6] The EC resisted pressure to liberalize agriculture and to impose tight disciplines on the 'non-tariff barriers' because most EC member states made use of industrial policy-type instruments.[7] Both the United States and EU included textiles and clothing on the agenda. Japan and the NICs were keen to see more discipline of contingent protection by the EC and United States in the form of antidumping or voluntary export restraint (VER) agreements, but resisted the EC's idea that the GATT safeguard provisions should be reformed to allow for selective safeguards.

Progress in the negotiations was held up by international events. Following the Yom Kippur War of October 1973 and the Arab oil embargo, there followed the first oil crisis, a fourfold increase in oil prices in late 1973. The rising tide of 'new protectionism' in the form of voluntary export restraint agreements against exports from the NICs, however, strengthened the desire to conclude an agreement. The G7 summits, established in 1975, provided political support and, in the run up to the 1978 Bonn summit, a nine-page outline of an agreement was tabled. The end result was modest compared to the Kennedy Round. There were tariff reductions averaging 35 per cent over eight years to 1988 based on the Swiss formula favoured by the EC because it helped bring down US tariff peaks.[8] But 'sensitive' sectors were excluded from cuts. Codes were agreed on subsidies and countervailing duties, customs valuation,[9] technical barriers to trade and a government procurement agreement (GPA), but these were too weak to have much effect. Likewise the revised

---

[6]   The US Secretary of State Kissinger sought to include scope to offer the Soviet Union MFN status in the trade legislation as part of the US détente policy, but this ran into problems in Congress which, in the Jackson–Vanik amendment, effectively linked trade to the performance of the USSR on human rights.

[7]   The 1974 Trade Act in the United States provided for a number of contingency measures including the use of countervailing duties against subsidized imports. It also introduced the infamous Section 301 fair trade provision that was to find later application in the 1980s. On the other hand the 1974 Act established Fast Track and modernized US trade policymaking.

[8]   The Swiss formula used was $y = 14x/(14+x)$ which meant for example, that a 20 per cent tariff was reduced to 8 per cent and a 50 per cent tariff to just under 11 per cent (see also Chapter 4).

[9]   Customs authorities designate a customs code for each product. As tariffs vary from product to product, how products are allocated can determine the tariff. The Brussels Tariff Nomenclature of 1950 had been adopted by all GATT members in 1970, but some issues remained, such as the continued use of the American Selling Price (ASP) according

provisions on antidumping failed to impose much discipline, with the US Congress resisting more effective rules on how to determine 'material' injury as a condition for applying duties. There was no agreement on a safeguards code, which meant in effect no discipline of VERs. Following the precedent of the previous negotiations the EC was able to exclude agriculture. Agreement was, however, reached on a Multi-Fibre Arrangement (MFA) that provided an extensive system of protection against textile and clothing imports from NICs and developing countries.

Developing countries were still not inclined to lower tariffs and spent much of the 1970s arguing for a New International Economic Order (NIEO) that would give them a greater say in policy, more development aid, debt relief and access to OECD markets. Under these conditions the two-tier system based on Part IV continued, but now included the Generalized System of Preferences (GSP) that permitted developed economies to offer (autonomous, that is to say, unbound) tariff preferences for developing country exports as another exception to MFN. Qualified MFN was also used for the non-tariff barrier codes that were signed only by the developed OECD economies. The Tokyo Round therefore witnessed the emergence of a form of 'club model' in which the agenda and negotiations were shaped by the leading OECD economies rather than the United States. But the 'multilateral' system still excluded the Soviet bloc and, effectively, the developing countries of the South.

The Uruguay Round 1986–94:
Towards an Inclusive, Rules-based System

The period of the Uruguay Round (UR) negotiations marked a significant *broadening* of the trading system in the form of a more active participation by more countries and an associated increased heterogeneity of the trading system, as well as a *deepening* with the most significant increase in the scope of the trade regime to date. There was also a shift to a significantly more rules-based international trading system.[10] As in previous decades it was the United States that pressed for this agenda from the early 1980s (Bergsten and Cline 1982). Although no agreement on launching a new comprehensive round could be reached at the 1982 GATT Ministerial meeting, mainly because of European reluctance, work on an agenda including agriculture, services and intellectual property began in the OECD. By the middle of the decade the reform in the European Community in the form of the single European market for goods and to a lesser degree services and a move

---

to which tariffs on chemical imports into the United States were based on the selling price of the chemical.

[10] For general histories of the Uruguay Round see Golt (1988) for the early stages, Croome (1995) and Stewart (1993) for a detailed negotiating history.

away from promoting national champions, brought about a shift in the EC towards a more liberal, rules-based approach to external trade and investment.

The decision to establish a Preparatory Committee for the new round was effectively taken by a club of OECD members in April 1985 (Preeg 1970: 54). As the negotiation progressed it became clear that it was the Quad (United States, EC, Japan and Canada) – and within this, the US–EC duopoly – that shaped the agenda and determined progress (Woolcock 1990). The most important developing countries in the Preparatory Committee, Brazil and India which led the so-called 'Group of 10' (G10), opposed a new comprehensive round. The G10 was not able to block progress towards a new round because a number of NICs were keen to see a strengthening of the rules to contain EC and US protectionism. The G10 of the 1980s could be seen as a rather less successful forerunner of the G20 established under similar leadership in 2003 (Narlikar 2010). The G10 aside, the UR was not characterized by the type of North–South divisions seen in the Tokyo Round. Issue-based coalitions were formed, such as the Cairns group of agricultural exporters and the Café au Lait group, led by Colombia and Switzerland. Japan and the Asian NICs, such as Hong Kong, were also more active.

The UR resulted in a more inclusive WTO with the ending of Part IV, of the qualified MFN codes and of the two-tier trading system by means of a 'Single Undertaking'. This was an aim of developed countries that wished to deal with free riding and to ensure that the stronger NICs graduated to full membership of the trading system. Special and differential treatment (SDT) for developing countries remained, but in the form of expectations of less-than-full reciprocity in commitments or longer transition periods to adopt rules. By the end of the round in 1994 the Cold War had ended and many transition economies, though not Russia, were joining the WTO. Thus although the Round was shaped by the OECD Club or the Quad, the outcome created a far more inclusive international trading system. Indeed by the time China joined in 2001 one could say the WTO was a global organization in a way that the GATT never was.

Reaching Further Beyond Market Access

The UR was the most comprehensive round of negotiations to date. Not only were all the agenda items inherited from the Tokyo Round revisited, but significant new issues were added in the form of services, investment and intellectual property rights (initially limited to counterfeit goods). Tariff reductions were based on targets for average cuts and zero-for-zero agreements in which tariffs were removed in certain sectors. The result was an overall average reduction of 30 per cent in tariffs, but tariff peaks, the higher tariffs for certain more sensitive products, remained. Developed countries average bound MFN tariffs in manufactures were reduced to between 4–5 per cent, with average tariffs in agriculture of around 15 per cent. Developing country bound MFN tariffs in manufactures were higher in a range between 15 and 50 per cent, with higher rates again for agriculture.[11] Developing countries also bound fewer tariff lines.

Agriculture was brought back under GATT discipline in the UR in the face of dogged EC resistance thanks to pressure from the United States and the Cairns group, but the level of actual liberalization was fairly limited (see Chapter 8). Agriculture was generally the issue that determined the pace of progress in the negotiations as a whole, and the (slow) pace of reform of the CAP in Europe determined the pace of progress in agriculture. There were three pillars to the agriculture negotiations: reductions in export and domestic subsidies and market access (tariff liberalization). After many years of negotiation and many crises, agreement was reached on agriculture between US and EC negotiators in Blair House in Washington in November 1992. After further internal debate and controversy within the EU, the final outcome was a reduction of 21 per cent in the volume of exports benefiting from export subsidies, a 20 per cent reduction in domestic subsidies and a 36 per cent reduction in tariffs, an outcome that was rather nearer the EC than the declared US aim of elimination of all subsidies.[12]

Of the new issues the Trade-Related Intellectual Property Rights (TRIPs) proved to be the most controversial. This constituted a significant shift towards establishing positive obligations on WTO members. The GATT tends to require governments to not do things, but the TRIPs, which was favoured by research-intensive industries, such as pharmaceuticals in the United States, Europe and Japan, requires all signatories to the WTO to comply with a number of international conventions covering protection of patents, literary and other rights (see Chapter 16). Noncompliance with these conventions opens the country concerned to the threat of trade retaliation. TRIPs was opposed by DCs because it was seen as benefiting the developed economies and limiting the ability of DCs to access technology and essential medicines at a reasonable price. But ultimately the developing countries accepted the TRIPs agreement when offered the carrot of liberalizing textiles and clothing and threatened with the stick of US unilateral trade sanctions for non-enforcement of IPRs under Section 337 of the US Trade Act.

The General Agreement on Trade in Services (GATS) was, in comparison, less controversial. This consisted of a framework agreement and a series of commitments to apply MFN and national treatment to foreign suppliers of services, whether these services were supplied across borders (Mode 1), by means of the consumer moving to another country to obtain a service (Mode 2), by investment or establishment of the service provider in the host country (Mode 3) or by workers entering the host country market (Mode 4) (see Chapter 9). The GATS outcome has been seen as a glass half empty, because 'liberalization' was generally little more than a

---

[11]   Bound MFN tariffs are the rates that WTO members cannot exceed. Many countries and especially developing countries generally have lower applied tariffs. For example, developing country average applied tariffs are nearer the range of 10–15 per cent for manufactures. The difference between the applied and bound tariff rates provides countries with flexibility to increase tariffs and is termed the 'water' in the tariff.

[12]   On the outcome of the Uruguay Round see Schott (1994).

commitment to bind what had in any case been liberalized unilaterally. Mode 3 commitments in the GATS constitute commitments to provide pre-establishment national treatment for foreign service providers, in other words access for foreign investment. Commitments are made in schedules using positive listing to specify sectors that are included, but also negative listing within these sectors to exclude certain activities. For example, a positive listing could mean business services are covered, but a negative listing could then exclude lawyers. Investment in the Round also came in the shape of Trade-Related Investment Measures (TRIMs) negotiations. The TRIMs covered 'performance requirements' on investors by host governments, such as those specifying local content or export requirements. Host governments require these in an effort to ensure that foreign investment contributes to value added in their economy. The TRIMs agreement prohibited six core performance requirements, but stopped a long way short of a full investment agreement covering liberalization and investment protection.

The negotiations in the 1980s also produced more effective GATT rules on non-tariff barriers. The Tokyo Round codes were replaced with fully fledged agreements. In some cases, such as antidumping, a good deal of discretion was left for national governments, but the agreements generally strengthened multilateral disciplines. On safeguards, multilateral discipline was effectively re-established over VERs one of the main instruments of new protectionism. The non-selective character of Article XIX was largely retained and all VERs had to be notified to the WTO and phased out. On subsidies GATT rules were made more operational by reaffirming the ban on selective state subsidies, but permitting support for general R&D, regional development and environmental policies. To this end a 'traffic light' system was introduced that classified aid as totally banned (red), potentially trade distorting and thus subject to countervail (amber) and permitted (green).[13] The rules for applying countervailing duties were also tightened.

A more sophisticated approach to technical barriers to trade (TBTs) was also developed that followed the EU model by distinguishing between mandatory technical regulations, conformance assessment and voluntary standards. National treatment remained the norm for (mandatory) regulations and conformance assessment and a voluntary code was established for standards-making bodies. EU experience was also followed with provisions promoting mutual recognition and the use of agreed international standards. In the related field of sanitary and phytosanitary (SPS) measures, the agreement reached was one that permits controls on imports that threaten human, animal or plant health, but only when these are based on scientific evidence and are not disguised forms of protection. In cases where there is a potential risk, but not yet sufficient scientific evidence, the Agreement on SPS allows for the use of precautionary measures until such evidence is available. When this agreement was negotiated European consumers had not yet been exposed to 'mad cow disease' (Bovine Spongiform Encephalopathy or BSE). Under consumer pressure following the case of 'mad cow disease' in which scientists had assured consumers that beef with BSE was safe to eat when it was

---

[13] The 'traffic light' regime was due for review in 1999 but was not extended.

not, a number of European governments moved, in conflict with the SPS rules, to ban certain products regardless of existing scientific evidence.[14]

Finally the negotiations reached beyond the border in adopting a plurilateral Government Procurement Agreement (GPA) that formed part of a political package with the UR rather than part of the Single Undertaking. The GPA (1994) strengthened the framework rules agreed in the 1979 GPA and included in particular a 'bid challenge' provision that enables aggrieved tenderers to challenge decisions by (public) purchasing entities that they consider to be illegal. It also introduced tighter, more extensive rules on transparency and contract award procedures. The second element of the GPA is a set of bilateral, reciprocity-based 'liberalization' negotiations on coverage specifying which government departments, levels of government and public enterprises are required to comply with the rules. Thanks in part to an extension of the EU regime to include public utilities, the 1994 GPA had broader coverage but not many more signatories than the 1979 agreement.

The UR therefore constituted the most significant extension of the scope of the international trade regime to date. Included in its definition of trade were many measures that reached well beyond border measures and into areas that had previously remained under national policy autonomy. The UR also moved beyond national treatment to require positive action by signatories to the WTO to comply with certain agreed international standards.

Institutional Strengthening

The UR strengthened the multilateral institutions. In 1988 as part of an 'early harvest' the Trade Policy Review Mechanism (TPRM) was established. The TPRM provides for regular peer reviews of all WTO members' trade policies, based on reports produced by both the WTO member concerned and the WTO Secretariat. The UR also established the World Trade Organization (WTO). Based on a Canadian proposal in 1990, the idea of creating a stronger institution found widespread support, with the most vocal opposition coming from the US Congress that feared it would encroach upon its sovereignty. The agreement establishing the WTO largely codified existing GATT practice, such as one member one vote, but with consensus of all countries present and not objecting as normal practice. The WTO incorporates the GATT (1994) the revised GATT, the GATS and TRIPs agreements. In order to ensure that the Single Undertaking was effective, GATT 1947 was wound up and all countries wishing to benefit from the strengthened rules-based system that is the GATT/WTO were obliged to sign up to the WTO. One innovation with the WTO was the creation of regular biennial Ministerial meetings.

Last but by no means least, the UR included the Understanding on Dispute Settlement (UDS) (Jackson 1998) (see also Chapter 21). This finally ended the ability of individual countries to veto the adoption of dispute settlement panel reports,

---

[14] There then followed a number of actions against the EU under WTO dispute settlement on beef hormones and genetically modified products.

something the United States had been seeking for decades. Henceforth panel reports were considered adopted unless there was a consensus against doing so. An Appellate Body (AB) was also added in order to ensure that panel decisions were coherent and consistent with established GATT/WTO principles. The UR negotiations, concluded by D-G Peter Sutherland in December 1993, therefore produced a comprehensive, rules-based and global trade regime.

The Doha Development Agenda (DDA): Modest Ambition for the WTO

The assumption among the trade policy community after the completion of the UR was that the next stage would be an extension of the trade regime to cover investment. Given the nature of international markets and the close links between trade and investment, the absence of comprehensive multilateral rules on investment was seen as an anomaly. At the first WTO Ministerial meeting in Singapore investment was therefore included on the agenda.[15] Other topics for discussion were competition policy and government procurement which, together with investment and trade facilitation, became the 'Singapore issues' most strongly promoted by the EU and Japan. Indeed, it was around this time that the EU emerged as the main proponent of a new round of comprehensive negotiations. But the balance of influence in the WTO was shifting. Having joined 'the club' with the Single Undertaking, developing countries expected to have a say in shaping the rules. Economic growth, combined with relatively high tariffs, in a number of emerging markets also gave these WTO members more leverage than the G10 had had in the previous decade. In comparison, the OECD markets, although still much bigger were growing more slowly and had already liberalized much of their economies.

The EU lead had only lukewarm support from the United States and faced opposition from many developing countries. In 1998, at the second WTO Ministerial meeting that marked 50 years of the GATT, the United States agreed to support efforts to launch a new round, but these failed in Seattle in late 1999 due to differences between the OECD economies, opposition from developing countries, which believed an agenda was again being imposed upon them by the OECD countries and a lack of resolve on the part of national governments in the face of growing civil society opposition to 'globalization' (Schott 2000).

The DDA was finally launched in Doha in December 2001, thanks in part to the use of 'constructive ambiguity' in the wording of the *communiqué*. Failure in Seattle had also been, in part, due to efforts to agree on a very detailed text. The EU remained the main *'demandeur'* for a new comprehensive round, in which it sought

---

[15]   For a discussion of the priorities for the new round as seen in 1996 see Schott (1996) and OECD (1996).

progress on the Singapore issues and market opening for services and manufactures in the larger emerging markets, in return for concessions on agriculture. The EU strategy favoured multilateral negotiations over preferential agreements and adopted a de facto moratorium on new preferential trade negotiations in 1999. In contrast to previous rounds, the United States provided only qualified support for a comprehensive round from 2001 when it obtained new Trade Promotion Authority. The US Administration began pursuing an active policy of 'competitive liberalization'. This was a pragmatic approach in which bilateral, regional or multilateral approaches to liberalization were to be pursued depending on which offered the best prospects of results. Developing countries illustrated their intention to have a greater say by first making the launch of the DDA conditional upon a statement interpreting the TRIPs agreement in a way that favoured developing country interests. This was the Doha Declaration on TRIPs and essential medicines. Secondly, the developing countries led by India insisted on an 'explicit consensus' on the final agenda. As smaller DCs or least developed countries (LDCs) are sometimes not present in negotiations and often remained silent when they were, specifying explicit consensus clearly gave the DCs a stronger veto power.

Between 2001 and 2003 a limited commitment to a new round combined with a general economic slowdown in 2001 slowed progress on the 'modalities' for negotiation. In an effort to move things along the EU and United States produced a joint text on agriculture in the run up to the 2003 WTO Ministerial Meeting in Cancun. Given that transatlantic differences on agriculture had determined the pace of the UR there was a belief, not shared by all policymakers in the EU, that an EU–US agreement would help. In effect the reverse was the case. The joint text was seen by the major developing countries as a bid to sustain a transatlantic duopoly over the trade agenda and continued protection for EU and US special agricultural interests, while pushing for DC concessions on other issues, such as services, non-agricultural market access (NAMA) and the Singapore issues. Brazil and India, joined now by China and other developing countries, formed the G20 and came forward with alternative proposals that made the overall ambition of the round dependent on the willingness of the EU and United States to make concessions on agriculture. The Cancun meeting, which was supposed to map out a course for the DDA, failed even though the scale of ambition had been reduced by the EU effectively taking the three most controversial Singapore issues (investment, competition and government procurement) off the table.

A more modest agenda was put together in the shape of the August 2004 Framework Agreement. This excluded the Singapore issues, except trade facilitation, and focused on the traditional topics of agriculture and NAMA. Even services slipped to a less than central position and although other topics were included in the negotiations, such as rules on regional trade agreements, antidumping and some aspects of intellectual property rights such as geographic indications (GIs), it became clear that the main substance of the negotiations concerned agriculture and NAMA. In these the G20 sought progress on agriculture from both the United States (reductions in domestic support) and the EU (elimination of export subsidies and lower tariffs). In return the EU and United States sought reductions in tariffs on manufactures in the major emerging markets as well as progress on services. As always this simple depiction of the G20 against the EU and United States or perhaps the OECD countries is inaccurate. In reality the picture was much more complex with tensions within both 'blocs'. For example, there was certainly some concern among China's G20 partners as well as within the United States and EU about lowering tariffs on products in which China was already very competitive.

The DDA stumbled on through times when there appeared to be some progress, such as at the Hong Kong 2005 WTO Ministerial meeting, and times when negotiations were 'on life support' (Lee and Wilkinson 2007). In 2007 and especially in 2008 major efforts were made in the various negotiating groups in Geneva and in high-level meetings away from the glare of the news media that had accompanied the big WTO ministerial conferences. In 2008 an agreement was near after progress was made on the modalities for tariff and subsidy reductions in agricultural and tariff reductions in NAMA.[16] But the negotiations failed, ostensibly on the issue of a special safeguard mechanism (SSM) for agriculture in which India with support from China wanted scope to re-impose tariffs in the event of import surges of agricultural products in order to protect its subsistence farmers. The United States in particular saw the proposals as a means of maintaining or even increasing protection, rather than safeguarding food security. In reality however, the main hindrance to agreement was a lack of domestic political support among key WTO members (see also Chapter 2).

The Rise of Bilateralism

As noted above, a number of WTO members were already considering active free trade agreement (FTA) policies before and as the DDA was launched. There had been a strengthening of EU integration in the mid-1980s and the adoption of the Canada–US FTA (CUSFTA) in 1988. In 1990 negotiations began on a wider North American Free Trade Agreement (NAFTA) to include Mexico. Arguably FTA activity began even before the end of the UR. At the time this was seen as facilitating multilateralism, but it could also be argued that by early 1991, the broad outlines of the UR could be seen in the Dunkel Text.[17] So that those interests seeking more in terms of access or rules would turn their minds to alternative negotiating fora, such as bilateral agreements, given that the next chance of getting satisfaction from the multilateral agenda was clearly going to be years away. In the early 2000s FTA activity increased and as the DDA began to falter and the ambition of the multilateral approach was reduced, FTAs began to be seen as alternatives to

---

[16] For details of the Chair's negotiating texts and progress reached in the various negotiating groups at this stage see WTO documents at www.wto.org/english/tratop_e/dda_e/dda_e.htm.

[17] The GATT Director General Arthur Dunkel produced what was intended to be a compromise final text in December 1990.

multilateral negotiations. Indeed, one could argue that the option of the bilateral alternative reduced the incentive to negotiate multilaterally. Whatever the motives, FTAs became a central feature of the international trading system during the 2000s. This has raised questions concerning the compatibility of FTAs with a multilateral trading system and whether FTAs are 'building blocks or stumbling blocks' for a wider system (Heydon and Woolcock 2009). As time progressed and it became clear that the increase in FTAs was not a temporary phenomenon the debate shifted more to whether it would be possible to 'multilateralize regionalism' (Baldwin and Thornton 2008). Whilst the terms regionalism and regional trade agreements continued to be used, the trend during the 2000s was very clearly towards bilateralism.

The number of FTAs increased but so did their scope, with agreements involving the major OECD economies being especially more comprehensive.[18] For example, the US agreements all included comprehensive investment provisions and TRIPs plus provisions on intellectual property rights. The EU agreements often included, in one form or another, the Singapore issues as did Japan's agreements (Heydon and Woolcock 2009). Bilateral agreements were in most cases North–South agreements negotiated between the developed and developing countries. In practice the spread of comprehensive regional and bilateral agreements began to establish de facto international norms on investment and other Singapore issues even though these had been excluded from the multilateral agenda. As the regional and bilateral agreements were generally rules-based with developed dispute settlement procedures, they also led to a further consolidation of a rules-based order.

The balance between multilateral and regional or bilateral approaches will in the future depend on progress in multilateral negotiations and whether bilateral and regional approaches can be made compatible with a wider international system. At the WTO level there have been efforts to enhance the multilateral rules on FTAs starting with improved transparency, but operational rules under Article XXIV GATT have remained elusive (WTO 2006). The threat of bilateral agreements may, however, not be as great as is sometimes stated. Although they create preferences in terms of tariffs and discrimination in some other areas of market access and policy, more comprehensive bilateral and regional agreements may be less distorting if they promote transparency, regulatory best practice and the use of agreed international standards.

Conclusions

What lessons can be drawn from this summary of the evolution of the trading system? First, if the evolution is compared to the debate on substantive policy issues

---

[18] Many FTAs especially between developing countries appeared, at least when first concluded, to serve more of a signalling function than agreements that would be rigorously implemented and enforced.

and topics, it should be clear that the vast majority of issues in the current debate are not new. International trade policy and the construction of an international trading system is an iterative process. The current debate can therefore be informed by knowledge of what went before.

Second, the international trading system has accommodated significant shifts in relative economic or market power during the post-1947 era. It has also found ways of accommodating large numbers of countries and countries at different levels of development. This suggests that the shift in the relative market power towards the large emerging markets and the inclusion of a large number of developing countries in the WTO need not be an insurmountable problem. If it was possible for the trading system to adapt to shifts in influence in the past it may be possible to do so again.

Third, the coverage of the international trade regime has been defined by the dominant trading nations or regions or the period. The definition of what is 'trade' has changed over time. There is no reason to believe that this will not continue to be the case. The GATT 1947 was shaped by the United States as was the trade agenda right into the 1980s. Once the EU established an internal consensus on trade it then began to seek to shape the trade agenda. As new trade powers emerge they can be expected to have an increasing influence on the nature of the agenda. But much will depend on the level of negotiation. Within the WTO the DDA negotiations pitted the EU view of the multilateral trade regime, and to a lesser degree that of the United States and other developed economies, against that of the G20. But in bilateral FTAs the EU and United States still retain their asymmetric power.

Fourth, the international trading system has never been a purely multilateral system, if by multilateral we mean a trading system in which there is no discrimination and one that is shaped by all trading nations. The application of the MFN principle to tariff liberalization and other trade barriers is close to a multilateral order, but there have been many exceptions to MFN over the years, such as the qualified MFN codes of the Tokyo Round, the use of various exceptions and continued use of plurilateral agreements. The evolution of the international trading system has also been shaped by a limited number of major economies. This is likely to continue even if the membership of the 'club' varies.

References

Baldwin, R. and Thornton, P. 2008. *Multilateralising Regionalism: Ideas for a WTO Action Plan on Regionalism*. London: Centre for Economic Policy Research.

Bergsten, C.F. and Cline, R.W. 1982. *Trade Policy in the 1980s*. Washington, DC: Institute for International Economics.

Croome, J. 1995. *Reshaping the World Trading System: A History of the Uruguay Round*. Geneva: World Trade Organization.

Diebold, W. 1952. The end of the ITO. *Princeton Essays in International Finance*, No. 16. Princeton: Princeton University Press.

Evans, J.W. 1971. *The Kennedy Round in American Trade Policy: The Twilight of the GATT?* Cambridge, MA: Harvard University Press.

Golt, S. 1988. *The GATT Negotiations 1986–90: Origins, Issues and Prospects.* Washington, DC: British North American Committee.

Heydon, K. and Woolcock, S. 2009. *The Rise of Bilateralism: Comparing American, European and Asian Approaches to Preferential Trade Agreements.* Tokyo: United Nations University Press.

Hoekman, M. and Kostecki, B. 2001. *The Political Economy of the World Trading System.* 2nd Edition. Oxford: Oxford University Press.

Jackson, J.H. 1998. *The World Trade Organization: Constitution and Jurisprudence.* Chatham House Papers, Royal Institute of International Affairs. London: Pinter.

Jackson, J.H. 2000. *The World Trading System: Law and Policy of International Economic Relations.* 2nd Edition. Cambridge, MA: MIT Press.

Jones, K. 2010. *The Doha Blues: Institutional Crisis and Reform in the WTO.* Oxford: Oxford University Press.

Lee, D. and Wilkinson, R. 2007. *The WTO after Hong Kong: Progress in, and Prospects for, the Doha Development Agenda.* London: Routledge.

Narlikar, A. (ed.). 2010. The new power in the club: the challenge of global trade governance. *International Affairs*, 86(3): 717–728.

OECD. 1996. *Market Access after the Uruguay Round: Investment, Competition and Technology Perspectives.* Paris: OECD.

Preeg, E. 1970. *Traders and Diplomats: An Analysis of the Kennedy Round of Negotiations under the General Agreement on Tariffs and Trade.* Washington, DC: Brookings Institution.

Schott, J.J. 1994. *The Uruguay Round: An Assessment.* Washington, DC: Institute for International Economics.

Schott, J.J. 1996. WTO 2000: setting the course for world trade. *Policy Analysis in International Economics*, No. 45 (September). Washington, DC: Institute for International Economics.

Schott, J.J. 2000. *The WTO after Seattle.* Washington, DC: Institute for International Economics.

Stewart, T.P. 1993. *The GATT Uruguay Round: A Negotiating History (1986–1992).* Deventer: Kluwer Law & Taxation.

Sutherland Report. 2007. *The Future of the WTO.* Geneva: World Trade Organization.

Trebilcock, M.J. and Howse, R. 1995. *The Regulation of International Trade.* London and New York: Routledge.

Warwick Commission. 2007. *The Multilateral Trade Regime: Which Way Forward?* The Report of the First Warwick Commission. Coventry: University of Warwick.

Woolcock, S. 1990. *The Uruguay Round: Issues for the European Community and the United States*, Discussion Paper No. 31. London: Royal Institute of International Affairs.

World Trade Organization. 2006. Negotiating Group on Rules, Transparency Mechanism for Regional Trade Agreements, Job(06)/59/Rev 5.

PART II
Outstanding Issues in
Key Policy Areas

Do Import Tariffs Still Matter?

Przemyslaw Kowalski[1]

Introduction

Despite strong theoretical and empirical arguments for free trade, most countries interfere with trade flows, and import tariffs are one of the oldest known trade controls used for this purpose. Tariffs have traditionally been used to achieve multiple goals, such as protecting local industry, raising public sector revenue, correcting market distortions, improving terms of trade, redistributing income, achieving certain macroeconomic objectives (for example balanced trade) or even as an instrument of foreign policy. Efficiency of tariffs in pursuing these goals depends on which of them are targeted, as well as on specific economic circumstances. However, if a country decides to include trade controls in its policy toolkit, tariffs are to be favoured because of their transparency and relatively benign character as compared to other trade controls. Indeed, tariffs have been emphasized as a principal means of trade protection in multilateral trade negotiations under the auspices of the General Agreement on Tariffs and Trade (GATT) and the World Trade Organization (WTO). At the same time these negotiations have achieved substantial cumulative reductions in tariffs.

This chapter considers selected economic effects of tariff protection. At the outset it briefly summarizes what economic theory has to say about the effects of tariffs. Next, it examines the principal features of tariffs today and outlines the various approaches to tariff reduction used in successive rounds of multilateral trade negotiations, including in the ongoing negotiations on tariffs under the Doha Development Agenda (DDA). Finally, a sample of the recent literature assessing the effects of various further trade liberalization scenarios is discussed with the aim of broadly establishing the relative importance of the remaining tariffs for the world economy today. It is evident that significant reductions in applied tariffs have already been achieved through unilateral, preferential and multilateral

---

[1]   The author is an economist at the Organisation for Economic Cooperation and Development (Przemyslaw.Kowalski@oecd.org). The views presented are strictly those of the author and do not represent the views of the OECD or its member countries.

reforms and while this is one of the key drivers of economic globalization in recent decades, additional non-negligible benefits can be realized. This can be done relatively easily by locking in the tariff reductions that have already been largely agreed in the DDA negotiations.

What Economic Theory Tells Us About the Effects of Tariffs

Similarly to other trade controls, tariffs influence trade, production, consumption patterns and welfare of not only the countries that impose them, but also of their trading partners. They do so through both the absolute levels of protection they impart and through distortions associated with their structure. In a country which is too small to influence world prices with its trade policy instruments, an import tariff creates a wedge between domestic and world prices, making foreign commodities more expensive to both domestic producers and consumers. This results in a reduction in consumer surplus, an increase in producer surplus and yields tariff revenue for the government while also leaving the economy with a net loss, consisting of consumer loss after both government and producer gains (Caves et al. 2002).[2]

The welfare costs associated with import protection reflect distortions in both production and consumption patterns. On the production side, import tariffs make the imported commodities relatively more expensive and thereby shift the allocation of productive resources within the economy towards domestically produced commodities. In turn, this results in a pattern of specialization that does not maximize the aggregate value of production at world prices. Consumption choices are also distorted since the cost to society of obtaining another unit of imported commodity (at world relative prices) is lower than the value to society of consuming another unit of this commodity (at after-tariff domestic relative prices). Both these mechanisms prevent trading countries from capturing gains associated with their comparative advantage and result in a welfare loss.

Tariff liberalization is thus generally expected to improve the allocation of resources, result in more favourable consumption patterns and bring benefits to countries implementing the reform, as well as to their commercial partners, especially if accompanied by appropriate complementary policies (for example, macroeconomic, social and labour market policies).

It is important to bear in mind that while tariff protection is likely to make a country as a whole worse off, different groups within it may be affected either positively or negatively. This is readily revealed, for example, by the opposing effects on consumers and producers (or importers and exporters). These redistributive

---

[2]   One well-known case for the use of import tariffs is the optimal tariff argument that advocates the use of tariffs by a large country to improve its terms of trade either by raising the relative world price of its exports or by driving down the relative price of its imports (Johnson 1954).

properties of tariffs highlight important political economy aspects of tariff policy and tariff liberalization when certain interests groups may lobby in favour of tariffs while others are against.

Importantly, whilst import tariffs have a negative effect on imports, it has been demonstrated that they also have negative effects on the export sector of the economy. In fact, Lerner (1936) showed that, with balanced trade, import tariffs are equivalent to export taxes.[3] This undermines the popular argument for tariff protection which points to the positive employment effects in tariff-protected import competing sectors without mentioning the negative employment effects in the export sectors.

Tariffs are just one type of instrument governments can employ to affect the economy and their effectiveness depends on the nature of policy objectives (see below for a discussion of tariffs as a means of raising revenue or of promoting developmental goals). It is uncontroversial to say that instruments that focus directly on the policy goal itself are usually more efficient in delivering results. In this respect, production subsidies/taxes or consumption taxes/subsidies, for example, would generally be more efficient than tariffs in targeting, respectively, production or consumption goals (Caves et al. 2002).

Yet, if trade controls are to be used, tariffs are generally preferred to other trade policy instruments. Firstly, welfare losses associated with tariffs can be smaller than those associated with trade quotas or other non-tariff measures (NTMs) that would generate an equivalent decrease in import volume. For example, some of the rents associated with quotas may accrue to specific interest groups while in the case of tariffs the generated government revenue can in principle be distributed according to society's needs, for example, in the form of public goods.[4] In fact, some trade measures may generate neither a rent nor government revenue, creating a welfare loss to society that is larger than that associated with an equivalent import tariff. Tariffs also have more pro-competitive effects as compared to quotas when market participants have monopoly power.

An additional argument for the use of tariffs is their relative transparency. Tariffs are usually expressed as a proportion of the price of imported merchandise that is paid to the authorities at the moment that the merchandise crosses the border.[5] This proportion is the wedge between the world and the domestic price and, in itself, is an approximation of the magnitude of the trade distortion that it triggers. This contrasts with quotas or other NTMs, the effects of which are less comparable across products and usually need to be estimated with the use of additional techniques and economic models.

---

[3]   This result is referred to as Lerner's symmetry theorem and has been derived under the assumption of balanced trade.

[4]   Quotas can be auctioned in which case they can also generate government revenue.

[5]   This is the case with the so called ad valorem tariffs. Non-ad valorem tariffs can be expressed as an amount to be paid per unit or kilogramme, for example. There is effort to reduce the incidence of non-ad valorem tariffs which are today mainly used in agricultural trade.

Tariffs as a Source of Government Revenue

Notwithstanding their welfare implications, tariffs have traditionally been used in less developed countries to raise public sector revenue. Collecting a tariff at the border or the port of entry of imported merchandise is much simpler than raising income or consumption taxes. Even today, import tariffs are still an important source of government revenue in many developing countries[6] and the potential loss of tariff revenue has been raised as one of the obstacles to the conclusion of DDA negotiations on tariffs (Kowalski 2006). Indeed, while the removal of quantitative restrictions, 'tariffication' of quotas or reduction of non-tariff barriers all have the advantage of preserving or even increasing government revenue without a major reform of the tax system (for example Ebrill et al. 1999), in general the same cannot be assumed about tariff reduction.

The importance of tariff revenue concerns is reinforced by the fact that countries at lower stages of development are often struggling to sustain a stable macroeconomic environment (of which fiscal sustainability is an important aspect) and face potentially adverse effects of revenue reduction on poverty reduction redistribution and development strategies.[7]

Welfare gains associated with tariff reforms and higher efficiency of other forms of taxation could be a viable incentive for countries to reform the tax system. However, the simple economics of tariff protection suggests that if countries are consistently using tariffs either to raise revenue or to protect import-competing industries, severe revenue losses may not necessarily mean significant welfare gains. Indeed, the fiscal and protective roles of tariff policy are to some extent two competing policy objectives. For example, revenue collections associated with an *ad valorem* import duty of a certain size are maximized when its impacts on trade and welfare are minimized. In particular, there are sectors with low price elasticity of import demand where the tax base (or the value of imports in this case) does

---

[6]   Recent estimates of reliance on tariffs as a source of revenue show that, on average, trade tax revenues accounted for around 4 per cent of low- and middle-income countries' GDPs in 1995–2000 while the equivalent estimate in high-income countries was below 1 per cent. In low-income countries tariff revenues were estimated to account for on average 18 per cent (and in some cases more than 50 per cent) of total government revenue. In Least Developed Countries (LDCs) in Africa, import duties represented about 34 per cent of total government revenue over the period 1999–2001, exceeding a 50 per cent share in a number of countries (UNECA 2003).

[7]   Hertel and Winters (2005) indicate that key determinants of the national poverty impacts include the incidence of national tax instruments used to replace lost tariff revenue. UNECA (2003) reported that the pace of implementation of more outward-oriented development strategies in some African countries has been to a significant extent hindered by fiscal considerations associated with heavy reliance on trade taxes. Failure to take fiscal constraints into consideration can be one of the principal causes for unsuccessful trade reforms (IMF 2003).

not deteriorate by much as a result of higher import duty.[8] This could mean that countries which have been using import tariffs for revenue purposes (that is to say setting high tariffs on products with inelastic import demand) would experience relatively low welfare effects of tariff reforms, while those countries that have been using tariffs predominantly for protective reasons (setting high tariffs on products with elastic import demand) would experience large welfare gains and small tariff revenue losses.

Whether this would actually be the case depends, however, on how countries use their tariff policies. Kowalski (2006) examined tariff profiles and juxtaposed them with estimates of import demand elasticity and found that in many developing countries, price-elastic goods are mostly tariffied at high levels implying the pursuit of the trade protection objective. Nevertheless, he also found a considerable dispersion of tariff rates imposed on goods with similar elasticities of demand. These findings led Kowalski (2006) to conclude that, on balance, there was considerable scope for freeing trade (and realizing welfare gains) without significantly compromising tariff revenue.[9] In this way, efficiency and welfare could be increased through a more uniform tariff profile with a relatively small effect on collected tariff revenue.

Even if the revenue effects of tariff reforms are small, the reform package needs to replace the lost revenue, ideally in a less distorting manner. Recent policy advice in this area stresses the use of other taxes as compensating measures (WTO 2003a, 2003b; Kowalski 2006). In fact, the shift away from trade taxes towards other forms of taxation such as income, sales or value-added taxes has been taking place for some time in many countries (Kowalski 2006) and the need to offset revenue losses from trade liberalization by strengthening domestic taxation has in many cases been a key consideration in the adoption of value-added tax (VAT) (IMF 2003).

The recommendation to shift away from trade taxes towards domestic consumption and income taxes reflects the view that trade taxes are a relatively inefficient way of raising revenue. As Whalley (2002) explains, trade taxes distort both consumption and production decisions and apply to a relatively narrow base. Since at the aggregate-level net trade must close the gap between domestic production and consumption, taxes applied to either domestic production or consumption or both would have the advantage of being relatively broadly based as compared to trade taxes. It is therefore possible, in principle, to switch from trade taxes towards consumption or income taxes in such a way that domestic

---

[8] If price elasticity is high, demand for imports would fall significantly thereby hampering or even overturning the impact of an increase in the tax rate. If imports are price inelastic, the change in tariff does not affect imports, and increases in the tariff rate will translate fully into higher revenues.

[9] For example, currently high tariff rates on price elastic goods could be lowered significantly, boosting trade flows (and welfare) and having a minimum impact on revenue. At the same time, applied tariff rates on price-inelastic products could be raised within the bound limits to compensate for any revenue loss that might have occurred from lowering rates on price-elastic products.

production, consumption and trade are less distorted, and in which the allocation of resources and welfare are improved and revenue unchanged or even increased (see for example Keen and Ligthart 2002).

Tariff Preferences

Tariffs are often used to grant a trading partner more favourable conditions of market access. This is mainly done in the context of reciprocal free trade agreements or customs unions or, non-reciprocally, by industrialized countries seeking to encourage exports by countries that would otherwise be unable to access their markets. Viner (1950) demonstrated that a tariff preference has a trade-creating and a trade-diverting effect. The preference creates additional trade with the beneficiary country and this is associated with a welfare gain in both the beneficiary and the preference-giving country. However, tariff preference can also have a trade diverting effect whereby more efficient suppliers from third countries may be crowded out of the market in the preference-giving country. The latter effect is associated with loss of welfare in both the preference-giving and the third country.

Recent estimates suggest that most world trade occurs under some form of preferential arrangement and so multilateral tariff reductions would necessarily involve a reduction in these advantages. However, the issue of erosion of preferences afforded to developing countries by major preference-giving countries such as the United States or the European Union became a particular concern during the DDA negotiations. These concerns were associated with the risk of negative economic impacts from erosion of tariff advantages upon which certain developing countries depend. A number of studies collected in Hoekman et al. (2009) analysed the extent of reliance on trade preferences afforded by major industrialized economies. Others compared the negative effects of preference with potential gains from new opportunities associated with the most favoured nation (MFN) liberalization (Lippoldt and Kowalski 2005a, 2005b). Importantly, this literature suggests that, on balance, for a majority of developing regions, MFN tariff liberalization by preference-granting countries would, by opening up new opportunities for trade, result in positive welfare gains, notwithstanding the effects of preference erosion. And for those countries that would be worse off, the answer is not to forgo the benefits of MFN liberalization but rather to seek ways, including via technical assistance, to broaden the export base.

The Economic Significance of Tariff Bindings

While thus far the discussion has focused on applied rates that directly affect trade flows, and on the basis of which tariff revenue is collected, it is crucial to distinguish them from the bound tariffs that are the basis of the WTO market access negotiations. The distinction is important owing to the considerable differences between bound and applied rates (the so-called binding overhangs) as these have implications for the trade, welfare and revenue impacts of any potential tariff reduction agreed in the WTO. While applied tariffs are usually considerably lower than bound tariffs and large cuts to the bound rates would be required to lower the applied rates, these bindings have an economic value in themselves. Francois and Martin (1998) and Hertel and Martin (1999) demonstrate that a cut in the binding overhang reduces the uncertainty about the future level of protection by compressing the margin within which the applied rates can fluctuate and reduces both the mean and the variance of the tariff rate. They also show that the relationship between the mean and the standard deviation is a nonlinear one and that the marginal impact increases as the introduced binding approaches the current mean. These insights suggest that the variance of protection maps directly into the welfare impact of protection and that GATT-type restraints on protection policy with tariff bindings are preferred to protection that is free to vary in an uncontrolled manner. In this context, Francois and Martin (1998) suggest rewarding countries with negotiating credit for tariff bindings at or in the neighbourhood of the currently applied rates.

The Structure of Remaining Tariffs in a Nutshell – Where Do We Stand?

Successive rounds of multilateral trade negotiations have achieved substantial cumulative reductions in tariffs. The full implementation of the Uruguay Round (1986–94) commitments was estimated to reduce the average (trade-weighted) applied MFN tariff rate on industrial goods in the OECD countries to 4 per cent (OECD 2001).

In spite of these developments, market access remains one of the most important issues for both the industrialized and developing countries in the DDA negotiations and has been identified as the area with the potential for generating most significant and balanced global gains.

An overview of the structure of remaining tariffs is presented in Annexes 4.1–4.3. Three important facts stand out. Firstly, there are significant differences between the applied and the bound rates and these differences have deepened since the conclusion of the Uruguay Round in 1994 as a result of unilateral liberalization reforms as well as through proliferating preferential trading agreements. We see a particularly large binding overhang on agricultural products as a result of the 'tariffication' process in the Uruguay Round and pronounced differences between bound and applied rates in the case of Least Developed Countries (LDCs).

Secondly, we see that levels of tariffs are negatively correlated with income levels. LDCs have a simple average applied tariff of 13.4 per cent in 2008 compared to 8.8 per cent and 2.6 per cent for low- and middle-income countries and high-income countries respectively. The gap in tariff rates between developed and developing countries was reinforced by the Uruguay Round, as average MFN tariff reductions among OECD countries were 45 per cent, compared to 30 per cent among non-OECD countries (OECD 2001). This outcome was partly the result of the failure or inability of some developing countries to engage fully in the negotiating process. Additionally, in the early 2000s tariffs imposed by developing countries on imports from other developing countries (so-called South–South trade) were particularly high and harmful (Kowalski and Shepherd 2006). This tendency seems, however, to have been reversed as tariffs imposed by poor countries on imports from other poor countries are now lower than those imposed on imports from high-income countries (Annex 4.3).

Thirdly, both in developing and developed economies, tariffs tend to be higher on imports of agricultural products compared to industrial products. The world average agricultural bound (applied) tariff in 2008 was estimated at 49 per cent (9 per cent) compared to 27 per cent (6 per cent) for industrial products. High tariff rates on agricultural imports are a consequence of the exclusion of agriculture from multilateral trade negotiations prior to the Uruguay Round (UR) and the fact that the UR converted agricultural non-tariff barriers (NTBs) into tariff barriers (WTO 2003c).

Estimated average tariffs imposed on industrial products by low- and middle-income countries (8.5 per cent) and LDCs (13.2 per cent) are also much higher than those imposed by developed economies (2.5 per cent). However, in contrast to the agricultural sector, where almost all tariff rates are bound, the binding of tariffs for industrial goods remains a negotiating issue. For example, many African and Asian countries have bound only a limited number of tariff lines (WTO 2003c). Industrial tariffs are generally lower than agricultural tariffs, but there is a considerable degree of heterogeneity within the industrial product categories; simple average bindings in textiles and clothing, leather, rubber, footwear and travel goods, transport equipment, and fish and fish products are significantly higher than those on other industrial products (Bacchetta and Bora 2001). As far as applied rates are concerned, textiles and clothing have the highest or the second-highest applied tariff averages in most countries (Kowalski and Molnar 2009). This sector is also reported to have the highest incidence of international tariff peaks (WTO 2003c).

Formula Approaches to Tariff Reductions

Although tariff reductions can be achieved by negotiating concessions for individual countries, products or sectors, the practice of multilateral trade negotiations indicates that there is a greater probability of success when using a formula approach to obtain concessions.[10] This dilutes the force of special interest groups, facilitates monitoring of the balance of concessions and enables the more effective participation of smaller countries that would be otherwise unable to negotiate bilateral deals.

---

[10] Francois and Martin (2003) examine the effectiveness of a formula approach.

A number of approaches to tariff cuts were used or discussed (Table 4.1) in past rounds of trade negotiations. The initial tariff negotiations under the GATT followed the *request-and-offer* procedure where members negotiated bilateral market access concessions and subsequently extended them to all members following the MFN principle. A *linear formula* approach was introduced in the Kennedy Round (1963–7) where a 50 per cent cut was agreed on all manufactured goods, with exceptions for sensitive goods including steel, clothing, textiles and footwear. The linear formula had the property of yielding higher absolute cuts (that is, in terms of percentage point reductions) of initially high tariffs as well as higher proportional reductions of duty-paid prices on high tariff items. Nevertheless, with the linear formula both high and low rates were cut in the same proportion thereby carrying over the initial tariff dispersion across sectors and countries.

The *Swiss formula* adopted in the Tokyo Round (1973–9) and chosen as the benchmark for reductions of industrial tariffs in the DDA negotiations has a number of desired properties. It maintains the advantage of the linear formula of decreasing high tariffs by more in absolute terms but it also does so in relative terms offering a more effective reduction of tariff dispersion.[11] Additionally, the coefficient *a* in the *Swiss formula* (Table 4.1) provides an upper ceiling on the maximum post-reform tariff rate.

The Uruguay Round approach involved setting broad tariff reduction goals such as a 30 per cent average reduction on industrial products, but leaving the distribution of the cuts across sectors up to negotiations. This approach brought about substantial tariff reductions but was less successful in achieving higher proportional cuts in higher tariffs and in lowering dispersion (Francois and Martin 2003). The Uruguay Round agreement on agriculture also included a range of formula-type elements such as average cuts in tariffs, a minimum cut in each tariff line, formulas for establishing bindings and ceiling bindings options.

Other formulas discussed in the literature include the so-called *flexible Swiss formula* (Francois and Martin 2003) and the formula that defines liberalization in terms of the forgone tariff revenue (Panagariya 2002) and takes into account both the initial tariff rate and the share of the country's trade in the world market (Table 4.1 and Figure 4.1).

What is at Stake in the DDA Negotiations?

Nineteen years after the conclusion of the Uruguay Round and over ten years into the DDA negotiations there is still, at the time of writing, considerable uncertainty about what the final DDA deal will imply for tariff cuts.

---

[11] Another approach that leads to higher proportional cuts in higher tariffs which was considered in the Tokyo Round is the general linear approach. Unlike the Swiss formula, this approach implies that some low rates may actually be increased. Proponents of this approach in the Tokyo Round advocated that it be applied only to tariffs greater than 5 per cent (Francois and Martin 2003, citing Laird and Yeats 1987).

Table 4.1   Selected formula approaches to tariff cuts

	Formula	Description
Simple linear approach	$T_{i1}=aT_{i0}$	T_{i1} and T_{i0} are the final and initial tariff respectively and $0<a<1$, subject to negotiation, is a percentage reduction in tariff which is constant for all initial tariffs $T_1/T_0=a$.
General linear approach	$T_{i1}=d+aT_{i0}$	d is a positive constant and $0<a<1$. This approach leads to larger percentage reductions in highertariff rates but could also lead to increases in the lowest rates.
Swiss formula	$T_{i1}=aT_{i0}/(a+T_{i0})$	a is the negotiated coefficient and the level of maximum resulting tariff. This formula implies higher percentage cuts for high rates but does not require increases in the lowest rates.
Flexible Swiss formula	$T_{i1}=aT_{i0}/(a*b+T_{i0})$	This formula maintains the attribute of the standard Swiss formula where a sets a maximum resulting tariff but it also permits additional flexibility through b: as b increases the formula tends to increase the reduction in the lower tariffs allowing for higher maximum rates with the same target reduction in the average tariff (source paper: Francois and Martin, 2003)
Tariff revenue formula	$T_{i1}=c/T_{i0}*V_{i0})$	c is a constant and V_{i0} is the value of initial imports at world prices

Source: Kowalski (2006).

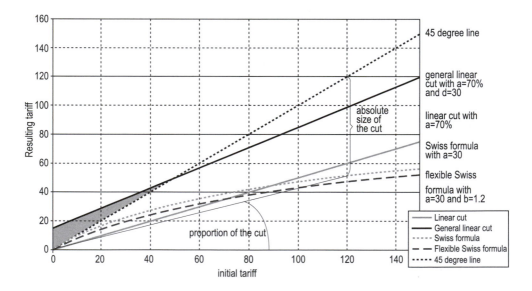

Figure 4.1   Formulas for tariff cuts:
Relationship between initial and resulting tariffs
Source: Kowalski (2006).

The DDA was declared a development round at its birth. Yet, from the outset it was not clear what this meant, for example, with respect to the extent of tariff reductions that was expected to be assumed by developing countries. Nor is it clear what is meant by the provision, agreed during negotiations, that developing countries will be allowed to offer 'less than full reciprocity' in their liberalization. Is it the developing countries that are to undertake the ambitious reforms and reap economic gains or should they be given an option of reducing their trade barriers by less (or more slowly) than required by the general formula? It became clear during negotiations that even within the developing countries group opinions on these issues were divided.

After protracted negotiations (for details see WTO 2003c, 2008a, 2008b; Lippoldt and Kowalski 2005a, 2005b; Hoekman et al. 2009) draft negotiating texts were tabled in December 2008. These texts (summarized in Table 4.2) provide a frame of reference for the discussion below on estimating the gains from liberalization. Key elements of the modalities for agricultural tariff reductions include a tiered formula for bound tariff cuts where tiers are defined differently for developed, developing and recently added members. The tiers and the required tariff cuts are set so that tariff cuts by developing countries are less aggressive and so that they can exclude from the cuts a larger percentage of tariff lines as compared to developed countries.

Table 4.2   December 2008 formulas for reductions of tariffs on agricultural and non-agricultural products

Tiered formula for reductions of agricultural tariffs								
Developed countries			Developing countries			Recently added countries		
Tier	Reduction	% of sensitive tariff lines excluded	Tier	Reduction	% of sensitive tariff lines excluded	Tier	Reduction	
0=20	50	4-6%	0=30	33.5	up to 33%	0=10	0	
>20=50	57		>30=80	38		>10=20	25.5	
>50=75	64		>80=130	43		>20=50	30	
>75	70		>130	47		>50=75	35	
						>75	39	

Swiss formula for reductions of non-agricultural tariffs							
Developed countries			Developing countries			Recently added countries	
Formula coefficient	& of sensitive tariff lines	depth of cut on sensitive products	Formula coefficient	& of sensitive tariff lines	depth of cut on sensitive products		
8	0	na	20	14% but less than 16% of total value of NAMA imports or 6.5% of tariffs unbound if they do not exceed 7.5 of total value of NAMA imports	half of agreed formula cut	not required to undertake tariff reductions	
			22	10% but less than 10% of total value of NAMA imports or 5% of tariffs unbound if they do not exceed 5% of total value of NAMA imports	half of agreed formula cut		
			25	no exceptions			

Source: WTO (2008a, 2008b).

Some other important parameters not detailed in Table 4.2 include a 54 per cent minimum average cut on bound tariffs for developed countries and 36 per cent maximum cuts required of developing countries (see WTO 2008a for details).

The main features of draft modalities for non-agricultural tariff cuts which concern the majority of world merchandise trade are also summarized in Table 4.2. The modalities specify that a simple Swiss formula for tariff cuts be applied with a separate coefficient of 8 per cent for developed countries and three optional coefficients of 20, 22 and 25 per cent for developing countries. The three different coefficients are associated with different levels of flexibility on exclusion of sensitive products with lower coefficients associated with higher flexibilities, and vice versa. The tariff reductions would be implemented gradually over a period of five years for developed countries and ten years for developing countries. Other important elements include anti-concentration provisions which prevent excluding entire sectors from tariff cuts and modalities for special groups of developing countries such as, among others, the LDCs which would be exempt from tariff reductions. Provisions are also included to alleviate the effects of preference erosion, mostly through more gradual tariff reductions on items where tariff preferences are of vital export importance for certain developing countries.

Estimates of Economic Effects of Further Multilateral Trade Liberalization and the Relative Importance of Tariffs

Continuing enhancements in economic theory, modelling approaches and data quality have resulted in analysts providing ever more integrated views of the implications of changes in the world trading system and levels of trade protection. While the modelling frameworks have become more complex and less readily accessible to non-specialists, progress in information technology has reduced the costs of developing and maintaining modelling frameworks. This has generated a large number of disparate estimates of gains from further liberalization which in turn has resulted in confusion about what is at stake. In this context, concerns were also expressed about the usefulness of quantitative analysis for trade policymaking (see Piermartini and Teh 2005 for a summary of this debate).

Kowalski (2009) argued that the richness of modelling approaches and alternative estimations of gains from further liberalization is not necessarily undesirable and can in fact be seen as a part of an organic analytical process. He argues that the differences in results from alternative modelling approaches are often linked to diverging views about economic realities (for example, the likelihoods of alternative negotiation outcomes) or assumptions about specific economic mechanisms (for example, so-called model closures) or estimates of behavioural parameters (such as trade elasticities). The differences can also sometimes be associated with differences in data sources or data quality. More worryingly, however, in a limited number of instances the differences in existing results can be artefacts of the employed methodology with, for instance, different regional or sectoral aggregations of the same model generating quantitatively, and occasionally qualitatively, different predictions. Modelling assessments are therefore a rigorous way of informing the negotiators and the public of the stakes and the distribution of costs and benefits of various options, but there are many reasons why they should not be treated as precise estimates of benefits of freer trade.

For example, as we have seen in the third section, even with the most advanced 2008 draft modalities on market access in agricultural and non-agricultural products, there is considerable uncertainty about their actual economic meaning. Most notably, this uncertainty is associated with the issue of sensitive products.[12] This uncertainty is reflected in the existing modelling literature where a wide range of policy changes have been modelled as 'realistic' DDA scenarios. Table 4.3, which summarizes the most important features of a selected set of modelling assessments of gains from the DDA published in the period 1999–2009, makes it clear that assumptions differed widely with respect to the relative depth of cuts in agricultural and non-agricultural sectors, as well as with respect to the relative depth of cuts in developing and developed regions or the likely outcome of trade facilitation negotiations.

These disparities clearly reflect differences in appreciation of what a realistic outcome of the negotiations would be and they are one of the main reasons why the estimates of welfare gains from further trade liberalization differ so widely. Many existing studies do include a 100 per cent liberalization scenario across all considered sectors and this scenario is often a better benchmark for comparing results across different models and datasets, while also remaining relevant post-DDA. Such a scenario is also a natural comparator for other, perhaps more realistic, scenarios as it captures the overall potential gains from dismantling the remaining trade barriers and bypasses the problem of whether the conjectured cuts are specified with respect to applied or bound rates.

Notwithstanding the differences in assumptions and modelling approaches, one striking feature of estimates generated by this literature is their overall size. Depending on the scenario and model used, welfare gains range from around 50 to close to 700 US$ billion or from approximately 0.1 to just above 1 per cent of world GDP. This is a small number but it should be seen as indicative only since the majority of existing studies focus on the so-called static gains from trade which are generated based on the assumption of an unchanged resource base (for example labour, capital), and an unchanged productivity level or productivity growth rate. Indeed, current applied general equilibrium models tend to focus on the static gains because they are easier to model but in fact trade economists strongly suspect that

---

12 Anderson, Martin and Van Der Mensbrugghe (2005), for example, argued that allowing all countries to exempt 2 per cent of their tariff lines as sensitive products would remove most of the gain out of a potential agricultural deal. Similar estimates have been made for non-agricultural products.

Table 4.3   Results obtained from CGE studies of trade liberalization

Study	Model and database	Liberalization scenario	Notes	Global welfare gains USD billion		
				Agriculture	Other	Total
Decreux and Fontagné (2009)	MIRAGE GTAP database 2004 base year	July 2008 drafts circulated by the WTO involving liberalization of goods and services trade and a trade facilitation scenario	Dynamic, imperfect competition in some sectors	n/a	n/a	57
Decreux and Fontagné (2008)	MIRAGE GTAP database 2004 base year	May 2008 drafts circulated by the WTO	Dynamic, imperfect competition in some sectors	n/a	n/a	43
OECD (2006)	GTAPEM GTAP database 2001 base year	50 per cent cut in domestic agricultural support and 50 per cent cut in applied tariffs – all sectors and regions		26	18	44
Kowalski and Shepherd (2006)	GTAP GTAP database 2001 base year	Elimination of tariffs, all sectors, all regions		35	33	68
Polaski (2006)	Carnegie Model [Wang (2003)], GTAP database 2001 base year	Reduction of tariffs and subsidies in agriculture and tariffs in manufacturing	Perfect competition with a particular treatment of clearing in labour market	n/a	n/a	168
Bouet et al. (2005)	MIRAGE GTAP database 1997 base year	Provisions included WTO draft compromise proposal of March 2003	Dynamic, imperfect competition in some sectors	29	n/a	n/a

Study	Model/Data	Description	Notes			
Anderson, Martin and Van Der Mensbrughhe (2005)	LINKAGE, dynamic GTAP database 2001 base year data	Elimination of domestic agricultural support and trade protection in all sectors	Dynamic version	173	105	278
Beghin et al. (2002)	LINKAGE, dynamic GTAP database 1997 base year data	Elimination of agriculture support and protection in high-income OECD countries		108	n/a	n/a
Francois et al. (2005)	GTAP 1997 base year data	Elimination of tariffs, all sectors, all regions	Increasing returns to scale, med. run increasing returns to scale, long run	109	107	*367.1 *670.0
Hertel and Keeney (2005)	GTAP 2001 base year data	Elimination of domestic agricultural support and tariffs – all sectors and regions		56	28	84
OECD (2003)	GTAP 1997 base year data	Elimination of tariff protection, all sectors		34	63	**174
Tokarick (2005)	GTAP 1997 base year data	Elimination of domestic agricultural support and trade protection		128	n/a	n/a
UNCTAD (2003)	GTAP 1997 base year data	50 per cent cut in applied agricultural tariffs	Incorporates tariff preferences	20	n/a	n/a

					n/a	n/a
USDA (2001)	CGE, dynamic	Elimination of domestic agricultural support and tariffs, all sectors	Static version	31		n/a
			Dynamic, productivity gains	56	n/a	n/a
World Bank (2003)	LINKAGE, dynamic 1997 base year data	Near 100 per cent reduction in domestic agricultural support and applied tariffs	Static version	193	98	291
			Dynamic version	358	156	518

Note: * Includes gains from services liberalization; ** Includes gains from trade facilitation.
Source: Kowalski (2009) and OECD (2010).

the so-called dynamic gains are very important.[13] Some existing applied studies consider supplementary increases in levels of total factor productivity on top of the static gains and these studies generate higher estimates of gains but technical constraints impede a satisfactory modelling of trade-related productivity growth (Kowalski 2009).[14] Thus, most likely, percentage increases in welfare associated with further trade liberalization scenarios are much larger than the currently estimated 1 per cent.

One important feature of the literature summarized in Table 4.3 is that, overall, tariffs are a very important element of future trade policy reforms. A number of studies separate the effects of further tariff reductions from other forms of trade liberalization. One point of comparison is the importance of tariffs relative to domestic support and export subsidies in agriculture. Anderson, Martin and Valenzuela (2005), for example, estimated that up to 93 per cent of the global cost of barriers to agricultural trade is due to tariffs. Similarly, in OECD (2006) approximately 20 out of US$26 billion of estimated welfare gains from a 50 per cent cut in domestic agricultural support and a 50 per cent cut in applied tariffs in the agricultural sector has been attributed to tariff reductions.

Conclusions

The evidence presented in this chapter suggests that import tariffs still play an important role in the world economy. While significant reductions in applied tariffs have been achieved through unilateral, preferential and multilateral reforms in recent decades, there are still significant differences between applied and bound rates and these binding overhangs have increased since the conclusion of the Uruguay Round in 1994. These overhangs create space for potential protectionism – a fact that has been particularly evident in the aftermath of the 2008–9 economic crisis when many individual counties took specific measures to increase tariffs or otherwise increase protection (OECD 2010).

Moreover, while average applied tariffs are low in high-income countries, many developing countries continue to impose significant tariffs, including on imports from other poor countries. The higher levels of tariffs in poorer countries suggest

---

[13] Nordas et al. (2006) analysed and summarized the various arguments of the debate and Kowalski (2009) focused on the treatment of links between trade liberalization and productivity in the computable general equilibrium models.

[14] Kowalski (2009) explains that this is related to the difficulty of unifying the concepts of specialization and structural change present in multisector comparative static trade models with the concept of balanced growth in literature on long-run economic dynamics. Ngai and Pissarides (2004) argue that 'structural shifts are usually studied in models that do not satisfy the conditions for balanced aggregate growth. Conversely, balanced aggregate growth is normally studied in models that do not allow structural change'. See Kowalski (2009) for more details.

that they are particularly well positioned to benefit from further tariff reforms through improvements to the allocation of resources, enhanced competition, wider product variety and benefits of scale economies. Indeed, tariff reduction modelling shows the bulk of liberalization gains going to developing countries, with a general tendency of these gains increasing with countries' commitment to own-liberalization. This would create a better base for implementing development and poverty reduction strategies and contribute to the objectives set for the DDA, especially if government revenue and preference erosion concerns are adequately addressed. Furthermore, agricultural tariffs are generally higher than industrial tariffs and there is a considerable degree of heterogeneity of protection within these broad product categories, creating further welfare costs, particularly for developing countries.

Existing estimates of gains from further tariff reductions suggest that they have the potential to generate significant and balanced additional gains, in absolute terms and as compared to other areas of negotiation. In short, tariffs still matter.

Annex 4.1 Structure of world import tariffs in 1995 and 2008: Simple average

	1995				2008			
	All products	Agriculture	Industry	Textile and Clothing	All products	Agriculture	Industry	Textile and Clothing
	Bound rates				**Bound rates**			
All countries	28.0	44.7	25.4	28.0	29.8	48.9	26.5	28.7
High income	5.7	12.8	4.8	11.2	16.3	22.5	15.3	21.2
Least developed countries	29.6	39.7	26.2	17.1	55.8	74.9	50.5	48.5
Low and middle income economies	35.3	53.9	32.4	33.9	34.4	56.6	30.6	31.7
East Asia & Pacific	30.8	40.4	29.2	28.4	28.8	33.4	28.1	28.2
Europe	16.8	48.1	12.1	15.4	8.3	16.5	7.1	10.4
Latin America and Caribbean	35.4	42.1	34.5	36.5	36.7	49.9	34.8	37.2
Middle East and North Africa	38.8	84.0	32.2	46.4	30.4	58.1	26.8	30.3
South Asia	60.2	95.9	56.0	24.3	50.7	89.8	44.2	25.8
	MFN rates				**MFN rates**			
All countries	13.7	16.5	13.3	20.2	9.3	13.2	8.7	13.8
High income	5.6	9.6	5.1	10.0	3.9	4.4	3.8	5.8
Least developed countries	20.3	25.3	19.7	40.1	13.5	16.1	13.1	19.2
Low and middle income economies	15.6	18.1	15.2	22.7	9.1	13.1	8.5	11.2
East Asia & Pacific	21.3	27.3	20.6	35.7	6.3	10.7	5.7	9.2
Europe	7.2	11.0	6.7	9.4	9.7	13.7	9.1	14.8
Latin America and Caribbean	12.0	13.0	11.8	18.1	17.7	34.3	15.5	28.3
Middle East and North Africa	28.5	40.4	27.2	42.0	12.9	19.3	12.0	14.8
South Asia	50.7	45.3	51.3	68.1	10.6	15.4	10.0	16.0
	Applied rates				**Applied rates**			
All countries	11.3	12.8	11.2	15.5	6.7	9.2	6.5	10.0
High income	5.1	7.4	5.0	10.6	2.6	3.0	2.5	5.3
Least developed countries	18.8	23.7	18.4	39.3	13.4	15.5	13.2	19.0
Low and middle income economies	15.0	16.5	14.9	20.0	8.8	12.7	8.5	13.1
East Asia & Pacific	18.6	24.7	18.1	30.5	8.8	13.6	8.4	11.4
Europe	7.0	9.9	6.7	10.5	4.8	8.4	4.5	6.8
Latin America and Caribbean	12.0	12.2	11.9	17.0	8.0	9.7	7.9	13.2
Middle East and North Africa	27.1	34.6	26.6	39.2	13.7	28.1	12.6	21.6
South Asia	50.1	43.3	50.6	66.7	13.0	20.8	12.3	15.8
	Preferential rates				**Preferential rates**			
All countries	2.9	5.7	2.7	6.9	1.7	2.6	1.6	2.4
High income	2.8	6.9	2.3	6.2	0.6	1.7	0.5	0.9
Least developed countries	2.1	2.6	2.0	2.3	4.9	4.2	5.0	5.9
Low and middle income economies	3.5	4.9	3.3	6.2	2.3	3.1	2.2	3.1
East Asia & Pacific	13.9	14.2	13.9	21.3	6.2	6.7	6.2	6.7
Europe	3.0	7.0	2.6	8.9	1.0	3.8	0.7	1.4
Latin America and Caribbean	2.7	2.6	2.7	3.7	1.4	2.1	1.3	1.6
Middle East and North Africa					5.4	7.1	5.3	7.1
South Asia	41.8	41.3	42.0	22.5	11.3	13.0	11.1	18.3

Note: values refer to simple averages, MFN rates come from the UN TRAINS and based on HS 6-digit tariffs. Applied rates come from the UN TRAINS and are effectively applied rates, taking into consideration applicable (and available) preferential rates, based on HS 6-digit tariffs fact table.

Source: UN TRAINS extracted from the World Integrated Trade Solution (WITS) database.

Annex 4.2 Structure of world import tariffs in 1995 and 2008: Trade-weighted average

	1995				2008			
	All products	Agriculture	Industry	Textile and Clothing	All products	Agriculture	Industry	Textile and Clothing
	Bound rates				Bound rates			
All countries	7.9	20.5	6.9	12.5	8.1	19.8	7.4	13.1
High income	3.8	15.8	3.0	10.5	4.0	9.0	3.8	11.6
Least developed countries	27.4	41.3	20.3	16.9	49.5	58.2	46.9	32.6
Low and middle income economies	30.4	49.3	28.1	30.6	19.4	40.4	17.9	22.3
East Asia & Pacific	25.3	45.0	23.3	26.7	4.8	13.3	4.5	9.5
Europe	15.2	48.2	10.8	14.2	10.9	26.1	9.6	14.2
Latin America and Caribbean	33.9	47.4	32.4	34.2	33.0	43.5	32.2	34.2
Middle East and North Africa	30.1	29.8	30.2	50.3	29.8	42.5	27.7	34.0
South Asia	60.0	81.1	56.4	18.9	38.0	95.9	34.6	23.4
	MFN rates				MFN rates			
All countries	6.1	9.1	5.9	12.3	3.7	8.7	3.4	9.9
High income	4.2	8.9	3.9	11.6	2.1	4.5	2.0	8.2
Least developed countries	14.1	19.7	12.9	30.8	10.5	12.4	10.2	19.6
Low and middle income economies	12.8	12.2	12.8	17.9	6.7	14.6	6.1	13.5
East Asia & Pacific	13.7	14.3	13.6	24.0	4.1	12.4	3.8	9.3
Europe	6.6	8.2	6.4	6.6	5.3	9.5	5.1	8.8
Latin America and Caribbean	11.8	11.7	11.8	16.8	9.6	23.6	8.5	16.5
Middle East and North Africa	21.0	11.4	23.7	38.0	13.3	15.5	13.0	28.4
South Asia	43.5	28.5	45.2	60.6	6.9	12.9	6.6	9.7
	Applied rates				Applied rates			
All countries	5.2	7.8	4.9	10.4	2.4	4.7	2.2	6.9
High income	3.4	7.9	3.1	9.5	1.3	2.8	1.2	8.5
Least developed countries	13.8	19.1	12.7	30.5	9.4	10.8	9.2	18.6
Low and middle income economies	11.6	10.7	11.7	16.2	4.8	8.2	4.6	10.3
East Asia & Pacific	13.7	14.3	13.6	24.0	3.9	11.4	3.6	8.1
Europe	5.6	6.9	5.5	6.4	3.8	6.8	3.6	6.7
Latin America and Caribbean	9.5	8.7	9.6	12.7	4.2	4.3	4.2	9.8
Middle East and North Africa	21.0	11.4	23.7	38.0	11.2	14.0	10.7	22.9
South Asia	43.5	28.5	45.2	60.8	6.7	11.8	6.5	9.6
	Preferential rates				Preferential rates			
All countries	2.4	3.9	2.2	7.1	1.0	1.9	1.0	3.4
High income	1.2	3.5	1.1	5.1	0.4	1.8	0.3	1.0
Least developed countries	2.0	2.8	1.7	2.2	3.7	2.8	3.9	6.1
Low and middle income economies	4.6	3.2	4.8	7.9	1.7	2.0	1.6	2.7
East Asia & Pacific	6.9	12.2	6.2	15.4	5.0	2.1	5.2	4.7
Europe	1.8	3.8	1.5	8.0	0.6	2.5	0.4	2.2
Latin America and Caribbean	4.8	2.8	5.1	7.9	0.8	1.3	0.7	0.7
Middle East and North Africa					4.1	8.7	3.7	7.8
South Asia	28.1	30.3	26.1	22.5	5.7	6.7	5.6	14.8

Note: values refer to simple averages, MFN rates come from the UN TRAINS and based on HS 6-digit tariffs. Applied rates come from the UN TRAINS and are effectively applied rates, taking into consideration applicable (and available) preferential rates, based on HS 6-digit tariffs fact table.
Source: UN TRAINS extracted from the World Integrated Trade Solution (WITS) database.

Annex 4.3 Structure of import tariffs by importing and source country

1995

Bound rates

Importer	All countries	High income	Least Developed Countries	Low and middle income economies	East Asia & Pacific	Europe	Latin America and Caribbean	Middle East and North Africa	South Asia
All countries	7.9	8.1	8.0	7.6	6.5	6.0	11.1	5.5	9.2
High income	3.8	3.6	6.8	4.4	4.5	3.8	3.9	6.1	6.1
Least developed countries	27.4	27.6	14.8	26.0	41.9	37.5	52.4	27.2	31.5
Low and middle income economies	30.4	29.4	31.6	34.4	34.8	24.2	36.0	33.1	37.8
East Asia & Pacific	25.3	24.2	24.0	31.0	28.7	30.3	36.2	33.3	38.1
Europe	15.2	14.7	19.6	17.9	16.7	16.5	37.9	8.3	17.4
Latin America and Caribbean	33.9	33.6	34.4	34.9	33.4	30.3	35.4	33.2	33.0
Middle East and North Africa	30.1	29.3	38.1	29.2	25.8	27.3	29.0	41.9	25.2
South Asia	60.0	57.7	54.9	63.7	70.3	56.6	76.0	51.5	55.7

Applied rates

Importer	All countries	High income	Least Developed Countries	Low and middle income economies	East Asia & Pacific	Europe	Latin America and Caribbean	Middle East and North Africa	South Asia
All countries	5.2	5.5	2.8	4.4	4.8	4.7	3.7	3.6	6.1
High income	3.4	3.4	4.9	3.3	3.6	3.3	2.3	4.3	5.3
Least developed countries	13.8	15.0	16.1	10.9	16.9	15.2	12.9	11.1	10.2
Low and middle income economies	11.6	12.3	9.2	9.2	15.8	4.5	7.4	8.7	14.5
East Asia & Pacific	13.7	14.4	7.7	10.7	13.4	8.4	8.7	4.3	11.7
Europe	5.6	6.6	1.3	3.9	6.4	2.7	9.0	7.3	5.9
Latin America and Caribbean	9.5	9.9	7.6	8.0	13.3	8.1	7.1	8.3	13.8
Middle East and North Africa	21.0	20.8	13.6	17.7	19.0	17.9	14.3	15.5	22.1
South Asia	43.5	46.1	25.0	38.9	50.1	31.9	44.0	25.5	32.8

2008

Bound rates

Importer	All countries	High income	Least Developed Countries	Low and middle income economies	East Asia & Pacific	Europe	Latin America and Caribbean	Middle East and North Africa	South Asia
All countries	8.1	9.1	8.3	7.3	6.45	5.3	11.0	4.7	10.0
High income	4.0	4.1	10.4	4.1	3.54	6.7	3.8	7.9	8.3
Least developed countries	49.5	47.7	54.8	51.3	45.87	50.6	49.4	40.5	43.5
Low and middle income economies	19.4	20.6	12.2	19.0	17.54	12.5	26.4	13.5	19.5
East Asia & Pacific	4.8	5.9	0.9	3.3	4.21	4.2	2.4	0.8	4.8
Europe	10.9	11.9	16.7	10.0	10.74	8.9	19.0	17.4	14.1
Latin America and Caribbean	33.0	33.4	32.3	32.5	32.75	23.2	33.1	31.2	32.7
Middle East and North Africa	29.8	29.5	8.8	29.0	28.97	25.4	41.6	34.0	19.7
South Asia	38.0	35.6	74.6	42.7	36.17	46.8	48.9	48.1	63.3

Applied rates

Importer	All countries	High income	Least Developed Countries	Low and middle income economies	East Asia & Pacific	Europe	Latin America and Caribbean	Middle East and North Africa	South Asia
All countries	2.4	2.6	1.4	2.1	2.93	1.5	1.1	0.7	4.0
High income	1.3	1.1	2.0	1.5	1.98	2.1	0.3	1.0	3.1
Least developed countries	9.4	9.4	5.7	9.4	13.65	8.5	9.3	6.6	9.3
Low and middle income economies	4.8	5.3	1.9	4.2	6.3	3.0	2.7	1.7	6.0
East Asia & Pacific	3.9	5.0	0.6	2.4	2.83	3.1	1.8	0.6	4.2
Europe	3.8	4.4	2.5	3.2	6.13	1.9	6.7	1.5	4.5
Latin America and Caribbean	4.2	4.0	3.5	4.4	8.29	3.9	2.0	1.2	9.3
Middle East and North Africa	11.2	11.4	1.8	10.5	16.83	9.2	9.8	4.5	8.0
South Asia	6.7	6.8	3.8	6.7	7.29	6.8	5.4	5.8	5.8

Note: values refer to simple averages, MFN rates come from the UN TRAINS and based on HS 6-digit tariffs. Applied rates come from the UN TRAINS and are effectively applied rates, taking into consideration applicable (and available) preferential rates, based on HS 6-digit tariffs fact table.

Source: UN TRAINS extracted from the World Integrated Trade Solution (WITS) database.

References

Anderson, K., Martin, W. and Valenzuela, E. 2005. The relative importance of global agricultural subsidies and market access, unpublished. [Online] Available at: http://siteresources.worldbank.org/INTRANETTRADE/Resources/RelativeIm portanceOfGlobalAgriSubsidies&MarketAccess.pdf [accessed 28 March 2011].

Anderson, K., Martin, W. and Van Der Mensbrughhe, D. 2005. Doha policies: where are the pay-offs? In *Trade, Doha, and Development: A Window into the Issues*, edited by R. Newfarmer. Washington, DC: World Bank, 43–57.

Bacchetta, M. and Bora, B. 2001. Post-Uruguay round market access barriers for industrial products. *Policy Issues in International Trade Commodities*, Study Series No. 12. Geneva: UNCTAD.

Beghin, J.C., Roland-Holst, D. and van der Mensbrugghe, D. 2002. Global agricultural trade and the Doha Round. What are the implications for north and south? *Working Paper 02-WP 308*, Center for Agricultural and Rural Development, Iowa State University, June. [Online] Available at: www.iastate.edu.

Bouet, A., Bureau, J.-C., Decreux, Y. and Jean, S. 2005. Multilateral agricultural trade liberalization: the contrasting fortunes of developing countries in the Doha Round. *The World Economy* 28(9): 1329–54.

Caves, R.E., Frankel, J. and Jones, R.W. 2002. *World Trade and Payments*. 9th Edition. New York: Addison Wesley.

Decreux, Y. and Fontagné, L. 2008. An assessment of May 2008 proposals for the DDA. *Rapport d'Étude No. 2008-01*, July. Paris: CEPII-CIREM.

Decreux, Y. and Fontagné, L. 2009. Economic impact of potential outcome of the DDA. *Rapport d'Étude No. 2009-01*, May. Paris: CEPII-CIREM.

Ebrill, L., Stotsky, J. and Gropp, R. 1999. *Revenue Implications of Trade Liberalisation*. Washington, DC: International Monetary Fund.

Francois, J.F. and Martin, W. 1998. Commercial policy uncertainty, the expected cost of protection, and market access. *Tinbergen Institute Discussion Paper No. 98-059/2*. [Online] Available at: http://ideas.repec.org/p/dgr/uvatin/19980059.html [accessed 28 March 2011].

Francois, J.F. and Martin, W. 2003. A formula for success? Potential approaches to market access negotiations. *World Economy* 26(1): 1–28.

Francois, J.F., Van Meijl, H. and Van Tongeren, F. 2005. Trade liberalization in the Doha Development Round. *Economic Policy* 20(42): 349–91.

Hertel, T.W. and Keeney, R. 2005. What is at stake: the relative importance of import barriers, export subsidies and domestic support. In *Agricultural Trade Reform and the Doha Development Agenda*, edited by K. Anderson and W. Martin. Washington, DC: World Bank, 37–62.

Hertel, T.W. and Martin, W. 1999. Would developing countries gain from inclusion of manufactures in the WTO negotiations? *GTAP Working Paper No. 07*.

Hertel, T.W. and Winters, L. 2005. Estimating the poverty impacts of a prospective Doha Development Agenda. *World Economy* 28(8): 1057–71.

Hoekman, B., Martin, W. and Braga, C.A.P. 2009. *Trade Preference Erosion; Measurement and Policy Response*. Washington, DC: The World Bank.

IMF. 2003. *Changing Customs. Challenges and Strategies for the Reform of Customs Administration.* Washington, DC: International Monetary Fund.

Johnson, H.G. 1954. Optimum tariffs and retaliation. *Review of Economic Studies* 21(2): 142–53.

Keen, M. (ed.) 2003. *Changing Customs, Challenges and Strategies for the Reform of Customs Administration.* Washington, DC: International Monetary Fund.

Keen, M. and Ligthart, J.E. 2002. Coordinating tariff reduction and domestic tax reform, *Journal of International Economics* 56(2): 489–507.

Kowalski, P. 2005. Impact of changes in tariffs on developing countries' government revenue. *OECD Trade Policy Working Papers No. 18.* Paris: OECD.

Kowalski, P. 2006. Impact on government revenue of tariff liberalisation in developing countries. In *Trading Up: Economic Perspectives on Development Issues in the Multilateral Trading System,* edited by Douglas Lippoldt. Paris: OECD, 109–32.

Kowalski, P. 2009. *Estimates of Gains from Further Multilateral Trade Liberalisation: Should They Differ.* From proceedings of OeNB Workshop on International Trade and Domestic Growth: Determinants, Linkages and Challenges, Oesterreichische National Bank, Austria, 27 September 2007.

Kowalski, P. and Molnar, M. 2009. Economic impacts of the phase-out in 2005 of quantitative restrictions under the agreement on textiles and clothing. *OECD Trade Policy Working Papers No. 90.* Paris: OECD.

Kowalski. P. and Shepherd, B. 2006. South-South trade in goods. *OECD Trade Policy Working Papers No. 40.* Paris: OECD.

Laird, S. and Yeats, A. 1987. Tariff cutting formulas – and complications. In *The Uruguay Round: A Handbook for the Multilateral Trade Negotiations,* edited by J.M. Finger and A. Olechowski. Washington, DC: World Bank, 89–100.

Lerner, A.P. 1936. The symmetry between import and export taxes. *Economica* 3(11): 306–13.

Lippoldt, D. and Kowalski, P. 2005a. Trade preference erosion: potential economic impacts. *OECD Trade Policy Working Papers No. 17.* Paris: OECD.

Lippoldt, D. and Kowalski, P. 2005b. Trade preference erosion: expanded assessment of countries at risk of welfare losses. *OECD Trade Policy Working Papers No. 20.* Paris: OECD.

Ngai, L.R. and Pissarides, C.A. 2004. *Balanced Growth with Structural Change.* Centre of Economic Performance, London School of Economics. [Online] Available at: http://cep.lse.ac.uk/pubs/download/dp0627.pdf [accessed 28 March 2011].

Nordas, H.K., Miroudot, S. and Kowalski, P. 2006. Dynamic gains from trade. *OECD Trade Policy Working Papers No. 43.* Paris: OECD.

OECD. 2001. *The Development Dimensions of Trade.* Paris: OECD.

OECD. 2003. *Doha Development Agenda: Welfare Gains from Further Multilateral Trade Liberalisation with Respect to Tariffs.* Paris: OECD.

OECD. 2006. *Agricultural Policy and Trade Reform; Potential Effects at Global, National and Household Levels.* Paris: OECD.

OECD. 2010. *Trade and Economic Effects of Responses to the Economic Crisis.* OECD Trade Policy Studies series. Paris: OECD.

Panagariya, A. 2002. Formula approaches to reciprocal tariff liberalisation. In *Development, Trade and the WTO*, edited by B. Hoekman, P. English and A. Matoo. Washington, DC: World Bank, 535–9.

Piermartini, R. and Teh, R. 2005. Demystifying modelling methods for trade policy. *Discussion Paper No. 10*. Geneva: WTO.

Polaski, S. 2006. *Winners and Losers: Impact of the Doha Development Round on Developing Countries*. Washington, DC: Carnegie Endowment for Peace.

Tokarick, S. 2005. Who bears the cost of agricultural support in OECD countries? *The World Economy* 28(4): 573–93.

UNCTAD. 2003. *Back to Basics: Market Access Issues in the Doha Agenda*. Geneva: United Nations Conference on Trade and Development.

UNECA. 2003. *Ad-hoc Expert Group Meeting on Maintaining the Government Fiscal Base in the Context of a Trade Liberalisation Regime*, Aide Memoire of the Conference held in Addis Ababa, on 1– 2 October 2003.

USDA. 2001. The road ahead: agricultural policy reform in the WTO (summary report). *Agriculture Economy Report No. 797*. Washington, DC: US Department of Agriculture.

Viner, J. 1950. *The Customs Union Issue*. New York: Carnegie Endowment for International Peace.

Wang, Z. 2003. The impact of China's WTO accession on patterns of world trade. *Journal of Policy Modelling* 25(1): 1–41.

Whalley, J. 2002. *Taxes and Trade*. [Online] Available at: www.worldbank.org/wbi/publicfinance/documents/taxpolicy/Whalley.pdf [accessed 28 March 2011].

World Bank. 2003. *Global Economic Prospects: Realizing the Development Promise of the Doha Agenda 2004*. Washington, DC: US Department of Agriculture.

WTO. 2003a. Communication from the International Monetary Fund: trade and safeguarding public revenues, *WT/TF/COH/16*, 14 February. Geneva: WTO.

WTO. 2003b. Revenue implications of trade liberalisation: communication from the United States, *TN/MA/W/18/Add.2*, 11 April. Geneva: WTO.

WTO. 2003c. *World Trade Report 2003*. Geneva: WTO.

WTO. 2008a. Revised draft of modalities for agriculture, *TN/AG/W/4/rev.4*, 6 December. Geneva: WTO.

WTO. 2008b. Fourth revision of draft Modalities for non-agricultural market access, *TN/AG/W/4/rev.4*, 6 December. Geneva: WTO.

Non-Tariff Measures

Michael J. Ferrantino[1]

Introduction

Tariffs have declined substantially throughout the world from the high levels observed prior to the Great Depression. These declines, implemented unilaterally, multilaterally in the GATT/WTO system, and through preferential trade agreements (PTAs), have made non-tariff measures (NTMs) increasingly more important for the international trading system. Few would question that NTMs have increased in importance relative to tariffs as a means of restricting trade. They may well have increased in absolute importance also. This is because many NTMs are outgrowths of national regulation of economic activity, most notably technical barriers to trade (TBT) and sanitary and phytosanitary measures (SPS) in agriculture. As national economic regulation has become progressively more extensive, the interface between such regulations and international trade has similarly grown.

A variety of definitions have been offered for NTMs, or alternately for non-tariff barriers (NTBs). While 'non-tariff barrier' is often taken to be synonymous with 'non-tariff measure', there is a difference in connotation. The term 'non-tariff barrier' suggests a policy imposed by governments that is in violation of an agreement, or at least inconsistent with it. 'Non-tariff measure', by contrast, denotes the existence of a policy, other than tariffs, that may affect trade, without prejudgment as to the legal status of that policy, or its appropriateness from a welfare standpoint. Many NTMs, such as inspection of food at the border, are intended to protect public health or safety, and are specifically allowed for in the text of the WTO agreements and the various PTAs. The choice of 'NTM' rather than 'NTB' in the present chapter is intended to draw focus to the economist's question, 'What are the economic effects of this measure?' rather than the lawyer's question, 'Can this measure be challenged at dispute settlement as being in violation of an agreement?'.

The Multi-Agency Support Team (MAST), an international group of experts convening in support of the United Nations Conference on Trade and Development's

---

[1] This chapter represents solely the views of the author and is not intended to represent the views of the US International Trade Commission or any of its Commissioners.

(UNCTAD) work on NTMs, proposed the following definition: 'Non-tariff measures are policy measures, other than ordinary customs tariffs, that can potentially have an economic effect on international trade in goods, changing quantities traded, or prices, or both' (MAST 2008). This definition focuses on the economic effects of NTMs, rather than their legal status. Legally, NTMs are only described as 'policy measures', that is, they are undertaken by governments. Defining NTMs in this way excludes private standards, such as the international buying practices of large retailers like Carrefour or Walmart, or private labeling schemes such as RugMark, which aims to certify that no child labour has been used in the manufacture of carpets. From an economic standpoint, private standards may have effects similar to policy-imposed NTMs, particularly for exporters in developing countries who find such standards costly to implement, and some researchers may consider private standards to be NTMs. The definition also excludes other difficulties that traders may face that are not directly caused by government policies, such as lack of information about foreign markets, problems in obtaining finance, or linguistic and cultural differences. Such impediments to trade have practical effects that are analogous to government-imposed NTMs.

Even by the definition above, the universe of NTMs may appear unmanageably broad. In a world of interconnected markets, any policies undertaken may have indirect effects on trade, even if the policies are purely domestic and not targeted specifically at imports or exports (think of income taxes). In order to limit the scope of inquiry, resort is often sought to an enumerated list of policies considered to be NTMs, usually having the feature that they are intentionally directed at trade in some way. The next section of this chapter will discuss specific types of NTMs using the list recently developed by MAST. Even so, there are a wide variety of issues in international trade policy that are not about tariffs, usually considered as separate from the topic of NTMs, but related to NTMs in some way. It may be helpful to attempt to delineate a bit further the boundaries between NTMs and some of these other trade policy issues.

From the standpoint of the economist, the topic of NTMs overlaps broadly with trade facilitation. Trade facilitation is usually conceived as measures governments can take to make trade easier, such as providing easy electronic submission of trade documents or reducing inefficiency or corruption in the customs service (see Chapter 7). NTMs are actions undertaken by governments to make trading more difficult. Seen this way, a trade facilitation measure is in effect a negative NTM, and the removal of an NTM can be considered trade-facilitating. Measures used to quantify the effects of NTMs, such as those discussed later in this chapter, generally can also be applied to the analysis of trade facilitation.

Both goods and services face barriers and impediments to their international exchange. Since services do not clear customs and do not pay tariffs, any measures restricting services trade are by definition NTMs. However, trade in services has particular features that make it analytically distinct from exchange in goods. Most services cannot be delivered effectively by cross-border means such as the post or Internet. Services trade usually requires some physical human presence – either the buyer or the seller usually moves to be face-to-face with the other. In many cases, service firms accomplish this by establishing affiliates in foreign countries through FDI. Barriers to FDI, though non-tariff in nature, thus affect trade in services. FDI barriers also affect goods trade, since a significant proportion of goods trade takes place within the boundaries of multinational firms. For example, in 2008 approximately 46 per cent of all US exports of goods and 36 per cent of all US imports of goods were associated with multinationals (Barefoot and Mataloni 2010).

Issues regarding intellectual property rights (IPRs) often appear in inventories of non-tariff measures, especially when such inventories are constructed based on complaints and concerns of traders. It is true that weak enforcement of IPRs can influence trade flows, and that IPRs are not tariffs. However, concerns about IPRs are very different analytically from most concerns about NTMs. Most NTMs have the effect of restricting trade and raising the prices of traded goods. However, weakly enforced IPRs have the opposite effect – they tend to lower the price of goods and may actually increase trade flows, since some exported and imported goods are counterfeits (OECD 2008). Thus, the analytical tools generally used for NTMs are usually not well suited for questions involving IPRs.

Types of NTMs and Their Operation

The UNCTAD–MAST Categorization Scheme

Historically, UNCTAD has provided information on NTMs for various countries on a tariff-line basis in its Trade Analysis and Information System (TRAINS) database. Following on the work of MAST in 2006–8, UNCTAD has substantially revised its categorization scheme for NTMs, to be used both in future versions of TRAINS and in surveys of market participants. In the current classification, the main headings are as follows:

1. sanitary and phytosanitary measures;
2. technical barriers to trade;
3. other technical measures (including pre-shipment inspection and special custom formalities not related to SPS/TBT, and other measures);
4. price control measures;
5. quantity control measures;
6. para-tariff measures (including customs surcharges, additional taxes and charges, internal taxes and charges levied on imports, decreed customs valuations, and other measures);
7. finance measures;
8. anticompetitive measures;
9. export measures;
10. trade-related investment measures;

11. distribution restrictions*;
12. restriction on post-sales services*;
13. subsidies*;
14. government procurement restrictions*;
15. intellectual property*;
16. rules of origin*.

This scheme reflects recent changes in the ways governments use NTMs. The regulatory policies (SPS and TBT) are given first place. These policies, which were lumped together in the previous classification as 'technical barriers', are separated out to reflect the special features of agricultural NTMs. The emphasis given to SPS and TBT measures reflects their actual significance in the experience of traders: in UNCTAD surveys of exporters and importers in six developing countries about their experience with NTMs, the share of complaints pertaining to SPS or TBT ranged from about 65 per cent in India, Tunisia and Uganda to 93 per cent in Thailand (Basu 2009). The categories marked with an asterisk (*) are not used by UNCTAD to collect official data, but are reserved for use in surveys of traders' complaints.

The practical difficulties traders face with NTMs do not always relate to the *de jure* content of the measures, but to the way in which they are administered. Previous reports on NTMs, such as the National Trade Estimate of the United States Trade Representative (USTR),[2] the EU's Market Access Database[3] and the members' comments on the WTO's Trade Policy Reviews[4] have identified a variety of procedural issues with the way NTMs are implemented. These issues are reflected in UNCTAD's survey work as 'procedural obstacles', which include such problems as arbitrariness or inconsistency; discriminatory behaviour favouring specific producers or suppliers; inefficiency or obstruction; non-transparency (including 'informal payment expected or required', legal issues and unusually high fees and charges).

Related to such practical problems with NTMs as arbitrariness, obstruction and non-transparency is the tendency in many cases for countries to apply an ever-changing variety of policies to the same product. This means that if traders succeed in surmounting one NTM, either through dogged adherence to administrative procedures or by the efforts of trade negotiators to eliminate particular NTMs, new ones pop up in their place.

The operation of each of the main types of NTMs will now be described, including some of the asterisked items above since they refer to important topics in trade policy not discussed at length elsewhere in this volume.

---

[2]   A historical series of these reports are available at: http://tcc.export.gov/Country_Market_Research/National_Trade_Estimates/index.asp.

[3]   Available at: http://madb.europa.eu/.

[4]   Available in English at: www.wto.org/english/tratop_e/tpr_e/tpr_e.htm.

Sanitary and Phytosanitary Measures and Technical Barriers to Trade

Both SPS and TBT represent the extension of government regulation to the realm of exports and imports. SPS can be thought of as a special category of technical barriers to trade applying to agricultural products. Both SPS and TBT measures are generally designed to protect public safety, health or the environment, and thus arise as part of the routine regulatory activities of governments. The international system has long recognized the potential tension between the regulatory objectives of governments and trade liberalization. Article XX of GATT 1947 implicitly recognizes that legitimate domestic regulatory purposes may require the adoption of measures at the border, so long as such measures do not act as a 'means of arbitrary or unjustifiable discrimination between countries where the same conditions prevail, or a disguised restriction on international trade'.

As an example of this tension, governments can refuse entrance at the border to agricultural goods containing pests or contaminants. But governments may also stop such goods at the border for long enough that the inspection causes them to spoil, or refuse to explain to traders the steps necessary to have their goods certified as pest-free or uncontaminated. In such cases, suspicion of a disguised restriction on international trade may arise. The balance between the interests of regulation and the desire not to unduly impede trade is further elaborated in the Uruguay Round SPS and TBT Agreements of 1994. For example, the SPS Agreement states that SPS measures should be 'based on scientific principles' and 'not maintained without sufficient scientific evidence'. While TBT provisions are generally thought of as applying to manufactures, both SPS and TBT issues can arise for agricultural goods.

The legal analysis as to whether a given SPS or TBT measure is in compliance with the WTO or a PTA is distinct from the economic analysis as to whether the benefits arising from a regulation exceed its costs, including any costs arising from the restriction of trade. While dispute settlement bodies must make bright-line distinctions about whether or not regulations and standards comply with trade agreements, economists must wrestle with the practical difficulties in measuring both costs and benefits. The benefits to consumers are often harder to measure than the costs induced by distortions to trade, but measuring the costs is not always easy either. One celebrated case involves the question of whether the health benefits of a tightening of European health regulations on aflatoxin in groundnuts is worth the loss in exports to African groundnut producers. Measures of lost exports associated with the regulatory change turn out to be highly sensitive to the statistical methods employed (Otsuki et al. 2008; Xiong and Beghin 2010).

One hot-button issue frequently arising in the context of SPS is that of genetically modified organisms (GMOs). Crops grown from seeds using recombinant DNA techniques have increased yields as well as improved the physical attributes of food, and have been widely adopted in many countries. However, they have been banned in many other countries because of concerns about safety. The question of whether bans on GMOs are based on scientific principles, or instead constitute trade-restricting NTMs, has taken up a good share of the SPS matters under dispute settlement, along with issues surrounding labelling (Walkenhorst 2003). Another frequently arising question comes from measures affecting trade in beef products, arising from concerns with bovine spongiform encephalopathy (BSE) (also known as mad cow disease), the use of hormones to accelerate the growth of cattle or related issues (USITC 2008). In the case of BSE, disputes arise from the fact that measures taken by countries to deal with BSE outbreaks, such as slaughtering large number of cows in the vicinity of an affected cow, are often not accepted as evidence of safe meat by a country's trading partners even when the affected country certifies the meat as safe for its own consumers.

Technical barriers to trade include product and process standards, technical regulations such as labelling, traceability requirements or tolerance limits for residues or restricted use of substances, as well as the conformity assessment procedures involved in certifying that imported goods correspond to national technical standards. Like food safety rules, standards are often meant to address practical issues. Standardized products allow for interoperability of goods made by different producers, as well as network economies arising from the ability to engage in transactions among a large group of individuals or firms. Standards can also be burdensome and duplicative. A power supply for a personal computer often contains markings from well over a dozen governmental and private standard-setting bodies, often imposing duplicative tests for such properties of the good as radio non-interference. The costs of obtaining the certification from each standard-making body, represented by a particular market, are borne by the manufacturer and ultimately the consumer of such goods. Such approaches as mutual recognition agreements among trading partners, unilateral recognition by one country of a trading partner's testing results, and increased acceptance of suppliers' declarations of conformity (SDoC) in which businesses self-certify their cooperation with standards, are approaches that can reduce the likelihood that certification procedures for health and safety become onerous TBTs (Johnson 2008).

Product standards can also potentially be used by governments to favour domestic firms in industries undergoing technological change. In the early stages of the development of a technology, products are often offered in non-compatible formats, such as the competing Betamax and VHS formats for video cassette recorders in the 1980s. While the marketplace is capable eventually of settling on a standard, in principle governments can use an official choice of standard for a technology in flux to exclude imports of competing goods. For example, in the market for mobile telephones and telephone service, it has sometimes been claimed that official choice of standards has impeded market access. Since a standard may be embodied in a group of patents which must be licensed in order to implement the standard, there are complex relationships between certain TBT issues and issues involving intellectual property.

Customs Measures

Delays in clearing customs are a frequently voiced complaint of traders. The Trading Across Borders data, compiled for the World Bank's *Doing Business* project, show that in developing countries such delays are comparable in magnitude to those associated with bad roads and slow water transport. In a world of rapid logistics, with increasing emphasis on supply chains with just-in-time manufacturing processes and quick response to changes in consumer demands, time is money. Methods relying on the willingness of shippers to pay a premium for faster air transport show that the 'tariff equivalent' of delays at customs is on the order of 1 per cent per day for the most time-sensitive products (Hummels 2007). Multiple border crossings add further burdens to traders exporting from or importing to landlocked countries (Arvis et al. 2010).

Improvements in customs procedures can take a variety of forms. Changing from paper to electronic processing of documents can both speed up clearance and reduce corruption. Appropriate risk assessment techniques, targeting specific shipments for more attention by the authorities, can reduce delays associated with opening every single shipment at the border as if they were all of equal concern.

Quantity Control Measures

Traditional quantity control measures are less common in international trade than previously, especially since the phasing out of the Agreement on Textiles and Clothing in 2005. The provisions of GATT 1947 are meant to rule out most quantitative restrictions except in the case of balance of payments emergencies. Nonetheless, NTMs of other types often have practical effects resembling quantitative restrictions, such as policies of non-automatic licensing, or exemptions from strict product standards up to a certain quantitative limit, which in effect act as a quantitative limit at the exemption level.

Quantitative restrictions can in principle be designed to mimic the effects of tariffs, limiting imports or raising import prices by a comparable amount. In practice, though, their economic effects are different. In the case of a tariff, the rents resulting from import restriction are received by the importing country's government, while in the case of a quota they accrue to the holder of the license to import, unless these licenses are auctioned off. Similarly, in cases where supply and demand are variable, quotas can contribute to price volatility in excess of what would be observed under a tariff which allows some of the variability of market conditions to be manifested in changes in import quantities.

Trade Remedies

Antidumping duties and countervailing duties (AD/CVD policies) often appear in catalogues of NTMs, as do trade safeguards. These measures are forms of administered protection codified in the WTO agreements, largely following historical precedents in US law. Antidumping policies allow the imposition of duties upon the finding of 'unfair pricing' (usually, a price lower than the price charged in the exporter's home market) coupled with a finding that the dumping is causing material injury to the competing domestic industry or is threatening to do so. Countervailing duties can be charged against subsidized imports that are found to be harming domestic producers. Temporary safeguard measures can be imposed if a country's domestic industry is injured or threatened with injury as the result of a surge in imports.

The various categories of trade remedy policies have been the subject of significant controversy. A finding of unfairly priced imports is often easier to obtain than a finding of predatory pricing under domestic antitrust law, even though the rhetorical descriptions of dumping and predatory pricing often sound similar. However, from the standpoint of quantitative analysis, AD/CVD policies can often be analysed with traditional tools. As price control measures, the economic analysis of AD/CVD policies is similar in many respects to the analysis of tariffs, though their administration raises some additional points for analysis. Safeguard measures can be implemented either by tariff-like policies or by quantitative restrictions.[5]

Rules of Origin[6]

In the strict sense, rules of origin are part of tariff policy, but they are often classed among NTMs for their potential to influence trade in a way not readily apparent from a simple examination of the published tariffs. Rules of origin are particularly important in the case of free trade agreements, customs unions or other preferential arrangements. If country A and country B each decide to grant imports from the other duty-free treatment, then it is necessary to have rules to determine whether such imports in fact originate in either A or B, as opposed to in country C, whose imports are intended to pay an MFN duty but which might be simply transshipped through A to B and relabelled 'Made in B'. Rules of origin may be based on a change in tariff classification, a percentage of value originating in the free-trade area, or a technological transformation criterion (for example, the 'yarn forward' rule in the North American Free Trade Agreement (NAFTA) requiring that the yarn, fabric and garment all be made in North America for a garment to qualify for duty-free status).

Rules of origin tend to vary greatly from product to product within the tariff code, requiring specialized legal attention and tracking of materials within the production process to insure compliance. For sectors such as textiles, apparel and autos, rules of origin can have significant impact on trade flows. Rules of origin

---

[5]   For a more detailed discussion of antidumping and other commercial instruments, see Chapter 6.

[6]   For a detailed examination of the economic effects of rules of origin, see Cadot et al. (2006).

can raise the cost of production, since more costly inputs satisfying the rule may be substituted for cheaper inputs outside the region in question in order to qualify for a duty reduction. Rules of origin can also serve as a form of subsidy to exports, since they may promote trade in higher-cost inputs within a free trade area. Failure to take rules of origin into account may lead to overestimates of the trade-creating effects of a free trade agreement.

Multiple NTMs and the 'Whack-a-Mole' Problem

Countries wishing to restrict the import of particular goods often use multiple methods to accomplish this objective. For example, high tariffs, restrictive SPS and TBT rules, non-automatic licensing and complex rules of origin may all be applied to the same product. This creates a problem for exporting firms, or national negotiators acting on behalf of such firms, trying to achieve market access. When one impediment is satisfied or negotiated away, another may arise to take its place, thus frustrating attempts at entering the market. This problem is often referred to as the whack-a-mole problem, after the children's arcade game in which a rubber mallet is used to bang down the heads of rodents which keep popping up again.

The existence of multiple NTMs for the same product also creates challenges for economic analysis. It may be possible to estimate a total amount of market distortion associated with NTMs, in terms of high import prices or low import quantities. However, it is not obvious how to assign partial effects of such a market distortion to different NTMs. It could be that each contributes a part of the distortion, that all must be removed to have any impact on the market at all, or that only one out of the multiple NTMs is truly binding. This makes it more challenging to provide policymakers with appropriate guidance on which of the multiple policies to prioritize in negotiations.

Quantifying the Effects of NTMs[7]

Potential Importance

While there are no global estimates of the effects of NTMs, several available partial estimates suggest that their impact on global trade is large. Andriamananjara et al. (2004) estimated that removal of certain categories of NTMs could have yielded global welfare gains of US$90 billion in 2001. This estimate involved compiling an inventory of NTMs that might have potentially affected trade, quantifying their

---

[7] See Deardorff and Stern (1998) and Ferrantino (2006) for more detailed treatment of quantification of NTMs. This discussion is adapted from Ferrantino (2010), which also contains a discussion of sources of data for the quantitative analysis of NTMs.

effects on prices using econometric methods and simulating the effects of removing the resultant price gaps in a CGE model. A recent study of NTMs affecting EU–US trade and investment estimates that an ambitious programme of NTM reduction and regulatory convergence would generate short-term real income gains of about US$85 billion and longer-term gains of US$210 billion (Berden et al. 2009).

A few studies also attempt to quantify the effects of NTMs relative to tariffs, usually finding that NTMs are relatively more important. Fugazza and Maur (2008) report that in 14 of 26 global regions, the *ad valorem* tariff equivalent of NTMs calculated using the results of Kee et al. (2009) is higher than the average tariff. In studies focused on particular products and markets, the impact of NTMs is often found to be as high as, or higher than, that of tariffs. For example, the impact of SPS measures on US beef exports from 2004–2007 (US$11 billion) has been estimated to be almost twice the impact of tariffs and tariff rate quotas which are estimated to be US$6.3 billion (USITC 2008). In another study focusing on US agricultural exports to India, the effects of removing India's NTMs on US exports were found to be in about the same order of magnitude as those removing India's tariffs (USITC 2009). The results were dominated by the effects on a single product, wheat, for which NTMs cut off trade completely.

Price Gaps versus Quantity Gaps

Non-tariff measures, if they have an impact in the marketplace, are likely to reduce the quantity of imports, increase their price, or both. Measures of the quantity or price effects of NTMs can be used to compare the degree of distortion for one product with another, or for the same product in different countries. Such measures of distortion can also be introduced into simulation models to estimate effects on welfare, GDP or inter-industry effects.

For purposes of simulation modelling, it is often convenient to express these effects as price gaps or tariff equivalents. The difference between the high price of imports induced by the NTM and the lower or 'world' price that would prevail in the absence of distortions can be treated as a tariff equivalent. Tariff equivalents have the advantage of providing easy comparisons between NTMs and tariffs. The removal of NTMs can be simulated in a partial equilibrium or CGE framework using familiar methods for simulating the effects of tariff changes.

One can also measure the quantity or value effect[8] of NTMs or other import restraints as the difference between the observed (lower) imports under the NTM and the higher level of imports that would have been observed without the NTM.

---

[8]   While ideally one would like to contrast quantity gaps with price gaps, in practice what are often estimated as quantity gaps are really value gaps, in which the analyst contrasts the dollar value of imports constrained by an NTM with a normal value. This is no doubt because data on trade values are more easily obtained than data on trade quantities (such as number of units, kilogrammes). Since value = quantity*price, analysis based on values may be influenced by variations in the level of prices, across trading partners or across time.

This requires the analyst to estimate a level of 'normal' imports in the absence of the NTM. One widespread technique for doing this is gravity modelling. It is well known that a high degree of the variation in the value or volume of trade between partners can be explained by the size of economies of the trading partners (more trade between partners with higher GDPs) and by the economic distance between partners (less trade between more distant partners, more trade between partners sharing a common border or a common language). Estimates of the gravity model can be used to generate out-of-sample estimates of what normal trade would be between country pairs for which the trade value is usually lower.

There are several reasons for preferring price gaps to quantity gaps in most cases. First, price gaps measure the difference between two observed values, a distorted (NTM-ridden) price and a non-distorted price. Quantity or value gaps measure the difference between an observed (distorted) value and an estimated normal value of trade, and are thus influenced by the quality of the estimated value, which is subject to the various uncertainties surrounding econometric specifications. Even when price gaps are 'mass-produced' using an econometric framework, such as the one presented by Dean et al. (2009), the econometric properties of these estimates are likely to be preferable to estimates of quantity gaps, since there is generally less cross-country variation in prices than in trade flows (Ferrantino 2006: 20, Annex 2).

Quantity gaps may be preferred in cases where the NTM is prohibitive and stops trade altogether. In such cases, there is no price of imports on which to base a price gap. They may also be used in cases where trade data are relatively abundant and prices are difficult to measure, for example for highly differentiated products of the same general type.

Cost–Benefit Analysis

Many NTMs arise from regulatory policies which are intended to provide benefits to consumers and producers, and not simply to be trade-restrictive. In many cases, they provide benefits such as protecting food from contamination, crops from disease, electronic devices from electromagnetic interference, and so on. The design of regulatory policies to achieve a set of stated objectives, while at the same time minimizing distortion of trade patterns, is a matter of ongoing interest for both policymakers and researchers.[9] A further implication of the regulatory nature of NTMs is that the relevant counterfactual for policy analysis may not be to eliminate the policy altogether, but to replace it with a policy which achieves the same regulatory objective with a less trade-distorting effect.

Analysts examining such policies from both the regulatory and the trade perspective may wish to explore cost–benefit analyses which weigh the potential

---

Analysis based on values is often reported as if it were based on quantities, making the unstated assumption that prices are constant in the relative dimension.

[9]   This point is a recurring theme of an analysis of NTMs affecting EU–US trade recently commissioned by the European Union (Berden et al. 2009).

regulatory benefits to producers and consumers against any trade-distorting effects. Recent progress has been made in identifying appropriate theoretical frameworks for different special cases for agro-food trade (van Tongeren et al. 2009). Gathering appropriate data is especially challenging in this area. The required information on the policies themselves may often go beyond what is currently provided in official data. Also, the measurement of benefits is particularly challenging, though recent advances in experimental economics with respect to the willingness-to-pay approach appear to offer promise in some cases (van Tongeren et al. 2009).

Supply Chain Analysis

Appropriate price comparisons for NTM analysis require the identification of a point in the supply chain where prices are to be compared. When there are multiple policies present, a single estimated price gap summarizes their effects but does not provide information on the effects of individual policies. Supply chain analysis offers potential for disentangling the effects of multiple policies.

The movement of goods from the exporter to the ultimate consumer involves numerous transactions costs, which take the form of markups. Anderson and van Wincoop (2004) suggest that the typical cost increase for developed country exports between the factory and the retailer is approximately 170 per cent. In many cases the markup from factory to consumer may be even higher. Feenstra (1998), citing Tempest (1996), reports data which imply that the markup on Barbie dolls produced in China and sold in the United States is approximately 900 per cent.

Thus, any comparison of distorted and non-distorted prices needs to specify at what point in the supply chain the price comparison is being made. If the non-distorted world price is measured at a different point in the supply chain than the distorted price affected by NTMs, corrections need to be made for those transport costs, tariffs and wholesale and retail markups which are added at each point of the movement of products. Products move from the farm or factory to the port of exportation, are loaded onto ships or planes, move internationally by ocean or air, are unloaded at the port of importation, pass through customs where tariffs may be charged and move into the internal distribution system in the importing country where they are subject to wholesale and retail markups.[10]

It is often the case that the difficulties faced by traders attempting to export or import goods consist of multiple policies applied to the same transaction, or to a mix of official and private practices (see Tilton (1998) for a case study of the whack-a-mole problem in Asian cement trade). The classic price gap or tariff-equivalent method is only able to express the summary effect of all policies in place, and is not able to apportion the effect among multiple policies.

---

[10] Some formulae that can be used for breaking down the various markups in the supply chain can be found in Ferrantino (2006; Annex 1), which follows closely Deardorff and Stern (1998; Appendix 3).

A supply chain perspective can help in the analysis of multiple NTMs. By isolating the individual locations in the supply chain where different policies can take place, it may be possible to obtain a better understanding of which policies act as absolute constraints and which are not constraining, but may increase costs. Breaking down the supply chain is especially useful for the analysis of trade facilitation as well. For example, the process of importation in a seaport can be broken down into a number of steps (Londoño-Kent and Kent 2003). Survey instruments can also be designed from the perspective of the costs or time associated with different parts of the supply chain.[11]

Measuring the impact of NTMs is never going to be easy, but given the growing importance of such measures it is a task that will require continued attention.

References

Anderson, J.E. and van Wincoop, E. 2004. Trade costs. *Journal of Economic Literature* 42: 691–751.

Andriamananjara, S., Dean, J.M., Feinberg, R., Ludema, R., Ferrantino, M.J., and Tsigas, M. 2004. The effects of non-tariff measures on prices, trade, and welfare: CGE implementation of policy-based price comparisons. *US International Trade Commission Office of Economics Working Paper*, EC2004–04–A. Washington, DC: USITC.

Arvis, J., Raballand G. and Marteau, J. 2010. *The Cost of Being Landlocked: Logistics Costs and Supply Chain Reliability*. Washington, DC: World Bank.

Barefoot, K.B. and Mataloni, R.J. 2010. US multinational companies: operations in the United States and abroad in 2008. *Survey of Current Business* 90(8): 205–30.

Basu, S.R. 2009. *Non-Tariff Measures: Results from Firm Surveys and Official Sources*, presentation to the UNESCAP/UNCTAD/WTO–OMC Research Workshop on Rising Non-Tariff Protectionism and Crisis Recovery, Macau, December 2009. [Online] Available at: www.unescap.org/tid/projects/ntp_s3_sudip.pdf [accessed: 22 December 2010].

Berden, K.G., Francois, J., Tamminen, S., Thella, M. and Wymenga, P. 2009. *Non-Tariff Measures in EU–US Trade and Investment: An Economic Analysis*. Rotterdam: ECORYS Nederland BC for the European Commission, Directorate–General for Trade. [Online] Available at: http://trade.ec.europa.eu/doclib/press/index.cfm?id=501 [accessed: 22 December 2010].

Cadot, O., Estevadeordal, A., Suwa–Eisenmann, A. and Verdier, T. 2006. *The Origin of Goods: Rules of Origin in Regional Trade Agreements*. Oxford: Oxford University Press.

---

[11] Examples of this include the 'Trading across Borders' component of the World Bank's Doing Business surveys (available at: www.doingbusiness.org), and the survey of logistics impediments in USITC (2005).

Dean, J.M., Signoret, J.E., Feinberg, R.M., Ludema, R.D. and Ferrantino, M.J. 2009. Estimating the price effects of non-tariff barriers. *The BE Journal of Economic Analysis and Policy: Contributions* 9(1): 1–39.

Deardorff, A.V. and Stern, R.M. 1998. *Measurement of Nontariff Barriers*. Studies in International Economics series. Ann Arbor: University of Michigan Press.

Feenstra, R. 1998. Integration of trade and disintegration of global production in the global economy. *Journal of Economic Perspectives* 12(4): 31–50.

Ferrantino, M.J. 2006. Quantifying the trade and economic effects of non-tariff measures. *OECD Trade Policy Working Papers No. 28*. Paris: OECD.

Ferrantino, M.J. 2010. Quantitative strategies for non-tariff measures: methodological approaches and ways forward with the pilot project data. In *Developing Countries in International Trade 2010: Non-Tariff Measures: Evidence from Selected Developing Countries and Future Research Agenda*. New York and Geneva: UNCTAD, 79–94.

Fugazza, M. and Maur, J. 2008. Non-tariff barriers in CGE models: how useful for policy? *Journal of Policy Modeling* 30(3): 475–90.

Hummels, D. 2007. *Calculating Tariff Equivalents for Time in Trade*. Nathan Associates for US Agency for International Development.

Johnson, C. 2008. Technical barriers to trade: reducing the impact of conformity assessment measures. *USITC Office of Industries Working Paper, ID–19*. Washington, DC: USITC.

Kee, H., Nicita, A. and Olarreaga, M. 2009. Estimating trade restrictiveness indices. *The Economic Journal* 119(534): 172–99.

Londoño-Kent, M. and Kent, P. 2003. A tale of two ports: the cost of inefficiency. *Research Report Submitted to World Bank: Office of the Chief Economist for Latin America and the Caribbean*. Washington, DC: World Bank.

MAST. 2008. *First Progress Report to the Group of Eminent Persons on Non-tariff Barriers*. Geneva: UNCTAD.

OECD. 2008. *The Economic Impact of Counterfeiting and Piracy*. Paris: OECD.

Otsuki, T., Wilson, J. and Sewadeh, M. 2008. What price precaution? European harmonization of aflatoxin regulations and African groundnut exports. *European Review of Agricultural Economics* 28(2): 263–83.

Tempest, R. 1996. Barbie and the world economy. *Los Angeles Times*, 22 September, A1 and A12.

Tilton, M.C. 1998. Japanese group boycotts and closed government procurement procedures as barriers to trade. In *The Economic Implications of Liberalizing APEC Tariff and Non-tariff Barriers to Trade*, 3101. Washington, DC: USITC.

USITC. 2005. *Logistic Services: An Overview of the Global Market and Potential Effects of Removing Trade Impediments*, 3770. Washington, DC: USITC.

USITC. 2008. *Global Beef Trade: Effects of Animal Health, Sanitary, Food Safety, and Other Measures on US Beef Exports*, 4033. Washington, DC: USITC.

USITC. 2009. *India: Effects of Tariffs and Nontariff Measures on US Agricultural Exports*, 4107. Washington, DC: USITC.

Van Tongeren, F., Beghin, J. and Marette, S. 2009. A cost–benefit framework for the assessment of non-tariff measures in agro-food trade. *OECD Food, Agriculture and Fisheries Working Papers No. 21*. Paris: OECD.

Walkenhorst, P. 2003. Agro-food products and technical barriers to trade: a survey of issues and concerns raised in the WTO's TBT committee. *OECD Joint Working Party on Agriculture and Trade Working Paper,* COM/TD/AGR/WP(2002)70/FINAL. Paris: OECD.

Xiong, B. and Beghin, J.C. 2010. Aflatoxin redux: does European aflatoxin regulation hurt groundnut exporters from Africa? *Iowa State University Department of Economics Working Paper No. 10013.* Iowa: Iowa State University.

Commercial Instruments

Patrick Messerlin and Stephen Woolcock[1]

Introduction

This chapter covers commercial instruments in the shape of antidumping (AD), anti–subsidy and safeguard measures. These instruments are provided for under the GATT 1994 and give the WTO members willing to use them some degree of freedom (under some specified conditions) with respect to the trade concessions they undertook in GATT and WTO Rounds. 'Commercial instruments' is a reasonably neutral term. Politicians and lawyers often use the term 'trade remedies', which tends to imply that there is some failing or unfairness in the trading system. By contrast, economists usually call them 'contingent protection', which implies that they have been generally used to limit import competition.

Commercial instruments are used in two general cases: to face allegedly unfair trade practices as (somewhat imprecisely) defined in the GATT or to provide some form of 'safety valve'. Alleged unfair practices can take the form of the dumping of products on a market or of the use of subsidies. The fact that these practices are said to be unfair suggests that the behaviour of the foreign competitors is the main source of the problem. By contrast, safeguard actions were (at least initially) conceived as a 'safety valve' to deal with 'unforeseen' import surges resulting from liberalization. In other words, they recognize that it is the domestic industry that has difficulty adjusting to foreign competitors.

Despite these different backgrounds, it is crucial to view all these commercial instruments as linked. During the late 1970s and 1980s, when increased import competition from Japan and the Newly Industrializing Countries (NICs) was fairly intense, the United States and the European Union (then called the European Community) sought a 'safety valve' as a means of mitigating the pressures. Safeguards were not an attractive instrument because their use was subject to strict conditions, such as the obligation to apply them in a non-discriminatory manner and to provide compensation. The 'safety valve' used was therefore a GATT illegal

---

[1]   We would like to thank very much K.A. Dickstein, M.K. Nevin and J. Suh for their excellent support.

practice, the so-called 'voluntary export restraints' (VERs). However, VERs have a downside: they allow foreign exporters to increase their prices and to grab the rents generated by the artificially created scarcity of imports. In the mid-1970s, the United States and the EU realized that antidumping duties, although not intended as a safety valve, could achieve the same result as VERs (they could be applied selectively) while retaining the rents in the form of antidumping duties. This use – abuse – of antidumping measures was possible because of the loose wording of the GATT Article VI, which regulates them. In 1995, the Uruguay Round banned VERs, but it also made the rules on safeguards less strict. Figure 6.1 does indeed show an increase in safeguard actions since then – a clear illustration of the potential substitution between the various commercial instruments depending on their relative capacity to provide protection and their costs for achieving this result.

It is often expected that the pressure for relief goes up when industries are under strain from the economic cycle, hence that the use of commercial instruments may be influenced by economic downturns. However, as shown by Figure 6.2, the expected inverse relationship between economic downturns and an increase in the use of commercial instruments, though present, is not very strong, particularly in recent experience. Indeed, the global financial crisis of 2008–9 has not witnessed significant increase of the use of commercial instruments. There are at least two explanations for this. As explained below, commercial measures (particularly antidumping measures) are largely triggered by large firms that want to use them for 'shaping' world competition; that is, for introducing anticompetitive behaviour in specific sectors, as best illustrated in steel or chemicals. The downward trend since 2002 may then reflect the fact that such firms have been successful in establishing a sustainable level of 'restrained' competition. The alternative explanation is that during the past two decades these large multinational firms have increasingly relied on production networks based in other countries. As a result, commercial instruments enforced by one country at the request of a firm could hurt the production processes of this firm in other countries. Indeed, there is evidence that some large firms have been hurt by antidumping measures that they were advocating.

Antidumping

Figure 6.1 clearly shows that antidumping actions have been the most used commercial instrument, followed (at some distance) by safeguards and anti-subsidy actions. However, it should be stressed that safeguard actions have a much wider coverage in terms of products and countries targeted, so that one safeguard action is often equivalent to many antidumping actions.

Annual initiations of AD, CVD and safeguard investigations

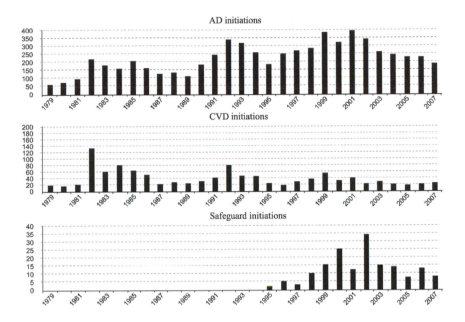

Annual number of new AD, CVD and safeguard measures

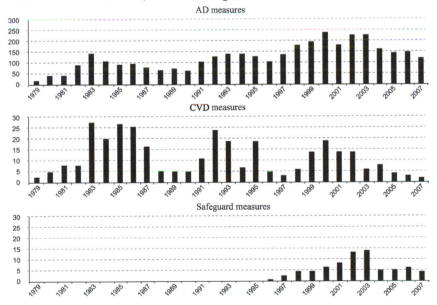

Figure 6.1   AD, CVD and safeguard investigations
Source: WTO Secretariat.

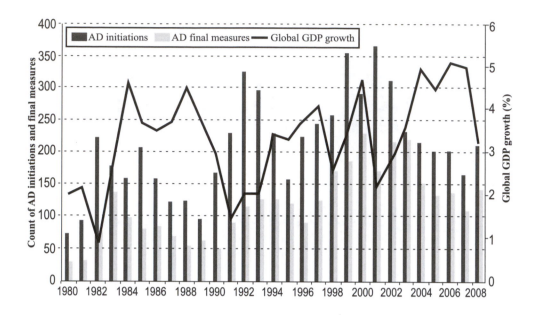

Figure 6.2   Trade contingent measures and the global business cycle

Note: Global GDP growth is from the IMF World Economic Outlook Database (April 2009).
Source: WTO (2009: 130). Chart illustrates the pattern for all the countries which, according to the WTO antidumping database, had at least one AD initiation from 1979 to 2008. 'CVD' refers to 'countervailing duty'.

A Brief Economic Analysis

Dumping is said to occur when the price of a good in an importing country is below the price of that good in the exporting country's home market. It should be underscored that, from an economic perspective, a mere price differential is an insufficient justification to take antidumping action. Economic analysis shows that selling below the full cost of a product is often economically sound and might occur naturally throughout the production cycle. It also shows that 'predatory pricing' (the act of cutting prices initially in order to eliminate competitors and thus to enjoy a monopoly in the subsequent period) is self-defeating if, during the following period (when the 'predator' raises prices in order to enjoy its expected monopoly) competitors can enter or re-enter the market. In this case, the predator would have made losses during the first period without being able to recoup them during the second period. Indeed, evidence shows that the only economic rationale of antidumping – fighting pricing practices that could ultimately be detrimental to competition – represents at most 5 per cent of the total number of EU and US antidumping cases (Bourgeois and Messerlin 1998; Shin 1998).

Shifting from the motives to the consequences, imposing antidumping duties on foreign imports could of course lead to the expansion of domestic production although evidence shows that it is seldom the case. But antidumping duties increase domestic prices and decrease welfare, since the domestic firms are not as efficient as some foreign firms eliminated from the market. As products under antidumping measures are often inputs (semi-processed goods), antidumping measures tend to penalize domestic firms that are consumers of such goods, before hurting the end-users of the products concerned.

These usual consequences of protection are magnified in many antidumping cases by the fact that the large firms, which initiate the complaints that lead to antidumping measures, operate in imperfectly competitive markets. Antidumping measures targeting key foreign competitors can then make the markets at stake even more imperfectly competitive, with such unintended effects as trade diversion and tariff-jumping foreign direct investments (Bloningen and Prusa 2003). In such cases, the protectionist impact of antidumping measures is compounded by an increase of collusion among firms in the markets concerned. Indeed, there is evidence that antidumping cases have led to such collusive behaviour (Messerlin 1990; WTO 2009).

History and Political Economy

Antidumping has a long history. The first explicit antidumping law was enacted by Canada in 1904, which defined it as occurring 'whenever it appears to the satisfaction of the minister of customs ... that the export price ... is less than the fair market value thereof, as determined according to the basis of value for duty provided in the Customs Act'. Australia and New Zealand promptly followed and, by 1921, the United States, France, Britain and the British Dominions all had antidumping laws in place.

Today, antidumping regulation is an administrative function of national governments in which discretion plays an important role, despite the GATT–WTO guidelines provided by the 1979 Tokyo Antidumping Code and the 1994 Uruguay Antidumping Agreement. The key development in antidumping policy since the mid-1970s has been its constant and ever deeper extension beyond the concept of imports priced 'below value' (which is empirically difficult to ascertain) to the concept of imports priced below fully allocated costs. All the changes have had the effect of enabling prices to be determined at such a level as to greatly facilitate a finding of dumping and to produce quite large dumping margins (Lindsey and Ikenson 2003; Thai 2003). Similar changes are still ongoing, as most recently illustrated by those proposed by the Obama administration (Ikenson 2010).

Once used exclusively by four developed countries (the EU, the United States, Australia and Canada), antidumping has been increasingly incorporated into the protection arsenals of the emerging and developing countries, as liberalization has eliminated or reduced traditional tools like tariffs, quotas and restrictive import-license schemes (see Figure 6.3). Between 1995 and 2000 India came top of the list of antidumping users ahead of the United States and EU, with South Africa, Brazil and China all joining the likes of the EU, United States, Australia and Canada as

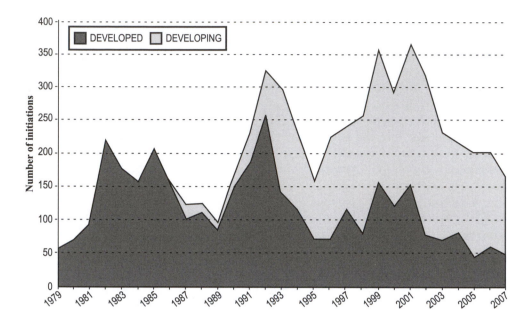

Figure 6.3   AD initiations, by level of development
Source: WTO Secretariat.

major users (Stevenson 2009). Indeed, there is evidence that antidumping (and the other commercial instruments) are increasingly a South–South phenomenon (Bown 2010).

In political economy terms, antidumping regulations were often 'sold' by the international institutions (World Bank, World Trade Organization, and so on) as a means of appeasing the concerns in a country beginning a liberalization process and as a way of 'venting protectionist steam' that might otherwise result in a more general challenge to trade liberalization. However, there is evidence of such a substitution effect only for the heavy users of antidumping actions among the developing economies (Moore and Zanardi 2008).

Legal Aspects: Antidumping in the GATT

GATT Article VI allows WTO members to employ antidumping measures under certain conditions even if this leads to a global level of protection (applied tariff plus antidumping duty) higher than the bound tariff and discriminatory with respect to certain trading partners. The conditions imposed by GATT Article VI deal mainly with definitions and procedures (investigation, determination and application of antidumping duties). It should be stressed that these conditions are expressed in terms vague enough to be open to interpretation and to give rise to practices

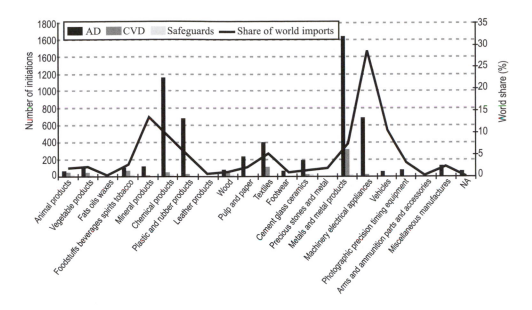

Figure 6.4 Number of initiations and world import share, by HS section

Note: Period of coverage: (1) Anti-dumping: 1979–2007; (2) Countervailing: 1975–2007; (3) Safeguards: 1995–2007.

Source: WTO Secretariat, UN COMTRADE (WTO 2009: 137).

increasingly more favourable to the firms lodging complaints, as described in more detail below.

First of all, Article VI specifies the range of calculations that can be used to determine the intensity of dumping. It provides three options for calculating a product's 'normal value': using the exporter's domestic market price, the price charged by the exporter in another country, or a combination of the exporter's production costs, expenses and typical product margins. Second, it outlines how to compare a normal price with an export price. Third, it sets out procedural guidelines on how to determine whether 'material injury' is actually being caused, including how to initiate, conduct and present evidence in any investigation. Finally, it imposes a five-year time limit on all antidumping measures found to be justified from the date of their imposition.

Efforts were made in the Kennedy Round to clarify all these conditions, particularly by including more precise criteria for determining the existence of 'material injury'. However, the US Congress opposed tighter disciplines on antidumping. As the United States never signed this agreement, it had no practical significance. A decade later, the Tokyo Round tried again to clarify the key concepts (dumping, injury, and so on) and the procedures for how the national competent bodies should conduct investigations, giving birth to the Tokyo Antidumping Code.

However, the Tokyo Antidumping Code did not prevent a boom in antidumping actions (see figures above). As a result, the Uruguay Round reopened the negotiations in order to clarify further the key guidelines on how to assess dumping margins, to identify the 'normal value' of the targeted product, and to provide further details on the methodology of injury investigations, giving birth to the Uruguay Antidumping Agreement. But it also provides for so-called 'price undertakings' (voluntary undertakings from any exporter to revise its prices or to cease exports to the area in question at dumped prices) so long as they eliminate the injury associated with the dumping. Exporters exposed to the threat of potentially disruptive and uncertain antidumping investigations can opt to either raise prices domestically or to cut back supply to reduce the injury to their export market. As noted above, there are strong links between commercial instruments. Price undertakings can have effects similar to VERs: they ease import competition at the cost of welfare losses in the importing market and enable exporters to capture some of the rents created when they reduce supply. In other words, price undertakings could be used to circumvent the ban on VERs which was imposed by the Uruguay negotiations on safeguards. However, the data on price undertakings in Figure 6.5 leave scope for different interpretations. The peaks in their use could be due to cyclical factors or to a lag effect since VERs had to be phased out up to 2000.

The 2001 Doha Ministerial Declaration included antidumping in the mandate of the Doha Round. Negotiations are held in the so-called 'Rules Negotiating Group'. A group of WTO members called the 'Friends of Antidumping Negotiations'

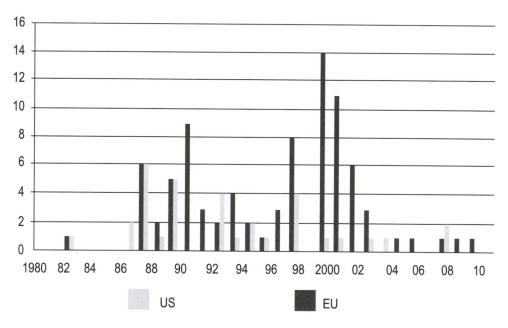

Figure 6.5   Comparison between US and EU price undertakings (1980–2010)
Source: Authors, based on data from the United States and EU.

(FANs) – consisting of developed WTO members, such as the EU and Switzerland, major exporters that have in the past or are currently subject to most antidumping actions, such as Japan, Korea and China, and other emerging markets and developing countries, including India – have made the case for modest detailed revisions of the GATT antidumping provisions.

It is not possible to include discussion of all the detailed reform proposals here, which cover the whole antidumping procedures.[2] What follows gives a brief illustration for each of the various steps of the procedure: defining the 'like product', calculating the dumping margin ('zeroing' and 'nonmarket economies'), determining the measure ('public interest clause') and closing the case ('sunset review').

One of the first steps of an antidumping investigation is to identify the domestic 'like product'. The Uruguay Antidumping Agreement defines this as 'a product which is identical, that is, alike in all respects to the product under consideration or, in the absence of such a product, another product which, although not alike in all respects, has characteristics closely resembling those of the product under consideration'. It has been argued, however, that examining a product simply by its physical characteristics is inadequate. Some argue that a better criterion would be whether any material change has occurred (Yu 2008). Economists would favour the concept of the 'relevant market', a concept widely used in competition cases in order to assess whether the prices of two products interact, or not.

A prominent issue in calculating the antidumping margin is 'zeroing'. Typically, such a calculation requires two steps. The first is to determine the dumping margin of each type or model of the targeted merchandise, which are then aggregated into subcategories. The second step is to combine all of these margins into an overall dumping margin. Some subcategories may show a negative dumping margin, indicating no dumping. However, rather than including a negative number in the overall summation, some authorities simply add a zero and justify this by arguing that, if the subgroup with a negative margin represents a substantial portion of the total sales, the overall margin would be skewed. However, other countries counter that zeroing inflates dumping margins to an unreasonable extent, and might even create artificial dumping where none exists (Thai 2003). Two WTO dispute settlement cases (against the EU in 2004 and against the United States in 2008) ruled that their practices of zeroing were illegal. However, the United States is resisting any reform to antidumping in the Doha Round unless zeroing is permitted.

Another crucial issue at stake when determining the dumping margin is the case of 'nonmarket economies'. This is important because China can be considered as a nonmarket economy by its trading partners until 2017 under China's Accession Protocol to the WTO. In such a case, antidumping investigators can use proxies to estimate the home market prices or costs of the (Chinese) foreign exports in

---

2   For a comprehensive discussion see Chair's Report of the Negotiating Group on Rules of March 2011, WTO TN/RL/24 available from WTO Documents Online at www.WTO.org. or the relevant Consolidated Chair's Text for the Antidumping and Subsidies and Countervailing Duty Measures dates from December 2008 TN/RL/w/236.

determining whether dumping takes place. Such proxies are defined in such a way that they make it easier to prove dumping than for market economies, and they inflate the dumping margin. This is shown by data from 208 EU and US antidumping cases initiated between 1995 and 1998. These show average dumping margins of 15–20 per cent when calculations are based on pure price comparisons and to 25 per cent when they are based on various constructed-value (costs) methods but an average of more than 40 per cent in the case of the nonmarket economies (Messerlin 2004).

The FANs also argue for a mandatory 'public interest clause' for all WTO Members (such a clause already exists in some WTO Members). Public interest clauses require authorities to assess who in the domestic economy will benefit from the proposed action and who will lose and by how much, before imposing antidumping duties. It is argued that such a provision would help prevent regulatory capture by protectionist interests and help ensure that antidumping duties do not have net adverse welfare effects. In fact, such a clause aims to give a voice to the consumers (consumers can be firms as well as households) in the antidumping procedures, which nowadays are totally dominated by domestic producers. In other words, it aims to cope with the political economy of trade where the gains from the imposition of duties are concentrated and the costs dispersed (see Chapter 2). But such clauses have not been very effective in practice because of the difficulty determining what the 'public interest' actually is. For instance, it did not prevent the EU applying dumping duties when only one firm remained in the relevant sector, thus giving it a monopoly position, which could hardly be said to be in the public interest.

Finally, 'sunset reviews' are another issue that pits the FANs against the United States. The Uruguay Antidumping Agreement calls for all measures to be terminated after five years, subject to a review. These sunset reviews determine whether dumping and the material injury to the industry concerned is likely to continue, if so then antidumping duties can be maintained. In the United States, sunset reviews of antidumping measures resulted in a 53 per cent continuation rate (Jones 2006). Countries whose exporters are often hit by such actions therefore advocate either a mandatory termination of measures after five years or stricter conditions for continuation of duties.

Safeguards

Safeguards were initially conceived as a form of insurance mechanism that should help to promote liberalization by allowing 'policymakers to make far-ranging commitments taking into account the uncertainty over future events that may require a change in policy' (WTO 2009: 65), hence by allowing WTO members to restrict imports when liberalization leads to import surges. This initial conceptualization of safeguards lies in US trade policy (Sykes 2006). As the United States moved to promote multilateral trade liberalization, 'the Congress confronted the US President with concerns about possible injury to US industries as a result of trade concessions'. The president agreed to push for an 'escape clause' in future trade arrangements. This initiative then shaped Article XIX of the GATT 1947 devoted to the safeguard instrument.

As noted in the introduction, this initial concept behind safeguards is very different to that behind antidumping or anti-subsidy actions. While antidumping actions deal with situations where the behaviour of foreign firms is seen as unfair, safeguard actions deal with situations where domestic firms are perceived as unable to cope with foreign competition (Messerlin 2000).

This concept, definitively much less favourable to the domestic firms, largely explains the stricter conditions imposed on the use of safeguards compared to those on the use of antidumping (WTO 2009: 54). Import surges must have been caused by 'unforeseen developments'. 'Serious injury' (a higher threshold than the 'material injury' in antidumping and anti-subsidy actions) to a domestic industry must be demonstrated and there must be a causal link between the increase in imports and the injury. Second, once these conditions have been met, a country can establish 'temporary' (an at-the-time undefined term) protectionist measures, such as tariffs or quotas. GATT Article XIX stipulates that these protectionist measures must be nondiscriminatory and that countries enacting safeguards must provide compensation to the exporting countries.

Until 1994, these stricter conditions were unchallenged, with two consequences. Safeguards were infrequently used until the mid-1990s: from 1948 to 1994, only 150 safeguard-related actions were taken in the GATT. VERs and antidumping measures became the dominant commercial instruments of the 'new protectionism' of the 1970s–1980s.

However, as so often in the domain of commercial instruments, the conditions on the use of the safeguard instrument have been progressively challenged. For instance, what is the acceptable threshold for import 'surges'? Does it require increases in absolute or in relative terms? Until when can developments be said to be 'unforeseen'? A couple of years after a liberalization seems a reasonable answer. But is it still the case when 'unforeseen' development occurs a decade after the related liberalization?

The Recent Evolution of the Safeguard Instrument

The increasing use of VERs during the 1970s and 1980s led to a political push to restore and enhance disciplines over safeguard measures in order to contain VERs (Sykes 2006). The attempt made during the Tokyo Round to strengthen both the use of safeguards and the scope of international control over them was unsuccessful (Rodriguez 2007). The 1995 Agreement on Safeguards (ASG) included in the Uruguay Round looked more favourable. It required VERs and other 'grey area' measures to be phased out by 1999. Sunset provisions were introduced for the first time: safeguards can be in place for a maximum of two periods of four years, in between which they can be renewed. Safeguards in the form of quantitative restrictions should also not reduce imports below the average level of imports over the previous three years. Safeguard measures could only be applied to a developing country's product if that country is supplying over 3 per cent of the imports of that product for a country.

However, at the same time, other elements of the ASG relaxed several key disciplines on safeguard actions, making them more attractive compared to antidumping (Messerlin 2000). Immediate provisional safeguards are allowed in 'critical circumstances' while the ASG makes no mention of GATT Article XIX condition that a relationship between ongoing liberalization and the import surges must exist. It also allows safeguard users not to compensate the exporting country for three years, unless investigation shows that no serious injury was caused by imports, at which point provisional duties must be reimbursed. While GATT Article XIX allows for immediate retaliation when a safeguard measure is taken, the ASG requires a three-year period after the safeguard's implementation before retaliation is allowed. Finally, quotas could now be used as safeguard measures in a more discriminatory way, with in particular the possibility to exempt preferential trade area partners and small developing countries.

As illustrated in Figure 6.1, the changes brought by the ASG led to a greater use of safeguards since the Uruguay Round. But antidumping actions remain still 'the trade remedy of choice' (Heydon and Woolcock 2009: 48). A reason may be a statistical artifice: by their legal nature, antidumping actions have a narrower scope in terms of products and firms – hence need to be more numerous than safeguards to achieve the same protectionist impact. That said, antidumping actions clearly allow a stronger discriminatory treatment of the foreign firms.

The Doha mandate does not include discussions on safeguards. Moreover, the Appellate Body has taken no clear steps to interpret ambiguity in the agreement (such as serious injury, unforeseen developments). Many safeguard actions that have been brought to WTO dispute settlement have been found to be inconsistent with WTO law. As Grossman and Sykes (2007) observe, the 'legal requirements for the use of safeguards are largely incoherent, and no nation can employ them without the near certainty of defeat in the dispute resolution process should they be challenged'.

A key debated issue is that safeguard measures can sometimes violate the most favoured nation (MFN) principle (Bown and McCulloch 2007). Small developing countries and preferential trade agreement (PTA) partners of the countries that use safeguards are on occasion excluded from these measures. But should PTA partners be excluded when safeguards are only intended for dire emergencies? It should be added, however, that most PTAs provide for the use of safeguard actions against PTA partners during the preferential liberalization. If most PTAs provide less scope for safeguards than under the ASG, by for example specifying two or three years as the maximum duration of a safeguard or a higher threshold for injury, some of them include 'special' safeguards which tend to enlarge the use of this instrument.

With the liberalization of services there also arises a question of whether there should be a safeguards provision within the General Agreement on Trade in

Services (GATS). As of today, GATS Article X on 'emergency safeguard measures' in services has no clear content (Messerlin 2000), despite it being under negotiation for a number of years. On one hand, a safeguard might encourage more service-related commitments, but on the other 'the trade-off between expected gains in liberalization and (safeguards-related) losses in predictability appears more precarious than in the area of goods' (WTO 2009: 51).

Special Safeguards

Where the 'risks' of liberalization have been seen to be especially high, or when the need to placate opposition to liberalization is especially strong, special safeguards have been introduced. An important example of the first motive is the special safeguard included in China's Accession Protocol to the WTO. Section 16 of the Protocol provides for 'WTO-minus' rules on so-called 'transitional product-specific safeguard' measures. This is WTO-minus in the sense that it requires proof of the lower level 'material injury' rather than the 'serious injury' required in the ASG (Lee 2005; Messerlin 2004).This has some systemic consequences in that as soon as one country has undertaken a safeguard measure against China under Section 16, the criteria for the other countries to adopt a similar measure are even less constraining.

An example of the second motive (especially strong opposition to liberalization) is the Special Safeguard Mechanism (SSM) considered in the Doha Round. The SSM would allow for a more generous use of safeguards than that allowed under Article XIX of the GATT or arguably under the existing Special Safeguards already available for agriculture under the Uruguay Agriculture Agreement. Essentially, the proposal for the SSM is intended to allow developing and recently acceded countries to protect their subsistence farmers against import surges. The mechanism, first proposed by developing countries in 2001, has put countries (including India and China) favouring greater scope to use the SSM in opposition to the United States, which favours a higher threshold for import surges to trigger an action (WTO 2009: 50). As any safeguard, the SSM requires the definition of the threshold allowed to trigger the action as well as the type and magnitude of the safeguard measure. Discussions on these issues have failed (Wolfe 2009) and have become the official reason for the collapse of the whole Doha negotiations in the July 2008 mini-Ministerial. By contrast, the Doha draft text scraps the 'special safeguard' created by the Uruguay Agreement for developed Members, hence contributing to the elimination of the 'reversed special and differential treatment (SDT)' enjoyed by the developed countries under the Uruguay Agreement.

Subsidies and Anti-Subsidy (Countervailing) Actions

Anti-subsidy (often called countervailing) actions are commercial instruments used to counter the distortions in competition caused by subsidies provided by the government of a trading partner. Subsidies must involve both financial contributions by the government and benefit conferrals (Hoda and Ahuja 2005). They can take many forms, such as direct payments, tax concessions or soft loans to firms. They can be generally available or firm-specific. While subsidies can be used for social welfare purposes or to correct market failures, they are seen as having an 'adverse effect' on countries importing subsidized goods through causing 'injury to a domestic industry, nullification or impairment of tariff concessions, or serious prejudice or threat thereof to the country's interests' (Hoekman and Kostecki 2009: 221). Economists argue that lower (subsidized) prices are beneficial to the foreign consumers of the subsidized goods. But the political economy of subsidies means that the cries of 'unfair' competition from those more directly affected by the costs, namely the competing industry in the importing country, tend to drown out such an argument.

Countervailing duties aim to offset the subsidy provided to exporters by raising the price of the imported good from its 'artificially' low to its alleged 'unsubsidized' price level. As they are also regulated by GATT Article VI (as antidumping actions) they also utilize the rhetoric of unfair trade to justify their use: the purpose of such duties is to counter trade-distorting subsidies in order to restore 'fair' competition. Countervailing duties are the least common of the commercial instruments, and they have predominantly been used by the United States. As China has emerged as a major export competitor and one that is seen to provide various subsidies for its exporters, there has been a rapid increase in the number of countervailing duties against China, as shown by Figure 6.7. Between 2007 and 2010, the United States launched 14 anti-subsidy duties against various allegedly subsidized Chinese exports.

Contrary to antidumping actions, which are aimed at firms, countervailing duties are aimed at countries, particularly developing countries (see Figure 6.6). This makes them more politically sensitive and likely to result in retaliation, as the Bombardier–Embraer case illustrated. In 1996, Canada complained that Brazilian subsidies to foreign purchases of Embraer were illegal export subsidies. This was confirmed by a 1999 WTO panel report. Brazil retaliated quickly in kind, pointing out illegal export subsidies by Canada.

When the country adopting countervailing duties is large, this may dissuade retaliation, which may explain why it is the United States that has to date been the main user of countervailing duties.

Number of CVD initiations, by user and target, 1975-2007

Users	Targets		
	Developed	Developing	Total
Developed	228	387	615
Developing	57	172	229
Total	285	559	844

Safeguard initiations, by user, 1995-2007

Users	Initiations	Measures
Developed	20	9
Developing	143	74
Total	163	83

Figure 6.6   Number of CVD and safeguard initiations
Source: WTO Secretariat.

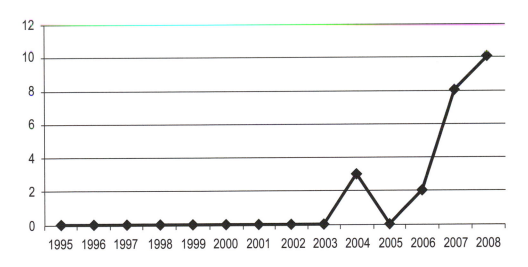

Figure 6.7   Percentage of CVD investigations against China
Source: Stevenson (2009: 15).

Subsidies and Anti-Subsidy Duties in the GATT

Subsidies have been addressed in increasingly stringent terms in the GATT. GATT 1947 only permitted action against subsidies if they caused 'serious prejudice' (Hoda and Ahuja 2005: 1009). Several years later, in the 1955–6 Review Session, a provision was introduced which prohibited all export subsidies on manufactured goods. A declaration that gave effect to this provision was adopted in 1962 by several developed countries. However, this provision was weak and ineffective (Hoda and Ahuja 2005: 1010). The Tokyo Round witnessed the adoption of a plurilateral Subsidies Code aimed at a tightening of the disciplines on export subsidies for manufactures and extended the prohibition of export subsidies to primary mineral products. It also addressed countervailing duties, introducing detailed procedural rules for investigation and imposition of countervailing duties.

The Uruguay Round led to the adoption of a stricter Agreement on Subsidies and Countervailing Measures (SCM) because the mood of the early 1990s was marked by strong opposition to the use of subsidies, which had shown too often their limited and/or perverse impact during the three previous decades.

The SCM Agreement regulates simultaneously the use of subsidies and the countervailing duties. The rules of the Agreement are intended to limit or preclude the adverse effects of subsidies on WTO Members and to prevent subsidies from counteracting concessions that have already been made during trade liberalization. The 1995 version of the SCM Agreement distinguished three types of subsidies with a 'traffic light' approach (non-actionable, actionable if they distort trade, prohibited). This approach was valid until 1999 and it could have been extended if there had then been a consensus. This consensus was not reached: as a result, there are no more 'non-actionable' subsidies.

A complainant country has thus two choices under the current SCM. First (the most frequent case) is to take a unilateral approach by investigating the subsidy and charging an additional (countervailing) duty on the subsidized imports that are having an adverse effect on domestic producers. To use countervailing duties, a country must meet requirements similar to those required for antidumping actions. It must provide proof that the exporting country is utilizing measures that can be considered as subsidies (financial contribution granting some benefits and distorting trade). It must show material injury to a domestic industry producing the like products. It must also provide evidence of a causal link between the exporter's subsidy and the material injury incurred. Alternatively, the country can pursue a multilateral response by taking the subsidizing country to the WTO dispute settlement panel in an attempt to bring about the withdrawal of the subsidy or its painful effects. The SCM imposes a sunset provision of five years for countervailing duties, subject to the detailed requirements and deadlines for investigations being met. Currently, export subsidies are also prohibited in the WTO for all but the least-developed countries (LDCs) and very low-income countries.

Subsidies and countervailing actions are included in the Doha Round mandate. The 2001 Doha Ministerial Declaration underscores the need to 'clarify and improve disciplines under the Agreements on Implementation of Article VI of the GATT

1994 and on Subsidies and Countervailing Measures'. As for antidumping, the basic concepts and objectives will be preserved, while there are some efforts to clarify them. At the same time, the Doha Round develops in an environment markedly different from the anti-subsidy mood of the Uruguay Round in the sense that it recognizes that 'subsidies may play an important role in developing countries and in the transformation of centrally planned economies to market economies'. In this context, it will be interesting to see what will be the impact of a recent Appellate Body ruling on several Chinese products which found that 'double remedies' (a countervailing duty combined with an antidumping duty) are inconsistent with WTO rules when subsidies are part of the cause for the dumping (the foreign firms are alleged to dump partly because they benefit from subsidies).[3]

Subsidies (Domestic Support) in Agriculture

The Uruguay Round Agreement on agriculture has witnessed the first efforts to discipline subsidies (often called 'domestic support') in agriculture. It defines three types of subsidies: the Amber Box ('aggregate measure of support' or AMS) covers the domestic support that is the most distorting because it is tightly linked to prices (price-support mechanisms) and/or to production; the *de minimis* Box covers measures of similar nature as those of the Amber Box, but in smaller amounts (they should not exceed 5–10 per cent of farm production); and the Blue Box includes domestic support considered as less distorting than the Amber Box because it is subjected to some restrictive conditions (such as imposing production limits curbing potential overproduction on direct payments based on the number of animals or on the area planted).

The Doha draft text in agriculture defines a complex set of cuts, caps on cuts and exceptions to these cuts. Cuts should be undertaken within each of these boxes at two levels: the country's aggregate agricultural output, and the level of the country's outputs of specific products. This two-level system aims at preventing the circumvention of the Doha disciplines on the global domestic support through transfers between different products.

Rather than describing all the cuts, caps and exceptions in detail, it is more important to get a sense of the impact of the Doha draft text on the farm production of the EU and the United States, the two major providers of subsidies. Calculations show that the Doha Round would essentially bind the EC and US farm policies expected to prevail by 2013 (Messerlin 2012, forthcoming).

This result may seem minor, but this is not the case. First, it means that the vast drifts in farm support of the 1950s–1990s will become impossible, or at least extremely costly. Second, it means that the Doha commitments would reduce the share of domestic support in agricultural output value to 12–14 per cent in the United States and EC – a percentage close to the NAMA average post-Doha tariff of emerging economies such as Brazil or India. This similarity suggests that the

---

3   Bridges Weekly Trade Digest, 16 March 2011.

criterion of 'a comparably high level of ambition in market access for Agriculture and NAMA' imposed by the negotiators in the context of a 'Doha Development Agenda' would be met.

Conclusions

There is a clear view among economists and some practitioners that 'contingent protection measures' are more of a political instrument than measures based on any sound economic or legal criteria. Safeguards, countervailing measures and above all antidumping duties have tended to be used as a form of (protectionist) 'political safety valve' when sensitive sectors face increased import competition. In the past, such measures were mostly used by the key major developed economies as they faced competition from low cost and more efficient producers in the NICs. In recent years there appears to have been a decline in the use of contingent protection by these developed countries and a relative shift towards greater use by developing countries. This could well be due to the growth in the use of value chains and the dispersal of different production functions across a range of countries. Such dispersed, global production patterns could well have changed the political economy of contingent protection because the costs of duties or restrictions on imports impact many firms, including the complainants. This would mean that contingent protection would be increasingly sought more by industries that are relatively less internationalized.

The prospects for major reforms of antidumping and anti-subsidy actions in the Doha Round are low and the proposals tabled so far are unlikely to have a significant impact. In an awkward way, drastic reforms would have the unintended – but expected – counterproductive consequence of triggering a boost in the safeguard actions which unfortunately are not fully included in the Doha Round mandate.

In such a difficult context the best policy prescription could be to promote greater transparency with regard to the costs and benefits of contingent protection. Investigations should reveal the 'wide variety of potentially distorted market outcomes' (Messerlin 1996, Bloningen and Prusa 2003) by providing information on the market structure of the goods under scrutiny, the market shares of the complainants and of the defendants, who owns whom as well as technological or production links between firms and the risks of collusive behaviour in case of measures being taken. Reviews could also assess the effectiveness of the commercial instruments to reach the targets they are supposed to achieve: how many jobs have been protected? Which have been the best protected interests (domestic or foreign ones, owners or workers)? Changing the minds of all the interests involved in commercial instruments is crucial for deep reforms in the future.

References

Bloningen, B. and Prusa, T. 2003. Anti-dumping, in *Handbook of International Trade Volume 1*, edited by K. Choi and J.C. Hartigan. Oxford: Basil Blackwell: 251–85.

Bourgeois, J. and Messerlin, P. 1998. The European Community's experience, in *Brookings Trade Forum 1998*, edited by R.Z. Lawrence. Washington, DC: The Brookings Institution: 127–45.

Bown, C. 2010. Taking stock of antidumping, safeguards and countervailing duties, 1990–2009, *World Bank Policy Research Working Paper 5436*. Washington, DC: World Bank.

Bown, C. and McCulloch, R. 2007. Trade adjustment in the WTO system: are more safeguards the answer? *Oxford Review of Economic Policy* 23: 415–39.

Grossman, G. and Sykes, A. 2007. United States: definitive safeguard measures on imports of certain steel products. *World Trade Review* 6(1): 89–122.

Heydon, K. and Woolcock, S. 2009. *The Rise of Bilateralism: Comparing American, European and Asian Approaches to Preferential Trade Agreements*. Tokyo: United Nations University Press.

Hoda, A. and Ahuja, R. 2005. The agreement on subsidies and countervailing measures: need for clarification and improvement. *Journal of World Trade* 39(6): 1009–70.

Hoekman, B.M. and Kostecki, M.M. 2009. *The Political Economy of the World Trading System: The WTO and Beyond*. 3rd Edition. Oxford: Oxford University Press.

Ikenson, D. 2010. Protection made to order: domestic industry's capture and reconfiguration of US anti-dumping policy. *Trade Policy Analysis No.44*, Washington, DC: Cato Institute.

Jones, V.C. 2006. WTO: anti-dumping issues in the Doha Development Agenda. CRS Report for Congress. Washington, DC: Congressional Research Service, Library of Congress.

Lee, E.K. 2005. *Transitional Product Specific Safeguard Mechanism: A WTO–Minus Measure of the Protocol on the Accession of the People's Republic of China and its Implication on the WTO Legal System*, LLM dissertation 2002. Seoul: Seoul National University.

Lindsey, B. and Ikenson, D.J. 2003. *Antidumping Exposed: The Devilish Details of Unfair Trade Law*. Washington, DC: CATO Institute.

Messerlin, P. 1990. Anti-dumping regulation or procartel law? The EC Chemical Cases. *The World Economy* 13(4): 465–92.

Messerlin, P. 1996. Competition policy and anti-dumping reform: an exercise in transition, in *The World Trading System: Challenges Ahead*, edited by J.J. Schott. Washington, DC: Institute for International Economics: 219–46.

Messerlin, P. 2000. Anti-dumping and safeguards, in *WTO After Seattle*, edited by J.J. Schott. Washington, DC: Institute for International Economics: 159–83.

Messerlin, P. 2004. Anti-dumping and safeguards, in *China in the WTO: Accession, Policy Reform and Poverty Reduction*, edited by D. Bhattasali, S. Li and W. Martin. Washington, DC: Palgrave Macmillan and the World Bank: 29–48.

Messerlin, P. 2012. The Doha Round, in *Handbook of Trade Policy for Development* [forthcoming], edited by A. Lukauskas, R.M. Stern and G. Zanini. Oxford: Oxford University Press.

Moore, M. and Zanardi, M. 2008. Trade liberalization and anti-dumping: is there a substitution effect? *ECARES Working Paper 2008–024.* (July). Brussels: ULB.

Rodriguez, P.M. 2007. Safeguards in the World Trade Organization 10 years after: a dissociated state of the law? *Journal of World Trade* 41(1): 159–90.

Shin, H.J. 1998. Possible instances of predatory pricing in recent US anti-dumping cases, in *Brookings Trade Forum 1998*, edited by R.Z. Lawrence. Washington, DC: The Brookings Institution: 81–97.

Stevenson, C. 2009. Global Trade Protection Report 2009: a review of global trade protection activity in 2008 (anti-dumping, countervailing duty and safeguards). [Online] Available at: www.antidumpingpublishing.com/info/free-resources/gtp-report.aspx [accessed: 29 March 2011].

Sykes, A.O. 2006. *The WTO Agreement on Safeguards: A Commentary.* Oxford: Oxford University Press.

Thai, B.A. 2003. *Zeroing Practice in the Calculation of Dumped Margins in the United States of America.* Lagos: BAO & Partners Report.

Wolfe, A. 2009. *The Special Safeguard fiasco in the WTO: The Perils of Inadequate Analysis and Negotiations.* Paris: Groupe d'Economie Mondiale at Sciences Po (GEM).

WTO. 2009. *World Trade Report 2009: Trade Policy Commitments and Contingency Measures.* Geneva: WTO.

Yu, Y. 2008. *Circumvention and Anti-circumvention Measures: The Impact on Anti-dumping Practice in International Trade.* The Netherlands: Kluwer Law International.

Trade Facilitation

Andrew Grainger

Introduction

Complaints about excessive red-tape and bureaucracy are frequent in international trade operations. The volume of paperwork and hurdles in ensuring compliance with set trade and customs procedures can be extensive.[1] Efficient and timely trade operations are all too often made dependent on the ability to manage trade and customs compliance effectively – preferably electronic and automated. The potential gain to be had from procedural reform is significant. Each 1 per cent reduction in trade-related transaction costs is estimated by the OECD to yield a worldwide benefit worth US$43 billion (OECD 2003). In countries with high levels of perceived bureaucracy, opportunity for trade facilitation-focused reform is particularly great. Trade facilitation promises improved business competitiveness, accelerated trade-led growth, a more streamlined and service-orientated public administration, as well as more efficient revenue collection and tighter security.

Described in the simplest of terms, trade facilitation is about making international trade operations as simple and easy as possible. As such, trade facilitation is nothing new. Many ideas underlying trade facilitation are as old as trade itself. Keen observers of administrative and commercial practice can easily find evidence of trade facilitation throughout history. For example, many medieval market towns in Europe kept public displays of applicable weights and measures to which, in the event of any dispute between traders, authoritative reference could be made.[2] Providing access to such public standards is free; they can significantly reduce the cost of conducting business transactions. Another example of early trade facilitation is the ancient customs stone at Ephesus,[3] which describes the customs regulations that were applicable during Roman times (Cottier et al. 2008).

---

[1]   For example, see George et al. 2009.
[2]   In the city of Bern in Switzerland such weights and measures are still on display today.
[3]   It is commonly referred to by historians as 'the Monument from Ephesus', which is now kept at the Ephesus Archaeological Museum in Sleçuk, Turkey.

Like today, public access to applicable trade and customs regulations ensures that traders know how to comply. In contrast, the absence of published rules and procedures creates uncertainty, provides unnecessary opportunity for the solicitation of bribes, greatly increases commercial risk and inhibits any trader's appetite for trade across borders.

Moving on from history, the topic of trade facilitation has, over the last decade, established itself as a central theme within mainstream trade policy (Grainger 2011). In light of falling tariff levels and a shift in trade policy towards the non-tariff area, this trend is probably not surprising. The World Trade Organization (WTO) formerly started discussing trade facilitation in 1996 as one of the four Singapore Issues; although, as stated in the General Agreement on Tariffs and Trade (GATT) preamble (GATT 1947), the substantial reduction of non-tariff barriers has always been a key objective. While three of the original four Singapore Issues have been dropped,[4] appetite for negotiating trade facilitation remains strong. Formal negotiations commenced in November 2004 with initial focus on Articles V, VIII and X of the GATT (1994), covering Freedom of Transit, Fees and Formalities, and Publication and Administration of Trade Regulations. Negotiation text is now in a reasonably advanced form (WTO 2010), though negotiations are closely linked to trade development and capacity-building type concerns. Subsequent sums allocated to narrowly defined trade facilitation capacity-building programmes have risen from US$100 million in 2001 to US$392 million in 2006 (WTO/OECD 2010). While detailed figures are difficult to compile, sums spent on closely related trade infrastructure and modernization programmes, which in themselves contain substantial trade facilitation–related components, are likely to be in the order of many billion dollars (OECD 2006).

Similar policy momentum towards trade facilitation can also be observed within regional as well as national trade and customs modernization programmes. For example, the European Union is currently in the process of radically overhauling its customs infrastructure with the aim of bringing together national customs administration systems more efficiently through use of modern technology (TAXUD/477/2004), generally referred to as the electronic customs initiative. Equally ambitious is the commitment by ASEAN leaders to develop interoperable Single Window systems (ASEAN 2005) that, if fully implemented, will radically reduce the cost of exchanging information such as trade and customs declarations between traders and regulatory authorities (UN/CEFACT 2004). Some national trade and customs systems, such as Singapore's TradeNet (Applegate et al. 1993; Teo et al. 1997) or Korea's uTradeHub[5] are often cited as being particularly inspirational. Motivation for such projects is to modernize current administrative systems and increase trade competitiveness by reducing the cost of complying with trade and customs procedures.

---

[4]   The three issues dropped from the original Singapore package were transparency in government procurement, investment and competition policy.

[5]   See www.utradehub.or.kr.

Supply chain security is another topic closely linked with trade facilitation (IMO 2003; WCO 2007). Relatively recent terrorist events that have fuelled public concern, such as the Lockerbie Bombing in 1988 or 9/11 in 2001, are now forcing policymakers to revisit the effectiveness of controls and procedures at national borders. They fear that the transport infrastructure carrying goods could be misused for terrorist purposes; be it, for example, to deliver destructive weapons or in the context of smuggling and clandestine cross-border movements (Flynn 2002). Many regulatory agencies now want to identify risks before goods move (Grainger 2007a). Trade facilitation is viewed as a means to make tighter controls more palatable to business communities (UNECE 2003). The debate between security and facilitation is often presented as an 'either-or' to which policymakers need to find the right balance. An alternative and more appropriate view is that the application of trade facilitation concepts – such as audit-based controls, risk management control techniques (Widdowson 2005) and preferential treatment of trusted, authorized economic operators (WCO 2007) – can improve overall enforcement and reduce compliance cost (Grainger 2008b).

To some extent trade facilitation may also be described as a trade policy agenda item made necessary by exponentially growing volumes in trade over the last few decades, thanks in part to ever-falling trade tariffs. This jars somewhat with the fact that inspection resources remain finite. To accommodate growing trade volumes with finite inspection resources, control strategies have to be made more effective and smarter. The traditional control paradigm, rooted in the image of a boom barrier and inspectors rummaging through cargo, has become somewhat outdated, especially in light of growing demands for tighter security without disrupting global production. In consequence, greater collaboration between the public and private sector is one of the key ingredients in any trade facilitation strategy (Grainger 2010).

At present there is no single definition for trade facilitation. As highlighted by the OECD (2001) a number of international organizations have made suggestions. For example, the WTO in an online training package once defined it as 'the simplification and harmonisation of international trade procedures' where trade procedures are the 'activities, practices and formalities involved in collecting, presenting, communicating and processing data required for the movement of goods in international trade' (WTO 1998). Procedures might be official in nature, for example in relation to complying with governing rules and regulations, or commercial in nature, for example the arrangements relating to payment between two contracting business parties. For most proponents of trade facilitation it is a topic that looks at how procedures and controls governing the movement of goods across national borders can be improved to reduce associated cost burdens and maximize efficiency while safeguarding legitimate regulatory objectives (Grainger 2011). Brian Staples very appropriately describes trade facilitation as the plumbing of international trade (Staples 2002); or as SITPRO, the former UK trade facilitation agency, once clarified in its tagline: trade facilitation is about 'cutting "red-tape" in international trade'.

Trade Operations

Indeed, there is a lot of red-tape in international trade. As most freight forwarders are likely to assert, the document in-tray can all too easily present itself as the most disruptive bottleneck in international transport operations. Mismatched reference numbers, missing supporting documentation, incomplete declarations and congested inspection facilities can easily bring shipments to a halt – even in the best managed economies. Cross-border operations tend to be complex, requiring a multitude of parties to work together. Amongst contracting business parties these can include:

- Traders, such as buyers, sellers, their agents and distributors.
- Transport operators, such as shipping lines, airlines, railway companies, logistics and trucking companies.
- Providers of trade services, such as banking, finance and insurance.
- Operators of transport infrastructure, such as port terminals, airports, stevedores and handling agents, warehouses and electronic information systems.
- Specialist service providers, such as freight forwarders, shipping agents and logistics service providers.

The regulatory side of trade is equally diverse. While most trade and customs procedures are specific to the control of goods, related controls targeting the vehicles moving the goods (transport) and people operating the vehicles (drivers, seafarers, flight crews) or running the companies (owners, directors and employees) can be equally – if not more – disruptive. Typically, regulatory procedures with an impact on cross-border operations can be classified into five groups: (1) Revenue Collection; (2) Safety and Security; (3) Environment and Health; (4) Consumer Protection; and (5) Trade Policy (see Figure 7.1).

Institutional arrangements for applying regulations vary greatly from country to country. Although the lead body is frequently customs, immigration and quarantine inspectors are often equally visible. There are however many other, usually less visible, executive bodies and agencies, too. Ministries, apart from customs, with a direct or indirect interest in trade facilitation typically include: finance, trade, transport, industry, home or internal affairs, police, immigration, forestry,[6] agriculture, fishery, planning and investment, information and communications, trading standards, health and safety, and statistics. In the United Kingdom, to give an example, it is easy to count more than 60 rules and procedures that can potentially apply (Grainger 2007a). Depending on how one counts the operational steps necessary for complying with each of the procedures, this number is probably much higher (Grainger 2007b). Figure 7.2 highlights some

---

[6]   Timber is one of the most prevalent packaging materials in international trade, frequently used as dunnage, for crating, and palletization. Forestry inspectors are likely to worry about parasites and diseases carried in untreated wood products.

Regulatory Category	Examples of Related Activity
Revenue Collection	Collection of Customs duties, excise duties and other indirect taxes; payment of duties and fees; management of bonds and other financial securities
Safety and Security	Security and anti-smuggling controls; dangerous goods; vehicle checks; immigration and visa formalities; export licences
Environment and Health	Phytosanitary, veterinary and hygiene controls; health and safety measures; CITES controls; ships' waste
Consumer Protection	Product testing; labelling; conformity checks with marketing standards (e.g. fruit and vegetables).
Trade Policy	Administration of Quota restrictions; Agriculture refunds

Figure 7.1   Regulatory categories and examples
Source: Grainger (2011).

of the documentary requirements that may be relevant to imports into the UK. Important to add is that trade and customs procedures do not only apply at home; they are equally prevalent in both source and destination countries (George et al. 2009). For landlocked countries transit procedures add a further dimension to potential complexity and cost. Figure 7.3 provides a brief overview of some of the procedures that may apply in any given landlocked country.

For businesses the act of compliance with regulatory requirements has both direct and indirect cost implications (OECD 2003). Direct costs are those that apply immediately when collecting, producing, transmitting and processing documents as well as the information necessary to complete those documents (or their electronic equivalent). Further costs include associated charges and fees, including the costs of setting up bonds and guarantees, laboratory tests and test certificates, inspection fees, and stamp charges. Commercial organizations frequently add their own service fees, including labour and handling charges for moving goods to inspection and storage facilities, demurrage charges, and out-of-hours surcharges. Many companies are likely to instruct third parties to manage compliance operations on their behalf. These types of specialist service providers include freight forwarders, customs brokers, logistics service providers and IT vendors (supplying electronic data management solutions); they, too, will add to their fees.

Indirect costs are subsequent to direct costs. These are often less tangible, but nevertheless very real – and often a greater barrier to trade than the direct costs. They include the costs resulting from delay at the border, missed business opportunities and undermined business competitiveness. It may be a cliché, but the damages for a shipper of turkeys who misses Christmas will be dire. Indirect costs are often the result of missing or contradictory documentation (for example

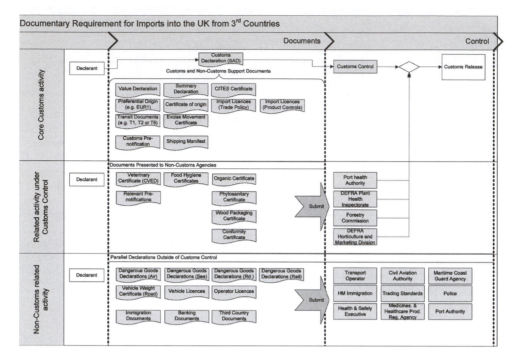

Figure 7.2   Documentary requirements for imports into the UK
Source: Grainger (2007b).

non-matching reference numbers amongst accompanying documents), delay by government authorities, congestion at inspection facilities, or overall heavy-handedness applied by executive agencies. Trade facilitation seeks to reduce the direct and indirect costs for business; though efficiency gains can be of equal benefit to regulatory authorities, too.

Key Institutions

A wide range of international institutions are applying themselves to the topic of trade facilitation. Their output of trade facilitation recommendation is long (Grainger 2011; UN/CEFACT and UNCTAD 2002) and extends from standards for trade documents and electronic communications to best-practice administrative systems (UN/CEFACT 2004), private sector consultation arrangements (UN/CEFACT 1974) and control practices (WCO 2007). Guiding principles underlying all trade facilitation measures tend to be the simplification, harmonization, standardization and modernization of trade procedures. Trade facilitation ideas can

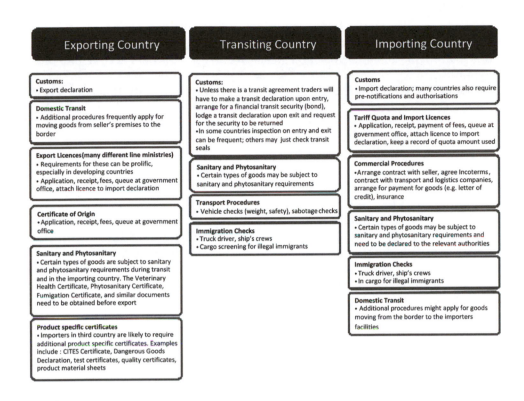

Figure 7.3   Illustrative example: Trade and customs procedures for exports from a landlocked country

Source: Author.

be categorized into four interdependent elements. They are: '1) the simplification and harmonization of applicable rules and procedures; 2) the modernization of trade compliance systems, in particular the sharing of information and lodgement of declarations between business and government stakeholders; 3) the administration and management of trade procedures; and 4) the institutional mechanism to safeguard the effective implementation of trade facilitation principles and the ongoing commitment to reform' (Grainger 2011).

Particularly prolific at the international level is the United Nations Centre for Trade Facilitation and Electronic Business (UN/CEFACT). It currently looks after 35 trade facilitation recommendations. UN/CEFACT is located in Geneva within the United Nations Economic Commission for Europe[7] (UNECE). Other groups within the UNECE also concern themselves with trade facilitation. For example, together with the International Road Transport Union the UNECE is responsible for the Road Transit Convention and UNECE's Working Party 7 looks after

---

[7]   Irrespective of its location, UN/CEFACT's remit is global.

agriculture quality standards that are relevant to the enforcement of horticulture and marketing standards. Standardized procedures for the transport of dangerous goods (flammable, toxic, corrosive, explosive[8]) also form part of the UNECE's work programme.

In view of the prominent role played by customs administrations, the World Customs Organisation (WCO), based in Brussels, is of particular significance. It maintains and supports a number of international instruments that seek to harmonize, simplify and modernize customs procedures. Noteworthy instruments include the Harmonised Commodity Description and Coding System for tariff classification (commonly referred to as the HS code) and the Revised Kyoto [Customs] Convention on the Simplification and Harmonisation of Customs Procedures. Working with the WTO, the WCO is also responsible for the interpretation of valuation rules under GATT Article VII and the non-preferential origin rules under the WTO Agreement on Rules of Origin. Specific to security and trade facilitation is the WCO's SAFE framework of standards (WCO 2007).

Sector-specific international organizations of note that have an interest in trade facilitation include the International Organization for Standardization (standards for handling equipment, but also for management systems such as ISO 28000), the International Maritime Organization (IMO 2011), the International Chamber of Shipping (shipping documents), the International Civil Aviation Organization and the International Air Transport Association (Smith and Moosberger 2009), the International Road Transport Union (transit procedures) and the International Chamber of Commerce (ICC). The ICC is particularly active in the area of commercial procedures, such as those governing trading terms (ICC 2010) and the use of letters of credit (ICC 2006).

The WTO, as outlined earlier, has been looking at trade facilitation in greater detail since 1996. Member proposals (WTO 2009) and the subsequent negotiating text (WTO 2010) are now reasonably mature and draw heavily on the work prepared by the organizations referred to above. The negotiating text includes ideas such as measures to ensure that rules and regulations are published and publically accessible, for instance via a website; the establishment of national enquiry points; commitments to active consultation with public and private sector stakeholders (Grainger 2010); use of advance rulings that cannot be overturned by executive officers at the border;[9] the right to appeal rulings and decisions taken by executive agencies; discipline relating to the setting of fees (such as for stamping documents or testing goods) and the scale of penalties (including provisions to correct inadvertent mistakes); pre-arrival processing; risk-based controls (Widdowson 2005); simplified customs procedures (WCO 2006); preferential procedures for authorized businesses (WCO 2007); cooperation between WTO members to reduce duplication (such as between import and export controls); use of international

---

[8]   This can include seemingly innocent and common products such as alcohol, hay, flour, pressurised gasses, and hospital waste.

[9]   The Binding Tariff Information as used in the European Union, provides one such example.

document standards or their electronic equivalent (UN/CEFACT 1981); the use of single window systems (UN/CEFACT 2004); to draw on commercial documents (such as the invoice) in lieu of official control documents; and the freedom of transit with minimal disruption.

Economic bodies with a remit in development or cooperation play a role, too. The World Bank for instance has provided substantial intellectual capital as well as financial resources. Noteworthy background publications include the World Bank's Customs Modernisation Handbook (De Wulf and Sokol 2005) and the Border Management Modernization guide (McLinden, et al. 2010). The Organization for Economic Cooperation and Development (OECD 2003, 2009; WTO/OECD 2010) and United Nations Conference on Trade and Development (UNCTAD 2006a, 2006b) have also provided valuable research. Further contributions with a more regional focus on the trade facilitation debate have been provided by the United Nations Economic and Social Commission for Asia and the Pacific (UNESCAP 2004, 2009), Asia–Pacific Economic Cooperation (APEC) (Wilson et al. 2003), the Asian Development Bank (ADB) (ADB 2009; Ujiie and ADB 2006) and the Greater Mekong Subregion (UNESCAP 2002), amongst others. The website of the Global Trade and Transport Facilitation Partnership[10] provides helpful links to a long list of further documents.

Trade Facilitation in Practice

The prevalence of international recommendations and instruments might suggest that the topic is very much driven by an orchestrated international effort. The truth however is that trade facilitation has its roots in the operational frustrations experienced by traders. It is about reducing and eliminating the operational frustrations and costs that they experience. As such there are two approaches to trade facilitation. The first is top-down and the second is bottom-up. They are both equally relevant.

The top-down approach to trade facilitation is largely driven by international recommendations and instruments as outlined above. It is about implementing perceived 'best practice' rather than overcoming experienced operational frustrations and tends to be directed from above. The donor community often adopts top-down approaches to trade facilitation, allocating significant sums for the implementation of specific trade facilitation measures that are in compliance with set international recommendations and standards.

The bottom-up approach to trade facilitation takes its premise from the operational frustrations experienced by the business community. It begins at the 'grassroots' level and escalates issues to a level where they can be effectively resolved. For example, some remedies to operational problems require national, regional or international coordination – such as, for example, the recognition

---

[10]   See www.gfptt.org.

of official certificates issued by different countries, the harmonization and standardization of trade documents and data elements to enable the development of electronic systems, and cooperation between enforcement agencies on both sides of the border to reduce the number of inspections (such as in the form of jointly operated inspection posts). Where suitably followed through, for example within the UN/CEFACT committees, such lobbying can on occasion lead to the draft of an international recommendation. Many operational issues are however of a more local nature and do not need to be escalated to higher policy levels. These can, to give a few examples, relate to how the queue is managed at a port gate, the opening times of a particular customs office, the performance and service provided by executive officers at a particular location, or technical specifications for an electronic customs system.

Given the complexity of the trade environment and its many public and private sector stakeholders, obstacles to reform are frequent. In fact, one question worth asking is why has trade facilitation taken so long to establish itself as a mainstream agenda item? The answer is likely to lie with the many obstacles that any trade facilitation initiative will face. Obstacles include: (1) conflicting or opposing interests; (2) institutional limitations; and (3) lack of knowledge (Grainger 2008a).

Given the diversity of stakeholders in the trade environment, conflicting or opposing interests are inevitable. For example, the implementation costs for trade facilitation measures are unlikely to be evenly distributed. For instance, an electronic customs system that could produce significant cost savings for a business that trades frequently may prove prohibitive for a business that only trades occasionally. For the latter old-fashioned paper documents may still be the cheapest way of submitting and sharing information with government authorities. Sometimes benefits are not distributed evenly either. For instance, benefits conferred to a port operator may not necessarily be passed on to freight forwarders or traders further down the supply chain. Another example involves the more old-fashioned breed of enforcement officers, who have been trained to be suspicious of every movement. They may find collaborative enforcement strategies, as postulated by many supply chain security programmes, less palatable. Then there are those human elements that give rise to conflicting interests, especially the fact that one person's simplification can easily be another person's redundancy. Vested interests can add yet a further dimension to the potential cocktail of conflicting and opposing interests. Vested interests may be derived from opportunities for rent-seeking behaviour, for example where legislation requires declarations to be submitted by nominated licensed individuals; gold-plating by commercial service providers, for example by exploiting customers' difficulties in fathoming true trade-compliance costs; or, the solicitation of 'facilitation monies' by officials to shortcut bureaucratic inefficiency.

Institutional limitations largely relate to the conflict between the very dynamic nature of commercial activity and subsequent business requirements, and the much slower mechanisms that are available to reform trade and customs procedures. While operational practice or requirements can change rapidly, the process to amend rules and regulations is usually less dynamic. It does not help that trade facilitation is often viewed by policymakers as a technical issue – especially where IT is concerned – and is often delegated to ranks that are unable to effect necessary changes to governing legislation, rules and procedures. The practice of delegation to technical ranks can be equally frustrating where trade facilitation projects, such as the implementation of a Single Window (UN/CEFACT 2004), require budgetary coordination at the ministerial level. Another limitation might be the distance between the capital and the borders. While policy may be guided by top-down international recommendations, their implications at the operational level may not be understood. Similarly, operational frustrations experienced at the border may not necessarily be effectively communicated back to the capital.

The lack of knowledge is a particularly grave issue, especially where reform is dependent on robust cost–benefit analysis. Even for practitioners the assessment of costs and benefits can be a challenge, especially given the dynamic nature of business requirements and conflicting interests. At present there is comparatively little research to draw on. Most research is dependent on economic models (OECD 2003; Wilson et al. 2005) and fails to look at the operational practices in any great detail. This can make prioritization of reform initiatives particularly problematic, especially in instances where policymakers fail to appreciate the complexity and intricacies of conflicting or opposing stakeholder interests. In contrast, there is a large supply chain management literature that looks at international production networks – including the quality and transaction costs between business partners – but with very few exceptions (Appels and de Swielande 1998; Grainger 2007b; Haughton and Desmeules 2001; Jones and Crum 1995; Sheu et al. 2006; Verwaal and Donkers 2002, 2003) this literature has not yet applied itself to looking at the interfaces with government executive agencies.

Overcoming Obstacles

While international pressure to address trade facilitation is growing (thanks in part to the WTO but also in response to emerging supply chain security initiatives in major export markets), trade facilitation measures still need to be developed and implemented. As outlined, there is a top-down and bottom-up approach to trade facilitation. The real challenge is to be able to make informed decisions about implementing trade facilitation measures and overcoming obstacles. The economic prize is high. The OECD (2003), for example, calculates that each 1 per cent reduction in trade-related transaction costs equates to a worldwide benefit of US$43 billion, and estimates that trade transaction costs can be anywhere between 2 per cent and 15 per cent of the value of imported goods. Apart from transaction cost savings and improved business competitiveness, countries that succeed in implementing trade facilitation measures are likely to gain efficiencies in administrative practice, too; crucial for customs duty dependent developing countries is that by making compliance with procedures easier, revenue collection yields can be improved (Geourjon and Laporte 2005).

A national trade facilitation strategy is a good starting point for rolling out a trade facilitation programme – informed by international best practice and the operational frustrations experienced by business stakeholders. The role of policymakers is then to balance the conflicting interests between stakeholders and the multiple policy levels (national and international). Of course obstacles such as institutional limitations and lack of knowledge need to be overcome, too. A pragmatic approach includes the establishment of a national trade facilitation body as well as a coordinated effort towards ensuring that trade facilitation is mainstreamed.

National trade facilitation bodies are invaluable for elevating operational frustrations to the right policy level, or for consulting with the private sector about how international recommendations can be best applied. More specifically, the purpose of such national trade facilitation bodies as outlined in UN/CEFACT Recommendation 4 (UN/CEFACT 2001) is to identify issues affecting the cost and efficiency of their country's international trade; develop measures to reduce the cost and improve the efficiency of international trade; assist in the implementation of those measures; provide a national focal point for the collection and dissemination of information on best practices in international trade facilitation; and participate in international efforts to improve trade facilitation and efficiency. Such bodies can also help fill in gaps about knowledge and become in themselves centres of expertise about the operational and institutional specifics governing the trade environment.[11]

Mainstreaming of trade facilitation is another necessary step to ensure that concepts are understood across government departments responsible for trade policy and operations. At present there is no international recommendation about how mainstreaming should be achieved, but pragmatic elements include the training of executive staff about commercial practices and trade facilitation measures, the appointment of champions (to promote trade facilitation within their ministries and departments), and a coordinated effort towards identifying operational problems and solutions – for instance through extensive consultation and working with the national trade facilitation body (Grainger 2010).

Conclusion

As shown in this chapter, trade facilitation is nothing new; the momentum gained currently in trade policy, however, is. Although trade facilitation ideas have often manifested themselves in the form of international recommendations by the likes of UN/CEFACT and WCO, it remains a topic that is essentially rooted in the operational experiences (and frustrations) of internationally operating businesses. The trade environment has many stakeholders. These include traders, transport

---

[11]   This chapter's author was the Deputy Director Trade Procedures at SITPRO, the UK's former trade facilitation agency.

operators, transport and logistics service providers as well as operators of transport infrastructure. On the regulatory side, customs is often the lead agency, but many other government agencies are likely to have an equal, if not more disruptive, impact on efficient cross-border operations. Trade facilitation seeks to make improvements. While obstacles to implementing trade facilitation measures can be considerable, their resolution yields competitive advantages for the business community as well as efficiency gains for the administrations. This makes the topic of trade facilitation particularly pertinent to developing countries who wish to attract foreign investment and pursue strategies of trade-led growth.

Important to note is that given the dynamic nature of the business environment trade facilitation should be viewed as a continuous effort where operational frustrations provide the impetus for reform (Figure 7.4). International recommendations and instruments are helpful, especially where coordination and cooperation between countries is required. However, many operational problems have a local element and do not necessarily need to be escalated to higher policy levels. Very few countries currently have established strong national trade facilitation bodies. Given the operational nature of trade facilitation (as opposed to the economic analysis traditionally associated with trade policy) setting up and strengthening suitable national trade facilitation bodies is something that will have to be addressed.

The research community also has a responsibility; as outlined earlier, the lack of knowledge does present a major obstacle. However, addressing trade facilitation as an economic problem alone (and reliance on economic models) will not suffice. The devil is, like so often, in the detail and any body of research will have to be of an interdisciplinary nature – as argued by Tom Butterly (2003), trade facilitation is

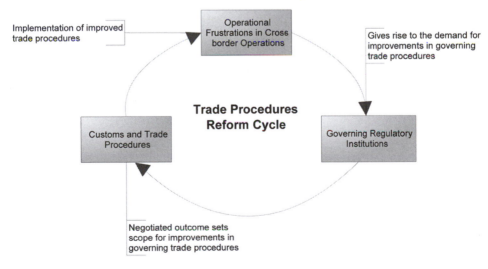

Figure 7.4   Trade procedures reform cycle
Source: Grainger (2007a).

at once a political, economic, business, administrative, technical and technological issue. The topic of trade facilitation provides much opportunity for aspiring researchers!

References

Appels, T. and de Swielande, H.S. 1998. Rolling back the frontiers: the customs clearance revolution. *International Journal of Logistics Management* 9(1): 111–18.

Applegate, L.M., Neo, B.S. and King, J. 1993. Singapore TradeNet: the tale continues. *Harvard Business School Cases*, 29 June.

ASEAN. 2005. *Agreement to Establish and Implement the ASEAN Single Window*. [Online] Available at: www.aseansec.org/18005.htm [accessed: 15 April 2010].

Asian Development Bank (ADB). 2009. *Designing and Implementing Trade Facilitation in Asia and the Pacific*. Manila: ADB.

Butterly, T. 2003. Trade facilitation in a global trade environment, in *Trade Facilitation: The Challenges for Growth and Development*, edited by C. Cosgrove-Sacks and M. Apostolovne. New York and Geneva: UNECE: 345.

Cottier, M., Crawford, M.H., Crowther, C.V., Ferrary, J.-L., Levick, B.M., Salomies, O. and Wörrle, M. 2008. *The Customs Law of Asia*. Oxford: Oxford University Press.

De Wulf, L. and Sokol, J.B. (eds). 2005. *Customs Modernization Handbook*. Washington, DC: World Bank.

Flynn, S.E. 2002. America the vulnerable. *Foreign Affairs* 81(1): 60–74.

GATT. 1947. The General Agreement on Tariffs and Trade. Geneva: WTO.

GATT. 1994. The General Agreement on Tariffs and Trade. Geneva: WTO.

George, C., Kirkpatrick, C., Dardaine, M.L., Grainger, A., Masi, F. and Servin, M.B. 2009. *Trade Sustainability Impact Assessment (SIA) of the Association Agreement under Negotiation between the European Community and Mercosur: Sector Study for Trade Facilitation*. Brussels: European Commission.

Geourjon, A.M. and Laporte, B. 2005. Risk management for targeting customs controls in developing countries: a risky venture for revenue performance? *Public Administration and Development* 25(2): 105–13.

Grainger, A. 2007a. Supply chain security: adding to a complex operational and institutional environment. *World Customs Journal* 1(2): 17–29.

Grainger, A. 2007b. Trade facilitation and supply chain management: a case study at the interface between business and government. PhD Thesis. London: Birkbeck College, University of London.

Grainger, A. 2008a. Customs and trade facilitation: from concepts to implementation. *World Customs Journal* 2(1): 17–30.

Grainger, A. 2008b. *Trade Facilitation and Import–Export Procedures in the EU*. Brussels: European Parliament.

Grainger, A. 2010. The role of the private sector in border management reform, in *Border Management Modernization*, edited by G. McLinden, E. Fanta, D. Widdowson and T. Doyle. Washington, DC: World Bank: 157–74.

Grainger, A. 2011. Trade facilitation: a conceptual review. *Journal of World Trade* 45(1): 39–62.

Haughton, M.A. and Desmeules, R. 2001. Recent reforms in customs administration. *International Journal of Logistics Management* 12(1): 65–82.

ICC. 2006. *ICC Uniform Customs and Practice for Documentary Credits – UCP 600*. Paris: ICC.

ICC. 2010. Incoterms. Paris: ICC.

IMO. 2011. Facilitation convention (FAL). London: IMO.

IMO. 2003. ISPS (The International Ship and Port Facility Security) Code. London: IMO.

Jones, C.M. and Crum, M.R. 1995. The US Customs modernization act and informed compliance act: implications for the logistics pipeline. *International Journal of Logistics Management* 6(2): 67–81.

McLinden, G., Fanta, E., Widdowson, D., and Doyle, T. (eds). 2010. *Border Management Modernization* Washington, DC: World Bank:

OECD. 2001. Business benefits of trade facilitation. *Working Party of the Trade Committee, TD/TC/WP(2001) 21*. Paris: OECD.

OECD. 2003. Quantitative assessment of the benefits of trade facilitation. *Working Party of the Trade Committee, TD/TC/WP(2003)31/Final*. Paris: OECD.

OECD. 2006. OECD/DAC Project on trade facilitation. *Phase 1: A Review of Technical Assistance and Capacity Building Initiatives for Trade Facilitation*. Paris: OECD.

OECD. 2009. *Overcoming Border Bottlenecks: The Costs and Benefits of Trade Facilitation*. Paris: OECD.

Sheu, C., Lee, L. and Niehoff, B. 2006. A voluntary logistics security program and international supply chain partnership. *Supply Chain Management: An International Journal* 11(4): 363–74.

Smith, S. and Moosberger, M. 2009. IATA e-freight: taking the paper out of air cargo, in *The Global Enabling Trade Report 2009*. Geneva: World Economic Forum: 53–8.

Staples, B.R. 2002. Trade facilitation: improving the invisible infrastructure, in *Development, Trade, and the WTO: A Handbook*, edited by B. Hoekman, A. Mattoo and P. English. Washington, DC: World Bank: 139–48.

Teo, H.H., Tan, B.C.Y. and Wei, K.K. 1997. Organizational transformation using electronic data interchange: the case of TradeNet in Singapore. *Journal of Management Information Systems* 13(4): 139.

Ujiie, T. and ADB 2006. *Trade Facilitation*. Manila: ADB.

UNESCAP. 2002. *Trade Facilitation Handbook for the Greater Mekong Sub Region, ST/ESCAP/2224*. Bangkok: United Nations.

UNESCAP. 2004. *ESCAP Trade Facilitation Framework: A Guiding Tool, ST/ESCAP/2327*. Bangkok: United Nations.

UNESCAP. 2009. *Business Process Analysis Guide to Simplify Trade Procedures, ST/ESCAP/2558*. Bangkok: United Nations.

UN/CEFACT. 1974. Recommendation 4 – national trade facilitation bodies CEFACT, *ECE/TRADE/352*. Geneva: United Nations.

UN/CEFACT. 1981. Recommendation 1 – United Nations layout key for trade documents, *ECE/TRADE/137: 11*. Geneva: United Nations.

UN/CEFACT. 2001. Recommendation 4 – national trade facilitation bodies, *ECE/TRADE/242*. Geneva: United Nations.

UN/CEFACT. 2004. Recommendation 33 – single window recommendation, *ECE/TRADE/352: 37*. Geneva: United Nations.

UN/CEFACT and UNCTAD. 2002. Compendium of trade facilitation recommendations, *UN/CEFACT, ECE/TRADE/279*. Geneva: UNCTAD.

UNCTAD. 2006a. Trade facilitation handbook part II – technical notes on essential trade facilitation measures, *UNCTAD/SDTE/TLB/2005/2*. Geneva: UNCTAD.

UNCTAD. 2006b. Trade facilitation handbook part I – national facilitation bodies: lessons from experience, *UNCTAD/SDTE/TLB/2005/1*. Geneva: UNCTAD.

UNECE. 2003. *Sharing the Gains of Globalization in the New Security Environment*. Geneva: United Nations.

Verwaal, E. and Donkers, B. 2002. Firm size and export intensity: solving an empirical puzzle. *Journal of International Business Studies* 33(3): 603–13.

Verwaal, E. and Donkers, B. 2003. Customs-related transaction costs, firm size and international trade intensity. *Small Business Economics* 21(3): 257–71.

WCO. 2006. WCO revised Kyoto convention enters into force. *WCO Press Release*. Brussels: WCO.

WCO. 2007. *WCO SAFE Framework of Standards*. Brussels: WCO.

Widdowson, D. 2005. Managing risk in the customs context, in *Customs Modernization Handbook*, edited by L. deWulf and J.B. Sokol. Washington, DC: World Bank: 91–9.

Wilson, J.S., Mann, C.L. and Otsuki, T. 2003. Trade facilitation and economic development: a new approach to quantifying the impact. *World Bank Economic Review* 17(3): 367–89.

Wilson, J.S., Mann, C.L. and Otsuki, T. 2005. Assessing the benefits of trade facilitation: a global perspective. *The World Economy* 28(6): 841–71.

WTO. 1998. *WTO Training Package: What is Trade Facilitation?* Geneva: WTO.

WTO. 2009. WTO negotiations on trade facilitation: compilation of members' textual proposals. *Negotiating Group on Trade Facilitation, TN/TF/W/43/Rev.19*. Geneva: WTO.

WTO. 2010. Draft consolidated negotiating text. *Negotiating Group on Trade Facilitation, TN/TF/W/165/Rev.4*. Geneva: WTO.

WTO/OECD. 2010. Doha Development Agenda Trade Capacity Building Database (TCBDB).

PART III
Sectoral Challenges

Agriculture

Stefan Tangermann

Introduction

Why is there a chapter on agriculture in a book on international trade, while there are none on automobiles, electronic equipment or any other sector producing specific goods? Is trade in agricultural products such an important part of world trade? Certainly not. In 2008, agricultural products accounted for no more than 8.5 per cent of world merchandise trade (WTO 2010), and that share is on a secular declining trend. It is the potential of agriculture to cause trouble in trading relations among otherwise friendly nations that tends to place agriculture high on the trade agenda. That trouble does not derive from any inherent characteristics of agricultural products – they are neither explosive nor toxic, and most of them are easily tradable. The trouble that agriculture tends to cause in international trading relations originates from the fact that many governments interfere heavily with markets for agricultural products and by doing so distort trade and international competition. Of course, agriculture is not the only sector where governments pursue policies that distort trade and create problems for other nations. However, the degree to which policies interfere with markets and trade is particularly pronounced in agriculture. What is more, there is a tendency for many governments to consider their agricultural policies a matter of national sovereignty which cannot easily be subjected to international disciplines. As a result, international trade negotiations, as pursued multilaterally in the World Trade Organization (WTO) or bilaterally, typically face particularly difficult issues when it comes to negotiating the treatment of agriculture.

When taking a closer look at agricultural trade issues it makes sense to start with at least a brief overview of the intensity of government policies in the agricultural sector. This is what the first section of this chapter will do. The question then immediately arises as to why governments pursue these policies, and that is what the following section will be devoted to. Some, if not all, of what governments try to achieve in agriculture may well be justified, but that does not say that interference with markets and trade is the most effective and efficient way of pursuing these objectives. We shall therefore turn, in the central section of this chapter, to a discussion of possible policy alternatives that may both perform better domestically and create fewer distortions in international trade.

Obviously, the nature of policy issues in agriculture and the specific characteristics of the instruments used in agricultural policies differ widely from country to country. However, there are certain similarities across many industrialized countries, and in discussing the fundamental issues in their agricultural trade one can, to some extent, generalize. The nature of issues and policies in many developing countries, though, is different from the situation in developed economies, and hence requires a separate treatment. Given the limited space available for this chapter, its focus will be primarily on the situation in the rich countries, not least because they account for the bulk of distortions in world agriculture.

The Nature of Agricultural Policies

From a trade perspective, the first point to make about agricultural policies is that tariffs in agriculture continue to be high, in both absolute terms and relative to tariffs on non-agricultural goods. As shown in Figure 8.1, the averages of all agricultural tariffs levied by the Organization for Economic Cooperation and Development (OECD) countries, be it on basic agricultural commodities or on processed agricultural products, are multiples of the average of tariffs in the textiles and clothing sector (typically also highly protected) or for manufactures. Developing countries outside the OECD area on average charge somewhat lower tariffs on primary agricultural commodities, and at the same time they charge higher tariffs on textiles/clothing and on manufactures than the rich countries. Hence, in developing countries tariff protection in agriculture is not as far above the level of tariffs on non-agricultural goods as in the developed countries. Behind these tariff averages across countries and products there is wide variety. In agriculture there are still many mega tariffs, often above 100 per cent and in some cases several hundred per cent (Jales et al. 2005). Moreover, agriculture tariff structures are often complex, with a mix of specific and *ad valorem* tariffs, seasonal variation and other complicating features. In addition, there are many cases of tariff rate quotas, with lower tariffs up to a given volume of imports and higher tariffs for quantities beyond that threshold.

Tariffs are clearly a major impediment to international trade, and their high level in agriculture is already an indication of the extent to which international trade in agriculture suffers from distortions. However, tariffs are but one dimension of the policy picture in agriculture. There are also ample subsidies to farmers, in particular in the developed countries. The OECD provides regular estimates of the totality of all transfers to farmers, whether they come in the form of price protection as provided through border measures or in the form of domestic payments from the public purse. The overall amount of transfers, called the producer support estimate (PSE), is best expressed as a percentage of all farm receipts (%PSE). As shown in Figure 8.2, the %PSE stood at close to 40 per cent in the mid-1980s and

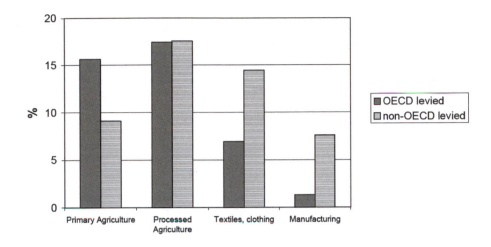

Figure 8.1   Average applied import tariffs by sector and country group, 2001
Source: OECD (2006).

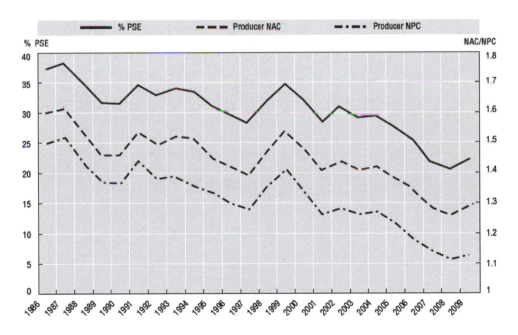

Figure 8.2   Indicators of agricultural support, OECD area
Source: OECD (2010).

has then exhibited a declining trend. However, it still is above 20 per cent, meaning that out of each dollar in gross receipts of the average farmer in the OECD area, more than 20 cents come through policies while only the remaining less than 80 cents originate from the market. The nominal protection coefficient (NPC), at 1.13 in 2009, indicates that domestic producer prices received by farmers in the OECD countries are 13 per cent higher than the equivalent prices in international trade.

It is clear that such output price support for domestic farmers can only be maintained if trade is prevented from flowing freely across borders. While tariffs are the major form of border protection, in agriculture the WTO rules also still allow the granting of export subsidies. The overall sum of export subsidies notified to the WTO has declined significantly after the Uruguay Round, but is still large, in both absolute terms and as a share of the total value of agricultural production in some individual countries (Table 8.1 and Figure 8.3).

Table 8.1   Export subsidy outlays in agriculture

Million dollars and percentages

	1995		1996		1997		1998		1999		2000	
	Value	%	Value	%	Value	%	Value	%	Value	%	Value	%
European Union (15)	6314	88.8	6748	89.7	4797	87.7	5676	90.1	5628	89.6	2462	87.1
Switzerland	446	6.3	369	4.9	295	5.4	292	4.4	290	4.6	189	6.7
Norway	83	1.2	78	1.0	102	1.9	77	1.2	128	2.0	45	1.6
United States	26	0.4	121	1.6	112	2.1	147	2.2	80	1.3	15	0.5
Other countries	243	3.4	202	2.7	166	3.0	144	2.2	151	2.4	116	4.1
Total	7112	100.0	7519	100.0	5473	100.0	6636	100.0	6278	100.0	2826	100.0

Source: WTO (2006).

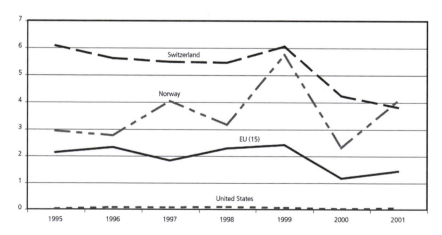

Figure 8.3   Export subsidies as share of total value of agricultural production, selected countries
Source: WTO (2006).

Regarding the nature of agricultural policies there are, however, wide differences across countries. In the OECD area, %PSEs vary between close to zero in New Zealand and Australia and around 50–60 per cent in Japan, Korea, Iceland, Switzerland and Norway (Figure 8.4).

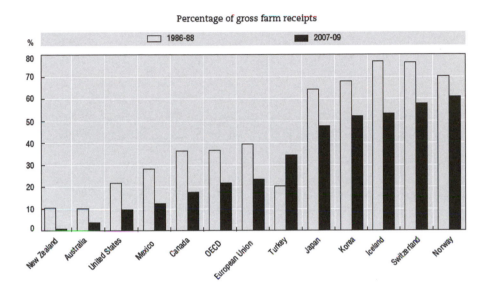

Figure 8.4   Producer support estimate by country in the OECD area
Source: OECD (2010).

Outside the OECD area, farm support is typically far below the level in many rich countries. In major emerging economies, the %PSE is in the order of magnitude of 5 to 10 per cent (Figure 8.5). In developing countries with lower living standards, the agriculture sector is often taxed, rather than supported. Import subsidies and export taxes are used to keep domestic food prices low in the interest of poor consumers, and other forms of taxation are used to channel transfers from agriculture to the rest of the economy, supposedly in the interest of a more dynamic overall development. Thus the global picture of agricultural policies is one of support to farmers in the rich countries and taxation of agriculture in developing countries as shown in Figure 8.6, where the nominal rate of assistance (NRA) provides largely the same information as the %PSE, except that its denominator is producer receipts valued at border prices (rather than gross farm receipts at domestic prices inclusive of support payments as in the case of the PSE).

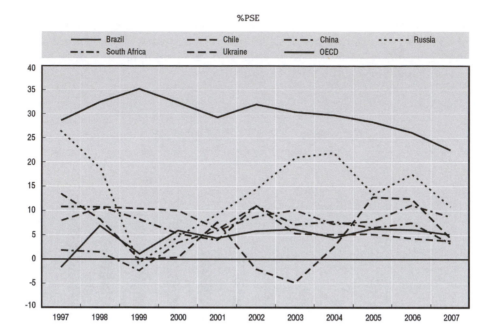

Figure 8.5   Producer support estimates for selected countries outside the OECD area

Source: OECD (2009).

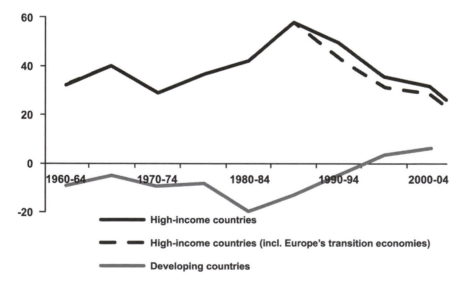

Figure 8.6   Nominal rates of assistance to farmers

Source: Lloyd et al. (2009).

From the statistics shown here it is evident that the level of farm support in the rich countries has declined over the last 25 years or so. Also, the composition of farm support from different categories of policy measures has changed over time (Figure 8.7). Support based on the quantities of output produced and inputs used, as well as support based on area (A), number of animals (An), revenue (R) or income (I) with production required has declined, as a share of both producer receipts and total support. This is welcome news as these forms of support are most distortive of markets and international trade, because they provide direct incentives to expand agricultural production. However, these most distorting agricultural policies still account for around three-quarters of all farm support in the OECD countries. Why are the governments of so many rich countries engaged in such policies, and is there any way the resulting distortions in international trade could be reduced? This is what will be discussed in the remainder of this chapter.[1]

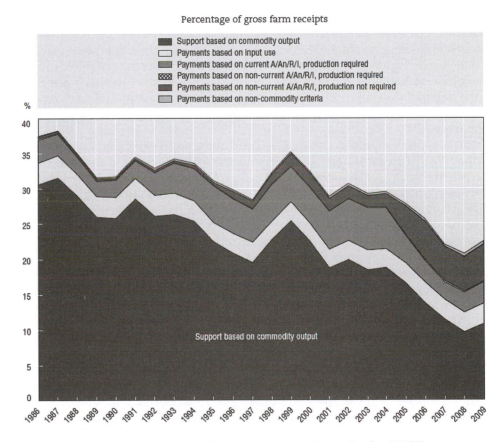

Figure 8.7   Composition of producer support estimate in the OECD area
Source: OECD (2010).

What are Agricultural Policies Trying to Achieve?

There must be reasons why governments in the rich countries provide so much support to agriculture. Some of these reasons may be purely political, and they will not be discussed here. But there are also very concrete objectives that policymakers identify when engaging in measures that address agricultural issues. With a minor degree of simplification, these objectives can be categorized into two groups: those concerned with equity, and those related to market failure. The equity issue in agricultural policies has to do with farm incomes. Market failure may occur in areas such as the relationship between agriculture and the environment.

As far as the farm income issue is concerned, the economic background is the secular adjustment process going on in agriculture. Demand for agricultural products, for both food and non-food uses, grows less than overall income in modern societies. People in the rich countries are well fed and have a limited capacity to eat. In developing countries, food demand grows more rapidly than in the rich countries, but even there the income elasticity of demand for food is generally below one as suggested by Engel's law (Abler 2010), with the implication that even in that part of the world expenditure on food lags behind overall economic growth. The situation is similar for non-food agricultural products. These characteristics of the demand side, taken by themselves, would already mean that farm revenue and hence farm income overall tends to grow less than overall income in most economies.

But a typical supply-side factor in agriculture aggravates the situation even further. Productivity of agriculture around the world tends to grow fast, due to successful breeding of crops and animals, improvements in agricultural production practices, innovation in farm machinery, and a continuous updating of farmers' skills. Productivity growth in world agriculture is more rapid than on average in the economy, and it has been so for more than a century. The combined result of these trends in demand and supply on agricultural markets is that there is a secular tendency for farm product prices to decline in real terms, and this decline can actually be empirically observed on many markets for agricultural products. This price development puts additional pressure on income of the farm sector overall.

At the macroeconomic level this is shown by the fact that the share of agriculture in GDP is in secular decline. At the sectoral level, this development requires a downward adjustment of the overall resources employed in agriculture. Combined with the secular increase in the (opportunity) cost of labour relative to the cost of capital and intermediate inputs, there is strong pressure for labour to leave agriculture. This reduction in the number of people working in agriculture has indeed taken place universally, and it continues. However, as in all similar cases, it is typically triggered by a situation in which incomes of the individuals concerned lag behind the incomes in other sectors, a development that is particularly noticeable in wealthy nations. This is the essence of the farm income issue, and the economic core of one particularly strong factor motivating agricultural policy in rich countries.

Market failure, as a second motivation for agricultural policy, may occur where externalities and public goods are involved (Arrow 1969). In agriculture, externalities may take the form of positive or negative effects that farm production can have on the environment. Agriculture in the OECD area accounts for a large share of total land and water use and, in many countries, dominates and shapes the landscape. Contrary to many other economic activities, agriculture has both harmful and beneficial effects on the environment through changing the quality or quantity of soil, water, air, biodiversity and landscapes. Increasing food demand, together with policies encouraging production, and technological and economic changes, has often led to a marked intensification of agriculture (more output per unit of land or labour) and to farming on environmentally sensitive land, which in some cases has led to environmental harm. These harmful effects include mainly water and air pollution, but also the loss of wildlife, habitats and landscape features. Soil degradation and water depletion are also serious concerns in some areas.

On the other hand, environmental benefits may in some circumstances include contribution to water accumulation, flood control, nutrient recycling and fixation, soil formation, carbon sequestration by trees and soil, wildlife and biodiversity protection and providing recreational services and aesthetic values. Landscape characteristics can also be a public good provided by agriculture. For example, livestock grazing on pasture may well be considered a desirable feature of the countryside in certain regions. However, tourists or other visitors cannot be made to pay for this benefit as individuals, because they cannot be excluded from the pleasure of viewing an agreeable landscape while walking through it. In a case like that, the government may have a role to play in making sure that farmers provide this public good. Similarly, maintenance of a thriving rural economy may require government activity. For some countries, food security is a concern, in the sense of making sure that the nation overall always has access to sufficient food supplies.

Are Current Agricultural Policies Doing a Good Job?

There is no point in debating the fundamental validity of such policy objectives, relating to farm incomes and market failure. However, the policy analyst may well ask whether current policies are most effective and efficient in obtaining these objectives, and whether there are alternatives that could achieve the same domestic outcome with less distortions of international trade.

In this regard, there are good reasons to argue that many agricultural policies in the rich countries are not doing the best possible job. This is particularly true for those policy measures that provide support directly coupled to farm products, such as price support and payments based on quantities of outputs and inputs, or payments based on other criteria but requiring production of agricultural commodities. As we have seen above, these policies strongly dominate agricultural policymaking in the OECD area, still accounting for around three-quarters of all support provided to farmers.

As far as support for farm incomes is concerned, providing price and output support is an approach that is unnecessary, inefficient and inequitable. It is unnecessary as there is not in reality a general problem in all OECD countries regarding the income level of people living on farms. In many OECD countries, incomes of farm households are well in line with, if not above, household incomes in the overall economy (OECD 2003a). In some other OECD countries, incomes of farm households are somewhat below the average level in the economy, but generally not by a large margin. Does this empirical finding not contradict the argument advanced above, that secular developments in the agricultural sector tend to generate a farm income problem? It does not, for two reasons. First, incomes of farm households include income from non-farm sources. In many cases, these incomes earned outside agriculture make up for a rather large share of total household income. In a way, they represent one element of an actual solution to what otherwise might have been a farm income problem: farmers and their families adjust to deteriorating on-farm incomes by looking for alternative sources of income. More generally, as adjustment processes in terms of farmers actually leaving agriculture, partially or completely, occur, the income gaps that induce them are closed.

Second, incomes of farm families include not only income from their labour, but also income derived from their land and capital assets. Thus, while actual labour income in agriculture may indeed be depressed, family income overall may do reasonably well. But where this is the case, are governments not called upon to provide support to agriculture, such that farmers can earn a 'fair' remuneration for all their resources employed on the farm, including their labour? If governments actually were to try and do this, they would completely undermine all adjustment processes, with the implication that the underlying farm income problem becomes worse and worse and at some point reaches an order of magnitude that is beyond the capacity of even the richest government to cure. An appropriate return to factors of production, that is labour, capital and land, is an issue of resource allocation, best left to market forces. Equity concerns must relate to family incomes, because they determine the standard of living. In this sense, there is not a general problem in rich country agriculture, and from that point of view broad-based support measures such as price and output support are unnecessary.

Price support is also a rather inefficient way of trying to raise farm incomes. This is because for each extra dollar spent, by consumers and taxpayers, on price support for agriculture, no more than 25 cents tend to end up in farmers' pockets, as remuneration for farm-owned labour and land, while the rest is capitalized in land values, goes to input suppliers or evaporates in inefficient resource use (OECD 2003a).

There are alternative agricultural policies that exhibit much higher transfer efficiency. For example, payments based on historical entitlements, such as production in a past reference period, can raise farm operator income by close to 50 cents for each extra dollar spent on this form of support – a transfer efficiency that is still not huge, but already twice that of price support. Policies of this nature, which are more decoupled from current production decisions taken by farmers, have more recently been introduced in some OECD countries.

Finally, providing farm income support through price and output-related measures is an inequitable approach. This is a most serious comment on a policy that is arguably motivated by equity concerns, related to the particular income situation in agriculture. But it is easy to see why transferring money to farmers through price and output support creates inequities. If governments keep domestic market prices high, or provide payments per tonne of output, then of course farms with large volumes of output receive more support, in terms of the absolute sum of money transferred, than farms producing a small amount. Typically, farmers owning farms with large output volumes have higher incomes than their colleagues producing less. In other words, price and output support favours the richest farmers more than the poorest.

To sum up, support that is directly coupled to agricultural production, such as price support and payments based on output and input, does a poor job of assisting farm incomes. In addition to not being necessary as a general policy, it is inefficient in transferring income to farmers, and the transfer that finally ends up in farmers' pockets goes to the wrong recipients. But can these policies do a better job in dealing with market failures, in addressing externalities and public goods related to agriculture?

Consider typical cases of negative environmental externalities resulting from agricultural production (OECD 2008a). Fertilizers in agriculture and animal effluent from livestock account for as much as 40 per cent of nitrogen and 30 per cent of phosphate emissions in surface water in some OECD countries, contributing significantly to the problems of eutrophication due to the depletion of oxygen in water. Nitrate leakage into groundwater is a significant problem in some areas with high concentration of livestock production. Pesticide runoff from agricultural land also impairs drinking water quality and harms water-based wildlife. Certainly these problems cannot be cured through policies such as price support that result in an expansion, and often also intensification, of agricultural production. On the contrary, price and output support aggravates such negative externalities. But what about positive externalities of agriculture, say flood control going along with rice production on paddy fields, or the preservation of cultural heritage through the maintenance of farm buildings in rural villages? There may be a tendency for such positive externalities to expand when agricultural output grows, but the linkage between the quantity of rice, wheat or milk produced and the provision of such positive services is weak at best. In many cases, a certain low level of agricultural activity is sufficient to make sure that the positive effects are achieved. Any policy-induced production beyond that level does not contribute to the desirable effect, but adds to economic costs. Moreover, typically the service required from agriculture is location-specific, while price and output support at the national level cannot differentiate among local conditions. The situation is similar regarding public goods that agriculture may provide, such as a pleasing landscape: most observers would agree that the beauty of a given countryside does not improve, and may actually deteriorate, if agricultural production is expanded and intensified beyond a certain point. Food security, too, does not improve beyond a given level of domestic production, if trying to expand domestic production beyond what market forces generate is at all considered the right approach to provide for a secure supply of food (OECD 2003b, 2008b).

With regard to the positive externalities that may go with agricultural production, and any public goods that agriculture may provide, reference is often made to the multifunctional character of agriculture (OECD 2001b). In the same context, the term 'non-trade concerns' has been coined in international trade negotiations. Agriculture is certainly not the only economic sector that has multifunctional characteristics, but the nature and variety of the services that agriculture can provide beyond commodity production may indeed be somewhat special. There may well be a role for government policies in this context. However, price and output support can rarely do a good job to promote the multifunctional performance of agriculture, and may indeed be counterproductive in a number of dimensions (OECD 2003b).

Policy Reform in Agriculture: Better Performance, Less Trade Distortion

If three-quarters of farm support provided in the OECD area is not sufficiently effective and efficient in helping to reach the most important objectives of agricultural policy, and may sometimes even be counterproductive, what can be done to improve the situation? The way forward consists of three strategic components, which can also be considered, in a time dimension, as three successive steps towards reform of agricultural policies: decoupling, targeting and reducing support to agriculture. Reform along these lines would not only improve the domestic performance of agricultural policies, but also greatly reduce trade distortions.[2]

Decoupling Support from Production

Decoupling means breaking the link between support and producer decisions in agriculture. This can be done by moving from price support, or payments based on current output or input quantities, in the direction of direct payments to farmers that are based on parameters which the farmer cannot change through production decisions. For example, the payment can be based on the monetary value of transfers through 'old' policies that a given farmer used to receive in a historical reference period. Why make such payments, rather than simply do away immediately with all existing forms of farm support?

---

[2]   For a more extensive treatment of the options for agricultural policy reform in developed countries, see OECD (2002, 2008c).

In most OECD countries, farm support has been provided for decades. Farmers have got used to the expectation that governments will continue to engage in these policies. Based on these expectations, they have decided to become farmers, take over the farm from their parents, make investments and forgo other opportunities outside agriculture. Once policy embarks on a new course, they should be given time to adjust, as a matter of fairness and equity. Also, and closely related to this reasoning, political resistance to policy reform would be difficult to overcome if farmers could not be compensated. Direct payments decoupled from production can allow the process of reform to start, and buy time for everybody involved.

But what is, then, the advantage of decoupling support from production, while the level of support may not yet decline? There are four fundamental benefits to decoupling, all related to the fact that policy-made production incentives for farmers are reduced. First, where price and output related support was counterproductive in reaching policy objectives, this drawback disappears. For example, negative environmental externalities going along with an expansion and intensification of agricultural production are redressed. Second, with a given amount of transfers to the agricultural sector, farm incomes rise, because decoupled payments are more transfer-efficient than output-related policies. Third, overall economic welfare of the nation is enhanced as production structure is brought more in line with comparative advantages. And fourth, distortions of international trade, and hence international spillover effects of agricultural policies, are reduced.

This fourth benefit is worth commenting on further. When major problems of current agricultural policies in many OECD countries were discussed in the preceding section, the focus was on the domestic functioning of these policies, from the perspective of the objectives that agricultural policies are supposed to pursue. But there is one additional big problem with many current policies, occurring at the international level. As policies relying on price and output support, dominant in most OECD countries, induce domestic farmers to produce more, they take markets away from farmers in other countries. Viewed from the angle of the secular trends of supply and demand for agricultural products, such policies can be interpreted as an attempt of governments to protect domestic farmers against adjustment pressures by simulating additional demand for their products. After all, the higher prices on domestic markets, resulting from government intervention, create the impression for farmers that there is more demand for their output than what the market actually generates. However, these government policies cannot really expand demand at the global level, as they do not add to purchasing power worldwide. The result is that the extra output generated by these farm policies, pushed onto the world market, depresses prices for farm products in international trade. This means that, in effect, the apparent additional demand for domestic farm output in the high-support countries is in reality nothing less than market share taken away from farmers in other countries. In other words, well-intentioned assistance to domestic farmers, delivered through market-distorting policy measures, effectively exports adjustment pressure to farmers in other parts of the world.

This seemingly somewhat abstract interpretation of the international repercussions emanating from price and output support policies in OECD agriculture has a very concrete counterpart in the tensions that these policies create in international trade. For a long time in the history of the General Agreement on Tariffs and Trade (GATT), agriculture proved so difficult a subject that it effectively remained outside operational rules and disciplines (Josling et al. 1996). It was not until the Uruguay Round that agreement was finally reached on how to integrate agriculture into the overall regime governing international trade. But tensions over agricultural issues continue to plague trade relations, both among OECD countries and between developed and developing nations. Among OECD countries, there was a tendency to respond to other countries' support policies by shielding domestic farmers through matching policies. Of course, while several countries' policies moved up the spiral of subsidies and tariffs, international market prices were driven down even further. Farmers in those OECD countries that have essentially opted out of this vicious cycle, such as Australia and New Zealand, feel left out in the cold. Similarly, farmers in developing countries that produce temperate zone products, or have the potential to do so, are left behind. Their governments do not have the economic means to provide matching subsidies, and because food consumers in these countries are poor, they also cannot engage in policies that raise the domestic price levels for farm products.

Surely these negative global repercussions of domestic price and output support policies in major OECD countries are unintended international spillover. But they are nevertheless real. Decoupling, and the resulting reduction in market and trade distortions, can make a major contribution to putting a break on the problematic implications for international trade that result from current domestic support policies. This is true even if decoupling of support from farm production does not completely eliminate all distortions to farmers' incentives. OECD research has shown that any support that is provided to farmers on condition that they are farmers has some effect on production decisions (OECD 2001a). However, the distortion effects of support that is decoupled, in the sense that it is not based on variables that farmers can affect through their production decisions, are orders of magnitude smaller than those of price and output-based support.

In a very practical way, the international trade dimension of moving towards domestic decoupling comes in the form of less reliance on tariffs and export subsidies. Price support to domestic farmers requires border measures. Tariffs are needed to prevent imports from undercutting domestic support prices. When production incentives to domestic farmers are strong enough to generate a surplus on the home market, export subsidies are also required to bridge the gap between high domestic and low international prices for quantities shipped to the world market. When decoupling takes place and price support is converted into direct payments, tariffs and export subsidies are no longer needed. In other words, decoupling can also make a major contribution to bringing tariffs and export subsidies down in international trade negotiations.

Targeting Support to Objectives

The second strategic ingredient into the reform of agricultural policies is targeting measures directly to the policy objectives pursued. This essentially means tackling each policy issue at its source, rather than dealing with the symptoms. As argued above, broad-based support policies, such as price support and payments based on output and input quantities, are neither effective nor efficient in solving income problems in agriculture and dealing with externalities and public goods. Targeted policies that directly address these issues do a much better job. This is common sense, but also a direct application of the Tinbergen (1956) principle that in order for a policy regime to be effective there must be as many independent policy instruments as there are targets to be pursued.

With respect to farm incomes, such targeted measures include assistance to improve on-farm performance, through enhancing farmers' skills and upgrading technology. They can also help farmers to diversify their income sources, through strengthening rural development outside the agricultural sector. Severe risks, in terms of farm income fluctuations over time, can be targeted through measures that improve the functioning of commodity markets, and any remaining income risks can be dampened through government-assisted income insurance. Finally, systemic problems of poverty in agriculture, to the extent they are not covered by generally available social safety nets, can be addressed by specific assistance to the individuals concerned, and through programmes that enhance their ability to adjust.

Regarding the effects of agriculture on the environment, negative externalities are best addressed by an appropriate combination of taxes and regulations specifically targeted to the individual environmental issue concerned. Positive contributions of farmers to improving the environment and biodiversity can be encouraged through specific payments based on the service desired. For example, payments can be made per metre of hedge planted, or for cutting grass late on a meadow where rare birds tend to nest. Public goods that farmers can provide would typically be best dealt with by paying per unit of service rendered. In some cases, it may even be possible for governments to create markets for what at first glance may appear to be public goods (OECD 2003b). Clearly, targeted payments can involve considerable transaction costs, for identifying the performance of the farmers concerned and administering the programme. However, in the overwhelming majority of cases, these transaction costs are likely to be significantly less than the economic losses resulting from unspecific and broad-based policies such as support to farm output that may provide the required service as a by-product. Only in rare cases may such transaction costs be high enough to justify general support to farm output (OECD 2003b). In order to strengthen rural communities, programmes that cover a wide array of economic activities do better than measures that focus exclusively on the agricultural sector. Farm support contributes less to rural development than measures that target any systemic policy bias against rural and remote areas, relating to the provision of infrastructure and public services.

Reducing Support

As decoupling of support from farm production, and targeting policies directly to the issues at hand, is more effective and avoids inefficiencies, it is possible to reduce support levels while still enhancing the degree to which policy objectives are achieved. The larger income transfer efficiency of decoupled payments, as explained above, is a typical example of why the reform strategy outlined here can go along with a reduction in support without any loss in farm incomes. In other words, this strategy can result in gains on all sides: farm incomes improve; the environment is better served; tensions in international trade are reduced; and the burden on consumers as well as taxpayers declines. From this perspective, there is no reason why all three elements of the reform strategy, that is decoupling, targeting, and reducing support, should not be pursued simultaneously.

However, in actual policymaking it may be easier to consider them as three successive steps. Reform can start with a move towards decoupling, by reducing price and output support and introducing decoupled payments instead. A second step can convert some part of the decoupled payments to all farmers into specific targeted payments directly based on specific services. And while this process is underway, the general decoupled payments can be gradually reduced and finally eliminated. In this context it is useful to remember that the central justification of decoupled payments is to allow farmers time to adjust to the new conditions under a reformed policy. In the long run, the focus can completely shift to payments that are targeted to specific objectives. Of course this strategy demands a precise and operational definition of the objectives pursued, and a careful analysis of which specific measures work best in achieving them. But these requirements are anyhow fundamental criteria for any public policy.

Are agricultural policies in the OECD area moving in the direction indicated by this reform strategy? The extent to which this is the case differs from country to country. Figure 8.8 provides an impression of developments over the last 20 years or so in selected countries, for the two dimensions of decoupling and reducing support. In this graph, a movement to the south signifies an improvement in policy structure towards more decoupled and hence less distorting instruments (as measured by the share of support on output and unconstrained inputs in the PSE), while a movement to the west indicates a reduction in the overall level of farm support (as measured by the %PSE). The length of the arrow for the individual country can be taken as an indication of the depth of change. For the OECD aggregate, the movement points in the right direction, that is south and west. Most individual countries also have made progress in policy reform, to varying degrees.[3] But a lot remains to be done before all farm policies in OECD countries have reached a large degree of decoupling and are firmly embarked on the path towards lower

---

[3]   The movement of New Zealand towards north-west may look odd, but its northward component has little importance given that the overall level of support in New Zealand has declined to close to zero.

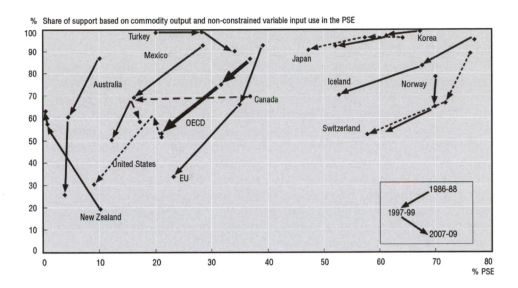

% Share of support based on commodity output and non-constrained variable input use in the PSE

Figure 8.8   Changes in level and composition of farm support in the OECD area

Source: OECD (2010).

levels of support. Moreover, much improvement can still be achieved in terms of better targeting policies towards specific objectives.

Agriculture in the WTO

Agricultural policy reform, in the direction described above, is in the enlightened interest of the countries still pursuing outdated policies. As indicated, it is indeed taking place, though the political economy involved makes reform a slow and partial process. International pressure can accelerate progress, and that is precisely what has happened, in particular through negotiations in the GATT/WTO. As mentioned above, agriculture has for a long time escaped effective disciplines in the GATT, though the letter of the General Agreement applied fully to the farm sector as well (Josling et al. 1996). The Agreement on Agriculture concluded in the Uruguay Round (URAA) has ended that agricultural exceptionalism, ironically through establishing a rather specific framework of rules and disciplines for agriculture (Josling 2010).

Creating a special sectoral regime for agriculture in the Uruguay Round was, though, the price that obviously had to be paid for ending what effectively was a non-treatment that agriculture had 'enjoyed' under the GATT before the Uruguay Round. From an economic perspective, what really counts is not so much the legal and institutional approach chosen, but an effective reduction of the large distortions that had plagued world trade in agriculture for decades. And it can well be argued that the URAA opened up a road leading in that direction.

The core achievement of the Uruguay Round in agriculture was that vague qualitative rules of the 'old' GATT gave way to reasonably well defined quantitative commitments which WTO member countries are now expected to honour in pursuing their agricultural policies.[4] Most important, in the domain of *market access* the host of non-tariff barriers (NTBs) that were so characteristic of agricultural trade before the Uruguay Round underwent 'tariffication' and were replaced by bound tariffs. In this regard, agriculture is now special in a rather welcome way as it is the sector with the highest share (100 per cent) of bound tariffs. On the side of *export competition*, the non-workable GATT rule of the 'equitable share' in world trade was replaced by quantified limits to the quantities of subsidized exports and budgetary outlays on those subsidies, and the commitment to reduce these limits over time. Regarding *domestic support*, the qualitative rules of the Subsidies Code were complemented by a newly defined yardstick for support levels (the Aggregate Measurement of Support, AMS), quantified maximum amounts of support and reduction commitments, and rules regarding the implementation of these new elements (Orden et al. 2011).

The URAA was progress in one sense but not in another (Tangermann 2002). It was certainly a huge step forward in the historical evolution of the trading order for agriculture as it established completely new and largely effective rules of the game where none had existed before. The URAA did not, though, directly force a break in actual agricultural policies of WTO member countries as the quantitative commitments agreed were set such that they contained too much water. However, there is no doubt that the Uruguay Round was effective in promoting the process of agricultural policy reform.

Its impact on actual policymaking in agriculture began already before the Round was concluded and the Agreement on Agriculture entered into force. The most notable case is that of the MacSharry reform of the Common Agricultural Policy (CAP) which was enacted in order to create the conditions under which the EU could agree to an agricultural accord in the Round (Daugbjerg and Swinbank 2009; Moyer and Josling 2002). After the URAA was concluded, the existence of the new disciplines began to be one of the arguments that played a role in the debate about agricultural policy settings in quite a number of countries. To be sure, all sorts of domestic concerns continued to be the major driving forces in agricultural policy making in most cases, but considerations relating to the WTO in one way or another also began to have some effect.

Perhaps even more important than the impact of the URAA commitments as such is the effect that expectations regarding future WTO disciplines in agriculture have had on agricultural policymaking. The EU and recent reforms of its CAP are clearly a case in point, in particular the Agenda 2000 decisions and, even more so,

---

[4]   For an extensive account of the agricultural negotiations during the Uruguay Round, as well as an outline and analysis of the URAA, see Josling et al. (1996).

the 2003 Fischler reform of the CAP (Swinnen, 2008 and 2010). These changes to the CAP were, to some extent, conditioned by the expectation that the enlarged EU would probably have to accept further reductions of the limits to its domestic support in the Doha Development Agenda (DDA) negotiations, and by a desire to avoid, through anticipatory action, a repeat of the situation in the Uruguay Round where the EU realized that it had to effectively interrupt the negotiations, do its policy reform homework, and only then come back to the negotiating table prepared for a conclusion of the round. As a result of the post-URAA adjustments to the CAP, the EU can indeed now reasonably easily accept rather large cuts to its domestic support commitments in the ongoing DDA negotiations, as envisaged in the draft modalities of December 2008 (Orden et al. 2011). The EU is also, in principle, prepared to agree to an elimination of export subsidies. On the other hand, the EU continues to protect its farmers through high tariffs and finds it difficult to accept the tariff cuts considered in the DDA negotiations, in particular for 'sensitive' products such as dairy products, beef and sugar.

Another real world impact of the URAA will also materialize only in the future, but it may be its most important achievement. The rules and commitments agreed in the Uruguay Round have provided a wholly new basis for the talks in subsequent rounds of WTO negotiations. Negotiations can now move straight to the reduction rates for the various types of commitments. Market access is particularly important in that regard. There is no need any more to debate the acceptability or otherwise of various kinds of NTBs. The core negotiating business is now the scale of reduction rates to be agreed. Clearly, all sorts of other issues are also on the negotiating table, not the least the provisions to be applied to 'sensitive' and 'special' products, as well as the treatment of the (regrettably still existing, and possibly even new) tariff rate quotas. However, the URAA has allowed the focus of future negotiations to be clearly on reduction rates, and that offers the hope that all water will eventually be squeezed out of the commitments agreed under the URAA, and that further reductions can then be agreed that truly bite into the flesh of existing policies.

As far as provisions of major significance to agricultural trade are concerned, in addition to the Agreement on Agriculture, the Uruguay Round also yielded progress in the area of food regulation, through the Agreement on the Application of Sanitary and Phytosanitary Measures, the Agreement on Technical Barriers to Trade and the Agreement on Trade Related Aspects of Intellectual Property Rights (Josling et al. 2004). Important progress was also made through the Understanding on Rules and Procedures Governing the Settlement of Disputes, and a number of agricultural disputes under these new rules have reinforced the impact of the URAA on national policies (Daugbjerg and Swinbank 2009).

Conclusion

Agriculture remains a particularly controversial sector in international trade relations, not because of inherent characteristics of the products it produces, but as a result of government farm policies pursued in many rich countries. Policymakers identify important objectives, having to do with equity issues regarding farm incomes, and relating to market failures in areas such as the relationship between agriculture and the environment. There is no point in questioning these objectives – it is for the political process to decide on them. Moreover, there is no doubt that the pursuit of such objectives may justify, and indeed require, government action.

However, there are good reasons to argue that much of current agricultural policy in the OECD area is not the most effective and efficient approach towards achieving the objectives relating to agriculture. In particular, policies that have the effect of providing strong incentives to farmers to expand production are not doing a good job, neither in improving equity nor in dealing with market failures. Yet, three-quarters of all farm support in OECD countries still come in this form. These policies are not only less than satisfactory in their domestic performance, they also generate problematic spillover at the international level. In trying to solve agricultural problems at home, many current policies make life more difficult for farmers in other countries, including developing countries.

The solution is not to do away with all agricultural policies. There are concerns in agriculture that cannot be left to markets. However, there is an important issue of policy choice: which measures work best domestically, with least spillover at the international level? The OECD has designed a positive agenda for reform that meets these criteria. It rests on the three pillars of decoupling farm support from production, targeting support to well specified objectives, and reducing support as reformed policies become more effective. At the international level, this strategy also facilitates reduced tariffs and export subsidies.

Overall, the development of agricultural policies in the OECD area is gradually moving in this direction, and some countries have more recently made significant steps towards reforming their agricultural policies in line with this strategy. However, reform progress is uneven and can be accelerated. International debate and multilateral trade negotiations can make a significant contribution to moving the reform process forward. Joint reform efforts across countries can facilitate policy change, because they help to reduce the burden of economic adjustment and to share the political pain. The time has come to move forward on agricultural policy reform. The WTO negotiations on the Doha Development Agenda provide an excellent opportunity to do this in a multilateral context, and to defuse the tensions that continue to plague international trade in agriculture.

References

Abler, D. 2010. Demand growth in developing countries. *OECD Food, Agriculture and Fisheries Working Papers, No. 29*. Paris: OECD.

Arrow, K.J. 1969. The organization of economic activity: issues pertinent to the choice of market versus non-market allocation, in *Analysis and Evaluation of*

Public Expenditure: The PPP System. Washington, DC: Joint Economic Committee of Congress: 59–73.

Daugbjerg, C. and Swinbank, A. 2009. *Ideas, Institutions, and Trade. The WTO and the Curious Role of EU Farm Policy in Trade Liberalization*. Oxford: Oxford University Press.

Jales, M., Josling, T., Nassar, A. and Tutwiler, A. 2005. Options for agriculture: from framework to modalities in market access, in *International Agricultural Trade Research Consortium, Trade Policy Issues*, Paper 2. Washington, DC: International Agricultural Trade Research Consortium.

Josling, T. 2010. Reflections on the exceptional treatment of agriculture in the WTO, in M. Banse and H. Grethe (eds), Perspectives on International Agricultural Policy – In Honour of the Retirement of Professor Stefan Tangermann. *German Journal of Agricultural Economics*, Vol. 59, Supplement.

Josling, T., Roberts D. and Orden, D. 2004. *Food Regulation and Trade: Toward a Safe and Open Global System*. Washington, DC: Institute for International Economics.

Josling, T., Tangermann, S. and Warley, T.K. 1996. *Agriculture in the GATT*. Houndmills, London and New York: Macmillan.

Lloyd, P.J., Croser, J.L. and Anderson, K. 2009. Welfare- and trade-based indicators of national distortions to agricultural incentives. *Agricultural Distortions Working Paper 72*. Washington, DC: World Bank.

Moyer, H.W. and Josling, T. 2002. *Agricultural Policy Reform: Politics and Process in the EC and the USA in the 1990s*. Burlington and Aldershot: Ashgate.

OECD. 2001a. *Market Effects of Crops Support Measures*. Paris: OECD.

OECD. 2001b. *Multifunctionality – Towards an Analytical Framework*. Paris: OECD.

OECD. 2002. *Agricultural Policies in OECD Countries: A Positive Reform Agenda*. Paris: OECD.

OECD. 2003a. *Farm Household Income – Issues and Policy Responses*. Paris: OECD.

OECD. 2003b. *Multifunctionality – The Policy Implications*. Paris: OECD.

OECD. 2006. *Agricultural Policy and Trade Reform – Potential Effects at Global, National and Household Levels*. Paris: OECD.

OECD. 2008a. *Environmental Performance of Agriculture in OECD Countries since 1990*. Paris: OECD.

OECD. 2008b. *Multifunctionality in Agriculture – Evaluating the Degree of Jointness, Policy Implications*. Paris: OECD.

OECD. 2008c. *Agricultural Policy Design and Implementation – A Synthesis*. Paris: OECD.

OECD. 2009. *Agricultural Policies in Emerging Economies – Monitoring and Evaluation*. Paris: OECD.

OECD. 2010. *Agricultural Policies in OECD Countries – At a Glance*. Paris: OECD.

Orden, D., Blandford, D. and Josling, T. (eds). 2011. *WTO Disciplines on Agricultural Support – Seeking a Fair Basis for Trade*. Cambridge: Cambridge University Press.

Swinnen, J.F.M. (ed.). 2008. *The Perfect Storm. The Political Economy of the Fischler Reforms of the Common Agricultural Policy*. Brussels: Center for European Policy Studies.

Swinnen, J.F.M. 2010. Political economy of agricultural distortions: the literature to date, in K. Anderson (ed.), *The Political Economy of Agricultural Price Distortions*. Cambridge: Cambridge University Press: 141–61.

Tangermann, S. 2002. Agriculture on the way to firm international trading rules, in D.L.M. Kennedy and J.D. Southwick (eds), *The Political Economy of International Trade Law*. Essays in Honor of Robert E. Hudec. Cambridge: Cambridge University Press: 254-282.

Tangermann, S. 2004. Agricultural policies in OECD countries: an agenda for reform, in A. Lopez-Claros (ed.), *The Global Competitiveness Report 2004–2005*. Houndmills and London: Palgrave Macmillan, for the World Economic Forum: 173-186.

Tinbergen, J. 1956. *Economic Policy: Principles and Design*. Amsterdam: North Holland.

WTO. 2006. *World Trade Report 2006 – Exploring the Links between Subsidies, Trade and the WTO*. Geneva: WTO.

WTO. 2010. *International Trade Statistics 2009*. Geneva: WTO.

Trade in Services

Christopher Roberts and Kenneth Heydon

Services make a major contribution to the economy and employment in all countries, whatever their stage of development. Yet they contribute a significantly smaller share of international trade than goods. Part of the reason for this is that only modest progress has so far been made to guarantee open markets for trade in services. This chapter sets out the importance of services in international trade, and assesses the gains that can be made from liberalization. It describes the structure and impact of the key international agreement on trade in services – the General Agreement on Trade in Services (GATS). It explains how far governments have committed themselves, both multilaterally in the World Trade Organization (WTO) and through preferential agreements, to keeping their markets open to foreign suppliers of services.

Some Definitions

Just what is meant by services and international trade in services? This is best illustrated by distinguishing goods and services. Unlike goods, services are not physical objects which you can touch or see, or drop on your toe. Yet goods and services are often closely interlinked: you cannot run a railway service without trains, or sell shirts around the world without the help of marketing and distribution services. Services include some of the oldest activities in the world, like teaching and construction, and some of the newest, like software design and satellite communications.

International trade in goods is relatively straightforward in that the producers are in one country and the goods travel across an international border to another. For services the position is more complex. While some services can be supplied across national boundaries, and digital transmissions are making this easier, others require the supplier and customer to be in the same location. This is why, for the purposes of negotiations under the GATS Agreement in the WTO, services are divided into four modes of supply. These four modes are *cross-border supply* (as with goods), *consumption abroad* where the consumer, such as a tourist, crosses the border, *commercial presence*, for example where a bank sets up an office overseas to handle local customers, and *movement of natural persons* where the supplier of the service such as a consultant goes abroad to work (Sampson and Snape 1985; Wunsch-Vincent 2005).

For negotiating purposes the WTO Secretariat, drawing on UN statistical work, has divided services into 12 sectors and some 150 sub-sectors (WTO 1991). These include all the well-known areas, like banking, insurance, telecommunications, transport and construction, as well as less traditional services like electronic data interchange or trading in futures and options. Services provided directly by government are excluded: these are defined as services 'supplied in the exercise of governmental authority' and 'supplied neither on a commercial basis, nor in competition with one or more service suppliers' (Adlung 2006; Chanda 2003; Krajewski 2003). There are other comparatively minor exclusions, of which the most significant is air traffic and landing rights. Outside these exclusions any WTO government is free to ask another to commit itself to allowing foreign providers to compete in any service sector; and the other government is free to agree or refuse.

The Economic Importance of Services

The economic importance of services can be clearly illustrated from European experience. Services account for over 77 per cent of European GDP and employment. In the UK the services share of employment is now as high as 81 per cent. In the late twentieth and early twenty-first centuries millions of European jobs were lost in agriculture and manufacturing, and were created in services. Germany and Italy are the only big European economies where a quarter of the working population are still in the business of making things. In the UK, financial and business services contribute more than twice as much to the British economy as the whole of manufacturing. In external trade Europe runs a current account deficit in trade in goods, and a surplus in trade in services.

Thus Europe depends increasingly on services for exports. Europe will continue to have an important capability for manufacturing exports, especially at the high technology, specialist end of the market – aerospace is an obvious example. But products like textiles, footwear, steel and other basic manufacturing, where the technology is relatively simple and labour is a substantial component of production, are already largely sourced from developing countries. Given the competitive advantage of these countries in labour costs, that is inevitable and right.

The position in the United States and other developed countries is broadly similar to that in Europe. In their World Development Indicators Online the World Bank give figures showing that the services share of GDP in high income countries (effectively developed countries) is 72 per cent, in middle income countries 53 per cent, and in low income countries 52 per cent. In all three cases the trend is progressively upwards. So while, as you would expect, services are more prominent in the economies of richer countries, they also represent at least half the wealth of the developing world, and as much as agriculture and industry together.

If however we look at services' share of exports the figures are less impressive. International trade in services is currently only about 20 per cent of global trade. The figure for European exports of services – 26 per cent of total exports – is a bit higher, but still low in relation to services' share of GDP. Of course many services are and will continue to be bought locally: most of us buy our groceries from a local supplier, and most journeys are within national boundaries. But retailers like Tesco, Carrefour and Walmart have developed substantial overseas business, and many of us travel by train or air services which are in foreign ownership. While it is probably unrealistic to expect services to be traded internationally to the extent that goods are, there is considerable scope for expansion.

The Economic Case for Liberalization

Developed Countries

There are clear economic advantages from liberalizing services, although individual interests may lose out (Jones and Kierzkowski 1990; OECD 2002, 2010). For Europe, North America and other OECD countries, the argument is fairly straightforward. Here services are much the largest sector of the economy, as they are in smaller, sophisticated economies like Hong Kong and Singapore. As jobs at the more labour-intensive end of manufacturing (and to some degree also of services) continue to move offshore to emerging markets, workers and managers need to find new jobs in services for which rich country wage levels remain competitive.

Significant numbers of internationally competitive manufacturing jobs will remain in developed countries, but many of them will be in capital intensive niche sectors where quality and skill matter more than price. Fashion textiles, certain advanced electronics, pharmaceuticals and whisky are four diverse examples. Nor will the developed countries have it all their own way in services. The strength of Indian competition in IT and business services is already evident, and over time more back office work in areas like financial, legal and accountancy services will move offshore, especially to countries where English and other European languages are well understood. But across the board it is to services, and to the new service products which are constantly being developed and extended, that the developed world must look for many of the jobs needed in the future. This is their area of greatest competitive advantage.

A further argument for opening up and developing the service sector is that it tends to be less prone to economic cycles than is manufacturing (Borchert and Mattoo 2009).

Developing Countries

Less obvious, perhaps, but no less valid, is the case for open markets for services in developing countries, whatever their stage of development. The economic arguments for liberalizing trade in services include the familiar arguments of comparative advantage which apply to trade generally, and which have been demonstrated by the contribution which more open trade in goods has made to world prosperity over the past 60 years. Over time, developing countries will become more significant producers and exporters of services, drawing on their cost advantages. They will develop new strengths to add to their existing success in IT and business services, construction and tourism (Cattaneo et al. 2010; Nielson and Taglioni 2004). But the case can probably best be made in terms of developing countries as importers and consumers of services. Access to modern, efficient services is as important to business consumers as it is to households and individuals: preventing or delaying such access is often tantamount to a covert tax on economic development. Developing countries cannot grow their economies and overseas sales without the support of efficient services, which will not be available in the necessary quality and quantity from domestic sources.

There will of course be some losers from this process. Any opening up of markets is likely to mean that, even when total demand increases, some of the less competitive local players lose market share or go out of business. However, there is one very good reason why indigenous service providers benefit from overseas companies coming into the market. It is often difficult or impossible to market services in a foreign country without some kind of local presence. Such an investment is usually best made in cooperation with a local partner who understands local conditions and customs, and involves the transfer of skills and technology to local people. A foreign insurance company, for example, can hardly sell policies which are unfamiliar to local customers without a local office and local representatives, familiar with local risks, engaged in marketing and selling on the spot.

So services liberalization opens the way for foreign investment, and the jobs which flow from that. In turn this provides vital support for exports, not least in some of the poorest countries. Countries in West Africa like Benin and Mali produce some of the finest cotton in the world, and pressed for the reduction of US subsidies so that they can compete on more even terms. But another necessary condition for making West African cotton competitive is access to banking finance, insurance, transport (roads and shipping), distribution services in overseas markets and so on. Some of these services may be available, or partially available, from local sources. Many of them will not be. Successful exports from developing countries rely on access to foreign services.

It is sometimes argued that developing countries should be free to take advantage of foreign services when they wish, but should not commit themselves indefinitely to granting access to such services, thus depriving themselves of the opportunity to protect domestic interests in the future. But one of the great strengths of the WTO system is that member countries give confidence to their trading partners, and to global trade in general, by guaranteeing a certain level of market access, whether by tariff bindings under GATT or market access commitments under GATS. They do so in return for broadly similar commitments undertaken by their partners. They compete for inward investment by the range of commitments they offer. If those commitments could be withdrawn overnight, confidence in future trading stability would be lessened, with damaging effects on trade. Moreover, because much international trade in services is linked to a presence and an investment in another country, companies would be reluctant to expend the effort and sunk costs required for a successful investment if the conditions on which that success depended could be changed overnight. For this reason, although many service sectors in key markets are at present relatively open, the long-term guarantee provided by GATS commitments to market opening is reassuring to both buyers and sellers.

How Far Can the Benefits of Services Liberalization be Quantified?

In seeking to quantify the gains from services liberalization there are three reasons to expect the numbers to be large. As we have seen, the service sector has the biggest share of GDP in all country groupings. That large sector tends to be highly protected in all countries. And gains are magnified to the extent that services liberalization acts as a proxy for the improved mobility of factors of production – capital via GATS Mode 3, and labour via Mode 4 (Chanda 2004; Whalley 2003).

It is thus found, in ex post analysis, that NAFTA had a strong positive effect on US service exports to Mexico. Similarly, EU service exports to Chile grew strongly as a result of the EU–Chile free trade agreement (Heydon and Woolcock 2009: 208).

The expectation of high gains is also borne out by computable general equilibrium (CGE) modelling – the only measurement technique that furnishes an economy-wide ex ante assessment of service barriers, and the main focus here. It is thus estimated that services liberalization would account for between 72 per cent (Hertel et al. 1999) and 82 per cent (Chadha et al. 2000) of total gains in welfare (GDP) from full Uruguay Round implementation and a successfully completed Doha Round. Services gains would thus far exceed those in agriculture and manufacturing. The modelling work also points to some important practical implications: that multilateral liberalization yields bigger gains than unilateral opening (Chadha et al. 2000); that gains are greater when barriers to both foreign and domestic service providers are reduced (Market Access in GATS terms) than when only barriers to foreign providers are reduced (National Treatment) (McGuire 2003); and that economies with high initial protection levels tend to gain most from liberalization (Dihel 2003; OECD 2003a).

Another important finding of the modelling work is that developing countries are major beneficiaries of services liberalization. Chadha et al. (2000) thus estimate that services opening yields a 2.5 per cent increase in GDP in developing countries, compared with a 2.0 per cent increase in developed economies. This is due in large measure to the fact that developing countries tend to have high barriers to trade in services. But it also reflects developing countries' growing competitiveness as services exporters.

Valuable though this modelling work is, it needs to be interpreted with great care. Measuring the gains from services liberalization faces two major challenges. The first results from the fact that national data on trade in services are much less comprehensive than data on trade in goods. The second challenge is methodological and results from the fact that services barriers are essentially domestic regulations that do not lend themselves to quantification in the way that tariffs do. In fact, the CGE modelling work relies on estimates of 'tariff equivalents' of services barriers that unavoidably have a considerable element of subjectivity. The modelling is also highly sensitive to underlying assumptions and scope. Thus while Chadha and Hertel reach broadly comparable results on the *relative* importance of services liberalization, compared with goods opening, they differ greatly on the *absolute* size of total welfare gains – USD 836 billion for Chadha and USD 493 billion for Hertel. The discrepancy arises because Hertel does not seek to estimate gains from increased competition and economies of scale.

But all of these challenges are being addressed. Data deficiencies are being tackled through collaborative work between the IMF, Eurostat, the WTO, OECD and UNCTAD. And the methodological underpinning of modelling work, the trade restrictiveness index, is being refined and developed by the OECD (Conway and Nicoletti 2006; OECD 2009), building on the pioneering work of Bernard Hoekman on tariff equivalents (Hoekman 1995).

Current modelling work is also focussed less on broad estimates of prospective gains in welfare and more on measuring the impact of barriers to trade in services on downstream users. It is thus found that if account is taken of service barriers, the effective rate of protection[1] for some agricultural and manufacturing sectors actually turns negative; in effect as we saw earlier, these sectors are being taxed (Dihel 2005; Dihel and Dee 2006). Put positively, countries will strengthen their comparative advantage in manufacturing following trade liberalization in services (Nordas 2010). Moreover, in the framework of intra-industry trade, which is driven by product differentiation, high trade costs in business services are found to be associated with a low level of product differentiation in downstream industries, particularly in the motor vehicle industry. An important policy implication of this finding is that open markets in business services will help industrial upgrading in developing countries (Nordas 2011).

In short, notwithstanding limitations of data and methodology, modelling work is valuable in demonstrating that the liberalization of trade in services yields

---

[1]   The effective rate of protection is the measure of net protection given when the cost of restrictions on imported inputs (say banking services) for the production of a particular product (say a motor vehicle) is subtracted from the protection given to that product.

major potential gains in welfare and in economic efficiency, not least for developing countries.

The Move for an International Agreement on Services

By the 1970s and early 1980s there was an increasingly strong view among those active in international trade policy that a General Agreement on Tariffs and Trade, focussing on goods, was not enough. There were other trade issues, notably agriculture, which in the opinion of many should be subject to international rules; and services were prominent among these issues. The switch of more labour-intensive manufacturing from developed to developing countries was becoming more apparent; new and important services, for example in information technology and satellite communications, were coming into being; and business leaders were becoming more aware that they did not have the same guarantees of open markets for services as they had for goods. When the scope of the Uruguay Round was under discussion, business groups in the United States argued for the inclusion of services. Europe was slower to take up the cause, although the City of London, with its strong interest in financial, professional and other services, lobbied actively. Some developing countries, on the other hand, feared that liberalization would swamp their small and not always competitive service industries; and were reassured that their concerns would be respected. When the Uruguay Round was launched in 1986, services were firmly on the agenda.

The Negotiation of the General Agreement on Trade in Services

So negotiation of a services agreement became a major part of the Uruguay Round (Croome 1999; Drake and Nicolaides 1992; Heydon 2011; OECD 1987; Sampson 2005). Together with the creation of the World Trade Organization and the dispute settlement system it was among the most notable achievements of that Round. The negotiators had to produce a comprehensive new agreement, comparable in scale to the General Agreement on Tariffs and Trade (GATT). This new agreement was in three parts. First, and much the largest part, a framework agreement containing the general rules and disciplines governing trade in services. Second, a number of annexes governing specific sectors. Third, the national schedules which list individual countries' specific commitments on access to their domestic markets by foreign service suppliers.

The GATS agreement has many features in common with the GATT. For example, both have provisions on most-favoured nation treatment, under which governments cannot treat one foreign supplier more favourably than another. Both have (somewhat different) provisions for national treatment, under which governments must treat foreign service suppliers in the same way that they treat their domestic suppliers, for example in relation to tax or regulation. The new dispute settlement arrangements agreed in the Uruguay Round apply to services as they do to goods.

There is, however, one major difference between GATT and GATS. The former can be described as a top-down agreement, in the sense that the starting point is the existing level of Customs tariffs, which can be negotiated down either individually or (now more usually) by the application of a formula such as a cut of x per cent, with exceptions to be agreed between the participants. GATS, on the other hand, is a bottom-up system. Each WTO member state lists in its national schedule those services, and only those services, for which it wishes to guarantee access to foreign suppliers. In addition to the services committed, the schedules can either grant completely free access, or limit the degree to which foreign suppliers of a particular service can operate in the market. For example, a country making commitments to allow foreign insurance companies into its market can restrict the number of such companies it allows in, or the number of sales outlets they may operate (Hoekman and Kostecki 2009).

The GATS agreement was not a completely finished product. A number of issues – not the most important, but still significant – were left for further negotiation, and in due course became part of the Doha Round. These included domestic regulation, emergency safeguards, government procurement and subsidies. All have proved difficult to resolve. However, the negotiation of the GATS itself, although requiring a great deal of complex and detailed work in an area hitherto unfamiliar to trade negotiators, was relatively uncontroversial in the context of the Uruguay Round. The work was almost entirely carried out by the GATT secretariat and specialist negotiators from the member states, and rarely engaged ministers. The structure of the GATS agreement made it less controversial, not least by allaying some of the concerns of developing countries. Governments knew that they would only have to include in their schedules those services for which they were content to liberalize or bind the existing regime, and that less extensive commitments would be expected from developing and especially least developed countries.

The inclusion within GATS of provision for negotiation on the movement of natural persons – the fourth of the service modes listed at the beginning of this chapter – was welcomed by developing countries. However, agreement has been difficult to achieve, mainly because of fears in developed countries, notably in the United States but also elsewhere, that workers from the developing world who come to undertake a particular task may stay permanently. Business opinion in developed countries is often sympathetic to measures designed to make it easier for them to move key staff around the world on a temporary basis. The opposition comes from trades unions, concerned about the job opportunities for their members, but particularly from politicians under pressure over levels of immigration. Some agreement on this issue is probably necessary if significant progress is to be made in GATS as a whole. The solution may lie in focussing on skilled workers travelling abroad who return home when their task is complete, and on checks to make sure that they do so (OECD 2004).

Sectoral Negotiations on Specific Services

The focus of service negotiations in the Uruguay Round was on the framework agreement. Such specific commitments as were made during the Round were largely to bind existing arrangements, and there were relatively few commitments to new market opening. It was envisaged that major negotiations to liberalize services would take place later. Indeed GATS Article XIX envisages, quite ambitiously, that 'successive rounds of negotiations' would begin not later than 2000 (five years after GATS entered into force in January 1995) 'with a view to achieving a progressively higher level of liberalisation'.

Meanwhile in the late 1990s negotiations took place in the WTO on three specific services sectors, telecommunications, financial services and maritime services. The most successful was the WTO Agreement on Basic Telecommunications, which came into force in 1998 with the support of 69 member countries. The results can now be seen. In almost all regions of the world, countries with WTO telecoms commitments have experienced a more rapid rate of growth in revenue from this sector than countries without such commitments. Access to both fixed line and to mobile services is higher in countries with commitments than in countries without. In Brazil and India, as elsewhere, liberalization has coincided with, and contributed to, dramatic increases in Internet and mobile phone use, and to price reductions.

The other sectoral negotiations were less successful. That on financial services produced little beyond bindings of the existing regime, although the insurance sector in India has grown rapidly since it was partially opened up to foreign suppliers in 1999. A parallel negotiation on maritime services was a failure.

Service Negotiations in the Doha Round

In accordance with GATS Article XIX fresh negotiations on services were started in 2000, but were soon subsumed into the Doha Round which was launched in the following year. Because the Doha Round is seen as a single undertaking, under which nothing is finally agreed until the Round as a whole is complete, it has been possible for the services negotiations to be held hostage to other parts of the Round, and specifically to the lack of progress on agriculture and on manufactured goods (known in WTO jargon as non-agricultural market access or NAMA). As a result hardly any in-depth negotiations on services were engaged over the first ten years of the Doha Round, and no significant results were secured. However, as long as the Doha Round remains alive, hope must remain that this long drawn out process will eventually yield a positive outcome in terms of improved market access for services.

Reasons for the Reluctance to Liberalize

A range of different reasons for the slow pace of services liberalization can be identified, some relating to pressure groups outside governments, some to the negotiating mechanics of GATS, and some to policy preferences within government (Gootiiz and Mattoo 2009; Sutherland 2010).

Pressure groups outside governments

A range of different pressure groups exert influence on different governments. There are local business interests, both in developing and developed countries, who fear loss of market share to more competitive outsiders but often present their case in terms of maintaining quality of service to local consumers. Examples are Indian lawyers keen to maintain their dominance of the local market for legal advice; and European audiovisual industries (film, broadcasting) wanting to reserve market share for local productions. Interestingly in both cases the industry is not unanimous. Some Indian lawyers want to team up with foreign firms to offer a global service from offices in India; and much of the European music industry opposes protection for the audiovisual sector.

Another set of pressure groups are trades unions and NGOs, often operating across national boundaries in developed and developing countries. The unions are particularly concerned to protect public ownership of services like health and education, and have persuaded the European Commission to say that they will not make offers in these two sectors. Other campaigning groups are concerned about the control of water supplies, or claim that consumers will suffer from the liberalization of services which ought to remain closely regulated. In the latter case it is important to distinguish between liberalization and deregulation, which are quite different. If there is a case for regulating a service, as for example in financial services or transport, there is a case for doing so whether or not that service is open to foreign providers. There is nothing in GATS which stands in the way of reasonable and impartial regulation (Nordas 2006; OECD 2002; Trachtman 2003; WTO 1999).

A third source of pressure, but on the other side of the account, is the private sector service lobbies. These have been rather less effective than their economic strength might entitle them to be. Indeed it is widely argued that they were more effective in the Uruguay Round than in the Doha Round. What are the reasons for this? Historically, the industries which have put most time and money into lobbying on WTO issues have been those concerned to preserve the status quo – European and Japanese farmers, US cotton producers. Many modern, successful service industries have been reluctant to devote much CEO time or corporate resources to lobbying on GATS, perhaps because, while their businesses are prospering and markets remain relatively open, they do not see the securing of GATS commitments as a major priority. Another factor is the long time scale over which GATS negotiations are conducted: many businesses are reluctant to spend time and money on a process which will take several years to show any benefit for their bottom line and are more inclined to support bilateral or regional initiatives.

Negotiating mechanics

For a number of reasons the complex structure of the GATS, for example by comparison with the GATT, makes it difficult for many governments, especially those with limited resources, to engage with GATS issues. Such governments can find it difficult to decide where their national interest lies in services, and in changing domestic regulation to allow market opening. A variety of ministries will have interests in different services and the rules governing them, and normally these will not be the trade or foreign ministries – the ministries which are familiar with the WTO. Some domestic service providers will not welcome competition, and may have the ear of local politicians. And changes in rules may involve legislation and legislators, who face political pressures: those sectors of an economy which feel threatened by liberalization often exert more influence than those who gain from it (see Chapter 2).

Another source of difficulty reflects the detailed, bottom-up, character of GATS negotiations, as noted earlier. Sector by sector, governments request the market opening measures which they want from their trading partners, and then make offers in response to the requests made of them. This is a slow process, and often difficult for governments to explain to their local constituencies.

Both the 1997 financial services negotiations and the GATS offers so far made in the Doha Round do little more than bind existing regimes. There are some useful offers of liberalization, but not many. This experience suggests that the way negotiations are conducted in GATS may encourage agreements that freeze the status quo, but lead to only very modest new market opening. GATS commitments would thus give countries international blessing for services reforms which they were carrying out anyhow for domestic reasons, but provide little incentive to go beyond this. If this is correct, the institutional structure of GATS may serve to inhibit faster liberalization (OECD 2001).

Priority for manufacturing and agriculture

However, the most immediate cause of delay to the services negotiations in the first ten years of the Doha Round was the preference given by some governments to agriculture and manufacturing (NAMA). Leading agricultural exporters like Brazil and Argentina, supported by India, insisted that, before they engaged seriously in negotiations on services, the basic framework of a deal on agriculture must be settled. When trade ministers came together in substantial face-to-face negotiations, in Geneva in July 2008, they failed to make progress primarily because of an unresolved dispute between the United States and the more prosperous developing countries on the level of commitment by the latter to reductions in tariffs on manufactures. The United States did not push as strongly for early progress on services as might have been expected. The European Union and some other developed countries who would like to see services treated as one of three big pillars of the Doha Round have been frustrated by the insistence of other major players on settling the framework for agriculture and manufacturing before getting down to serious business on services. At the time of writing (March 2012) this dispute remains unresolved, and seems unlikely to be settled quickly. Meanwhile the growth of preferential trade agreements (PTAs) continues unabated.

Services in Preferential Trade Agreements

Since 1994, some 180 preferential agreements including trade in services rules have come into existence, compared with only 38 in the previous 40 years (Heydon and Woolcock 2009). Over 40 per cent of the cumulative total has come into existence since 2000, involving mainly bilateral agreements between countries increasingly further apart and more diversified in levels of development. The most active countries have been identified as Mexico, Chile, Singapore, the United States, Australia and New Zealand, with the EU, EFTA and ASEAN standing out as the most active regional groupings (Houde et al. 2007).

Three factors help explain the increased attention to trade in services in bilateral and regional trade agreements: the size of the potential liberalization gains on offer, the failure to make progress in the Doha Round, and the opportunity presented to go beyond the WTO in the pursuit of deeper integration.

Liberalization Gains

The broad scope for welfare gains from the liberalization of trade in services has been discussed earlier. As would be expected, gains are also apparent when liberalization is being conducted bilaterally or regionally. It is estimated, for example (Copenhagen Economics and Francois 2007), that in the recently negotiated PTA between the EU and Korea no less than 70 per cent of EU gains are attributable to the liberalization of trade in services and that EU exports will increase by 40 to 60 per cent in the areas of wholesale and retail trade, transport services, communications, financial services and other business services.[2]

---

[2]   The relative importance of services gains is explained by Korea's growing demand for service inputs to economic growth and the fact that the Korean service sector is highly protected by non-tariff barriers. Also in the modelling, barriers to trade in services are

Slow Progress in the Doha Round

In recalling the reasons for lack of progress in the DDA, it is possible to see why many countries feel that PTAs offer more hope of progress, albeit with discriminatory elements.

As we have seen, the attainment of services liberalization in the Doha Development Agenda has been held hostage to the lack of progress in other areas, notably agriculture and non-agricultural market access (NAMA). It may be felt that the greater scope in bilateral deals to exclude sensitive products, and in some cases whole sectors, offers less risk of stalemate.

Progress in the Doha Round has also been impeded by stand-offs within the services negotiations, with some parties, mainly developing countries, reluctant to liberalize commercial presence (GATS Mode 3) until others, predominantly developed countries, show a willingness to liberalize the movement of service providers (Mode 4). Again, bilateral arrangements may be seen as offering better opportunities for breakthrough, such as with the provisions on the movement of nurses contained in the Japan–Philippines and Japan–Indonesia PTAs, and EU commitments under Mode 4 in the EPA with CARIFORUM.

GATS negotiators, mindful of the central GATT principle of non-discrimination, have tended to focus on improved national treatment (which yields benefits only to foreign service providers), whereas most estimates of the gains from liberalization suggest relatively greater opportunities arising from improved market access (which brings benefits to both foreign and domestic service providers). PTAs, by their nature, will be less focussed on the principle of non-discrimination.

Finally, as noted earlier, progress in the GATS has been impeded by concerns (understandable, though largely unfounded) about threats to regulatory sovereignty in sensitive public services. While PTAs offer little beyond the extensive provisions in the GATS for carve out, bilateral agreements have not so far attracted the intense attention of NGOs seeking to put a brake on liberalization.

WTO-Plus

There is no doubt that many preferential agreements, in the pursuit of deeper integration, have achieved a measure of liberalization of trade in services not so far seen in the GATS. The opportunities to be WTO-plus will be discussed in more detail in the following section, with a particular focus on the agreements to which the United States and the European Union are parties.

---

assumed to be real resource costs, compared with tariffs and quotas in other sectors which generate tariff revenue and quota rents.

Going beyond the WTO[3]

United States: NAFTA, the model for all US PTAs, is based on a negative list (or top-down) approach, whereby everything is liberalized unless explicitly excluded, compared with the predominantly positive list (or bottom-up) approach of the GATS, as described earlier. The negative list approach is generally regarded as being more transparent than positive listing and as affirming an upfront commitment by signatories to an overarching set of general obligations. This approach, pioneered by the United States, Canada and Mexico, has since been spread by these countries in the agreements they have signed in Central and South America.

NAFTA was also a pioneer in providing for the right of non-establishment (i.e. no local presence requirement as a precondition to supply a service) as a means of encouraging greater volumes of cross-border trade in services. This right, for which no GATS equivalent exists, is particularly well suited to promoting electronic commerce (Sauvé 2003).

Moving beyond the NAFTA, all US agreements, apart from the PTA with Jordan, advance on WTO rule making in financial services and telecommunications. In financial services, US PTAs advance on transparency measures, senior management (Mode 4) requirements and dispute settlement procedures. For telecommunication services, US PTAs go beyond the GATS in the treatment of access to public telecommunication transport networks and services, licensing processes, scarce resources, enforcement, dispute settlement issues, and independent regulation and privatization.

The United States' PTAs also tend to be GATS-plus on mutual recognition issues – of particular importance for the (Mode 4) movement of natural persons. Movement of natural persons is furthered beyond the GATS in the agreements with, for example, Chile and Singapore that define minimum education requirements and alternative credentials in several professions. Under these agreements, the United States has committed to accept quotas of 1,400 and 5,400 business entry applications, respectively, from Chile and Singapore.

European Union: the desire to match US successes in negotiating significantly GATS-plus commitments in services has been one of the factors behind the EU's more aggressive push for better market access in services since 2006.

The Euro-Med Agreements are WTO-plus in services to the extent that for Mediterranean countries that are not Members of the WTO and therefore not signatories to the GATS, a basic framework agreement similar to that of the GATS is established.

The EU Neighbourhood Policy sets the basis for future PTAs in services with Mediterranean non-Member Partners and will upgrade the current provisions on services found in the Association Agreements. The EU-Moroccan Action Plan calls for opening of negotiations on a PTA in services, as well as exchange of information with a view to regulatory convergence with the EU, capacity building, and e-commerce development. Specific actions in the field of financial services are

---

[3]   Material in this and the following section draws on Heydon and Woolcock (2009).

aimed at upgrading Morocco's regulatory system in line with that of the EU and with international standards.

The EU has recently negotiated an Economic Partnership Agreement (EPA) with the CARIFORUM, seen by the EU as a model for EPAs with other regions. The EU has made commitments on 90 per cent of sectors and has in particular made more generous commitments in Mode 4 than it was ready to do in the Doha negotiations. The EU's concessions in Mode 4 must of course be seen against other policy areas, such as government procurement where the EU was able to make progress towards its own aims.[4] The EPA with CARIFORUM includes competition provisions in the tourism sector that seek to ensure no abuse of market dominance by large EU investors in the Caribbean. The EPA also follows the EU–Chile model of including significant sections aimed at the promotion of e-commerce.

A common feature of both US and EU PTAs is the extent to which the agreements advance beyond the GATS in financial and telecommunication services. This contrasts with an earlier finding (OECD 2003b) that progress in these infrastructure services was more likely in a multilateral setting, where critical mass is more present. It may in fact be the case that, in a form of reverse engineering, progress in the GATS has provided a stimulus to liberalization at the bilateral and regional level.

WTO-minus?

It may well be that the WTO-plus features outlined above are implemented on a non-discriminatory basis. This will frequently be the case where the measures are achieved through increased transparency or flexibility in domestic regulation. But non-discrimination is by no means guaranteed. Mutual recognition agreements in services (or elsewhere) are inherently discriminatory (Zarrilli 2005).

Moreover, though there is abundant evidence of both US and EU agreements going beyond the GATS, there are important qualifications to the notion that their PTAs are necessarily more ambitious.

For the United States, their ambition is seriously dented by the increasing tendency for US PTAs to contain negative-list reservations that exclude all measures affecting services maintained at the sub-national level.

Moreover, the much-vaunted negative-list feature of US PTAs is not without debate. While negative listing is usually associated with greater liberalization than positive listing, this says nothing about causality. It may simply be that countries that are prepared to open up significantly are more likely to use a negative list. Nor is the balance of advantage always clear. This is nicely illustrated by Japan's

---

4   The Mode 4 commitments by the EU include fairly generous provision for temporary entry of professionals and contract workers from the CARIFORUM states and even include access for Caribbean artists in the cultural industry, where the EU has been especially defensive in the GATS with its insistence on a 'cultural exclusion'. See Chaitoo (2008).

agreements (Fink and Molinuevo 2007). Positive listing (as in Japan-Malaysia) can offer advantages, like status quo bindings, usually ascribed only to negative listing. While negative listing (as in Japan-Mexico) can bring disadvantages, like effectively denying application of the agreement to future service activities, usually ascribed only to positive listing.

In the case of the EU, the Protocol on the Liberalisation of Trade in Services that will provide the basis of services liberalization with Euro-Med partners contains features that will need handling with great care by developing country partners. For example, the provision in the Protocol (Article 13) that in order to achieve National Treatment, treatment of the other Party may be formally different to that afforded nationals needs to be approached with care where this might involve treating foreign entities, say in the area of tax, more favourably than domestic entities. A similar consideration may arise with the GATS, though here the Exceptions provisions in Article XIV appear to grant considerable latitude with respect to tax policy.

It should also be noted that the pursuit of services provisions in PTAs does not necessarily serve the interests of multilateral negotiations to the extent that the motivation for a broad WTO agreement can be undermined by PTAs satisfying the offensive interests of key sectors of the major traders. Moreover, sensitive sectors will remain sensitive – bilaterally as well as multilaterally – and there is likely to be a growing disparity between the treatment of those sectors subject to liberalization commitments and those (such as health, education and audiovisual) that preferential accords, no less than multilateral negotiations, tend to exclude.

Finally, notwithstanding the tendency for EU and US regulatory standards to become the de facto norm in bilateral agreements to which they are a Party, the proliferation of PTAs nevertheless means a proliferation of standards. This has been identified as a particular challenge for developing countries (OECD 2005).[5]

Conclusions

A powerful case can be made for liberalizing services globally in terms of growth and employment creation. The potential gains in terms of world trade and national welfare from opening up services are greater than in agriculture or manufacturing. Yet progress on services has been disappointingly slow in the GATS negotiations, mostly for reasons not directly arising from the services negotiations themselves. Yet if the Doha Round is eventually concluded, there is reason to hope that, with the support of at least some influential developing countries, it will include a substantial services element. Meanwhile preferential trade agreements can offer pointers to the way to go, though as a second-best to a successfully completed, non-

---

[5]   Where countries are economically and socially disparate, the conditions for regulatory harmonization may be less than optimal (see work undertaken at the World Bank to establish criteria for 'optimum regional harmonization areas'; Mattoo and Fink 2002).

discriminatory, Doha Round. If this is to happen, however, governments which understand and support the case for services liberalization will have to show greater political will and determination on this front than they did in the first ten years of the Doha Round.

References

Adlung, R. 2006. Public services and the GATS, *Journal of International Economic Law*, 9(2): 455–485.

Borchert, I. and Mattoo, A. 2009. The crisis resilience of services trade. *Policy Research Working Paper, No. 4917*. Washington, DC: World Bank.

Cattaneo, O., Schmid, L. and Walkenhorst, P. 2010. Engineering services: how to compete in the most global of the professions, in *International Trade in Services: New Trends and Opportunities for Developing Countries*, edited by O. Cattaneo, M. Engman, S. Saezand and R. Stern. Washington, DC: World Bank: 293–318.

Chadha, R., Brown, D., Deardorff, A. and Stern, R. 2000. Computational analysis of the impact on India of the Uruguay Round and forthcoming WTO trade negotiations. *Discussion Paper No. 459*, School of Public Policy, University of Michigan. Ann Arbor, Michigan.

Chaitoo, R. 2008. Services and investment in the Cariforum-EC Economic Partnership Agreement. ComSec/CALC Workshop, St Lucia, 27–28 May 2008.

Chanda, R. 2003. Social services and the GATS: key issues and concerns, *World Development*, 31(12): 1997–2001.

Chanda, R. 2004. Inter-modal linkages in services trade. *OECD Trade Policy Working Paper No. 30*. Paris: OECD.

Conway, P. and Nicoletti, G. 2006. Product market regulation in the non-manufacturing sectors of OECD countries: measurement and highlights. *OECD Economics Department Working Papers, No. 530*. Paris: OECD.

Copenhagen Economics and Francois, J.F. 2007. *Economic Impact of a Potential Free Trade Agreement Between the European Union and South Korea*.

Croome, J. 1999. *Reshaping the World Trading System: A History of the Uruguay Round*. The Hague: Kluwer Law International.

Dihel, N. 2003. Quantifying costs to national welfare from barriers to services trade: a review of the literature, in *Quantifying the Benefits of Liberalising Trade in Services*. Paris: OECD: 113–145.

Dihel, N. 2005. The impact of services barriers on effective rates of protection in agriculture and manufacturing, in *Enhancing the Performance of the Services Sector*. Paris: OECD: 127–132.

Dihel, N. and Dee, P. 2006. Services as outputs and intermediate inputs: the impact of liberalization, in *Trading Up: Economic Perspectives on Development Issues in the Multilateral Trading System*. Paris: OECD: 231–275.

Drake, W.J. and Nicolaides, K. 1992. Ideas, interests and institutionalization: trade in services and the Uruguay Round, *International Organization*, 46(1): 37–100.

Fink, C. and Molinuevo, M. 2007. *East Asian Free Trade Agreements in Services: Roaring Tigers or Timid Pandas*. Washington, DC: World Bank.

Gootiiz, B. and Mattoo, A. 2009. Services in Doha: what's on the table? *Journal of World Trade*, 43(5): 1013–1030.

Hertel, T., Francois, J. and Martin, W. 1999. Agriculture and non-agricultural liberalisation in the Millennium Round. Paper presented at the Global Conference on Agriculture and the New Trade Agenda from a Development Perspective: Interests and Options in the WTO 2000 Negotiations, sponsored by the World Bank and WTO, Geneva, 1–2 October. Summary of work available in OECD (2003a).

Heydon, K. 2011. The OECD: lessons from investment and services, in *The New Economic Diplomacy*, third edition, edited by N. Bayne and S. Woolcock. Aldershot: Ashgate: 231–248.

Heydon, K. and Woolcock, S. 2009. *The Rise of Bilateralism: Comparing American, European and Asian Approaches to Preferential Trade Agreements*. Tokyo: United Nations University Press.

Hoekman, B. 1995. Assessing the General Agreement on Trade in Services. *World Bank Discussion Paper No. 307*. Washington, DC: World Bank.

Hoekman, B. and Kostecki, M. 2009. *The Political Economy of the World Trading System*, third edition. Oxford: Oxford University Press.

Houde, M.-F., Miroudot, S. and Kolse-Patil, S. 2007. The interaction between investment and services chapters in selected regional trade agreements. COM/DAF/INV/TD(2006)40 FINAL. Paris: OECD.

Jones, R. and Kierzkowski, H. 1990. The role of services in production and international trade: a theoretical framework, in *The Political Economy of International Trade*, edited by R. Jones and A. Krueger. Oxford: Basil Blackwell: 31–48.

Krajewski, M. 2003. Public services and trade liberalisation: mapping the legal framework, *Journal of International Economic Law*, 6(2): 341–367.

Mattoo, A. and Fink, C. 2002. *Regional Agreements and Trade in Services: Policy Issues*. Washington, DC: World Bank.

McGuire, G. 2003. Methodologies for measuring restrictions on trade in services, in *Quantifying the Benefits of Liberalising Trade in Services*. Paris: OECD.

Nielson, J. and Taglioni, D. 2004. Services trade liberalisation: identifying opportunities and gains. *OECD Trade Policy Working Paper, No. 1*. Paris: OECD.

Nordas, H.K. 2006. Services trade and domestic regulation. TD/TC/WP(2006)20 FINAL. Paris: OECD.

Nordas, H.K. 2010. Trade in goods and services: two sides of the same coin? *Economic Modelling*, 27(2): 496–506.

Nordas, H.K. 2011. Opening markets for business services: industrial perspective for developing countries. *Journal of Economic Integration*, 26(2): 306–328.

OECD. 1987. *Elements of a Conceptual Framework for Trade in Services*. Mimeo. Paris: OECD.

OECD. 2001. *Trade in Services: Negotiating Issues and Approaches*. Paris: OECD.

OECD. 2002. *GATS: The Case for Open Services Markets*. Paris: OECD.

OECD. 2003a. *Quantifying the Benefits of Liberalising Trade in Services*. Paris: OECD.

OECD. 2003b. *Regionalism and the Multilateral Trading System*. Paris: OECD.

OECD. 2004. *Trade and Migration: Building Bridges for Global Labour Mobility*. Paris: OECD.

OECD. 2005. *Standards and Conformity Assessment: Minimising Barriers and Maximising Benefits*. Summary report of Workshop, 21–22 November 2005, Berlin. Paris: OECD.

OECD. 2009. Methodology for deriving the Services Trade Restrictiveness Index. *Paper prepared for an OECD Experts Meeting, 2–3 July.* Available at: www.oecd.org.

OECD. 2010. Responding to the economic crisis: implications for trade policy. Document TAD/TC/WP(2010)11. Available at: www.oecd.org/topic/0,3373, en_2649_37431_1_1_1_1_37431,00.html.

Sampson, G. 2005. *The WTO and Sustainable Development*. Tokyo: United Nations University Press.

Sampson, G. and Snape, R. 1985. Identifying issues in trade in services, *The World Economy*, 8(2): 171–181.

Sauvé, P. 2003. Services, in *Regionalism and the Multilateral Trading System*. Paris: OECD: 23–43.

Sutherland, P. 2010. ECIPE Jan Tumlir Lecture. Brussels: European Centre for International Political Economy.

Trachtman, J. 2003. Lessons for the GATS from existing WTO rules on domestic regulation, in *Domestic Regulation and Service Trade Liberalisation*, edited by A. Mattoo and P. Sauvé. Washington, DC: World Bank: 57–81.

Whalley, J. 2003. Assessing the benefits to developing countries of liberalization in services trade. *NBER Working Paper No. 10181*. Cambridge, MA: National Bureau of Economic Research.

WTO. 1991. MTN.GNS/W/120, 10 July, available at: www.wto.org.

WTO. 1999. Article VI: 4 of the GATS: Disciplines on Domestic Regulation Applicable to All Services: Note by the Secretariat, Document S/C/W/96.

Wunsch-Vincent, S. 2005. Cross-border trade in services and the GATS: lessons from the WTO US-Internet Gambling Case. *Working Paper*, Institute of International Economics, Washington, DC. Available at: www.iie.com.

Zarrilli, S. 2005. Moving professionals beyond national borders: mutual recognition agreements and the GATS. Paper prepared for UNCTAD Expert Meeting on Trade and Development Aspects of Professional Services and Regulatory Frameworks, Geneva, 17–19 January 2005.

Changes in the Value Chain of Manufacturing Industries: A Japanese Perspective

Risaburo Nezu

Introduction

This chapter examines, from a Japanese perspective, the key trends that have come to dominate global production and trade in manufactures. The first section briefly addresses the relative decline in manufacturing within the developed economies. The second section examines the contrasting experience of Japan in two key sectors – the vertically integrated automobile sector and the horizontally fragmented electronics industry. The third section highlights some keys to success in the global value chain. The fourth section touches on a number of future challenges likely to be faced by global manufacturing activity. The fifth section concludes.

Declining Manufacturing Industry in Developed Countries

Over a long period of time, manufacturing sectors have lost their relative importance in the economies of developed countries (see Figure 10.1). The proportion of manufacturing sectors, measured as the ratio of value added to gross domestic product (GDP), shows steady declining trends, although such declines are more pronounced in the two Anglo-Saxon countries, the United Kingdom and the United States, while in Germany and Japan there seems to be some flattening in the second half of the last decade until the international financial crisis of 2008.

However, this crisis hit the manufacturing sector even harder than the financial sector, which was the epicentre of the crisis. Some industrial sectors, particularly automotive and consumer electronics, experienced a contraction in production levels by some 40 per cent to 50 per cent. Judging by massive plant closures during the past two years and modest economic growth recovery prospects of developed

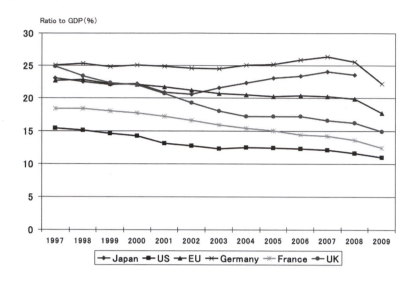

Figure 10.1 Share of manufacturing in most industrialized countries
Source: OECD, Eurostat, USDOC.

countries, it is highly likely that these manufacturing sectors in developed countries will never return to the pre-crisis level of production. Expansion of markets for these sectors will be largely in the emerging economies. In terms of employment, this decline of the manufacturing sector is even more noticeable (see Figure 10.2).

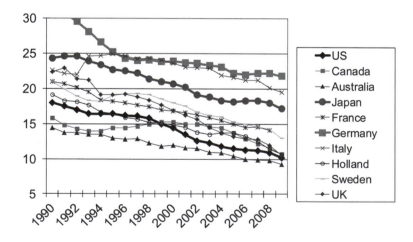

Figure 10.2 Share of manufacturing sectors in employment
Source: US Bureau of Labor Statistics.

In Organization for Economic Cooperation and Development (OECD) countries, proportions of employment in manufacturing sectors have followed straight lines of decline almost without exception. Even Germany, which identifies itself as the industrial base of Europe, could not escape this trend.

Due to this relative contraction of manufacturing industries in the OECD economies, and also due to the sharp rise in manufacturing in the emerging economies, the combined share of the United States, EU and Japan has declined, although the European Union (EU) has suffered a relatively smaller decline (see Figure 10.3).

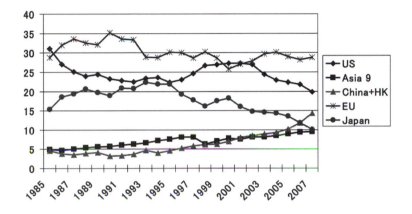

Figure 10.3 Share of major countries in global manufacturing sectors
Source: Produced by the Fujitsu Research Institute based on the US National Science Foundation database.

This is perhaps due to relocation of plants and factories to the former Eastern European area that is now a part of the EU. During this period, emerging Asian countries have gained greater proportions of the global manufacturing pie. This relative expansion and contraction of manufacturing sectors can be confirmed by comparing GDP and the index of industrial production (IIP) of individual countries. GDP helps to measure the growth rate of the economic activity of the total economy, while IIP tracks only the manufacturing sector. In most OECD countries, the growth rate of IIP is slightly lower than real GDP, while in emerging Asian economies, the opposite is the case (see Figure 10.4).

This shift to emerging economies seems to be following a well-known pattern of how multinational companies shift their production sites to developing countries according to the theory of the product life cycle proposed by Vernon (1971). The shift started with labour-intensive, mature industries like textiles, garments, shoes and toys which by now have disappeared from most OECD countries, except for some high quality brands. Steel and material industries have also moved offshore.

	US		Japan		EU15		China		India		Korea	
	Real GDP	IIP	Real GDP	IIP	Real GDP	IIP	Real GDP	IIP	Real GDP	IIP	Real GDP	IIP
2005	3.1	3.9	1.9	1.3	1.8	1.2	11.3	16.4	9.5	8.2	4	6.4
2006	2.7	2.4	2	4.3	3.1	4.1	12.7	16.6	9.7	11.6	5.2	8.4
2007	2.1	3	2.4	3	2.7	3.5	14.2	18.5	9.2	8.5	5.1	6.9
2008	0.4	-4.5	-1.2	-3.4	0.5	-1.8	9.6	12.9	6.7	2.8	2.3	3.4
2009	-2.4	-11	-5.2	-21.9	-4.1	-13.9	9.1	11	7.4	10.5	0.2	-0.8
Average	1.2	-1.2	0	-3.3	0.8	-1.4	11.4	15.1	8.5	8.3	3.4	4.9

Figure 10.4   Changes of GDP and IIP for major countries
Source: OECD Economic Outlook, CEIC database.

Production of capital goods, such as machine tools, robotics and construction equipment are moving more slowly due to the high level of technology content, lack of skilled workers in the developing world to operate plants and factories, and high capital costs in these sectors. But even in these sectors, most capacity expansions are seen in non-OECD countries.

Broad Trends in Manufacturing Production and Trade: A Comparison Between Automotives and Electronics

Accelerating Offshore Shift after the Global Financial Crisis of 2008

Shifts in manufacturing to the developing world are accelerating in the wake of the global financial crisis of 2008. Although the global economy, including OECD countries, recovered more quickly in 2009 than at first feared, it never reached the pre-crisis level of production. Major contraction is still continuing in automotive and consumer electronics. The case of General Motors (GM) in the United States testifies to the magnitude of such movements. After years of poor performance, GM went bankrupt and came back to the stock market only in November 2010. During the period of government ownership, the company closed ten factories in North America, sold out a number of product lines and brands and laid off tens of thousands of workers. At the same time, the company invested heavily in China, which has become the biggest automobile market in the world. In Europe, since late last century, major automobile companies like Fiat and Volkswagen have closed factories at home and moved their plants to Eastern Europe. In the electronics industry, Philips and Siemens have either terminated production of consumer goods like audiovisual products, let alone white goods, or are moving their production base to emerging countries. At home, they are now concentrating their resources on medical technology, environmental equipment and infrastructure businesses.[1]

However, it is important to note that while OECD countries are losing their share to emerging countries in the conventional industrial sectors, they are successfully maintaining their positions in the high-tech areas, composed of information and communication equipment, biotech, aerospace and precision measurement equipment. As Figure 10.5 shows, the combined world market share of the United States and EU has remained at around 60 per cent over the last ten years. And there seems to be no sign of weakness. Here, the high-tech industry is characterized by the OECD having a high ratio of research and development (R&D) expenditure to sales. The only exception is Japan, which has lost its position to China. This happened because Japan poured vast amounts of several resources into information and communication technology (ICT) and failed to establish a stronghold in other high-tech sectors. China could erode the dominant position of Japan by attracting foreign direct investments from US and European ICT companies.

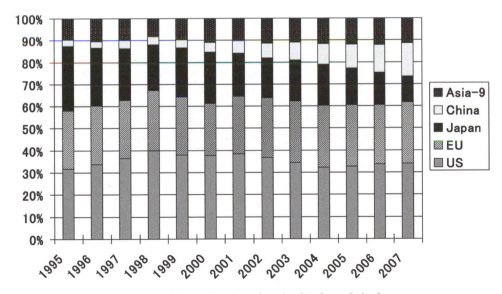

Figure 10.5 Shares of world production for the high-tech industry
Note: High-tech refers to ICT, biotech, aerospace, precision measurement equipment.
Source: Created by FRI based on National Science Foundation data.

---

[1]   Annual reports of Siemens and Philips (2008, 2009, 2010).

A similar decline in competitiveness is evident in Japan's share of world exports, which has slipped from 8 per cent in 1995 to 4 per cent at present. While this downward trend is inevitable to some extent given the increasing roles of China and other newly emerging Asian economies, the problem is the rate of decline, which is fast even compared to that of Germany or the United States. The major factors which explain this rapid shrinkage of Japanese industry are to be found in two key industrial sectors, automotive and electronics. These sectors used to be the main driving force behind Japanese economic growth.

The nature of the problems faced by these two sectors differs fundamentally. Japanese automobile companies have retained their positions as global leaders, by relocating their factories and reorganizing their supply chains on a global scale. In contrast, the electronics industry has not been able to transform its value chain globally in a timely fashion and accordingly has lost its competitive position.

The Automotive Story – Shifting Vertically Integrated Factories to Emerging Countries

The automotive industry is a mature sector, with a history of more than 100 years since the first commercialization of the car in Europe. The key concepts of a vehicle, which consists of an internal combustion engine, wheels and a transmission, are all mature technologies. Innovations go in a continuous manner at a constant speed (Fujimoto 2002; Tanaka 2009). In this environment, Japanese companies have developed unique production methods like the *kaizen* (continuous improvement) quality control circle, or what is known more broadly as 'lean production' (Womack and Jones 1992). Another success factor for the Japanese auto industry has been its insistence on energy efficiency. Originally, efficiency was a domestic concern for Japanese consumers, as gasoline prices were higher in Japan and air pollution was an acute problem. The oil crises in the 1970s, which quadrupled crude oil prices, made Japanese cars the most preferred cars in the world.

At first, Japanese auto companies responded to this situation only by increasing exports, but this strategy soon proved to be a major cause of trade friction with the United States and Europe. Under pressure from the governments of Japan, the United States and Europe, Japanese companies decided to produce in the host countries in order to create jobs there. Such overseas production came much later than that of their European and US counterparts, because initially the Japanese companies were not sure if the Japanese way of production would be possible on foreign soil. They moved cautiously at first, then more boldly in subsequent years. This was the starting point of a long process of creating a global value chain. In order to maintain high quality and a lean production system, Japanese companies maintained close relations with their parts and components suppliers in Japan, with whom the assemblers had shared experience and know-how for several years. They maintained a vertically integrated production system, which enabled them to fine-tune and coordinate hundreds of thousands of parts and components. There was outside criticism that Japanese companies had exclusive buyer–supplier relations and were refusing to buy from local suppliers, but there is no denying that these long-term relationships were the key to the success of the Japanese auto industry (Fujimoto 2002).

This cohesive relationship between auto assemblers and parts suppliers came to a sudden turning point in 1999, when Nissan, the second-largest auto company in Japan, was acquired by Renault. In order to reduce costs, Carlos Ghosn, the newly appointed chief executive of Nissan, decided to change the company's long-standing policy to buy only from its affiliated suppliers and began to purchase from open sources at more competitive prices. Other companies began to move in the same direction, albeit more cautiously. Thus, the vertically integrated *keiretsu* system began to unwind. But such unwinding never went as far as seen in the electronics sector. In car-making, each part and component must be carefully fine-tuned and tailored to fit the others. It is not like buying products at a supermarket.

The Successful Japanese Automotive Industry and Hollowing Out of the Japanese Industrial Base

During the 1990s, Japanese auto companies built more factories abroad, at first in the United States and Europe, then in neighbouring Asian countries. During this period, overseas production consistently increased until the global financial crisis of 2008. With time, Japanese auto companies learned how to apply the Japanese way of producing automobiles abroad, namely lean production. More companies began to adopt the policy of building their cars where there is demand. Their domestic production declined from 14 million vehicles in 1990, to less than ten million in 2009. But overseas production, which started from scratch 30 years ago, now surpasses domestic production. The number of workers employed in the automotive industry in Japan decreased from 956,000 in 1991 to 787,000 in 2002. Japanese companies now employ more than one million workers outside Japan.

At the same time, such moves boosted exports of parts and intermediaries from Japan, leaving an important part of the value chain at home. This export of parts is now gradually being replaced by local or third country production which raises the ratio of local procurements even higher. But, because of the rapidly expanding local production of cars in Asia, the overall export of parts from Japan is steadily increasing, with a positive effect on the balance of Japan's international payments.

The Agony of the Japanese Electronics Industry – a Case of Horizontal Fragmentation of the Value Chain

In recent years, the Japanese electronics industry, once the overwhelming global leader, has been faced with serious structural and strategic problems. Unlike the automotive industry, this industry has undergone a fundamental shift from analogue to digital technology. In particular, the advent of the Internet has forced many existing electronics companies to leave the market, making way for entirely new venture-type companies (Sato 2006).

Regardless of the country or industry, it is generally correct to say that successful companies tend to be bound by existing methods of production and can move only slowly to take advantage of new technologies. In the information technology (IT) sector, composed of such technologies as semiconductors, personal computers, mobile telephones, software and computer solutions businesses, Japanese companies like Sony, Hitachi, Toshiba, Matsushita and Fujitsu lost their international competitive edge and were forced to retreat to the domestic market. They did not lose to the existing foreign firms, however, but rather to new companies like Microsoft, Dell, Cisco Systems, Apple and Oracle. These companies all started up during the 1980s, except for Microsoft which was founded in 1977. Google was founded in 1998 but, within less than ten years, it became the largest search engine company in the world. In Japan, such young entrepreneurs were non-existent. Instead, the new challenge fell on the shoulders of old but large companies. Of course, these large companies were fully aware of the magnitude of the impact of digital technology, particularly the Internet. Many taskforces were created and serious efforts were made to bring this technology to the market. But these companies were slow, bureaucratic and averse to risk. In the end they lost out not only to the young US companies, but to strategically focused Korean and Taiwanese companies as well.

Concern over Japan's industrial competitiveness is mounting. Particularly in the electronics industry, including the Japanese mainstay of consumer electronics, losing world share in a succession of product areas to Korean and Chinese firms is increasing pressure on the government to present some solid solutions in its growth strategy. An oft-raised example is Korea's Samsung Electronics which, up until 20 years ago, was regarded as incapable of anything more than imitating Japanese firms. Now, Samsung dominates those same firms in high-tech areas such as semiconductors, flat-panel TVs and mobile phones (Noguchi 2010; Sato 2006).

The situation in Japan for electronics and electrical machinery is dire. Japanese firms suffered across the board in the 1990s, in some cases because they had the wrong corporate strategies and in others because they were unable to take effective steps when their strategies became outmoded in the face of change. These changes were epitomized by the IT industry. The 1990s saw a string of changes that profoundly affected corporate strategy: digitalization, downsizing and horizontal specialization. For example, mainframe computers gave way to personal computers, the core parts of which are chips called microprocessing units (MPU), and the software which runs on these operating systems (OS). Japanese and US firms both picked up on personal computers at virtually the same time, with all firms initially making proprietary models. In the United States, however, IBM decided to stop producing complete units in-house and instead outsourced MPU production to the chip company Intel and OS production to Microsoft, which were at the time almost completely unknown venture firms. IBM's performance subsequently suffered almost to the point of bankruptcy, but the firm succeeded in rehabilitating itself by shifting its business focus. The cause of Japanese firms' apparent inability to turn their technologies into successful business was essentially structural. Venture firms and new companies that have nothing to lose are conversely much better at developing and commercializing new products.

Intel and Microsoft ended up virtually monopolizing the rapidly growing personal computer market. Particularly, as computers came to be used for access to the Internet, international connectivity became critical, and because only Intel and Microsoft products provided this, Japanese firms were obliged to sell computers containing 'Wintel' (Windows and Intel) elements, with Japanese computers per se disappearing from the market. Computers are obviously composed of more than just MPUs and OSs, but because memory chips and other small parts are easily manufactured, these markets were captured by firms in Korea and Taiwan where wages were low. The same thing happened with routers and mobile phones, the other Internet 'switching systems'. Japanese firms had all their parts made in-house or by their affiliates, and not one became a strategic Wintel-style company using a focus on core competencies to monopolize world markets in a particular part of the value chain.

Some Keys to Success in the Global Value Chain

The Challenge of Destructive Technology

Digital technology is a completely new field, previously unseen in the commercial business of electronics production. Nobuyuki Idei, former chief executive of Sony, once said, 'The Internet came like a meteorite' (Idei 2002), like that which eliminated the dinosaur from the earth 65 million years ago. It is a typical destructive innovation that presents a major break from earlier technologies. Many Japanese IT companies with a broad business domain found it difficult to take on the challenges as the new technology would cannibalize existing business. This is the typical situation which Christensen (2003) called the innovators' dilemma. Samsung, on the other hand, chose to specialize in a simple memory chip technology: dynamic random access memory, or DRAM. Japanese firms also had outstanding DRAM technologies, but overcrowding in the domestic market prevented individual firms from achieving the scale necessary to bring down costs sufficiently. In addition, because firms used their chips in their end products – consumer electronics – rather than selling them on the open market, unit prices crept up. Operated by its founder, Samsung took a bold decision to make massive capital investments at the right moment so that it was positioned to seize markets ahead of Japanese firms during periods of economic expansion. Capital investment by Japanese firms was always too little, too late, causing them to gradually fall behind. With fierce price competition from Korean and Taiwanese firms stripping away profits, almost all major Japanese electronics companies eventually withdrew from the market with the exception of Elpeda, a dedicated memory chip manufacturer. It is often said today that 'Japanese companies won technology competition, but lost market competition' (Seno 2009).

Winning a Global Standard

Japanese problems with mobile phones point to yet another challenge. Mobile phones penetrated faster in Japan than anywhere else in the world. Telecommunications connectivity depends on common technical standards. NTT, the biggest Japanese telephone operator, led the way in developing the world's most advanced technical standard. In Europe, meanwhile, the realization that individual national standards would limit market scale saw Global System for Mobile Communications (GSM) created as a single European standard and efforts were made to have this adopted internationally. The GSM drive was spearheaded by Northern Europe and the United Kingdom. Japanese firms, however, appear to have believed that they should first control Japan's massive domestic market of 100 million people, and then it would be possible to capture the global market. Japanese firms underestimated the strategic importance of capturing the world standard. As a result, most countries, including those in Asia, adopted GSM as their technical standard, leaving Japanese mobile phones effectively trapped at home. Conversely, because GSM phones cannot be used in Japan, Japan has become one of the world's most isolated and inconvenient markets – the so-called Galapagos phenomenon (Nomura Research Institute 2008). With ten manufacturers vying for Japan's limited market, the production volume for each company cannot go much above ten million units. On the world market, Finland's Nokia alone produces 300 million units a year. Naturally, most of these units are made in Asia where labour costs are low, so Japanese firms cannot compete on price. Defeated on mobile phones too by global firms such as Nokia and Samsung, Japanese firms have vanished from the world market. The chips in mobile phones are made by US firms such as Qualcomm and Texas Instruments, which design the chips themselves but outsource production to Asian firms. US and Asian firms are thus prospering from a pattern of specialization that plays to their respective strengths. Dividing up among different companies the various stages of the production process, from development through to sales and after-sales service, is known as horizontal fragmentation, and US and Asian firms' active pursuit of this is boosting their competitiveness. In the case of Japanese firms, however, their desire to do everything in-house seems to obstruct the development of relationships whereby each firm focuses on its own core competencies and teams up with other firms for everything else. Out of 1.2 billion units produced in 2008 across the world, only 3 per cent of mobile handsets are produced by Japanese makers for Japanese domestic users.

The Power of Modularity

A key concept in understanding the difference between horizontal fragmentation and vertical integration is modularity. This concept is introduced in the book Design Rules by Baldwin and Clark (2000: 6), who state:

> At the level of engineering design, computers proved amenable to an approach we call 'modularity in design'. Under this approach, different parts of the computer could be designed by separate, specialized groups working independently of one another. The 'modules' could then be connected and (in theory at least) would function seamlessly, as long as they conform to a predetermined set of design rules.

This is precisely what happened in the 1990s to the global electronics industry with such force that it altered the landscape of the industry fundamentally. The key to the success of this module approach is that design rules are predetermined and made accessible to anyone who wishes to produce certain parts to be connected with other parts and modules. Both Intel and Microsoft made public their interfaces, enabling any potential supplier to produce parts that can work with them. The earlier mentioned GSM and the Transmission Control Protocol/Internet Protocol (TCP/IP) are yet other examples of such design rules. This opened doors for young specialized venture companies to enter into the computer business. This is the primary reason why in the computer and telecommunications industries there were so many new start-up companies.

This module approach did not occur in the automotive industry to the same extent as in electronics. Individual modules could not be produced without consideration of other modules. There is a need for close coordination and fine-tuning among producers of different modules. This makes it impossible for an assembler to buy parts from independent suppliers. While Japanese automobile companies are well known for their long-term relationships with their suppliers, more or less the same relations exist in the American and European automotive industries. Assemblers buy from a limited number of suppliers with whom they have long-term relations. Unlike with electronics, there is no entry into the automotive industries of OECD countries.

A Focus on Parts and Raw Materials

While electronics and electrical machinery manufacturers might have lost out on finished products, many Japanese companies are in fact doing well in the less visible areas of parts and raw materials. For example, Japanese companies dominate the markets for small parts such as the condensers and small motors that turn the hard disk drives in computers. With raw materials, too, Japanese firms have an overwhelming presence in the centipede-like lead frames and silicon wafers on which chips are built and the glass substrate and chemical surface coating for flat-panel TVs. Looking at industrial sectors in what were previously described as sunset industries – chemicals and ceramics, for example – firms have been working quietly to develop products and improve quality, earning the trust of their clients. These are sectors where new Asian firms have barely ventured. In Korea, electronics firms like Samsung and LG have grown successfully, but the more their sales rise, the more exports of raw materials from Japan to Korea also increase, with Korea's deficit to Japan failing to diminish at all. In that sense, Japanese and Korean firms have established a good pattern of specialization and collaboration.

Even steel, the archetypal materials industry, is doing unexpectedly well. Since the 1970s, resource constraints and environmental problems have caused the steel industry to be viewed as a sunset industry. In fact, production levels continued to fall throughout the 1980s and 1990s, and all steel firms started exploring avenues other than steel, but most of these ventures ended in failure. Together with steel itself, however, auto steel exports and exports to Southeast Asia have been growing since 2000, while production levels have bounced back to above 100 million tonnes per annum. There have been no major technological breakthroughs, however, in recent years; Japanese firms have managed to maintain their competitiveness through a string of small efforts such as cutting personnel costs, boosting product quality and reducing energy consumption to meet customer demands.

Trade in Technology

Technology trade is an important subset of global value chains, where Japan has reason to be optimistic. The net receipt of technology trade, that is export minus import of technology, turned to surplus for Japan in the 1990s, but the surplus has constantly widened since then. This comprises fees from patent licensing, royalties, technical service, software programming and information processing. In 2008, Japanese export of such services was 2.2 trillion yen while its payment was 0.6 trillion yen, with a net surplus of 1.6 trillion yen (nearly US$16 billion) in technology trade. This is a rather small amount relative to Japan's GDP, but it is the second-largest surplus in the world after the United States, whose surplus was US$37 billion. The UK ranks more or less the same as Japan, but Germany is a distant fourth in this ranking. About 70 per cent of technology export is undertaken by the overseas subsidiaries of Japanese companies. The automotive industry plays the most important role in this technology export. This surplus of technology trade will continue to grow as more and more Japanese companies move their factories abroad and more of them regard R&D as an independent business domain rather than a subsidiary to manufacturing.

The Smile Curve as a Useful Means to Understanding Value Chains

It is generally believed that the concept of the smile curve was first proposed by Stan Shih, chief executive of Acer, a personal computer manufacturer in Taiwan, to explain the structure of the value chain for a personal computer. But this concept seems applicable to many other IT products. As shown in Figure 10.6, if we plot different stages of production on a horizontal axis, starting with R&D, key parts and essential materials, to be followed by assembly, sales and after-sales service, and then plot value-added on a vertical axis, we get a curve high at either end but low in the middle. Hence the term 'smile curve'.

In the case of personal computers, the lion's share of the profit goes to R&D and after-sales service, leaving very little for assemblers to take.

In semiconductors, there are companies like Qualcom and Texas Instruments which concentrate on researching and developing new semiconductors, but do not produce anything themselves. Experts call such companies 'fabless', which means 'without fabrication'. They draw up blueprints and circuit designs, but contract out manufacturing to Asian producers such as Taiwan Semiconductor Manufacturing Company (TSMC), the largest maker of semiconductors in the world. Such contract manufacturers can also make reasonable profit if they can maintain large scale operations and a high rate of capacity utilization. Taiwanese manufactures have been successful in this regard.

The cost structure of iPods resembles that of personal computers. As is shown in Figure 10.7, a large proportion of the price is profit for Apple and its distribution network. Another important part is the hard disk drive, which takes a quarter of the entire value. Only one-fifth of the price goes to all other remaining parts, and assembly gets almost nothing. Clearly the most profitable parts of the value chain

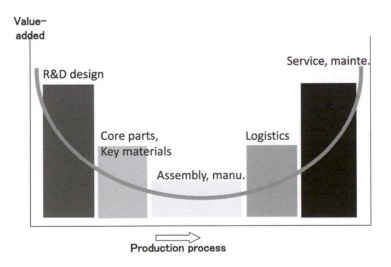

Figure 10.6   Value chain of manufacturing industry

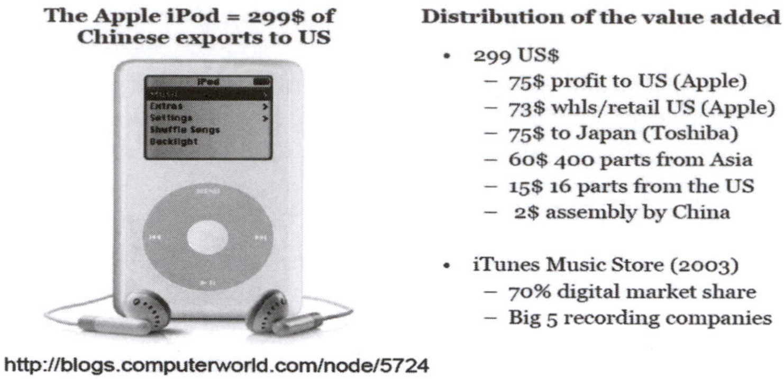

The Apple iPod = 299$ of Chinese exports to US

Distribution of the value added

- 299 US$
  - 75$ profit to US (Apple)
  - 73$ whls/retail US (Apple)
  - 75$ to Japan (Toshiba)
  - 60$ 400 parts from Asia
  - 15$ 16 parts from the US
  - 2$ assembly by China

- iTunes Music Store (2003)
  - 70% digital market share
  - Big 5 recording companies

http://blogs.computerworld.com/node/5724

Figure 10.7   Who really makes money on the iPod?

are the R&D and design stage and the retail shops, which are at the far end of the chain. None of the hardware inside the iPod, which is all easily available on open markets, is of particular value. The flash memory chip is made by Samsung; the stainless body frame is manufactured by a small company in a remote village of Japan. There is not much that Apple fabricates, as far as hardware is concerned. What makes the iPod different from other handsets is its design and the services made available on it, and this is what creates value for iPods. Its distribution channel also provides unique product-attraction and satisfaction to customers.

Smile curves exist in sectors other than IT. Uniqlo, a Japanese clothing retail shop, is another example where the value chain looks like a smile curve. In Japan, the company focuses on designing inexpensive, but still fashionable, casual clothes, as well as running fancy retail shops. The company concentrates on producing in countries where the labour cost is lowest, like China, but more recently Cambodia and Bangladesh. One of the defining features of the company is its capacity to maintain high quality through rigorous training of workers and tight quality control even in countries where worker skills are low. The speed with which they bring new designs to the market is another factor of the company's success. Its outlets are located at the best sites in large cities or in wealthy residential areas.

Some Future Challenges and Opportunities

Electric Vehicles: Threat or Opportunity for the Auto Industry?

Returning to cars, among Japanese firms Toyota has stood out for its insistence on Japanese-style skilled manufacturing. While there remains some concern as to whether this style can be competitive in offshore markets, overall the Japanese auto industry appears to have globalized successfully. The challenge lies ahead. There is no doubt that Asia will be the growth market in the future, but no matter how much Asia is growing, its income level is still a tenth of Japan's. One strategy would be to target the extremely rich segment of the population, but looking at the market as a whole, firms need to make cars commensurate with overall Asian income levels. In other words, 200,000–300,000 yen per car, compared with two million to three million yen in Japan. This will not be achieved through any mere cost-cutting exercise, and may well require transformation of the entire value chain. The experience and know-how accumulated to date will be of very little help. Competition will begin from a blank slate. What worries Japanese automotive experts is that the rise in environmental problems could trigger a shift from gasoline-driven cars to electronic vehicles, which will encourage the same kind of horizontal specialization and international collaboration that has occurred in the electronics industry, leaving Japanese firms out in the cold again. It is said that making an electronic car is possible for anyone with a motor and a battery, both of which are readily available on the market. Many electric vehicle ventures are emerging in the United States, and it is even possible that currently unknown venture firms may be the world's biggest auto firms in ten years' time.

Infrastructure Business as the New Growth Industry

The 'Lehman shock' in the fall of 2008 clearly brought to light the weakness of Japan's industrial structure. In other words, a narrow focus on selling consumer durables such as cars and consumer electronics to developed-country markets has its limits because it leaves firms extremely vulnerable to economic fluctuations. These two industrial sectors follow very different paradigms, but they have a lot in common: they both involve the mass production of standardized products and companies' competitiveness is determined by their ability to produce a large number of the same product as speedily as possible with the least variance in quality. This type of industry is prone to price competition with low-cost countries.

Attention has instead shifted to the so-called infrastructure business – water, power and transport. Profits in this type of business are recovered over a long 20–30 year timeframe, but with the promise of long-term, stable revenues. At the same time, the long recovery period, the sheer amount of capital involved, and the involvement of host country governments place infrastructure businesses beyond purely private sector means; state support is vital. Further, while Japanese firms have strong individual technologies, their poor overall project management capacity causes them to miss out on projects. In particular, most firms that are engaged in telephone, power, railway or water supply businesses in Japan enjoy a virtual state-run monopoly at home and have little experience or even interest in operating offshore. Consequently, they are not capable of any immediate offshore expansion. However, if these companies with their many skilled engineers and the pent-up energy derived from confinement in a saturated domestic market could be skillfully guided, they too could find new growth opportunities offshore. Ironically, since the change of administration in 2009 from the Liberal Democratic Party to the Democratic Party of Japan, bureaucrats have begun moving actively to capture this kind of infrastructure business. In France and Germany, the state became actively involved in infrastructure businesses from a very early point, and China and Korea too have recently been strengthening moves in this direction. Japan was once described as 'Japan, Inc.' and variously praised or criticized for its cooperative government–business relationship. Since the 1980s, however, the government has become increasingly inclined to stay out of private sector marketing efforts and has consequently neglected to back private sector business. Now it seems that the government will again be playing a more active role. From the viewpoint of value chains, this is yet another attempt by Japan to reap more value from the downstream of the value chain, namely operating, maintaining and running total infrastructure systems through such activities as collecting tolls from highways, running trains on railroads and supplying water. Such total operation of infrastructure is far more profitable than just selling steel bars and concrete, trains, pumps, pipes and power generators. In order to be successful in infrastructure businesses, however, a holistic project management capacity is called for. Whether Japan has it or not is yet to be tested.

Preferential Trade Agreements:
A Springboard for Asia-wide Value Chains

Since the turn of the century, Asian economies have begun to be deeply integrated by bilateral or regional preferential trade agreements (PTAs). This development is similar to the establishment of the EU or the North American Free Trade Agreement (NAFTA). In Asia, this came later. The first PTA in this region, signed in 1992, aimed to remove tariffs and non-tariff barriers among the six ASEAN countries. But now, all major countries in the wider Asia region have signed PTAs with the ASEAN countries and beyond, involving Japan, Korea, China, Australia, New Zealand and India. An even more ambitious proposal is under discussion to create a broad free trade zone in the Asia-Pacific region.

Trade under the Asian PTAs is characterized by a deepening production network that spreads across borders. One of the benefits generated by liberalization is the optimization of production and distribution systems on a regionwide scale. As different markets have become open to others, business strategies for production networks have changed. Concentration of production in one country has been replaced with more fragmented production that is spread across several different countries with more favourable conditions. The effect of such divisions of labour and horizontal production networks is observed most clearly in the case of the automotive industry.

With the introduction of the ASEAN Industrial Cooperation scheme of 1996, tariffs on some intraregional and intra-industry trade were reduced and eventually eliminated. Accordingly, automotive production blocks in Southeast

Asia came to differ from country to country. For example, the production of automobiles by Japanese automakers in Thailand grew rapidly in the late 1980s after the appreciation of the yen. It then accelerated in the early 1990s due to an unprecedented economic boom and the Thai government's liberalization policy. The Thailand–Australia FTA, which came into force in 2005, affected the pattern of automobile imports into Australia. Imports of cars from Thailand have been increasing steadily, while those from Japan have decreased markedly. This implies that Japanese auto manufacturers began to use Thailand as the centre of production not only for Thailand but for Australia as well, thus benefitting from the preferential tariff treatment under the Thailand–Australia FTA.

Analysis of the production of car engine parts points to increasingly clear-cut trends towards relocation to and centralization in certain countries. Indonesia, Singapore and Thailand have picked up the lion's share of production. By 2007, this industry had grown up to 38 times from 1990-levels in Thailand and 148 times in Indonesia. In contrast, Malaysia, which once had a relatively large share, has lost its position. Other types of components makers, such as those producing steering wheels and gearboxes, show trends different from the engine parts industry. The steering wheel industry has become concentrated in Thailand and Malaysia and the gearbox industry in Indonesia and the Philippines.

Conclusion: The Changing Pattern of Trade of Finished and Intermediate Products in Asia

In response to a variety of changes that have occurred over the last two decades, Japanese manufacturing companies have reorganized their value chains across the Asian region. Their key strategy is to keep the most value-adding part of the value chain at home and move the least profitable part to Asian countries. This has been most noticeable in the electronics sector. In electronics, Japanese companies lost much of the world market to Chinese, Korean and Taiwanese manufacturers, but companies that produce key components and materials still maintain dominant positions. China is now the largest importer of electronic parts and intermediate products, as well as the largest exporter of finished electronic products. This is discernible in the trade flow in Asia (Figure 10.8).

Japan still maintains a trade surplus, but today more than 90 per cent of its exports to Asia are in intermediates and high grade raw materials, not finished products. Contrary to the widespread perception that China commands complete control over the entire length of the value chain, the fact is that it controls only the assembly stage and imports most of the parts, components and raw materials from neighbouring Asian countries, including Japan. When it comes to finished products, China practically dominates the world production of personal computers, with its share now running at 96 per cent. It is by far the biggest exporter to the United

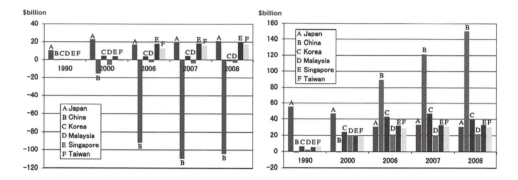

Figure 10.8a Trade of electronic parts in East Asia (net export)

Figure 10.8b Trade of finished electronic products in East Asia (net export)

Source: Created by FRI from WTO data.

States and EU. However, much of such production and export is executed under the brand names of large multinational companies like HP, Dell and Acer.

In contrast with the electronics industry, the horizontal fragmentation in the automotive industry is less visible and slow moving. But as a result of the decision by Japanese companies to produce in the vicinity of the market, and also as a result of PTAs that eliminate or reduce barriers to the free movement of parts and finished products, the production of automobiles in Asia is booming. Some vehicles are shipped back to the Japanese market. Not only do they increase local production, but they are also accelerating the horizontal division of labour across borders. Local production of parts is also on the rise. Overall, the Japanese manufacturing industry will continue to adapt to the ever-changing structure of the global value chain.

References

Baldwin, C.Y. and Clark, K.B. 2000. *Design Rule-Power of Modularity*. New York: MIT Press.

Christensen, C. 2003. *Innovators' Dilemma*. New York: Harvard University Press.

Fujimoto, T. 2002. *Japanese Style Supplier System and Modularity – A Case Study of Automobile Industry*. Tokyo: Tokyo Keizai University.

Idei, N. 2002. *The Era of Discontinuity*. Tokyo: Shinchousha.

Noguchi, T. 2010. Fearsome Korean companies – why Japan cannot win over Samsung. Tokyo: Fuyoshashinnsho. Available in Japanese only.

Nomura Research Institute. 2008. *Japan That Looks like Galapagos*. Tokyo: Nomura Research Institute. Available in Japanese only.

Sato, F. 2006. *A Scenario for Reorganization of Japanese Electronics Industry*. Tokyo: Kankishuppann.

Seno, K. 2009. *Why Does Japan Lose Out, in Spite of its Technology?* Tokyo: Diamond Press. Available in Japanese only.

Tanaka, T. 2009. *The End of Modularity*. Tokyo: NTT Press.

Vernon, R. 1971. *Sovereignty at Bay – The Multinational Spread of US Enterprises*. New York: Harvard University Press.

Womack, J.P. and Jones, D.T. 1992. *The Machine That Changed the World*. Cambridge, MA: MIT Press.

PART IV
Trade-related Complexities

Trade and Investment

Sébastien Miroudot

Introduction

The Growth of Trade and Investment

Over the past two decades, the volume of world trade has tripled and the stock of foreign direct investment (FDI) has multiplied almost six times in real terms. By comparison, world gross domestic product (in volume) has multiplied 1.5 times.[1] This expansion of trade and investment at a higher rate than output characterizes the globalization of production (Figure 11.1). Importantly, this is a combination of trade and investment.

Figure 11.1 illustrates the 'second wave of globalization' or 'second unbundling' (Baldwin 2006). The 'first unbundling' refers to the decrease in transportation costs that occurred between 1850 and 1914, resulting in an important increase of trade at the same time that the industrial revolution was triggering modern growth in Western Europe and the United States. Lower transportation costs made it possible to produce goods far from the location where they were consumed. The 'second unbundling' is within firms with the production of goods and services being geographically split. The fragmentation of production started in the 1980s in Japan and the United States. Geographically separating various production stages became more and more attractive in the 1990s with the continuing decline in trade costs due to the information and communication technology (ICT) revolution and policy initiatives to further liberalize trade, such as the conclusion of the Uruguay Round, the creation of the World Trade Organization (WTO), the signing of the General Agreement on Trade in Services (GATS) and, as a second best, a new wave of preferential trade agreements following the adoption of the North American Free Trade Agreement (NAFTA). Trade became much more than just a simple exchange of merchandise across borders. It developed into a constant flow of investment,

---

[1] WTO International Trade Statistics (2010) and UNCTAD World Investment Report (2010). Calculated for the period 1990–2009, using US GDP deflator for world FDI stock.

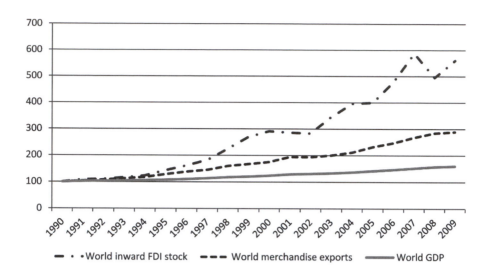

Figure 11.1 The growth of trade, FDI and GDP (1990–2009, volume, 1990 = 100)
Source: *WTO International Trade Statistics* (2010) and *UNCTAD World Investment Report* (2010).

technologies, goods for processing, and business services, in what has been called 'the global value chain' (Sturgeon and Gereffi 2009).

Trade policies have adapted to this new context and trade agreements tend to incorporate provisions on investment that were previously found in Bilateral Investment Treaties (BITs). In 1994, NAFTA was the first preferential trade agreement (PTA) to combine provisions on the protection and promotion of investment with provisions on the liberalization of foreign investment and comprehensive trade in services disciplines. Less than ten PTAs had deep investment provisions in 2000. Their number increased to 56 (out of 190 PTAs notified to WTO) at the end of 2009.[2] The number of new BITs concluded has, on the contrary, been slowing down since 2001 (UNCTAD 2008).

This chapter first looks at the economic determinants of trade and investment to understand the relationship between flows of goods and services and the movement of capital. The second section reviews the recent economic literature on the fragmentation of production, vertical specialization and offshoring to explain why trade and investment are increasingly intertwined. It explains also why investment has grown at a higher rate than trade. The third section describes how trade agreements are catching up with new production models and more often incorporate investment chapters and services chapters that cover Mode 3 trade

---

[2]   Calculation from the author on the basis of the WTO database. A PTA with 'deep investment provisions' is defined as a PTA with provisions on the liberalization and/or protection of investment. Some PTAs have just provisions on the promotion of investment with no real legal binding and are not regarded as investment agreements in this chapter.

in services. The section first reviews multilateral rules on trade and investment and then examines why it is in preferential trade agreements that the interaction between trade and investment is mainly dealt with. The fourth section concludes with policy lessons and challenges for the future.

Trade and Investment: From Substitutes to Complements

In traditional trade theory, trade and investment are regarded as substitutes. In the Heckscher–Ohlin–Samuelson model, the movement of goods is a substitute for the movement of production factors. Capital is assumed to be internationally immobile and through trade capital-scarce countries can benefit from relatively cheaper capital-intensive goods produced in capital-abundant countries. This assumption that trade and investment are substitutes is also the basis of the standard theoretical framework described in the 'proximity–concentration tradeoff' (Brainard 1997).

The Proximity–Concentration Tradeoff

The tradeoff is the following: when multinational firms engage in FDI and produce abroad in the destination market, they can escape trade costs (all the costs incurred when exporting the good from the country of the parent company to the destination market). But while they save on trade costs, firms producing abroad split their production and lose the advantage of scale economies. It is cheaper to produce all the goods in the firm's home plant. The theory thus suggests that FDI occurs only when the benefits of producing abroad (no trade costs) outweigh the loss of economies of scale from producing exclusively in the home country. Trade liberalization (that is, reduced trade costs) should lead to less FDI.

However, the paradox is that since the 1990s FDI has increased much more than trade in the context of trade liberalization (Neary 2009). While there is evidence in favour of the proximity–concentration tradeoff, the theory corresponds to one type of FDI – horizontal FDI – where the firm reproduces abroad the full production process (and thus loses scale economies). In the context of vertical specialization and vertical FDI, firms achieve efficiency by slicing up the production process in a global value chain.

Fragmentation of Production and Vertical Specialization

Once trade costs are low enough to allow the fragmentation of production, firms can minimize the total cost of production by organizing the production into several blocks, each block being produced in the country where the marginal cost is the lowest (Jones and Kierzkowski 1990). Services inputs are needed to link the blocks, such as communication, transport and logistics services, as well as financial and

211

business services. Setting up affiliates to produce abroad also implies investment costs. As long as the cost advantage of an internationally fragmented production offsets the additional fixed costs of the services inputs and investment costs, the production process is more efficient than if performed in a single country. This is how trade and investment become complements in the context of vertically-integrated firms and how trade liberalization (especially in services sectors) leads to both an increase in trade and in investment flows.

Setting up distribution networks and organizing production internationally also involves more complex firm structures than the one described above. International investment is motivated by strategies that can be 'resource-seeking', 'market-seeking', 'efficiency-seeking' or 'strategic asset-seeking' (Dunning and Lundan 2008) and global firms typically pursue multiple objectives combining several of these motives. Moreover, the location and organization of global value chains is not static. Multinational enterprises (MNEs) constantly adapt their strategies and redefine their boundaries (Mudambi and Venzin 2010). More recently, global firms have also increasingly relied on outsourcing (that does not involve investment) and headquarter activities are more often offshored (Desai 2009).

If trade and investment flows are complements, one can wonder about the causal relationship. Is increasing trade a consequence of FDI or is investment promoted by the liberalization of trade? Several empirical studies have applied causality tests to the complementary relationship between trade and investment. While results vary from one study to another, what is usually found in the literature is that it is FDI flows which increase trade flows, a result consistent with firms' strategies described above. But the causality can run in the other direction as well. For example, Aizenman and Noy (2006) decompose the feedback effects and find that 50 per cent go from FDI to trade and 31 per cent from trade to FDI. The rest represent two-way linkages. Therefore, trade and investment can be described as mutually reinforcing and this is why they are best described as complements.

The Rise of Investment Relative to Trade

As emphasized by Bergstrand and Egger (2010), an important aspect of the growth of trade and investment is that FDI has a higher growth rate than trade. Between 1995 and 2005, the ratio of FDI to trade in Organization for Economic Cooperation and Development (OECD) countries has increased from 48 per cent to 86 per cent (Miroudot et al. 2009). An initial explanation is that FDI includes international mergers and acquisitions (changes in ownership inflate the data even when no new productive capacity is added). This is however not enough to explain the growth of FDI relative to trade and does not explain why FDI was preferred to trade by the foreign investor.

Recent trends in the growth of trade and investment have been prompted by new firm strategies that combine horizontal and vertical FDI. This can be illustrated with the example of the automotive industry (Sturgeon et al. 2008). Political pressure for local production and market demand considerations have driven automakers to set up final assembly plants in their main markets. For example, in the mid-1980s, Japanese car manufacturers established plants in the United States and European Union. This form of horizontal FDI has reduced trade flows of final goods (less cars exported to these markets) and increased FDI (the substitution effect). But at the same time, automakers have outsourced the production of auto parts and created affiliates to build regional networks and clusters for specialized activities such as automotive design. Horizontal FDI was thus combined with vertical FDI. Traditional suppliers were also asked to establish next-to-final assembly plants and in consequence the global reorganization of the automotive industry has led to more FDI than trade. As FDI is a stock with an important initial movement of capital and lower flows in subsequent years, this increase in FDI characterizes the transition to new production networks and is not likely to be sustained over time.

The rise of investment versus trade is even more pronounced in services industries. In the case of services, the ratio of FDI to trade has increased from 140 per cent in 1995 to more than 250 per cent in 2005. The banking industry illustrates that global value chains are not limited to manufacturing and that the combination of horizontal and vertical FDI described for goods also applies to services. Banks are now highly internationalized and need affiliates for the face-to-face contact with their customers. International banks have developed through horizontal FDI important networks to serve their customers worldwide. But only the end of the value chain requires commercial presence. As most banking activities are services that can be supplied across borders due to their high degree of digitalization (Mudambi and Venzin 2010), vertical specialization has also increased with services provided from financial hubs such as London or New York, as well as from offshore competence centres. The globalization of the banking industry accounts for a significant share of the increase in FDI with many cross-border acquisitions and mergers in the 2000s and more recently in the aftermath of the financial crisis. Cross-border trade in financial services has increased but to a lesser extent.[3]

Another explanation of the rise of investment relative to trade lies in policies. Notwithstanding moves towards trade liberalization, trade costs for goods and services remain high (Miroudot et al. 2010; Novy 2010) while FDI has been widely liberalized and services reforms have decreased FDI costs. Most FDI flows remain between OECD countries that maintain strict disciplines on international investment through the OECD Code of Liberalization of Capital Movements and the Code of Liberalization of Current Invisible Operations. FDI has also been increasingly liberalized in emerging countries. In the OECD FDI restrictiveness index, eight non-OECD economies are now more open to investment than the OECD average (Kalinova et al. 2010). In contrast, multilateral trade negotiations have been stalled at the WTO for the past 15 years. This discrepancy between FDI liberalization and trade liberalization could be another explanation for the rise of investment relative

---

[3] In the case of financial services, one should also take into account that cross-border trade statistics cannot fully capture the service inputs traded. The rise of investment relative to trade is likely to reflect both the reality of vertical specialization and specific issues in the measurement of trade in services in balance of payments statistics.

to trade. Moreover, in the case of services trade, multilateral and preferential liberalizing commitments are more prevalent for Mode 3 (commercial presence) than for cross-border trade (Marchetti and Roy 2008). For services, the rise of investment relative to trade corresponds to the rise of sales of foreign affiliates relative to cross-border transactions.

Complementary Gains from Trade and Investment

The complementary relationship between trade and investment can also be extended to their positive effects on productivity, growth and development. While the debate on the impact of FDI on development has been controversial in the past, there is a growing body of evidence that FDI benefits the host economy, in particular because of potential productivity spillovers to local firms. FDI spillovers have been found particularly significant in the case of vertical relationships between foreign affiliates and their local suppliers, but the evidence is mixed regarding horizontal spillovers in the same industry.[4] Moran et al. (2005) provide many examples of the positive externalities of FDI but also explain why empirical studies have not systematically found evidence of the positive impact of investment on growth and development. FDI spillovers are not automatic and depend on the conditions into which FDI is introduced. To maximize the gains from FDI, developing countries need an 'absorptive capacity', which can be defined as the propensity of local firms to benefit from foreign presence through adequate human resources and production capacities (Blalock and Simon 2009). There is also a set of policies that determine the ability of foreign investors to enhance productivity in the host economy and the first one is trade liberalization.

Using firm-level data, Lesher and Miroudot (2008) highlight the role of trade openness in the realization of FDI spillovers. In addition to the fact that vertical FDI can happen only if trade costs are low, there are also competitive effects that explain why foreign affiliates are more likely to transfer knowledge in an open trade environment. Protectionism attracts foreign companies seeking rents while shielded from foreign competitors with, at the end, little incentive to innovate and share knowledge with local partners. An open trade regime on the contrary fosters efficiency-seeking FDI and partnerships with local companies.

Trade and Investment in Trade Agreements

As trade and investment are more and more intertwined in the context of international supply chains, countries are increasingly incorporating investment

---

[4]   Foreign affiliates have obviously less incentives to transfer technology to their competitors. Regarding vertical spillovers, a meta-analysis conducted on 57 empirical studies confirms that spillovers to suppliers are positive and economically significant (Havranek and Irsova 2011).

provisions in PTAs instead of BITs. By combining trade liberalization provisions with investment liberalization and protection, these agreements emphasize the complementary relationship between trade and FDI and are empirically found to have a stronger impact on investment than BITs (UNCTAD 2009).

Investment Provisions in Multilateral Agreements

The importance of international investment has long been recognised in multilateral trade negotiations but all attempts to sign a comprehensive agreement on investment have failed so far. The Havana Charter of 1947 included a commitment for the International Trade Organization (ITO) to negotiate an agreement on international investment but the idea was abandoned when the ITO was rejected and the more modest General Agreement on Tariffs and Trade (GATT) came into force. Trade and investment were back on the agenda with the creation of the WTO in 1995. At the Ministerial Conference of Singapore in 1996, it was decided to set up a working group on the relationship between trade and investment and the issue became part of the negotiations in the Doha Development Agenda. However, in 2004, trade and investment comprised one of the Singapore Issues dropped from the negotiations. Another example of aborted effort to reach consensus on international investment is the Multilateral Agreement on Investment, negotiated within the OECD between 1995 and 1998.[5] After three years of negotiations, conflicting ambitions and lack of political will among the protagonists, exacerbated by NGO activism, led to the project being abandoned (Henderson 1999).

These unsuccessful attempts to promote investment in the context of multilateral trade negotiations explain why many countries have now turned to PTAs to address investment issues. However, despite there being no multilateral framework on investment, WTO agreements do include investment-related provisions.

The Agreement on Trade-Related Investment Measures (TRIMs) introduces disciplines regarding the use of investment measures that can restrict or distort trade in goods. The agreement provides an illustrative list of TRIMs that are inconsistent with Article III of GATT (national treatment) or Article XI (quantitative restrictions), such as local content requirements or export requirements. Also called 'performance requirements', these measures consist of government-assigned objectives to firms linked to the authorization of their investment. Trade-related objectives include for example the use of local inputs rather than imported intermediate goods (local content requirement) or a percentage of output to be exported and not sold on the domestic market (export performance requirement). The motivation for governments is to protect domestic producers and the impact of TRIMs is similar to any protectionist measure. In addition, TRIMs were generally not found to be very effective in the context of developing economies where the rationale was to encourage nascent local capabilities (Moran 1998). This is why the

---

[5]   While the text was negotiated among OECD countries, the agreement was open to the signature of other countries and the ambition was to create a true multilateral agreement.

occurrence of trade-related performance requirements has been reduced both in developed and developing countries (UNCTAD 2003).

While the GATS does not mention investment in its scope, this is certainly the multilateral agreement that comes the closest to an international investment accord. GATS Article I defines as trade in services the supply of a service by a service provider from one country, through commercial presence in the territory of any other country (Mode 3 trade in services). 'Commercial presence' is then defined as any type of business or professional establishment. GATS does not introduce rules on investment per se (which is a movement of capital) but on the establishment and provision of services through commercial presence of service providers. As two-thirds of investment flows are in services sectors and there is an overlap between services providers and investors with respect to Mode 3, GATS provides important disciplines on investment that compete with other international investment rules in BITs and PTAs. In particular, GATS offers WTO members the possibility of two types of commitments for Mode 3: market access commitments and national treatment commitments. Market access is defined through a list of limitations that are prohibited if a services market is to be regarded as open (such as no foreign equity limits). National treatment consists of according to foreign services providers a treatment no less favourable than that granted to domestic suppliers.

As a services trade agreement, GATS covers only investment issues related to services but also has a relatively narrow definition of investment. GATS relies on an 'enterprise-based' definition consisting of any type of business or professional establishment where the investor has majority ownership or exercises control (direct investment). In contrast, bilateral rules on investment generally refer to a broader 'asset-based' definition that in addition covers portfolio investment and different forms of tangible and intangible property (such as real estate). By covering both goods and services and being based on a broader definition of investors and investment, some PTAs have more extensive provisions on investment than those found in the GATS and offer a type of trade and investment agreement with no equivalent at the multilateral level. With respect to TRIMs, PTAs also go further in the type of prohibited performance requirements and have stricter disciplines.

Investment Provisions in Preferential Trade Agreements

As we saw earlier, most recent PTAs now include investment provisions. Their number is modest however as compared to the more than 2,500 BITs in force. The major difference between PTAs and BITs is in the type of investment provisions covered. With the exception of agreements signed by the United States and in some cases by Canada and Japan, BITs do not include non-discrimination provisions on pre-establishment. They grant national treatment and most-favoured-nation (MFN) treatment in the post-establishment phase (that is once the investor is established) but lack the essential dimension of market access (that is how the investor first establishes in the market). PTAs, in contrast, focus on national treatment and

MFN treatment in the establishment phase itself and can thus be understood as agreements liberalizing investment. From a political economy perspective, there is a case for dealing with investment liberalization at the same time as trade liberalization. Concessions on investment can be balanced with concessions on trade and countries can deal in a more comprehensive way with market opening issues that today involve both trade and investment.

Two models of PTAs have been identified, one inspired by the provisions found in NAFTA and one following the provisions of GATS. The fact that the scope of GATS is limited to services creates complex interactions between investment and services chapters in PTAs (Houde et al. 2007).

NAFTA-inspired agreements

The architecture of NAFTA-inspired PTAs is characterized by a clear separation between the investment chapter and the cross-border trade in services chapter. Provisions relevant to investment in services are part of the investment chapter. The definition of investment is far-reaching and also covers some types of portfolio investment as well as property. Non-discrimination disciplines (national treatment and MFN treatment) apply with respect to 'the establishment, acquisition, expansion, management, conduct, operation, and sale or other disposition of investments'. In addition, the standard of treatment provision grants the better of national and MFN treatment, while the 'minimum standard of treatment' clause provides for 'fair and equitable treatment and full protection and security'. NAFTA-inspired PTAS generally cover all relevant protection disciplines such as the free transfer of funds, provisions on expropriation and compensation, as well as provision for investor–state dispute settlement.

The far-reaching nature of NAFTA-inspired agreements can also be seen in the negative list approach to liberalizing commitments. National treatment and MFN treatment are granted for all sectors with two lists of reservations, one for existing measures that are non-conforming at the date of the agreement, and another for future measures that gives governments discretion to maintain or to introduce restrictive measures after the agreement has entered into force. The negative list approach is generally seen as being more favourable to liberalization in the sense that commitments are taken for investments in all sectors and only the exceptions listed at the time the agreement is signed can be maintained. There is nonetheless still some discretion left for governments because of the practice of introducing reservations for future measures (that is, new restrictive measures not listed in the agreement). NAFTA-inspired agreements nevertheless not only lock in the investment regime but also include as commitments under the PTA any new measure taken unilaterally by the counterparties. This creates a ratchet effect as, once removed, investment restrictions cannot be reintroduced.

Preferential trade agreements signed by Canada, Mexico and the United States (the three parties to NAFTA) are not surprisingly NAFTA-inspired but the approach has also been exported to Asia where a significant number of bilateral agreements follow the NAFTA model (for example Chile–Korea FTA, Korea–Singapore FTA and Singapore–Australia FTA).

GATS-inspired agreements

GATS-inspired agreements also have an investment chapter that covers all investments (including in services industries) and provides for the protection of investment with disciplines as far-reaching as in NAFTA-inspired agreements. The difference is however that the market-access provisions of national treatment and MFN treatment of the investment chapter apply only to goods. For services, the analogous non-discrimination principles are found in a separate chapter that deals with trade in services. The treatment of investment in services is therefore influenced by concepts that come from the GATS, with a narrower definition of investment. As in GATS, the MFN principle is a general obligation and applies to all services sectors covered in the agreement. Exemptions can be listed in a negative list. For market access and national treatment, GATS-inspired agreements reproduce the format of GATS schedules of commitments. There is a positive list of sectors where specific commitments are made and then limitations are listed for these commitments. This could explain why the GATS approach has been popular among PTA negotiators. They are on familiar ground when working with GATS-like schedules of commitments and they can more easily strike a deal on the basis of existing multilateral commitments augmented with preferential commitments.

While most agreements can be clearly identified as GATS-inspired or NAFTA-inspired, there are agreements that depart from these two models or try to combine them in a hybrid approach. For example, most of the agreements signed recently by Japan (with the exception of Japan–Chile) deal both with commercial presence and investment in services and include at the same time a GATS-like schedule of commitments as well as a NAFTA-inspired negative list of non-conforming measures. The ratchet mechanism is transposed into the GATS-inspired schedule of commitments with an additional column where Japan commits to bind any new liberalization measure in specific sub-sectors.

Despite important differences, NAFTA-inspired and GATS-inspired agreements offer the same degree of protection for investment and can equally liberalize investment, even if empirically NAFTA-inspired agreements are found to be more ambitious in their scope and sectoral coverage (Fink and Molinuevo 2008; Houde et al. 2007).

Economic Impact of Investment Provisions

The economic impact of investment provisions in trade agreements has been examined in various empirical studies.[6] There is generally a positive relationship

---

[6] See Miroudot (2009) for a review.

between the negotiation of PTAs with deep investment provisions and increased trade and investment flows. For example, Lesher and Miroudot (2006) examine 24 North–South PTAs and find that the more extensive the investment provisions, the higher the positive impact on investment and, to a lesser extent, trade flows. In the case of Asia, Dee (2007) argues that patterns of investment are already explained by fundamentals rather than by investment provisions of PTAs. When FDI and trade are not driven by the size, income and other market characteristics, Dee finds positive PTA effects for some economies.

Berger et al. (2010) focus on specific types of provisions and point out that guarantees of market access for foreign investors as well as state–investor dispute settlement mechanisms have a positive impact on bilateral FDI flows. PTAs not offering liberal admission or effective dispute settlement leave bilateral FDI unaffected (or can even induce a substitution of trade for FDI).

The literature on the economic impact of BITs has more mixed results. Aisbett (2009) finds no robust relationship between participation in BITs and investment flows, while Busse et al. (2010) have a positive correlation to report when controlling for unilateral investment liberalization. BITs may hence be seen as a substitute for weak institutions by providing protection for investors but not as a substitute for the liberalization of investment. This result is consistent with the fact that most BITs are limited to disciplines in the post-establishment phase and do not deal with market access. The more significant impact of PTAs with investment provisions on FDI can be explained by provisions on market access, national treatment and MFN treatment in the pre-establishment phase. PTAs provide economic incentives for investors (that is, access to the market) in addition to legal incentives (the protection of investment once established). While Berger et al. (2010) highlight the role of liberal admission rules and dispute settlement mechanisms in increasing bilateral FDI flows in PTAs, they find that in the case of BITs investors react to the mere existence of agreements. Their content matters less.

Another economic impact to highlight is that PTAs with deep investment provisions do not seem to introduce severe economic distortions among investors nor do they create a 'spaghetti bowl' as described for trade in goods (Baldwin et al. 2009). Because of leaky rules of origin, the preferential treatment granted in investment PTAs can to some extent benefit investors from third parties. For juridical persons (that is, companies), being established and having substantive business in a country is sufficient to benefit from the more preferential treatment granted to this country. MNEs can therefore invest through their affiliates located in countries that have negotiated the best investment provisions. However, this strategy can be costly and only large MNEs have a network of affiliates that enables them to cherry-pick investment preferences in PTAs. One should not underestimate the risk of economic distortions when there is no level playing field among investors. Investment liberalization through PTAs remains a 'second best' as opposed to the 'first best' of multilateral liberalization.

Conclusion

Main Policy Lessons and Challenges for the Future

As there is evidence that investment provisions can play a positive role in trade agreements, the following question arises: why is there no multilateral effort to harmonize and deepen the liberalization of investment in relation to trade? While trade and investment was one of the Singapore Issues left out of the Doha Development Agenda, the key issue of market access for Mode 3 trade in services is still part of the negotiation. Moreover, the lack of trade liberalization (high trade costs in key sectors, including services industries) may today be one of the most important barriers to FDI now that barriers to the movement of capital have been removed in most countries. While there is a compelling case for discussing investment issues in the WTO, the success or the failure of any such negotiation depends on the tradeoffs and cross-issue linkages between investment and other policy areas. Linking investment to environment or labour issues could be detrimental to the expected welfare gains, but a broader agenda that would include other policies affecting the location of firms could help to achieve consensus (Hoekman and Kostecki 2001).

With the proliferation of PTAs, what could not be achieved multilaterally has to some extent been achieved bilaterally and regionally. There is, however, a risk for developing countries of missing the opportunity of being part of global production networks when they have not negotiated trade agreements with deep investment and services commitments. With the shift of demand and production networks to the South, investment provisions in South–South PTAs should be further developed, as observed in recently signed PTAs in Asia. The multilateralization of investment disciplines – through strengthened MFN provisions, liberal rules of origin or consolidation of PTAs in larger regional trade agreements – could help the least developed countries who lack resources and may be at a disadvantage in bilateral negotiations.

One important lesson from recent changes in world production is that attracting firms to the domestic economy is key to maximize the gains from trade and investment. In the context of vertically specialized value chains, imports are not competing with domestic production. Imports are more often inputs of intermediate goods and services that increase the competitiveness of local firms. Foreign firms are no longer competitors, from whom domestic companies should be protected, but buyers or suppliers that can enhance local capabilities and work with local firms to create an export capacity. The attractiveness of the local economy relies on a variety of policies, where trade policy is only one (important) element, but it also encompasses policies dealing with investment, taxation and competition, as well as the regulation of infrastructure services.

For trade policymakers, the rise of investment relative to trade and the complementary relationship between trade and investment highlight three new policy issues. First, the interests of domestic-owned affiliates located abroad and foreign-owned companies in the domestic economy are likely to change the political economy of trade negotiations and can provide new incentives for trade liberalization. Blanchard (2007) argues that taking into account the revenue of foreign-owned affiliates and the impact of tariffs on inputs that domestic producers import from their subsidiaries lowers the optimal tariff of countries. An important implication is that opening markets to foreign investors from a partner country should reduce the tariff barriers faced by domestic firms exporting to that country (because the optimal tariff of the partner country becomes lower). FDI liberalization can thus be the driver of trade liberalization from a political economy perspective.

Second, the importance of vertical specialization in the new organization of firms should draw attention in trade agreements to the buyer–supplier relationship. Bargaining issues have been highlighted in the literature in the context of specialized inputs where the supplier has to make relationship-specific investments. The 'hold-up problem' refers to the situation where the parties to a contract (either the buyer or the supplier) underinvest because they fear that the other party will not comply with the contract, as the specialized input is so specific that it has no value outside of the contract. Bargaining issues suggest that trade agreements should go beyond traditional market access concerns and also address domestic measures that influence the relationship between suppliers and buyers (Antràs and Staiger 2008).

Our third policy implication is that standards have an important impact on global value chains and on the relationship between trade and investment (Kaplinsky 2010). Whether public or private, local or international, standards influence the entry of firms into new markets. On the one hand, meeting standards represents a cost and can be a barrier to entry or rule out local producers. On the other hand, standards play a positive role in firm upgrading and can help companies to participate in global production networks. There are policy challenges in harmonizing standards and ensuring that they do not represent trade or FDI barriers, not least for developing countries that are seeking access to global markets.

Because we are in a transition to a world where production is more geographically fragmented and vertically integrated, trade and FDI have markedly increased and created new opportunities for firms in developed and emerging economies. The future of global supply chains is however not assured. Their fragility was revealed in the aftermath of the 2008–2009 financial crisis (Escaith et al. 2010) and as coordination costs increase along the supply chain, an optimal level of fragmentation is ultimately achieved. Firms are also confronted with new challenges, such as environmental concerns related to trade and offshoring.

As previously emphasized, firms constantly have to adapt their strategies and redefine their boundaries. An open trade and investment regime is the best way for policymakers to minimize distortions and facilitate the response of firms to economic and social change. Open markets have a key role to play in helping sustain the dynamism of global supply chains to secure for all consumers the benefits of globalization.

References

Aisbett, E. 2009. Bilateral investment treaties and foreign direct investment: correlation versus causation, in *The Effect of Treaties on Foreign Direct Investment: Bilateral Investment Treaties, Double Taxation Treaties and Investment Flows*, edited by K. Sauvant and L. Sachs. Oxford: Oxford University Press: 395–436.

Aizenman, J. and Noy, I. 2006. FDI and trade – two-way linkages? *The Quarterly Review of Economics and Finance*, 46(3): 317–37.

Antràs, P. and Staiger, R. 2008. Offshoring and the role of trade agreements. *NBER Working Paper No. 14285*. Massachusetts: The National Bureau of Economic Research.

Baldwin, R. 2006. Globalization: the great unbundling(s). Contribution to the project *Globalization Challenges for Europe and Finland*, Economic Council of Finland.

Baldwin, R., Evenett, S. and Low, P. 2009. Beyond tariffs: multilateralizing non–tariff RTA commitments, in *Multilateralizing Regionalism: Challenges for the Global Trading System (World Trade Organization)*, edited by R. Baldwin and P. Low. Cambridge: Cambridge University Press: 79–145.

Berger, A., Busse, M., Nunnenkamp, P. and Roy, M. 2010. Do trade and investment agreements lead to more FDI? Accounting for key provisions inside the black box. *Staff Working Paper ERSD–2010–13*. Geneva: WTO.

Bergstrand, J.H. and Egger, P. 2010. A general equilibrium theory for estimating gravity equations of bilateral FDI, final goods trade, and intermediate trade flows, in *The Gravity Model in International Trade: Advances and Applications*, edited by P. van Bergeijk and S. Brakman. Cambridge: Cambridge University Press: 29–70.

Blalock, G. and Simon, D.H. 2009. Do all firms benefit equally from downstream FDI? The moderating effect of local suppliers' capabilities on productivity gains. *Journal of International Business Studies*, 40(7): 1095–112.

Blanchard, E. 2007. Foreign direct investment, endogenous tariffs, and preferential trade agreements. *The B.E. Journal of Economic Analysis & Policy*, 7(1): 1–50.

Brainard, S.L. 1997. An empirical assessment of the proximity–concentration tradeoff between multinational sales and trade. *American Economic Review*, 87(4): 520–44.

Busse, M., Königer, J. and Nunnenkamp, P. 2010. FDI promotion through bilateral investment treaties: more than a bit? *Review of World Economics*, 146(1): 147–77.

Dee, P. 2007. Multinational corporations and Pacific regionalism, in *Multinational Corporations and the Emerging Network Economy in Asia and the Pacific*, edited by J.J. Palacios. London: Routledge: 114–38.

Desai, M.A. 2009. The decentering of the global firm. *The World Economy*, 32(9): 1271–90.

Dunning, J. and Lundan, S. 2008. *Multinational Enterprises and the Global Economy*. 2nd Edition. Cheltenham: Edward Elgar.

Escaith, H., Lindenberg, N. and Miroudot, S. 2010. Global value chains and the crisis: reshaping international trade elasticity? in *Global Value Chains in a*

Postcrisis World. A Development Perspective, edited by O. Cattaneo, G. Gereffi and C. Staritz. Washington, DC: World Bank: 73–123.

Fink, C. and Molinuevo, M. 2008. East Asian preferential trade agreements in services: liberalization content and WTO rules. *World Trade Review*, 7(4): 641–73.

Havranek, T. and Irsova, Z. 2011. Estimating vertical spillovers from FDI: Why results vary and what the true effect is. *Journal of International Economics*, 85(2): 234-244.

Henderson, D. 1999. *The MAI Affair: A Story and its Lessons*. London: Royal Institute of International Affairs.

Hoekman, B. and Kostecki M. 2001. *The Political Economy of the World Trading System*. 2nd Edition. Oxford: Oxford University Press.

Houde, M.F., Kolse-Patil, A. and Miroudot, S. 2007. The interaction between investment and services chapters in selected regional trade agreements. *OECD Trade Policy Working Paper 55*. Paris: OECD.

Jones, R. and Kierzkowski, H. 1990. The role of services in production and international trade: a theoretical framework, in *The Political Economy of International Trade*, edited by R. Jones and A. Krueger. Oxford: Basil Blackwell: 31–48.

Kalinova, B., Palerm, A. and Thomsen, S. 2010. OECD's FDI restrictiveness index: 2010 update. *OECD Working Papers on International Investment 2010/3*. Paris: OECD.

Kaplinsky, R. 2010. The role of standards in global value chains. *World Bank Policy Research Working Paper 5396*. Washington, DC: World Bank.

Lesher, M. and Miroudot, S. 2006. Analysis of the economic impact of investment provisions in regional trade agreements. *OECD Trade Policy Working Paper No. 36*. Paris: OECD.

Lesher, M. and Miroudot, S. 2008. FDI spillovers and their interrelationships with trade. *OECD Trade Policy Working Paper No. 80*. Paris: OECD.

Marchetti, J.A. and Roy, M. 2008. Services liberalization in the WTO and in PTAs, in *Opening Markets for Trade in Services, Countries and Sectors in Bilateral and WTO Negotiations*, edited by J.A. Marchetti and M. Roy. Cambridge: Cambridge University Press: 61–112.

Miroudot, S. 2009. Impact of investment provisions in Asian RTAs, in *Expansion of Trade and FDI in Asia. Strategic and Policy Challenges*, edited by J. Chaisse and P. Gugler. London: Routledge: 186–211.

Miroudot, S., Lanz, R. and Ragoussis, A. 2009. Trade in intermediate goods and services. *OECD Trade Policy Working Paper 93*. Paris: OECD.

Miroudot, S., Sauvage, J. and Shepherd, B. 2010. Measuring the cost of international trade in services. *GEM Working Papers*. Paris: SciencesPo, Groupe d'Economie Mondiale.

Moran, T.H. 1998. *Foreign Direct Investment and Development: The New Policy Agenda for Developing Countries and Economies in Transition*. Washington, DC: Peterson Institute for International Economics.

Moran, T.H., Graham, E.M. and Blomström, M. 2005. *Does Foreign Direct Investment Promote Development?* Washington, DC: Institute for International Economics and Centre for Global Development.

Mudambi, R. and Venzin, M. 2010. The strategic nexus of offshoring and outsourcing decisions. *Journal of Management Studies*, 47(8): 1510–33.

Neary, J.P. 2009. Trade costs and foreign direct investment. *International Review of Economics and Finance*, 18(2): 207–18.

Novy, D. 2010. Gravity Redux: measuring international trade costs with panel data. Coventry: University of Warwick. [Online] Available at: www2.warwick.ac.uk/fac/soc/economics/staff/academic/novy/fast.pdf [accessed 28 March 2011].

Sturgeon, T. and Gereffi, G. 2009. Measuring success in the global economy: international trade, industrial upgrading, and business function outsourcing in global value chains. *Transnational Corporations*, 18(2): 1–36.

Sturgeon, T., Van Biesebroeck, J. and Gereffi, G. 2008. Value chains, networks and clusters: reframing the global automotive industry. *Journal of Economic Geography*, 8(3): 297–321.

UNCTAD. 2003. *Foreign Direct Investment and Performance Requirements: New Evidence from Selected Countries*. New York and Geneva: United Nations.

UNCTAD. 2008. *International Investment Rule-Making: Stocktaking, Challenges and the Way Forward*. UNCTAD Series on International Investment Policies for Development. New York and Geneva: United Nations.

UNCTAD. 2009. *The Role of International Investment Agreements in Attracting FDI to Developing Countries*. UNCTAD Series on International Investment Policies for Development. New York and Geneva: United Nations.

Trade and Competition Policy

Kamala Dawar and Peter Holmes

Introduction

As governments open up markets to foreign trade through reducing or eliminating tariff barriers at the borders of countries, it is widely understood that the persistence of domestic market failures behind the border can work to undermine the efficiency and growth effects associated with liberalization (Bhagwati et al. 1971). Competition can be obstructed for a variety of structural and behavioural reasons and governments address the different restrictions of competition through different policies and legal instruments because, as this chapter notes, competition policy can also be used to promote a range of different trade and social policy objectives.

The first section of this chapter defines competition, competition policy and competition law, and the relevant economic and legal concepts related to competition before introducing a discussion of the nature of anticompetitive practices in the second section. The third section provides an overview of the development of different domestic competition policies and laws, drawing on the existing body of literature that is concerned with the legal rather than economic aspects of competition policy. The fourth section examines the issue of competition policy at the international level, identifying the various perspectives and the positions of developed and developing countries.

The chapter concludes by noting that the existence of multiple objectives in national competition laws prevents harmonization of competition policy at a multilateral level. For despite a strong economic rationale for multilateral agreements to deal with the increase in cross-border anticompetitive practices that have not been eradicated by, and in some cases may be facilitated by, global trade liberalization, most governments continue to express ambivalence about negotiating such a legal instrument.

Definitions and Terminology

What is Competition?

Competition is the dynamic force created by firms attempting to gain advantage over their market rivals (OECD 1993). In a competitive market, firms seek to be market leaders by striving to produce superior products in terms of price, choice, quality and service with the aim of consumer satisfaction. A competitive market is contestable;[1] in the event that market prices (and therefore profits) rise above normal levels, there are no barriers to the entry into the market of new suppliers (Graham 1999). Contestable markets create opportunities for new businesses to enter a lucrative market, putting pressure on existing firms to innovate and be more efficient in order to maintain their market position.

Governments face difficulties when trying to create and maintain competitive markets for a variety of reasons. As discussed in the next section, some obstacles to competition are structural, for example, the existence of so-called 'natural monopolies' such as the transmission of electricity or water, while some obstacles are behavioural, as with the deliberate attempts of firms to make greater profits through restrictive business practices such as by creating barriers to new entry. These attempts are considered to be 'unfair' or 'anticompetitive' because the objective of a firm is to gain advantage by limiting competition in order to increase profits. Anticompetitive behaviour is generally considered detrimental to the welfare of other firms (unless they are part of a cartel too), to consumers, and to economic efficiency by contributing to the misallocation of resources (Hoekman and Holmes 1999; Levenstein and Suslow 2001; OECD 2002a). There is a strong body of economic analysis to suggest that competition allows the benefits of trade reform, deregulation and privatization to be realized, which in turn creates a better commercial environment and attracts greater foreign direct investment (FDI). Further, promoting inter-firm rivalry enhances dynamic economic performance, promoting economic growth and development (Jenny 2005; Lipimile 2004; OECD 2000).

Competition Policy

Competition policy comprises the entire set of measures and instruments used by governments to regulate or determine the conditions of competition and the contestability of markets (Hoekman and Holmes 1999). The scope of competition policy includes both private and public markets. Competition policy is related to industrial, investment and trade policy because they all aim to promote national

---

[1]   Contestability is a measure of the extent to which a market is open to new entry. William Baumol argued that the threat posed by the possibility of new firms entering the market is taken to be a key determinant of the behaviour of existing firms.

economic growth. Competition policy can therefore encompass privatization and deregulation measures, cutting firm-specific subsidy programmes, reducing discrimination against foreign business activities, in addition to regulating the behaviour of businesses. Despite agreement on what competition is and its desirability, domestic competition policies vary because different governments do not treat the same types of business practices similarly. What is considered to be an anticompetitive or restrictive business practice not only varies in different jurisdictions but on a case-by-case basis within countries. One frequently cited objective of competition policy is to maximize economic welfare through achieving allocative efficiency (Kolasky and Dick 2003).

Allocative efficiency is achieved by ensuring that the competitive process is not distorted or impeded by the restrictive business practices of firms that have a detrimental effect on economic welfare. This notion of welfare sidesteps the issue of income distribution, and economists usually argue that the distribution of income is best addressed through direct measures. That is, while the aim of redistributing opportunities towards, for example, small businesses or traditionally disadvantaged groups may be a legitimate objective for a domestic government, using competition laws to achieve such a goal may detract from achieving overall allocative efficiency. As discussed later in the chapter, countries vary in the emphasis that is placed on efficiency. Many domestic competition laws also include 'fairness considerations' or social objectives (Kerber 2008). Nevertheless, the decision to prioritize distributive or sectoral goals of competition policy such as fairness and justice, the protection of small- and medium-sized firms, or the promotion of national champions, are commonly viewed critically by economists (for example Motta 2004: 18).

This is not to say, however, that the pursuit of competition cannot be tempered by other considerations. Competition policies recognize that specific agreements between firms that may reduce competition can occasionally be efficiency enhancing, and consequently competition laws make allowance for such agreements. Similarly, some competition policies choose to design competition laws to ensure that environmental standards are not relaxed for economic efficiency concerns. Article 174 of the Treaty of the European Communities, (now Article 191 of the Treaty on the Functioning of the European Union) for example, states that environmental factors may also be taken into account in competition law enforcement. This Article allowed for the European Commission to permit an agreement between European washing machine producers to discontinue manufacturing the least energy efficient washing machines, which also happened to be the cheapest. As Motta points out, in this case the Commission felt the producer agreement would benefit society environmentally because it would reduce energy consumption and individual consumers cannot be relied upon to factor these environmental externalities into their purchasing decisions (Motta 2004: 26).

Competition and Consumer Welfare

A tension arises between competition considerations and trade law when the former are just seen as driven by the rights of producers to be protected from unfair competition or exclusion. If foreign firms are not seen as having such rights, their ability to exercise countervailing power may be constrained.

Competition and consumer policies and laws are complementary because while the former addresses the supply of competition by removing structural obstacles and preventing the restrictive behaviour of businesses, consumer policies address the ability of the individual customer to demand competition. There is a body of research that suggests that consumer laws and competition policies need to act together to enhance the competitive environment, enabling consumers to make appropriate choices and send the correct market signals to producers about their needs and preferences (Dawar 2007). As a result, some competition laws explicitly reference consumer policy and others, such as in Australia, also create competition bodies where consumer policy and law is given an equivalent status to competition law.[2]

Competition Law

The term competition law used throughout this chapter refers to the set of legal instruments created and maintained by governments to regulate the behaviour of firms that restrict competition in the market. Domestic competition law systems differ because they operate under different and often short-term economic and political pressures. This reflects the fact that competition decisions can directly shape the strategic and tactical choices of businesses as well as national economic interests. Competition laws may be applied on the basis of the effects of conduct as well as on the basis of its physical location, which means that several national laws may be applicable to the same conduct. This 'extraterritorial' effect of competition laws brings them into contact with different legal systems. Despite the variety of competition laws, they typically tend to address the following business practices (OECD Framework for Competition Law; UNCTAD 2002).

- Measures relating to agreements between firms in the same market to restrain competition. These measures can include provisions banning cartels as well as provisions allowing cartels under certain circumstances.
- Measures relating to attempts by a large incumbent firm to independently exercise market power by raising prices or artificially creating barriers to market entry (sometimes referred to as an abuse of a dominant position).

---

[2]   Review of Australia's Consumer Policy Framework Inquiry 2008. [Online] Available at: www.pc.gov.au/projects/inquiry/consumer/docs/finalreport [accessed: 27 March 2011].

- Measures relating to firms that, acting collectively but in the absence of an explicit agreement between them, attempt to exercise market power. These measures are sometimes referred to as measures against collective dominance.
- Measures relating to attempts by a firm or firms to drive one or more of their rivals out of a market. Laws prohibiting predatory pricing are an example of such measures.
- Measures relating to collaboration between firms for the purposes of research, development, testing, marketing and distribution of products.
- Mergers and acquisitions which may reduce competition.

The different anticompetitive practices that competition laws are designed to prevent are now examined in more detail. A further aim included in EU competition policy is the control of distortionary state aids, but in the international context this is generally dealt with in separate rules, for example the GATT Subsidies code.

The Nature of Anticompetitive Practices

Agreements Among Firms – Collusion

There are two main categories of collusion between firms that are defined as horizontal and vertical agreements. Generally speaking,[3] horizontal restraints on competition primarily entail other competitors in the market while vertical restraints tend to entail supplier–distributor relationships.

Collusion or cartels are often viewed as the worst types of anticompetitive conduct because they rarely offer any economic or social benefit to justify their negative effects. Research into the cartels prosecuted by the United States Department of Justice (USDOJ) has shown that cartels tend to form across all sectors and industries and that they raise prices by a conservative estimate of 10–25 per cent (Levenstein and Suslow 2001). The ready mix concrete cartel in Germany generated damages of 112 million Euros, the hydropower electricity case in Norway led to damages of 140 million Euros and the hotel association cartel in Spain caused 180 million Euros in estimated harm (OECD 2002a). The OECD Recommendations relating to hardcore cartels[4] consider them unacceptable and recommend that they

---

[3]   The OECD Glossary (1993) points out that the distinction between horizontal and vertical restraints on competition is not always clear-cut and practices of one type may impact on the other.

[4]   The OECD defines hardcore cartels in its Recommendations as 'An anticompetitive agreement, anticompetitive concerted practice, or anticompetitive arrangement by competitors to fix prices, make rigged bids (collusive tenders), establish output restrictions or quotas, or share or divide markets by allocating consumers, suppliers, territories, or lines of commerce' (OECD 2002b).

be actionable; indeed, as discussed later in the chapter, in some jurisdictions they fall under the scope of criminal law.[5]

The existence of international cartels with anticompetitive effects in several markets brings greater regulatory problems because there are limits to the effectiveness of national enforcement efforts against international hardcore cartels, notably when action and the evidence of it is in one jurisdiction and the impact in another. One estimate puts the value of total imports by developing countries of 16 cartelized products at over $80 billion. This is equivalent to 6.7 per cent of all imports by developing countries and to 1.2 per cent of their combined gross domestic product (GDP). The cartels controlling the markets for vitamins, heavy electrical equipment and graphite electrodes used in steel were seen to have a significant impact on some developing countries (Levenstein and Suslow 2001).

National competition authorities have difficulties enforcing the law prohibiting international cartels because of the challenges involved in collecting evidence abroad, interviewing witnesses overseas, and extraditing persons from other jurisdictions. Furthermore, national corporate leniency programmes[6] become less attractive due to the possibility that applications for leniency in one jurisdiction result in the company being exposed to investigations and potential punishments in other jurisdictions. Further, fines for cartelization are a function only of the cartel's effects within a jurisdiction. Most competition laws do not penalize anticompetitive behaviour affecting foreigners and do not allow evidence to be handed over to other countries (Evenett 2002).

Vertical restraints seem more esoteric but they pose problems for trade when firms try to use them to segment markets or to create import bottlenecks. Differences in approaches across jurisdictions have made international agreement harder in this area, particularly with the EU holding market integration as an objective, while the United States stresses efficiency.

The fourth section of this chapter examines the debate surrounding the reasons why international competition laws to address international hardcore cartels have not emerged, despite the powerful economic evidence in favour of action.

The Deliberate Anticompetitive Actions of a Single Firm: Monopoly and Abuse of Dominance

Monopoly is the ability of a firm to act without fearing the response of rivals, notably to raise and maintain prices above the level that would normally prevail

---

[5]   In the United States, Section One of the Sherman Act of 1890 criminalizes 'Hard-core cartel activity, price-fixing, bid-rigging and market allocation agreements'.

[6]   Leniency programmes are sophisticated fine schemes which grant total or partial immunity from fines to firms that collaborate with the authorities. They are based on the principle that those who break the law might report their illegal activities if the proper incentives are created. See Motta (2004: 192–202) on ex post competition policies against collusion.

under a situation of competition. The origin of the term refers to a seller with 100 per cent of its market. The term is more widely, if not consistently, used to refer to firms with unassailable market power. Monopoly as such is rarely illegal but abuses are. The exercise of market power by a monopoly firm leads to reduced output and loss of economic welfare, unless the markets are highly contestable. Without the dynamic of competition, a monopoly firm is able to charge higher prices while being less innovative, less productive and less responsive to consumer preferences. In such a situation, income (and wealth) are transferred from consumers to the monopoly firm. Increasingly, competition authorities pay attention to entry conditions (contestability) rather than profit margins as evidence of monopolistic abuse.

There is no universal definition of abuse of dominance; different governments view the exercise of market power differently. As noted later in the chapter, in some jurisdictions, a firm that charges unreasonably high prices may be seen to be in violation of an abuse of dominance law, while in others this is viewed as an essential market-based incentive. Most jurisdictions focus on issues such as price discrimination, predatory pricing, price squeezing by integrated firms, a firm's refusal to deal or sell its product or the opposite – tied-selling or product-bundling – and pre-emption of facilities (Schmidt 1983: 417–60).

Structural Factors Preventing Competition

In addition to regulating the behaviour of firms operating in the market, competition policy can also address structural features that emerge in a market to hinder the competitive dynamic. Such features not only include aforementioned natural monopolies but also include the creation of commercial entities through the merging of firms that have sufficient market power and intent to prevent fair competition. This again will lead to higher prices, lower quality and less innovation and a transfer of income from the consumer to the commercial entity. Most competition law thus includes merger-control assessment tests. This test involves characterizing competing products and firms, along with their market strength with respect to the product markets and scope for entry, including by foreign firms. Merger control includes notification requirements that allow for an investigation of market conditions and barriers to new entry.

The degree to which merger laws allow acquisitions by foreign firms varies widely from country to country. A recent comparative study of the EU and the United States argued that since 2004 the two regimes have converged significantly, but that there are still differences. The EU is less likely than the United States to accept an efficiency defence but, where it does act against a merger, the EU is more likely to accept weak rather than strong remedies (Bergman et al. 2010).

Domestic Competition Law

Both governments and economists have a long tradition of denouncing the anticompetitive behaviour of firms.[7] Adam Smith is noted for his prescience about the harmful effects of monopolies and collusion among businesses. He feared that 'people of the same trade seldom meet together even for merriment and diversion, but the conversation ends in a conspiracy against the public or in some contrivance to raise prices' (Smith 1904 [1776]). Yet, despite the contribution of economists as far back as Smith, it has taken several centuries for the widespread enactment of domestic competition laws, the latest greatest surge taking place in the 1990s. For many years there was a dissenting current within economics based on Schumpeter's argument that large monopolistic firms were necessary to generate the profits needed for research and development (R&D). Other economists argued that the pressure of competition was the best way to promote innovation. This debate crystallized at the international regulatory level in the controversial Trade Related Aspects of Intellectual Property Rights (TRIPs) agreement which forced countries at all stages of development to adopt US/EU-style patent and copyright rules, albeit with scope for these to be amended in the case where patents were used to create monopolistic abuses (Nguyen 2008: 558–86).

The evolution of national competition policy has produced domestic competition systems which differ in their legal responses to particular problems. This section examines the main models operating in the United States and in Europe, before discussing the domestic legal systems that are emerging in other parts of the world, particularly in developing countries.

US Antitrust Law

Although not the first,[8] US antitrust law is usually considered to be the pioneer of competition law (Gerber 2006). The Sherman Act (1890) was introduced in the United States at a time when state acquisition laws were being liberalized, allowing for an increase in firm size to capture economies of scale and scope[9] in growing US markets. During the second half of the nineteenth century, price instability and price wars led some of these firms to try to make agreements and trusts with rivals

---

[7]   Braithwaite and Drahos (2000: 185), for example, cite Emperor Zeno's edict to the Praetorian Prefect of Constantinople in 483 AD: 'We command that no one may presume to exercise a monopoly of any kind of clothing, fish, or of any other thing serving for food or for any other use … Nor may any persons combine or agree in unlawful meetings, that different kinds of merchandise may not be sold at a less price than they have agreed upon among themselves'.

[8]   Canada introduced antitrust legislation in 1889.

[9]   Economies of scale occur when unit costs of production fall with the quantity produced, economies of scope emerge when unit costs fall because two or more goods are produced jointly.

to fix prices and maintain profit margins. The growing negative effect of these cartels and trusts on consumers, small firms and small farmers was sufficient to produce a strong lobby in favour of introducing antitrust laws (Motta 2004: 3–9).

Motta provides a history of the development of the Sherman Act which indicates that antitrust in the United States has been primarily enacted with the aim of promoting economic efficiency. By the 1990s, Gerber (2010) notes that many legal policymakers viewed US economic success as a confirmation of the superiority of US economic policy. US antitrust has been closely associated with 'US-style capitalism', which is typically critical of government intervention in the economy and with business. The United States has signed a number of bilateral agreements on competition policy but generally prefers the freedom of manoeuvre of being able to act unilaterally.

European Competition Law

The competition law of the EU is based on a general framework provided since 1957 by the EU Treaty which applies to matters that affect cross-border trade among the member states. Article 102 of the Lisbon Treaty prohibits abuse of dominance while Article 101 prohibits decisions by associations of undertakings and concerted practices which may affect trade between member states and which have as their object or effect the prevention, restriction, or distortion of competition within the common market. There is an efficiency defence permitted in Article 101 – exemptions can be given if such agreements contribute to improving the economic environment, while allowing consumers a fair share of the resulting benefit. Article 101 TFEU (earlier Article 81 TEC) was extensively used by the Commission to promote integration by preventing agreements between firms for market sharing or exclusionary purposes within the Common Market.

In 2004, major reforms were introduced that, *inter alia*, required that EU competition law generally be applied in all cases other than those whose effects are limited to one state. Restrictive trade practice issues come within the jurisdiction of the European Commission; individual member states are not permitted to apply rules that deviate from EU law. However, European member states are permitted to apply the law of their national statutes with respect to abuse of dominance if that law is more restrictive than that of the EU.[10] Domestic member state law also controls private rights of action. Thus, despite the harmonizing impact of EU competition law, domestic regimes retain domestic policy concerns and characteristics.

As the EU became a more integrated market it became anomalous to allow different principles to apply for domestic and cross-border practices, hence the more harmonized approach since 2004. As we shall see, the EU's experience in promoting intra-European trade via competition policy has influenced its attitude

---

[10] Council Regulation 1/2003 of 16 December 2002, regarding the implementation of competition rules laid down in Articles 81 and 82 of the EC Treaty, Article 3(2), 2003 O.J. (L1) 1,8.

to the global system. The European Commission has long considered its powers to address private barriers to entry, which results in distorting trade between member states, a vital counterpart to the Treaty-based prohibitions on government measures and has seen the removal of trade barriers at the WTO a necessary but not sufficient condition for freeing trade.

Competition Policy in Developing Countries

Singh (2002) has characterized the structure of markets in developing countries as generally having limited competition, due to high barriers to entry and low contestability, and the tendency for a small number of firms to have large concentrations of market power. Many of the conditions in developing countries allow anticompetitive practices to thrive, and can provide a safe haven for international cartels (Evenett et al. 2001; Levenstein and Suslow 2004). This has led policymakers in these countries to 'recognise the importance of implementing an effective competition policy and law, to achieve the maximum benefit from the process of liberalisation' (CUTS 2003: 17). A body of opinion now exists which supports implementing competition law in developing countries because 'strong competition policy is not just a luxury to be enjoyed by rich countries, but a real necessity for those striving to create democratic market economies' (Stiglitz 2001). There is no empirical evidence to show that restraining competition strengthens developing countries' firms (UNCTAD 2004). This is reflected in the number of developing countries that are in the process of establishing competition laws. Until 1990 only 16 developing countries had a formal competition policy, yet 50 countries completed legislation for competition laws in the 1990s and, by 2002, another 27 were in the process of doing so (Singh 2002 cited in UNCTAD 2004).

Despite the growing number of developing countries with competition policies and laws, a significant number still have not enacted any form of competition law. There are development analysts who argue that competition law may be less relevant in developing countries which might not have the resources to set up an effective competition regime and where the economy tends to be characterized by small- and medium-sized enterprises, many operating outside the formal sector, limiting the ability of formal laws and institutions to regulate their behaviour. Effective competition laws and policies rely on the prior existence of strong and stable institutions and institutional powers if they are to avoid creating greater market failures. It has also been argued that when the institutions designed to promote competition policy are weak, corruption can flourish (Pope 2000).

Gal (2003) notes that while for many developing countries the enactment of a competition law has been seen as one of the cornerstones of their liberalization and pro-market reforms, such enactment requires some important preconditions to be effective. She argues that developing countries' low level of economic development, which is often accompanied by institutional design problems and complex government regulation and bureaucracy, must be addressed before the successful implementation of an antitrust regime. Several developing countries have had antitrust laws for several decades, but until recently none appears to have been regularly enforced to further the aims generally associated with competition law.

In light of the lack of a fertile institutional and ideological environment for competition law in some developing countries, there are analysts who argue that for smaller economies, open trade and FDI policies are enough to ensure sufficient domestic competition at this stage of their economic development (Graham 1999: 418; see also Kronthaler et al. 2005; OECD 2003, 2004). Hylton and Deng's (2007) analysis of whether the presence of a competition law has an impact on the intensity of competition in a country's economy suggested that the effects were ambiguous or not significant enough to have an economic impact. Liu (2004) too has noted in the case of Asia, that fostering competition is harder than enacting competition laws. He argues that calling these 'fair trade laws' causes immediate confusion because 'fairness can mean many things and anything but efficiency, the dominant goal of antitrust laws'. Much of the problem lies in the transplantation of competition laws from other jurisdictions, without the accompanying ideological environment, as Gal has noted. As a result, competition laws are not prioritized in the political arena and competition authorities are not respected. Governments are not always able to provide sufficient legislative push to enact or implement an effective competition law. This observation has led, on the one hand, to proposals for an international agreement on competition, increased competition advocacy and capacity-building from international bodies such as the OECD, International Competition Network (ICN),[11] WTO and World Bank, and, on the other hand, a commensurate increase in opposition to such proposals from various non-governmental organizations.

The next section will look at the proposals for and against a multilateral competition agreement, along with the various organizations and actors engaged in this debate.

International Competition Rules and Cooperation

The protracted debate surrounding the need to introduce international competition laws has a longer history than most domestic competition laws. Competition disciplines were included in the draft constitution of the International Trade Organization (ITO) after the Second World War. This included provisions to address 'restrictions imposed by private combines and cartels' on the grounds that private agreements that divided markets undermined any trade liberalizing

---

[11] The ICN aims to provide competition authorities with an informal structure for maintaining regular contacts and addressing practical competition concerns. This should serve to build consensus and convergence towards sound competition policy principles across the global antitrust community. The ICN is unique in being as yet the only international body devoted exclusively to competition law enforcement. See: www.internationalcompetitionnetwork.org.

measures governments were implementing. Chapter V of the Havana Charter set out to specifically address restrictive business practices with a requirement that governments police anticompetitive practices with an international dimension (Anderson and Holmes 2002: 536). Due to opposition from the US Congress the Charter was not ratified and its replacement, the General Agreement on Tariffs and Trade (GATT 1947), omitted Chapter V. Yet the relevance of international provisions to address restrictive business practices remained.

UNCTAD subsequently became a focus for the issue of competition in developing countries. In 1980, after nearly a decade of negotiating, an agreement was reached and adopted by the UN General Assembly on a nonbinding code of conduct relating to competition and international trade, commonly known as 'The UN Set of Multilaterally Agreed Equitable Principles and Rules for the Control of Restrictive Business Practices'. Since 1994, the Asia Pacific Economic Cooperation (APEC) forum's Collective Action Plan has been developed in order for member economies to 'consider developing non-binding principles on competition policy and/or laws in APEC'.[12]

At the OECD, the Competition Law and Policy Committee has investigated a number of aspects of national competition law and policy and the convergence of such national laws and policies. As regards developed countries, the OECD Council has adopted a number of Recommendations relating to the international dimensions of competition law, including a series of Recommendations from 1967 relating to bilateral cooperation in competition law enforcement and the adoption in 1998 of the Recommendations Concerning Effective Action Against Hard Core Cartels. The OECD Joint Group on Trade and Competition has also investigated the interaction between trade and competition policies, and an annual Global Forum has been established to further outreach and promote cooperation and understanding between and among developing and developed country competition authorities.

Work at the OECD developed the concepts of negative and positive comity, which are essentially a formal commitment to take others' interests into account when one applies one's own laws. Positive comity is sometimes incorporated into bilateral or regional competition agreements. Under such agreements, when the anticompetitive business effects of a cartel or boycott cut across the boundaries of more than one jurisdiction, the country affected may request the competition authority in which the cartel or boycott originates to take action vis-à-vis this cartel in its territory. However, the effectiveness of positive comity often is limited to instances when the anticompetitive effects of conduct affect both the requesting state and requested state; otherwise, the requested party has little capacity to prohibit the conduct, perhaps even the reverse may be the case if the party permits export cartels.[13] There are cases of effective positive comity, such as when the

---

[12]   The objective was a part of the response to the Bogor Declaration committing all APEC member economies to free trade and investment by 2010 for the developed economy members or 2020 for the developing economy members.

[13]   For example, the US Webb Pomerene Act, 15 USC, 61–6 (1994) and the Japanese Export and Import Transactions Law, Law No. 299 of 1952 as amended.

US and Canadian authorities successfully cooperated in their investigation of a Japanese fax paper cartel to bring criminal charges against the cartel. However, Japan was not the requested party in this example. Nevertheless, despite the limited effects of positive comity currently (Marsden 2010), it is argued that a positive comity approach ultimately may prompt the parties to push forward the eventual harmonization of most, if not all, of their respective competition laws (Matsushita 1999: 463).

Negative comity occurs when a party to the agreement refrains from applying its competition law to the conduct of an enterprise if such application conflicts with governmental policy of the other party. This can happen if one state applies its competition laws to prohibit an international merger that is permitted by the government of another state, resulting in conflicting jurisdictions. Under negative comity, the former state would refrain from applying its competition law to that merger out of respect for the governmental policy of the latter state. Again, this is an interesting approach but with limited effects to date.

And in addition to the establishment of soft competition law in the form of recommendations and guidelines by different intergovernmental organizations, the issue of a multilateral competition agreement in the WTO has continued to bubble under the negotiating table, acting as a reference point for those for and against binding multilateral competition laws.

A Multilateral Competition Regime?

In December 1996, during the first Ministerial meeting of the WTO in Singapore, a decision was taken to establish a working group to study the interaction between trade and competition policy, including anticompetitive business practices. The Ministerial Declaration stated that any future negotiations regarding multilateral disciplines in this area would take place only after an 'explicit consensus decision' was reached by WTO members. This mandate was confirmed at the Doha Ministerial in 2001. As with the ITO, a lack of consensus has prevented the negotiation of any type of multilateral competition agreement in the WTO. The July 2004 Framework Agreement formally dropped the issue of trade and competition policy from the Work Programmes of the Doha Round. This was primarily due to the consistent opposition of most developing countries and the opposition of the United States to the proposals pushed by the European Union.

The EU sought a general commitment to a competition law by every WTO member, but was seemingly unwilling to commit itself to disciplining the behaviour of its own firms in the rest of the world. The resource-short developing world saw little interest in it for them and suspected a hidden market access agenda. The United States meanwhile was quite content with the extraterritorial reach of its own laws and proclaimed the sufficiency of its own voluntary offers of assistance to other partners.

Bhattacharjea (2006) argues that developing countries objected to the EU proposal – that would at a minimum prohibit hardcore cartels and require members to enact competition laws incorporating the fundamental principles of non-discrimination, national treatment and transparency – for a variety of reasons. While developing countries acknowledged the harm caused by international cartels, they emphasized the need to respect their diversity in terms of stages of development, socioeconomic circumstances, legal frameworks and cultural norms. There was vocal opposition from many NGOs, such as Third World Network and ActionAid, to a so-called 'one size fits all' agreement, transplanting a foreign competition policy framework into environments lacking in experience, expertise and institutional memory. Yet no other proposals were tabled and the 'no new issues' campaign ultimately dominated the WTO negotiating agenda. This suggests that many developing countries had policy objectives that were seen as more important than promoting efficiency and competition. Nevertheless, somewhat paradoxically, many of these same dissenting developing countries have entered into bilateral and regional trade agreements – where arguably they have less bargaining strength than in the multilateral setting of the WTO – that include competition provisions, although such provisions are rarely binding (Bourgeois et al. 2008).

But before focusing on bilateral and regional competition provisions, it is worth briefly mentioning the view that multilateral or preferential agreements on competition policy could in practice provide a means to reduce the use of antidumping. In reality however, antidumping duties are not systematically targeted at monopolistic predatory pricing (Bourgeois and Messerlin 1998) and there is little connection between these policy instruments. Hoekman (1998) has argued that there is no correlation between inclusion of competition provisions in preferential trade agreements (PTAs) and provisions to limit antidumping.

There are nevertheless a number of PTAs in which signatories have agreed to use domestic competition policy – instead of antidumping sanctions – to address concerns about dumping. This applies for example to the Canada–Chile FTA, the Australia–New Zealand agreement and most agreements involving European Free Trade Association (EFTA) countries. Nordstrom (2009) recently argued that the EU should include competition instruments in its PTAs and preclude antidumping. But it would be unrealistic to assume that this notion could significantly reduce resort to antidumping action.

Bilateral and Regional Competition Provisions

The ongoing rejection of any sort of competition framework within the WTO coincides with the increasing negotiation of competition provisions in bilateral and regional trading agreements, as a halfway house or stepping stone towards an agreement at the international level. This development has not been unanimously welcomed, partly because of the costs of negotiating and implementing the bilateral or regional competition provisions when the economic and welfare effects of such regimes are as yet inconclusive. The alternative option of negotiating a Mutual Legal Assistance Treaty (MLAT) is preferable to some commentators. MLATs set the terms for competition authorities in the two countries assisting one another in securing and sharing evidence that is not readily obtainable.

Clearly, improving interagency relationships and cooperation mechanisms will facilitate greater coordination of competition investigations and prosecutions. However, MLATs cannot be applied to jurisdictions without competition agencies, and are less effective among agencies with different levels of expertise, resources and enforcement mechanisms.

The more comprehensive PTA competition regimes negotiated can potentially overcome some of these challenges and discrepancies. In principle, the economic benefit of including competition law and provisions within PTAs is to ensure that liberalization will not be undermined by anticompetitive business practices within the member countries, to the disadvantage of consumers and firms. Beyond this rule of thumb, there is little evidence to make definitive conclusions about the economic benefits of the different types of competition-related provisions found in PTAs. However, the inclusion of competition provisions in trade agreements is potentially beneficial, particularly for developing countries who tend to lose more from the anticompetitive practices of multinational corporations, which have especially detrimental consequences in a context of economic scarcity.

In regional groupings like MERCOSUR, the Andean Pact and COMESA (Common Market for Eastern and Southern Africa), where the individual Members of the agreement are at very different states of economic development – some without a competition law or a functioning enforcement agency and with different approaches to sovereignty pooling – there are benefits to establishing a strong regional enforcement mechanism. MERCOSUR is an example of an intergovernmental ministerial approach to regional competition law that has not been implemented effectively. This failure is usually attributed to the unwillingness of some of the member states to pass national laws or domestic regimes giving effect to external regional obligations. The lack of effective regional competition remedies has contributed to a degrading of the free trade schedules for this common market. And while some MERCOSUR members have developed competition law and policy, without an effective domestic law in all members of the agreement there can be no legal basis for a member to take any action against practices organized in another member state in respect of the effects upon its own territory. The reasons for the poor implementation of regional competition provisions are both institutional and behavioural, however, due to a lack of competition culture or political will to promote implementation domestically. A well designed regional competition agreement needs to takes account of these local realities and act as a policy tool to create the national structural and behavioural environment necessary to benefit from regional competition provisions.

North–South agreements have greater development benefits and better implementation records when the more developed party offers appropriate technical assistance and capacity-building, and therefore increases the ability of the less developed regional partner to benefit from the provisions. For those members with nascent or non-existent competition regimes, technical assistance provisions should aim to impart the necessary expertise and experience over the long term. This promotes the behavioural changes necessary for a competition culture. Indeed, while PTA competition provisions can offer the legislative push and policy lock-in necessary for sustained reform, it can be more beneficial initially to focus on establishing a culture that values competition at the national or sub-regional level in the region. The provisions can focus primarily on the exchange of information, technical assistance and capacity-building. Subsequent negotiations can expand the agreement. More general commitments should only be implemented after the necessary expertise and cooperation mechanisms have been developed. Provisions could be included that oblige members, over a specified period of time, to adopt competition laws that can address the full range of private and state-created anticompetitive practices and outcomes. Regional laws can act as a temporary alternative to the expense of establishing and implementing domestic competition laws.

Conclusion

This chapter has aimed to provide an introduction to the main features of competition law and policy, and the policy context in which they are framed. Competition law and policy are now seen as important tools to underpin trade liberalization and ensure that the benefits of open markets are not undermined by the restriction of competition between firms in developing as well as developed countries.

At a domestic level, not only have governments increasingly addressed the restriction of competition through different policies and legal instruments, they have also used competition law to promote a variety of other trade and social policy objectives. The result is that there is very little uniformity in domestic competition laws, and very little consensus on how best to tackle cross-border anticompetitive business practices collectively. This divergence has been gradually eroding over time, but not enough to secure agreement on an international framework. Such a framework seems likely to remain elusive for the foreseeable future. Developing countries have been sceptical of EU motives in advocating it. They are backed by the United States, which prefers its own unilateral and selective bilateral approaches. But there are signs that the ground is not entirely frozen. The willingness of developing countries to agree to include competition provisions in bilateral agreements is in marked contrast to the refusal to allow trade and competition discussions to proceed after the Cancun WTO Ministerial. As practical cooperation evolves and custom and practice emerge, we may eventually see a codification at the WTO of best practice as it materializes in bilateral agreements and in fora such as the International Competition Network.

References

Anderson, R. and Holmes, P. 2002. Competition policy and the future of the multilateral trading system. *Journal of International Economic Law*, 5(2): 536.

Bergman, M.A., Coate, M.B., Jakobsson, M. and Ulrick, S.W. 2010. Merger control in the European Union and the United States: just the facts. *Working Paper Series*. [Online]. Available at: www.springerlink.com/content/n5u8362433u0q254.

Bhagwati, J., Jones, R.W., Mundell, R. and Vanek, J. (eds). 1971. *The General Theory of Distortions and Welfare, in Trade, Balance of Payments and Growth: Essays in Honour of C.P. Kindleberger*. Amsterdam: North Holland.

Bhattacharjea, A. 2006. The case for a multilateral agreement on competition policy: a developing country perspective. *Journal of International Economic Law*, 9(2): 293–323.

Bourgeois, J. and Messerlin, P 1998. The European Community's experience, in *Trade, Competitiveness, Global Economics, Antidumping: The Brookings Trade Forum 1998*, edited by R.Z. Lawrence. Washington, DC: The Brookings Institution: 127–45.

Bourgeois, J., Dawar, K. and Evenett, S. 2008. A comparative analysis of selected provisions in free trade agreements. [Online] Available at: trade.ec.europa.eu/doclib/docs/2008/march/tradoc_138103.pdf [accessed: 16 March 2011].

Braithwaite, J. and Drahos, P. 2000. *Global Business Regulation*. Cambridge: Cambridge University Press.

CUTS. 2003. *Pulling Up Our Socks: A Study of Competition Regimes of Seven Developing Countries of Africa and Asia: The 7-UP Project*. Jaipur: Jaipur Printers.

Dawar, K. 2007. Establishing consumers as equivalent players in competition policy, in *Competitive Advantage and Competition Policy in Developing Countries*, edited by P. Cook, P. Fabella and C. Lee. United Kingdom: Edward Elgar Press: 79–92.

Evenett, S.J. 2002. National competition policies in an era of integrating markets, in *Development, Trade and the WTO: A Handbook*, edited by B.M. Hoekman, A. Mattoo and P. English. Washington, DC: The World Bank: 456–62.

Evenett, S.J., Levenstein, M. and Suslow, V. 2001. International cartel enforcement: lessons from the 1990s. *The World Economy: Special Global Trade Policy*, 24(9): 1221–45.

Gal, Michal S. 2003. *Competition Policy for Small Market Economies*. Cambridge, MA: Harvard University Press.

Gerber, D.J. 2006. Competition law, in *The Oxford Handbook of Comparative Law*, edited by M. Reimann and R. Zimmermann. Oxford: Oxford University Press.

Gerber, D.J. 2010. *Global Competition: Law, Markets and Globalization*. Oxford: Oxford University Press.

Graham, E.M. 1999. Approaches to competition policy, in *Trade Rules in The Making*, edited by M. Rodriguez Mendoza, P. Low and B. Kotschwar. Washington, DC: The Brookings Institute Press: 421.

Hoekman, B. 1998. Free trade and deep integration: antidumping and antitrust in regional agreements. *Policy Research Working Paper Series No.1950*. Washington, DC: The World Bank.

Hoekman, B. and Holmes, P. 1999. Competition policy, developing countries and the WTO. *The World Economy*, 22: 875–93.

Hylton, J.K.N. and Deng, F. 2007. Antitrust around the world: an empirical analysis of the scope of competition laws and their effects. *Boston University School of Law Working Paper No. 06-47*.

Jenny, F. 2005. *Cartels and Collusions in Developing Countries*: submission by France. Presentation to the 5th UN Review Conference, Antalya, Turkey; 14–18 November.

Kerber, W. 2008. Should competition law promote efficiency? Some reflections of an economist on the normative foundations of competition law, in *Economic Theory and Competition Law*, edited by J. Drexl, L. Idot and J. Moneger. Cheltenham: Edward Elgar: 8–9.

Kolasky, W. and Dick, A. 2003. The merger of guidelines and the integration of efficiencies into antitrust review of horizontal mergers. *Working Paper 31. Wilmer Cutler Pickering Hale and Dorr Antitrust Series*. [Online] Available at: http://law.bepress.com/wilmer/papers/art31 [accessed: 27 March 2011].

Kronthaler, F., Stephan, J. and Emmert, F. 2005. Competition policy foundations for trade reform, regulatory reform and sustainable development. [Online] Available at: www.cpftr.org/cpftr/deliverables/Deliverable34.pdf [accessed: 27 March 2011].

Levenstein, M. and Suslow, V. 2004. International price-fixing cartels and developing countries: discussion of effects and policy remedies. *Antitrust Law Journal*, 71(3): 801–52.

Levenstein, M.C. and Suslow, V.Y. 2001. Private international cartels and their effect on developing countries. *Background Paper for the World Development Report 2001*. Washington, DC: World Bank.

Lipimile, G.K. 2004. Competition as a stimulus for enterprise development, in *Competition, Competitiveness and Development: Lessons from Developing Countries*. *Unctad/Ditc/Clp/2004/1 (2004)*.

Liu, L.S. 2004. *In Fairness We Trust? Why Fostering Competition Law And Policy Ain't Easy In Asia*. [Online] Available at: http://papers.ssrn.com/sol3/papers.cfm?abstract_id=610822 [accessed: 27 March 2011].

Marsden, P. 2010. The curious incident of positive comity – the dog that didn't bark, in *Regulation and Competition in the Global Economy: Cooperation, Comity and Competition Policy*, edited by A.T. Guzman. Oxford: Oxford University Press: Chapter 15.

Matsushita, M. 1999. International cooperation in the enforcement of competition policy. *Washington University Global Studies Law Review*, 1: 463.

Motta, M. 2004. *Competition Policy: History Objectives and the Law*. Cambridge: Cambridge University Press.

Nguyen, T.T. 2008. Competition rules in the TRIPS agreement: the CFI's ruling in Microsoft v. Commission and implications for developing countries. *International Review of Intellectual Property and Competition Law*, 39(5): 558–86.

Nordstrom, H. 2009. Antitrust instead of antidumping in the Community's bilateral trade agreements, in *The Contribution of Trade to a New EU Growth Strategy*. Stockholm: Kommerskollegium. [Online] Available at www.kommers.se/upload/Analysarkiv/In%20English/Analyses/LS%20Antitrustandantidumping_1.pdf [accessed: 27 March 2011].

OECD. 1993. *OECD Glossary of Industrial Organisation Economics and Competition Law*. Paris: OECD. [Online] Available at: www.oecd.org/dataoecd/8/61/2376087.pdf [accessed: 27 March 2011].

OECD. 2000. *The OECD Background Report on The Role Of Competition Policy in Regulatory Reform*. [Online] Available at: www.OECD.Org/Dataoecd/46/23/32407554.Pdf [accessed: 16 March 2011].

OECD. 2002a. *Competition Policy and Economic Growth and Development Ccnm/Gf/Comp*. Paris: OECD.

OECD. 2002b. *Report on the Nature and Impact of Hard Core Cartels and Sanctions Against Cartel Laws Under National Competition Law*. Paris: OECD.

OECD. 2003. OECD Global Forum on Competition. Malaysia, 6 February.

OECD. 2004. OECD Global Forum on Competition. Thailand, 4 February.

Pope, J. 2000. Confronting corruption: the elements of a national integrity system. *Transparency International Source Book*. London: Transparency International.

Schmidt, I. 1983. Different approaches and problems in dealing with control of market power: a comparison of German, European and US policy towards market-dominating enterprises. *Antitrust Bulletin*, 28: 417–60.

Singh, A. 2002. *Competition and Competition Policy in Emerging Markets: International and Developmental Dimensions, UNCTAD*. [Online] Available at: www.unctad.org/en/docs/gdsmdpbg2418_en.pdf [accessed: 16 March 2011].

Smith, A. 1904 [1776]. *An Inquiry into the Nature and Causes of the Wealth of Nations*. 5th Edition, edited by E. Cannan. London: Methuen and Co.

Stiglitz, J.E. 2001. Competing over competition policy. *Project Syndicate* [Online] Available at: www.project-syndicate.org/commentary/stiglitz [accessed: 16 March 2011].

UNCTAD. 2002. *Closer Multilateral Cooperation on Competition Policy: The Development Dimension*. Consolidated report on issues discussed during the Panama, Tunis, Hong Kong and Odessa regional post-Doha seminars on competition policy. New York and Geneva: 21 March–26 April 2002 and 15 May 2002.

UNCTAD. 2004. *Competition, Competitiveness and Development: Lessons from Developing Countries*. Edited by P. Brusick, A. Alvarez, L. Cernat and P. Holmes. Geneva: United Nations Conference on Trade and Development.

Environmental Protection, International Trade and the WTO

Robert Falkner and Nico Jaspers

Introduction

The expansion of international trade since the Second World War has gone hand-in-hand with global economic growth on an unprecedented scale. It has also coincided with a dramatic rise in global environmental degradation, in the form of increased air and marine pollution, desertification and deforestation, loss of biological diversity and climate change.

Two sets of questions arise from this. The first concerns the general link between trade and environment: is the liberalization and expansion of international trade in some way responsible for what many now refer to as the global ecological crisis? Or do freer trade, increased global competition and greater wealth help to promote environmental protection and a more efficient use of scarce resources? The second is about the specific institutional context of international trade and environmental policy: do the rules of the international trading system, primarily those of the General Agreement on Tariffs and Trade (GATT) and the World Trade Organization (WTO) system but also bilateral and regional trade agreements, help or hinder efforts to protect the environment? Furthermore, are international environmental agreements consistent with the rules and obligations of the WTO order?

These and other questions about the trade–environment nexus have been intensely debated for decades, and especially since the 1990s (for a general overview, see Sampson 2005). They remain critical to the future of the trading system. This chapter reviews the debate and recent scholarship on this topic. It begins with a brief discussion of the general relationship between trade and environment and then focuses more closely on the institutional context for trade and environmental policymaking: the rules of the WTO and how they relate to environmental matters; the relationship between the WTO and multilateral environmental agreements; recent WTO jurisdiction on trade–environment conflicts; and political efforts to resolve such conflicts within the WTO's Committee on Trade and Environment (CTE) and the Doha Round.

Links Between Trade and the Environment

Are international trade and environmental protection compatible or in conflict? This question has provoked a lively debate between academics, environmental campaigners and free trade advocates. It has focused on two types of causal links between trade and environment: the first concerns the effect that trade liberalization has on environmental quality in a given country or worldwide; the second reverses the perspective and addresses the impact that environmental protection policies have on international trade. At the risk of oversimplifying a complex debate, free trade supporters generally argue that liberalizing trade has a mostly positive effect on the environment, but some environmental measures pose a protectionist threat to the free trade order (Bhagwati 2004; Bhagwati and Srinivasan 1996; Hettige et al. 1998). In contrast, environmentalists assert that free trade is one of the main causes of the global environmental crisis, and that environmental policy should rightly limit free trade where it harms environmental quality (Daly 1993; Goldsmith and Mander 2001).

Closer examination of the empirical evidence behind these claims reveals a more nuanced picture (for an overview, see Neumayer 2001). Under certain circumstances, free trade can lead to more polluting production and greater consumption of natural resources. This is the case in countries that specialize in the production of pollution-intensive goods in response to trade liberalization, such as China which has seen a dramatic rise in air and water pollution caused by the expansion of export-oriented manufacturing (Economy 2004). In other contexts, free trade can promote greater efficiency in production and the diffusion of environmental technologies and standards throughout the world. For example, more globally oriented companies in the chemical and steel industries tend to adopt and promote higher environmental standards than national companies (Garcia-Johnson 2000; Reppelin-Hill 1999).

The empirical record is also mixed when it comes to the impact of environmental policies on trade. Environmental protection efforts can disrupt international trade and often give rise to accusations of disguised protectionism. Many developing countries, in particular, have accused advanced economies of using environmental standards to protect their domestic markets against foreign competition (OECD 2005). Other measures, however, can be compatible with the international trading system. Abolishing subsidies for fossil fuel use, for example, would not only help in the fight against global warming; it would also promote a level playing field in international energy markets (Anderson and McKibbin 2000).

Overall, therefore, generalizations about the trade–environment nexus are problematic. Trade liberalization and environmental protection can, but need not, be in conflict. Much depends on the specific circumstances of the industrial sectors and national economies concerned, and the specific environmental policies pursued by governments.

A more useful way to think about these connections is, therefore, to consider context-specific causalities and to identify particular mechanisms by which trade impacts on the environment. Grossman and Krueger (1993) propose three such mechanisms: scale, composition and technique. The *scale* effect occurs when liberalized trade stimulates economic growth, which in turn leads to an increase in environmentally harmful activities including increased resource consumption. The *composition* effect leads to greater specialization between countries and, as a consequence of the shift in economic activity, differential rates of environmental degradation. Countries with lower environmental standards will see an expansion of environmentally harmful activity in response to this trade-induced specialization effect. The *technique* effect involves changes in the technologies for production and resource extraction. Where increased trade and competition leads to improvements in the efficiency of production or the transfer of advanced technologies to less developed economies, trade can raise the level of environmental protection worldwide.

Environmentalists add to this two further mechanisms, which are generally not well captured by economic models. One such mechanism can be found in the *cultural change* in society which is caused by an opening up to international trade. In this view, trade liberalization creates shifts not only in production technologies but also in consumption patterns, due to a spread of consumerist values and the greater availability of goods, leading to an ever-rising spiral of consumer needs. Rising consumption may even outstrip any efficiency gains from more trade (Princen et al. 2002). Another mechanism is the so-called *distancing* effect. International trade creates longer and more complex chains between geographically dispersed economic actors, from resource extraction and manufacturing to international trade and retailing. As a consequence, consumers are less able to identify and accept the responsibility for the consequences that their decisions have on the environment in evermore distant locations (Princen 1997).

While free trade advocates and environmentalists continue to argue over the right way to conceptualize the linkages between trade and the environment, international policymakers are keen to stress the mutual supportiveness of trade and environmental policies, as was the case at the 2002 World Summit on Sustainable Development. But whether trade and environmental policymaking support each other or clash depends on how existing international norms and rules are to be interpreted. We need to consider in particular how the rules of the GATT/WTO trade system affect environmental policy and vice versa. Other bilateral and regional trade agreements (such as NAFTA) also affect the trade–environment relationship (Gallagher 2004; Heydon and Woolcock 2009), but the subsequent analysis focuses on the relationship between multilateral trade rules and environmental policies and regimes.

International Trade Rules and Environmental Protection

At the time of the creation of the GATT in the late 1940s, there was no international environmental agenda to speak of. Apart from a small number of treaties and institutions dealing with transboundary environmental concerns, environmental protection was predominantly seen as a domestic policy issue. Understandably, therefore, the creators of the GATT did not include in the agreement any special provisions on the relationship between trade and environmental policy. Still, they recognized that governments might occasionally need to restrict trade in the interest of public health or nature conservation.[1]

The GATT's main objective has been to reduce the overall level of tariffs and other trade barriers through a series of multilateral negotiations. Its legal structure is based on a number of fundamental norms, of which reciprocity and non-discrimination are the most important. Reciprocity in the GATT system is evident from the way in which negotiations on tariff reductions have been conducted. Rather than lower trade barriers unilaterally, GATT members, in multilateral negotiations, have only agreed to reduce their levels of protection in return for reciprocal concessions from other trading partners. Non-discrimination is expressed in two principles in the GATT agreement: the most-favoured-nation (MFN) principle (Article I), which requires each GATT member to accord to all other members the same privileges it has granted to its 'most-favoured-nation'; and the national treatment principle (Article III), which demands that GATT members treat 'like products' imported from foreign producers in the same way as those of domestic producers. The concept of like products is an important one in the context of trade–environment debates, even though no definite interpretation of it exists in GATT/WTO law and jurisdiction (Sampson 2005). Internationally traded goods may be different in some respects, for instance reflecting different designs or production techniques; but they are to be considered as like products if they share important physical characteristics or are functionally equivalent (such as cars by different manufacturers).

Article XX is the only provision in the GATT that specifically mentions environmental concerns. It sets out the conditions for restricting international trade in the interest of human, animal or plant life or health (Article XX(b)) and the conservation of natural resources (Article XX(g)). Such measures are allowed if they do not arbitrarily and unjustifiably discriminate between countries with similar conditions or constitute a disguised protectionist measure; if (in the case of subclause b) they can be considered necessary, that is no other, less trade-intrusive, measures are available; and if (in the case of subclause g) equivalent domestic restrictions are imposed as well. The GATT thus allows exceptions from its trade disciplines where environmental objectives are concerned, but seeks to ensure that these measures do not give rise to discrimination or protectionism (Neumayer 2001: 24–25).

Like many other elements of the GATT, the conditions set out in Article XX are ambiguous and have given rise to conflicting interpretations. A number of disputes have arisen that centre on the use of Article XX as a rationale for imposing trade restrictions. We review some of these cases and the evolution of GATT/WTO jurisdiction below. It is worth noting in this context, however, that Article XX contains provisions that are bound to come into conflict with a wide range of

---

[1]   A comprehensive guide to WTO law and jurisdiction in relation to environmental matters can be found in Bernasconi-Osterwalder et al. (2006).

environmental policies. This is most clearly the case with the non-discrimination rule for like products. As a general rule, GATT provisions prohibit member states from restricting trade based on the way in which goods have been produced, so-called process and production methods (PPMs). From an environmental perspective, however, it is often the production process that gives rise to concern and that is targeted by environmental measures (for example greenhouse gas emissions of manufacturing processes). Indeed, many international environmental agreements are about restricting the environmentally damaging side-effects of global economic activities, and environmentalists have long complained about the GATT's 'chilling' effect on taking out trade measures focused on polluting production methods (Eckersley 2004).

More recently, the creation of the WTO at the end of the Uruguay Round has signalled a greater willingness in the trading system to recognize the legitimacy of environmental policies (Charnovitz 2007). This is most clearly evident in the preamble of the Marrakesh Agreement Establishing the WTO, which lists sustainable development and environmental protection as explicit objectives for the trading system. Although not legally binding, the preamble represents an important departure from the GATT's previous philosophy of a strict separation of trade and environmental policy. Furthermore, because the WTO also strengthened the GATT's dispute settlement mechanism and made its rulings legally binding, the evolving WTO jurisdiction on cases involving environmental trade measures has assumed greater importance in balancing the competing perspectives of trade and environmental protection.

Other notable achievements of the Uruguay Round that are of relevance to the trade–environment link include the Agreements on Technical Barriers to Trade (TBT) and on the Application of Sanitary and Phytosanitary Measures (SPS). The TBT agreement sets rules for the use of technical regulations and standards with a view to minimizing their trade-distorting effect (Stein 2009). It recognizes the right of countries to impose such measures to protect human health and the environment, but stipulates that these should not be more trade-restrictive than necessary. For example, an environmental label that informs consumers about the potential health risks associated with a particular product could be considered acceptable under WTO rules if it is applied in a non-discriminatory manner. However, a label that aims solely at PPM characteristics of a product (such as carbon-intensity of car manufacturing) might fall foul of the TBT agreement. This applies particularly to mandatory standards and regulations imposed by governments, whereas measures such as voluntary eco-labels, which are created by private actors, do not fall under WTO jurisdiction.

The SPS agreement, which deals with measures to protect human, animal or plant life or health, similarly allows states to take such measures where they don't lead to discrimination or disguised restrictions on international trade (Charnovitz 1999). Both the TBT and SPS agreements encourage the harmonization of standards or the creation of international standards, such as through multilateral environmental agreements. Article 2.2 of the Agreement further specifies that SPS measures are to be based on scientific principles of risk assessment and sufficient scientific evidence. This requirement can be temporarily suspended where 'relevant scientific evidence is insufficient', but additional scientific information is to be obtained to carry out a full risk assessment 'within a reasonable period of time' (Article 5.7). The SPS Agreement is the only trade agreement that formally recognizes precaution as a justification for taking trade measures where there is scientific uncertainty but some evidence of potential harm. The question that has repeatedly pitted the WTO against environmentalists is whether such uncertainty is only a temporary phenomenon or a more persistent and thus long-term problem that pervades many areas of environmental policymaking, such as food safety and genetically modified organisms (Isaac and Kerr 2007; Post 2006).

Multilateral Environmental Agreements, Trade Measures and the WTO

Well over 200 multilateral environmental agreements (MEAs) have come into existence since the first United Nations (UN) environment conference in 1972. Some treaties, such as the UN Framework Convention on Climate Change (UNFCCC), have achieved near-universal membership, while others are of a more regional nature or represent small clubs of countries. A small but growing proportion of these MEAs include trade measures among their regulatory instruments. As trade restrictions become more popular in global environmental policymaking, concern is rising that these measures will increasingly come into conflict with WTO rules.

The definition of trade measures in MEAs is fairly wide and often imprecise. It most commonly refers to various forms of restrictions on trade for environmental purposes, such as bans on the trade of certain polluting substances or embargoes on specific countries that are in breach of environmental obligations. It may also include other measures that have an indirect trade impact, such as reporting requirements, labelling systems, prior consent requirements, or fiscal instruments (such as taxes, subsidies) (Brack and Gray 2003: 5–6). Some MEAs are designed to regulate trade. The Convention on Trade in Endangered Species (CITES), for example, uses trade restrictions to control and, where necessary, ban the transboundary movement of animal and plant species that are close to extinction. It also uses trade restrictions as a form of punishment for those parties that do not comply with its provisions. Other treaties use trade restrictions as one of many instruments to support their main environmental goal. One such example is the Montreal Protocol on ozone layer depletion, which imposes a phase-out schedule for certain chemical substances that harm the stratospheric ozone layer. The treaty also includes a ban on trade in these substances with countries that have not ratified the Protocol, the so-called non-parties (Brack 1996).

Trade measures have become popular instruments in MEAs for a number of reasons. They broadly serve three purposes (see Brack and Gray 2003: 13–15):

- Target environmental harm: Most trade measures in MEAs seek to tackle environmental problems by restricting the international movement of products or species that are potentially harmful or endangered (such as CITES, Basel Convention on the Control of Transboundary Movements of Hazardous Wastes and Their Disposal, Cartagena Protocol on Biosafety).
- Promote compliance and regime effectiveness: some MEAs use trade measures to ensure the effective operation of an environmental regime. For example, restrictions may be imposed to punish countries that do not fully comply with a regime's provisions, or to prevent industrial flight to non-parties, so-called 'leakage'.
- Encourage participation in environmental regimes: trade restrictions are also seen as a form of pressure on countries that are reluctant to join an environmental regime. For example, the Montreal Protocol's prohibition of trade with non-parties encouraged some countries to join the Agreement to prevent being excluded from the international trade in regulated substances and products containing them.

While trade measures have become a central element of international environmental treaties, they pose certain problems from a trade perspective. As discussed above, WTO rules require environmental trade measures to be non-discriminatory, that is they should not discriminate between like products from different WTO members or between domestic and international production. Where environmental treaties target products because of the underlying process and production methods rather than environmental quality of the product itself, any resulting trade interference could be seen to be in breach of WTO obligations. A further area where MEAs and the WTO rules could clash is where one party to an MEA uses trade sanctions against a non-party, but both parties are members of the WTO. In such cases, the party that suffers a trade sanction could take action under the WTO alleging breach of trade rules. As yet, no WTO member has challenged an MEA in the WTO's dispute settlement mechanism. However, as the number of environmental treaties with trade restrictions grows and the value of the affected trade increases, a future conflict over the application of MEA-based trade restrictions cannot be ruled out.

One area where WTO–MEA tensions may surface in the not too distant future is climate change. Indeed, the potential use of climate regulation to justify restrictions on trade in carbon-intensive goods has raised considerable interest and concern in the academic and policy community (for an overview, see UNEP 2009). Overlaps between trade and international policies aimed at reducing carbon emissions are inevitable, given the centrality of fossil fuel-based energy to international shipping and manufacturing. As yet, the international climate regime does not include explicit trade measures. But a successor agreement to the Kyoto Protocol, which expires in 2012, may include such measures, and if no comprehensive climate regime is agreed for the post-2012 era, then national or regional climate policies may include some form of border tax adjustment to deal with the competitiveness effects of an uneven regulatory environment (Houser et al. 2008). One way or the other, climate policy is bound to come into contact, and potentially conflict, with WTO rules.

What do recent WTO dispute settlement cases tell us about the evolution of WTO jurisdiction on trade–environment conflicts? The next section reviews the most high-profile environment-related trade disputes of the last 20 years, before considering the current state of play in multilateral negotiations.

Trends in WTO Jurisprudence

So far, only a very small fraction of the over 500 disputes that have been considered under the GATT/WTO dispute settlement mechanism relate to environmental issues, and virtually all of them occurred over the past two decades. Despite their small number, environment-related trade disputes have attracted a great deal of public attention. A closer examination of the most important cases reveals important developments in international trade jurisdiction.[2]

The Tuna–Dolphin Case

One of the earliest and most controversial trade–environment disputes concerned a US ban on certain tuna imports as part of a wider effort to protect dolphins. The 1972 Marine Mammal Protection Act (MMPA) required US fishermen to use dolphin-safe fishing methods to prevent the unwanted trapping of dolphins in purse seine nets used by tuna fishing fleets. In 1984, the US Congress added a Direct Embargo Provision to the MMPA that allowed the US to impose import bans on tuna from countries that did not employ dolphin-safe fishing methods. This trade measure was designed to prevent foreign competition from circumventing the MMPA's provisions and gaining an unjustified competitive advantage over US fishermen. When the United States implemented an embargo on tuna imports from Mexico and a few other countries in 1990, Mexico filed a complaint with the GATT arguing, among others, that the US ban was illegal as it was focused on process and production methods (type of nets that trap dolphins), rather than the product itself (tuna). Mexico further argued that the United States was not allowed to use GATT Article XX to force other countries to abide by its domestic environmental laws (extraterritoriality). The GATT panel that heard the case decided in Mexico's favour in 1991, but the ruling never became legally binding. In light of the upcoming negotiations on the North American Free Trade Agreement (NAFTA), Mexico decided not to demand the formal adoption of the decision. In any case, the GATT rules gave any party, such as the United States, the right to veto

---

[2]   An overview of these and other environment-related cases, as well as panel and appellate body reports, can be found at: www.wto.org/english/tratop_e/dispu_e/dispu_status_e.htm.

a panel decision. The decision caused uproar among environmentalists and led to a protracted debate in the 1990s about whether the GATT was fundamentally hostile to environmental concerns (Esty 1994).

The US–Gasoline Case

In 1990, the United States amended the Clean Air Act (CAA) in an effort to improve air quality by reducing adverse emissions from gasoline use. The law mandated the sale of reformulated (that is, cleaner) gasoline in heavily populated urban areas but permitted the continued sale of conventional gasoline in more rural areas. To prevent a shift in inexpensive but highly polluting gasoline ingredients from urban to rural areas, the law also stipulated that conventional gasoline must remain as clean as it was in 1990 (the baseline). By and large, domestic refiners were allowed to use individual baselines that were actually in use in 1990, while foreign producers had to follow an average baseline set by the Environmental Protection Agency. This, Venezuela and Brazil argued, was in conflict with Article III of the GATT as it discriminated against imported products. In 1996, the WTO Appellate Body decided that the baseline establishment methods were indeed inconsistent with Article III and could not be justified by Article XX, as the United States had claimed. However, the Appellate Body found that the US measures were aimed at the conservation of natural resources, and that WTO members were free to set their own environmental objectives, provided they do so in conformity with WTO rules, in particular with regard to the treatment of domestic and foreign products. The dispute settlement body, now operating under the strengthened rules of the WTO agreement, thus took a broader view of the environmental purpose of the trade measure and did not focus solely on the discriminatory nature of the measure (Trebilcock and Howse 2005).

The Shrimp–Turtles Case

A similar case to the *tuna–dolphin* dispute emerged in 1997, when India, Malaysia, Pakistan and Thailand filed complaints at the WTO against a US decision to force foreign shrimp trawlers to use so-called 'turtle excluder devices' (TEDs) when fishing in areas where sea turtles are present. The plaintiffs argued that this measure, which was based on the US Endangered Species Act of 1973, was in breach of WTO rules as it threatened foreign producers with a trade ban if they did not comply with US environmental law. Again, the case was decided under the enhanced powers of the WTO agreement and in the context of the WTO's greater emphasis on balancing free trade with environmental sustainability. In 1998, the dispute settlement body (DSB) ruled that the US import ban was generally a legitimate policy with regard to provisions under Article XX related to 'exhaustible natural resources'. However, it also found that the way the ban operated and the fact that the United States had previously negotiated treaties on sea turtle protection with some but not all affected countries, constituted 'arbitrary and unjustifiable discrimination' between WTO members. The United States subsequently changed its rules to be targeted at individual shipments rather than at countries – a practice that the WTO decided was justified under Article XX. While the United States technically lost the initial case, the decision marked an important shift in WTO jurisdiction as it essentially acknowledged that in certain circumstances, countries can use trade measures with the aim of protecting natural resources. The United States lost the case not because it aimed to protect the environment but because it had designed the measure in a discriminatory way – similar to the above gasoline case. Critically for the debate on whether the WTO and environmental policies are compatible, the ruling also pointed to the possibility that trade restrictions can be based on process and production methods in another country if these restrictions do not arbitrarily and unjustifiably discriminate between different countries (Howse 2002).

The EC–Biotech Case

A series of food and feed safety scares in Europe in the late 1980s and in the 1990s created considerable public pressure for more stringent food safety measures at the European level. In the second half of the 1990s, NGO campaigns and consumer hostility against genetically modified organisms (GMOs) led the EU to impose a de facto moratorium on GMO approvals and imports. Under pressure from their farming and biotechnology sectors, the United States, Canada and Argentina in 2003 brought a WTO case against the EU's restrictions on the marketing of GMOs. At the heart of the dispute was the question whether the EU was entitled to act in a precautionary manner even though a high degree of scientific uncertainty surrounded the GMO safety debate. The use of the WTO as a forum to settle a dispute over the appropriate use of precaution in environmental risk regulation proved controversial, not least since the Cartagena Protocol on Biosafety had been adopted in 2000 against US resistance (Falkner 2007). In 2006, the WTO ruled against the EU on procedural grounds, finding that the de facto GMO moratorium was in violation of WTO law, but did not pass a substantive judgment on the WTO consistency of the EU's precautionary GMO legislation as such. By the time the ruling was announced, the EU had already revised its regulations on GMOs and lifted its moratorium at least partially, even though its GMO approval process remains complex and prone to substantial delays due to domestic resistance to agricultural biotechnology (Lieberman and Gray 2008).

The Brazil–Retreaded Tyres Case

In late 2004, Brazil decided to strengthen its import restrictions on retreaded tyres (reconditioned old tyres for further use) from non-MERCOSUR countries, arguing that the disposal of such tyres creates environmental and human health problems. A year after Brazil imposed these restrictions, the EU asked for a WTO panel to consider whether they conformed to WTO rules. Brazil claimed that its import restrictions were justified under Article XX and that it was obliged to exclude MERCOSUR countries from the restrictions according to the rules of the customs union. The EU countered that the exemption of MERCOSUR countries from the import restriction constituted a breach of the WTO's non-discrimination rule, among others. Both the Panel and the Appellate Body ruled in 2007, albeit for different reasons, that Brazil's import restrictions were inconsistent with WTO rules and could not be justified by Article XX. Similar to earlier rulings such as *US–gasoline* or *shrimp–turtles*, the Appellate Body argued that import bans can be justified on environmental grounds, but that the chapeau (introductory provisions) of Article XX stipulates that they must not lead to 'arbitrary and unjustifiable discrimination between countries'. Brazil complied with the DSB's request to revise its laws to make them conform to WTO rules.

Overall Trends in WTO Jurisdiction

Over the past two decades, GATT/WTO jurisdiction on environment-related trade measures has changed considerably. Earlier rulings as in the *tuna–dolphin* case insisted that trade restrictions must not be aimed at process and production methods (PPMs) outside a country's own jurisdiction, a position that threatened to undermine many trade-related environmental policies. Soon after this decision, however, the *US–gasoline* case marked the cautious beginning of a less restrictive interpretation of environmental measures. While the WTO panel stressed that trade measures must not discriminate among countries, it acknowledged that they can be based on grounds of environmental protection. The *shrimp–turtle* case is widely seen as a watershed in the WTO's interpretation of environmental trade measures. The decision almost reversed the earlier *tuna–dolphin* decision by arguing that a trade measure based on PPMs *can* be directed at other countries under Article XX, and that animals can qualify as an 'exhaustible natural resource' that may be protected through trade bans. In the *EC–biotech* case, the WTO Panel reinforced the importance of non-discrimination and the proper application of regulatory procedures, but acknowledged the importance of scientific uncertainty in justifying trade restrictions, arguing that a moratorium amidst scientific uncertainty need not necessarily violate international trade law.

Thus, WTO jurisdiction has gradually come to accept that trade-restricting measures under Article XX can be justified for environmental reasons, but continues to insist that they must not constitute an arbitrary and/or unjustifiable discrimination. Indeed, the primary reason for why environmental measures in *gasoline*, *shrimp–turtle*, and *retreaded tyres* were found to be in breach of WTO rules was not the ultimate objective of these measures but the way in which they had been applied. As DeSombre and Barkin (2002) argue, the WTO ruled against these measures not because they were inherently bad, but because they 'were either clear attempts at industrial protection dressed up in environmentalist clothes, or they were poorly thought through and inappropriate tools for the environmental management intended'.

The Committee on Trade and Environment and the Doha Round

One of the outcomes of the Uruguay Round was the creation of the Committee on Trade and Environment (CTE) in 1995, which was tasked to consider the relationship between environmental and trade measures, and to formulate recommendations on how to modify WTO rules with regard to environmental policy if modifications are required. The CTE's initial work programme covered an extensive policy terrain, ranging from the relationship between MEAs and WTO rules to issues related to transparency, market access, intellectual property rights, and arrangements with NGOs.

To date, the CTE has made only minimal progress in trying to resolve the issues on its agenda. At best, it produced a series of background studies and annual reports on trade–environment matters and provided a forum for different stakeholders from national and international bodies to exchange their views (Charnovitz 2007; Neumayer 2004). At the heart of the CTE's failure to resolve any of the issues on its agenda are deep-seated differences in national interests, particularly between developed and developing countries, but also a more general unwillingness among participants to address the underlying tensions between WTO norms and principles and those of environmental regimes (Gabler 2010).

The role of the CTE in the WTO framework changed with the launch of the Doha Round in 2001, when it was given a negotiating mandate at the WTO Trade Negotiations Committee (TNC). The 2001 WTO Doha Ministerial Declaration recognizes the importance of 'enhancing the mutual supportiveness of trade and environment' (paragraph 31) and calls for 'the reduction or, as appropriate, elimination of tariffs and non-tariff barriers to environmental goods and services' (paragraph 31). Other elements of the negotiation mandate include the relationship between the WTO and MEAs and procedures for information exchange between MEAs and WTO committees. Little progress has been made in any of these areas. Notwithstanding the potentially large gains from the liberalization of environmental goods and services (Steenblik et al. 2005), because 'environmental goods' were not defined in the Doha mandate, much of the focus in negotiations has been on competing attempts to arrive at a workable definition. This task is further complicated by the fact that technological progress makes it difficult to establish definite lists of goods that fall into this category.

Conclusion

The trade–environment nexus remains a controversial and challenging issue on the international trade agenda. Some progress has been made in identifying the circumstances in which international trade and environmental protection can be mutually compatible, but several areas of contention and conflict remain.

The first area relates to the WTO's general approach to environmental policy. Some observers call on the WTO to become more engaged with environmental issues, not least since the WTO already adjudicates cases that involve conflicts between environmental measures and international trade law. Given the WTO's de facto impact on global environmental policy, they argue that the WTO should take on more formal environmental responsibilities, even though details of such a closer engagement with the global environmental agenda remain sketchy. On the other hand, concerns have been raised that environmental protection might actually take a backseat on the international trade agenda due to an increasing use of bilateral agreements instead of multilateral ones and a generally low interest among some countries on issues related to environmental protection (Neumayer 2004). The WTO has so far trod a careful path through this debate, stating repeatedly that, while it aims to contribute to sustainable development, it does not consider itself as an environmental protection agency (WTO 2004).

The second area relates to the interpretation of existing legal provisions. Despite an evolving mandate and institutional framework, the WTO has had significant impact on certain environmental measures, as outlined above. Past decisions have clarified what a 'necessary' environmental measure is; what is meant by 'exhaustible natural resource'; whether measures can extend extraterritorially; and how 'arbitrary' and 'unjustifiable' should be interpreted under the chapeau of Article XX. Disagreement still exists, however, with regard to environmental measures aimed at PPMs, especially when they are 'unincorporated', that is when they cannot be detected in the final product. The definition and use of precaution remains equally contested, as has been illustrated by the *EC–biotech* case and the question of 'sound' science as a criterion for policymaking versus a broader interpretation of the evidence basis for risk assessment.

The third area relates to the question of inclusiveness and transparency of decisionmaking. While the CTE has been tasked with addressing the relationship between MEAs and the WTO, both in institutional and jurisdictional terms, there remains considerable debate on how to integrate the two, especially when the former continue to employ trade-restricting measures that remain vulnerable to challenges under WTO law (Eckersley 2004; Palmer and Tarasofsky 2007). Another contentious point is the access of external stakeholders, especially civil society and NGOs, to WTO decisionmaking processes. While the WTO has promoted dialogue with interested organizations, NGOs continue to raise concerns about the lack of transparency in the WTO's deliberations and negotiations, especially with regard to environmental issues.

The fourth and final area relates to the increasingly important impact of the climate change debate on international trade. As states explore different options for reducing greenhouse gas emissions, it is becoming increasingly clear that trade measures will be part of the international effort to combat global warming. This could be in the form of border tax adjustment to address international competitiveness issues, preferential treatment of climate-friendly goods and services, renewable energy subsidies and product labels indicating carbon content, among others (Brewer 2010). Efforts to enforce international climate policy through trade measures may severely test the scope of Article XX (Frankel 2009), and a push to target carbon-content in internationally traded goods may test the WTO's willingness to accept trade measures that are based on PPMs (Hufbauer and Kim 2009). The WTO itself recognizes its responsibility in the international community to address climate change as part of its sustainable development agenda, but sees its role primarily as an arbiter of conflicts. The challenge will be to avoid the trap of green protectionism where general trade restrictions are used to seek compliance with quite distinct climate goals. Climate policy may yet prove to be the biggest challenge for the WTO's ability to manage the trade–environment relationship.

References

Anderson, K. and McKibbin, W.J. 2000. Reducing coal subsidies and trade barriers: their contribution to greenhouse gas abatement. *Environment and Development Economics* 5(4): 457–481.

Bernasconi-Osterwalder, N., Magraw, D., Oliva, M.J., Orellana, M. and Tuerk, E. 2006. *Environment and Trade: A Guide to WTO Jurisprudence*. London: Earthscan.

Bhagwati, J. 2004. *In Defense of Globalization*. Oxford: Oxford University Press.

Bhagwati, J. and Srinivasan, T.N. 1996. Trade and environment: does environmental diversity detract from the case for free trade?, in *Fair Trade and Harmonisation: Prerequisites for Free Trade?*, edited by J. Bhagwati and R. Hudec. Cambridge, MA: MIT Press: 159–199.

Brack, D. 1996. *International Trade and the Montreal Protocol*. London: Earthscan.

Brack, D. and Gray, K. 2003. *Multilateral Environmental Agreements and the WTO*. London: The Royal Institute of International Affairs.

Brewer, T.L. 2010. Trade policies and climate change policies: a rapidly expanding joint agenda. *The World Economy* 33(6): 799–809.

Charnovitz, S. 1999. Improving the agreement on sanitary and phytosanitary standards, in *Trade, Environment, and the Millennium*, edited by G.P. Sampson and W.B. Chambers. Tokyo: United Nations University Press: 171–194.

Charnovitz, S. 2007. The WTO's environmental progress. *Journal of International Economic Law* 10(3): 685–706.

Daly, H.E. 1993. The perils of free trade. *Scientific American* 269(5): 50–57.

DeSombre, R. and Barkin J.S. 2002. Turtles and trade: the WTO's acceptance of environmental trade restrictions. *Global Environmental Politics* 2(1): 12–18.

Eckersley, R. 2004. The big chill: the WTO and multilateral environmental agreements. *Global Environmental Politics* 4(2): 24–50.

Economy, E.C. 2004. *The River Runs Black: The Environmental Challenge to China's Future*. Ithaca: Cornell University Press.

Esty, D. 1994. *Greening the GATT*. Washington, DC: Institute for International Economics.

Falkner, R. 2007. The political economy of 'Normative Power' Europe: EU environmental leadership in international biotechnology regulation. *Journal of European Public Policy* 14(4): 507–526.

Frankel, J.A. 2009. Addressing the leakage/competitiveness issue in climate change policy proposals, in *Climate Change, Trade, and Competitiveness: Is a Collision Inevitable?*, edited by I. Sorkin and L. Brainard. Washington, DC: Brookings Institution Press: 69–91.

Gabler, M. 2010. Norms, institutions and social learning: an explanation for weak policy integration in the WTO's Committee on Trade and Environment. *Global Environmental Politics* 10(2): 80–117.

Gallagher, K.P. 2004. *Free Trade and the Environment: Mexico, NAFTA, and Beyond*. Palo Alto: Stanford University Press.

Garcia-Johnson, R. 2000. *Exporting Environmentalism: U.S. Multinational Chemical Corporations in Brazil and Mexico*. Cambridge, MA: MIT Press.

Goldsmith, E. and Mander, J. (eds). 2001. *The Case Against the Global Economy: And for a Turn Towards Localization*. London: Earthscan.

Grossman, G.M. and Krueger, A. 1993. Environmental impacts of a North American Free Trade Agreement, in *The US–Mexico Free Trade Agreement*, edited by P. Garber. Cambridge, MA: MIT Press: 13–56.

Hettige, H., Mani, M. and Wheeler, D. 1998. Industrial pollution in economic development: Kuznets revisited. *World Bank Development Research Group Working Paper No. 1876*. Washington, DC: World Bank.

Heydon, K. and Woolcock, S. 2009. *The Rise of Bilateralism: Comparing American, European and Asian Approaches to Preferential Trade Agreements*. Tokyo: United Nations University Press.

Houser, T., Bradley, R., Childs, B., Staley, B., Werksman, J. and Heilmayr, R. 2008. *Leveling the Carbon Playing Field: International Competition and US Climate Policy Design*. Washington, DC: The Peterson Institute for International Economics.

Howse, R. 2002. The Appellate Body rulings in the Shrimp/Turtle Case: a new legal baseline for the trade and environment debate. *Columbia Journal of Environmental Law* 27(2): 491–521.

Hufbauer, G.C. and Kim, J. 2009. *The World Trade Organization and Climate Change: Challenges and Options*. Washington, DC: The Peterson Institute for International Economics.

Isaac, G.E. and Kerr, W.A. 2007. The biosafety protocol and the WTO: concert or conflict?, in *The International Politics of Genetically Modified Food: Diplomacy, Trade and Law*, edited by R. Falkner. Basingstoke: Palgrave Macmillan: 195–212.

Lieberman, S. and Gray, T. 2008. The World Trade Organization's report on the EU's moratorium on biotech products: the wisdom of the US challenge to the EU in the WTO. *Global Environmental Politics* 8(1): 33–52.

Neumayer, E. 2001. *Greening Trade and Investment: Environmental Protection Without Protectionism*. London: Earthscan.

Neumayer, E. 2004. The WTO and the environment: its past record is better than critics believe, but the future outlook is bleak. *Global Environmental Politics*, 4(3): 1–8.

OECD 2005. Environmental requirements and market access, *OECD Trade Policy Studies*. Paris: OECD.

Palmer, A. and Tarasofsky, R. 2007 *The Doha Round and Beyond: Towards a Lasting Relationship Between the WTO and the International Environmental Regime*. London: Chatham House.

Post, D.L. 2006. The precautionary principle and risk assessment in international food safety: how the World Trade Organization influences standards. *Risk Analysis* 26(5): 1259–1273.

Princen, T. 1997. The shading and distancing of commerce: when internationalization is not enough. *Ecological Economics* 20: 235–253.

Princen, T., Maniates, M. and Conca, K. (eds). 2002. *Confronting Consumption*. Cambridge, MA: MIT Press.

Reppelin-Hill, V. 1999. Trade and environment: an empirical analysis of the technology effect in the steel industry. *Journal of Environmental Economics and Management* 38(3): 283–301.

Sampson, G.P. 2005. *The WTO and Sustainable Development*. Tokyo: United Nations University Press.

Steenblik, R., Drouet, D. and Stubbs, G. 2005. Synergies between trade in environmental services and trade in environmental goods. *OECD Trade and Environment Working Paper* 2005–1. Paris: OECD.

Stein, J. 2009. The legal status of eco-labels and product and process methods in the World Trade Organization. *American Journal of Economics and Business Administration* 1(4): 285–295.

Trebilcock, M.J. and Howse, R. 2005. *The Regulation of International Trade*. 3rd Edition. New York: Routledge.

UNEP. 2009. *Climate and Trade Policies in a Post-2012 World*. Nairobi: UNEP.

WTO. 2004. *Trade and Environment at the WTO*. Geneva: WTO.

Trade and Risk Assessment

David Robertson

Introduction

There is more risk evident in the international trading system today than at any time since the end of the Second World War. The difficulties surrounding the WTO Doha Development Agenda since it was launched in November 2001, and the widespread resort to preferential trade arrangements since the closing stages of the Uruguay Round are evidence that the multilateral trading system is under stress. Activist non-government organizations (NGOs) are pursuing anti-trade agendas at international meetings and conferences, while promoting environment protection agendas, social programmes and global governance, and attacking multilateralism and globalization. The uncertainties created are introducing new and unforeseen risks into international commerce.

The adoption of the GATT after the Second World War was intended to avoid the ruinous beggar-my-neighbour economic policies of the depressed pre-war decade, comprising increasing trade protection and competitive exchange rate depreciation. Post-Second World War recovery took time, but the economic disruptions that had occurred after the First World War were avoided. Global trade grew three times faster than GDP in the five decades after 1945. The GATT rules gave reassurance to international traders, and insurance costs of freight and transport covering trade risks soon adjusted. Unit costs of insurance (like transport costs) declined as a proportion of traded values as confidence returned and transport and communications technologies advanced.[1]

The Final Act of the Uruguay Round trade negotiations (1994) established the World Trade Organization, which incorporated the GATT (1947) and included many new agreements, decisions and declarations on trade in goods and services. The complexity of WTO agreements, decisions and declarations increased the need for arbitration and interpretation of complex accords and new commitments. This has been referred to as *the lawyers' revenge* because whereas GATT disputes had

---

[1]   For a description and analysis of post-Second World War international economics see Robertson (2006).

been resolved by negotiations between officials, the new WTO processes often require legal judgements to enforce and interpret decisions.

The fall of the Berlin wall in 1989 restored political freedom in Eastern Europe and the role of 'civil society' in easing the process to democracy enhanced the status of NGOs in western countries. The interference from NGOs, however, complicated the closing stages of the Uruguay Round negotiations, although little account was given to their concerns in the Uruguay Round Final Act (1994). Unfortunately, the special economic interests of new developing country members were similarly ignored. This allowed a natural alliance to form in international meetings between NGOs promoting their interests in areas such as the environment, health and safety standards and social justice and income disparities, and interests of developing countries.

The closing decade of the twentieth century produced contrasting successes. 'Globalization' brought economic prosperity, enhanced by the dispersion of new technologies, and their rapid adoption across the world. However, antipathetic groups formed that, for a variety of motives, opposed 'globalization'. These NGOs represented interests stretching from insular nationalism to advocacy of global governance, built around the United Nations (UN).

As the 1990s progressed, NGOs began to combine their activities to achieve greater impact, sometimes resorting to violence. International meetings became key targets, including the GATT (and later WTO) meetings. NGO activists demanded participation in GATT/WTO meetings, alongside governments, and proposed that trade measures should be used to prevent 'damage to the environment', to assist development in poor countries, and in other ways to improve the world. Among the more extreme groups, it is doubtful if they saw any virtue in trade liberalization raising living standards. The NGOs demanded that they should be permitted to attend and to speak at WTO meetings, alongside governments. That the WTO (GATT) is an inter-government agency was lost on these protesters. Apparently, NGO definitions of 'democracy' require that anyone who wants to speak – or protest – at any forum should be able to do so at any international meeting.

These independent voices have complicated international agencies and their agendas. Moreover, their 'actions' make good copy for the 'media'. Minority opinions are broadcast not only through legitimate journals and programmes, but any sensational statement on the Internet (true or not) is likely to be repeated – and exaggerated. Official responses from governments and international agencies are then evaluated against the NGO's claims. Blocking official action by governments and international agencies is the driving force for many NGOs, which much of the media encourages.

The Precautionary Principle

One of the most effective instruments in the NGOs' armoury is 'the precautionary principle', which was inflicted on the world in the chaos of the UN Conference on Environment and Development (UNCED), held in Rio de Janeiro in 1992 ('The Earth Summit'). This gathering exposed the whole world to fears about damage to the global environment from economic growth. It forced many ill-prepared governments to accept far-reaching commitments that were not properly understood at the time. This was a triumph for the United Nations Secretariat, but above all for the well-organized 'green movement'. The meeting generated several new UN agencies, which have provided convenient platforms for NGOs.

'The precautionary principle' became the foundation of many new agreements that imposed restrictions on economic and scientific activities. Since it was incorporated into the UN Environment Programme (UNEP) in 1994,[2] the precautionary principle has been reiterated in UN circles at every opportunity.

The Rio meeting in 1992 granted thousands of 'green' activists free access to meeting rooms, where they could contact and influence national delegations. Such NGO intrusions into UN conferences became common. When some national governments objected, the UN Secretariat had to intervene, but some official delegations continue to include NGO representatives in their delegations as advisers.

Formulations of the precautionary principle had appeared in general discussions since late in the 1960s. By the 1980s it was appearing in UN documents, which suggested that when potential adverse effects are not fully understood, activities should not proceed. The European Community adopted the Precautionary Principle in 1990 (later revised to match the UN definition).

In 1998, the EC definition was revised again and made stronger:

> The precautionary principle is an approach to risk management that is applied in circumstances of scientific uncertainty, reflecting the need to take action in the face of potentially serious risks, without awaiting the results of scientific research. (EC Commission, Feb. 2000 COM(2000)1)

This seems to authorize action even without due cause.

Cass Sunstein (2005) suggests there are 20 or more definitions of the precautionary principle in use, stretching from the cautious versions where lack of decisive evidence of harm should not be grounds for refusing to regulate or to act even if cause and effect relationships are not established scientifically. The risk of trading with the EU when environmental agencies are free to act in such peremptory fashion is disturbing. Sunstein claims that European courts have no uniform definition, and some require that risks should be reduced 'to the lowest level reasonably imaginable'.

GATT article III states that 'measures to discriminate against products in international trade because of the manner in which they are produced' are not permitted. Yet this is precisely what NGOs seek to achieve; to differentiate and

---

[2]   The precautionary approach should be applied where there are threats of serious or irreversible damage; lack of full scientific certainty shall not be used as a reason for postponing cost-effective measures to prevent damage to the environment.

to target selected products, processes and producers they consider might damage the environment, often without presenting satisfactory evidence or scientific assessments. In GATT terms, an imported product must not be treated differently from an equivalent product made in the home market, regardless of production methods.

Many governments are under pressure from their consumers and resident 'green' groups (such as Greenpeace, WWF) to ban imports or trade dealings with 'offending' companies. These 'moralist' campaigns can damage international relations. Unfortunately, where their propaganda proves to be wrong, supporting media ignore the error and unfavourable incidents slip from the community memory.

GM Foods and Crops

In the closing years of the twentieth century, European governments and consumers were alerted by news that substantial proportions of US farmers' staple crops were produced using genetically modified (GM) seeds and that GM substances were used in some food processes. GM plant varieties had been progressively introduced into North American agriculture during the 1990s and these crops were harvested and treated as equivalent to traditional harvests. Frequently, these GM crops were stored with conventional varieties. No harmful consequences had been identified.

When this news that GM seed was being used reached the European media, the 'green' NGOs pounced on this opportunity to attack US farmers, with support from protectionist EU farmers, who were denied the benefits of the new technology. European environment ministers introduced bans on trial plantings of GM crops. EU consumers succumbed to the green propaganda quickly, because food safety standards in several EU countries had been inadequate to deal with previous food scares.[3] Imports that might contain so-called 'Frankenstein foods' were banned, and complaints arose over European food labelling. The hysteria generated by alarmist and unsubstantiated reactions in the EU spread quickly to other countries frightened of facing new EU trade discrimination. Farmers in EU countries that were trialling GM crops were threatened and their crops destroyed during a period of media madness.

The hysteria generated by NGO propaganda – and supported by the media – invoked 'the precautionary principle' without any genuine attempt to assess risks. Green groups forced commonly used processed foods that might contain imported GM ingredients to be withdrawn from shelves (such as tomato paste, soya breads). Consumer groups joined with 'the greens' to demand tougher labelling regulations.

---

[3] These included dioxins in Belgian pork and chicken, the Bovine Spongiform Encephalopathy (BSE) outbreak in Britain (causing hysteria in France) and swine fever in the Netherlands.

GM refers to modern techniques of genetic enhancement which allow improvements in desirable properties beyond those that can be readily achieved by natural selection and breeding. This genetic engineering is more certain and quicker than traditional breeding methods, but not fundamentally different at the molecular level.

The media dug up some insignificant (and irrelevant) evidence of damage from GM seeds,[4] but no firm evidence of harm from GM-modified plants or animals was found. In fact, GM experiments have benefitted mankind immensely. Plants and animals have been selectively bred for centuries, and without such experiments the world's population would be much smaller and poorer. Without the Green Revolution in the 1970s,[5] many Asian developing countries would not have been able to feed their populations and to sustain their industrialization. Concerns over rising food prices increased in 2007–8 as living standards in middle–income economies increased, only to be curtailed by the global financial crisis. However, according to US Department of Agriculture forecasts, food prices in 2011 would return to 2008 levels, even with good harvests that year.[6]

Mankind depends on microorganisms for everyday staples such as bread, wine, cheese and beer. These products were derived centuries before anyone heard of microbiology or genetic manipulation. Since the 1970s, biotechnology has created commercial industries and medicines (such as insulin), as well as enhancing agricultural and food processing. Many biotechnology inventions are used in fields such as chemical and textiles industries, mineral industries, and so on. Opponents of genetic manipulation tend to condemn all GM activities as a group. Yet GM is crucial to modern techniques of genetic enhancement for desirable properties, which improve life for everyone. It is not sorcery!

'Transgenic' refers to genes transferred between species that cannot be achieved using traditional breeding methods; such as inserting genes from bacteria into plants to make them resistant to insect attack. The infinite variety of such transfers could bring risks to food safety, but proper testing controls that. Unfortunately, anti-GM lobbies deny that they have similarities with normal breeding methods. Toxicologists know that there are no effective methods for testing conventional foods, some of which are known to be poisonous if not properly prepared (for

---

[4] A cause célèbre was a claim that American monarch butterflies that breed in the US mid-west corn-belt were affected by plantings of GM maize that carried a natural insecticide. After several months of academic dispute and Greenpeace invective, this link was rejected (Losey et al. 1999). Similarly, experiments where laboratory rats were force-fed raw GM potatoes to prove harmful effects were also discredited (Ewen and Pusztai 1999, cited by Robertson and Kellow 2001).

[5] Dr Norman Borlaug (Nobel Laureate 2006) invented short-stem grain varieties used to enhance food production.

[6] To some extent this relates to another 'green' neurosis. Corn prices have almost doubled in the past year because of increasing demand for ethanol (*The Financial Times*, 25 February 2011, 'US forecasts rising food prices').

instance kidney beans, almonds, manioc), while many plants that have natural protections against pests can be toxic (potatoes, fruits).[7]

Environmental lobbies seem most concerned about third-party damage; for example pest-resistant pollen escaping to cross-breed with weeds and create varieties resistant to weed-killers. The opportunity cost of not adopting the genetic alternatives is the continuation of serious environmental problems (and higher prices for popular consumables). Moreover, incorporating pesticide and insect-resistant genes into plant species reduces the quantities of chemicals applied to crops, most of which end up in waterways.[8]

The disruption and anxiety caused by this EU precautionary programme over GM revealed the consequences of precipitate action by authorities when faced with untested demands from NGOs. One of the principal barriers to marketing GM varieties in the EU was the insistence of member countries' governments that they should enforce their own rules on food safety. In consequence, the EU Commission could not enforce on EU member governments the WTO's 2006 Dispute Settlement Panel ruling against EU restrictions – a ruling dismissed as irrelevant by the EU trade commissioner Peter Mandelson.[9] (This was a convenient cop-out for the Commission because EU member governments cannot appear before WTO committees. As a result, the United States and Canada did not pursue their dispute further.)

The consequences of NGOs' campaigning to block GM products from EU consumers have not, of course, been evaluated. Moreover, the income losses of US and Canadian farmers (and others) have not been addressed. NGOs, and the irresponsible press and electronic media, produced no tangible evidence of dangers. Gradually, European farmers and food companies have begun to trial GM crops as the turmoil has receded.[10] Consumer activists were reduced to pursuing mandatory practices such as food labelling. (Green NGOs have found another campaign to pursue; to regulate all chemicals employed in EU production and consumption called REACH.)

---

[7]   The Royal Society (1998). Also, Professor Nancy Millis (chapter 14 in Robertson and Kellow 2001) assesses health risk effects of GM foods as extremely low.

[8]   Other objections to GM crops relate to the use of antibiotic marker genes (regarded as reducing effectiveness of medicines) and the search for terminator genes, which would require fresh seed to be purchased for each season.

[9]   The Financial Times, 9 February 2006, 'EU shrugs off WTO censure over curbs on modified food'.

[10]   Total land planted with GM crops across the globe in 2010 increased to 148 million hectares (10 per cent of total cropland). The three largest producers were the United States, Brazil and Argentina; maize, soya beans, cotton and canola dominate; developing countries are adopting GM crops readily; drought-tolerant maize and biotech rice are pending. (The Financial Times, 23 February 2011, 'Rapid growth in GM cropland'.)

Quarantine and Food Labelling (SPS–TBT)

The sanitary–phytosanitary agreement (SPS) (quarantine standards) was incorporated into the WTO to cover the application of food safety and animal and plant health regulations into the broader 'standards code' contained in the WTO Technical Barriers to Trade (TBT) agreement. These agreements, administered by WTO committees, are designed to prevent industrial standards (including labelling standards) and technical regulations being used as impediments to trade.

Measures to protect the environment, consumer interests and animal welfare are not mentioned in the SPS agreement[11] but may be addressed under GATT article XX (general exceptions). NGOs complain that GM products are not covered by the SPS. The SPS agreement, however, is intended to prevent misuse of the quarantine regulations, and judgements are based on scientific evidence. It does not apply to properties of plants or animals.

On the other hand, article XX provides for 'general exceptions' in special circumstances but they may not be used to discriminate between countries. NGOs argue that two provisions in article XX are relevant to environmental matters as a public concern:

- XX(b) allows exceptions 'necessary to protect human, animal or plant life or health';
- XX(g) allows exceptions 'relating to the conservation of exhaustible natural resources'.

In both cases, any measures introduced using these clauses would cause discrimination and encourage complaints. The EU favours global environmental agreements that take priority over WTO rules. Any member government may challenge specific measures introduced under article XX, but where disputed, they must be resolved according to the Dispute Settlement Undertaking.

There are still some gaps in the SPS agreement that offer opportunities for environmental arguments to be made, in terms of risk assessments or the design of standards for food safety and quarantine regulations, which are defined by standards organizations (such as FAO/WHO Codex Alimentarius, IPPC). The TBT agreement incorporates quality and labelling requirements, but it does not specifically provide a solution to controversies over GM foods.

The Committee on Trade and the Environment, established by WTO Ministerial Decision in Marrakesh (1994), has considered special measures to identify GM foods and crops for special treatment. However, specific labelling and bans on GM

---

[11] Key provisions of the SPS agreement: measures must be applied where necessary to achieve their purpose, based on scientific principles; measures must be non-discriminatory among countries where similar conditions apply, be transparent and not a disguised restriction on trade; measures must be based on international standards, unless justified by scientific judgement; risk analysis should be used to establish appropriate protection.

foods are not regarded as trade issues according to TBT and SPS provisions. The GM issue is skulking in the background.

The modern approach to risk assessment exposes weaknesses in the SPS agreement's insistence on scientific principles. Scientific evidence is not enough for some self-appointed NGO critics, unless it supports their political prejudices. As far as GM foods are concerned, respect for scientists among NGOs seems to be selective! Belief outweighs science when public outrage and moral indignation can be mobilized.

'Civil Society' as the EU Conscience

The latest NGO intervention in EU affairs is REACH – Registration, Evaluation, Authorisation and Restriction of Chemicals. This was adopted into EU legislation in November 2010. It has still to be approved by EU governments, but the REACH text has been under discussion with EU governments since 2003, so rejection is unlikely. It is intended to replace current legislation and will require reassessment of over 30,000 chemicals that were introduced into EU markets before 1981. It follows the same approach and has the same weaknesses as the GM programme; namely, it casts doubts in the minds of consumers about familiar chemicals, without presenting any evidence of damage or harm. Such scare campaigns tie up scarce resources (particularly scarce skilled labour).

Industries inside and outside the EU have disputed the need for this comprehensive testing and retesting of all chemicals, because it switches the onus of proof from regulators proving a chemical is dangerous to manufacturers proving they are safe.[12] The compromise was that safety of chemicals would be judged regardless of whether they are used in mass consumer products or in restricted laboratories. This was accepted to avoid even stricter measures proposed by green groups.

In 2006, EU officials managed to get this policy accepted as a 'Global Plan of Action' at a UN conference on international chemicals management in Dubai. So the UNEP can be expected to pursue a global acceptance of REACH. EU 'greens' are leading the world into expensive programmes of caution, and denying that market mechanisms are able to judge the costs and benefits of new technologies. The adoption of 'the precautionary principle' removes responsibilities from entrepreneurs, whose interests are at stake, into the realm of bureaucrats, who have nothing at stake. No attention seems to be given to the costs of delaying the arrival of new chemicals on the EU market, for the sake of precaution. It is, of course, possible to regard this as protectionist.

---

[12] This EU decision shows no recognition of the disasters caused when wrong decisions are made. For example, the ban on the use of DDT sprays in developing countries where mosquito-borne malaria was rife. This arose from pseudo-science in Rachel Carson's Silent Spring (1962), which was refuted within months (Kellow 2007: 153).

The protectionism inherent in the REACH programme will impact on international trade, especially if it is adopted only in the EU. Undoubtedly, the REACH process will delay new chemicals (or new uses of approved chemicals) from being used in EU industries until they are cleared. This is another intervention by EU officials at the behest of 'green' NGOs, without recognition of the costs imposed on EU consumers and producers. Delays in approving new chemical products and in recruiting qualified staff for official testing laboratories will impose unnecessary costs and delays on industries subject to market disciplines, which themselves ensure product safety. (According to reports, some green groups (such as Greenpeace, WWF, Friends of the Earth) believe the REACH agreement does not go far enough!)

The European Commission is one of the most prolific sources of new legislation and new requirements to control trade. The Commission insists that its trade partners should adhere to its regulations and repeatedly calls for other WTO members to adopt its rules. For example, in the lead up to a meeting on 'Trans-Atlantic market harmonisation', *The Financial Times* (19 February 2007) reported EU officials declaring:

> The single market gives the EU the potential to shape global norms and to ensure that fair rules are applied to worldwide trade and investment. The Single Market of the future should be the launch pad of an ambitious global agenda.

The EU Commission has frequently ignored or avoided WTO rules. Various findings by Dispute Settlement Panels, and upheld by the Appellate Body, have declared EU trade measures illegal according to WTO rules (for example banana imports from Latin America,[13] the US 'beef–hormones' case). The EU has resisted these rulings. Further recent examples are the imposition of 'the precautionary principle' and the REACH legislation, which are without doubt inconsistent with accepted WTO practice.

The EU is not alone in evading or ignoring WTO rules, of course. The United States has long avoided its antidumping commitments to GATT article VI; 'antidumping has evolved from an instrument of law aimed at preserving competition to a bureaucratic apparatus devoted to restricting it'.[14] In August 2010, the US Commerce Department proposed tightening antidumping rules, possibly to incorporate effects of 'misaligned currencies', targeting imports from China. So far no decision has been taken.

When the environment became a controversial international issue in the 1990s, the GATT, and later the WTO, came under attack from NGOs (and some governments) because they had no specific provisions to deal with environment protection. The first major disputes arose when US fishing fleets demanded embargoes on

---

[13]   One of the longest running trade disputes ended 3 February 2010, when the European Parliament ratified an EU–Latin American banana accord, which will be completed in 2020.

[14]   Ikenson (2010).

imports of foreign-caught shrimp and tuna, on grounds of endangering turtles and dolphins, respectively (see also Chapters 13 and 21). The Earth Island Institute, a US environment NGO, had sued the US government under US environment law and succeeded.[15] That US court decision was reversed after reviews by WTO dispute settlement panels and the Appellate Body, and resulted in intense criticism from environmental NGOs.

Dispute Settlement Understanding

The DSU incorporated into the WTO during the Uruguay Round negotiations was a significant step towards resolving disputes. The Secretariat's role in the GATT was to serve the Council of the Contracting Parties and the WTO Secretariat has the same limited independence. The member governments in Council initiate negotiations and approve decisions. If the Council could not reach a decision in the GATT, there was no means of redress. Yet serious disputes between members need to be resolved or the capacity to manage the trading system is lost.

In these circumstances, the Uruguay Round negotiators realized that rules and procedures were required to resolve disputes, using expert panels. And, in case of continuing disagreement between the disputing parties, an Appellate Body was needed to review disputed findings or conclusions from panel hearings. This provided a means to resolve disputes with a quasi-legal process, which opened opportunities for NGOs to participate.[16]

In the post-Uruguay Round discussions on the role of NGOs, there were different opinions. Some saw NGOs as bringing valuable insights and expertise, while most members saw the WTO as an intergovernmental treaty and a forum for negotiation, implying that the responsibility for consulting with 'civil society' should be at the national level. Under pressure, concessions were made for some NGOs to attend periodic WTO Ministerial Council meetings as observers. Gradually the Secretariat has increased its consultations with NGOs, at the official and the casual level. These were not all sweetness and light because NGOs themselves have conflicting interests.

The Dispute Settlement Body administers the dispute rules. A member claiming that benefits from a WTO agreement are nullified or impaired by failure of another member to meet their obligations under the agreement can request a dispute panel. A panel of trade experts is assembled to hear the case, and it can call witnesses to give evidence and/or to give technical advice. This enables NGOs to present

---

[15] These two cases aroused intense international interest among WTO members, NGOs and international lawyers, when the WTO Appellate Body made its decision on interpretation of GATT article XX and the Settlement of Disputes.

[16] Some NGO advocates present themselves as 'intellectual competitors' with governments in the search for optimal policies (Esty 1998 and 2002; for a reasoned response, see Henderson 2002).

amicus briefs to the panels, but these should not include legal opinion. Legal matters are the concern of the Appellate Body, and, where appropriate, *amicus briefs* are forwarded to the Appellate Body in the event of an appeal. However, the Appellate Body contains only legal experts, though technical experts can be summoned to give advice.

When early dispute settlement panels and the Appellate Body viewed environment issues sympathetically (for instance US cases on accidental damage to turtles and dolphins), some 'green' groups anticipated using trade regulations to restrict environmental damage, while some industries saw opportunities to reduce foreign competition in their domestic markets. However, NGOs argued that 'compliance processes' rather than 'confrontational litigation' should settle disputes. In other words, mediation, conciliation and arbitration techniques should be used to resolve disputes – a talking shop without end! (The Appellate Body is comprised of lawyers who, eventually, exercise their judgement.)

The operation of the Uruguay Round dispute settlement mechanism has provided a means to interpret WTO agreements in the light of changing circumstances. The line between interpretation and clarifying rights and obligations in these agreements is a fine one, and changes with the circumstances. Lawyers point out that dispute panels focus on trade and scientific evidence, but Appeals focus on legal procedures and ethical and social perceptions as they affect trade. Cottier (2001) blames 'the lack of a proper methodology referring to the social sciences, [which] should be developed to allow legal assessment of risk management; in particular, to include inquiries into the social and political acceptance of existing risk'. The entry of lawyers into dispute settlement has exposed economics to social scepticism, because lawyers introduce the precautionary principle into their judgements. (For the lawyers' view see McCall Smith (2003).)

Most trade and economic literature promotes strengthening the Dispute Settlement System (DSS) to increase security and predictability, and to reduce risk and uncertainty (Cottier 2001; Pauwelyn 2001). Some believe opening panel meetings and the Appellate Body to the public and allowing the WTO Secretariat to seek outside experts to assist the settlement process would enhance support for the process. On the other hand, GATT/WTO supporters declare that the DSS is to serve the rule of law in the WTO, and to ensure security and predictability in global trade; that is, to reduce risk.

Some disputes between major players have been difficult to resolve. The Latin America dispute over banana exports to the EU and the US–EU dispute over 'hormone-treated' beef, each lasted for more than a decade. The opening of WTO procedures to NGO participation would increase uncertainties over rules and outcomes. (Other disputes, such as the shrimp/turtle case and tuna/dolphin case, were returned to appeal panels in the 1990s before they were resolved under the DSS.)

Fortunately, dispute panels and appeal processes take time to reach their conclusions, so businesses are forewarned. But uncertainties about the global trading system are increasing with preferential trade agreements multiplying, while faith in the multilateral system and prospects for successful multilateral negotiations are receding.

The Brittle Trading System

Opening WTO processes to influences from 'civil society' (NGOs) increases risks for businesses, consumers and social structures. Weak coalition governments in OECD economies seem to be hostage to propaganda from 'green' NGOs. Even sources of information become unreliable when authorship of their reports is disguised.

For example, late in 2009, WTO and UNEP issued a joint report, *Trade and Climate Change*. It was described as 'A report explaining the connections between trade and climate change', and it was released without notice. The WTO Secretariat should have been embarrassed because, apparently, member countries were not made aware of its release. Even so, WTO member governments seem to have ignored the report. The report's cover declared it was a 'WTO–UNEP Report', yet the inside cover declared that the views expressed did not necessarily represent the views of the WTO Secretariat or UNEP (or member governments, presumably). So how and why was this report released? And why have member governments not commented on this renegade document?[17]

Newspapers reported the release of this document in the following terms:

- 'WTO declares backing for border taxes';
- 'WTO supports climate protection goals';
- 'WTO admits trade limits necessary to stop climate change';
- 'UN, WTO call for trade shift to halt climate change'.

The media interpretation of this report was misleading, and it enhanced public perceptions that priority should be given to 'global warming' claims over trade matters, without an international mandate.

An academic review of this renegade report criticized the mode of its release (Charnovitz 2010). Charnovitz acknowledged that WTO rules do not require that governments' trade liberalization should accord with social or environmental objectives. However, 'risk' is associated with international trade if countries change laws/rules as part of new environment protection procedures.

---

[17] The report was released just before the December 2009 Copenhagen meeting of the UN Framework Convention on Climate Change.

International Law has Changed

At the end of the Second World War, sovereignty was the dominating force for economic repair and reconstruction. Economic recovery depended on collaboration and good will, and financial generosity from the United States as far as Europe was concerned. Over the past 30 years or so, governments have faced new challenges in international relations. Many former dependencies have become independent, while sovereignty is now under siege from new political agents, at home and offshore. NGOs represent largely non-economic interests, such as environment groups with diverse concerns, 'civil society' promotes 'global governance' pursued through UN agencies, while development agencies seek to overcome poverty and disease.[18] There are complex questions over harmonization of international and domestic laws, especially in terms of extraterritorial applications of laws in international waters and in the atmosphere, where many environmental issues arise.

Besieged from all angles, governments have grown weaker and sought alliances that involve compromises. To meet new demands and to change preferences, new international organizations have evolved and non-state actors are claiming rights and obligations under international law. These developments increase risks and uncertainties facing traders. Weakening government sovereignty makes international cooperation more difficult. GATT/WTO was a leading example of effective cooperation, but evidence of its present weakness is apparent in the subsidiary role of trade matters in the G20 leaders' meetings on the continuing global financial crisis.

In many ways, GATT/WTO commitments of national governments are being usurped and the role of the WTO weakened by initiatives taken within the WTO Secretariat.[19] In particular, the GATT experiment to collaborate in trade liberalization led to negotiations that recognized fully the benefits of self-interest. The elementary model that reducing tariffs benefitted liberalizers was too simple. But governments did understand that tariffs could be used internally to divert rents from exporters to importers using 'optimum tariffs'.[20] This ensured that market power was employed to raise national living standards. The extent that tariffs were lowered by bilateral negotiations within the GATT, multilateralized by the most-favoured-nation commitment and economic benefits redistributed to raise living standards, was a genuine demonstration of 'the invisible hand' at work.

These issues are central to John Jackson's review of international economic cooperation and the role of law (Jackson 2006). It is evident that although

---

[18] See Robertson (2000).

[19] In December 2006, the WTO Council decided that new Preferential Trade Agreements (PTAs) should be notified to the WTO Secretariat for confidential review. These reviews are voluntary and held in confidence. This process was announced in Bangalore (17 January 2007), when the Director General, Pascal Lamy, praised PTAs as instruments of trade liberalization. This is a matter of opinion.

[20] Johnson (1953–4).

governments retain a role in the international order, they no longer have a monopoly over international events. When NGOs became disillusioned with governments, it implied rejection of democracy and markets. Technological advances in transport and communications, which stimulated changes in rules and institutions and allowed new processes to develop, brought globalization.

Jackson (2006) believes the GATT/WTO has the capacity to adapt to changes by using the powers of the Dispute Settlement Understanding. This process has not confined itself to application of GATT/WTO law, because its judicial decisions (DSB Appellate Body) involve an evolution of trade law by the acceptance of *amicus briefs* to resolve disputes between trade and environment interests. This raises the question of how far this mixture of interests could be developed without undermining the effectiveness of the WTO. How can economic costs be assessed against damage to rare species or forest clearing? Lawyers believe in 'justice', but comparing scenic beauty or rare species with gold in the bank is another matter!

Advances in many technologies have driven rising living standards and prosperity during the past 40 years. However, the success of market economics has created an anti-globalization backlash, based on identifying 'outsiders' among those disillusioned or neglected by governments and the globalization process. Globalization brought new political challenges, as well as economic changes. It brought into the international sphere issues that, traditionally, had been covered by national laws. That required rewriting international law into domestic law, and adapting domestic law to deal with international application. These adaptations require extreme cooperation between governments, which bring more challenges.

How can a new, strengthened international law be negotiated among contrary philosophies? International economic law has been weakened by 20 years of active opposition from the 'anti-globalization' NGOs, and the intervention of international lawyers.

Jackson's proposal to resolve the dilemma between WTO authority, national sovereignty and NGO independence is to intensify interaction among nations to safeguard globalization and to use compromises to achieve cooperation. This requires governments to surrender some independence and some authority to international agencies to achieve mutually beneficial cooperation (Low 2007). This would seem to be the only route to reducing risks and uncertainties, but it will need to be navigated with great care if national authority is not to be seriously eroded, leading to breakdown of international cooperation.

Risk and Uncertainty

Commercial risk is assessable for insurance, and an everyday event for businesses whether trading at home or overseas. Premiums are increased when uncertainties apply to participating institutions (government or private), or where political risks are threatening. In the past 20 years, however, general uncertainties have appeared that insurance agencies are unable to assess in advance, and substantial losses may occur as political circumstances change.

For example, the EU decision to ban GM crops affected decisions on North American farms that had planned to sow GM wheat or corn. Similarly, US ranchers using hormone treatments could not sell their beef in EU markets. Moreover, when many other countries followed the EU example, without any testing, this also affected farm exports. These import restrictions have been before WTO dispute panels for many years. Even if EU import bans are removed, however, the 'US first' advantage will have been lost. Some EU members are reviewing their positions, though they will have to overcome 'green' NGOs' trenchant opposition. Forward-looking EU farmers are doubtless already trialling GM crop varieties, realizing that an opportunity might have been missed while the embargo was in place. Nevertheless, the first entrepreneurs were denied 'rents' by intervention from 'green' NGOs that are not part of the market.[21] This is a new and uncertain force in markets that cannot be anticipated by innovators, traders or insurers.

The power of NGOs is intimidating governments. The press (and media generally) can report any kind of nonsense and rarely be required to retract mistakes or untruths, while governments seldom confront their tormenters.[22] This reluctance to confront the NGOs is evident in governments' attitudes to 'climate change', probably the most significant issue they face. Many questions are raised about the projected apocalypse. None are honoured with a response, only contempt. In many countries, governments have become multiparty coalitions, causing impotence and compromise which NGOs exploit using propaganda and fear of electoral losses. This is particularly evident in EU countries, where NGOs are financed from national and Community budgets, but not subject to the discipline of tax returns or general board meetings (Kellow 2007).

International institutions are alert to the growing weaknesses of national governments and they recognise the opportunity this provides to strengthen 'global governance'. UN agencies cooperate assiduously with NGOs as 'advocacy' groups and support their 'operational' functions in order to promote UN influence over national governments. The term 'global civil society' indicates their political ambition to bypass national governments and to promote 'global governance' (Robertson 2000). The UN charter provides for UNESCO to consult with NGOs, if they operate in two or more countries. National and international bureaucracies have expanded rapidly as government budgets have grown with administration of expensive social welfare programmes. Similarly, UN agencies and other international organizations (privately funded or depending on government

---

[21]   There are many examples of false or incomplete experiments that damaged businesses without any recompense or acknowledgement from 'green' protesters. Farmers cultivating GM crops were victims (Robertson and Kellow 2001; chapter 15, 16 for examples).

[22]   The UN–IPCC is a case in point. Several prominent members of IPCC have been exposed for manipulating climate data or repeating obvious errors. Yet the integrity of IPCC reporting is not questioned (Henderson 2009; Kellow 2007: chapter 3).

contributions) are promoted by burgeoning NGOs, which have prospered as a result of globalization and integration.

'Risk' increases as reformers and their critics confuse benefits with comprehensive objectives and institutional expansion. Proliferation of rules in international agreements cause clashes over alternative interpretations of international law, and clarity is lost. This competition tends to undermine the authority and effectiveness of law, and plays into the hands of anti-globalization groups. If the courts and tribunals established under agreements come into conflict, the authority and the effectiveness of the law and the tribunals will suffer. The WTO system is already under pressures from NGOs, especially from 'green' NGOs. In the interest of stability in international rulemaking and governance, international tribunals and inquiries into trade, investment, environment, and so on must adopt methods to agree jurisdiction over issues in conflict.

Conclusion

The world economy is always in transition. However, the present conflicts between weakening OECD governments in ageing international agencies, and truculent NGOs with individual programmes (supported by some invidious political forces) that make no allowances for economic consequences, are confusing and worrying. These confrontations are complicated by the rise of China and the other 'new' dynamic economies that have their individual ambitions. In these circumstances, there are many economic and political uncertainties that raise trade risks and the costs of insuring contracts.

Risk assessments on international trade transactions now have to consider many non-commercial issues that might impinge on contracts. The circumstances surrounding transactions are becoming subject to increasing numbers of intergovernmental and environmental challenges. Insurance costs must be expected to take account of these uncertainties.

References

Carson, R. 1962. *The Silent Spring*. London: Houghton Miffin.

Charnovitz, S. 2010. Review of trade and climate change: a report by UNEP and WTO. *World Trade Review*, 9(1): 273–88.

Cottier, T. 2001. Risk management experience in WTO dispute settlement, in *Globalization and the Environment: Risk Assessment and WTO*, edited by D. Robertson and A. Kellow. Cheltenham: Edward Elgar: 41–62.

Esty, D.C. 1998. Linkages and governance: NGOs at the WTO. *Journal of International Economic Law*, 1(4): 295–329.

Esty, D.C. 2002. The World Trade Organization's legitimacy crisis. *World Trade Review*, 1(1): 59–90.

European Commission. 2000, 2 February. The precautionary principle, Communication from the Commission. COM (2000) 1. Brussels: European Commission.

Ewen, S.W.B. and Pusztai, A. 1999. Effects of diets containing genetically modified potato expressing Galanthus nivalis lectin on rat small intestine. *The Lancet*, 354(9187): 1353–4.

Henderson, D. 2002. WTO: imaginary crisis, real problems. *World Economics*, 3(4): 277–96.

Henderson, D. 2009. Economists and climate science: a critique. *World Economics*, 10(1): 59–90.

Ikenson, D. 2010. *Protection Made to Order*. Washington, DC: CATO Institute.

Jackson, J. 2006. Sovereignty, the WTO and changing fundamentals of international law. *World Trade Review*, 6(3): 3–15.

Johnson, H.G. 1953–4. Optimum tariffs and retaliation. *Review of Economic Studies*, 21(2): 142–53.

Kellow, A. 2007. *Science and Public Policy*. Cheltenham: Edward Elgar.

Losey, J.E., Rayor, L.S. and Carter, E. 1999. Transgenic pollen harms monarch larvae. *Nature*, 399: 214.

Low, P. 2007. Comment on Jackson, 2006. Sovereignty, the WTO and changing fundamentals of international law. *World Trade Review 2007*, 6(3): 485–90.

McCall Smith, J. 2003. WTO dispute settlement: the politics of procedure in Appellate Body rulings. *World Trade Review*, 2(1): 65–100.

Pauwelyn, J. 2001. Applying SPS in WTO disputes, in *Globalization and the Environment: Risk Assessment and WTO*, edited by D. Robertson and A. Kellow. Cheltenham: Edward Elgar: 63–78.

Robertson, D. 2000. Civil society and the WTO. *The World Economy*, 23(9): 29–44.

Robertson, D. 2006. *International Economics and Confusing Politics*. Cheltenham: Edward Elgar.

Robertson, D. and Kellow, A. (eds). 2001. *Globalization and the Environment: Risk Assessment and WTO*. Cheltenham: Edward Elgar.

The Royal Society. 1998. *Genetically Modified Plants for Food Use*. Expert group report. [Online] Available at: www.royalsoc.ac.uk/st_htm.

Sunstein, C.R. 2005. *Laws of Fear: Beyond the Precautionary Principle*. Cambridge: Cambridge University Press.

Trade and Labour Standards[1]

Göte Hansson

Introduction

Demands for international labour standards have been advanced in international economic relations for more than 200 years. The diplomatic efforts have taken various forms, from minor initiatives by individual philanthropists in the form of memoranda and petitions, to the actual formation of organizations and agreements (Hansson 1983, 2003: 1–5 and references therein). A frequent argument in these activities has been the assumed or witnessed relationship between working conditions and international competitiveness. As labour costs are essential for competitiveness, it is obvious that increased requirements for working conditions in an individual country can easily result, at least in the short term, in higher costs of production and therefore in reduced international competitiveness. As a result, trade unions and governments in some 'old' industrial countries have found great incentives to invest in various types of political activities for establishing internationally valid labour standards that are linked to the rules of international trade.

The Diplomatic Struggle for International Labour Standards

As far back as at least 1788, the French banker and Minister of Finance, Jacques Necker, pointed to the fact that if one country changed its working conditions (in this case the abolition of the weekly day of rest), it would affect the country's relative international competitiveness (Fyfe and Jankanish 1997: 84). However, he also argued that if the same change was to occur in all countries, there would be no effect on the relative competitiveness (Fyfe and Jankanish 1997). As a result, it

---

[1]   This chapter is a slightly revised version of a chapter, 'Diplomacy, trade, aid, and global working conditions', first published in Aggestam and Jerneck (2009), here published with permission from Liber.

soon became common to demand international labour standards and legislation, and to link them to the rules of international trade. According to these demands, once the legislation took effect it would be possible to improve working conditions, notwithstanding the existence of international competition.

Among the most active persons in the struggle for international labour legislation were the English manufacturer and philanthropist, Robert Owen, Charles Frederick Hindley who was the Member of Parliament for Ashton-under-Lyne, and the French liberal economist Jerome Blanqui (Follows 1951; Krawtschenko 1910; Mahaim 1934). While Owen is frequently mentioned as the founder of the idea of international labour legislation, Follows (1951: 10) argues that Hindley is the person who deserves to be given this recognition. Hindley argued for international labour legislation citing: 'There is only one way of accomplishing it [the reform of manufacturing working conditions] while avoiding its disastrous consequences: this would be to get it adopted simultaneously by all industrial nations which compete in the foreign market' (J.A. Blanqui, *Cours d'économie industrielle, 1838–1839* [Paris 1939], here quoted from Mahaim 1934: 4).

However, the first person who, in a publication from the International Labour Organization, is mentioned as 'the principal originator of the idea of international labour legislation, and precursor of the work of the International Labour Organization' is Daniel Legrand, who was an Alsatian manufacturer (ILO 1978: 3; Mahaim 1934: 4).

The work of Karl Marx in the 1860s, drawing up the Provisional Rules of the International Workingmen's Association should also be mentioned among the early efforts to internationally improve working conditions and achieve greater emancipation of the working class (Follows 1951: 60). After a not-so-successful period, labour leaders in Europe succeeded in 1889 in forming the 'Second International' that aimed at paving the way for social reforms through labour market legislation, nationally as well as internationally. They also agreed to proclaim 1 May as a worldwide labour holiday that is still recognized and respected in large parts of the world today (US Department of Labor 1920: 50f.).

The struggle continued and conferences were held at the start of the twentieth century and during the First World War. Eventually, in 1919, diplomatic and trade union efforts resulted in the inclusion of the issue of working conditions, and thus the protection of workers, in the Treaty of Versailles (Shotwell 1934: 424ff.). A further step was taken in the preamble to the Constitution of the International Labour Organization (ILO) which says:

> Whereas also the failure of any nation to adopt humane conditions of labour is an obstacle in the way of other nationals which desire to improve the conditions in their own countries. (ILO 1980: Preamble)

However, even though this can be seen as an important step on the way towards international labour legislation, it is important to stress that the ILO does not include any explicit trade sanctions in the case of noncompliance. Therefore the struggle for linking working conditions to international trade agreements continued. In the statutes of the ITO, drawn up after the Second World War in 1948, it is stated that:

> The Members recognize that … all countries have a common interest in the achievement and maintenance of fair labour standards related to productivity, and in the improvement of wages and working conditions as productivity may permit. (UN 1948: Article 7(1))

Even though an agreement on international trade was greatly needed, the statutes of the ITO were never ratified. In 1947, however, as a part of the ITO discussions, the General Agreement on Tariffs and Trade (GATT) had been agreed upon in Geneva. In the GATT there is no other explicit link between trade and working conditions than Article XX on actions against products produced by prison labour. In some ways, however, the ideas of the ITO remain alive in the GATT under Article XXIX where it is stated that:

> The contracting parties undertake to observe to the fullest extent of their executive authority the general principles of Chapters I to VI inclusive and of Chapter IX of the Havana Charter. (GATT 1986: Article XXIX)

In 1954, the work on linking working conditions to international trade continued, and in Europe the work on a Social Charter for the members of the Council of Europe began. In 1961 the final text, largely based on ILO conventions and instruments, was agreed upon (European Social Charter and International Labour Standards, 1961).

The issue of labour standards in trade policy was given increased attention in the 1970s, alongside globalization, the increased competitiveness of the Newly Industrialized Countries and the problems relating to the 'first' oil crisis at the beginning of the decade. Thus, a number of proposals demanding the inclusion of labour standards (a social clause), into the rules governing international trade were presented by trade unions in the 'old' industrial countries, for example, the International Metalworkers' Federation (1976), the Executive Council of The American Federation of Labour and Congress of Industrial Organizations (AFL-CIO) in the United States (US Department of Labor 1978: 16), and the International Confederation of Free Trade Unions (ICFTU) (1979). The Department of Labour in Canada (1979) was also active and presented a document that emphasized solidarity with workers in developing countries, stating:

> A fair labour standards system would help those of the developing countries which are seeking to improve their labour standards but may be deterred by the threat of competition from countries which are less scrupulous. (Department of Labour, Canada 1979: 4)

It is interesting to note the great similarities between this statement and the wording of the Preamble to the ILO Constitution back in 1919. The explicit link with developing countries was also present in the European Economic Communities (EEC) proposal to include labour standards in the Lomé Convention by stating that the trade preferences offered by the EEC should be (are) conditioned by requirements on working conditions. It should be noted that this proposal was rejected by the developing countries. However, the EEC (1980: 4) continues to stress the relationship between working conditions and trade.

Among other sources in which the link between working conditions and trade is explicitly mentioned we note the Brandt Report from 1980 (The Independent Commission on International Development Issues 1980: 176) and the regional trade agreements in North America, NAFTA, or more precisely, the supplementary North American Agreement on Labour Cooperation (NAALC) in 1993 (Leary 1996: 206).

In Europe a 1985 white paper on the creation of the Single European Market also discussed the labour standard issue and in 1988 a charter on fundamental social rights for workers was adopted by all member states apart from the United Kingdom. The UK continued its resistance when the Social Charter was agreed upon by the other EEC members. It should, however, be noted that the Charter was to be implemented on a voluntary basis and was not included in the Maastricht Treaty (Brown et al. 1996: 233).

In the last decade of the twentieth century, the issue of working conditions was vigorously debated in Europe (Sapir 1996: 555f.). One such issue that has been much discussed during the second half of the twentieth century relates to the enlargement of the European Union and the increased focus on the four fundamental freedoms (free movement of goods, services, capital and labour). Working conditions for non-permanent short-term migrants in particular have created severe tensions within the trade union movement. It should, however, be noted that the underlying philosophy behind both temporary and permanent migration is the same as the philosophy behind international trade in goods and can thereby be seen as an important source of economic growth.

The European Union Generalized System of Preferences (GSP) towards developing countries also includes requirements on working conditions. It is especially worth noting that the EU GSP-plus system deals with the core labour standards, that is, the freedom of association, the right to organize and to collective bargaining, non-discrimination in employment and occupation, prohibition of forced labour and of child labour.

At the GATT negotiations in Marrakesh 1994 and at the WTO Ministerial Conference in Singapore 1996 the issue of linking labour standards to the rules of international trade was on the agenda, but was left largely unresolved (see the press brief from the Singapore meeting, www.wto.org/english/news_e/pres96_e/pob.htm).

One of the conclusions drawn by the then WTO Director-General was that there was a wide support for the opinion that 'All WTO member nations oppose abusive work place practices, through their approval of the United Nations Universal Declaration of Human Rights'. But he also found wide support for the opinion that: 'Trade sanctions should not be used to deal with disputes over labour standards'.

And in 1996, the OECD countries published *Trade, Employment and Labour Standards* (OECD 1996), updated by *International Trade and Core Labour Standards* (OECD 2000), without concluding that labour standards should be linked to international trade rules.

Towards the end of the twentieth century the United Nations Secretary-General Kofi Annan presented a challenge to the global business society in announcing the Global Compact, consisting of ten principles of business behaviour. Among the ten principles, four relate directly to the issue of labour standards:

- Principle 3: business should uphold the freedom of association and the effective recognition of the right to collective bargaining.
- Principle 4: the elimination of all forms of forced and compulsory labour.
- Principle 5: the effective abolition of child labour.
- Principle 6: eliminate discrimination in respect of employment and occupation.

Another interesting concept, which was launched by the ILO in the publication *A Fair Globalization: Creating Opportunities for All* (ILO 2004), is the concept of 'decent work'. The ILO defines 'decent work' in the following way:

> Employment must be freely chosen and provide an income sufficient to satisfy basic economic and family needs. Rights and representation must be respected, basic security attained through one form or another of social protection, and adequate conditions at work assured. (ILO 2004: 64)

It is this concept of working conditions that has been at the very centre of the various demands for international labour standards to be linked to international trade and that has continued to be debated, in different forms, ever since the end of the eighteenth century.

From the above analysis, we can conclude that the everlasting struggle for international labour standards and their link to international trade, and thus globalization, has successfully survived as an important issue on the diplomatic agenda. One reason is that the trade unions have kept the issue alive and also received support from some governments in the 'old' industrial world that have feared the increased competition from 'new' exporters of manufactures that are said to have achieved parts of their competitiveness by means of less stringent working conditions. It is also clear that some industrial countries have complemented this view by arguing that international labour standards linked to trade rules can be seen as an act of solidarity with workers in foreign countries where the requirements of working conditions are less demanding.

In conclusion, diplomatic efforts to establish international labour standards have been quite successful in at least two respects: firstly, in succeeding to create an international labour organization, the ILO, that supervises global working conditions, and secondly, in keeping open the debate about linking such working conditions or labour standards to the international trade system. One important part of that long-lasting debate has been to relate the demands for improved working conditions or decent working conditions to threats of trade sanctions. Let us therefore turn to this aspect and ask ourselves why such links have not been established to any significant degree.

Trade Policy Threats – a Failed Strategy

Based on the brief history above of international labour standards, we have noted that the demands for such standards have frequently, but largely unsuccessfully, been linked to threats in the form of trade sanctions. One reason for the lack of success has been the fact that opponents of such a link have been quite successful in arguing that this link would constitute an act of protectionism (Brown 2000; Hansson 1983: 29ff., 2003: 6ff.; Maskus 1997; OECD 2000 and references therein for a discussion of the political economy and the appropriateness of labour standards in trade policy). Let us here present some of the arguments that have been advanced against labour standards in international trade agreements.

Firstly, even though it would be possible to introduce labour standards into the rules that govern international trade, for example via GATT Article XXIX, referred to above, or Article XX dealing *inter alia* with exceptions to protect human life or health, the practical difficulties of implementing such standards efficiently would be great. The use of the WTO's teeth – the advocates' principal argument given their perception of the ILO as a toothless tiger – would prove problematic in practice. The use of the WTO's enforcement authority would require that, in invoking the WTO dispute settlement mechanism, a plaintiff would need to prove that injury had occurred and that it was directly the result of a country's noncompliance with core labour standards and not, for example, simply the result of lower labour costs. Drawing such a distinction and establishing the causal link between labour standards and injury would not be easy. We should add to this the difficulties in gaining acceptance of a global standard of implementation since countries differ with respect to the level of economic development, climate and culture (Hamilton 1978a, 1978b; Sanger 1920).

Secondly, and this is a significant part of the argument, at least among economists, there is no general economic justification for the sanction-driven incorporation of labour standards. There is abundant analysis indicating that compliance with core labour standards serves to stimulate rather than impede economic development and that, accordingly, compliance is seen to increase as countries grow (OECD 2000). Stiglitz (2000), for example, finds that the 'high road' to economic development, which he takes to include the right to collective bargaining, can enhance the overall efficiency of the economy by facilitating income redistribution that would not otherwise occur or which would be more costly to implement through the tax/welfare system. For its part, the ILO (1998) finds that collective bargaining and tripartite dialogue are necessary elements for creating an environment that encourages innovation and higher productivity, attracts foreign direct investment and enables society and the economy to adjust to external shocks such as financial crises and natural disasters. Rodrik (1997) reaches a similar conclusion. And Palley (1999) finds that countries which improved rights of freedom of association experience an increase in GDP growth of between 1.2 and 1.4 percentage points in the ensuing five-year period.

Thirdly, and perhaps most importantly from the point of political economy, such an incorporation would mean an open deviation from the free trade principle that, at least in wording and in various agreements, is widely accepted in large parts of the world. Thus, deviating from this principle and thereby also breaking existing international agreements can be expected to have quite high political costs in the form of loss of political prestige and through the risks of protectionist capture, and consequential retaliation.

Fourthly, it is relatively easy for less developed countries to argue against the incorporation of labour standards in trade policy by claiming that it is a way for developed countries to try to place the burden of domestic problems on poorer countries, thereby hampering their possibilities of growth and development through trade. Sanctions would not address the underlying reasons for noncompliance and would run counter to the principle we owe to Nobel laureate Jan Tinbergen that there should be as many independent policy instruments – here trade policy and social policy – as there are distinguishable goals (Tinbergen 1956).

Finally, it is also quite easy to claim that their incorporation would be a severe interference in other countries' sovereignty, and especially for the less developed countries, an interference with their ability to form their own society and their own policies.

On the other hand, the advocates of linking labour standards to the rules of international trade sometimes state that such a link would constitute a force against increased protectionism in the form of traditional trade barriers. This argument is based on the presumed success in introducing traditional trade barriers based on poor working conditions. Such arguments receive support easily, but can be difficult to test and verify empirically (Hansson 1983).

To conclude, we can note that the issue of linking working condition requirements to the multilateral trade system by threatening noncompliant countries with trade sanctions has been on the international agenda for more than 200 years. However, such a link is more or less absent in multilateral trade relations (except the clause on prison labour). Thus we conclude that the strategy to introduce labour standards into the multilateral rules that govern global trade relations has largely failed when using the argument that labour standards help to combat protectionism.

What is happening by default, however, is that in the absence of multilateral provisions via the WTO, bilateral and regional preferential trade agreements (PTAs) are coming increasingly to incorporate provisions dealing with core labour standards – particularly agreements involving the United States and, to a lesser extent, the EU (Heydon and Woolcock 2009: 138). The problem here of course is that each of the pitfalls identified above is equally applicable to social provisions incorporated into PTAs. Hence the need for continued vigilance and caution.

Aid Policy – a Promising Strategy?

In the previous section we found that the strategy based on trade policy threats has been largely unsuccessful. We have found various reasons behind the successful opposition to the incorporation of labour standards into the rules of international trade. Besides being a politically costly strategy, the higher costs of production have strengthened political opposition in countries with poor working conditions.

One alternative to press for improved working conditions using trade threats can be by introducing external pressure as a positive incentive. This can be done by offering foreign assistance, conditional on the acceptance of standards and the process of successive improvements in working conditions. This policy can, in principle, be designed in two alternative ways, which will lead to differing effects. The differences will arise as a consequence of whether the foreign assistance takes the form of direct support to the specific sectors that are required to improve their working conditions, or whether the aid is introduced as direct budget support.

In the first case, with sector-specific support, the cost increases that arise as a consequence of the improvements in working conditions will be partly or completely offset by the aid to the sector. This means that the net costs of the changes will be reduced or even eliminated. Thus, in this case we can expect political opposition in the recipient country to be diminished or removed entirely.

In the second case of labour conditioned foreign assistance, aid takes the form of national budget support – the whole economy, in addition to the public sector, will be stimulated through the increased budget of the country. Thus, in addition to the improved working conditions, the price of (and thereby the allocation of resources to) the public sector tends to increase.

Taken together, the introduction of aid-conditioned international labour improvements can be expected to meet less opposition in countries subject to external pressure to improve working conditions than has been the case when various trade policy measures, such as social clauses, have been suggested.

Conclusion

The issue of including labour standards in trade policy has a long history, and it is interesting to note the change in focus of the debate during the course of history. Early on, the demands focused on hours of work and working time for women. By the time of the formation of the ILO, the focus was on what can be called human rights-based labour standards, such as the rights of association and collective bargaining, child labour, forced labour and non-discrimination in the labour market. Then, in the 1960s and 1970s, the increased competitive strength of the Newly Industrialized Countries (NICs) brought wages to the fore of the 'fair competition' debate. The 1980s saw the debate focus on the circumstances in which some countries see their export sectors and geographically separated zones (export processing or free zones) favoured as regards the liberal and low requirements on various labour standards. Finally, during the last couple of decades, the fair labour standards debate has once again come to focus on the core, or human rights-based, labour standards. This is the case particularly with the highly emotional and sensitive issue of child labour, an issue that has been part of the debate more or less continuously ever since the beginning.

During the post-war period the advocates of linking labour standards to the international trade system have emphasized international solidarity and human rights arguments rather than protectionist arguments for such standards. However, the argumentation has gained limited success. The changeover to human rights-based labour standards during the past decades can be seen as an attempt to make the insertion of labour standards or a social clause into the rules that govern international trade more morally acceptable and efficient in the international debate. It can also be seen as a way of reducing the opposition of economists to labour standards in trade policy by emphasizing human rights motives.

This chapter has shown that the traditional way of looking at trade-related labour standards has been far from successful, even though diplomatic efforts have been significant for many decades, as most clearly shown in the establishment of the International Labour Organization in 1919. By shifting the focus from trade policy measures to aid policy, a better chance of success can be expected, provided that donor countries really are willing to pay the price, not only in terms of potentially increased commodity prices but also in the form of tax-based aid financing. Thus, the suggested change can be seen as a test of the seriousness of the solidarity argument that has been advanced frequently in the international labour standards debate. To some extent consumer support for and engagement in the fair trade movement and fair trade labelling can be seen as a sign of such a willingness to pay for global improvements in working conditions. Such willingness is also apparent in the form of government policies to finance improvements abroad.

References

Aggestam, K. and Jerneck, M. (eds). 2009. *Diplomacy in Theory and Practice*. Malmö: Liber AB.

Brown, D.K. 2000. International trade and core labour standards: a survey of the recent literature. *OECD Labour Market and Social Policy Occasional Papers, No 43*. Paris: OECD.

Brown, D.K., Deardorff, A.V. and Stern, R.M. 1996. International labour standards and trade: a theoretical analysis, in *Fair Trade and Harmonization: Prerequisites for Free Trade? Vol. 1: Economic Analysis*, edited by J. Bhagwati and R.E. Hudec, Cambridge, MA and London: The MIT Press: Chapter 3.

Department of Labour, Canada. 1979. *International Fair Labour Standards: Some Issues*, mimeo, April 1979.

EEC Economic and Social Committee. 1980. *Report of the Section for External Relations on Development Cooperation and the Economic and Social Consequences of Applying Certain International Standards Governing Working Conditions*. Brussels: EEC.

The European Social Charter and International Labour Standards I and II. 1961. *International Labour Review*, 84: 354–75.

Follows, J.W. 1951. *Antecedents of the International Labour Organization*. Oxford: Clarendon Press.

Fyfe, A. and Jankanish, M. 1997. *Trade Unions and Child Labour: A Guide to Action*. Geneva: International Labour Office.

GATT. 1986. *The General Agreement on Tariffs and Trade*. Geneva: GATT.

Hamilton, C. 1978a. SkaSverigeexportera sin arbetslöshet till u?länderna? *Tiden*, 3.

Hamilton, C. 1978b. Argumentenförfrihandelnkvarstår, *Tiden*, 6.

Hansson, G. 1983. *Social Clauses and International Trade – An Economic Analysis of Labour Standards in Trade Policy*. New York: St. Martin's Press.

Hansson, G. (ed.). 2003. *International Labour Standards – A Conference Report*, Expert Group on Development Issues (EGDI). Stockholm: Almqvist & Wiksell International.

Heydon, K. and Woolcock, S. 2009. *The Rise of Bilateralism: Comparing American, European and Asian Approaches to Preferential Trade Agreements*. Tokyo: United Nations University Press.

ICFTU. 1979. *1980 Review of the World Economic Situation*, Appendix. Brussels: ICFTU.

ILO. 1978. *International Labour Standards*. Geneva: ILO.

ILO. 1980. *Constitution of the International Labour Organisation and Standing Orders of the International Labour Conference*. Geneva: ILO.

ILO. 1998. *Labour and Social Issues Relating to Export Processing Zones*. Geneva: ILO.

ILO. 2004. *A Fair Globalization: Creating Opportunities for All*. The World Commission on the Social Dimension of Globalization. Geneva: ILO.

The Independent Commission on International Development Issues. 1980. *North-South: A Programme for Survival* (The Brandt Report). London: Pan Books.

The International Metalworkers' Federation. 1976. *Proposal Concerning a Social Clause to be Inserted in the G.A.T.T. Treaty*, International Metalworkers' Federation, February 1976.

Krawtschenko, N. 1910. J.A. Blanqui – der erste Verkuender der Idee des internationalenArbeiterschutzes, *Jahrbucher fur Nationalekonomie und Statistik*, 40.

Leary, V.A. 1996. 'Workers' rights and international trade: the social clause (GATT, ILO, NAFTA, U.S. Laws), in *Fair Trade and Harmonization: Prerequisites for Free Trade? Vol. 2: Legal Analysis*, edited by J. Bhagwati and R.E. Hudec. Cambridge, MA and London: The MIT Press: 177–230.

Mahaim, E. 1934. The historical and social importance of international labor legislation, in *The Origins of the International Labor Organization*, Vol. I, edited by J.T. Shotwell. New York: Columbia University Press: 5–22.

Maskus, K.E. 1997. Should core labor standards be imposed through international trade policy? *Policy Research Working Paper Number 1817*. Washington, DC: World Bank.

OECD. 1996. *Trade, Employment and Labour Standards: A Study of Core Workers' Rights and International Trade*. Paris: OECD.

OECD. 2000. *International Trade and Core Labour Standards*. Paris: OECD.

Palley, T.I. 1999. *The Economic Case for International Labor Standards: Theory and some Evidence*. Mimeo. Washington DC: AFL-CIO.

Rodrik, D. 1997. *Has Globalization Gone Too Far?* Washington, DC: Institute for International Economics.

Sanger, S. 1920. Practical problems of international labour legislation, in *Labour as an International Problem*, edited by E.J. Solano. London: Macmillan: 135–60.

Sapir, A. 1996. Trade liberalization and the harmonization of social policies: lessons from European integration, in *Fair Trade and Harmonization: Prerequisites for Free Trade? Vol. 1: Economic Analysis*, edited by J. Bhagwati and R.E. Hudec. Cambridge, MA and London: The MIT Press: 544–70.

Shotwell, J.T. 1934. *The Origins of the International Labor Organization*, Vol. I. 8th Edition. New York: Columbia University Press.

Stiglitz, J. 2000. Democratic Development as the Fruits of Labor. Keynote Address, Industrial Relations Research Association, Boston, January.

Tinbergen, J. 1956. *Economic Policy: Principles and Design*. Amsterdam: North Holland.

UN. 1948. United Nations Conference on Trade and Employment in Havana, 1948. *UN Doc. E/Conf. 2/78 (1948), Article 7(1)*.

US Department of Labor, Bureau of International Labor Affairs. 1978. *Labor Standards and Trade Distortions*. Washington, DC: Government Printing Office.

US Department of Labor, Bureau of Labor Statistics. 1920. *Historical Survey on International Action Affecting Labor*. Washington, DC: Government Printing Office.

Intellectual Property Rights and Trade

Meir P. Pugatch[1]

Introduction

Twenty-five years ago, when the Uruguay Round negotiations had just begun, many people asked whether intellectual property rights (IPRs) had anything to do with international trade agreements. The common view among trade experts at the time was that, while trade agreements ultimately focus on the liberalization of international trade in goods and services, IPRs do just the opposite; that is, they increase the propensity for protectionism.

Although few denied the importance of international treaties dealing with IPRs (such as those discussed at the World Intellectual Property Organization – WIPO) there was little support for – and even antagonism against – the inclusion of this odd bird in the new international trading architecture of the World Trade Organization (WTO).

Are IPRs trade-related? Should IPRs be regulated by international, regional and bilateral trade agreements? These are important theoretical questions that will be summarized later in this chapter. But, practically speaking, IPRs are now an inseparable part of the international trade agenda, not least because the agreement on Trade Related Aspects of Intellectual Property Rights (TRIPS) is an integral part of WTO agreements and institutions. Furthermore, preferential trade agreements – such as those negotiated between the United States and the European Union on one hand and their various trading partners on the other – now also include extensive provisions relating to IPRs. Whether we like them or not, IPRs are closely linked to the international trading system, both affecting it and being affected by it. It is therefore important to address the major questions and debates concerning IPRs and how IPRs relate to the world trading system.

---

[1]   Dr Meir Pugatch (PhD) is Senior Lecturer at the University of Haifa, Israel.

A Brief Discussion on IPRs and Their Complex Economic Nature

Any discussion on trade-related intellectual property agreements is far from being straightforward. Unlike other trade agreements, the international regulation of IPRs deals with a unique commodity – knowledge. Therefore, it is subject to a set of constraints and interests that differ substantially from the 'conventional' challenges of international trade agreements. Suffice to say that while trade liberalization agreements aim to reduce protection, international intellectual property (IP) agreements aim to increase it. As such, there is merit in considering some of the theoretical aspects and challenges associated with the creation, exploitation and distribution of IPRs.

IPRs in a Closed Economy

Economists explore ways of efficiently allocating scarce resources to unlimited wants and find that private property rights are a plausible way of dealing with scarcity in an efficient manner. Knowledge, however, is a unique resource that is not inherently scarce. Theoretically, the potential use of existing knowledge is unlimited and may be diminished only when such knowledge becomes obsolete. Thus, the use of an invention by one individual does not reduce its accessibility to others, but rather is more likely to increase it. Patents, copyrights, trademarks and other forms of IPRs establish exclusive ownership of varying types of knowledge, allowing their owners to restrict, and even prevent, others from using that knowledge. The result, as Hindley (1971) puts it, is that 'the establishment of private property rights in these cases artificially creates the symptoms of scarcity; they do not derive from it'.

Consider, for example, the case of patents. The structural tradeoff built into the patent system – that in order to increase the amount of available knowledge in the future, the efficient use of existing and available knowledge is inhibited in the present – is probably its most problematic aspect (Arrow 1962). On the one hand, there would be underproduction in inventive activities due to free-riding (Arrow 1962). This represents a particular situation of market failure in which the incentive to innovate is diminished as work is copied without any reward for the innovator. Establishing property rights, that is patents, therefore allows inventors – both firms and individuals – to secure commercial returns for their work and thus provides an incentive to invest in future inventive activities. On the other hand, a patent system inhibits the free and rapid dissemination of existing knowledge because an inventing firm that has been granted a patent essentially gains monopoly powers through its exclusive right to control both the quantity and the price of its invention.

In principle, economists should be able to say whether protection of IPRs generates a net loss or a net benefit to society, or what is more important to society: does more available knowledge in the future justify less accessible knowledge in the present? As yet, no conclusive answer to these questions is available notwithstanding the availability of a rich and in-depth literature on the economics of IPRs.[2] In this context, the term 'paradox of patents', which was coined by Joan Robinson as early as 1956, seems to capture the true nature of the patent tradeoff: 'by slowing down the diffusion of technical progress, patents insure that there will be more progress to diffuse' (1956: 87).

Economists disagree about the effects of patents on the allocation of resources to inventive activities, the allocation of resources within the sphere of inventive activities and on the allocation of inventions as a factor of production (Hindley 1971: 1–31). The optimum term of protection is also disputable. A longer patent term increases the incentive to invent but also prolongs the restriction on the use of existing knowledge. Therefore, not only is it difficult to establish a single optimal patent term, but it is also likely that different inventions require different terms of protection. Thus, since a decision on a specific patent term for all inventions is bound to be arbitrary, for different inventions there may be a term that is more socially desirable than the current period of 20 years (Nordhaus 1969; Scherer 1972). Back in the 1950s, Machlup (1958) argued that 'no economist on the basis of present knowledge could possibly state with certainty that the patent system, as it now operates, confers a net benefit or a net loss to society'. This statement also seems to be true today.

IPRs and Trade

Different countries may find it in their interests for various reasons to either support or reject a stronger international IP system. Of central importance are the effects of such a system on trade in IP-related products and its impact on the rate and magnitude of technology transfer and FDI.

Regarding trade in IP-related products, there is a divergence between the interests of developed and developing countries. Countries with strong IP capabilities will benefit from membership of a strong international system of IPRs thanks to improved terms of trade as an exporter of IP-related products and from additional income thanks to the higher prices IP owners can charge by virtue of their monopolistic position (Chin and Grossman 1990; Penrose 1951; Vernon 1990). On the other hand, countries with weak IP capabilities are likely to benefit most from trade in IP-related products when they are not part of such a system. Remaining outside an international system of IPRs will enable such countries to freely exploit and imitate IP-related products in their own domestic economies. Where they are successful, these countries may even be able to compete with the original IP owners, thus becoming exporters of such products themselves (Penrose 1951: 95–6).

---

[2]   For an in-depth economic review of the patent system, see Arrow (1962); Machlup (1958); Primo-Braga (1990).

Empirical data confirm the above theoretical statements. The global ownership and commercial exploitation of IPRs is still dominated by developed countries and a select number of emerging economies. For example, the *World Intellectual Property Indicators Report* for 2010 shows that the lion's share of worldwide patent filings (using the Patent Cooperation Treaty – PCT System[3]) is concentrated in the hands of applicants from a select group of countries, notably the United States, which still accounted for the largest share (29.6 per cent) of PCT applications in 2009, followed by Japan (19.1 per cent) and Germany (10.7 per cent). These top three countries thus accounted for 59 per cent of all PCT filings in 2009 (though their share has decreased from 64 per cent in 2005). Moreover, applicants from the business sector accounted for the majority (83.2 per cent) of PCT applications published in 2009. Universities and public research institutions jointly accounted for 7.7 per cent of published PCT applications, and individuals made up the remaining 9 per cent. In terms of the distribution of 'rents' from trade in IP-related goods and services, there is therefore a clear tension between 'north' and 'south'.

On the other hand, there is growing statistical evidence suggesting that a stronger environment of IPRs contributes to an enhanced level of economic development, foreign direct investment (FDI) and technology transfer in developing countries. Based on the most comprehensive empirical research to date, an OECD study of the relationship between IPRs, technology transfer and FDI in 115 countries found that in developed countries an increase of 1 per cent in the strength of patent rights resulted in an increase of 0.5 per cent in FDI flow (based on licensing deals), which in turn resulted in the transfer of know-how, that is, innovative capabilities (Park and Lippoldt 2008). The study found that in developing countries, including least developed countries (LDCs), the effect is even stronger so that an increase of 1 per cent in the strength of patent rights could be associated with an increase of 1.7 per cent in FDI flows.

Léger (2006) has conducted a similar study of developing countries only, in which he estimates the link between innovation and IPRs and corrects for other determinants of innovation such as market demand, past innovative activities, economic conditions, political stability, human capital, financial capital and openness to trade. Comprising observations from 36 developing countries over 26 years (1970–1995), Léger reports that IPRs have a strong positive impact on investment and innovation in developing countries. Robbins (2006, 2008) also finds that countries that have increased the level of patent protection over time, including developing countries such as Taiwan and South Korea, become larger recipients of income from IP-based activities in the form of FDI and technology transfer, as compared to other countries. Robbins finds that these countries benefit considerably from activities that are based on the licensing of patents and trade secrets.

---

[3]   The PCT makes it possible to seek patent protection for an invention simultaneously in each of a large number of countries by filing an 'international' patent application. For an overview of the PCT, see the Wipo website, at: www.wipo.int/pct/en/treaty/about.htm.

While the above studies establish a more positive link between the strengthening of IPRs and FDI activity in developing countries, this does not tell us much about the level of IPR protection. As it is not possible to say at what point IPR protection becomes counterproductive, the main focus of the above studies is on the effect on FDI flows and technology transfer of narrowing IP gaps between north and south. In terms of IPRs and trade, there remains therefore a built-in tension between the static and dynamic costs and benefits, the distribution of rents from trade in IP-related products and the gains generated by increased levels of FDI and technological inflows.

If economic theory and research therefore provides no clear-cut answers, it is necessary to look at how IPRs are being regulated and managed in the international trading system.

IPRs and the Multilateral Trading System

Generally speaking, international IP agreements aim to achieve two major goals. The first is to level the playing field and establish the ground rules according to which trade in IP-related products will take place. The second is to standardize the level of IP protection granted by signatories to international IP agreements.

In this context, the most significant step towards the harmonization of international trade in IP-related goods and services was the creation of the Agreement on Trade Related Aspects of Intellectual Property Rights (TRIPS) by the WTO.

A Short Overview of the TRIPS Agreement

Signed in Marrakesh (15 April 1994) as Annex 1C to the Final Act establishing the WTO, the TRIPS Agreement came into effect in January 1995. At the time, it was one of the most innovative and important subjects to be included in the multilateral negotiations of the Uruguay Round. With respect to IPRs specifically, the TRIPS Agreement represented a significant increase in the global level of IP protection. Some scholars, such as Reichman (1998), considered it to be a 'revolution in international intellectual property law'.

The negotiating process leading to the establishment of the TRIPS Agreement proved to be one of the most controversial and complicated tasks in the Uruguay Round.[4] The inclusion of IPRs in the Uruguay Round negotiating agenda in the form of the ministerial declaration of 20 September 1986, was primarily initiated by the United States, backed by the European Community (EC), Switzerland and Japan. These countries, particularly the United States and the EC, exerted heavy pressure, including threats of unilateral trade retaliation in the case of the United States, on

---

[4]   For the history of TRIPs see: Abbott (1989); Stewart (1993); Emmert (1990).

some key developing countries such as India, Korea and Brazil to get them to agree to negotiate on a comprehensive IP agreement under the auspices of the General Agreement on Tariffs and Trade (GATT). There were also disagreements within the north, such as between the United States and the EC on more detailed issues such as specific elements of the patent system, but it is safe to say that negotiations – both on the essence of TRIPS and on its practical outcome – were shaped by the north–south divide.

As described above, the TRIPS Agreement aimed to increase and harmonize the global protection of IPRs (at the national, regional and international levels) in five main areas, namely international principles of National Treatment (NT) and Most Favoured Nation (MFN) treatment, minimum standards of protection, enforcement, dispute settlement and technical assistance.

First, as part of the WTO agreements, the TRIPS Agreement incorporated the principles of NT and MFN (Blakeney 1996). The former (TRIPS, Article 3) requires all members to treat nationals of other members no less favourably than their own nationals, on all issues concerning IPRs, subject to the exemptions laid down in previous IPR conventions and treaties. The MFN principle (Article 4) requires that any advantage, favour, privilege or immunity granted by a member to the nationals of any other member must be extended unconditionally to the nationals of all other members.

Second, the TRIPS Agreement specified the minimum protection standards that member countries must adopt under their domestic IP legislation (Article 1.1). In this context, the TRIPS Agreement incorporates four major international treaties: the 1883 Paris Convention for the protection of industrial property, as revised by the Stockholm Act of this convention (14 July 1967), the 1886 Berne Convention for the protection of literary and artistic works, as revised in the Paris Act of this convention (24 July 1971), the Rome Convention for the protection of performers, producers of phonograms and broadcasting organizations (26 October 1961) and the Treaty on intellectual property in respect of integrated circuits (IPIC) of 26 May 1989.[5] More importantly, the TRIPS Agreement provided a detailed 'technical guide' for member countries with regard to the protection of IPRs. TRIPS articles refer specifically to copyright and related rights (Article 9–14), trademarks (Article 15–21), geographical indications (Article 22–4), industrial designs (Article 25–7), patents (Article 27–34), layout designs of integrated circuits (Article 35–8) and the protection of undisclosed information (Article 39).

Third, the TRIPS Agreement specified minimum provisions on enforcement (Article 41–61) (Blakeney 1996: 123–39). According to these, each WTO member is required to introduce civil and judicial procedures in order to prevent, or at least inhibit, the infringement of IPRs (Article 41). Members' remedies must include injunctions – 'to prevent the entry into channels of commerce in their jurisdiction of imported goods that involve the infringement of an intellectual property right'

---

[5]   See: TRIPS Agreement, Article 2 and Arrow (1962); Text of the agreement between WIPO and WTO, Geneva (22 December 1995); WTO Dispute Settlement Body; Blakeney (1996: 20–4).

(Article 44), damages for injuries (Article 45) and the destruction of infringed goods without compensation of any sort (Article 46). Member countries are also required to adopt adequate border measures, aimed at preventing the importation and circulation of counterfeit and pirated IP-related goods (Article 51–60). Finally, in order to combat the illegal trade in pirated products involving copyright or trademark rights infringements, WTO members are required to provide for criminal actions under their domestic IP legislation (Article 61).

Fourth, the TRIPS Agreement also relies on the WTO's Dispute Settlement Body (DSB), which is responsible for settling disputes between member countries (Dispute Settlement Understanding, Article 1).[6] The DSB has the sole authority to establish panels of experts for each and every dispute, to accept or reject panel findings and decisions and to monitor member states' compliance with the WTO dispute rulings. If and when a member country chooses not to comply with a given ruling, the DSB has the power to authorize trade-retaliation measures against that member (DSU, Article 22).

Finally, there is the provision of technical assistance to developing and least developed countries (LDCs) to help them implement IPRs in general and the TRIPS agreement in particular. It is well established that LDCs, as well as some developing countries, are bound to face considerable obstacles in meeting their international IP obligations. As a result, TRIPS Article 67 clearly states that developed countries should provide technical and financial assistance to developing countries and LDCs. Accordingly, international organizations and institutions, such as WIPO, the World Bank, the WTO, as well as some of the developed countries, such as the United States and the EU, provide technical, educational and, to some extent, technological, assistance to developing countries and LDCs in order to promote TRIPS benefits in these countries. But there is also criticism that such assistance has not fully taken into account the special needs and circumstances of developing countries and LDCs (Kostecki 2006).

The Rise and Fall of the TRIPS Framework

The 17-year life of the TRIPS can roughly be divided into three periods. The first period – 1995 to early 1999 – may be described as the period of 'determination'. Developed countries were convinced that TRIPS could provide a long-term platform for the protection and enforcement of their IP rights worldwide. One need only look at the different WTO disputes between the United States/EU and India/Pakistan on the so-called patent 'mail-box' provisions in order to understand such optimism (WTO Dispute Settlement Body 1998). But developed countries underestimated the growing opposition to TRIPS among developing countries, and particularly the LDCs.

The second period – November 1999 to November 2001 – may be described as the period of 'resentment'. Developing countries, backed by a new wave of anti-IP

---

6   In fact, when reviewing disputes the General Council functions as the DSB.

sentiment within the NGO community, expressed a growing sense of antagonism towards their implementation of the TRIPS as of 2000. Many developing countries felt that the TRIPS Agreement was too one-sided in favouring developed countries and offered little to their own nationals. This resentment was fuelled, in part, by two separate events; the colossal failure of the Seattle WTO Ministerial Conference in late 1999 and the debate on patented AIDS medicines in South Africa.

The third period – November 2001 to date – may be described as the period of 'flexibility', though not necessarily in a positive sense for all parties concerned. This period has brought two major changes. First, the discussion on TRIPS has narrowed to an almost exclusive focus on pharmaceutical IPRs. Second, the focus is no longer on the implementation, but rather on the 'flexible' interpretation of TRIPS, in other words on the manner in which developing and least developed countries could essentially avoid or bypass the agreement. Most representative of this period are the 2001 Declaration on the TRIPS Agreement and Public Health (as part of the Doha Development Agenda) and the August 2003 Agreement on the implementation of Paragraph 6 of the declaration (focusing on the manner in which LDCs with no manufacturing capacities can import generic substitutes to existing patented pharmaceutical drugs) (WTO 2003).

Flexibility, while celebrated in the media and by some NGOs as elevating concerns about the restrictive effect of TRIPS on the access to medicines, has had two important implications. The first is the (almost) complete stagnation in the negotiating agenda of TRIPS. In the past decade, we have experienced vast and rapid technological developments, such as in the World Wide Web and mobile and digital mediums. These fields encompass highly complex and important IP issues, most of which have not been incorporated into TRIPS, with the result that the resultant other global platforms, such as the Anti-Counterfeiting Trade Agreement (ACTA), are currently being considered.[7] In contrast, negotiations on TRIPS tend to focus today mostly on the possible creation of a multilateral geographical indications (GIs) register for wines and spirits (WTO 2010), although one can argue that the issue of GIs is of a lesser importance compared with the other pressing issues relating to the global IP architecture.

The second and perhaps more important outcome is inclusion of IPR protection in the regional and bilateral agreements initiated by the United States, the EU and other developed countries. These agreements are discussed in the next section.

IPRs and Regional/Bilateral Trading Agreements – Going for 'TRIPS Plus'

Despite the rather deep freeze at the multilateral level, developed and developing countries have, since 2000, been signing preferential trade agreements (PTAs)

---

[7] See: European Commission (2007).

at both the regional and bilateral levels that include IP provisions, and there is growing evidence that the agreements between the United States or the EU on the one hand and developing countries on the other have been based on TRIPS Plus provisions (Abbott 2004; OECD 2002; Vivas-Eugui 2003; World Bank Development Prospects Group 2005). To date, the US-led agreements seem to be more detailed and comprehensive than the EU-led ones, both in terms of their framework (that is, enforcement, administration, etc.) and specific provisions.

US-led PTAs

While the TRIPS Agreement specifies the minimum IP commitments of WTO members, US-led PTAs are in essence based on a 'to-do list' approach (some would argue, a 'nanny' approach) that specify IP amendments and actions that its trading partners should implement.

Chapter 15 of the Central American–Dominican Republic Free Trade Agreement (CAFTA–DR) of May 2004 is probably the clearest example of the manner in which the United States pursues its TRIPS Plus framework. CAFTA–DR requires its signatories to significantly strengthen their level of IP protection, as well as their civil, administrative and enforcement procedures. For example, Articles 26 and 27 require CAFTA–DR signatories to strengthen their criminal remedies by, for example, imposing 'sentences of imprisonment or monetary fines, or both, sufficient to provide a deterrent to future acts of infringement'.

Similar to this approach at the regional level, the United States also expects comprehensive IP protection in the bilateral agreements it negotiates, such as those in the US–Republic of Korea FTA (KORUS FTA, 2007), US–Chile FTA (2003), the US–Singapore FTA (2003), the US–Morocco FTA (2004), the US–Bahrain FTA (2004) and, to some extent, the US–Jordan FTA (2000).[8] Generally speaking, US agreements include TRIPS Plus provisions for both copyrights and trademarks by, for example, prohibiting the parallel importation of pharmaceutical products, a practice allowed under the international exhaustion regime of TRIPS (Heydon and Woolcock 2009).

US autonomous trade legislation in the shape of Section 301 (commonly referred to as Special 301) of the Trade Act of 1974 enables the United States Trade Representative (USTR) to identify Priority Foreign Countries which, according to US criteria, provide inadequate protection for IPRs and thereby cause the greatest adverse impact on right holders. The 301 process can eventually lead to a situation in which the United States may take unilateral action and possibly impose sanctions against countries found to be significant violators of IP rights. The Special 301 lists include two categories – the Priority Watch List and a Watch List – for countries whose actions meet some, but not all, of the criteria for increased bilateral attention concerning the problem areas.

---

[8]   Available at: www.ustr.gov.

EU-led Trade Agreements

Compared to those of US agreements, the IP provisions of new-generation PTAs, such as recent Association Agreements or the Economic Partnership Agreements (EPAs) between the EU and the African, Caribbean and Pacific (ACP) states are much more general in nature. Typical EU-led PTAs – both older agreements such as the EU–Israel FTA (2000), the EU–Chile FTA (2002), the EU–Jordan FTA (2002) or the EU–Mexico FTA, and more recent agreements, such as the Framework Agreement on Trade and Cooperation between the EU and South Korea (2007) – are characterized by 'objectives' and 'scope'. The objectives generally require signatories to 'grant and ensure adequate and effective protection of the highest international standards including effective means of enforcing such rights'. The agreements' scope enumerates the different types of IPRs that the agreement covers, such as copyrights, patents, industrial designs, GIs, trademarks, layout designs (topographies) of integrated circuits, and the protection of undisclosed information. Some recent agreements, such as EU–Caribbean Economic Partnership Agreement (CARIFORUM – 2007), do tend to be more detailed, but more towards the direction of identifying the developmental needs of the partnering countries (especially on issues of medicines, biodiversity and traditional knowledge). At the same time, for the more established forms of IPRs (copyrights, trademarks and patents) the Agreement adheres to the 'general approach' identified above (EC 2008).

Instead of specifying the IP requirements that signatories should implement (as in the US to-do list model), EU-led PTAs specify what international conventions and treaties signatories should implement, based on three stages of IPR protection.

The first stage relates to existing international conventions that require 'adequate and effective implementation', such as the TRIPS Agreement; the Paris Convention for the Protection of Industrial Property (Stockholm Act, 1967); the Berne Convention for the Protection of Literary and Artistic Works (Paris Act, 1971); the Rome Convention for the Protection of Performers, Producers of Phonograms and Broadcasting Organisations (Rome, 1961) and the International Convention for the Protection of New Varieties of Plants 1978 (the 1978 UPOV Convention) or the International Convention for the Protection of New Varieties of Plants 1991 (the 1991 UPOV Convention). The second stage relates to conventions that were to have been implemented and ratified by 2007 and 2009, such as the Nice Agreement Concerning the International Classification of Goods and Services for the Purposes of Registration of Marks (Geneva, Act 1977, amended in 1979); the World Intellectual Property Organization Copyright Treaty (Geneva, 1996); the Patent Cooperation Treaty (Washington, 1970, amended in 1979 and modified in 1984); and the Convention for the Protection of Producers of Phonograms against the Unauthorized Reproduction of their Phonograms (Geneva, 1971). The third stage concerns agreements that require implementation at 'the earliest possible opportunity', such as the Protocol to the Madrid Agreement concerning the International Registration of Marks (1989); the Madrid Agreement Concerning the International Registration of Marks (Stockholm Act, 1967, amended in 1979); and the Vienna Agreement establishing an International Classification of Figurative Elements of Marks (Vienna, 1973, amended in 1985).

Despite this general approach based on existing international standards of IPR protection, the EU seeks much more specific protection of GIs. For example, Roffe (2004) finds that, as regards the EU–Chile FTA: 'probably, the most significant intellectual property related provisions are contained in Annex v, on the "Agreement on the Trade in Wines" and Annex vi concerning Spirits. These annexes include provisions on the reciprocal protection of geographical indications related to wines and spirits, and the protection of traditional expressions [of both Parties]'.[9] He concludes that 'the Association Agreement between Chile and the EU is also a TRIPS–Plus Agreement especially on the protection of geographical indications'.

Finally, unlike the US model, EU-led PTAs do not have specific provisions on enforcement, civil and criminal remedies, or administration. Some, such as the EU–Jordan FTA, have a consultation mechanism, according to which: 'if problems in the area of intellectual, industrial and commercial property affecting trading conditions … occur, urgent consultation shall be undertaken, at the request of either Party, with a view to reaching mutually satisfactory solutions' (EU–Jordan Association Agreement, 2002, Article 56). But this more flexible approach has, however, made it difficult to ensure that the EU's trading partners implement their IP commitments in bilateral agreements. As a result, it appears that the EC is becoming more proactive in enforcing IPRs. This can be seen in several instruments that have been adopted by the EC, such as the *Strategy for the Enforcement of IPRs in Third Countries* (European Commission Directorate General for Trade 2004a, 2004b).

Implications

What are the implications of these trends? First, although the common view is that the current emphasis on the so-called TRIPS flexibilities would serve the interests of developing countries, the recent surge in US- and EU-led TRIPS Plus bilateral agreements, where the United States and EU can use their asymmetric bargaining strength, suggests that this strategy (particularly in pharmaceuticals) may have been counterproductive. Second, the US-, and now EU-led bilateral agreements, are both raising the level of protection in developing countries as well as strengthening implementation and enforcement provisions. These suggestions on the direction and pace that the North's global enforcement of IPRs will take are arguably controversial and need much more empirical research in order to be validated (or disproved).

---

[9]   Also see: Vivas-Engui (2003).

Conclusion

Seventeen years after the launch of the TRIPS Agreement, the debate about the desirability of international scale IPRs is far from being settled. On the contrary, future debates on IP issues promise to be both extensive and heated. They encompass issues across the board, such as incentives for innovation, industrial development, trade policy, access to available technologies and effective commercialization in the age of knowledge-intensive industries.

It would be unrealistic to expect policymakers to come up with the perfect policy toolkit that would address all the challenges and opportunities associated with the IP field. But a more efficient and practical IP policymaking process is needed. Such a process – conducted at the national, bilateral and multilateral level – should be based on three major pillars.

The first pillar concerns the preferred approach to policymaking in each given IP area, taking full account of different social, industrial, environmental and developmental needs. While there is an obvious case for taking all of these perspectives into account, the policymaker must eventually decide on relative priorities. For example, when it comes to making a decision about the scope and term of patent protection in pharmaceuticals, policymakers have, for example, to balance the aim of encouraging innovation against improved developing country access to medicines, while also balancing the aim of attracting FDI from multinational companies against policies in support of domestic industries. Whilst the policymakers' aim is to achieve such balances, in practice there is always a need to identify a strategic preference, towards one goal over the other. In order to make such decisions, policymakers need a clear understanding of the range of IP issues and objectives.

The second pillar concerns the need for coherence between the various elements of national IP policies and other relevant policy areas. Most of the focus here should fall on collaboration and coordination between the different ministries and agencies that are responsible for IP policies. For example, there is a need for much better coherence between policies that deal with IPRs from the perspective of *competition issues* (anti-trust) and policies that deal with IPRs from the perspective of *competitiveness* (that is, policies aimed at enhancing the global competitive position of one country vis-à-vis other countries). The IP-related aspects of different areas are often being dealt with by different entities (for example, DG Competition and DG Enterprise in the EU deal with the issue of competition and competitiveness respectively). These entities may well differ in how they perceive IPRs and the objectives and challenges that they choose to focus on. This can result in a lack of coherence, inconsistency or even conflict between the entities.

Finally, for each and every IP topic, there is a need for much better monitoring to ensure, throughout the entire policymaking process, that the strategic objectives identified by policymakers are indeed reflected in the final outcomes, for example in a given free trade agreement.

To sum up, when it comes to IPRs, there is no grand theory that can be followed. Policy formulation will remain an uphill struggle that reflects both the joint as well as rival interests of different parties as well as the underlying 'paradox of IPRs'. What is clear, however, is that given the growing importance of the so-called 'global knowledge economy', there is increasingly a need for skilled IP policymakers who understand the complexities within the uneasy marriage of IPRs and international trade.

References

Abbott, F.M. 1989. Protecting First World assets in the Third World: intellectual property in the GATT multilateral framework, *Vanderbilt Journal of Transnational Law*, 22(4): 689–744.

Abbott F.M. 2004. *The Doha Declaration on the TRIPS Agreement and Public Health and the Contradictory Trend in Bilateral and Regional Free Trade Agreements*, Occasional Paper. Geneva: Quaker United Nations Office.

Arrow, K. 1962. Economic welfare and the allocation of resources for invention, in *The Rate and Direction of Inventive Activity: Economic and Social Factors*, edited by National Bureau of Economic Research. Princeton: Princeton University Press: 609–26.

Blakeney, M. 1996. *Trade Related Aspects of Intellectual Property Rights: A Concise Guide to the TRIPs Agreement*. London: Sweet and Maxwell.

Chin, J.C. and Grossman, G.M. 1990. Intellectual property rights and North-South trade, in *The Political Economy of International Trade*, edited by R. Jones and A. Krueger. Oxford: Basil Blackwell: 90–197.

Emmert, F. 1990. Intellectual property in the Uruguay Round – negotiating strategies of the western industrialized countries, *Michigan Journal of International Law*, 11(1317): 1317–99.

European Commission. 2007. *European Commission, the Fact Sheet: Anti-Counterfeiting Trade Agreement* (updated November 2008). [Online] Available at: http://trade.ec.europa.eu/doclib/docs/2008/october/tradoc_140836.11.08.pdf.

European Commission. 2008. EU–Caribbean Economic Partnership Agreement–Innovation and Intellectual Property. [Online] Available at: http://trade.ec.europa.eu/doclib/docs/2008/october/tradoc_140978.pdf [accessed: 10 January 2011].

European Commission Directorate General for Trade. 2004a. *Strategy for the Enforcement of Intellectual Property Rights in Third Countries*. Brussels: EC.

European Commission Directorate General for Trade. 2004b. *EU Strengthens Fight Against Piracy and Counterfeiting Beyond its Borders*. Brussels: EC.

Heydon, K. and Woolcock, S. 2009. *The Rise of Bilateralism: Comparing American, European and Asian Approaches to Preferential Trade Agreements*. Tokyo: United Nations University Press.

Hindley, B.V. 1971. *The Economic Theory of Patents, Copyrights, and Registered Industrial Designs:Background Study to the Report on Intellectual and Industrial Property*. Ottawa: Economic Council of Canada.

Kostecki, M. 2006. *Intellectual Property and Economic Development: What Technical Assistance to Redress the Balance in Favour of Developing Nations?* Geneva: ICTSD.

Léger, A. 2006. *Intellectual Property Rights and Innovation in Developing Countries: Evidence from Panel Data.* Proceedings of the German Development Economics Conference in Berlin, 2006.

Machlup, F. 1958. *An Economic Review of the Patent System.* Study of the Subcommittee on Patents, Trademarks and Copyrights of the Committee on the Judiciary, US Senate, 85th Congress, Second Session, Study No. 15. Washington, DC.

Nordhaus, W.D. 1969. *Invention, Growth and Welfare.* Cambridge, MA: MIT Press.

OECD. 2002. *Regional Trade Agreements and the Multilateral Trading System.* Paris: OECD.

Park, W. and Lippoldt, D. 2008. Technology transfer and the economic implications of the strengthening of intellectual property rights in developing countries. *Working Paper No. 62.* Paris: OECD.

Penrose, E. 1951. *The Economics of the International Patent System.* Baltimore: Johns Hopkins Press.

Primo-Braga, C. 1990. Guidance from economic theory, in *Strengthening Protection of Intellectual Property in Developing Countries,* edited by W.E. Siebeck. World Bank Discussion Papers No. 112, Washington, DC: World Bank: 17–32.

Reichman, H.J. 1998. Securing compliance with the TRIPs Agreement after US v India, *Journal of International Economic Law,* 1(4): 585.

Robbins, C.A. 2006, 2008. *Measuring Payments for the Supply and Use of Intellectual Property,* Ottawa: International Association for Official Statistics (IAOS).

Robinson, J. 1956. *The Accumulation of Capital.* London: Macmillan.

Roffe, P. 2004. Bilateral agreements and a TRIPS-Plus world: the Chile-USA Free Trade Agreement, *TRIPS Issue Paper No. 4.* New York and Geneva: Quaker United Nations Office.

Scherer, F.M. 1972. Nordhaus' theory of optimal patent life: a geometric reinterpretation, *American Economic Review,* 62: 422–27.

Stewart, P.T. (ed.). 1993. *GATT Uruguay Round – A Negotiating History (1986–1992),* Vol. II. Boston: Kluwer.

Vernon, R. 1957. *The International Patent System and Foreign Policy.* Study of the Subcommittee on Patents, Trademarks and Copyrights of the Committee on the Judiciary, US Senate, 85th Congress, Second Session, Study No. 5, Washington, DC.

Vivas-Eugui, D. 2003. Regional and bilateral agreements and a TRIPS-Plus world: the Free Trade Area of the Americas (FTAA), *TRIPS Issue Paper No. 1.* New York and Geneva: Quaker United Nations Office.

World Bank Development Prospects Group. 2005. *Trade Regionalism and Development.* Washington D.C.: World Bank.

World Intellectual Property Indicators, 2010 Edition, Geneva, 51–2.

WTO. 2003. WTO Ministerial Declaration on the TRIPS Agreement and Public Health Adopted on 14 November 2001; Council for TRIPS, Implementation of Paragraph 6 of the Doha Declaration on the TRIPS Agreement and Public Health, 30 August.

WTO. 2010. *Geographical Indications Talks Gear Up For 2011 Endgame*. [Online] Available at: www.wto.org/english/news_e/news10_e/trip_10dec10_e.htm [accessed: 10 January 2011].

WTO Dispute Settlement Body. 1998. India – patent protection for pharmaceutical and agricultural chemical products: complaint by the European communities and their member states. *WT/DS79/R*, 24 August. Geneva: WTO.

PART V
Trade and Development

Trade Openness and Growth Miracles: A Fresh Look at Taiwan

Arvind Panagariya[1]

Introduction

Taiwan was one of the two original miracles – the other being the Republic of Korea – that first convinced many development economists of the superiority of outward-oriented policies over import substitution. But authors such as Wade (1990, 2004) and Rodrik (1995) subsequently challenged the view that the Taiwanese success represented the triumph of outward-oriented policies and reinterpreted it as the outcome of a set of government interventions. While a number of original converts to outward orientation as the preferred development strategy, including Little (1996) and Bhagwati (1999), have responded to these critics, not all of the criticisms have been laid to rest. Consequently, the importance of the Taiwanese experience towards validating the case for outward orientation as a means to sustained rapid growth remains less than fully recognized. The objective of this chapter is to correct this deficiency in the literature.

My focus is principally on the approximately 15-year period from the late 1950s to the early 1970s. This is the key period during which the Taiwanese economy took off and grew on a sustained basis at near double-digit growth rates and was transformed into an industrial powerhouse. I will argue that a switch to outward-oriented policies was the key to both catalysing and sustaining the rapid growth Taiwan achieved during this period. I will also discuss in detail why the contrary view that gives credit to the government for launching the country into a high-growth orbit by acting strategically or coordinating private investments lacks validity.

---
[1]   The author is indebted to Ken Heydon for excellent suggestions on tightening this chapter to meet the editors' constraints on length and to Gustav Ranis for comments on an earlier draft.

An Overview of Growth: 1952–80

Figure 17.1 shows annual gross domestic product (GDP) growth rates in Taiwan from 1952 to 1980. As the scope for easy import substitution was being exhausted, the annual growth rates in the second half of the 1950s had been declining. The trough at 6.3 per cent in 1960 was almost 5 percentage points below the average of 1962–73 and a full 7 per cent below the peak reached in 1972. A critical breakpoint occurs at the border between 1962 and 1963 since this is when the high-growth path appears firmly established.

The higher growth rates were accompanied by a rapid transformation of the economy. Trade became progressively more important, exports reoriented from agriculture to manufactures, the share of industry in GDP rose substantially and the workforce shifted out of agriculture into industry in significant volumes. Before turning to this transformation, it is useful to review the evolution of trade and industrial policy.

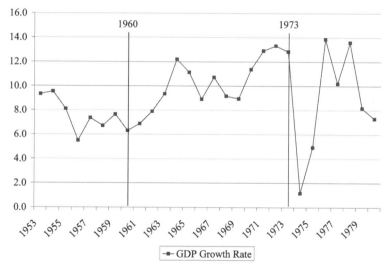

Figure 17.1 Annual GDP growth rates in Taiwan: 1953–80
Source: Author's construction based on data in Yu (1999).

Trade and Industrial Policies

The Import Substitution Phase: 1951–60

Analysts on both sides of the debate agree that the period 1951–7 was dominated by policies commonly associated with import substitution. Tariffs were high, strict import licensing was applied and, despite several devaluations, the domestic currency remained overvalued throughout the period. Strict quantitative restrictions implemented through licensing generated large quota rents even after netting out the high tariffs. Scott (1979: 315) refers to Lin (1973) as reporting quota premiums over CIF import price plus custom duties equalling 48 per cent on wheat flour, 33 per cent on cotton yarn, 150 per cent on cotton piece goods, 350 per cent on soda ash and 100 per cent on ammonium sulphate in 1953.

Switching to Outward Orientation: Key Reforms of 1955 and 1958–60

In his important book, Lin (1973) points out that some major manufacturing sectors such as textiles, wood products and rubber goods had slowed down after the early 1950s as 'easy' import substitution came to an end. In turn, this led to a slowdown in the growth of the manufacturing sector as a whole. GDP grew significantly more slowly during 1955–8 than during 1952–5 (Figure 17.1). After 1954, there was also a pronounced decline in the absolute level of gross private sector investment.[2]

In July 1955, the Executive Yuan passed the Regulation for Rebate of Taxes and Export Products. This measure provided for the rebates of commodity tax, import duty and defence tax paid on exports. In addition, for purposes of private sector exports, the domestic currency was devalued from NT$15.55 per US dollar to NT$25 per US dollar. Given the high rates of import duty and commodity taxes around this time, the rebates made some of the previously unprofitable exports profitable while the devaluation boosted the value of the profits in the local currency. The measures led to a perceptible impact on non-agricultural exports, which grew 33 per cent per annum during 1956–8. The effect could even be seen in a favourable movement in total exports translating into a mildly rising trend in the exports-to-GDP ratio after bottoming out at 5.8 per cent in 1954. By 1957, the ratio had returned to its early 1950s level.[3]

The key problem still confronting many potential exporters of manufactures was the following: given the poor resource base of Taiwan, most of the potential export products required imported inputs accounting for two-thirds or more of the value of the product at world prices. The catch was that imported inputs were subject to strict licensing that produced very large rents. These rents exceeded the sum of the border price, custom tariff, domestic indirect taxes and retailing costs by a sufficiently large amount that their processing for exports was unprofitable even taking into account the fact that the tariff and other indirect taxes were refundable under the 1955 reform. The only way to make exports profitable was to substantially eliminate quota rents and provide inputs at world prices to exporters.[4] The reforms initiated in April 1958 and implemented over the following two years accomplished

---

[2]   Scott (1979: 318).

[3]   I draw on Scott (1979: 324–5) for the discussion of the reforms described in this paragraph. The trends in trade flows described here are discussed in greater detail below.

[4]   Scott (1979: 321–4) provides empirical evidence supporting the argument in the text.

this task by the removal of quantitative restrictions on imports in many cases and streamlining the quota allocation in favour of exporters in others.

A further important reform, which complemented import liberalization, concerned the exchange rate. In November 1958, the domestic currency was devalued with the result that the exchange rate applicable to the bulk of the import and export transactions by private enterprises changed from NT$25 to approximately NT$40 per US dollar. This adjustment in the exchange rate greatly increased the profitability of processed exports achieved through the first reform.[5]

Additional reforms during this period included:

- the removal of export controls on more than 200 items, simplification of procedures for tax rebates, waiver of the 2 per cent harbour dues on exports and the provision of easier credit terms for exporters;
- the opening up of foreign investment, which brought multinational firms to the shores of Taiwan and helped expand the exports of electronic products; and
- tax holidays, accelerated depreciation, a ceiling on the corporate income tax rate and other remissions to encourage investment.

The Economic Transformation

In addition to the acceleration in growth previously discussed, the structure of trade, output and employment was dramatically transformed.

The Rise of Labour-Intensive Exports

The key reforms towards outward orientation took place in 1955 and during 1958–60. Against this background, Table 17.1 reports the shares of agricultural and non-agricultural exports along with the total value of exports on a continuous basis from 1952 to 1971. It can be seen that non-agricultural exports increased both in absolute and proportionate terms continuously. In 1959, the total exports fell due to a sharp decline in agricultural exports but non-agricultural exports, principal beneficiaries of the reform, showed a healthy growth. They rose from US$18.8 million in 1958 to US$32.1 million in 1959. The following year, agricultural exports fell again but the increase in non-agricultural exports more than made up for it. During 1959–63,

---

[5]   It is important to understand that devaluation alone unaccompanied by the first reform could not have worked. This is because it would have led to a proportionate increase in the prices of exports and imported inputs in the domestic currency. Therefore, if exports were unprofitable initially, they would have remained so post-devaluation. But once the first reform created positive profits, their value in the domestic currency proportionately rose with devaluation.

non-agricultural exports grew at the average annual rate of 50.3 per cent. In the process, the share of non-agricultural exports in the total exports rose from 11.4 per cent in 1958 to 39 per cent in 1963. The process of structural transformation of trade continued in the subsequent years with this proportion rising to 77.5 per cent in 1971. Table 17.2 offers more detailed composition of exports. Category 'others', which included such important labour-intensive exports as clothing and footwear, expanded from 8.1 per cent in 1955 to 39.8 per cent in 1970.

Table 17.1   Agricultural and non-agricultural exports of Taiwan: 1952–71

Year	Total ($Million)	Agricultural ($Million)	Non-agricultural ($Million)	Agricultural (as % of total)	Non-agricultural (as % of total)
1952	119.5	114.2	5.3	95.6	4.4
1953	129.8	121.2	8.6	93.4	6.6
1954	97.8	90.8	7	92.8	7.2
1955	133.4	124.4	9	93.3	6.7
1956	130.1	114.9	15.2	88.3	11.7
1957	168.5	155.4	13.1	92.2	7.8
1958	164.4	145.6	18.8	88.6	11.4
1959	160.5	128.4	32.1	80.0	20.0
1960	169.9	121	48.9	71.2	28.8
1961	214	131.9	82.1	61.6	38.4
1962	238.6	129.4	109.2	54.2	45.8
1963	357.5	218.2	139.3	61.0	39.0
1964	463.1	277.6	185.5	59.9	40.1
1965	487.9	286	201.9	58.6	41.4
1966	569.4	289	280.4	50.8	49.2
1967	649.9	296.9	353	45.7	54.3
1968	841.8	315.6	526.2	37.5	62.5
1969	1110.6	342.2	768.4	30.8	69.2
1970	1561.7	392.2	1169.5	25.1	74.9
1971	2135.5	480.1	1655.4	22.5	77.5

Source: Excerpted from Ranis (1999: Table 5.2, p. 117).

Table 17.2 Composition of exports of Taiwan (percent of total exports)

Item	1952	1955	1960	1965	1970	1975
Food, beverages and tobacco preparations	83.6	84.6	58.5	39.1	9.4	7.3
Textiles, leather, wood, paper and related products	0.9	2.4	17.1	26.2	30.3	24.4
Non-metallic mineral products	0.0	0.0	1.8	3.1	2.5	0.6
Chemical and pharmaceutical products	3.5	3.3	4.9	4.4	1.8	2.0
Basic metals	0.9	1.6	3.7	3.6	3.2	1.5
Metal products	0.0	0.0	0.6	1.1	1.4	1.6
Machinery	0.0	0.0	0.0	1.3	2.3	2.4
Electrical machinery and apparatus	0.0	0.0	0.6	2.7	8.8	9.6
Transportation equipment	0.0	0.0	0.0	0.4	0.6	1.4
Others	11.2	8.1	12.8	18.0	39.8	49.2
Total ($Million)	100.0	100.0	100.0	100.0	100.0	100.0

Source: Excerpted from Ranis (1999: Table 5.5, p. 122).

Rising Output and Employment Share of Industry

The structural transformation in exports was accompanied by a similar transformation in output and employment.

Table 17.3 reports the resulting shift in the composition of output across sectors. Between 1951–3 and 1958–60, the share of industry in the GDP rose from 26.2 per cent to 33.8 per cent. This shift accelerated during the outward-orientation phase with industry claiming 51 per cent of the GDP by 1971–3. Within industry, the share of manufacturing in the GDP rose even more sharply, increasing to 37.9 per cent in 1971–3 from just 15.5 per cent in 1951–3.

In parallel, the employment shares of various sectors shifted as well. According to Galenson (1979: Tables 6.2, 6.3), the proportion of the labour force in agriculture fell from 60.5 per cent in 1952 to 52.7 per cent in 1960, 36.8 per cent in 1970 and 29.9 per cent in 1975. Correspondingly, the employment share of industry rose from 18.4 per cent in 1952 to 25.2 per cent in 1960, 33.7 per cent in 1970 and 41.2 per cent in 1975.

Table 17.3 Composition of GDP in Taiwan

Period	Agriculture	Industry	Manufacturing	Services
1951–3	33.2	26.2	15.5	40.6
1954–7	27.8	31.8	19.6	40.4
1958–60	27.2	33.8	21.4	39
1961–3	24.9	36.1	23	39
1964–7	22.4	39.9	26.7	37.7
1968–70	16.5	46	32.3	37.5
1971–3	13.1	51.3	37.9	35.6

Source: Excerpted from Kuznets (1979: Table 1.10).

Connecting the Outcomes to Policies

In linking outcomes to policies, let us first look at the role of trade liberalization. I then turn to the complementary policies whose presence played a crucial role in ensuring that the benefits of openness were actually realized. Finally, I outline a stylized story of the growth process.

Link to Trade Policies

Following the reforms of 1958–60, Taiwan clearly became outward oriented while accelerating its growth rate to the double-digit range. The exports-to-GDP ratio, which stood at 8.6 per cent in 1958, rose to 21.4 per cent in 1969 and then shot up to 43.9 per cent in 1973.

Various interventions notwithstanding, it remains true that Taiwan specialized according to its comparative advantage, exporting labour-intensive products in return for capital- and skilled-labour-intensive ones. Little (1979: 478) makes this point in the following terms:

> Although the boom was extraordinary, it is not really surprising. The great increases in exports came in clothing, textiles, light electrical machinery, radio and television, electronic components, and shoes. All these (except synthetic textiles, fiber, and yarn) are labor-intensive activities. Taiwan had a disciplined, hard-working labor force, working for a small fraction of the wages, prevalent in the developed countries.

Additionally, several studies show that, on average, manufactures exports of Taiwan showed greater intensity of unskilled labour than its imports. For example, using data for 1966 and 1971, Liang and Liang (1976) show that export industries have 'significantly lower ratios of fixed assets per worker than import industries, and their skill ratio is on average somewhat lower'.[6] Studies by Lin (1973: 131–7) and Scott (1979: 355–7) obtain similar results.

Complementary Policies

Why was the opening up strategy successful in Taiwan while the same did not happen in many African and Latin American countries in the 1980s? The answer lies in the presence of complementary conditions and policies in Taiwan that were probably absent from the unsuccessful countries in Africa and Latin America. I consider the main ones below.

---

[6]   Quoted from Scott (1979: 354).

First, with a firmly established one-party rule and no opposition, Taiwan was politically stable during this period. This made policies credible and the policy environment predictable.

Second, Taiwan had an extremely flexible labour market during this period. The main social protection was in the form of a social insurance scheme (Little 1979: 469). This was a very different regime from that prevailing in a country like India where the level of protection to workers in the organized sector was and remains extremely high and exceeds that in the developed countries along many dimensions (Panagariya 2008: chapter 13).

Third, the government also provided a stable macroeconomic environment. Once the hyperinflation following the Second World War had been brought under control, inflation remained low. This was especially true during the export-orientation phase.

Fourth, as incomes rose, the savings rate rose as well. As in many other developing countries, household savings response to rising incomes in Taiwan was very substantial. The high interest rate policy pursued by the government perhaps played an important role in encouraging these savings.

Fifth, the government maintained and expanded infrastructure as needs arose. In the area of power, it not only made provision for industry at reasonable rates, it also brought electricity to rural areas. Of particular importance was the expansion of paved roads and linking of internal transport network to ports. The latter was especially crucial to facilitating the rapid expansion of trade that took place during the 1960s.

Sixth, the government also played an important role in ensuring the availability of an educated labour force that could quickly adapt itself to industrial production processes. According to Ranis (1999: 121), 'Most important to the success of the education system was the fact that vocational education was highly diversified, flexible and continuously responsive to changing market demands'.[7]

Finally, liberal rules relating to foreign investment also made a modest contribution to the growth of manufacturing. The reforms during 1958–60 had opened the door to direct foreign investment with no cap on the share of foreign investors and full repatriation permitted.

A Stylized Story of Growth

The earliest year to which the sustained spurt in the growth rate can be traced is 1961. However, the spurt in non-agricultural exports preceded it by three years. It is also important to recognize that the acceleration of growth itself was cumulative. The GDP growth rate rose from 6.3 per cent in 1960 to 6.9 per cent in 1961, reaching the double-digit level for the first time only in 1964. By this time, the total exports had already risen to 17 per cent of GDP and non-agricultural exports had climbed

---

[7] This paragraph is based solely on Ranis (1999: 121).

up to 40 per cent of total exports. In current dollars, these exports grew at the astonishing annual rate of 47.5 per cent from 1959 to 1964.

The proposition that the initial spurt in the growth rate in the early 1960s came from the switch to outward-oriented policies and the resulting increase in the profitability of existing as well as potential export sectors thus turns out to be quite robust. The remaining question then relates to the role of outward orientation in sustaining the high growth. Here one must confront the possibility of outward orientation leading to declining incentive to accumulate capital.

The Stolper–Samuelson theory (see also Chapter 1) tells us that opening to trade, which progressively raises the price received by labour-intensive exports, would push the real wages up (as indeed happened in Taiwan in the 1960s and early 1970s) and the real return to capital down. The latter fact would diminish the incentive to accumulate capital and thus choke off growth. This is a standard theoretical problem one confronts in explaining super-high growth rates over prolonged periods. A variety of endogenous growth models have been suggested to get around this problem.[8] My own view is that the most plausible explanation of the Taiwanese experience is in terms of a model postulating technological differences between the advanced and poor economies. High rates of growth in the poor, labour-abundant economies can then be accompanied by technological catch-up, which counteracts the Stolper–Samuelson effect and allows both real wages and the return to capital to rise for some time. The incentive to accumulate capital is thus preserved until technological catch-up is complete.

Within the context of such a model, the stylized story of the Taiwanese growth may be told somewhat as follows: the introduction of some major export incentives, including substantial devaluation of the domestic currency, made many actual and potential labour-intensive export products highly profitable. This led to the movement of resources including some fresh capital into these activities. Exports expanded and allowed the expansion of imports as well. More productive machinery, including older vintage and second-hand machinery suitable for labour-intensive production and often underpriced relative to their productivities in labour-abundant countries, could now be imported in larger volume. Improved resource allocation and technological upgrading through diffusion and imported machinery led to increases in incomes. With other complementary conditions present, the savings rate rose, allowing investment to grow. Flexible labour markets ensured that wages did not rise faster than labour productivity. The provision of vocational training by the government helped ensure the availability of adequate supply of skilled workers at wages that would leave the sectors intensive in the use of these skills competitive. Likewise, the provision of infrastructure by the government ensured that domestic and foreign trade flowed smoothly. Finally, foreign investors also aided the process since they too could take advantage of the export incentives and operate in the large world market rather than stay confined to the small domestic market, as would have been the case under an import-substitution regime.

---

[8]   For example, Ventura (1997) and Mulligan and Sala-i-Martin (1993).

To round up the discussion, let me reiterate that it is difficult to imagine how Taiwan could have sustained its rapid growth without the ability to exploit world markets. To put the matter starkly, even if all complementary policies mentioned above had been present, Taiwan could not have sustained rapid growth for long under a pure import-substitution strategy. Indeed, that was precisely the experience in the 1950s, which led the policymakers to rethink their strategy. Technological improvement, which was probably an important factor in maintaining high rates of return on capital, was itself tied to the country's ability to trade. But equally important, profitability and hence the incentive to accumulate capital would have been exhausted in a relatively short period of time if entrepreneurs had been confined to the small domestic market. India ran into this problem in the first four decades of its development even with a potentially much larger market (Panagariya 2008: chapters 1–4).

Critique and Response

Wade (1990) and Rodrik (1995) have offered major critiques of outward orientation as the key to explaining the Taiwanese miracle. I consider each in turn.

Robert Wade

In his 1990 volume, reprinted in 2004 with a new introduction, Wade argues that the view placing outward orientation at the centre of the success of Taiwan, which Ian Little and other economists have espoused, cannot be right because the government in that country extensively intervened in the making of the miracle. Characterizing the policies identified by Little (1979) as the key to the Taiwanese miracle as 'neoclassical', Wade articulates his argument thus (Wade 2004: 72):

> In short, Taiwan seems to meet the neoclassical growth conditions unusually well. Yet other evidence shows that the government has been intervening for decades, often quite aggressively, to alter the trade and industrial profile of the economy in ways that it judges to be desirable. We then face a formidable identification problem. How can we decide to what extent Taiwan's exceptional economic performance is due to the presence of many of the neoclassical growth conditions and to what extent the government's selective promotion policies? Ultimately, I cannot resolve the issue. But for my purpose it is enough to demonstrate that the government has indeed been guiding the market on a scale much greater than is consistent with neoclassical prescriptions or with the practice of Anglo-American economies. For the fact of such guidance has been almost completely overlooked by neoclassical economists. Recall Ian Little's claim that 'apart from the creation of [these neoclassical conditions] … it is hard to find any good explanation for the

sustained industrial boom...' (1979: 480). In 20 thousand-word essays on the mechanism of Taiwan's development, both Little and Gustav Ranis largely ignore the promotional role of government after the economic liberalization of 1958–62.

It should first be stressed that Wade is factually incorrect in asserting that these authors 'almost completely overlooked' government interventions. What they did was not play up the role of the interventions in the making of the miracle and the reason for it was that they did not consider the interventions as a central, positive element in the miracle. This is particularly evident, for example, in Little (1979).

Turning to the more substantive weaknesses, let me note that as a critic Wade's burden is twofold. First, he must provide clear reasons for why the precise explanation offered by the economists he criticizes is invalid. Second, he must provide an alternative explanation that is more persuasive. He fails to deliver on both counts.

In trying to discharge his first burden, Wade argues that the explanation offered by Little and others, which he characterizes as representing the neoclassical model, could not have been at work since the Taiwanese government intervened extensively. But this is a non sequitur for at least two reasons. First, if the government interventions push the economy in the same direction as markets would and the country achieves rapid growth, this proves the success, not failure, of the neoclassical model. As Gustav Ranis has often argued, the government in Taiwan essentially speeded up what the markets would have done anyway.

Second, Wade provides no clearly articulated set of sufficiency conditions whose presence or absence would render the neoclassical model ineffective or inoperative. The bottom line is that significant interventions may exist in one part of the economy while another part gives entrepreneurs free play under neutral incentives and serves as the driver of rapid growth.

Turning to the second burden, Wade states at the outset that he cannot determine the extent to which the government's selective promotion policies contributed to Taiwan's exceptional performance. Ranis (2003: 34), who actually considers import substitution at the initial stage of development as necessary for the eventual success of outward-oriented growth policy, expresses his dissatisfaction with the analysis by Wade in these terms, 'Wade's [1990 book] *Governing the Market* describes government interventions on Taiwan *ex post*; but I could find no primer on just how to "act strategically".'

The bottom line Wade offers is as follows:

> The fact of big leadership [meaning that the government leads private entrepreneurs through initiatives that significantly alter investment and production patterns] or big followership [meaning that the government follows the lead of private entrepreneurs in designing its interventions] does not mean that government intervention has been effective in promoting economic growth; it only means that government intervention cannot be dismissed as having made negligible difference to outcomes. But the balance

of presumption must be that government industrial policies, including sectoral ones, helped more than they hindered. To argue otherwise is to suggest that economic performance would have been still more exceptional with less intervention, which is simply less plausible than the converse.

The first point to note about this line of argument is that it suddenly drops the bar for judging the success of interventions. Recall that the criterion applied to the policies emphasized by Little and others was whether or not they offered a sufficient explanation of the Taiwanese miracle, not just whether they made a positive contribution to the economic outcome. Arguing that the interventions played a neutral or marginally positive role and simultaneously claiming that they represent a successful development strategy, as Wade seems to do in this paragraph, is like having your cake and eating it too.

But this is not the end of the story. In his response, Little (1996: 12) goes further, questioning the very logic underlying Wade's argument head on:

> Since the less interventionist Hong Kong, Singapore, and Taiwan grew faster than Korea, it is unclear why Wade thinks it simply less plausible that less intervention would have been better, given also the widespread failure of government industrial policies elsewhere. I find it simply more plausible that Korea grew fast despite its industrial policies, than because of them.

The final point concerns the direct involvement of the government in the production activity. The absolute level of interventions discussed by Wade in various sectors at various points in time notwithstanding, over time the government became less and less important to the production activity starting from the early 1950s all the way down to the early 1970s. According to data provided by Ranis (1979: Table 3.31), the output shares of the public sector in industry as a whole and in manufacturing declined steadily between 1953 and 1972 with the decline accelerating in the 1960s.[9]

Dani Rodrik

The critique by Rodrik (1995) can be divided into two broad parts. In the first part, he offers arguments why the outward-orientation thesis explaining the Taiwanese and Korean miracles is wrong. In the second part, he offers his own alternative thesis based on a coordination failure model. I will consider each part of the critique in turn.

With respect to the first part, Rodrik makes two key points. First, the timing of the introduction of incentives for exports and export response do not match. Related, exports follow rather than lead the spurt in growth. Second, when the

---

[9]   There was a small temporary reversal of this trend due to the initiation and completion of the Ten Major Projects between 1973 and 1978. Three of these projects were devoted to the development of heavy industry. For details, see Kuo (1999).

growth spurt came, exports were too small to pull the GDP ahead. Let me consider each argument in turn.

To make his first point, Rodrik compares the movements in two series: the total-exports-to-GDP ratio and a general measure of real exchange rate that begins in 1960. He notes that the former exhibited a spurt in 1963–4, which coincided with an appreciation of the real exchange rate. Evidently, exports could not have been responding to incentives, which had risen in 1958–60 but fell during 1963–4. The story of export incentives driving exports and exports driving growth, thus, simply does not work.

There are two serious problems with the data series Rodrik uses to drive his point home. First, unaware of the real effective exchange rate for exports, calculated by Lee and Liang (1982), he uses a general measure of the real exchange rate, which begins in 1960, to establish that incentives to export in 1963–4 could not have been behind a large expansion of exports during that period.[10] But this is a non sequitur. For one thing, with sufficiently large export-specific incentives, the real effective exchange rate for exports can show improved incentives even when a general measure of the real exchange rate does not do so. But much more importantly, to gauge the relative profitability in a post-reform year, one must compare the post-reform real effective exchange rate with the pre-reform rate. If the initial incentives to export granted by the reform are large, even a small subsequent reversal may leave exports highly profitable.

The second problem with Rodrik's analysis arises with respect to the specific measure of export performance he uses. Whereas the reforms during 1958–60 were designed to stimulate manufacturing exports, he uses total exports (as a proportion of GDP) to measure the export performance. But total exports may behave quite differently than manufactures exports, especially if they are heavily dominated by agricultural exports, as indeed was the case around this time (Table 17.1). Agricultural exports performed poorly during 1958–62, declining at an average annual rate of 3.4 per cent over the five years. This significant decline in agricultural exports, which accounted for 88.6 per cent of the total exports in 1958 and 54.2 per cent even in 1962, masked the large positive response of manufactures exports.

Once we consider the conceptually correct real effective exchange rate for exports calculated by Lee and Liang (1982), which covers both pre- and post-reform years, we find that even during periods of appreciation in the 1960s, the revenue in constant-price local currency for each dollar's worth of exports remained minimally 38.2 per cent above its level prior to the 1958–60 reform. More importantly, a major spurt in the growth of non-agricultural exports fully coincided with the 1958–60 reform. Both the reform and the surge in exports preceded the acceleration in the growth rate of the GDP. Rodrik's observation that total exports as a proportion of

---

[10]   From the statement 'Unlike in Korea, we do not have a synthetic measure of an effective exchange rate for exporters', I infer that Rodrik (1995: 65) was unaware of the work by Lee and Liang (1982). Curiously, he also makes no mention of the important paper by Scott (1979) who analyses the implications of the 1955 and 1958–60 reforms for the profitability of exports in great detail.

GDP did not respond until 1963–4 is entirely an artefact of the poor performance of agricultural exports, which the real exchange rate depreciation could not have helped in the short run in a major way. Symmetrically, the spurt in total exports in 1963–4 to which Rodrik alludes also resulted from huge expansion of agricultural exports. It had virtually nothing to do with investment boom requiring imports of machinery and therefore export expansion to pay for it, as Rodrik surmises.

Rodrik's second criticism of the thesis that exports were the key to Taiwan's success is that the level of exports in Taiwan in the early 1960s was simply too small to pull up the GDP at a faster pace. As Bhagwati (1999) has argued, this too is an incorrect argument. Even if exports are small, the exportable sector is not. When depreciation makes exports more profitable, it makes all exportable products, whether exported or sold at home, more profitable. It can also make some exportable products not initially exported profitable to export. Therefore, the depreciation increases investment in not just exports but the entire exportable sector including products that may not be exported at all in the initial equilibrium. Moreover, since the world markets are virtually limitless from the viewpoint of a small economy, demand is not a constraining factor in this sector.

To put the matter in an economist's jargon, it is the scope for expansion at the margin rather than the initial level of exports that determines the ability of a sector to spur growth. Besides, it needs to be emphasized that the miracle is made not just by catalysing growth but also by sustaining it. And, surely, given how rapidly manufactures exports grew and became a significant proportion of the GDP, it is implausible that growth could have been sustained without them.

Both of the major criticisms of Rodrik (1995) thus fail to stand up to close scrutiny. Let me next turn to his interpretation of the Taiwanese miracle. He argues that the government made the miracle by engineering a significant increase in the private return to capital by subsidizing and coordinating investment decisions. In his story, there existed investments subject to substantial scale economies that would yield high rates of return if undertaken jointly but low rates if undertaken individually. But an individual investor could not be sure that investments that raised the return to his particular activity would be undertaken and therefore would either under-invest in the activity or not undertake the activity at all. If the government offered investment subsidies that made the activity attractive to the investor even when undertaken in isolation, all investment activities would in fact be undertaken and the country would reap the high social rate of return.

To clarify, consider an example. Suppose the return to investment in toothbrush production would be high if investment takes place simultaneously in toothpaste but not otherwise. If there are no scale economies, an individual investor can, of course, invest in both activities and reap the high return. If there are very substantial scale economies, however, capital constraints may allow him to invest in only one activity, say toothbrushes. But without assurance that someone will invest in toothpaste as well, he may find the investment unprofitable. The coordination failure problem may thus arise. The government may break the logjam by underwriting the losses of both toothbrush and toothpaste manufacturers and thus help investors realize the high rates of return. Since no losses will actually be realized, the government will not even have to pay the two manufacturers anything. Rodrik argues that this is just what the government in Taiwan did, not by underwriting the losses but giving explicit investment subsidies.

Of course, we know that trade expanded very rapidly in Taiwan during the growth process. So what is the link of this story to the rapid growth in trade? Here Rodrik argues that investments required machinery, which had to be imported. But, beyond aid, which had been shrinking around this time, imports are not possible unless exports generate the necessary revenues. Rodrik concludes, 'Thanks to appropriate macroeconomic and exchange rate policies, export supply was adequate to meet the increase in import demand, and rose alongside imports'. In other words, exports were merely a passive response to the need for imports, which was itself a response to the investment boom the government had engineered.

There are several problems with this story. First, when the avenue to trade is open, the coordination failure argument has limited validity. In the toothpaste and toothbrush example above, the manufacturer of toothbrushes could either export toothbrushes or toothpaste could be imported. The higher return would be realized either way. To validate the argument, one must argue that there exist interdependent investment opportunities subject to scale economies in non-traded sectors. Rodrik (1995) is aware of this problem and argues that there indeed were such activities but offers few convincing examples. Private investment mostly grew in manufactures, which were by and large tradable and, therefore, not subject to the coordination failure problem.

Second, ignoring this problem, if the story offered by Rodrik is correct, we must observe an investment boom occurring first, followed by import expansion, growth acceleration and then export expansion. But as I have already argued, manufactures exports had begun to grow rapidly well before the growth spurt. As for the sequencing between exports and imports, in a comment on Rodrik's paper, Norman (1995) has already pointed out that it was the reverse of what Rodrik predicts even using Rodrik's aggregate data.

Third, in view of the activist policies to boost exports in both Taiwan and Korea, the argument that export expansion was a passive outcome of the investment boom is problematic as well. Both Taiwan and Korea consciously went after exports by instituting a free trade regime for exporters. The governments made a significant effort to create the necessary administrative machinery to implement the exemptions of custom duties and indirect taxes on direct as well as indirect imports. Korea went even further, setting export targets, which the government then carefully monitored on a regular basis. Westphal (1990: 56) describes the priority the Korean government assigned to exports in these terms: 'If nothing else, policies towards exports have created an atmosphere – rare in the Third World – in which businessmen could be certain that the economic system would respond to and subsequently reward their efforts aimed at expanding and upgrading exports.'

In turn, the study by Westphal and Kim (1982: 271), on which Westphal (1990) draws, assigns a central role to outward-oriented trade policy in stimulating growth in Korea. Westphal and Kim thus turn the Rodrik story on its head, partially attributing the growth in investment itself to export growth and the income increase stimulated by it.

Finally, even granting for the sake of argument that investment coordination catalysed growth, we must ask whether this growth could have been sustained without the outward-oriented policies the countries pursued. India's experience points to an unequivocally negative answer to this question. India intervened far more heavily to boost investment. But unlike Korea and Taiwan, it did so in an autarkic environment and achieved far poorer results until it changed course (Panagariya 2008: chapter 1). As far as trade openness is concerned, the prescription provided by Rodrik's story is no different than that offered by pro-free trade advocates.

Conclusion

The role of openness in the making and sustaining of the Taiwanese miracle has been seriously questioned by some analysts. The presence of interventions and protection during the high-growth period in this case is no more in question than in the cases of China and India. But it is also true that, as in China and India, the general movement of the economy was towards increased openness and reduced role of the government at least in manufacturing activities. There was a small surge in government activity during 1973 to 1978 in Taiwan but the country returned to more open and less interventionist policies soon after.

Though the government in Taiwan intervened heavily, at least until the early 1970s, it did not cause the outcome to deviate significantly from what a neutral policy regime would have produced. Sectors that showed the best performance on the export front were invariably labour-intensive and not subject to selective targeting. In Taiwan, the share of the public sector in industrial and manufacturing outputs also fell sharply.

In summary, growth in Taiwan was driven by rapid growth in private sector investment and characterized by rapid expansion of exports by private entrepreneurs. The composition of output was also consistent with what we would expect under neutral policies. Therefore, a reasonable conclusion is that the government interventions more or less followed the lead of the private sector, reinforcing what the market equilibrium under neutral trade policies would have produced in the first place.

In concluding, we may ask what lessons the Taiwanese experience has for countries that remain poor and are struggling to achieve sustained rapid growth, mainly in sub-Saharan Africa and South Asia. Apart from the obvious that small poor countries have little hope of achieving sustained rapid growth through inward-oriented policies, two points are worth emphasizing. First, in principle, countries can proceed as Taiwan did by providing a more or less free-trade regime for exporters while still maintaining, initially, substantial protection against imports. But in practice, this is not going to work. The Taiwanese government that followed this strategy was highly capable and enjoyed effective control of the administrative machinery. It was also able to respond quickly to changing circumstances. Therefore, it could efficiently administer what was a relatively complex set of measures without subversion by corrupt officials. Most governments in poor developing countries are going to find the literal emulation of the Taiwanese model a real challenge. Therefore, pragmatism dictates a more conventional approach involving clean import liberalization complemented by an exchange-rate policy that avoids overvaluation. Second, outward oriented policies by themselves will be insufficient. Complementary policies such as macroeconomic stability, labour-market flexibility, adequate infrastructure including the supply of electricity at reasonable prices and the provision of skills through vocational training are critical to the success of outward-oriented policies.

References

Bhagwati, J. 1999. The 'miracle' that did happen, in *Taiwan's Development Experience: Lessons on Roles of Government and Market*, edited by E. Thorbecke and H. Wan. Boston: Kluwer: 21–39.

Galenson, W. 1979. The laborforce, wages and living standard, in *Economic Growth and Structural Change in Taiwan: The Postwar Experience of the Republic of China*, edited by W. Galenson. Ithaca and London: Cornell University Press: 384–447.

Kuo, S.W.Y. 1999. Government policy in the Taiwanese development process: the past 50 years, in *Taiwan's Development Experience: Lessons on Roles of Government and Market*, edited by E. Thorbecke and H. Wan. Boston: Kluwer: 43–93.

Kuznets, S. 1979. Growth and structural shifts, in *Economic Growth and Structural Change in Taiwan: The Postwar Experience of the Republic of China*, edited by W. Galenson. Ithaca and London: Cornell University Press: 15–131.

Lee, T.H. and Liang K. 1982. Taiwan, in *Development Strategies in Semi–Industrialized Economies*, edited by B. Bela. Baltimore: Johns Hopkins University Press for the World Bank: 310–50.

Liang, K. and Liang, C. 1976. *Exports and Employment in Taiwan.Conference on Population and Economic Development in Taiwan*. Taipei: Institute of Economics, Academia Sinica.

Lin, C. 1973. *Industrialization in Taiwan: 1946–72*. New York: Praeger.

Little, I.M.D. 1979. An economic reconnaissance, in *Economic Growth and Structural Change in Taiwan: The Postwar Experience of the Republic of China*, edited by W. Galenson. Ithaca and London: Cornell University Press: 448–507.

Little, I.M.D. 1996. Picking winners: East Asian experience – The Social Market Foundation. Occasional paper, 1 February.

Mulligan, C. and Sala-i-Martin, X. 1993. Transitional dynamics in two-sector models of endogenous growth. *Quarterly Journal of Economics*, 108(3): 739–73.

Norman, V. 1995. Discussion. *Economic Policy*, 20: 101–3.

Panagariya, A. 2008. *India: The Emerging Giant*. New York: Oxford University Press.

Ranis, G. 1979. Industrial development, in *Economic Growth and Structural Change in Taiwan: The Postwar Experience of the Republic of China*, edited by W. Galenson. Ithaca and London: Cornell University Press: 206–62.

Ranis, G. 1999. The trade–growth nexus in Taiwan's development, in *Taiwan's Development Experience: Lessons on Roles of Government and Market*, edited by E. Thorbecke and H. Wan. Boston: Kluwer: 113–40.

Ranis, G. 2003. Symposium on infant industries: a comment. *Oxford Development Studies*, 31(1): 33–5.

Rodrik, D. 1995. Getting interventions right: how South Korea and Taiwan grew rich. *Economic Policy*, 20: 55–107.

Scott, M. 1979. Foreign trade, in *Economic Growth and Structural Change in Taiwan: The Postwar Experience of the Republic of China*, edited by W. Galenson. Ithaca and London: Cornell University Press: 308–83.

Ventura, J. 1997. Growth and interdependence. *Quarterly Journal of Economics*, 112: 57–84.

Wade, R. 1990. *Governing the Market: Economic Theory and the Role of the Government in East Asian Industrialization*. Princeton: Princeton University Press.

Wade, R. 2004. *Governing the Market: Economic Theory and the Role of the Government in East Asian Industrialization*. 2nd Edition. Princeton: Princeton University Press.

Westphal, L.E. 1990. Industrial policy in an export-propelled economy: lessons from South Korea's experience. *Journal of Economic Perspectives*, 4(3): 41–59.

Westphal, L.E. and Kim, K.S. 1982. Korea: incentive policies for exports and import substitution, in *Development Strategies in Semi-Industrialized Economies*, edited by B. Balassa. Baltimore: Johns Hopkins University Press: 212–79.

Yu, T. 1999. A balanced budget, stable prices and full employment: the macroeconomic environment for Taiwan's growth, in *Taiwan's Development Experience: Lessons on Roles of Government and Market*, edited by E. Thorbecke and H. Wan. Boston: Kluwer: 141–55.

The Evolution of Special and Differential Treatment and Aid for Trade

Matthias Meyer and Peter Lunenborg

Introduction

After the end of the Second World War, the main trading nations wanted to create an International Trade Organization (ITO). The effort was stillborn and, as a second best to a new international institution, the General Agreement on Tariffs and Trade (GATT) was concluded in 1947. Already in the negotiations for an ITO there were doubts that all countries could be treated equally in international trade.

Non-reciprocity is described for the first time in Part IV of GATT, introduced in 1965: the developed contracting parties do not expect reciprocity for commitments made by them in trade negotiations to reduce or remove tariffs and other barriers to the trade of less-developed contracting parties.[1] Less-than-full reciprocal market opening by developing countries has remained a core element of special and differential treatment (SDT) in GATT/WTO negotiating rounds. But other forms of SDT have also become part of global trade policy. We distinguish the following types of SDT: absence from market access commitments and non-tariff measures (NTM), new interpretations of intellectual property rights, differential rights and obligations with respect to non-tariff measures, non-reciprocal and reciprocal trade preferences, provisions to facilitate compliance with trade rules (such as simplifying notification of duties to the WTO Secretariat or easier access to dispute settlement) and best endeavour commitments. Finally, positive efforts by developed members to facilitate the trade integration of developing countries, including through technical assistance, constitute an important category of SDT.

---

[1]   Article XXXVI.8 GATT.

The Group of Developing Countries Becomes More Diverse Over Time

How are Developing Countries Defined at GATT/WTO?

Only developing countries benefit from SDT. Although the term 'less-developed countries' – later replaced by 'developing countries' – is used frequently in the GATT/WTO legal framework, it has been left open which WTO members belong to this group. The WTO Secretariat (2010) explains that: 'There are no WTO definitions of "developed" or "developing". Members announce for themselves whether they are "developed" or "developing" countries. However, other members can challenge the decision of a member to make use of provisions available to developing countries.' A case in point is China. It acceded to WTO as a developing country but its permissible base level of agricultural subsidies (*de minimis* clause, as percentage of domestic farm production) was set at an intermediate rate (8.5 per cent) between the one for developed (5 per cent) and developing countries (10 per cent).

In GATT/WTO texts, developing countries differ from developed countries because they have much lower 'standards of living',[2] a special 'need for rapid and sustained expansion of the export earnings',[3] and a 'dependence on the exports of a limited range of primary products'.[4] This is why efforts have to be made to 'secure a share in the growth of international trade commensurate with the needs of their economic development'.[5] In conclusion, they have different 'development, financial and trade needs'.[6] Possible indicators for being considered a developing country that could be derived from this country profile refer to income per capita, trade structure and international trade exposure. A few cases of dispute settlement and early industrialized member decisions on trade preferences confirm this general vision of what a developing country is (see GATT 1957, 1965; Guglielmo 1996).

Implicit in these partial images of development status is that developing countries are in a transition towards diversified, high-income developed economies. Those countries economically converging with developed countries should progressively assume the same rights and obligations. At some point in time, they would not have a need for SDT and graduate from developing status. This is the message of the seminal ministerial Enabling Clause of 1979.

---

[2]   GATT 1947, XVIII.1 (revised 1955) and XXXVI:1c (the text speaks of a 'wide gap of standards of living').

[3]   GATT 1947, XXXVI.2.

[4]   GATT 1947, XXXVI.4; Annex I (Notes and Supplementary Provisions), Ad Art. XVIII.1 and 4, mentions that the expression 'in the early stages of development' (the second element of Art. XVIII.1) includes economies in the process of industrialization to correct an excessive dependence on primary production.

[5]   GATT 1947, XXXVI.3.

[6]   Enabling Clause 1979, paragraphs 3(c) and 5.

No Graduation in Spite of Dynamic Emerging Market Economies

The share in world trade of developing countries has rapidly grown, from 39 per cent in 2006/7 to 43 per cent in 2009. At the same time, the disparities in trade and income among developing countries became more pronounced after the 1980s (UN 2006).

In spite of these substantial structural changes in the developing world, the only countries graduating from developing status at the WTO are new members of the European Union. This means that Singapore (GDP per capita of $36,537 in 2009), Korea (GDP per capita of $17,078 and OECD member) and Ghana (GDP per capita of $1,098) are all considered developing countries and benefit in the same way from SDT measures in GATT/WTO agreements.[7] In parallel to the growing heterogeneity of the developing world, the WTO has become a global institution in which developing countries are a vast majority. Of the 157 members of the WTO in March 2012, nine industrialized countries and the 27 EU members are considered developed. The remaining 121 members are classified developing or transition economies.

New Subgroups to Cope with Diversity

- *Least Developed Countries (LDCs)* are those with the greatest development challenges, as measured by a group of human development and poverty indicators.[8] Today, 48 countries are considered LDCs, 26 of which are from sub-Saharan Africa.[9]
- *'LDCs plus' countries* with GNP per capita below $1,000 are allowed continued use of export subsidies which have to be phased out by other developing countries.
- *LDCs plus net food-importing developing countries (NFIDC)* created to protect poor countries which depend on food imports from volatile or rising food prices.
- *Newly acceding countries.* Those countries that acceded after the conclusion of the Uruguay Round had to make significantly more commitments to be accepted than founding WTO members.

---

[7]   All GDP figures mentioned in this section relate to 2009, are expressed in current US dollars and are taken from the World Bank's World Development Indicators database. Bulgaria, the poorest EU country, has a GDP per capita of $6,423.

[8]   Three criteria are used for inclusion and graduation (same criteria but a higher threshold): gross national income (GNI) per capita, a composite human assets index and an economic vulnerability index.

[9]   Since the establishment of the category in 1971, three countries have graduated from the list: Botswana (1994), Cape Verde (2007) and Maldives (2011). Samoa is set to graduate in 2014.

- *Small and Vulnerable Economies (SVEs)*. The Doha Round is leading to a further fragmentation of SDT. The proposed SVE group, separate from the LDC group, was inspired by the concern about small economies and their vulnerability, independently from their income per capita level. The definition, exclusively based upon a very small participation in world trade, is not identical across negotiation areas, with the result that the SVE group counts around 70 marginal traders for negotiations on industrial goods and about 50 for agricultural negotiations (WTO 2005b, 2008: par. 157 and Annex I).

Milestones in the History of Special and Differential Treatment

In this section key changes in policies on SDT at GATT/WTO are summarized.

1954–7: A First Review of the GATT Focusing on Developing Countries

The 1954–5 GATT review session led for the first time to a special rule for developing countries. An amended Article XVIII made it easier for them to react to a persistent trade deficit and protect nascent industries through higher tariffs or import quotas.

1958–64: First Principles for Developing Countries

The 1958 Haberler Report concluded that export earnings of developing countries were insufficient for their economic development. In order to expand trade, the report recommended the opening of developed country markets to exports from developing countries. In 1961 a Declaration on the Promotion of Trade of Less-Developed Countries called for a 'sympathetic attitude' for non-reciprocity in trade relations between developed and developing countries, unilateral trade preferences and the elimination of duties for tropical products (GATT 1961: Annex). These proposals were not seriously acted upon immediately but became important decades later (Keck and Low 2004).

Many developing countries were of the view that their trade concerns were not effectively addressed in GATT, despite a number of reports and declarations to this effect. The United Nations Conference on Trade and Development (UNCTAD) was created in 1964 to address these concerns. It was in this forum that the principles for tariff preferences were laid down that each developed country was to grant to developing countries. This became later known as the Generalized System of Preferences (GSP). This deviation from the most-favoured nation (MFN) principle was made permanent through the Enabling Clause. Another early UNCTAD initiative was commodity agreements with a price band and buffer stocks to reduce price volatility (UNCTAD 2006). The writings of UNCTAD's first Secretary General, Dr Raul Prebisch, influenced the SDT provisions in the GATT/WTO framework, for instance the Development Chapter of GATT.[10] His research was also a main source for import substitution policies of Latin American countries (see Chapter 25 and IDB–INTAL 2006; Love 1980; United Nations 1950).

1964–7: A Development Chapter is Added to GATT

During the Kennedy Round (1964–7) Part IV of GATT was added, Article XXXVI to XXXVIII. Developed countries were encouraged to reduce or eliminate restrictive border measures on products from developing countries and to refrain from imposing internal taxes that discourage consumption of primary products from developing countries.

It also defines 'joint actions', to be pursued within GATT in collaboration with UNCTAD and other multilateral agencies. The concept of 'non-reciprocity' was codified and confirmed. Finally, through Part IV, the Committee on Trade and Development was created, the GATT/WTO body where SDT and other questions at the interface of trade and development are still discussed today. While an impressive array of provisions figures in Part IV, they are largely declaratory, 'best endeavour' clauses.

At the same time, a first technical agreement, the Anti-Dumping Code, was negotiated. It was called a code because almost only developed countries adhered to it, a 'plurilateral' agreement in GATT/WTO parlance. By giving developing countries the option to participate or abstain, their veto was avoided.

1973–9: The Enabling Clause as Centrepiece for SDT

In 1979, at the conclusion of the Tokyo Round, GATT ministers took a decision, considered a hallmark for SDT, titled 'Differential and more favourable treatment, reciprocity and fuller participation of developing countries'. This is commonly referred to as the Enabling Clause (GATT 1979b). It explains that SDT is a temporary right commensurate with the level of economic development. It will be attenuated and then disappear when developing countries will converge with developed countries. The Enabling Clause broadens and deepens SDT by:

- making non-reciprocal preferences for developing countries a permanent exception to MFN tariffs;

---

[10]   The Singer–Prebisch thesis posits that the terms of trade between primary products and manufactured goods tend to deteriorate over time. Countries that export commodities (such as most developing countries) would be able to import less and less for a given level of exports. For this reason, developing economies should not focus on producing primary products but should instead promote the development of manufacturing industry.

- recognizing that developing countries may be treated differentially and more favourably in agreements on non-tariff measures and not only in tariff reduction;
- authorizing preferential trade agreements among developing countries according to different criteria than those of Article XXIV GATT (the general exception for regional trade agreements), which however have not been determined since;
- recognizing the LDC group, established by the UN, as a distinct recipient of more extensive SDT than the developing country group.

In addition to the Enabling Clause, other Tokyo Round agreements strengthen SDT rights: the safeguard against balance of payments (BoP) imbalances and the protection of infant industries of Article XVIII GATT are enhanced and the appointment in dispute settlement of at least one developing country panel member is stipulated, if the dispute is between a developed and a developing country (GATT 1979a, 1979c, 1979d). Finally, the Anti-Dumping Code was renewed and six new codes on NTM were enacted.[11]

1986–94: The Single Undertaking

The Uruguay Round (1986–94), which led to the establishment of the WTO, introduced the notion of a single undertaking (see also Chapter 3). GATT members had to accept all agreements on NTM to accede to the WTO, in sharp distinction to the code approach of the Tokyo Round. This 'single undertaking' allowed for bargaining and exchange of concessions across agreements.

In the final negotiating package, developing countries had to participate in renewed former codes and new agreements on NTM. It included a separate agreement on agriculture, services and trade-related intellectual property rights (TRIPS). New domestic regulations had to be implemented which led to a costly adaptation to the norms of developed countries. The TRIPS Agreement has been considered imbalanced and primarily in the interest of industrial countries and their exporters of technology (Finger 2002; Finger and Nogués 2001).

SDT in the Uruguay Round consisted mainly of provisions to make it less onerous to assume obligations, for instance by postponing their effectiveness for some time or reducing paperwork. Small exporting countries got waivers to contingent market access barriers. Also, developed countries promised to support the building of capacities in developing countries to deal with the new agreements (non-binding 'best endeavour clauses'). Many developing countries had financial and institutional difficulties to implement these agreements.

---

[11] The codes covered the following areas: subsidies and countervailing measures, technical barriers to trade (the Standards Code), import licensing procedures, government procurement, customs valuation and trade in civil aircraft. Besides developed countries, only advanced developing countries joined them.

Also, they considered the Uruguay Round results as unbalanced. This is why developing countries initially opposed and then set conditions to start the Doha Round, launched in 2001.

Better Development Prospects Have Not Changed the Claim for SDT

The justifications used by developing countries for SDT have not changed significantly over time. The main reasons invoked are domestic industry protection, costs incurred and time required to build trade management capacity, fiscal revenue losses and food security.

The infant industry thesis states that enterprises can build a competitive advantage in manufacturing through an initial period of protection. Developing countries argue that they have the right to pursue such policies for economic growth, just as the now developed countries did in the past. This line of reasoning has been popularized among others by Ha-Joon Chang (2002).

Globalization has however transformed production conditions in the last 20 years. Cross-border transport and communications have become cheaper and faster; many final products are part of a complex value chain with elements being produced and services rendered in many countries. High tariffs lead to high input costs and render both domestic and foreign-invested companies uncompetitive on external markets (see Chapters 1 and 17).

Implementing global trade rules requires well-trained people, modern equipment and efficient trade institutions. This is exactly what poor countries lack. This is why priorities have to be set in developing the local trade infrastructure, privileging policies and institutions which have the biggest impact on lowering transaction costs and thereby increase the trade competitiveness of enterprises. This explains the many promises of technical assistance in GATT/WTO documents and the emergence of aid for trade as a major component of SDT. It also explains generous transition periods granted to LDCs before being bound by the obligations of the TRIPS Agreement.

Tariffs, import licenses and other border fees are important sources of government revenue. Tariffs still account for around 15 per cent, on average, of fiscal revenues in developing countries, with much higher rates in LDCs and low-income countries (Fisher 2006; OECD 2006; SouthCentre 2004). In the Doha Round this argument is somewhat mute since presently applied tariffs will often not decrease, or only to a limited extent, as a result of negotiations which take as point of departure the much higher bound rates (see also Chapter 4).

Food is invoked in the Doha negotiations to argue for keeping high import tariffs on basic food items (Special Products), having more flexibility in agricultural subsidies and creating a strong safeguard in case of shocks in import prices or volumes (the Special Safeguard Mechanism). Yet other policy tools are more effective than tariffs in ensuring food security in a world of rising prices. First, strong incentives should be created for domestic production of basic foodstuffs which need to be complemented by regulatory frameworks (for instance property rights).

Second, food price volatility could be reduced by increasing public information to farmers, introducing financial tools to manage risks, developing regional trade in basic foodstuffs and keeping open borders in times of crisis. Finally, efficient social safety nets should be established, including food banks, that allow poor people to buy or receive food in case of crisis (Schneiderman 2011).

Notwithstanding the continuity in the rationale for SDT, the single undertaking of the Uruguay Round represented a watershed, as developing countries became more engaged in multilateral trade negotiations. They did so in recognition that earlier limited engagement had led to a two-tier trading system (with higher barriers on exports of interest to them) in which developing countries failed to gain the full benefits of their own liberalization or have a significant say in the shaping of that system.

The Current Status of SDT

What Might We Expect From a Successfully Concluded Doha Round?

Full participation in the main WTO agreements. After 60 years of GATT/WTO's existence, developing countries – today dominant in membership – participate fully in the WTO for the first time. Almost all developing country members will bind substantially all their tariffs and will participate in all agreements on NTM. The only real exceptions are services, where trade is still limited, and many developing countries, particularly poorer ones, stand on the sidelines.

Less than full reciprocity. The right of developing countries to keep a wedge in tariff reductions with developed countries will lead to more open markets in the developed world while market access in developing countries will not change much. Yet, among developing countries, tariffs will be more harmonized after Doha than before, a positive result from a perspective of trade integration.

Only around 30 advanced developing countries participate in the tariff reduction formulas in agriculture and in Non-Agricultural Market Access (NAMA). The about 90 others will on average keep a higher protection of their domestic markets than their wealthier neighbours. This is how the Doha negotiations are creating de facto target groups for SDT which are different from the groups recognized in the GATT/WTO legal framework.

First inroads in intellectual property. The TRIPS Agreement has always been seen as protecting predominantly the economic interests of developed countries. This perception is changing in a number of dynamic developing countries that are diversifying rapidly their economic structure, thanks to foreign investment but also to a rapid strengthening of home-grown technological innovation. During the Doha Round a number of topics of interest to developing countries have been taken up, including importantly, access to medicines and the protection of genetic resources (see also Chapter 16).

Contingent border protection. Quotas and tariff surcharges to protect the BoP and infant industries were the first SDT measures to be introduced in the 1950s. Safeguard measures, introduced in the Uruguay Round and open to all members, could be used for similar purposes. All three clauses were used by developing countries – the BoP clause most frequently – mainly to protect domestic industries for some time. But these exceptions have been notified rarely in the 2000s. Antidumping measures are taken mainly by advanced developing countries. Proposals in the Doha Round to make access to these defensive tools easier for developing countries have not found a positive response by developed country members.

Non-tariff measures. It is hoped that as a result of the Doha negotiations, access to international markets will improve for agricultural exporters from developing countries because trade-distorting subsidies will be reduced for developed country producers together with import tariffs. This is a case of 'reverse SDT', which will become less pronounced. Industrial export subsidies for LDCs and low-income countries, a legacy of the Uruguay Round, will remain available. Together with Duty-free Quota-free (DFQF) preferences and non-reciprocal preferences for services, LDCs will have strong incentives to diversify their export base.

In recent negotiations on sector-specific technical standards, many developing country delegates seek to influence the discussions on the harmonization of standards and their transparency. It is probable that this will obviate strong defensive clauses for special treatment of developing countries.

A mixed prospect for trade preferences. The GSP has been the first and most important market access incentive among the tools of SDT. Many trade experts (see Low and Piermartini 2006; Paez et al. 2010) consider its impact to be slightly positive, at least for some developing countries and some export products. But its future is clouded because of the erosion of its preferential margins caused both by the expected results in tariff reduction of the Doha Round as well as an increasing number of North–South 'free trade agreements' based upon reciprocity of tariff reductions (even if the timelines for reduction may be much longer for developing countries).

The assessment is different for the new generation of DFQF preferences for LDCs. Their impact might be substantial; if 'sensitive goods' are not excluded from preferences, emerging market economies join the club of preference providers, and rules of origin give an incentive for investment in LDCs (as happened with textiles and garment investment in some African countries covered by the African Growth and Opportunities Act). With the broadening of the circle of preference providers to other advanced developing countries, DFQF preferences will replace a largely inefficient voluntary preference system among developing countries, established in UNCTAD, the General System for Trade Preferences.

Preferential regional trade agreements among developing countries, authorized by the Enabling Clause of 1979, have played an increasing role in the last ten years and are likely to become a major trade and economic integration tool in the future. The 'transparency mechanism', established for preferential trade agreements (PTAs) in the Doha Round, might become a forum where 'good practice' for PTAs will be better defined.

The reform of old SDT clauses: a tedious and frustrating process but some significant results. The strengthening of over 160 SDT clauses in the Uruguay Round and earlier agreements was a condition for developing countries to engage in the Doha Round negotiations. The initial expectations and ambitions were quickly dampened. Developing countries realized that most developed countries would oppose any significant change in trade principles and rules incorporated into the GATT/WTO framework over 50 years of organizational life. More than cosmetic changes could not be expected except for LDCs and possibly other marginal trading nations.

In retrospect, the results of this reform process, focused mainly on SDT in agreements on NTM, are more nuanced and, overall, have brought about significant changes. The summary below assumes that the Doha Round will confirm the negotiating results and trends discernible at present:

- Some initial proposals led or are about to lead to significant changes of SDT beyond facilitation, transparency and best endeavour. Of note are DFQF tariff preferences and General Agreement on Trade in Services (GATS) preferences for LDCs as well as measures to dampen the effect of preference erosion. Negotiations began on the protection of genetic resources and traditional knowledge and on geographical indications for goods other than wine and liquor.
- In several areas compulsory pre-decision consultation mechanisms with developing countries were created or are proposed. Good examples are dispute settlement, Sanitary and Phytosanitary (SPS) measures and antidumping. Participation of developing countries is also the key to new negotiations on technical non-trade barriers and sector tariff agreements in NAMA. The hope is that these agreements will sufficiently take into account developing countries' interests to make specific SDT measures superfluous or of minor importance, at least for non-marginal developing trading countries.
- The result of the negotiations on strengthening SDT is that delegates and trade experts of developing countries are much more familiar now with the formal intricacies and the relative importance for their economies of non-trade barriers, at home and in external markets. These agreements could not be changed but in many cases periodic reviews and monitoring of SDT measures were decided. A good example is the 'transparency mechanism' for preferential trade agreements. The committee discussions on these agreements have already led to some more clarity on how PTAs between developing countries, authorized by the Enabling Clause of 1979, can be distinguished from other PTAs authorized by Article XXIV GATT.
- A substantial majority of 'best endeavour' clauses ask developed countries, multilateral aid agencies, or the WTO Secretariat to provide 'technical assistance'. In the course of the Doha Round, technical assistance has become aid for trade and an essential form of SDT. This major achievement of the Doha Round is described later in this chapter.
- Finally, none of the proposals were accepted which intended to create 'policy space' for developing countries by changing basic trade rules or broadening

considerably exceptions already granted, except in the case of LDCs. This simply would have changed the common objective of the WTO, which is to abide by some core trade rules which support trade creation and integration.

Aid for Trade

WTO: A Mobilizing and Coordinating Agent for Aid in the Doha Round

In the late 1980s and 1990s, when many LDCs and other 'lesser-developed' countries joined GATT and then WTO, they were confronted with an avalanche of norms and procedures in the many new trade agreements they adhered to. At the same time, these two decades were lost for development in many poorer developing countries. Economic mismanagement, unmanageable debt, low export prices and political instability meant that poverty increased markedly. To ensure human security became a major if not the only development policy priority, at least in a number of LDCs, external cooperation agencies, including the World Bank, reacted by focusing their support in poor countries on social sectors and did not put a strong emphasis on agriculture, infrastructure and economic diversification more generally. Trade policy and Trade-Related Technical Assistance (TRTA) was put on the backburner. This changed with the Doha Development Agenda (DDA).

Ministers from developing countries insisted on including more effective SDT as a negotiating element of the Doha Round. Part of this understanding was to build up technical support to developing countries. Also, a special effort was to be made to reinforce special treatment more generally to LDCs and other marginal trading nations. These goals are reflected in the Doha Declaration of November 2001 (WTO 2001: par. 38–41). From then on, WTO has grown into a primary forum to mobilize additional aid commitments and review progress on aid for trade.

An essential next step in reinforcing the WTO's aid role were the recommendations of the Task Force on Aid for Trade, endorsed by the General Council in October 2006 (WTO 2006). The Hong Kong Ministerial Conference of December 2005 was at the origin of the Task Force. It called for the expansion of aid for trade to 'help developing countries, particularly LDCs, to build the supply-side capacity and trade-related infrastructure that they need ... to expand their trade' (WTO 2005a: par. 57). African countries had insisted on this broader concept of aid for trade arguing that better access of their enterprises to external markets was not enough as they were unable to produce competitive goods and services.

The Task Force also referred to good aid practice, namely developing country ownership, harmonization of external cooperation projects and alignment to the beneficiary country's priorities.[12] Finally, global aid reviews should take place

---

[12]   These are the main principles of the Paris Declaration on Aid Effectiveness of

periodically to monitor the quality and adequacy of aid for trade. Such review meetings had taken place since 2002 as a joint venture of the WTO and OECD. The difference now was that at the 2007 and 2009 global review meetings the heads of major international agencies participated while earlier meetings took place at senior level.

Important Steps in Strengthening the Aid for Trade Agenda

Positive changes in the aid environment. The international community had good reason to believe that its appeal to strengthen both the volumes and the quality of aid for trade would be heard. Four reasons support this view: first, in the 2000 decade hope returned that many poor developing countries had a good potential to catch up with successful neighbours. Investment and growth rates remained very high on average until the financial crisis and have picked up since (Meyer 2010). Second, external observers see clear signs of improving economic governance in low-income countries. Third, the pressure on donors to increase aid volumes in general has been quite high in the last decade for example through the monitoring of the Millennium Development Goals to be achieved by 2015 or the G-8 Gleneagles Agreement in 2005 to double aid to Africa. In fact, aid volumes have increased considerably in the last decade although not in the targeted proportions. Fourth, given the new effective demand of poor countries for support to create the fundaments of export-led growth and diversification, private sector development and economic infrastructure (often in partnership with private investors) have received important aid contributions. Thus, the climate was benign for a strengthened aid for trade. We will outline now the major aid initiatives taken.

The Enhanced Integrated Framework (EIF) of the early 2000s is an alliance of LDCs, a group of six multilateral agencies, and bilateral donors.[13] Its headquarters is at the WTO and its goal is to help LDCs to create action plans for the trade sector – Development and Trade Integration Studies (DTIS) – to coordinate trade project delivery and to mobilize donor resources to implement trade policy reforms and capacity-building and investment projects. Today, trade sector strategies and action plans of variable quality exist in most LDCs and are often reflected in the countries' poverty reduction strategies.[14] However, only in a limited number of LDCs have the identified priorities been fully transformed into tangible projects (Kaushik 2010).

2005, which was signed by donor countries, multilateral cooperation agencies and many developing countries.

[13]   The six agencies are UNCTAD, ITC, UNDP, WTO, IMF and the World Bank.

[14]   Since the turn of the century, low-income countries prepare Poverty Reduction Strategy Papers. These are then endorsed by the Executive Boards of the World Bank and the International Monetary Fund and become the reference for policy-based lending of these two institutions.

Capacity-building initiatives. Five agencies have established a capacity-building fund to address SPS trade barriers, focussing on low-income countries, named the Standards and Trade Development Facility (STDF).[15] Based at WTO, the STDF approves about ten projects per year. Its annual budget of some $5 million is financed entirely by a number of developed country donors.

United Nations Industrial Development Organization (UNIDO) has stepped up substantially its engagement in standards' development, reaching annual commitment levels beyond $50 million. WTO increased its training programmes, cooperating with training institutes in developing regions, and created an internal institute for training and technical assistance. Its annual budget of some 25 million Swiss francs is mainly funded by cooperation agencies of developed countries. Finally, the World Bank launched a fund to support reforms of customs and trade logistics, the Trade Facilitation Facility in 2008, again with funding from a group of developed country donors.

Cooperation agencies scale up their aid for trade programmes. The World Bank has accompanied the Doha negotiations with policy research studies and developed analytical tools for developing country negotiators. It has also established two grant funds, financed by bilateral donors, to initiate or strengthen its operational activities in low-income countries and LDCs.[16] It focused on trade-related private sector support, capacity-building in trade policy (such as in services and trade-impact models), infrastructure and the strengthening of technical trade institutions. By now, the trade sector has become an important part of the World Bank's country programme.

A promising way to associate aid with trade rules. Finally, in the negotiation of a trade facilitation agreement in the Doha Round, a consensus has emerged on an innovative link between the respect for new Customs management standards and technical assistance. Developing countries will have the option of postponing the implementation of some of the standards. They may request capacity-building assistance from donor countries that will enable them to achieve an adequate level of efficiency to master such standards. Reform progress will be monitored by the WTO committee in charge of trade facilitation and a date will then be set for the application of the postponed standards. This appears to be a method that could be applied also to acceding developing countries in other agreements and to future new agreements.

Achievements in Aid for Trade

A sea change has taken place in aid for trade during the Doha Round, justifying the epithet 'Doha Development Agenda'; aid for trade is paid attention to by the

---

[15]   The agencies are FAO, OIE, World Bank, WHO and WTO. See: www.standardsfacility. org/index.htm.

[16]   The two funds are a trade window of the Bank Netherlands Partnership Program and the Multi-Donor Trust Fund for Trade and Development.

international community at the highest levels. For the first time the majority of WTO members who are marginal traders are given support to integrate in the global economy. The scope of assistance has broadened to include not only trade policy skills and modernizing trade institutions but also export-led development. Volumes of aid have increased substantially, as detailed below. More importantly, the quality of aid and its impact on the development prospects of poor countries is starting to command attention. The knowledge about what should be considered good cooperation practice is deepening.

As evidenced by Table 18.1, aid for trade has expanded at high rates in the last decade. The most significant change has taken place in the core category of capacity-building to enable developing countries to defend their trade interests and lower trade transaction costs by modernizing technical trade institutions (that is for instance Customs, trade logistic services, and technical and food standards). Aid commitments have increased seven times (in current and not in real terms) to reach $1.3 billion in 2009. Export supply projects with private enterprises (such as investment credit, infrastructure for industrial parks and trade promotion) and investments in economic infrastructure have more than doubled. Aid for trade goes in its majority to LDCs and other low-income countries, and their share is increasing (OECD/WTO 2009).

Africa provides two tangible examples of how aid for trade can help. While pesticide residues once kept Kenyan flowers out of US and EU markets, a five million euro grant from the EU helped Kenyan industry phase out the pesticides and emerge as one of the world's leading exporters. And aid for trade funding is an important catalyst for the North–South Corridor transport project that will link Dar es Salaam with the southern ports of South Africa, via the copper belt (OECD/WTO 2009: chapter 5, The Regional Dimension).

Table 18.1 Annual aid for trade commitments (current USD, in billions)

Category	1995–2001 (average)	2002–5 (average)	2006	2007	2008	2009
Building productive capacity	6.96	8.92	10.45	12.90	16.39	17.84
Economic infrastructure	9.91	10.78	12.50	15.16	21.34	20.38
Transport policy	0.38	0.54	1.27	1.33	1.87	2.25
Energy policy	0.51	0.52	0.89	1.68	2	0.97
Trade policy and regulations	0.18	0.67	1.13	0.88	1.27	1.29
Trade-related adjustment	0	0	0	0	0.01	0.02
Total aid for trade	17.05	20.37	24.08	28.94	39.00	39.51

The Future of SDT

The Doha Round has been an occasion to identify specific SDT needs of developing countries and strengthen the corresponding trade rules. It also led to differentiating further subgroups of developing countries to benefit from SDT. All SDT provisions in the GATT/WTO legal framework were examined and reforms proposed. The expected results of these negotiations were presented in the previous section. Yet, these results also throw light on the SDT toolbox and pending reforms for the post-Doha future. This is what this last section is about.

SDT beneficiary groups: back to basics. As a result of the proliferation of SDT beneficiary groups witnessed earlier, an array of exceptions is conceded to different subgroups of developing countries while at the same time treating countries with starkly diverging development status as equals. Such a trade policy is arbitrary because no economic rationale is able to back it up and inequitable because some countries are discriminated against without valid reasons.

A return to the basic SDT rationale – treating countries differently if their trade and development needs are different – would be best respected by a three-tier formula:

- Developing countries who have substantially converged with developed countries are graduated from SDT status. As such graduation is usual in international financial institutions and in preference schemes, it should not be difficult to find objective indicators.
- The present 'base group' of countries benefitting from SDT should be consolidated. This would lead to an 'LDC plus' group that in addition to the LDC group would also include SVEs and low and lower-middle-income countries up to a certain population threshold. This group would include about 60 countries at present.[17] Taking into account new WTO accessions as well as passages to the 'advanced group' (below) in the next ten years, it would represent around half of WTO members in 2020 (90 out of 180).
- The group of advanced countries, defined as dynamic traders relying on a diversifying production structure and increasing trade competitiveness, should, in a next negotiating round, benefit from less-than-full reciprocity in tariff reductions and possibly from occasional support in capacity-building. This could be called 'SDT light'. In all other respects they would be equated to developed countries including the obligation to provide trade preferences to the base group. This group has about 30 members now and maybe 45 in 2020.

Passage from one subgroup to another should be simple and objective in the sense that it relies on one or several quantitative indicators, as is presently the case with the SVE and LDC plus groups. If categories of SDT beneficiaries and graduation

---

[17]   Thirty-one LDCs are WTO Members and around half of the 45 SVEs in agriculture negotiations are low or lower-middle-income countries.

criteria were unequivocally defined, negotiations of SDT benefits would become easier because less unjustified discrimination and unfair competition would result among developing countries. Exclusion from broader SDT benefits, available to the base group, and corresponding potential losses would only concern countries which have gone through positive structural change, have been able to create adequately performing trade institutions and are reasonably well integrated in international markets. To be reliable and predictable, a legal framework that distinguishes development stages has to make clear to which tiers countries belong.

Advantages and risks of an issue-specific approach. The Uruguay and Doha Rounds have not only led to more developing subgroups but also to several cases where an exception has been tailored to a new subgroup for a specific agreement or clause (such as the LDC plus group allowed to have export subsidies or the group of NFIDCs) or even to a small group of countries or even single countries. Keck and Low (2004) see such a tailoring of SDT provisions to 'economic needs that automatically identify the beneficiary members' as positive. The problem is that the identification of the needy beneficiaries is often tricky and risks being arbitrary. Stevens (2002) argues this point in the case of special provisions for NFIDCs: food insecurity is not necessarily linked to being a net-food importer but to having a sizable poor population in a country with an insufficient calorie intake. Such a country may be a net-food exporter. The concern of Keck and Low is fully justified. One should avoid deciding on the same standard exception for countries with different needs. Yet the solution to this dilemma lies probably more in consultations with developing countries that have very limited capacity to deal with technical rules before a decision is made. This group is in many cases quite big if not identical with the base group that we identified above. It is then possible to link the obligation to implement a provision with support in capacity-building, enabling a country to reach a higher level of performance. We will revisit this point below.

A new wave of plurilateral agreements: a return to exclusion? We mentioned earlier that at the end of the Doha Round all members will participate in core WTO disciplines – binding substantially all tariffs on goods and participating in non-tariff measures. Yet some variable geometry cannot be excluded. Some issues are not well understood. Plurilateral agreements might be concluded among a critical mass of large developing countries but excluding marginal traders. This could involve sector agreements in industry with the goal to reach zero tariffs (for instance for chemicals) and agreements on standards and conformity assessments for specific goods (for instance cars). In the post-Doha era, plurilateral service sector agreements are probable.

Some of these agreements could be of keen interest to subgroups of developing countries, as for example gems and jewellery proposed by Thailand and fish proposed by New Zealand (WTO 2011). But plurilateralism would have clear disadvantages particularly for poorer developing countries. Their interests and issues of concern would not be represented in the final outcome. In the future, if they were to join, they would have to accept the *acquis* and would not be able to force a renegotiation (Hoekman 2005). In the case of technical standards, this would be a return to the Tokyo Round Codes, but now limited to very specific areas.

The future of aid for trade. Aid for trade will be a strong enabling factor for an accelerated trade integration of low-income and marginal trading countries. It helps in reducing the recourse of poor countries to defensive policies and enables them to develop their trade interests in a constructive and participative way. Even more importantly, by helping to lower trade transaction costs and strengthen the trade competitiveness of enterprises, aid for trade contributes to high investment and growth and the product diversification of low-income economies. To be able to play fully this role, the planning processes of aid delivery have to improve both in the recipient countries as well as among the donor community. This is why monitoring by the international community with a leadership role of the WTO and international financial institutions is essential and should be given strong support by all concerned countries, developed and developing alike. Aid for trade should also embrace more comprehensively areas of support that have received scarce attention so far: regional integration, investment policies, regulation and trade of services, agricultural exports and food security, and capacity-building for trade negotiations.

This latter point reminds us – as a concluding observation – that however important, aid for trade, like SDT more broadly, is essentially a complement to the underlying goal of liberalizing trade and investment as tools for growth, development and improved human welfare.

References

Chang, H.J. 2002. *Kicking Away the Ladder: Development Strategy in Historical Perspective.* London and New York: Anthem Press.

Finger, J.M. 2002. The Doha Agenda and development: a view from the Uruguay Round. *ERD Working Paper No. 21.* Manila: Asian Development Bank.

Finger, J.M. and Nogués, J.J. 2001. The unbalanced Uruguay Round outcome. *Policy Research Working Paper 2732.* Washington, DC: World Bank.

Fisher, B. 2006. Preference erosion, government revenues and non-tariff trade barriers. *The World Economy,* 29(10): 1377–93.

GATT. 1957. Report of the Panel on Article XVIII application by Ceylon, *L/751, 1–2.*

GATT. 1961. Meeting of Ministers (Conclusion adopted on 30 November 1961). Contracting Parties – Nineteenth Session, *L/1657.*

GATT. 1965. Tariff preferences for less–developed countries – request for a waiver by Australia, *L/2443.*

GATT. 1979a. Declaration on trade measures taken for balance-of-payments purposes, *L/4904.*

GATT. 1979b. Differential and more favourable treatment reciprocity and fuller participation of developing countries. (Decision of 28 November 1979). *L/4903.*

GATT. 1979c. Safeguard Action for Development Purposes. (Decision of 28 November 1979). *L/4897*.

GATT. 1979d. Understanding regarding notification consultation, dispute settlement and surveillance. (Adopted on 28 November 1979). *L/4907*.

Guglielmo, V. 1996. The definition of developing countries under GATT and other international law. *German Yearbook of International Law*, 39: 164–97.

Hoekman, B. 2005. Operationalizing the concept of policy space in the WTO: beyond special and differential treatment. *Journal of International Economic Law*, 8(2): 405–24.

IDB–INTAL. 2006. Raúl Prebisch – power, principle and the ethics of development.

Kaushik, A. 2010. *Reassessing Scope and Mandate of the Enhanced Integrated Framework*. Eschborn: GTZ.

Keck, A. and Low, P. 2004. Special and differential treatment in the WTO: why, when and how? *Staff Working Paper*, Economic Research and Statistics Division. Geneva: WTO.

Love, J.L. 1980. Raul Prebisch and the origins of the doctrine of unequal exchange. *Latin American Research Review*, 15(3): 45–72.

Low, P. and Piermartini, R. 2006. Non-reciprocal preference erosion arising from MFN liberalization in agriculture: what are the risks? *WTO Staff Working paper ERSD–2006–02*. Geneva: WTO.

Meyer, M. 2010. LDCs' trade and investment challenges: a report and action plan of a group of NGOs in view of the Istanbul Summit of Least Developed Countries, May–June 2011. [Mimeo] Geneva: IDEAS centre, CUTS and ICTSD.

OECD. 2006. *Trading Up: Economic Perspectives on Development Issues in the Multilateral Trading System*. Paris: OECD.

OECD/WTO. 2009. *Aid for Trade at a Glance 2009: Maintaining Momentum*. Paris and Geneva: OECD/WTO.

Paez, L., Karingi, S., Kimenyi, M. and Paulos, M. 2010. A decade (2000–10) of African–US trade under the African Growth and Opportunity Act (AGOA): challenges, opportunities and a framework for post-AGOA engagement. Adis Ababa: UNECA.

Schneiderman, R.M. 2011. Davos: Zoellick on the world's challenges. *Newsweek*, 23 January.

South Centre. 2004. Revenue implications of WTO NAMA tariff reduction, *SC/TADP/AN/MA/1*. Geneva: SouthCentre.

Stevens, C. 2002. The future of special and differential treatment (SDT) for developing countries in the WTO. *IDS Working Paper No. 163*. Brighton: Institute of Development Studies.

UN. 1950. The economic development of Latin America and its principal problems, *E/CN.12/89/Rev. 1*. New York: United Nations.

UN. 2006. *World Economic and Social Survey 2006 – Diverging Growth and Development*. New York: United Nations.

UNCTAD. 2006. *UNCTAD: A Brief History*. New York: UNCTAD.

WTO. 2001. Doha WTO ministerial 2001: Ministerial Declaration, *WT/MIN(01)/DEC/1*.

WTO. 2005a. Ministerial Declaration. Ministerial Conference (sixth session). Hong Kong, *WT/MIN(05)/DEC*.

WTO. 2005b. Shares of WTO Members in world non-agricultural trade, 1999–2004. Negotiation Group on Market Access, *TN/MA/S/18*.

WTO. 2006. Recommendations of the task force on Aid for Trade, *WT/AFT/1*.

WTO. 2008. Revised draft modalities for agriculture. Committee on Agriculture – Special Session, *TN/AG/W/4/Rev.4*.

WTO. 2010. *Who are the Developing Countries in WTO?* [Online]. Available at: www.wto.org/english/tratop_e/devel_e/d1who_e.htm [accessed: 22 March 2011].

WTO. 2011. Sectoral negotiations in non-agricultural market access (NAMA). Room document 17.

Trade Preferences for Developing Countries: The Case of the European Union

Christopher Stevens

Introduction

All industrialized countries offer 'trade preferences' in the sense of multiple import regimes offering different levels of market access to different countries but those of the European Union (EU) and its predecessors are particularly complex. As such, the EU offers a valuable case study for a more general phenomenon. But detail is all important. The EU case illustrates the difficulty of calculating the economic effects of a particular change to a trade policy that already includes multiple layers of market access. But applying these lessons to other countries requires detailed information on the differentiated trade practice of each, which is a point to which we return in the conclusions.

The original Six inherited colonial trade preference schemes from France, Belgium and Italy, and the UK extended these when it joined. Originally these were reciprocal – the beneficiaries had to accord preferential access to the colonial power and, later, to the Six. During the 1970s–90s, these were largely replaced by non-reciprocal agreements requiring no trade quid pro quo. Since then two parallel systems (with porous borders) have emerged: on the one hand there has been a shift back to reciprocal accords, justified in the WTO as free trade areas (FTAs); on the other, the system of non-reciprocal preferences has been reinforced in certain respects.

This chapter covers both the reciprocal and non-reciprocal accords because the trade effects of Europe's actions under both systems are the same. The overall economic effects of reciprocal and non-reciprocal arrangements differ, since the former also involve policy changes by Europe's partner(s), but there is no difference on the EU side. Both systems give rise to a set of economic questions (do they, for example, create or divert trade?) and of political questions (are they, in Bhagwati's celebrated aphorism, 'building blocks or stumbling blocks' to multilateralism?).

We return to these questions at the end of the chapter and find that they are not straightforward to answer. The very complexity of the EU's preference system makes it a particularly illuminating case study for the way in which non-multilateral trade agreements create multiple (and sometimes conflicting) effects at different levels. The complexity (absolute and relative to other developed countries) can best be illustrated by reference to Africa. The EU has no fewer than 13 different preference agreements with Africa whilst the United States has four, while Australia, Canada, Japan and Norway have three apiece[1] (Stevens and Kennan 2011). Consequently, it is a country's position in the hierarchy relative to its competitors that is the fundamental determinant of the trade effects of its preferences. And, if the pack is shuffled, so are its trade effects. The last decade has seen a lot of shuffling.

The Evolution of the European System

Francophone states in North and sub-Saharan Africa were the principal beneficiaries of this system until 1975 when they were joined by some of the UK's former colonies and the Africa, Caribbean and Pacific (ACP) group was created (Lister 1988, 1997). The access of ACP goods exports to the European market was determined by the provisions of the Lomé Convention which was signed in 1975 and renegotiated three times until it was superceded in 2000 by the Cotonou Partnership Agreement (CPA). In its early years, Lomé was at the apex of Europe's 'pyramid of privilege' in the sense that a wider range of its actual and potential exports entered the European market at lower tariffs than did those of any other trade partner.

Alongside was a set of bilateral non-reciprocal preferential trade agreements with most Mediterranean countries which offered market access that was very liberal but more closely tailored than the Lomé Convention. The main restrictions were on access for products falling under the Common Agricultural Policy (CAP), which was limited broadly to traditional volumes of traditional exports, and the absence of the Lomé guarantee of unlimited tariff and quota-free access for non-CAP goods.

The third main plank in the EU's trade regime for developing countries was the Generalized System of Preferences (GSP). Following an initiative in the United Nations Conference on Trade and Development (UNCTAD) and justified in the

---

[1]   The EU has six interim Economic Partnership Agreements or EPAs (all of which are different) with some sub-Saharan African states, bilateral agreements with Algeria, Egypt, Morocco, South Africa and Tunisia, and trades with others under either EBA or the Standard GSP. Canada and Japan offer GSP to almost all African states (and most-favoured nation or MFN to those not eligible), with a special tranche for LDCs. Most but not all African countries are eligible for the United States' GSP (with the rest trading on MFN terms), and some benefit from the additional provisions for LDCs. In addition, a group of sub-Saharan states is eligible for The African Growth and Opportunity Act (AGOA), with some 'lesser developed' states benefitting for extra preferences on apparel.

General Agreement on Tariffs and Trade (GATT) and World Trade Organization (WTO) by the 1979 'Enabling Clause', all the developed countries have created a GSP that offers lower tariffs on some of their imports from developing countries. All of the GSPs are 'autonomous policies' of the developed countries concerned (that is they have been designed and agreed voluntarily by each state acting alone) and so all are different in their details.

Europe's GSP began life as the poor relation of its trade preferences for developing countries (Stevens 1981). It covered fewer products than either Lomé or the Mediterranean accords and often imposed higher tariffs. Moreover, some developing countries were 'graduated out' either of the whole scheme or of eligibility for goods in which they were deemed to be too competitive. Consequently, whilst all developing countries were eligible for the GSP it was used in day-to-day commerce only by those that did not have superior access under one of the other regimes.

History and trade pragmatism initially determined which countries were covered by which regimes. All of the parties to the more preferential regimes had been European colonies but not all former colonies were offered membership. The ACP states were mainly small (economically if not geographically) because Britain's larger and more competitive former colonies, primarily those in South and South East Asia, were ruled out of Lomé eligibility (as were the Commonwealth developed countries that had preferential access to the UK market before it joined the European Community). Also in the group of developing countries only eligible for the GSP were those that had not been colonies of the Six or UK, most notably all of Latin America. A consequence of this eligibility pattern was that the EU could claim a majority of the poorest *countries* were covered by its most liberal preferences whilst critics could argue that the majority of the poorest *people* were served only by the least liberal tier.

After the early 1990s this pattern began to change as the GSP developed internal differentiation. Initially, there was a scheme to offer extra preferences to Central American and Andean states. It was justified as support for their struggle against the narcotics trade, making it well received in Washington as well as Madrid. This tranche was wider than 'the Standard GSP' (more products were covered) and deeper (tariffs were lower). Then in 2001 the EU launched the Everything But Arms (EBA) scheme under the GSP. This provides duty-free and quota-free (DFQF) access for all exports from least developed states (LDCs), albeit with a transition period for bananas (to 2006), rice and sugar (to 2009).[2] Finally in 2005 the special tranche for the Central American/Andean states was transformed into a broader GSP+ regime available to a wider group of developing countries but still excluding MERCOSUR and most of South, South East and East Asia (Stevens 2007). Despite the differences, one common feature of all the regimes is that they are non-reciprocal, that is, the beneficiaries are not required to offer any special regime to European exports in return.

---

[2]   In addition, special tranches were introduced for countries adhering to international labour and environmental conventions but these were barely used until given a new lease of life by the incorporation of their broad approach into the GSP+.

The result was a more complex pattern of trade preferences. The non-reciprocal Lomé/Cotonou regime was joined at the apex by EBA, with GSP+ close behind and, in a parallel development, Europe began to negotiate reciprocal FTAs with its close neighbours and with South Africa, Chile and Mexico. It also did so with its Mediterranean partners to replace the non-reciprocal accords.

This created, in broad terms, a three-band inverted pyramid of privilege. At or near the apex were a large number of states that had liberal access to the European market for their goods exports under either a non-reciprocal preference agreement or an FTA. In the middle were those developing countries eligible only for the Standard GSP. The base comprised primarily the small number of Organisation for Economic Cooperation and Development (OECD) states not covered by an FTA,; these states export to the EU under the misnomer of the GATT/WTO 'most-favoured nation' (MFN) regime and pay the highest tariffs.

Most recently, there have been two changes resulting in a sharp move of states from the non-reciprocal to the reciprocal groups (but no great change in membership of the three bands). First, the CPA trade regime came to an end on 31 December 2007 (though the other aid and political aspects of the Agreement continue until 2020). The ACP split into a group of 36 states that initialled reciprocal Economic Partnership Agreements (EPAs) and the rest for which access remained non-reciprocal but under the GSP.[3] Second, as the Doha Development Round of multilateral trade agreements stagnated, the EU began actively to negotiate FTAs with a range of important developing country trade partners. These include the Central American and Andean states to replace their non-reciprocal GSP+ as well as countries like South Korea (that are not eligible for the GSP) and India, with the long-running negotiations with MERCOSUR also given a boost.

GATT/WTO Compatibility

The GATT and WTO have played a key role in the shaping of the EU's pattern of trade preferences. Some elements remain controversial because of an inherent feature of the multilateral system of trade rules. This is that the conformity of specific Member State policies is determined, if at all, *ex post* rather than *ex ante*. Only if one Member challenges the policy of another under the dispute settlement provisions will conformity be adjudged, and then only if the two parties fail to reach a compromise solution during the earlier, conciliation stages of the process. Until then, a Member may apply any policy that it believes, or chooses to believe, is in conformity without any official, independent assessment of the merits of the case.

---

[3]   Seventy-six of the ACP states took part in the negotiations. Of the 35 states that initialled, most have gone on to sign either full or interim EPAs but, at the time of writing, negotiations were continuing with seven initialling states plus South Africa, which failed to initial. There were also continuing negotiations with many of the other ACP states but without any strong indication that they would sign.

Until the mid-1990s, the EU justified the conformity of its preferences with multilateral rules by mere assertion that they were covered by the provisions dealing with special and differential treatment (SDT) in favour of developing countries. In this the EU was acting no differently than some other developed states: several North–South non-reciprocal preferential trade agreements are still justified by the parties in the same way. But for Europe this claim was put to the test in multilateral dispute settlement, in relation to the Lomé Convention, and ruled to be invalid. This has had a profound effect on the evolution of the EU's trade policy.

Banana Disputes

The trigger setting the process in motion was a 1993 GATT judgment on the legality of the European banana trade regime which was, in turn, 'collateral damage' from the completion of the Single European Market (Stevens 2000). Prior to 1992 the EU did not have a common trade regime for bananas. Separate regimes existed (largely reflecting colonial legacies) which resulted in markedly different prices in member states. They were made possible by a provision in the Treaty of Rome (Article 115) that permitted member states to restrict imports from their partners of goods that originated outside the Community. Coupled with the oligopolistic nature of the trade in bananas, this allowed the UK, France and Italy to restrict imports of cheaper Latin American bananas (both directly and via another member state) until their markets had absorbed all of the more expensive fruit exported by ex-colonies (and overseas Départements).

Because the Single Market allowed cheaper fruit imported into other EU states to be transhipped to UK/France in competition with the 'colonial fruit', the old regime had to be replaced with one that would impose sufficient restrictions on imports from the most efficient suppliers (in Latin America) to remove the incentive for such producers to take over the market share of the former colonies. The result was a three-tier tariff (zero for the ex-colonies, low for Latin America within a quota and high outside the quota) which became the subject of a series of GATT and WTO disputes, all of which the EU lost.

The Three WTO 'Pegs'

In the first of the adverse judgments, the GATT panel concluded not only that the banana regime was contrary to the rules but also that the same applied to the entire Lomé Convention. The search was on to find a regime that would be less open to multilateral challenge.[4] There are three 'pegs' on which GATT/WTO Members can

---

[4] In principle requests for a waiver had to be approved by 75 per cent of members, but in practice the GATT worked on the basis of consensus (as does the WTO), and so in reality all members must at least acquiesce in any request for it to go forward.

hang their justification for breaching the MFN principle and treating some trade partners more favourably than others. One is to obtain a waiver from the 'normal' rules. Up until and during the 1990s, waivers were the 'solution of choice' for North–South trade agreements like the United States' Caribbean Basin Initiative (CBI) and Canada's Caribcan regime, and the EU's first response to the adverse GATT panel ruling on Lomé was to seek one. A waiver was obtained initially for 1995–2000 and, then, until 2007 to cover a transitional phase under the CPA whilst EPAs were negotiated. But waivers which had been approved largely without contention in the GATT became increasingly difficult to obtain in the more litigious atmosphere of the WTO. It took the EU until 2002 to obtain the extension of the waiver as part of the deal to launch the Doha Development Round and it was required to 'compensate' Thailand, Philippines and Indonesia by offering them improved fisheries access. With the banana dispute rumbling on, DG Trade was very reluctant either to seek a new waiver or to allow the existing one to expire in 2007 without an alternative being in place.

The EU's strong preference was that the replacement for the CPA trade preferences should be a regime hung on the second WTO peg – the provisions for the creation of FTAs and customs unions in Article XXIV of GATT 1994 for trade in goods and Article V of the General Agreement on Trade in Services (GATS) for services. Two key provisions of Article XXIV stipulate how much trade must be liberalized and how quickly for an agreement to qualify as an FTA or customs union. In the case of FTAs, 'substantially all the trade' between the parties must be liberalized (paragraph 8) within a period that should be a 'reasonable length of time' (paragraph 5), which the Understanding on Article XXIV specifies should exceed ten years 'only in exceptional cases'. Article V of the GATS 1995 applies analogous rules on the extent to which services trade must be liberalized.

Whilst this phraseology may appear straightforward, Article XXIV actually poses considerable challenges of interpretation which means that unless and until a case reaches adjudication through the WTO's dispute settlement process, alternative interpretations can coexist. One thing seems to be clear: 'substantially all' trade is less than 'all trade'. Some products need not be liberalized – but how many? The European Commission interprets 'substantially all trade' as requiring a liberalization of around 90 per cent on average of the total value of trade between parties which can be achieved asymmetrically with one party liberalizing by more and the other(s) by less than this figure. Most recent EU agreements meet this threshold (see next section).

The final WTO peg is the 'Enabling Clause' which underpins the GSP because it allows developed countries to grant unilateral preferential treatment to all developing countries or to recognized subgroups. Whilst the requirements for fulfilling Article XXIV have not been established precisely through adjudication, the WTO's dispute settlement system has given some guidance in relation to the GSP. The least liberal 'Standard' tranche of the EU's GSP very probably meets the requirements since it is available to all developing countries as does EBA since the LDC group is a recognized WTO category of country. But there is uncertainty over GSP+ (Bartels 2007).

The GSP+ had its birth in a case brought against the EU in 2002 by India, provoked by the extension in 2001 of the GSP's antinarcotics tranche to Pakistan (EC 2001). The essence of India's case was that the antinarcotics regime violated GATT Article 1.1 (on non-discrimination) and that countries could not discriminate within their GSP schemes between different developing countries.[5] The EU's primary defence was that the discrimination was justified by the Enabling Clause. In its judgment, the WTO Appellate Body rejected one part of the Indian argument – and in so doing established important 'case law' on the allowable features of GSPs. It did not accept the Indian argument that the Enabling Clause required tariff preferences to be identical for all beneficiaries. Rather, it asserted the legitimacy of providing different preferences provided that the difference responded to a widely recognized 'development, financial [or] trade need' (WTO 2004a: paragraph 164). It gave as examples of such 'broadbased recognition' cases 'set out in the WTO Agreement or in multilateral instruments adopted by international organizations' (paragraph 163), a formulation that would seem to secure the legitimacy of the LDC group and, hence, EBA.

But the Appellate Body then went on to uphold the specifics of the Indian challenge to the EU's higher level preferences for Pakistan because the EU's antinarcotics regime failed to satisfy this criterion: the beneficiaries did not share a widely recognized trade need that bound them together as different from all non-beneficiaries. Subsequent arbitration resulted in the EU being asked to amend its trade policy by 1 July 2005 (WTO 2004b).

The principle result of this amendment was the creation of the GSP+ as the third tranche of the EU's GSP scheme. Like the preceding antinarcotics regime it offers preferences to a specific group of eligible states that are broader and deeper than those available under the Standard GSP. The key question – which may remain unanswered definitively unless and until a case is taken to WTO dispute settlement – is whether this eligible group shares 'a widely recognized trade need'. There are three eligibility criteria for GSP+. One is that beneficiaries must ratify and implement a set of international social, labour and environmental conventions; the EU argues that the 'extra' preferences assist countries to meet the costs incurred. The others are more controversial: exports must not be too 'diversified' and the economy must be relatively small. Both are established by a formula that effectively excludes from eligibility, regardless of their social, labour and environmental stance, a swathe of countries in South and South East Asia and MERCOSUR, including some with lower gross national products (GNPs) than those of beneficiaries. Since this formula is not used by any other developed country or by the EU in any of its other classifications of developing countries, there must be some doubt that it meets the Appellate Body's requirement of a 'widely recognized' category of countries.

---

[5] Initially India challenged all of the high level GSP preferences other than EBA, but it then concentrated on the antinarcotics regime and reserved its position on the other two.

Diversity Continues

At one level, the EU preference system has become simpler. With the end of the CPA trade regime and the renegotiation of the Mediterranean agreements there is now only one vehicle for non-reciprocal preferences: the autonomous, non-negotiated GSP. All other preferences are now reciprocal and have been negotiated. This sharp polarization between non-reciprocal and autonomous on the one hand and reciprocal, negotiated on the other did not exist before 2008.

At a deeper level, though, the diversity continues. There are differences between the reciprocal agreements, and a new set of rules of origin introduced in 2010 establishes further differentiation in the GSP.

The FTAs

The EU Commissioner for Trade, Karel De Gucht, has argued that:

> The EU has an active negotiating agenda with developing countries from all corners of the globe ... These agreements are not identical. There is no identikit model agreement that the EU seeks to impose on partner countries. (de Gucht 2010)

Whilst this is an accurate statement since all the FTAs are different in their details, there are some clear patterns on core features. One is that the scope and rigour of the agreements has tended to grow over time. The Euro–Med agreements negotiated mainly in the 1990s[6] are quite limited both in scope and enforceability. The 2000 Trade Development and Cooperation Agreement (TDCA) with South Africa liberalizes a large proportion of trade within a stated timeframe and has strong provisions on competition policy, but for most other areas of trade policy it offers only a framework for further negotiations; enforcement mechanisms are weak. The 2002 Chile agreement has more extensive coverage and more closely delineated enforcement provisions as well as operational provisions on sanitary and phytosanitary standards (SPS). The one full EPA (with a grouping of the Caribbean Community (Caricom) and the Dominican Republic, known as the Caribbean Forum or CARIFORUM) also has wide, enforceable provisions. The interim EPAs (with all the other signatory states) are also foreseen as covering more than trade in goods, but so far negotiations have not proceeded far (and may never do so).

Most, but not all, of the more recent agreements include enforceable dispute settlement. Even though they are rarely activated, the provisions on dispute

---

[6]   Association Agreements with Tunisia (1995), Israel (1995), Morocco (1996), Jordan (1997), the Palestine Authority (1997), Algeria (2001), Lebanon (2002), Egypt (signed 2001, entered into force 2004), Syria (initialled 2009).

settlement underpin the enforceability of any agreement. If they are weak or lacking, the agreement is no more than the expression of good intentions. Even if never actioned, the combination of measurable obligations with a system for imposing penalties for noncompliance is likely to have an impact at least on the extent of commitments made in the agreement. The provisions of the early Euro–Med agreements 'are very loosely formulated' (ECDPM 2004: 2). They combine wide discretion with an absence of time limits for specific steps to be taken, which provides considerable latitude to delay indefinitely the hearing of a complaint; even if adjudication does take place, there are no provisions for penalties in case of noncompliance. The TDCA sets clear (albeit leisurely) time limits for the adjudication process but it also fails to specify the remedies available to a complainant if the other party fails to take appropriate action following an adverse judgment. By contrast, the Mexico, Chile and Korea agreements as well as most of the EPAs provide detailed procedures, timeframes for the relevant steps, and sanctions in the form of a suspension of benefits from the agreement.[7]

The extent of EU liberalization on goods in these agreements is closely linked to the *status quo ante*. In all of the EPAs it has given DFQF immediately on initialling of the accords and in the Euro–Med agreements it has continued significant pre-existing access on sensitive products. In none of the other FTAs has it done so. In its statements concerning the TDCA the EU claimed that it was liberalizing 95 per cent of its imports. Although such a figure is unverifiable (since no base year is given) and needs to be interpreted in the light of a county's overall tariff pattern,[8] in this case it accurately reflects the fact that a relatively small number of sensitive agricultural, processed agricultural, industrial and manufactured goods are either excluded from liberalization altogether or subject to tariff quotas (TQs). In the Korea agreement, the EU's liberalization is complex and partial. Apparently substantial (and in many cases quick acting) removal of *ad valorem* EU agricultural tariffs is partly offset by a different calendar for the removal of excise duties and the entry price system. Similarly, the EU's agricultural liberalization is limited towards Chile and very limited for Mexico.

Although the liberalization made by the EU's partners varies widely, when seen alongside Europe's liberalization the picture appears broadly consistent with the EU position in the WTO that the Article XXIV requirement of 'substantially all' trade being liberalized is met if by the end of the implementation period tariffs have been removed on a basket of goods representing 90 per cent of the value of total trade.[9] By contrast, recent agreements are harder to reconcile with the Article

---

[7] The exceptions are the interim EPAs with the East African Community (EAC) and Eastern and Southern Africa (ESA).

[8] A point best illustrated by reference to a hypothetical state with only two tariff levels: zero and so high as to choke all imports. It could, theoretically, liberalize 100 per cent of imports without improving access for a single good since the excluded products would account for 0 per cent of imports.

[9] The position is only 'broadly consistent' as it takes no account of bilateral trade balances. If each party accounts for half of trade, the 90 per cent target is met by the EU

XXIV requirement that implementation should only exceed ten years in exceptional circumstances. The time allowed for completing liberalization in the EU's FTAs has been getting longer. In the Mexico and Chile FTAs both sides had up to ten years. In the TDCA the EU committed to completing its liberalization in ten years and South Africa to 12 years. But the implementation periods for the EPAs range from 15–25 years from the date of initialling.[10] In the Korea agreement the EU will complete its liberalization in five years but Korea has up to 20 years.

All of the recent agreements prohibit quotas (unless they are specifically listed and admitted in the document) and what can be called 'para-tariffs' (charges on imports not defined by the imposing country as a tariff but not fulfilling the criteria set out in the agreements for exempt taxes). Export duties are also restricted.

There are services and investment chapters in most of the EU's agreements (and also in the CPA) but only the Chile, CARIFORUM and Korea FTAs include substantial provisions that potentially go beyond GATS obligations and, in the case of the Mexico agreement, stand still.[11] The provisions are highly context-specific, which makes generalization about their scope impractical, but one common, structural feature of the FTAs is that they provide a single set of covers for what are, effectively, a set of bilateral commitments (40 of them in the case of the CARIFORUM EPA) that combine common general principles and provisions with a host of national exceptions. This flows from the EU's limited shared competences in non-goods trade that applied when these accords were negotiated (and may change as a result of the Lisbon Treaty) plus, in the case of the EPA, the non-shared competences of CARIFORUM.

There are provisions in several agreements that refer to one party offering improved treatment to the other if it negotiates an agreement with a third party. The section of the Mexico agreement on government procurement, for example, includes the commitment that 'In the case that the Community or Mexico offer a GPA or NAFTA Party, respectively, additional advantages with regard to the access to their respective procurement markets beyond what has been agreed under this Title, they shall agree to enter into negotiations with the other Party with a view to extending these advantages to the other Party on a reciprocal basis' (Article 37).

---

liberalizing on 100 per cent of its imports and the partner by 80 per cent of its imports. But, as calculations by the Commission during the course of the EPA negotiations made clear, some partners have a trade surplus with the EU and so need to liberalize on more than 80 per cent since their tariff cuts apply to over half of the value of trade (and vice versa for countries with a trade deficit). These calculations dropped out of Commission presentations during the course of the negotiations.

[10]   Unlike most of the other agreements which express the liberalization calendar in terms of number of years after the agreement comes into force, the EPAs use actual dates. A consequence is that the delay between initialling and signature has reduced the time available after the agreement comes into force. The members of the Southern African Customs Union will complete liberalization more quickly because they are affected either de facto or de jure by the TDCA implementation period, which expires in 2012.

[11]   There is provision in the other, interim, EPAs for the parties to negotiate services provisions but the outcome is uncertain.

It is in the EPAs, however, that the MFN clause is most fully developed – and exhibits some potentially important differences in the detail. The core standard provision for goods (using the CARIFORUM EPA as the source for quotes) is that 'With respect to matters covered by this Chapter, the CARIFORUM States or any Signatory CARIFORUM State shall accord to the EC Party' more favourable treatment resulting from 'the CARIFORUM States or any Signatory CARIFORUM State becoming party to a free trade agreement with any major trading economy after the signature of this Agreement' (Article 19.2).

Another common provision is the definition of a 'major trading economy' as being:

> Any developed country or any country accounting for a share of world merchandise exports above 1 per cent in the year before the entry into force of the free trade agreement referred to in paragraph 2, or any group of countries acting individually, collectively or through an free trade agreement accounting collectively for a share of world merchandise exports above 1.5 per cent in the year before the entry into force of the free trade agreement referred to in paragraph 2. (Article 19.4)

One area of difference is what happens when both sides of the new agreement are more favourable. Most of the MFN clauses specify what will happen in such cases, but the texts of the East African Community (EAC) and Eastern and Southern Africa (ESA) EPAs are silent. Where it can be demonstrated that the better-than-EPA treatment accorded by the ACP party is reciprocated by treatment from its partner that is 'more favourable' (in the CARIFORUM agreement) or 'substantially more favourable' (in the others) the procedure (using the Pacific EPA text Article 16.3) is that 'the Parties will consult and may jointly decide how best to implement the provisions'. No definitions are offered for either 'more favourable' or 'substantially more favourable'.

Another difference with potential importance if a case goes to dispute settlement lies in the definition (or lack of it) of a 'free trade agreement' (or 'economic integration agreements', which is the term used in the Central Africa and EAC texts). This remains undefined in the CARIFORUM and Southern African Development Community (SADC) texts but the others specify (citing the Ghana EPA Article 17.5) that the term

> 'free trade agreement' means an agreement substantially liberalising trade and providing for the absence or elimination of substantially all discrimination between or among parties thereto through the elimination of existing discriminatory measures and/or the prohibition of new or more discriminatory measures, either at the entry into force of that agreement or on the basis of a reasonable time frame.

These differences could prove to be important since it remains to be seen how these clauses will be applied in practice given that there exists considerable ambiguity.

What counts as 'more favourable treatment' by the ACP party in an agreement that may have some parts that are less good and some that are better? What happens in cases where the 'more favourable treatment' by the ACP party is in return for treatment by the other that is also more favourable than the EPA? Will it apply to South–South agreements notified to the WTO under Part IV (as expressions of SDT) rather than Article XXIV in those EPAs that do not contain a definition of a free trade/economic integration agreement? Answers to such questions will become clear only as the MFN clause is applied either autonomously by one party or following a dispute judgment.

Only the CARIFORUM EPA has enforceable provisions on environmental, labour and social standards, but it is hard to see any parts of the relevant text (Title IV Chapters 4 and 5) that are expressed in sufficiently precise terms for an infraction to be easily identifiable. Moreover, the use of trade remedies (that is the suspension of preferences) against an infraction is explicitly ruled out. There is a chapter on Trade and Sustainable Development in the Korea agreement but this states explicitly that it is not the intention of the parties 'to harmonise the labour or environment standards of the Parties' but only to strengthen their trade relations and cooperation in ways that promote sustainable development (Article 13.1.3). There are pledges to abide by named international conventions and for expert consultations in cases where one party has a problem. But, crucially, such consultation is instead of, and not additional to, the overall provisions on dispute settlement (from which this chapter is explicitly excluded – Article 13.6) and no provision is made for remedies.

New GSP Rules of Origin

Rules of Origin (RoO) are the 'small print' of preference agreements. They establish where a good is produced and therefore what tax is paid (or other rules applied) when it is imported. Any favourable treatment promised in a preference agreement applies only to goods that meet the rules. Changing the rules will change the benefits.

The current regimes have been under review since December 2003, when the European Commission presented a Green Book on the revision of the preferential RoO. Following consultations with the private sector and other stakeholders, the Commission presented, on 16 March 2005, a communication on the future of the RoO which aimed 'to make rules simpler and, where appropriate, more development friendly'. (EC 2005)

The structure of the current rules is the same in all of the EU's preference regimes although the detailed provisions differ (even between the EPAs). The GSP and all of the FTAs identify on a product-by-product basis the processing that must be applied to non-originating inputs in order for them to acquire originating status. No single criterion applies in all cases: the requirements are expressed as either a change of tariff heading, or a specific process/action to be undertaken, or a percentage contribution to the ex-works price or some combination of these.

After much internal wrangling within the EU, a set of changes to the rules was finally proposed in 2010 (EC 2010). The initial 2005 initiative would have applied the new rules to the GSP, the EPAs and, in due course, all of the EU's preferential agreements. But the 2010 regulation applies only to the GSP. This is because only the GSP can be amended unilaterally by the EU; all of its other accords are negotiated and any changes to the RoO would need to be agreed by its partners. Although originally billed as making the rules 'simpler', the new regulation actually extends the internal differentiation within the GSP by introducing some rules that are different for LDCs and non-LDCs. The former, for example, can now claim originating status for exports of clothing produced from non-originating imports of cloth – putting them in the same position as EPA signatories and lesser developed African states exporting to the United States under AGOA.

The most fundamental change would have been on the criterion for establishing originating status. The Commission proposed in the 2005 communication to replace the current mix of criteria for establishing whether an exporter has undertaken 'sufficient processing' by value added as the normal criterion. Depending on the level at which the value added threshold was set, this could have altered substantially the ease with which the rules could be met and, hence, the practical value of the GSP preferences. But the new regulation, whilst expressing a marked enthusiasm for the value added criterion, allows multiple criteria to continue.

Building or Stumbling Blocks?

How do the EU's preferences relate to multilateral rules and liberalization? Do they create or divert trade? Both questions require answers that are to a large extent qualitative and judgmental. That may seem more self-evident with the first question than the second. In the absence of a clear counterfactual, any assessment of what the EU *would have done* in the GATT/WTO had it not pursued so many bilateral and plurilateral accords must necessarily rely on informed inference from observation. Trade creation and diversion, by contrast, have been widely studied through rigorous quantitative analysis, and it is clear that even in respect of the EU's accords they provide a part of the answer. But the volume of detailed trade data and assumptions needed realistically to model the multilevel effects of changes to EU trade policy is so great that it is only a very partial guide.

The EU's Pragmatic Preference Making

The EU's pattern of preferences has all the hallmarks of having been created by a pragmatic reaction to events rather than a strong guiding strategy. A strategy has been apparent, inherited from colonial links and the EU's perception of itself as a champion of regionalism, but it has been overlain (heavily at times) by more pragmatic concerns. The creation of EBA and GSP+ provide two illustrative examples.

When EBA was developed by DG Trade, amid considerable secrecy (with DG Agriculture reportedly 'consulted' only at the end of the process), it was widely perceived as having as its target not only LDCs but also the European common agricultural policy (CAP), especially for sugar which, until then, had proved to be remarkably impervious to change. In the months following its launch, three normally competing lobbies made common cause to oppose the proposals on sugar: the EU beet producers, the cane refiners and the ACP cane exporters. By setting a deadline for DFQF imports of sugar from LDCs it made reform of the CAP for sugar (which was based on controlling supply into the European market) inevitable since a continuation of the old regime could have become financially unsupportable.

Without the CAP perspective, EBA appears to have been an exercise of pure idealism (to favour LDCs) and strategic incoherence (since it greatly weakened the EU's policy of replacing CPA preferences with EPAs). The EPA negotiations were unusual in the sense that they did not involve to any significant degree the exchange of trade concessions that is normal both multilaterally and bilaterally. Because the EU provided the ACP with liberal market access under the CPA, it had only limited scope to make substantial additional commitments on goods as part of an EPA deal in return for the ACP accepting reciprocity. At the heart of its negotiating strategy, therefore, was a threat to ACP non-signatories that they would suffer a deterioration in their access to the European market after the end of the CPA trade regime by being downgraded to the GSP. But EBA removed much of the sting from this threat for ACP LDCs. Not surprisingly, almost all of the states that have declined to initial an EPA are LDCs.[12]

The GSP+ was introduced rapidly to replace the antinarcotics regime following a WTO judgment. In order to make it reasonably broad-based, the Commission's communication of March 2005 gave countries wishing to be considered until end-October 2005 to ratify any 'missing' conventions and apply. But this would have led to a hiatus in higher level preferences for the Latin American beneficiaries of the antinarcotics regime after this ceased by the WTO's 1 July 2005 deadline. The EU therefore provided that 14 states would receive GSP+ immediately on a provisional basis even before applying – since they already fulfilled the criteria (European Council 2005: Preamble 8). Yet three of these states appeared not to have met at that time the criteria in terms of convention adoption whilst others that had done so were not included in the list of provisional beneficiaries.

The EU's higher level preferences are now so extensive that it would be more accurate to refer instead to a system of discriminations. Over the past two decades the EU has responded pragmatically to the pressures put upon it in a way that

---

[12] The non-LDCs that had failed to initial at the time of writing all export goods that mainly face low or zero EU MFN tariffs. There are country-specific reasons why each of the ten LDCs that initialled did so.

manages market opening to maintain greater restrictions on countries deemed to be most competitive than on others. Liberalization on sensitive goods has been undertaken initially for the least competitive global suppliers and then, over time, generalized to a wider and wider group. On this interpretation, multilateral liberalization occurs at the end of this process when the EU is willing to liberalize towards the largest or most competitive suppliers. One consequence is that the 'middle' tier of the inverted pyramid of privilege now comprises primarily countries in South and South East Asia and MERCOSUR, which face relative discrimination vis-à-vis almost all developing and many middle-income states. The EU is currently seeking to negotiate FTAs with most of these states that would offer reciprocal gains in return for, probably, carefully crafted liberalization.

Different Types of Trade Diversion

It is conventional when showing analytically their potential effects for FTAs and non-reciprocal preferences to be compared with a *status quo ante* in which preferred and non-preferred states are treated equally. Hence, the removal of barriers to imports from preferred states can either 'create trade' (if the now cheaper imports displace domestic production) or 'divert trade' (if they displace imports from more efficient suppliers that still face full tariffs). But very few of the EU's changes have taken place against such a *status quo ante*. When shuffling moves a country 'up' the pyramid, it creates (or extends) a relative advantage over countries that were previously at the same level (or lower down). At the same time, such a move reduces any discrimination vis-à-vis countries that are higher up. In other words, the change will produce both new trade diversion and remove earlier diversion.

Creating two additional categories, of positive 'diversion removal' (DR) and negative DR, helps to understand the range of likely effects. Positive DR occurs when a country moves up the pyramid and there is an erosion of the preference previously enjoyed by a competitor (and there is enhanced diversion against any competitor that has not been elevated). Most of the DR created by the shuffling over the past decade has been of the positive kind, but some has been negative. This occurs when a country is moved down the pyramid. So far it has occurred only in relation to the small number of non-LDC ACP states that have not initialled EPAs and now export to the EU under the standard GSP. More widespread negative DR has been avoided so far by the EU's unilateral extension of DFQF to all those states that have initialled an interim EPA. But negative DR may increase in 2014 as the Commission proposes to remove the unilateral preferences for ACP states that haven't signed an EPA and to graduate all upper middle income states out of the GSP.

Each type of effect will produce a different impact from a given trade policy change on the level of imports, adjustment by domestic competitors and consumer gains. By definition, a policy change that results only in trade creation will result in the largest relative increase in imports, domestic adjustment and consumer gain for any given level of tariff cut and price elasticity of supply and demand. The scale of trade diversion, as conventionally understood, and positive DR will be similar: there will be a relatively small increase in the level of imports and, hence, consumer gain. But whereas the loss for trade diversion is borne by competitive suppliers left out of the tariff change, under positive DR it is borne by uncompetitive exporters that previously enjoyed more favourable access. Negative DR, by contrast, will tend to result in a fall in imports (and no consumer gain). Those suppliers from which preferences have been removed will tend to reduce exports in the face of higher tariffs and there is no reason to expect any offsetting increase in imports from other suppliers given that their access terms have not changed.

Any specific trade policy change may encapsulate a bewildering combination of these different effects. Teasing out the various strands will often require knowledge of the market for very disaggregated product groups – who actually competes with whom, for example, on a specific type of grape juice that is treated significantly differently in GSP+ from the GSP? As with comparative advantage it may turn out to be easier to identify 'revealed' trade creation and diversion after the event by inferring measurable changes in flows to a previous change to trade policy. And for that, the large changes in EU preference policy are too recent to have fed through clearly into actual trade flows.

Conclusions

The complexity of the EU's preferential trade regimes for developing countries puts it at the extreme end of the spectrum, but it is not unique. Other developed countries also have overlapping regimes with a variety of esoteric qualifying criteria as well as, or instead of, income which are subject to frequent change. The United States has both a GSP and a set of other non-reciprocal regional agreements (such as the Africa Growth and Opportunity Act (AGOA) and several schemes known colloquially as the Caribbean Basin Initiative) as well as reciprocal FTAs. Canada has the Caribcan non-reciprocal regime for the Caribbean (and is currently negotiating an FTA) as well as its GSP. And some countries, whilst focussing preferences for developing countries on their GSPs, provide differentiation within it. Treating LDCs differently from other developing countries is commonplace but both Australia and Norway treat some non-LDC developing countries differently from others in their GSPs. As well as special provision for LDCs, Australia has a regime in its 2011 tariff schedules for most (but not all) LDCs plus 11 other countries most of which are Pacific states but which also include Botswana and Namibia. Similarly, Norway has since 2008 extended in principle a special regime for LDCs to 14 low-income countries (and has implemented this so far in eight of them).

Hence, the EU experience can be seen as having a broader significance for the analysis both of sub-multilateral trade policy change and for the development effects of preferences. But applying this guidance to the specificities of any particular country's trade policy requires detailed knowledge of its trade regimes. The picture of a single, MFN trade regime applying in all WTO members is a mirage.

Both this detailed analysis of the EU's regimes and brief glance at those of other states suggest that the questions normally posed – trade diversion versus creation, stumbling versus building blocks – are either unanswerable or too narrowly specified. Whether or not world trade would be more disciplined and global welfare higher had the EU (and other developed countries) not deviated so much from the MFN principle is not a question to which a definitive answer can be given. A plausible case can be made in favour of the 'building blocks' case – but the opposite opinion is also valid. If the focus is on incremental change (rather than the whole sub-multilateral edifice), it is more feasible to offer a strong answer – but *only* if the specificities of both the proposed change and of the most plausible counterfactual are taken fully into account (which, again, introduces a basis for differing opinions). As with any such system built up pragmatically over decades, analysis often requires the creation of a set of stylized facts since reality is too complex. But these stylized facts must be very carefully constructed to avoid gross distortion.

References

Bartels, L. 2007. The WTO legality of the EU's GSP+ arrangement. *Journal of International Economic Law*, 10: 869–86.

De Gucht, K. 2010. Speech to seminar on EU trade policy towards developing countries, Brussels, 16 March, mimeo.

ECDPM. 2004. Comparing EU free trade agreements: dispute settlement, *In Brief No6G*, Maastricht: ECDPM.

European Commission. 2001. Amended Proposal for a Council Regulation applying a scheme of generalised tariff preferences for the period 1st January 2002 to 31st December 2004, COM(2001)688 final, 2001/0131 (ACC), Brussels: EC.

European Commission. 2005. Communication from the Commission to the Council, the European Parliament and the European Economic and Social Committee. The rules of origin in preferential trade arrangements. Orientations for the future, COM(2005) 100 final, Brussels: EC.

European Commission. 2010. Regulation (EU) No 1063/2010 of 18 November 2010 amending Regulation (EEC) No 2454/93 laying down provisions for the implementation of Council Regulation (EEC) No 2913/92 establishing the Community Customs Code, L 307/1 Brussels: EC.

European Council. 2005. Council Regulation (EC) No 980/2005 of 27 June 2005 applying a scheme of generalised tariff preferences. *Official Journal L 169*, 48.

Lister, M. 1988. *The European Community and the Developing World*. Aldershot: Avebury.

Lister, M. 1997. *The European Union and the South*. London: Routledge.

Stevens, C. (ed.). 1981. *The EEC and the Third World: A Survey*. Sevenoaks: Hodder & Stoughton.

Stevens, C. 2000. Trade with developing countries: banana skins and turf wars, in *Policy Making in the European Union*, edited by H. Wallace and W. Wallace. Oxford: Oxford University Press: 401–26.

Stevens, C. 2007. Creating a development-friendly EU trade policy, in *EU Development Policy in a Changing World*, edited by A. Mold. Amsterdam: Amsterdam University Press: 221–36.

Stevens, C. and Kennan, J. 2011. Creating an appropriate trade regime for Africa. London, mimeo.

WTO. 2004a. European Communities – conditions for the granting of tariff preferences to developing countries, AB–2004–1. *Report of the Appellate Body, WT/DS246/AB/R*. Geneva: WTO.

WTO. 2004b. European Communities – conditions for the granting of tariff preferences to developing countries, AB–2004–1/17. *Arbitration under Article 21.3(c) of the Understanding on Rules and Procedures Governing the Settlement of Disputes, WT/DS246/14*. Geneva: WTO.

Developing Professional Services in Africa: How Regional Integration Can Help[1]

Nora Dihel, Ana M. Fernandes and Aaditya Mattoo

Introduction

Policymakers in Eastern and Southern African countries have recognized that weaknesses in their services sectors impede growth. Recent studies have revealed a strong relationship between African firms' productivity and their access to services (Arnold et al. 2006). In parallel with reform of backbone services like telecommunications, banking and transport, governments are beginning to prioritize reform of professional services, including by creating more integrated regional markets. However, relative to the process of regional integration in East Africa, regional integration in Southern Africa is much less advanced.

This chapter attempts to remedy the large gaps in information on policies and market conditions in professional services, using as case studies accounting, engineering and legal services in Kenya, Rwanda, Tanzania and Uganda in Eastern Africa, and in Botswana, Malawi, Mauritius, Mozambique, South Africa and Zambia in Southern Africa, with the objective of identifying the requirements for reform at the national level and accelerated integration at the regional level. The chapter places trade in services firmly within the broader context of sound domestic economic management.

---

[1] This chapter draws on the work on professional services developed in World Bank (2010b, 2011).

Importance of Professional Services for Growth in Eastern and Southern Africa

Professional services play an important role in the functioning of modern economies and are among the fastest growing services sectors in many developed and developing economies. Professional services contribute directly and indirectly to economic growth, including by lowering transactions costs and by creating spillovers of knowledge to other industries. Moreover, in common with services generally, professional services show greater resilience to economic downturns than do manufactures, in part because of their lower demand cyclicality (Borchert and Mattoo 2009).

Accounting, legal and engineering services contribute directly and indirectly to economic growth, including by lowering transactions costs, being key inputs and creating spillovers of knowledge to other sectors. Accountancy is critical for accountability, sound financial management and good corporate governance (Trolliet and Hegarty 2003). Effective legal and justice systems and access to legal services improve the predictability of the business environment, facilitate engagement in contracts and mitigate investment risks (Cattaneo and Walkenhorst 2010). Engineering is a knowledge-intensive sector essential to the productivity and sustainability of other economic activities. For example, civil engineering is critical for the development and maintenance of a country's physical infrastructure, while electrical engineering is important to the operation of public networks such as utilities or commercial facilities and communication systems (Cattaneo et al. 2010).

Greater usage of professional services is associated with higher labour productivity for firms – particularly small firms – across countries in Eastern and Southern Africa.[2] Moreover, professional services can become an important source for export diversification in Africa.

While professional services are among the fastest growing services sectors in Eastern and Southern Africa,[3] their weaknesses and underdevelopment are dwarfing their current contribution to growth in the region.

The analysis of professional services sectors in Africa has been hampered by the lack of information on demand and supply, including data on market conditions and policies and regulations in professional services. To address this gap, a comprehensive data collection exercise – including enterprise surveys covering users of services, enterprise surveys covering providers of services, regulatory surveys (covering entry and conduct regulation applied to domestic and foreign providers), and surveys of costs and procedures to become an accounting, engineering or legal professional – was undertaken by the World Bank in Eastern

---

[2]   See World Bank (2010b, 2011).

[3]   The available data for Eastern and Southern Africa indicate that the average annual growth rates of business services outputs (of which professional services constitute an important part) were 21 per cent in Zambia, 18 per cent in Uganda, 14 per cent in Tanzania, 8 per cent in Kenya and 7 per cent in South Africa over the 2000–2009 period.

and Southern Africa in 2009–2010. The diagnostics based on these different data sources are discussed next.

Level of Development of Professional Services Sectors in Eastern and Southern Africa

Across the markets for accounting, engineering and legal professionals in Eastern and Southern Africa, a heterogeneous picture emerges. While scarcity premia are generally observed across professions in all countries, there is a wide spectrum of perceived skills shortages, their nature and the underlying reasons with different policy implications for each country's reform agenda.

Availability Varies Across Countries and Professions

Eastern and Southern African countries show significant variation in the availability of professionals, with relative abundance in Mauritius, South Africa and Kenya and relative scarcity in Rwanda, Zambia, Malawi and Tanzania. But per capita availability in most Eastern and Southern African countries is only a fraction of that in the more advanced economies of Mauritius and South Africa (Figure 20.1).

Limited Availability of Middle–Level Professionals

Middle-level professionals who can provide services to under-served client segments and produce large economic gains are a sometimes underappreciated category of professionals. For example, accounting technicians can provide basic recordkeeping services needed by SMEs. Paralegals engage with clients on a variety of complex law-related tasks, including working with lawyers on criminal justice

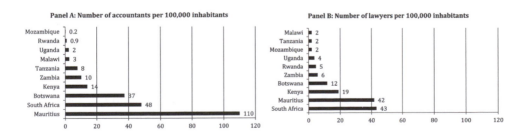

Figure 20.1 Professional density in Africa
Source: World Bank survey of providers of professional services in Africa, 2009 and 2010.

cases, advising clients on law-related issues, and mediating commercial disputes between parties. Indeed, there is a growing role for paralegals in the criminal justice space in Africa.

The existing data suggest that – with the exception of accounting technicians in Kenya – East Africa is facing a middle-level skills vacuum. Southern Africa is somewhat better endowed with middle-level professionals but they account generally for only half the total number of professionals in a given sector.

Skills Mismatches

Skills mismatches at technician and skilled professional levels are a serious issue across professions in all African countries. For example, accounting associations in Tanzania and Kenya reported that there are jobless accountants despite high demand for qualified accountants. Potential explanations include the absence of links between the education system, labour market and professional associations. Consultations with accounting sector stakeholders in Mozambique revealed that multinational auditing and accounting firms face shortages of

1. Entry-level accounting and auditing professionals despite many applications as most applicants do not have the requisite training quality (Fernandes and Mattoo 2009); and
2. Senior-level local professionals that could monitor the quality of financial reporting (World Bank 2008).

In Malawi, public and private sector stakeholders indicated that the country suffers from significant skills mismatches in accounting. Therefore, despite high demand for accounting professionals, there are many unemployed accountants in Malawi. In South Africa, mismatches in accounting result from private sector firms hiring chartered accountants (CA) registered with the South African Institute of Chartered Accountants (SAICA), because of their perceived quality, for work that could be performed by less highly qualified accountants.

Segmentation of Regional Markets for Professional Services in Africa

Data on the presence of foreign professionals in Eastern and Southern Africa (mode 4 in the GATS; see Sampson and Snape 1985) are scarce. Table 20.1 shows that in Kenya, Malawi, Tanzania, Uganda and Zambia foreign accounting professionals represent less than 10 per cent of the total, but that percentage is high in Botswana, Mozambique and Rwanda. Foreign engineers are an important proportion of total engineering professionals in Botswana, Mauritius and Zambia but a small proportion in Tanzania. In legal services (not shown in Table 20.1), there are virtually no foreign professionals practising in any of the African countries.

Table 20.1   Foreign professionals in Eastern and Southern Africa

	Accounting		Engineering	
	Total number of professionals	Share of foreign professionals	Total number of professionals	Share of foreign professionals
Kenya	5,266	6.1%	n/a	n/a
Rwanda	89	59.6%	n/a	n/a
Tanzania	3,121	5.3%	8,408	6.3%
Uganda	699	8.6%	n/a	n/a
Botswana	704	75.9%	543	40.0%
Malawi	360	2.8%	5	0.0%
Mauritius	1,389	n/a	685	24.5%
Mozambique	50	96.0%	913	4.6%
South Africa	22,846	n/a	14,474	n/a
Zambia	1212	2.1%	2535	35.4%

Source: Professional associations in the various countries and background reports.

Regarding commercial presence (mode 3 in the GATS), statistics from professional associations reveal some foreign participation in accounting and engineering services. In accounting/auditing services, firms with foreign affiliation (that is with foreign equity or with foreign partners) dominate the markets. In engineering, 25 per cent of registered firms in Mauritius and 35 per cent of registered firms in Tanzania have foreign participation. In Mozambique, there is some foreign ownership although most engineering consulting firms are domestically owned. In Zambia however, out of 298 engineering firms only two are foreign-owned. Foreign law firms are virtually absent in most African countries. In South Africa out of 8,200 registered law practices in 2008 only three are foreign-owned. But in Botswana, although few, foreign-owned law firms are among the five major law firms in the country and in Mozambique the same is verified. In Mauritius, where law firms are a recent development, the majority of law firms are actually foreign-owned.

The *World Bank Surveys of Users of Professional Services in Eastern and Southern Africa* show that only a small proportion of firms import accounting, engineering or legal services in Eastern and Southern African countries, which may be a consequence of high trade barriers in place.

Evidence compiled on World Bank-supported civil works procurement contracts between 1994 and 2009 reflects the lack of integration of Eastern and Southern African markets for engineering services. Domestic companies generally win most contracts, except in energy, mining and transportation, and, in some countries, industry, trade, water and sanitation, where non-African companies have the lion's share. Surprisingly, there is virtually no intra-East African foreign firm participation in these contracts, with the limited exception of Kenyan firms in some Tanzanian and Ugandan projects and Ugandan firms in some Rwandan projects. Similarly, there is virtually no intra-Southern African foreign firm participation in these contracts with the limited exception of South African firms in several Southern African countries and some Malawian projects in Mozambique.

Explaining Skills Shortages and the Segmentation of Markets for Professional Services in Eastern and Southern Africa

Explaining the Skills Shortages in Professional Services – Education Issues

Despite the demonstrated need for professional services from an economic development perspective and the demand for them by formal sector firms, Eastern and Southern African countries currently experience skills shortages and skills mismatches in professional services. Some key education-related reasons for these shortages are as follows.

First, professional education is very expensive in all Eastern and Southern African countries. While skills premia for professionals exist and internal rates of return to education are high in the region, the average cost of acquiring a professional degree across all countries and professions is more than US$22,000. These costs are more than four, often more than six, times larger than the countries' GDP per capita in 2008. This makes attaining professional qualification unaffordable for the majority of the population in these countries, especially given the underdeveloped nature of the markets for educational loans.[4]

Second, the weaknesses in secondary education witnessed across Eastern and Southern African countries limit the ability of students to acquire professional skills. The general erosion of mathematical skills in all countries explains the declining number of applicants in science, engineering and technology courses, leading to shortages in the engineering sector.

Third, the capacity and quality of professional education institutions are limited. In several Eastern and Southern African countries, institutions that offer specialized postgraduate courses, as well as institutions that offer academic and professional training courses for middle-level professionals, are entirely absent.

Fourth, there is an absence of links between educational systems, employers and users of services. This dynamic leads to unmet needs and unemployed professionals, explaining the attrition of skills in several professions in Eastern and Southern Africa. Stakeholders from the private sector emphasized the severe lack of coordination between employers, professional associations and education

---

[4]   See World Bank (2010b) for details on the calculations of costs and rates of return to professional education.

institutions with regards to the content of educational programmes for accountants and engineers.

Explaining the Segmentation of Markets for Professional Services – Domestic Regulation

Domestic regulation on the entry and operations of professional services firms often undermines competition and constrains the growth of strong professional services sectors in Eastern and Southern Africa. Domestic entry regulation, such as licensing and educational requirements, quantitative restrictions on the number of suppliers of professional services and exclusive rights granted to suppliers in certain activities, as well as regulations on the operations of firms such as restrictions on prices and fees, advertising, form of business, and inter-professional cooperation, are particularly heavy when compared to those in emerging economies and in OECD countries (Figure 20.2).[5]

In Eastern and Southern Africa, entry regulation is significant in all professional services sectors. The three professions are subject to qualitative entry requirements related to education and qualifications that do not vary significantly across African countries.

Other qualitative entry requirements are present in most African countries. Membership in the relevant professional association is mandatory in accounting and legal services in all countries. Compulsory licensing is a must in accounting in all countries but in legal services Mauritius and South Africa do not require licensing. In engineering, licensing requirements are also absent in South Africa, Botswana and Rwanda; in the last two countries because engineering boards have not been established yet. Continuing education is an obligation for accountants in all countries except Mozambique, for lawyers only in Kenya, Tanzania and Uganda, and for engineers only in South Africa and Zambia.

The regulation of middle-level professionals is much more heterogeneous across African countries. For example, the regulatory spectrum for engineering technicians ranges from total absence of entry requirements in Botswana and Rwanda to requirements to pass a professional exam, undertake compulsory training, and engage in continuing professional development in South Africa and Tanzania.

---

[5]   The indices shown in Figure 20.2 convert qualitative information on regulatory conditions into quantitative indicators for each sector using the OECD methodology described in Conway and Nicoletti (2006). Entry regulations include barriers to becoming a member of a profession taking the form of licensing and educational requirements, quantitative limits on the number of suppliers of professional services, and/or exclusive rights granted to suppliers in certain activities. Conduct/operation regulations include restrictions on prices and fees, advertising, form of business, and inter-professional cooperation. The qualitative information originates in our regulatory surveys. A detailed description of the methodology is provided in World Bank (2010b).

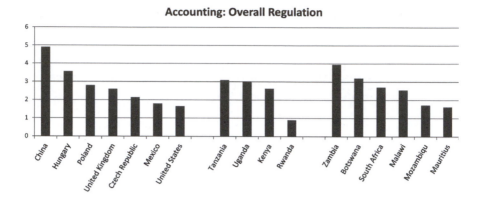

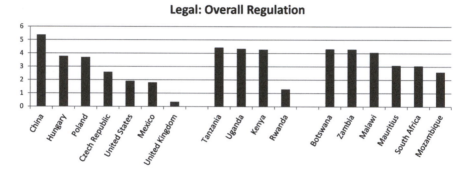

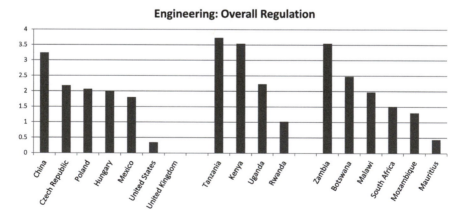

Figure 20.2 Overall regulatory indices for professional services
Note: A higher value of the index indicates a more stringent regulation. For countries with
no bars the index is equal to 0.
Source: OECD regulatory database on professional services and World Bank regulatory
surveys in Africa, 2009 and 2010.

Furthermore, restrictive qualitative requirements taking the form of restrictions on access to the profession, mainly due to the monopoly of professional associations over training institutions, were identified in legal services in Kenya and Zambia. The higher education institutions that provide the required law degrees are controlled by the professional associations which restrict the number of students. The Kenya School of Law, through which all legal professionals must pass, has a limited capacity of 600 students per year. The Zambia Institute of Advanced Legal Education is the only institution providing the postgraduate one-year course necessary for domestic and foreign candidates to become licensed lawyers in Zambia.

Qualitative entry requirements can thus limit the number of professionals and services available. This may be especially the case when entry restrictions are combined with exclusive tasks for the regulated profession (OECD 2007).

Highly skilled professionals in all sectors and countries have exclusive rights to perform certain activities: auditing for accountants; representation of clients before courts and advice on legal matters for lawyers; feasibility studies and design and planning for engineers. The scope of exclusive activities is wider in accounting and legal services.

Regulation affecting conduct/operations of legal and engineering services providers in Eastern and Southern Africa is heavier than in most other countries. This evidence is explained by price regulations, advertising prohibitions, restrictions on firms' business structure and on multidisciplinary activities.

In accounting and engineering, professional services' fees tend to be negotiated freely between practitioners and clients across African countries but accountancy fees are regulated in Zambia and engineering fees are regulated in Botswana, South Africa, Tanzania and Zambia. As opposed to most developed countries, legal services' fees are regulated in all African countries except Mozambique and Rwanda.

Several professional services in Eastern and Southern Africa are subject to advertising prohibitions: accounting in Botswana, Kenya, Tanzania and Uganda; legal in Botswana, Kenya, Malawi, Mozambique, Rwanda, Tanzania, Uganda and Zambia; and engineering in Tanzania and Zambia. In general, African countries impose more severe regulations on advertising than most developed and developing countries.

Restrictions on the business structure permitted are present in all professional services in most African countries. These regulations restrict the ownership structure of professional services companies, the scope for collaboration within the profession and with other professions and the opening of branches, franchises or chains.

Explaining the Segmentation of Markets for Professional Services – Trade Barriers

Trade barriers limit competition and the efficiency of professional service providers in Eastern and Southern Africa (for a broader discussion of the gains from services trade liberalization see Chapter 9 and Dihel and Dee 2006; OECD 2002; Trachtman

2003). Trade in legal services tends to be more heavily regulated and restricted than trade in accounting/auditing services in Africa and elsewhere. Kenya, South Africa, Tanzania and Zambia are characterized by more severe restrictions on trade in legal services than most countries in the sample. In contrast, South Africa and Rwanda have some of the least restrictive trade policies in accounting/auditing services (Figure 20.3).

The establishment of foreign law firms (mode 3 of trade in services in GATS) is substantially more difficult than that of foreign accounting/auditing firms in Africa, but also elsewhere in the world. A few of our examined African countries – Botswana, Mozambique, Rwanda and Uganda – exhibit the most open markets to the presence of foreign law firms across a large number of countries. However, the entry of foreign law firms is prohibited in South Africa while ownership by non-locally licensed professionals is prohibited in Zambia and limited in Mozambique. In Mauritius entry is allowed only if the foreign law firm sets up a joint venture

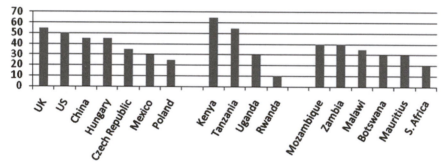

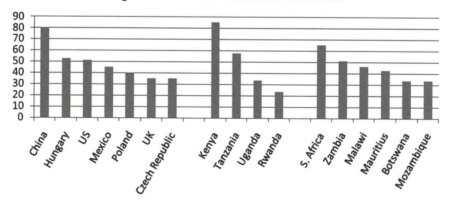

Figure 20.3 Overall restrictiveness indices for professional services
Note: A larger index value indicates a more restrictive trade policy.
Source: Gootiiz and Mattoo (2009).

with a local firm, while in Malawi branches are not allowed. Local members of international networks face restrictions on using the network's brand name or the foreign parent's name in Botswana, Kenya, Tanzania and Uganda.

In accounting and auditing, the establishment of foreign firms is permitted in all African countries but with restrictions. Malawi, Rwanda and Uganda have lower restrictions than those in many OECD countries. Kenya, Tanzania, Malawi, Mauritius, Mozambique and Zambia prohibit ownership or control by non-locally licensed professionals. In Kenya, Uganda and even the more liberal Rwanda, branches of foreign firms are prohibited. In Tanzania, ownership by foreign nationals is limited to 50 per cent. Botswana and Tanzania impose restrictions on the use of the foreign parent firm's name.

The movement of natural persons (mode 4 of trade in services in GATS) is substantially more restricted for legal professionals than for accounting/auditing professionals in Kenya, Tanzania, South Africa, Malawi and Zambia. These countries impose some of the most restrictive barriers to the practice of foreign lawyers in their jurisdictions, only equalled by the barriers imposed by China. In Kenya, Tanzania, Malawi, Mauritius, Mozambique and South Africa, *de jure* or *de facto* nationality requirements to practice domestic law exclude participation by foreign professionals.

The entry of foreign accountants and auditors is less restricted across African countries. In fact, Mauritius and Rwanda exhibit the most liberal trade policies towards the movement of foreign accountants among all countries. Except for Mauritius, all African countries impose discretionary limits on the presence of foreign accounting professionals.

Entry conditions through mode 3 and mode 4 are much more liberal for engineering. The establishment of foreign engineering firms is not prohibited in any African country and the form of entry is not restricted.

In terms of immigration policies, Eastern and Southern African countries apply stringent regulations to the movement of skilled workers into and out of their borders. In South Africa, the difficulties in obtaining work permits lead many international firms to set up partnerships with local firms instead of setting up commercial presence in the country (Black et al. 2006). The immigration law of 2007 in Mozambique is very restrictive and makes hiring foreign workers extremely difficult.

Implications for Policy Action

The national markets for professionals and professional services in most Eastern and Southern African countries remain underdeveloped with performance indicators below the averages of countries at a similar level of development. Also, the regional markets for professional services and professional education in Africa are fragmented by restrictive policies, such as nationality requirements and regulatory heterogeneity, relating to licensing, qualification and educational requirements. Strict domestic regulations combined with a lack of regional coordination among countries further constrain foreign investment and hinder economic growth and development in the region. These outcomes are the result of constraints that suggest policy action in the following areas: education, regulation of professional services, trade policy and labour mobility. While policy action at the national level will differ from country to country given diverse conditions and outcomes in the examined countries, international and regional cooperation would ideally complement domestic policy reform. Trade liberalization and regional integration can be used to reduce the scope for private interest regulation, enhance competition, and deal with labour mobility issues that are crucial in professional services.

Policy Action at the National Level

Reforms at the national level need to focus on the development of framework conditions that address skills shortages and skills mismatches and that attempt to facilitate the growth of professional services in the various African countries.

Education reforms need to focus on the following issues:

- Financial constraints prevent individuals from acquiring a professional education, so *developing new and expanded means of financing higher education* such as student loans schemes is a priority.

    Access to professional education could be increased by making financing more easily available for potential students. A central challenge with financing higher education in Africa is that the total number of students attending university outpaces the available funding support, leading to a large supply shortfall. Some countries have handled this challenge better than others: Botswana's funding resources have kept pace with student growth whereas Kenya's have lagged student growth by a factor of three (World Bank 2010a). Since it is unrealistic to expect governments to provide all necessary additional funding, the introduction or expansion of students' loan programmes could be useful to diversify the sources of funding for higher education while also addressing its affordability for individuals. Student loan schemes currently operate in more than 60 countries, including South Africa and 12 other African countries, and are becoming an increasingly important financing mechanism for higher education (World Bank 2010a).

- Weaknesses in African educational systems mean that students are poorly equipped to acquire professional skills, so *enhancing the quality and capacity of schools (especially in mathematics, sciences, and technical studies)* needs to be a key item on all countries' policy agendas.

    International and national experiences related to quality assurance of secondary and higher education could serve as a model for African countries. For example, in Europe a major step for improving the quality of higher education programmes has been the adoption of a common set of Standards and Guidelines for Quality Assurance in the European Higher Education Area (European Association for Quality Assurance in Higher Education 2005). The study Tuning Educational Structures in Europe[6] is another useful example. South Africa, whose quality assurance capacity is well ahead of that of its neighbours, can play a crucial role in enhancing the educational capacity in the region.

- Given the capacity constraints and quality limitations of professional education institutions, improving existing institutions and encouraging the creation of new ones is necessary.

  There is a need for both horizontal differentiation (for instance new educational providers in the same category operated by for-profit, non-profit, international or local government entities, to respond to the increased demand for higher education) and vertical differentiation (for example new types of institutions such as polytechnics, professional institutes, junior colleges for middle-level professionals, to respond to labour market needs for a greater diversity of skills and training levels). Malawi's development of middle-level legal professionals could be a useful model for the other African countries.[7]

Reforms need to focus on incremental, qualitative improvements in domestic regulation:

- Disproportionate cumulative entry requirements need to be relaxed. For example, narrowing the scope of exclusive tasks in certain professions would contribute to this goal. Exclusive rights can lead to increased specialization of professionals and guarantee a higher quality of service but if they create monopolies they can have adverse price and allocation effects, especially when granted for services for which adequate quality can be provided at a lower cost by less-regulated middle-level professionals.
- Disproportionate restrictions that limit competition need to be eliminated.

1. Price regulations are supported and introduced by professional associations who claim that they are useful tools to prevent adverse selection problems. Countries need to adopt less restrictive mechanisms such as better access to information on services and services providers to accomplish the same goals at lower economic cost.

---

[6]   See more information at http://unideusto.org/tuning/.

[7]   Some successful initiatives have encouraged the education, training and development of middle-level professionals. The Paralegal Advisory Service in Malawi is an innovative programme that offers paralegal aid in criminal cases and has so far trained 38 paralegals. Candidates receive training from NGOs working in partnership with key stakeholders including Malawi Prisons, Police Services and the court system. The paralegals are then able to work with these same institutions, making the arrangement beneficial for both sides. The programme has been so successful that the organization is being transformed into the Paralegal Advisory Services Institute and is introducing similar programmes throughout the Africa region and even further abroad in Bangladesh.

2. Countries impose restrictions on the ownership structure of professional services firms; the scope of collaboration within the profession and with other professions; and, in some cases, the opening of branches, franchises or chains. These countries need to eliminate regulations that are clearly anticompetitive and that may harm consumers by preventing providers from developing new services or cost-efficient business models.
3. Advertising prohibitions are imposed by most examined African countries on many of their professional services sectors. These countries need to allow advertising of professional services that facilitates competition by informing consumers about different products and that can be used as a competitive tool for new firms entering the market.

Policy Action at the International Level

The fragmentation of regional markets for professional services and professional education by restrictive policies and regulatory heterogeneity prevents countries from taking advantage of gains from trade based on comparative advantage, as well as gains from enhanced competition and economies of scale.

The potential benefits from regional integration in Eastern and Southern Africa are considerable.

- The differences in national endowments of professionals and in the capacity for professional training, reflected in differences in professionals' earnings and the costs of training across countries, suggest that there is substantive scope for trade based on comparative advantage and potentially large gains from eliminating trade impediments.
- Deeper regional integration would enhance competition between service providers, allow providers to exploit economies of scale especially in professional education, produce a wider variety of services, and increase the prospects for attracting domestic and foreign investment.
- Regionalization may make it possible to reap scale economies in regulation and supervision, particularly where national regulatory agencies face skill constraints; it could also reduce scope for capture of national regulation by private sector interests.

Policy action is called for in the following key areas:

i. *Steps need to be taken to relax the explicit trade barriers applied by African countries to the movement of natural persons and commercial presence of professional services.*

Examples of possible reforms are:

- articulating the economic and social motivation for nationality and residency requirements;

- developing transparent criteria and procedures for applying any quantitative restrictions on the movement of professionals, such as economic needs tests;
- minimizing restrictions on the forms of establishment allowed;
- developing a transparent and consistent framework for accepting professionals with foreign qualifications.

The reduction of explicit trade barriers needs to be complemented with the reform of immigration laws.

ii. *Trade liberalization needs to be coordinated with regulatory reform and cooperation at the regional level.*

Trade barriers ideally would be liberalized on a most-favoured-nation or non-preferential basis because that would generate the largest welfare gains. But such liberalization may not be technically feasible or politically acceptable, especially when impediments arise from differences in regulatory requirements. Deeper regional integration through regulatory cooperation with neighbouring partners who have similar regulatory preferences can usefully complement non-preferential trade liberalization. Regional integration would also enhance competition among services providers, enable those providers to exploit economies of scale in professional education, and produce a wider variety of services. Regional integration brings further benefits in that a larger regional market is able to attract greater domestic and foreign investment; and regionalization may help take advantage of scale economies in regulation, particularly where national agencies face technical skills or capacity constraints.[8]

Regulatory cooperation to overcome regulatory heterogeneity under the aegis of the Tripartite arrangement between the East African Community (EAC), the Common Market for Eastern and Southern Africa (COMESA) and the Southern African Development Community (SADC) would be particularly useful in the following areas:

Mutual recognition of professional qualifications and licensing

The model adopted by East Africa could be followed by Southern African countries. The five East African countries have taken the first steps towards mutual recognition in professional services in the context of the EAC Common

---

[8]   See World Bank (2010c) for a discussion on the role that international trade agreements, particularly the Economic Partnership Agreements (EPAs) that are currently being negotiated with the European Union (EU), can play in supporting coordinated trade and regulatory reforms in Africa. The study discusses the key issues that EPAs will have to address if they are to support the development of service sectors in Africa, while recognizing that EPAs might not necessarily be the most effective way to pursue service sector reform for all African countries.

Market negotiations. The Common Market Protocol, adopted by the Multi-Sector Council in 2009, includes an annex on a framework agreement on mutual recognition (MRA) of academic and professional qualifications. The implementation of a full-fledged MRA would need to cover areas such as education, examinations, experience, conduct and ethics, professional development and re-certification, scope of practice, and local knowledge.[9] If African countries adopted common criteria for professional qualifications or recognized (with no hassles) the qualifications and licenses obtained in other African countries, significant efficiency gains would be obtained. Kox et al. (2004) estimate that the stock of FDI in the European Union could increase by 20 per cent to 35 per cent if regulatory heterogeneity across countries was reduced as a result of a common services regulation directive.

Developing appropriate standards

Inappropriate standards can stifle demand for services. While uniformity of standards may improve the quality, completeness and comparability of the reported information, and international standards remain appropriate in specific cases, applying common international standards to large firms and SMEs can prevent smaller firms from using auditing and accounting services. A single standard may be appropriate if there is little demand for service variety and there is no anticompetitive risk from having a single standard. However, if the market requires variety to satisfy different types of users, then a single standard may not be appropriate.

The development of an appropriate standard may be desirable at a regional rather than national level in order to exploit economies of scale in regulatory expertise, prevent fragmentation of the market by differences in standards, and limit the scope for regulatory capture.

Removal of restrictions to free movement of labour

Regional cooperation in removing restrictions on the free movement of labour (including visa and immigration laws) is crucial for Africa. The mobility of businesspeople is a key factor in the promotion of free and open trade. While the EAC and the SADC have tried to regulate labour mobility, so far none of the groupings has adopted a regional labour mobility agreement, mostly due to disagreements among national governments.[10] The experience of the EU or the APEC Business Mobility Group that have made considerable progress in this area could provide practical guidance for the implementation of commitments related to the free movement of labour and harmonization of immigration policies in Africa.

---

[9]   See Peek et al. (2007) for NAFTA's experience with MRAs.
[10]   See Musonda (2006) and Shitundu (2006).

Financing higher education and improving professional education institutions

Regional cooperation in terms of sharing information and experiences to increase the recovery rate of loans while increasing students' access to higher education could improve the impact of student loan schemes in Africa. The recent partnership between the Kenya Higher Education Loan Board, the Tanzania Higher Education Students Loans Board and the Students Finance Agency for Rwanda, under the aegis of the African Higher Education Financing Agencies, to tackle students' loan schemes regionally is a useful example from East Africa that could be followed by Southern Africa.

The absence of institutions that offer specialized (postgraduate) courses (such as in legal and engineering services) was noted in many African countries, as was the absence of institutions offering academic and professional training courses for middle-level professionals. Where the market of a given country (such as Malawi, Mozambique, Rwanda) is too small to justify the creation of missing institutions or courses, policies to facilitate access to foreign training are needed – including portability of course credits and scholarships. The system of credits in higher education to be implemented within SADC is a right step in this direction.

Also, specialized courses for which a need was expressed in Eastern and Southern Africa (for instance legal courses focusing on e-commerce, technology transfer, etc.) could be designed and implemented at the regional level. Regional institutions could exploit economies of scale and recoup the large fixed costs of establishing training programmes in order to produce students with the necessary specializations for the EAC and SADC regions. South Africa has the highest potential to become a regional hub for higher and professional education.

Conclusion

Eastern and Southern African governments need to engage in deep regulatory cooperation at the regional level, use trade liberalization and regional integration to reduce the scope for private interest regulation, and enhance competition to facilitate the growth of their professional services sectors. The various governments could engage with donors to secure technical and financial assistance to strengthen the capacity of regulatory associations, and develop appropriate regulation (for example in the context of the European Partnership Agreement negotiations).

While the economic benefits from regional integration are evident, the pace of integration is largely dependent upon the members' political motivation and conviction that such liberalization is beneficial to their domestic constituencies. To improve such prospects, the promotion of more frequent and open dialogue between the key stakeholders involved in professional services – professional bodies, private sector providers and users of services, higher education institutions, trade negotiators – is important.

The Eastern and Southern African countries have committed themselves (at least on paper) to pursue regional integration in the context of the EAC, the COMESA and the SADC. The adoption by the five East African Heads of State of the Common Market Protocol in 2009 initiated the integration process in professional and other services in Eastern Africa. Kenya, Rwanda, Tanzania and Uganda have scheduled commitments in accounting and engineering services, and have adopted the annexes on removing restrictions on the free movement of workers and on the right of establishment, and the annex on mutual recognition of academic and professional qualifications.

The Southern African countries have also committed themselves to pursue regional integration in the context of the SADC that launched its Free Trade Agreement (FTA) in 2008 aimed at liberalizing intra-regional trade in goods and services. However, the FTA does not include any concrete measures for services liberalization. SADC negotiations on services have been ongoing for ten years centring on the framework agreement for the negotiations, that is, 'negotiating how to negotiate'. SADC has identified six backbone sectors which call for immediate trade liberalization in terms of the services protocol, including construction and related engineering services. But sectors such as business services (that include other professional services) are scheduled to be liberalized only in later rounds of negotiations.

While recognizing that there is a varying degree of political will and commitment among the Eastern and Southern African countries, the information provided in this chapter serves as a pointer towards more informed choices as countries contemplate reform and regional integration in professional services sectors.

References

Arnold, J., Mattoo, A. and Gaia, N. 2006. Services inputs and firm productivity in sub-Saharan Africa: evidence from firm-level data. *Journal of African Economies*, 17: 578–599.

Black, R., Crush, J., Peberdy, S., Ammassari, S., Hilker, L., Mouillesseaux, S., Polley, C. and Rajkotia, R. 2006. *Migration & Development in Africa: An Overview*. Southern African Migration Project.

Borchert, I. and Mattoo, A. 2009. The crisis resilience of services trade. *Policy Research Working Paper*, No. 4917. Washington, DC: World Bank.

Cattaneo, O. and Walkenhorst, P. 2010. Legal services: does more trade rhyme with better justice?, in *International Trade in Services: New Trends and Opportunities for Developing Countries*, edited by O. Cattaneo, M. Engman, S. Saez and R. Stern. Washington, DC: World Bank: 67–98.

Cattaneo, O., Schmid, L. and Walkenhorst, P. 2010. Engineering services: how to compete in the most global of the professions, in *International Trade in Services: New Trends and Opportunities for Developing Countries*, edited by O. Cattaneo, M. Engman, S. Saezand and R. Stern. Washington, DC: World Bank: 293–318.

Conway, P. and Nicoletti, G. 2006. Product market regulation in the non-manufacturing sectors of OECD countries: measurement and highlights. *OECD Economics Department Working Papers, No. 530*. Paris: OECD.

Dihel, N. and Dee, P. 2006. Services as outputs and intermediate inputs: the impact of liberalization, in *Trading Up: Economic Perspectives on Development Issues in the Multilateral Trading System*. Paris: OECD: 231–275.

European Association for Quality Assurance in Higher Education. 2005. *Standards and Guidelines for Quality Assurance in the European Higher Education Area*. Helsinki: ENQA.

Fernandes, A. and Mattoo, A. 2009. Professional services and development: a study of Mozambique. *World Bank Policy Research Working Paper Series, No. 4870*. Washington, DC: World Bank.

Gootiiz, B. and Mattoo, A. 2009. Services in Doha: what's on the table? *Journal of World Trade*, 43(5): 1013–1030.

Kox, H., Lejour, A. and Montizaan, R. 2004. The free movement of services within the EU. *CPB Documents* No. 69, CPB Netherlands Bureau for Economic Policy Analysis.

Musonda, F. 2006. Migration legislation in East Africa. *International Migration Papers No. 82*. Geneva: International Labour Office.

OECD. 2002. *GATS: The Case for Open Services Markets*. Paris: OECD.

OECD. 2007. Competitive restrictions in the legal profession. *DAF/COMP (2007)39*. Paris: OECD.

Peek, L., McGraw, E., Robichaud, Y., Castillo Villarreal, J., Roxas, M. and Peek, G. 2007. NAFTA Professional mutual recognition agreements: comparative analysis of accountancy certification and licensure. *Global Perspectives on Accounting Education*, 4: 1–24.

Sampson, G. and Snape, R. 1985. Identifying issues in trade in services. *The World Economy*, 8(2): 171–181.

Shitundu, J. 2006. A study on labour migration data and statistics in East Africa. *International Migration Papers*, 81. Geneva: International Labour Office.

Trachtman, J. 2003. Lessons for the GATS from existing WTO rules on domestic regulation, in *Domestic Regulation and Services Trade Liberalization*, edited by A. Mattoo and P. Sauvé. Washington, DC: World Bank and Oxford University Press: 57–82.

Trolliet, C. and Hegarty, J. 2003. Regulatory reform and trade liberalization in accountancy services, in *Domestic Regulation & Services Trade Liberalization*, edited by A. Mattoo and P. Sauvé. Washington, DC: World Bank and Oxford University Press: 147–166.

World Bank. 2008. *Report on the Observance of Standards and Codes: Mozambique*. Washington, DC: World Bank.

World Bank. 2010a. *Financing Higher Education in Africa*. Washington, DC: World Bank.

World Bank. 2010b. *Reform and Regional Integration of Professional Services in East Africa: Time for Action*. Washington, DC: World Bank.

World Bank. 2010c. *Africa's Trade in Services and Economic Partnership Agreements.* Washington, DC: World Bank.

World Bank. 2011. *Harnessing Regional Integration for Trade and Growth in Southern Africa.* Washington, DC: World Bank.

PART VI
The WTO and Multilateralism

The Structure and Function of the World Trade Organization

John H. Jackson and Steve Charnovitz[1]

Introduction

The World Trade Organization (WTO) is an international body, established by governments to provide rules for the commercial interface of national economies. The rules of world trade law apply to government policies that restrict or affect international trade. WTO law has a broad reach, covering international trade in goods and services and some trade-related issues including investment, government subsidies and intellectual property. Issues of private international law, such as the international convention of contracts for the international sale of goods, lie outside the scope of the WTO.

The WTO sponsors intergovernmental negotiations to progressively liberalize international trade and to further the underlying objectives of the multilateral trading system. The current round of comprehensive trade negotiations, known as the Doha Development Agenda, began in 2001 and extensive progress has been made in narrowing differences among governments (Hohmann 2008). Nevertheless, prospects for completing this round in the near future remain low (Pruzin 2010).

Although every international organization has some associated epistemic communities, the WTO seems to attract more passionate critics than many other organizations do (Irwin 2002). In part, this is surely a reflection of the broad reach of WTO law and the organization's perceived effectiveness. However, the animus towards the WTO in some quarters stems from some misconceptions about the role of the WTO vis-à-vis national policymaking and the purpose of world trade law. One of our goals in this chapter is to clarify some of the confusion about the WTO. Of course, fears about the WTO also stem from the way that international trade can affect the labour market. In our view the WTO will be more effective in enhancing economic welfare, while respecting social justice, if governments put

---

[1]   Portions of this chapter are drawn in part from previous writings by each of the authors.

in place appropriate domestic policies to help workers and communities adjust to economic change.

Whether economic policies which are based on market principles are the best approach for maximizing human satisfaction is, of course, controversial (Corden 1974; Jackson 1998; Kenen 1994; Krugman and Obstfeld 1994; Stiglitz 2002). Various alternatives have been much debated and many of those largely rejected, but substantial arguments are made in favour of some sort of mixture of policies, perhaps to temper the perceived negative effects of 'too pure market approaches'. Whatever mixture may appeal to certain societies, it seems reasonably clear that markets can be very beneficial (Sykes 1998). Even when not beneficial, market forces demand respect and can cause great difficulties when not respected.[2]

This chapter provides an overview of the structure and functioning of the WTO. Although the WTO was established in 1995, the roots of the world trading system go back many decades and so the current WTO structure and function reflects learning from a lengthy era of intergovernmental trade cooperation. Yet the WTO also contains many innovative features that were added in 1994 and thus were not present in the pre-WTO trading system. As a result of these 'constitutional' reforms occurring less than a generation ago, the WTO combines some of the most cutting-edge institutional features of any international organization with a jurisprudence and organizational culture going back over half a century.

The WTO is similar to other international organizations in some ways but dissimilar in many others. Like most major international organizations the WTO is founded by a multilateral treaty, has governmental members and contains an independent secretariat. Yet unlike most other international organizations, the WTO has an in-house dispute settlement system with compulsory jurisdiction over complaints by one WTO member against another. Another difference is that the WTO's membership is not limited to states but can also include autonomous customs territories, with Chinese Taipei (Taiwan) being the most notable example. The WTO's treaty is also different from the organic law of other major international organizations since the WTO contains a very detailed set of rules known as world trade law (Wouters and De Meester 2007).

The WTO's rules for trade were written by member governments for governments. Although the legitimacy of world trade law is sometimes questioned, the justification for legitimacy is strong. No government is forced to join the WTO and so when a government chooses to join, it consents to the rules and to the contractual obligation that it acts in accordance with those rules. Moreover, past and current rulemaking in multilateral trade negotiations operates on a consensus basis. Of course, it is also true that many governments have felt pressured to join the WTO and may have wished that they could have ratified the WTO Agreement with reservations concerning particular agreements or rules. Unlike many other treaties, however, the Marrakesh Agreement Establishing the World Trade Organization does not permit reservations.

---

[2]   For an overview of the economic principles which support policies of liberal international trade rules, see Sykes (1998 and Chapters 1 and 2).

Although the rights and obligations of WTO law operate among governments, the beneficiaries of the WTO also include private sector actors. Because of WTO rules, international trade gains more security and predictability and this economic condition benefits producers, consumers, traders and workers (Moore 2001). Perhaps the best example of how a government can reap the benefits of WTO membership has been China, which strengthened its reputation for honouring the rule of law when it joined the WTO in 2001 (Lamy 2010a).

The remainder of this chapter proceeds in five parts. The second part explains the background and history of the world trading system, the third discusses the basic structure and decision-making in the WTO, the fourth provides an overview of WTO dispute settlement and the fifth part addresses the ongoing agenda of the WTO. The final part offers some of our own conclusions about the challenges facing the WTO.

Background and History of the Trading System

The WTO is now the principal institution for international trade but to understand this institution it is necessary also to know something about its predecessor, the General Agreement on Tariffs and Trade (GATT). Indeed, the WTO Charter makes it clear that the GATT history is significant, prescribing in Article XVI that 'the WTO shall be guided by the decisions, procedures and customary practices followed by the CONTRACTING PARTIES [expressed in all caps to signify the Contracting Parties acting jointly under the GATT Agreement] to GATT 1947 and the bodies established in the framework of GATT 1947'.

The 1944 Bretton Woods conference in the United States established the charters for the World Bank and the International Monetary Fund, two pillars of the post-Second World War international economic institutional system. Because the Bretton Woods conference was directed and organized by the financial ministers of the governments concerned, it was not felt appropriate to address the trade questions which generally belonged to other ministries at that time. However, the Bretton Woods conference explicitly recognized the necessity of an international trade organization to complement the responsibilities of the financial organizations. Indeed, in some ways the WTO has at last provided the 'missing leg' of the Bretton Woods system.

The negotiations for an international trade organization were launched in 1946 by the United Nations (UN) Economic and Social Council. Besides the impetus from the Bretton Woods talks, the project to construct a trading system can be traced back to several strands of international cooperation and conflict. One strand was the programme of bilateral trade agreements negotiated by the United States after the enactment of the 1934 Reciprocal Trade Agreements Act championed by the then Secretary of State Cordell Hull. Between 1934 and 1945, the US government entered into 32 bilateral reciprocal trade agreements, many of which had clauses that later became models used in drafting the GATT. Another strand was the economic cooperation attempted in the League of Nations whereby a multilateral treaty to ban import restrictions had been negotiated in 1927 and subsequently abandoned. A third strand of thinking stemmed from the view that the mistakes made concerning economic policy during the interwar period were a major cause of the disasters that led to the Second World War. In the interwar period, particularly after the damaging 1930 US Tariff Act was signed, many other nations began enacting protectionist measures, including quota-type restrictions, which choked off international trade. Political leaders in the United States and elsewhere made statements about the importance of establishing postwar economic institutions that would prevent these mistakes from happening again.

At the end of the UN drafting conference in Geneva in November 1947, a complete draft of the GATT was readied but the charter for the new trade organization needed more work (Irwin et al. 2008). This added work was scheduled for a conference in Havana in 1948 and at the UN Conference on Trade and Employment, the Charter for an International Trade Organization (ITO) was finalized. The charter, however, became doomed after the Truman Administration was unable to secure sufficient political support for ratification in the US Congress.

Since the GATT, including the various tariff obligations, had already been completed in October 1947 by 23 nations, many negotiators believed that it should be brought into force quickly, even before the anticipated Havana conference. There were several reasons for this. One was a concern that the still-secret substance of the agreed-upon tariff reductions would leak out and that trade patterns could be seriously disrupted as traders waited for new rates to come into force. Another reason for early implementation involved the United States trade agreement implementation authority which was slated to expire in mid-1948. Yet there were political concerns in many countries that bringing the GATT into force through a treaty ratification process might then complicate the process of ratifying the ITO Charter.

The solution agreed upon was the adoption of the Protocol of Provisional Application (PPA) to apply the GATT treaty provisionally on or after 1 January 1948 pending the establishment of the ITO. The PPA was drafted to require that governments only implement the GATT 'to the fullest extent not inconsistent with existing legislative'. By using the PPA with its 'grandfathering' of existing law the negotiators allowed most governments, which would otherwise need to submit to the GATT for legislative approval, to approve the separate PPA by executive or administrative authority without going to their parliament.

When the ITO did not come into force, the GATT found its role changing dramatically as nations turned it into the forum in which an increasing number of problems of their trading relations could be handled. More countries became contracting parties to the GATT and a second round of tariff reductions was undertaken in 1949. Although the GATT was technically not an organization, it gradually stepped into the role of an organization. Committees and working parties were slowly set up and in 1960 the GATT parties established the GATT Council to provide governance. The Interim Commission for the ITO provided secretariat services to the GATT on a 'leased' basis and this makeshift procedure worked to enable the GATT Secretariat to function. Since the GATT operated in some ways like a members' club, the spontaneous lawmaking that can occur in small communities transpired in the GATT

The GATT should be praised for its considerable success, certainly beyond what would have been predicted following its flawed origins. By 1970 the GATT had overseen six major trade negotiations and succeeded in bringing about dramatic reductions in tariffs, at least for manufactured products imported into advanced industrial countries. As the GATT looked forward to its seventh round of negotiations, known as the Tokyo Round (1973–9), the focus expanded to include new regulations on non-tariff barriers. The Tokyo Round negotiators did not seek to change the GATT itself, but rather adopted a series of separate codes, each of which was a standalone treaty that a GATT party could choose to join or not. These codes addressed a number of troublesome non-tariff barriers that distorted trade flows, such as autarkic government procurement regulations and product standards that had the effect of thwarting imports.

The eighth and last trade round under the GATT umbrella was the Uruguay Round launched in Punta del Este, Uruguay in 1986 and which finally concluded at a ministerial-level negotiating conference in Marrakesh, Morocco in April 1994. The Uruguay Round was clearly the most ambitious of all of the GATT rounds and surely the largest and most complex completed economic multilateral treaty negotiation in history. A key achievement of the round was the establishment of the WTO itself. Setting up a new multilateral organization was not included in the agenda agreed to at Punta del Este and only rose to a high priority late in the negotiation. This turn of attention came about partly as a result of the views of the negotiators, who began to see that the Uruguay Round results were so extensive that a new institutional structure would be essential for the successful implementation of the new agreements. Happily, some GATT experts in governments and academia had been thinking about what institutional reforms were needed (Jackson 1990).

WTO Basic Institutional Structure and Decision-making Procedures

The WTO was established on 1 January 1995 when the massive treaty agreed to in the Uruguay Round came into force (Jackson 2006). The beginning portion of that 26,000-page treaty is a brief 14-page text that establishes the WTO as a proper (no longer provisional) organization. Although this text is often referred to as the WTO's Constitution or Charter, the WTO Agreement is technically a single undertaking, including four annexes and numerous sub-annexes, which contains the legal rules and bindings agreed to in the negotiations. Annex 1 contains the multilateral rules for goods, services and trade-related intellectual property. Annex 2 contains the rules for dispute settlement. Annex 3 governs the operation of the

Trade Policy Review Mechanism. Annex 4 contains the plurilateral agreements that bind only the WTO members who join them.

Within Annex I, Annex I A provides the rules on goods. The centrepiece of Annex I A is the GATT 1994 which is a new agreement based on the original GATT negotiated in 1947, the amendments to the GATT that occurred between 1947 and 1994 and six negotiated 'Understandings' of particular GATT provisions. The most extensive part of the GATT is the tariff schedules for each WTO member that set maximum tariff commitments. Annex I also contains 12 specialized agreements on trade in goods. They cover: agriculture, antidumping, import licensing, investment measures that are trade-related, pre-shipment inspection, rules of origin, safeguards, sanitary and phytosanitary standards, subsidies and countervailing measures, technical barriers to trade, textiles and clothing (now expired), and valuation. Since the GATT provisions were not renegotiated during the Uruguay Round, some GATT provisions are clearly superseded by these specialized covered agreements. A brief text at the end of the WTO Charter stipulates that if there is a conflict between GATT 1994 and one of these covered agreements, the latter shall prevail.

Annex I B provides the rules on services. The centrepiece is the General Agreement on Trade in Services (GATS) which is among the most creative lawmaking that emerged from the Uruguay Round in defining how services are provided in international trade and in applying trade law principles to this previously ungoverned means of international trade (Sauvé and Stern 2000). The GATS also contains subject specific annexes covering air transport services, financial services, maritime transport services and telecommunications. In addition, like the GATT, there are also detailed annexes providing country-specific negotiated commitments.

Annex 1 C provides the rules on intellectual property via the Agreement on Trade-Related Aspects of Intellectual Property Rights (TRIPS). In TRIPS, each government agreed to grant the included rights to the nationals of other members and to provide a means of enforcement of these rights under its own domestic law. TRIPS extends broad coverage to intellectual property, including copyrights, trademarks, geographic indications, patents and several others. For some of these areas, TRIPS incorporates by reference the provisions of major multilateral treaties on intellectual property.

Unlike the GATT, the WTO Charter establishes an international organization, endows it with legal personality and supports it with the traditional organizational clauses regarding 'privileges and immunities', a Secretariat, a Director-General (DG), budgetary measures and explicit authority to develop relations with other intergovernmental organizations and nongovernmental organizations (NGOs). The Charter prohibits staff of the Secretariat from seeking or accepting instructions from any government 'or any other authority external to the WTO'. The WTO has benefited from the leadership of several DGs, each of whom has brought unique talents and capacities to a very demanding job.

The governing structure of the WTO follows some of the GATT-era model, but it also departs from it substantially. At the top there is a 'Ministerial Conference', which is directed to meet not less than every two years. Below that are four additional councils. The General Council has overall supervisory authority, including responsibility for carrying out many of the functions of the Ministerial Conference between those conference sessions. In addition, there is a Council for each of the Annex I agreements, that is for goods, services, and intellectual property. Each of these Councils is open to membership for any WTO member who chooses to take it on.

When the General Council convenes to discharge responsibilities for dispute settlement, the Council transmogrifies into the Dispute Settlement Body (DSB) with identical membership (that is, all WTO members), but a different chairman. The role of the DSB in administering the WTO Dispute Settlement Understanding (DSU) will be addressed in the fourth part of this chapter.

The rules in the WTO Charter for decision-making are formally complex but simple in practice. They are complex because there are distinct voting requirements for each particular type of decision. The current practice of consensus decision-making (other than for dispute settlement decisions) makes the topic simpler, however. Article IX:1 of the WTO Charter states that 'The WTO shall continue the practice of decision-making by consensus followed under GATT 1947'. But this provision further states that 'Except as otherwise provided, where a decision cannot be arrived at by consensus, the matter at issue shall be decided by voting'. This clear language leaves the door open to non-consensus decision-making in the future.

The default voting rule under the WTO Charter is majority rules wherein each WTO member receives one vote. Yet decision-making by a simple majority of the votes cast does not apply when the WTO Charter specifies a higher requirement as it does for almost all areas of decision-making. An action by the Ministerial Conference or the General Council to adopt an 'interpretation' of the WTO Agreement requires a three-quarter majority of the members. (No interpretations have been adopted.) An action by the Ministerial Conference to grant a WTO member government a waiver requires three-quarter of the members, but certain obligations can only be waived by consensus.

The voting rule for amending the WTO Agreement depends on what provision is to be amended. Some provisions can be amended by two-thirds of the members, others by a three-quarter majority and some by universal acceptance. Some amendments only take effect for a member when that member accepts it while others are notionally effective without individual member acceptance.

Even in that case there is provision for a hold-out member to withdraw from the organization or negotiate a special dispensation. Since withdrawal by certain key members of the WTO would probably end the WTO's effectiveness, such key members probably effectively have a 'veto' regarding amendments.

Only one amendment to the WTO has been approved by the Ministerial Conference and that was on the topic of compulsory licensing of pharmaceuticals. This amendment has not been accepted by a sufficient number of WTO member countries to come into force. The substantive rulemaking in the amendment had been previously accomplished through a waiver that remains in effect.

The WTO Dispute Settlement System and its Important Achievements

The WTO's dispute settlement system (DSS) is unique in international law and institutions both at present and historically. This dispute settlement system embraces mandatory exclusive jurisdiction and virtually automatic adoption of dispute system reports. It has been described as the most important and most powerful of any international law tribunals, although some observers reserve that primary place to the World Court (International Court of Justice). Even some experienced World Court advocates, however, have been willing to concede that primacy under some criteria to the DSS.

Some statistics will aid understanding of the role of the DSS. During just over 15 years of existence (1 January 1995 to July 2010), the DSS has adopted over 158 reports. The approximate total number of pages of this 'adopted' jurisprudence is 60,000 pages, or the rough equivalent of 150 400-page volumes. The reports are carefully crafted, extremely analytical and very well reasoned, compared to the outputs of other excellent court systems – national and international.

This body of jurisprudence reflects the difficult issues confronting the WTO. A major part of these difficulties is directly related to the constant tension between the claims of authority and allocation of power by nation-state and other WTO members on the one hand, and the assertions of the WTO as an international legitimate authority requiring control of some issues in order to carry out its responsibilities on the other. This tension is manifested repeatedly in the vast jurisprudence of the DSS. The characterization 'boiler-room of international relations', used by one of us in a previous publication about GATT (Jackson 1995), is surely appropriate. This jurisprudence contains many lessons with many 'classical dilemma situations' that should instruct all participants and observers of international law in particular, and international relations in general (Sacerdoti et al. 2006).

The GATT had a well-functioning DSS, but its operation depended on the good-will of governments which sometimes was not present. For example, setting up a panel and approving its report both required a consensus of GATT Contracting parties. Another problem was that if a panel reached a decision that embodied legal error, there was no way to get it corrected short of blocking adoption of the panel report.

The new WTO Dispute Settlement Understanding vastly improves the dispute procedures:

1. It established a unified dispute settlement system for all parts of the GATT/WTO system, including the new subjects of services and intellectual property.
2. It clarified that all parts of the Uruguay Round legal text relevant to the matter in issue and argued by the parties can be considered in a particular dispute case.
3. It reaffirmed and clarified the right of a complaining government to have a panel process initiated, preventing blocking at that stage.

4. It established a 'reverse consensus' rule for adoption of a panel report, which results in almost automatic adoption with no chance for 'blocking'. However, an appeal can be made before adoption.

5. It established a creative new appellate procedure which will substitute for some of the former procedures of Council approval of a panel report. An appellate body of seven members acting independently of governments is constituted and three of these members act to provide conclusions, which are binding. The opportunity of a losing party to block adoption of a panel report is no longer available.

6. It established new procedures for setting a reasonable period of time for implementation, for adjudicating whether measures taken to comply do, in fact, constitute compliance, and for determining the amount of suspension of concessions or other obligations (SCOO) that can be imposed on a scofflaw country that fails to comply (Bown and Pauwelyn 2010).

The relationship of international law generally to the WTO has been commented on for a number of years under the GATT and was very prominently addressed at the very beginning of the existence of the WTO Appellate Body. The question in GATT times was sometimes stated to be whether the GATT was a 'separate legal regime' from international law, so that general international law norms would not necessarily be relevant or pervade the work of the GATT. In the very first case that the Appellate Body handed down, it addressed the question of the relationship of international law to the WTO and emphatically pronounced that, with respect to treaty interpretation, general principles of customary international law were binding on members of the WTO. The Appellate Body also noticed that many countries deemed the text of the Vienna Convention on the law of treaties to appropriately articulate the customary international law of treaty interpretation and the Appellate Body quoted Articles 31 and 32 of the Vienna Convention extensively.

Another important jurisprudence concept is the use of 'precedent'. Too often some observers and commentators ('publicists') have tended to discuss the use of precedent in judicial decision-making as involving a dichotomous choice between *stare decisis* and not relying upon precedent.[3] As with many dichotomous analyses, this is deeply flawed. The underlying problem is the question of how much influence a prior decision of a judicial body should have when considering new cases. In the WTO (like the GATT before it) we can detect a fairly strong use of precedent. Moreover, the Appellate Body has made it clear that panels are expected to adhere to judgments of the Appellate Body on the same subject matter.

One of the most important, indeed, perhaps the single most important, case of WTO jurisprudence so far, in the sense of fundamental and 'constitutional' concepts, is the *Shrimp Turtle* case (WTO 1998b). This case touches on a number of the concepts relating to interpreting the WTO constitution. The case was brought by

---

[3]   Stare decisis is a Latin term meaning 'to stand by decisions and not disturb the undisturbed'.

four developing country members of the WTO against the United States, arguing that the US regulator was violating the WTO in prohibiting the importation of shrimp from particular countries. The rationale for the US action was that the harvesting of shrimp in certain ways tends to kill sea turtles, almost all of which are endangered species. Consequently, the United States effectively required the exporting nation-state to take measures to ensure that turtle excluder devices, or other means to prevent harming the turtles, were utilized in the gathering of shrimp. The first-level Panel ruled with quite strong language against the United States, partly based on its view that the unilateral measures were inappropriate in a multilateral organization. The Appellate Body dramatically modified the language of the first-level Panel, but nevertheless concluded that, as applied, the US measures were not consistent with its obligations. After this report, the United States was able to change its practices by administrative changes (without seeking legislation from the Congress) and argued successfully that those changes brought its programme into consistency with the WTO.

This case is extraordinarily complex and nuanced and cannot be thoroughly reported here, but a few broad, brief ideas about the case can be set forth.

One such idea is the explicit invocation of the Appellate Body of an 'evolutionary' principle of interpretation, particularly relating to language speaking of 'exhaustible natural resources' as an exception under Article XX (g) of GATT. The basic question there was whether a living animal could be considered an exhaustible natural resource and the Appellate Body rendered its opinion that it could be, even though, at the time of the origin of this language, that term was considered to apply to minerals and other non-renewable resources.[4] The Appellate Body opinion was partly based on the idea that WTO member governments had accepted programmes to save endangered species.

Another feature of the *Shrimp Turtle* case is the idea that non-trade policies must be considered in connection with the trade policies of the WTO. The Appellate Body gave a number of reasons for including environmental policies as part of the policy landscape of the WTO, particularly when interpreting language of GATT Article XX 'Chapeau' (the preamble to Article XX).

The Appellate Body, in this, its first *Shrimp Turtle* opinion, reversed the panel conclusion that 'unilateral' measures were clear violations of the WTO treaty. The Appellate Body view was much more complex. In its consideration of interpretation of 'unilateral' measures, it found a series of specific problems in the United States measure, as those would be considered in the interpretation of the Article XX Chapeau language, relating to 'unjustifiable discrimination' and 'arbitrary discrimination'. The Appellate Body felt that it had to do this in a way that would take account of the environmental policies and thus had to develop a balancing approach between competing norms (Vranes 2009). The opposite approach, to be totally textual and not balance any non-trade policies, could ultimately lead to the

---

4   The Appellate Body appeared not to consider elements of the GATT negotiating history that showed references to animal life as exhaustible natural resources.

inability of the organization to maintain a degree of legitimacy that would enable it to carry out its broader objectives relating to trade liberalization.

In summing up the general conclusions about the WTO Appellate Body jurisprudence it is easy to see that treaty interpretation is, at times, much more complicated than thought by many of the individuals who are involved in the process. It is extraordinarily varied and it touches on a number of different institutional or 'constitutional' policies, as well as challenging the older 'consent' theory notions of Westphalian 'sovereignty'. In many ways, treaty interpretation illustrates important implications of detailed aspects of modern tensions between 'sovereignty' and 'international institutionalism.'

WTO Policy and Administrative Activities

Although the long-delayed WTO Doha Round negotiations have received considerable attention in the press and from scholars, the other achievements of the WTO do not receive as much attention even though they are important. The inability of WTO member governments to complete the Doha Round has put greater pressure on the dispute settlement system to clarify and fill the gaps in incomplete WTO rules. To be sure, the failure of the Doha Round so far shows a dysfunction in the WTO's legislative branch. Nevertheless, it is important not to assume that the exclusive legislative output of the WTO is completed trade rounds. The WTO Councils and Committees and the Secretariat have, over the past 16 years, accomplished a great deal that has furthered the interest of the trading system.

The most significant expansion in the reach of the WTO has been the accession process whereby 25 new member governments have joined the WTO. Accession negotiations are conducted between the applicant government and the WTO, which means that all incumbent WTO members must be satisfied with the negotiated terms of admission to the WTO. Over the past decade, these accession negotiations have become more drawn out with WTO members demanding that applicant governments provide a plan for bringing any WTO-inconsistent domestic measures into compliance with WTO rules. Sometimes bilateral trade concerns are also injected into the accession negotiation as, for example, between WTO member Georgia and the then applicant Russian Federation. When large economies apply for membership as, for example, China and Vietnam, they have been asked by the WTO to agree to country-specific rules that apply only to them and not to incumbent WTO membership. Such applicant WTO-plus obligations are unusual in international organizations (Charnovitz 2008). Applicant governments will also be asked to submit a schedule of commitments on goods and services. A government joining the WTO today will need to make more extensive commitments on trade in services than the same country would have needed to do if it had been an original member of the WTO in 1995.

Despite the difficulties of joining the WTO by accession, 29 governments are waiting to do so. The near-universal interest of governments to be part of the WTO is indicative of the fact that governments want a seat at the table in the WTO. Indeed, the importance for governments to fully participate in international law mechanisms has modernized the traditional meaning of the term 'sovereignty'.

Another important policy achievement is the Information Technology Products Agreement (ITA) negotiated by 29 WTO member governments at the Singapore Ministerial Conference in December 1996. The number of governments participating has now grown to 70, representing about 97 per cent of world trade in information technology products. The ITA provides for participants to completely eliminate duties on Information Technology products covered by the Agreement. In a recent complaint against the European Communities, a WTO panel ruled that concessions made pursuant to the Agreement apply to continuing product evolutions.

Review of national trade policies by the WTO's Trade Policy Review Mechanism (TPRM) is another important ongoing activity. This review is not specifically aimed at examining compliance with WTO obligations, but rather to range broadly over all issues relevant to a member's international trade measures and policies. The review is based on a combination of self-reporting by the subject government, a review by the WTO Secretariat and discussion by governments' representatives. All of these documents are promptly published on the WTO website and have become an important resource for those researching national trade policies.

The WTO has established cooperative relations with the international organizations most closely related to its work, such as the World Customs Organization, the World Intellectual Property Organization and other international organizations including some of the specialized bodies of the UN. Most of these activities occur within the pertinent WTO bodies or are carried out by the WTO Secretariat. For example, in 2009 the WTO and United Nations Environment Programme issued a joint report on international trade and climate change. The WTO Secretariat has also issued a report on how the WTO contributes to the UN Millennium Development Goals.

A decision made at the Singapore Ministerial Conference in 1996 led the WTO to take up the issue of trade facilitation, that is, the practical problems of the management of cross-border trade and the improvement of infrastructure for the delivery of goods (see Chapter 7). The WTO works with the UN Conference on Trade and Development and the UN Centre for Trade Facilitation and Electronic Business to address these problems. Some questions of trade facilitation are also being addressed in the Doha Round in parallel to steps being taken regionally in negotiations for free trade agreements.

The WTO has stepped up its training and capacity building for government trade officials. The WTO Committee on Trade and Development (CTD) oversees these activities, many of which are carried out by the Secretariat. For example, in 2009 the CTD devoted two sessions to the problems of small, vulnerable economies. The WTO also participates in the Enhanced Integrated Framework for Least Developed Countries (LDCs) which is a joint programme of the World Bank, the International Monetary Fund, the WTO and several other international organizations. Projects are supported through a trust fund. For example, 35 developing countries recently prepared Diagnostic Trade Integration Studies aimed at identifying bottlenecks and other problems handicapping trade expansion. The WTO also carries out training workshops in Geneva and in numerous regional locations. Some of these workshops are conducted in partnership with other organizations such as the International Development Law Organization. One recent creative initiative sponsored by the WTO and the Organisation for Economic Cooperation and Development (OECD) has sought case story write-ups on the success of aid-for-trade initiatives. The WTO Secretariat has also sponsored a WTO Chairs programme that supports trade-related research and teaching in 14 universities around the world.

Several WTO committees have engaged in what might be called administrative rulemaking. For example, in 2000 the WTO's Committee on Sanitary and Phytosanitary Standards (SPS) adopted 'Guidelines to Further the Practical Implementation of Article 5.5' (WTO 2000), a provision of the SPS Agreement regarding the consistency of national measures. In 1999 the Council for Trade in Services adopted 'Disciplines on Domestic Regulation in the Accountancy Sector' (WTO 1998a).

The norm-generating capacity of the WTO has been remarkable, especially given how weak the WTO's legislative branch has been due to the stalemate in the Doha Round. Let us give a few examples. In the recent financial crisis, there were strong protectionist pressures in many countries, some of which were succumbed to, but many of which were headed off by the constraining authority of WTO law. In November 2008 the G-20 countries made a commitment that 'we will refrain from raising new barriers to investment or to trade in goods and services, imposing new export restrictions, or implementing World Trade Organization (WTO) inconsistent measures to stimulate exports' (G-20 2008). Unfortunately, those commitments were broken and at the next summit (G-20 2009) the governments pledged 'to rectify promptly any such measures', and also called 'on the WTO, together with other international bodies ... to monitor and report publicly on our adherence to these undertakings on a quarterly basis'. Indeed, the WTO Secretariat had begun such monitoring a few months earlier. DG Pascal Lamy (Lamy 2009) explained in February 2009 that 'we have set up a radar tracking trade and trade-related measures taken in the context of the current crisis'. Thus the G-20 statement served to confirm the WTO's self-initiated role to monitor protectionist acts and to reinforce the norm that WTO rules were to be respected even during an economic crisis.

In the past decade the WTO has worked successfully to begin addressing the problem of distance between the WTO and the public. For most of the GATT era, the GATT had little direct contact with the public. This insular attitude had begun to change in the last years of the GATT system and has been transformed considerably in the WTO. To be sure, transparency has improved across the board in international organizations over the past decade in part because of the technology available for organizational websites. The WTO, however, embraced Internet access earlier and more comprehensively than other economic organizations. Today, the WTO website is among the most informative and interactive of any international organization.

The WTO has also carried out many other activities to improve transparency and public access. For example, the WTO holds a public forum each year where NGOs and business groups are given an opportunity to organize panel sessions in the presence of government delegates and Secretariat officials, among others. The WTO Secretariat has also participated in intergovernmental parliamentary activities considering trade issues such as those organized by the Inter-Parliamentary Union. Of course, WTO officials still cherish the idea that the WTO is a member-driven institution and therefore opportunities offered to NGOs to participate in the WTO have been circumscribed.

Conclusions

In a recent thoughtful article, WTO scholar Jeffrey L. Dunoff (2009) analysed the role of constitutional discourse regarding the WTO and called into question the suggestions that the WTO Agreement has constitutional dimensions. Professor Dunoff argues that there has been little WTO jurisprudence to mandate an internal separation of powers or to uphold fundamental rights of individuals and little evidence that WTO judicial decisions play a norm-generating role. Although we commend Professor Dunoff's exacting analysis and agree that there are no simple analogies between the international plane and national constitutions, we see many emerging features of the WTO and its relationship to national law, other international organizations and the world economy that reflect a constitutional structure. We also note that Dunoff's article is careful enough to state that 'To claim that the WTO today should not be understood as a constitutionalized entity is not to say that it could never be understood as such' (2009).

The WTO has a very difficult role to play because it must address issues that are being generated in the world, with particular reference to economic issues which constantly change, and involve problems over which governments and the international organization have relatively little control. So the WTO's task is the unenviable one of assisting governments to achieve a better solution for managing the problems of globalization and interdependence than could be achieved without the coordination techniques that can be carried out under the umbrella of a WTO. In many ways, the organization deserves recognition for its achievements in its very short history, more than it deserves criticism of its shortcomings. Nevertheless, the shortcomings exist and they certainly merit attention. Indeed, DG Pascal Lamy (2010b) says publicly that 'multilateral trade rules are still unbalanced in favour of developed countries'.

A number of trade experts (Ismail 2009; Kotera et al. 2009; Steger 2010) have called for a 'reform' of WTO rules and practices. The areas sometimes pointed to for reform are:

1. The WTO's flat governance structure in contrast to some other international organizations which have an elected governing body.

2. The perceived need to conduct decision-making with less than a consensus of WTO members in instances where a few governments engage in foot dragging.

3. A willingness to abandon the idea that each negotiation has to be conducted in a round leading to a single undertaking and instead to engage in more frequent lawmaking on particular issues.

4. Changes to the DSS to promote compliance and to prevent governments from using the time-consuming DSS as a three-year free pass to violate WTO law. So far, there is no widespread agreement as to how or whether any of these changes should be made.

In conclusion, the WTO provides a degree of governance for the world economy and in particular of the way that trade and domestic policies of one country can affect other countries. The success of the WTO so far can be attributed both to its remarkable structure and its function. The WTO's governance structure allows it to take legislative, judicial and executive/administrative actions. The WTO's multiple functions are increasingly important in an era of economic and cultural globalization.

References

Bown, C.P. and Pauwelyn, J. (eds). 2010. *The Law, Economics and Politics of Retaliation in WTO Dispute Settlement*. Cambridge: Cambridge University Press.

Charnovitz, S. 2008. Mapping the Law of WTO Accession, in *The WTO: Governance, Dispute Settlement & Developing Countries*, edited by M.E. Janow, V.J. Donaldson and A. Yanovich. Huntington, New York: Juris Publishing, 855–920.

Corden, W.M. 1974. *Trade Policy and Economic Welfare*. 1st Edition. Oxford: Clarendon Press.

Dunoff, J.L. 2009. The Politics of International Constitutions: The Curious Case of the World Trade Organization, in *Ruling the World? Constitutionalism, International Law, and Global Governance*, edited by J.L. Dunoff and J.P. Trachtman. Cambridge and New York: Cambridge University Press, 178–205.

G-20. 2008. Paragraph 13 in *Declaration of the Summit on Financial Markets and the World Economy*, 15 November. [Online] Available at: www.g20.utoronto.ca/2008/2008declaration1115.html [accessed: 30 March 2011].

G-20. 2009. *London Summit Leaders' Statement*, paragraph 22. 2 April. [Online] Available at: www.g20.utoronto.ca/2009/2009communique0402.pdf [accessed 30 March 2011].

Hohmann, H. (ed.). 2008. *Agreeing and Implementing the Doha Round of the WTO*. Cambridge and New York: Cambridge University Press.

Irwin, D.A. 2002. *Free Trade Under Fire*. 1st Edition. Princeton: Princeton University Press.

Irwin, D.A., Mavroidis, P.C. and Sykes, A.O. 2008. *The Genesis of the GATT.* Cambridge and New York: Cambridge University Press.

Ismail, F. 2009. *Reforming the World Trade Organization: Developing Countries in the Doha Round.* Jaipur: Consumer Unity and Trust Society.

Jackson, J.H. 1990. *Restructuring the GATT System.* Royal Institute of International Affairs. London: Pinter.

Jackson, J.H. 1995. International Economic Law: Reflections on the 'Boilerroom' of International Relations. *American Journal of International Law and Policy,* Vol. 10, 595–606.

Jackson, J.H. 1998. Global Economics and International Economic Law. *Journal of International and Economic Law,* Vol. 1, 1–23.

Jackson, J.H. 2006. *Sovereignty, the WTO and Changing Fundamentals of International Law.* Cambridge and New York: Cambridge University Press.

Kenen, P.B. 1994. *The International Economy.* Cambridge and New York: Cambridge University Press.

Kotera, A., Araki, I. and Kawase, T. (eds). 2009. *The Future of the Multilateral Trading System: East Asian Perspectives.* London: Cameron May.

Krugman, P.R. and Obstfeld, M. 1994. *International Economics: Theory and Policy.* 3rd Edition. New York: HarperCollins.

Lamy, P. 2009. *Trade is Part of the Solution to the Global Economic Crisis.* 3 February. [Online on WTO website] Available at: www.wto.org/english/news_e/sppl_e/sppl114_e.htm [accessed: 30 March 2011].

Lamy, P. 2010a. *China's WTO Membership is 'win-win'.* 22 July. [Online on WTO website] Available at: www.wto.org/english/news_e/sppl_e/sppl162_e.htm [accessed: 30 March 2011].

Lamy, P. 2010b. *Concluding the Doha Round will Level the Playing Field of Global Trade.* 31 August. [Online on WTO website] Available at: www.wto.org/english/news_e/sppl_e/sppl166_e.htm [accessed: 30 March 2011].

Moore, M. 2001. *Promoting Openness, Fairness and Predictability in International Trade for the Benefit of Humanity.* Speech to the Inter-Parliamentary Union meeting on International Trade, 8 June.

Pruzin, D. 2010. US Elections Throw Dark Cloud Over Doha Talks as Negotiators Regroup. *BNA Daily Report for Executives,* 13 September.

Sacerdoti, G., Yanovich, A. and Bohanes, J. (eds). 2006. *The WTO at Ten: The Role of the Dispute Settlement System.* Cambridge: Cambridge University Press.

Sauvé, P. and Stern, R.M. 2000. *GATS 2000.*Washington, DC: Brookings Institution.

Steger, D.P. (ed.). 2010. *Redesigning the WTO for the Twenty-first Century.* Ottawa: Wilfrid Laurier University Press.

Stiglitz, J.E. 2002. *Globalization and Its Discontents.* New York: W.W. Norton & Company.

Sykes, A.O. 1998. Comparative Advantage and the Normative Economics of International Trade Policy. *Journal of International and Economic Law,* Vol. 1(1), 49–82.

Vranes, E. 2009. *Trade and the Environment.* Oxford: Oxford University Press.

Wouters, J. and De Meester, B. 2007. *The World Trade Organization: A Legal and Institutional Analysis*. Antwerpen: Intersentia.

WTO. 1998a. *Disciplines on Domestic Regulation in the Accountancy Sector*. S/L/64, 17 December. [Online] Available at: www.wto.org/english/tratop_e/serv_e/sl64.doc [accessed: 30 March 2011].

WTO. 1998b. *US – Imports Prohibition of Certain Shrimp and Shrimp Products*. WT/DS58/AB/R, 6 November. [Online] Available at: http://docsonline.wto.org/DDFDocuments/t/WT/DS/58ABR.doc [accessed: 30 March 2011].

WTO. 2000. *Guidelines to Further the Practical Implementation of Article 5.5*. G/SPS/15, 15 July. [Online] Available at: http://docsonline.wto.org/DDFDocuments/t/G/SPS/15.DOC [accessed: 30 March 2011].

Preferential Agreements and Multilateralism

Mark Manger

Introduction

One of the most noteworthy developments since the creation of the WTO in 1994 has been the rapid proliferation of preferential trade agreements (PTAs). PTAs come in various forms and guises, but their common denominator is that they are exceptions to the most-favoured-nation (MFN) principle that underpins the GATT and the GATS, and that features prominently in many other commercial treaties. In a PTA the members grant better (hence preferential) market access to their partners than to non-members. As reciprocal agreements, they are not to be confused with programmes such as the 'Generalized System of Preferences', through which developed countries unilaterally concede better access for imports from developing countries.

Although preferential trade agreements have a long history going back to the nineteenth century, for most of the post-Second World War period they remained few. Since the early 1990s, however, the number of PTAs has grown at a stunning pace. In 1990, a mere 30 or so PTAs were legally in force.[1] By the summer of 2010, this number had reached 202, counting only agreements covering trade in goods and notified to the WTO by their members.[2] About an additional 100 agreements have been signed by non-members. Perhaps even more surprising is that almost 90 per cent of these agreements are bilateral, producing a complex network of treaties with different rules and tariffs.

---

[1]   Author's calculations based on data from the McGill RTA database ptas.mcgill.ca/, Tuck Trade Agreements Database www.dartmouth.edu/~tradedb/trade_database.html, and WTO regional trade agreements gateway http://rtais.wto.org/.

[2]   The WTO counts agreements covering goods and services as separate entities. In practice, more and more PTAs cover both forms of trade, but there are no free-standing services agreements between countries that do not already have a PTA covering goods.

Inevitably, a growing share of world trade is covered by preferential rather than non-discriminatory rules. The sizeable remainder is mostly trade between the major economic powers: the United States, the European Union (EU), Japan and China. Given the lack of progress in WTO negotiations, it is not an exaggeration to say that multilateral trade liberalization has become a sideshow.

The sudden, but all the more rapid, proliferation of PTAs has inspired a vast body of research in economics and international political economy. This chapter presents an overview of the key themes and findings of this research. At its centre is the question of how the multilateral trade system and preferential trade agreements interact, and what the implications of current trends are for the future of the WTO.

A Typology of PTAs

Before turning towards the analysis of PTAs, some definitions are in order. In GATT parlance, preferential trade agreements are referred to as 'regional trade agreements'. Governments give agreements various labels such as 'Association Agreements' (EU) or 'Economic Partnership Agreements' (Japan and the EU, although with substantially different meanings). For research purposes, it is more useful to classify PTAs in terms of the liberalization efforts required from their members.

Partial scope agreements, as the name suggests, only reduce the trade barriers for a small range of specific goods. A recent example is the Chile–India Preferential Trade Agreement. The agreement reduced (but did not eliminate) tariffs for 75 per cent of Chile's imports from India in terms of value, or 3.7 per cent of all different tariff lines, and eliminated duties on 0.5 per cent. The 'typical' reduction is from 6 per cent to just less than 5 per cent. India reduced (but did not eliminate) the tariffs on about 95 per cent of imports from Chile, but only by 1 or 2 per cent from a high baseline of 10 to 50 per cent in some instances. This outcome is not uncommon for partial scope arrangements. Often, they do not offer meaningful reductions of MFN tariffs.

South–South agreements, especially those involving low-income countries, fall mostly into this category. As they contribute little to the elimination of trade barriers, their effect on trade and the multilateral system is usually minimal. Creating trade institutions, however, can become an opportunity for patronage, so that these agreements are often a source of costs rather than benefits and are of questionable value for economic development (Gray 2010).

Most common among PTAs are Free Trade Agreements (FTAs). In an FTA, the partner countries eliminate tariff barriers between themselves, but retain different MFN tariffs vis-à-vis the rest of the world. Over 90 per cent of current PTAs fall into this category. The remainder of PTAs and partial scope agreements are customs unions (CUs). In a customs union, the members agree on a common external tariff. This is politically more demanding but has the advantage that no additional rules are required to determine through which country a good is first imported – a point we will return to later.

Preferential trade agreements can cover trade in goods only, but increasingly often also reduce barriers to trade in services and investment. Recently, PTAs have also incorporated chapters on investment rules that draw on bilateral investment treaties, trade facilitation and political cooperation.

Legally speaking, PTAs among WTO members that liberalize trade in goods are permitted under Article XXIV of the GATT and Article V of the GATS. Article XXIV prescribes that the agreement should: eliminate the tariffs on 'substantially all trade' between the partners, achieve this goal in a reasonable time of ten years (but 'exceptional cases' are possible), and not erect new barriers against those left outside. However, the latter is permitted provided the partners offer other WTO members 'compensation' in the form of reductions of other tariffs. The EU did so in 1995 when it admitted Sweden, as the country had to raise tariffs to bring its duties in line with the common external tariff of the European Union. GATS Article V gives equivalent clauses for trade in services, but as services trade barriers are mostly regulatory, its implications are unclear. It is noteworthy that although PTAs are regularly scrutinized by the WTO, no country or set of countries has been officially accused of violating Article XXIV of the GATT – perhaps because no one is willing to cast the first stone.

PTAs among developing countries do not have to adhere to these rules. The Enabling Clause, a product of the 1979 Tokyo Round, allows the partial liberalization under the rubric of 'special and differential treatment' at whatever pace the participants deem suitable. In practice, this means that developing countries can delay tariff reductions in a PTA indefinitely or not implement the provisions of a negotiated agreement at all.

The prescriptions of Article XXIV have a straightforward economic rationale. The very existence of the GATT stems from the experience of the interwar years, when the world economy was divided into competing trade blocs. With this experience in the background, the negotiators of the initial treaty faced the challenge of accommodating existing and proposed preferential arrangements such as the system of 'Imperial Preferences' proposed at the Ottawa conference of 1932, the US–Canada 'Auto pact' (effectively a partial scope agreement for auto parts), and the proposal for economic integration in Europe. Although these agreements would clearly violate the principle of non-discrimination, the GATT founders tried to limit their adverse effects.

The Economics of PTAs – Trade Creation and Diversion

PTAs that discriminate against the rest of the world may cause (net) *trade diversion*, that is, they can reduce imports from those outside the PTA by more than they *create trade* among the members.

Consider the following situation: prior to the formation of a PTA, a particular good is imported from a supplier in a third country. Once the tariffs in the PTA are eliminated, the suppliers in the partner country may become relatively cheaper. The imports from the third country still carry a most-favoured-nation tariff, while those from within the PTA are tariff-free. In principle, this is a good thing, as it creates trade. Imports are now cheaper, so consumption can increase. However, if the producers from within the PTA are less efficient than those outside, the PTA is inefficient since the producers within the PTA earn an economic rent. What is more, it can even make the importing country worse off because tariff revenue is forgone.

Although the basic mechanism of trade creation versus trade diversion was identified decades ago (Lipsey 1957; Viner 1950), only recently have the data become available to conduct econometric studies that shed light on how relevant these concerns are in practice. In theory it is easy to devise trade agreements that are Pareto-efficient, making the PTA partners better off and leaving those outside unaffected (Kemp and Wan 1976). In practice, such considerations are second to the political requirements for striking a deal. Whether an agreement is trade-diverting therefore largely depends on the existing tariffs vis-à-vis the rest of the world. The higher the initial tariffs, the more likely that trade diversion materializes.

How relevant are these concerns in practice? Because of the importance of the US market for many countries, several studies have investigated whether the North America Free Trade Agreement (NAFTA) has diverted trade (Fukao et al. 2003; Krueger 1999), but have only found very limited evidence for specific product groups. In general, PTAs do not divert as much trade in the aggregate as is often feared — with some notable exceptions such as MERCOSUR (Adams et al. 2003). But by definition, even without *net* trade diversion, any PTA that influences trade must have a negative effect on some exporters outside of a PTA and thus be second-best to multilateral liberalization. Because these exporters lose out, they often seek some form of compensation. PTAs may therefore trigger a political reaction.

All else being equal, excluded countries have three possible ways to react to a PTA: join the existing agreement, form a PTA with the more important member(s), or negotiate an agreement with alternative trade partners to secure new export markets. All of these will result in even more agreements, creating a dynamic whereby PTAs are becoming endogenous; each new agreement begets others (Baldwin 1996; Egger and Larch 2008; Katada et al. 2009; Manger 2005, 2009; Solís 2003).

It is worth remembering that we may observe this effect even though trade agreements are not net trade-diverting. All that is necessary is that third-party exporters make a convincing case to their governments that they are facing trade discrimination.

And yet, there are plenty of reasons why trade-diverting agreements should be easier to negotiate. Any agreement that reduces trade barriers exposes some producers to competition. Naturally, these import-competing actors will oppose the PTA. To muster enough political support for a PTA, they must be counterbalanced by some other interest group. The obvious candidates are producers who would benefit from trade diversion, that is to say those who can only compete if they have a preferential tariff margin. Considering that the excluded countries do not have a voice at the negotiating table, it is tempting for politicians to favour producers within the PTA at the expense of those in non-member countries (Grossman and Helpman 1995; Hirschman 1981: 271) – precisely the scenario that GATT Article XXIV is supposed to prevent.

The Political Economy of PTA Formation

Aside from the growing evidence that PTA formation is partly interdependent, why do countries sign PTAs in the first place? This is not a moot question — through the six decades of its existence the multilateral trade regime has been astoundingly successful in reducing barriers to trade. Today, developed-country tariffs on merchandise imports are usually below 5 per cent, and are often zero. Perhaps even more impressively, most countries in the world are now WTO members with the remainder either isolated for political reasons (for example, North Korea) or because they are exporters of natural resources, such as some Central Asian countries. Compared to even small tariff reductions on an MFN basis, the gains from complete liberalization within a PTA are often minute. So why the enthusiasm for preferential trade?

Reasons to form PTAs fall into three categories: purely political grounds; the goal to stabilize economic policy and therefore increase trade flows and foreign direct investment (FDI); and different aspects of gains from trade. Often, these factors combine to precipitate a PTA.

Politics First, Economics Second

Clearly, a number of PTAs have only a limited economic rationale. Some are policies to lend economic support to allies (the US–Israel FTA), while others are used by major powers to reward states for compliant behaviour (the US–Jordan FTA). Yet others are largely symbolical because the partners are so small and so distant that they hardly trade with each other. Another dimension is to encourage development in order to stem immigrant flows, as in the case of NAFTA. Of the PTAs formed between former socialist countries, many merely re-established free trade between countries that had previously been a single economic entity, such as the Czech and Slovak Republics.

A further, primarily political reason is that liberalization efforts at the WTO have slowed to a glacial pace, or rather have joined the 'Samuel Beckett school of iterative stasis: "Let's go." "We can't." "Why not?" "We're waiting for Doha"'.[3] This is the most often cited reason given by trade negotiators, perhaps also because in the absence of a WTO deal, PTA negotiations secure their jobs. There is, however,

---

3   Beattie (2009).

solid empirical evidence that an increase in the number of WTO members has promoted PTA formation, and that PTA negotiations are often initiated during ongoing multilateral negotiations (Mansfield and Reinhardt 2003).

For developing country governments, one of the most important motivations during the last two decades has been to underpin domestic economic reforms. In this context a preferential trade agreement serves a dual purpose. First, it can help overcome domestic resistance to liberalization, because the government can use the 'external pressure' of a larger negotiating partner as leverage (and as an excuse) to pursue market-opening policies. Second, and perhaps more importantly, a PTA with a bigger, more developed partner can be used to lock in policies so that succeeding governments cannot overturn them (Fernández and Portes 1998). This should in principle encourage domestic and foreign investment and boost economic growth.

Preferential trade agreements are therefore part of a larger shift in developing country economic policies. Until the late 1980s, most developing countries pursued an industrial strategy of substituting imports with domestic production to stimulate economic development, sheltered by high tariff walls (Krueger 1995). The dismantling of the tariff barriers began slowly after the Debt Crisis of the early 1980s, as countries sought to attract foreign investment to improve their balance-of-payments position, at first directly through capital inflows and then indirectly through export-oriented manufacturing investment. Many governments, however, faced considerable resistance to such reforms because domestic industries saw themselves (usually correctly) as incapable of competing with imports from developed countries and the more successful East Asian industrializing countries. Moreover, countries in Latin America had a history and reputation for vacillating between periods of liberalism and economic populism and foreign investors therefore questioned the continuity of reforms.

Given this situation, negotiating a PTA with a major economic power such as the EU, the United States or Japan solved several problems at once. First, the more powerful partner would demand liberalization of inefficient sectors, which would then receive inflows of foreign capital to become more efficient or otherwise simply disappear. In the negotiations, the government of the developing country would point at these demands to deflect the ire of domestic interest groups. Second, the commitments made in the negotiations would be written into an international agreement and would be monitored and, if necessary, enforced by the bigger partner by threatening to withdraw market access. In terms of contract theory, the PTA functions as a 'commitment device'. As a result, foreign and domestic investors would be reassured that the liberal economic environment was here to stay.

The poster child for reforms leading to an important PTA is Mexico, long a champion of import-substitution industrialization and disassociation from the economies of the developed world. Following its default on sovereign debt in 1982 that marked the beginning of the Third World Debt Crisis, successive Mexican administrations implemented austerity packages and radically lowered trade barriers (Pastor and Wise 1994). By 1990, however, domestic resistance prevented further market-opening, while foreign investment inflows continued to disappoint.

In a surprising move, President Salinas proposed the negotiation of a free trade agreement with the United States the following year (Cameron and Tomlin 2000). During the negotiations, the Mexican government made strategic 'concessions' to the United States that in reality were key policy goals, but impossible to sell at home (Cameron 1997). Most sectors were opened up to foreign investment, with the exceptions of petroleum extraction which was protected by the Mexican constitution and telecommunications, where domestic interests prevailed.

Although Mexico suffered yet another major financial crisis at the same time as NAFTA entered into force, its causes can be found in economic policy choices made unrelated to the PTA. If anything, NAFTA meant that the United States had an enormous stake in Mexico's well-being and quickly assembled a bailout package (Cameron and Aggarwal 1996). Moreover, the rapid depreciation of the peso made exports from Mexico even more lucrative and stimulated investment, in particular in the Mexican automobile industry.

Crises have promoted PTAs in other parts of the world, too. In Southeast Asia, the experience of the 1997 Asian Financial Crisis meant that many governments preferred stable direct investment to volatile portfolio capital and bank lending. Shortly after the crisis, Southeast and East Asian countries embarked on a policy to negotiate PTAs with each other (Dent 2003, 2006), to deepen existing agreements such as the ASEAN Free Trade Area and to secure access to major markets like the EU and the United States.

Economics First, Politics Second

The motivations for PTAs described up to this point should not obscure the fact that the agreements are fundamentally about gains from trade. On purely economic grounds, three mechanisms make free trade attractive: gains from trade due to comparative advantage; intra-industry trade based on economies of scale and product differentiation; and vertical specialization within the same industry, but with different factor prices (Krugman 1980). Comparative advantage does not privilege preferential trade agreements. The other two types of trade, however, potentially favour preferential over non-discriminatory liberalization. Horizontal intra-industry trade based on economies of scale tends to make liberalization relatively easier, because rather than being displaced by more competitive imports, firms can choose to produce a different variety of product. Adjustment costs are therefore not borne by the whole sector or industry, but are specific to each firm (Gilligan 1997). If the same industries in two countries forming a PTA manage to specialize in different product varieties, liberalization is almost painless. But even if there are competing industries, the governments can 'trade off scale economies' across these industries bilaterally to negotiate a PTA (Milner 1997). This route is likely to be taken by countries with comparable GDPs and level of economic development, and helps explain much of the support of manufacturing industries for European economic integration. Most importantly, it does not in any way create a bias against subsequent multilateral liberalization. In fact, firms that were initially opposed to global free trade, after having 'moved down the cost curve' of production, may now become supporters.

By comparison, vertical specialization favours preferential (and often bilateral) agreements because the partners make relation-specific investments. Vertical specialization occurs when firms in the same industry produce goods with different capital intensity. An example would be the production of compact cars by French and German companies in the Slovak Republic for export to France and Germany, while the same companies manufacture their luxury models at home and export them in small numbers to Slovakia.

In principle, PTAs between developed and advanced transition or developing economies are highly beneficial because they promote capital flows from a capital-abundant economy to a relatively capital-poor partner. Unfortunately for the signatories' firms, these PTAs also open the backdoor for the competition. Continuing with the same example, when the Slovak Republic gained free market access to the EU through the 'Europe Agreements', it became attractive for Japanese firms to invest there to sell cars into the EU market.

To prevent this, the firms within a PTA will often demand a high local content quota that discriminates against outsiders. In our example, German firms can count German and Slovak components towards fulfilling such a requirement. Japanese firms can only count the Slovak components, not imported Japanese parts. This forces firms from outside the PTA to behave like local firms.

A related argument is that it matters if firms expect a move towards non-discriminatory free trade. Countries will then specialize according to their comparative advantage. If preferential trade agreements appear feasible, however, they are more likely to support them because they permit specialization within the PTA – inefficient but lucrative for firms that do not have to face global competition. Unfortunately, this also makes them less likely to support global free trade once a PTA has been formed because they have made investments – PTAs become 'insidious' (McLaren 2002).

In the legal language of PTA texts, local content quotas are a type of 'rules of origin' (RoO). RoO stipulate whether a good produced from parts from within and without the PTA qualifies for tariff-free shipping across intra-PTA borders. Usually, this is implemented by requiring a transformation of a good in one tariff group to another (for example, from pork to ham), or prescribing certain parts that have to be from within the PTA (such as LEDs for computer screens), or by requiring a minimum percentage of value added in a member country of the PTA. Infamously, NAFTA prescribes that 62.5 per cent of a car's value must be produced in a NAFTA country to allow the vehicle to be shipped from one country to another without paying tariffs.[4] Below this threshold, the car would be treated as a non-NAFTA import and would incur the respective MFN tariff

---

4   Under NAFTA's predecessor, the CUSFTA, US customs officials found in 1991 that Honda Civics produced in Canada did not fulfil the applicable RoO and did not qualify for tariff-free exports from Canada to the United States.

of each country, ranging from 2.5 per cent for a Sedan to 25 per cent for a Sports Utility Vehicle in the United States.

Because RoO are relatively arcane, they have not attracted much attention among political economists until very recently. Theoretical exercises indicate that it is quite easy to structure RoO to become a form of 'hidden protectionism' (Duttagupta and Panagariya 2003; Krishna and Krueger 1995). And indeed, empirical research confirms that firms not only expend much time and energy on lobbying to obtain favourable RoO (Chase 2008), but that RoO also have quite strong effects on trade patterns (Anson et al. 2005). Perhaps most problematic, because RoO require elaborate documentation of what component comes from where, compliance with RoO is often only worthwhile for big firms producing large numbers of identical goods. Smaller firms and those from developing countries often do not use the tariff preferences available and chose to pay most-favoured-nation tariffs instead (Takahashi and Urata 2010).[5]

Efforts to simplify RoO by negotiating at the multilateral level have so far failed. However, there is a tendency among major economic powers to harmonize the RoO across their own PTAs. The leader is the European Union, having introduced a pan-European RoO regime for all 'Association' agreements. For decades, the EU Commission tolerated the absurd situation that inputs from one PTA partner could not be counted towards the RoO in another. Cloth from Morocco, for example, could not be used in garment production in Turkey, even though both had tariff-free access to the EU market. The new rules allow for 'cumulation', that is, the inclusion of inputs from other EU partners to meet a RoO threshold. Rules of origin represent one of the areas in which there is much variation across PTAs and which therefore cause concern for the negotiators who have to strike delicate bargains while keeping the developments of other PTAs in mind. This problem is less pronounced in other areas of PTAs.

The Economic Effects of PTAs

Although surely not an optimal policy choice on the path to global free trade, recent research shows that the economic benefits of PTAs are tangible. Whether it is because they offer access to large markets or because of the commitment device function of PTAs, countries that sign such agreements attract greater inflows of FDI, both from the partner country as well as from third countries (Büthe and Milner 2008). This effect may partly be driven by the reassurance that tariff rates are not going to change abruptly and so the volatility of trade volumes is reduced (Mansfield and Reinhardt 2008). Most importantly, preferential trade agreements often have surprisingly strong effects on trade — some estimates say that at the

---

[5]   The same applies to preferential schemes through which developed countries offer unilateral concessions to poorer countries. Brenton (2003) shows that the majority of preferences under the EU's 'Everything But Arms' initiative are not used.

end of the typical ten-year implementation period, PTAs on average double the members' bilateral trade (Baier and Bergstrand 2007).

What, then, is the main problem with the proliferation of preferential agreements? One area of concern is the multiplication of different rules, especially the aforementioned rules of origin. The devil, however, is in the detail. In general, PTAs tend to follow similar templates.

PTAs and Multilateralism

Legal Considerations

Despite the vast number of agreements, there is a degree of convergence in their fundamental principles. Most PTAs draw directly on the GATT and GATS and the specific legal definitions they have established. This tendency is unsurprising as the most active proponents of PTAs are also WTO members.[6] At the same time, it qualifies the claim that preferential trade agreements are a venue to develop and test new approaches to trade policy. The majority of PTAs have been negotiated after the WTO came into existence and so WTO members are required to make the policies implemented through PTAs consistent with WTO principles and obligations. The broad coverage of the Uruguay Round therefore implies that innovation takes place mainly in areas not covered by multilateral agreements. In practice, this means foreign direct investment, trade facilitation, and the establishment of links between trade policy and issues like labour and environment that are staunchly resisted at the WTO. However, even in the field of rules for FDI, most preferential trade agreements draw on existing rules negotiated in the over 2,500 bilateral investment treaties (BITs). The principal difference is that many recent PTAs incorporate chapters that liberalize the investment regimes of the partner countries.

One of the most prominent examples of innovative rule-making in a FTA is Chapter 11 on 'Investment' in NAFTA. Much of the text is taken directly from the template that the United States used for its bilateral investment treaties in the early 1990s, stipulating legal protection of foreign investments and investors. Beyond such standard language, however, Article 1106 bans the various kinds of performance requirements (for example, local content quota in production) that Mexico had previously applied. Article 1108 lists various exceptions and reservations. Finally, several annexes provide commitments to phase out regulations that limit foreign investment over time, especially those related to ceilings on foreign equity participation. By contrast, the Trade-Related Investment Measures (TRIMS) agreement only lists a small number of 'trade-related' performance requirements.

---

[6]   The similarity of fundamental principles in GATT, GATS and PTAs can also be seen as an example of 'nesting' of international regimes (Aggarwal 1998).

Throughout the NAFTA agreement, a 'negative list' approach prevails — only exceptions that are explicitly listed apply and what is not listed is deemed to be liberalized. Compare this with the approach in the GATS, still under negotiation at the time the NAFTA deal was sealed. In the GATS, only listed ('bound') sectors are liberalized, everything else is potentially subject to restrictions.

Subsequent FTAs negotiated by the United States have followed the same principle. It has not, however, been adopted at the WTO level, nor have the EU and Japan followed suit. Most developing countries prefer a 'positive list' approach, partly because it often allows for the retention of more restrictions, but also because cataloguing all restrictions 'in the books' is administratively challenging. In short, rule-making in PTAs tends to go beyond the WTO when a powerful actor (usually the United States or the EU) promotes these rules in a bilateral deal with a smaller, usually developing country, partner.

A further question is whether the tariff reduction that can be achieved in PTAs is more far-reaching than that in WTO rounds. Proponents of PTAs often argue that they can move ahead more quickly with 'willing partners'. In practice, however, there is evidence that PTAs fail to address the most entrenched protectionism, and that the 'gaps' in liberalization are much the same in PTAs and the WTO (Hoekman and Leidy 1993).

Policy Issues

Preferential trade agreements are here to stay. What are the implications for the multilateral trade regime? Will PTAs supplant the WTO, can they coexist, or can PTAs actually boost liberalization efforts?

Economists have usually framed this question as one of 'building blocks' or 'stumbling blocks' on the way to global free trade. In addition to the problem of trade diversion, domestic groups can often extend protection at the national level to protection within a PTA by using (or abusing) dispute settlement procedures and rules of origin. Moreover, as Levy (1997) shows, PTAs may make global free trade impossible to achieve. When a sufficiently large group inside each state that joins a PTA is satisfied with the economic gains, they will raise the bar for a global trade agreement so high that it becomes infeasible.

Others have countered that any trade agreement will exert some adjustment pressures and therefore strengthen pro-trade lobbies and weaken protectionists (Richardson 1993). Moreover, in a larger market, lobbies must organize at the regional level where they are relatively smaller and less geographically concentrated – although this only applies when the authority to set trade policy is transferred to a supranational body, as in the EU (Hanson 2003). Unfortunately, there is very little empirical research to investigate these claims – the exception being Kono (2007), who finds that PTAs between countries with similar comparative advantage promote free trade, while those between very different countries do not.

More complicated is the issue of whether PTAs impede or boost negotiations at the WTO. In the past, governments could craft coalitions of export-oriented sectors in line with the 'GATT-think' that 'exports are good, imports are bad' (Krugman 1991: 15). The key to achieve trade barrier reductions was then to link issues affecting different sectors, so that each country would lose a bit and gain a bit across the board (Davis 2004). These export sectors supported trade liberalization against import-competing sectors. Usually, the most active members were multinational firms (Milner 1988). These firms are also often the most important proponents of preferential trade agreements, whether because they achieve greater economies of scale within the PTA market or because they shift production into low-wage countries (Chase 2003).

Considering the rapid proliferation of North–South PTAs, bilateral and regional trade agreements may well satisfy the needs of these multilateral firms. This should be especially worrying when PTAs do not achieve broad liberalization of protected sectors such as agriculture – but given the asymmetries in North–South deals, it is unlikely that the smaller partner can obtain concessions that the more powerful partner is unwilling to make even in multilateral negotiations. And indeed, the exclusions and barriers to agricultural trade retained in North–South PTAs tend to mirror those in most-favoured-nation tariffs. Japan and the EU are notorious for maintaining protection that excludes the most competitive agricultural imports from their developing country partners. The United States does not impose such barriers, but instead heavily subsidizes exports (Manger 2009: 233). At the same time, as we have seen, such PTAs often move beyond WTO commitments in services and investment. This means that even those North–South PTAs that fully comply with GATT Article XXIV can diminish the chances of success in multilateral trade negotiations. In the past, progress in the liberalization of agricultural trade against Japanese and European resistance has only been achieved when the United States linked this issue with others where the EU and Japan had important export interests (Davis 2003). Such interests are now served by PTAs. As a result, the multilateral trade regime is saddled with the apparently intractable problem of liberalizing agricultural trade, but left with nothing that market-opening in protectionist countries could be traded off against. In this political sense, rather than because of the manifold economic concerns, the proliferation of PTAs is most likely to have an adverse effect on the multilateralism system in the short term.

In the longer term, multiple different rules of origin and divergent regulations in issue-areas not covered by WTO agreements will inevitably increase transaction costs, a point not lost on business leaders.[7] At this point, the WTO may be called upon to harmonize rules, or, as rules of origin lose their force when most-favoured-nation tariffs are eliminated, a new tariff round may come into sight. This has led to the observation that complementarity between PTAs and the multilateral trade system will only be achieved if that system is robust – strengthening rules and

---

[7]   See, for example, the critical views of Victor Fung, chairman of Li & Fung, Hong Kong's largest export trading company, in the *Financial Times*, 3 November 2005, and Michael Treschow, chairman of Ericsson, the Swedish telecommunications company, in the *Financial Times*, 18 October 2006.

reducing MFN tariffs – so that the distorting effects of PTAs are held in check (Heydon and Woolcock 2009: 260).

In the meantime, a division of labour between preferential and multilateral forums appears to be emerging. While trade barrier reductions mostly take place in PTAs at the moment, the WTO assumes the role of 'constitution' of the global trade system, with the dispute settlement procedure to support a 'rule of law' in international commerce. Although many PTAs include rules to arbitrate disputes, the most prominent cases are brought to the WTO. Preferential agreements and the WTO therefore coexist, but as stages for quite different shows.

References

Adams, R., Dee, P., Gali, J. and McGuire, G. 2003. *The Trade and Investment Effects of Preferential Trading Arrangements – Old and New Evidence*. Canberra: Australian Productivity Commission.

Aggarwal, V.K. 1998. *Institutional Designs for a Complex World: Bargaining, Linkages, and Nesting*. Ithaca: Cornell University Press.

Anson, J., Cadot, O., Estevadeordal, A., De Melo, J., Suwa-Eisenmann, A. and Tumurchudur, B. 2005. Rules of Origin in North-South Preferential Trading Arrangements with an Application to NAFTA. *Review of International Economics*, 13(3): 501–517.

Baier, S.L. and Bergstrand, J.H. 2007. Do Free Trade Agreements Actually Increase Members' International Trade? *Journal of International Economics*, 71(1): 72–95.

Baldwin, R.E. 1996. A Domino Theory of Regionalism, in *Expanding Membership of the European Union*, edited by R.E. Baldwin, P. Haaparanta and J. Kiander. Cambridge: Cambridge University Press: 25–48.

Beattie, A. 2009. Review of 'Misadventures of Most Favoured Nations' by Paul Blustein, *Financial Times*, 12 October.

Brenton, P. 2003. Integrating the least developed countries into the world trading system: the current impact of European Union preferences under 'Everything but Arms'. *Journal of World Trade*, 37(3): 623–646.

Büthe, T. and Milner, H.V. 2008. The Politics of Foreign Direct Investment into Developing Countries: Increasing FDI through International Trade Agreements. *American Journal of Political Science*, 52(4): 741–762.

Cameron, M.A. 1997. North American Trade Negotiations: Liberalization Games between Asymmetric Players. *European Journal of International Relations*, 3(1): 105–139.

Cameron, M.A. and Aggarwal, V.K. 1996. Mexican Meltdown: States, Markets and Post-NAFTA Financial Turmoil. *Third World Quarterly*, 17(5): 975–987.

Cameron, M.A. and Tomlin, B.W. 2000. *The Making of NAFTA: How the Deal Was Done*. Ithaca: Cornell University Press.

Chase, K.A. 2003. Economic Interests and Regional Trading Arrangements: The Case of NAFTA. *International Organization*, 57(1): 137–174.

Chase, K.A. 2008. Protecting Free Trade: The Political Economy of Rules of Origin. *International Organization*, 62(3): 507–530.

Davis, C.L. 2003. *Food Fights over Free Trade: How International Institutions Promote Agricultural Trade Liberalization*. Princeton: Princeton University Press.

Davis, C.L. 2004. International Institutions and Issue Linkage: Building Support for Agricultural Trade Liberalization. *American Political Science Review*, 98(1): 153–169.

Dent, C.M. 2003. Networking the Region? The Emergence and Impact of Asia-Pacific Bilateral Free Trade Agreement Projects. *Pacific Review*, 16(1): 1–28.

Dent, C.M. 2006. *New Free Trade Agreements in the Asia-Pacific*. Basingstoke: Palgrave Macmillan.

Duttagupta, R. and Panagariya, A. 2003. *Free Trade Areas and Rules of Origin: Economics and Politics*. Washington, DC: IMF.

Egger, P. and Larch, M. 2008. Interdependent Preferential Trade Agreement Memberships: An Empirical Analysis. *Journal of International Economics*, 76(2): 384–399.

Fernández, R. and Portes, J. 1998. Returns to Regionalism: An Analysis of Nontraditional Gains from Regional Trade Agreements. *World Bank Economic Review*, 12(2): 197–220.

Fukao, K., Okubo, T. and Stern, R.M. 2003. An Econometric Analysis of Trade Diversion under NAFTA. *North American Journal of Economics and Finance*, 14(1): 3–24.

Gilligan, M.J. 1997. Lobbying as a Private Good with Intra-industry Trade. *International Studies Quarterly*, 41(3): 455–474.

Gray, J. 2010. Politics and Patronage: The Function of Dysfunctional Regional Trade Agreements. Paper presented at the Workshop on The Politics of Preferential Trade Agreements: Theory, Measurement, and Empirical Applications. Niehaus Center for Globalization and Governance, Princeton University, Princeton.

Grossman, G.M. and Helpman, E. 1995. The Politics of Free-Trade Agreements. *American Economic Review*, 85(4): 667–690.

Hanson, B.T. 2003. What Happened to Fortress Europe? External Trade Policy Liberalization in the European Union. *International Organization*, 52(1): 55–85.

Heydon, K. and Woolcock, S., 2009. *The Rise of Bilateralism: Comparing American, European and Asian Approaches to Preferential Trade Agreements*. Tokyo: UN University Press.

Hirschman, A.O. 1981. *Essays in Trespassing: Economics to Politics and Beyond*. Cambridge: Cambridge University Press.

Hoekman, B. and Leidy, M.P. 1993. Holes and Loopholes in Integration Agreements: History and Prospects, in *Regional Integration and the Global Trading System*, edited by K. Anderson and R. Blackhurst. Hemel Hempstead: Harvester Wheatsheaf: 218–245.

Katada, S.N., Solís, M. and Stallings, B. 2009. *Competitive Regionalism: Explaining the Diffusion of FTAs in the Pacific Rim*. London: Palgrave.

Kemp, M. and Wan, H. 1976. An Elementary Proposition Concerning the Formation of Customs Unions. *Journal of International Economics*, 6(1): 95–97.

Kono, D.Y. 2007. When do Trade Blocs Block Trade? *International Studies Quarterly*, 51(1): 165–181.

Krishna, K. and Krueger, A.O. 1995. Implementing Free Trade Areas: Rules of Origin and Hidden Protection, in *New Directions in Trade Theory*, edited by A. Deardorff, J. Levinsohn and R. Stern. Ann Arbor: University of Michigan Press: 149–187.

Krueger, A.O. 1995. *Trade Policies and Developing Nations*. Washington, DC: Brookings Institution.

Krueger, A.O. 1999. *Trade Creation and Trade Diversion under NAFTA*. Cambridge, MA: National Bureau of Economic Research.

Krugman, P.R. 1980. Scale Economies, Product Differentiation, and the Pattern of Trade. *American Economic Review*, 70(5): 950–959.

Krugman, P.R. 1991. The Move Toward Free Trade Zones. *Economic Review of the Federal Reserve Bank of Kansas*: 5–25.

Levy, P.I. 1997. A Political-Economic Analysis of Free-Trade Agreements. *The American Economic Review*, 87(4): 506–519.

Lipsey, R. 1957. The Theory of Customs Unions: Trade Diversion and Welfare. *Economica*, 24(93): 40–46.

Manger, M.S. 2005. Competition and Bilateralism in Trade Policy: The Case of Japan's Free Trade Agreements. *Review of International Political Economy*, 12(5): 804–828.

Manger, M.S. 2009. *Investing in Protection: The Politics of Preferential Trade Agreements between North and South*. Cambridge: Cambridge University Press.

Mansfield, E.D. and Reinhardt, E. 2003. Multilateral Determinants of Regionalism: The Effects of GATT/WTO on the Formation of Preferential Trading Arrangements. *International Organization*, 57(4): 829–862.

Mansfield, E.D. and Reinhardt, E. 2008. International Institutions and the Volatility of International Trade. *International Organization*, 62(4): 621–652.

McLaren, J. 2002. A Theory of Insidious Regionalism. *Quarterly Journal of Economics*, 117(2): 571–608.

Milner, H.V. 1988. *Resisting Protectionism: Global Industries and the Politics of International Trade*. Princeton: Princeton University Press.

Milner, H.V. 1997. Industries, Governments, and the Creation of Regional Trade Blocs, in *The Political Economy of Regionalism*, edited by E.D. Mansfield and H.V. Milner. New York: Columbia University Press: 77–106.

Pastor, M. and Wise, C. 1994. The Origins and Sustainability of Mexico Free-Trade Policy. *International Organization*, 48(3): 459–489.

Richardson, M. 1993. Endogenous Protection and Trade Diversion. *Journal of International Economics*, 34(3–4): 309–324.

Solís, M. 2003. Japan's New Regionalism: The Politics of Free Trade with Mexico. *Journal of East Asian Studies*, 3(3): 377–404.

Takahashi, K. and Urata, S. 2010. On the Use of FTAs by Japanese Firms: Further Evidence. *Business and Politics*, 12(1): 47–69.

Viner, J. 1950. *The Customs Union Issue*. New York: Carnegie Endowment for International Peace.

ASHGATE
RESEARCH
COMPANION

PART VII
Trade Policymaking:
Regional Perspectives

The United States:
Trade Policy Sleeping –
Short Nap or Long Slumber?

Gary Hufbauer and Kati Suominen

Introduction: The Long View

Three long phases, each lasting about 70 years, can be discerned in US trade policy. Between the founding of the Republic in 1788 and the Civil War in 1861, trade policy was rather liberal. For a span of 73 years, the agrarian South, an exporting region, dominated the Congress; consequently, tariffs were imposed to raise revenue and not to protect Northern industry. After the Civil War ended in 1865 until the Smoot–Hawley Tariff of 1930, a span of 65 years, the general direction of trade policy was protection and more protection. With a very few exceptions (notably the Underwood Tariff of 1913), Northern and Midwestern industrial interests controlled Congress and the name of the game was to insulate American manufacturing firms from British and German competition.

Thanks to the sharp devaluation of the dollar, President Franklin Roosevelt raised the price of gold from US$20 per ounce to US$35 per ounce in 1933, depreciating the dollar by over 50 per cent. The US trade balance improved in the midst of the Great Depression and export interests gained a bigger say in trade policy. Secretary of State Cordell Hull harnessed these interests to enact the Reciprocal Trade Agreements Act of 1934 (RTAA), authorizing the President to cut US tariffs on a bilateral and reciprocal basis. The RTAA was successively renewed until it was superseded by the Trade Expansion Act of 1962. In the meantime, the RTAA served as the legal vehicle for the United States to accede to the General Agreement on Tariffs and Trade (GATT) in 1947 and to participate in the first five rounds of GATT negotiations. Under the auspices of the GATT, with vigorous US leadership, supplemented by bilateral and regional trade agreements, the United States and its main trading partners progressively cut their barriers until the Uruguay Round commitments were fully implemented in 2005. From 1934 until 2005, a span of 71 years, US trade policy sought and delivered open markets at home and abroad.

The central question we pose is whether, since 2005, US trade policy has entered another long phase, if not of outright protectionism reminiscent of the post-Civil War period, then of profound scepticism of open markets. After 2005, the American political system clearly balked at fresh liberalization. The Democratic Congress ignored the bilateral free trade agreements negotiated by President George W. Bush. Senator Barack Obama ran for the presidency on a platform of trade scepticism and, since taking office in 2009, President Obama has not disappointed his union supporters. But we must recall that the long era of trade liberalization after the Second World War was punctuated by pauses that can be characterized as 'short naps'. Is the period since 2005 another short nap, or is it the beginning of a long slumber – one that could turn into a nightmare for world trade?

Amazing Trade Expansion

Before turning to our central question, it is useful to explore the amazing expansion of trade since the Second World War, particularly in the last 30 years, and the policy initiatives that made this expansion possible.

Driven by Policy

US two-way trade has grown by more than 500 per cent in nominal terms since 1980, outpacing US Gross Domestic Product (GDP) growth of 370 per cent during the period. As a result, trade has become increasingly important for the US economy. The ratio of merchandise trade (imports plus exports) to US GDP grew from 17.4 per cent in 1980 and 24.6 per cent by 2008 according to World Bank World Development Indicators data. If the factors that have driven US trade in the past 40 years continue to hold for the next decade, the share of two-way US merchandise trade of GDP is bound to reach nearly 33 per cent.

The US trade profile has also changed qualitatively over the post-war decades. US commerce is increasingly oriented to emerging markets; while Canada remains the lead US trading partner, China and Mexico are second and third and some 40 per cent of US trade is carried out with middle-income nations. US trade in manufactured goods is already mostly with the emerging economies. Moreover, US trade is increasingly intra-industry rather than inter-industry, reflecting an era of vertical supply chains. Finally, services trade is growing as a share of total US commerce. Services exports more than doubled as a share of US exports between 1980 and 2008, from 17 per cent to 40 per cent, according to WTO Trade Statistics.

Three strong drivers have expanded US trade: policy liberalization, general economic growth and improvements in global communications and transportation. Hufbauer and Adler (2010) calculate that roughly one-quarter of US merchandise trade growth between 1980 and 2005 can be attributed to policy liberalization. The other three-quarters can be explained by the general expansion of the world economy (72 per cent) and falling transportation costs (3 per cent). In other words, over the past three decades, nearly all the expansion of US trade *relative* to GDP can be explained by policy liberalization.

Patterns of Trade Liberalization

When the dust settled on the Smoot–Hawley Tariff of 1930, the Congress had raised duties on thousands of imported goods to record heights, ignoring the pleas of hundreds of economists. The simple average tariff level reached 20 per cent and the American legislation precipitated a global closure of markets.

The tide changed and the next long phase of trade policy began when the Congress passed the Reciprocal Trade Agreements Act (RTAA) in 1934. The RTAA authorized the president to negotiate reductions of up to half of Smoot–Hawley duties on a reciprocal basis. By 1945 the United States had entered into 32 bilateral agreements under the RTAA with 27 countries; these cut average tariff rates by some 44 per cent and covered a total of 64 per cent of US dutiable imports (Jackson et al. 1984).

Under the auspices of GATT negotiations (supplemented by bilateral free trade agreements), the average US tariff level was reduced to 3.5 per cent in 2008, much below the 9.6 per cent for China, 13 per cent for India, 12.6 per cent for Mexico, 11.6 per cent for Argentina, 12.2 per cent for Brazil and the flat 6 per cent for Chile, and also well below the European Union's (EU) 5.5 per cent (WTO Tariff Profile database). US tariff cuts have been made unilaterally, in bilateral trade agreements and in multilateral trade rounds. US applied tariffs are on a par with the level of tariff bindings in the WTO. Agriculture and textiles remain the sensitive sectors, with more elevated tariffs than in manufactures (see Table 23.1). US trading partners have complemented the United States' own opening, furthering US trade expansion; the average most-favoured-nation (MFN) applied rates in the United States' major export destinations dropped from around 10.3 per cent in 1990 to about 7.4 per cent by about 2004 and weighted non-tariff barriers (calculated as *ad valorem* tariff equivalents) essentially halved (see Table 23.2).

After the Second World War, American leaders gave priority to the multilateral trade regime and the seven successive GATT rounds that culminated in the conclusion of the Uruguay Round and the formation of the WTO in 1994. In the 1990s, however, the United States made a consequential change in its trade policy by embracing regionalism and bilateral preferential trade agreements. In 1988, Washington signed a free trade agreement (FTA) with Canada, followed by launching the Asia-Pacific Economic Cooperation (APEC) forum with Canada and ten Asia-Pacific economies in 1989. These pacts were followed by the watershed North American Free Trade Agreement (NAFTA) with Canada and Mexico in 1994 and 12 additional FTAs with partners in the Americas, Asia and the Middle East, ratified between 2001 and 2007 (see Table 23.3).

Table 23.1   US tariffs and imports by product group in 2010

Product Groups	Bound duties AVG	Bound duties Duty-free %	Bound duties Binding	MFN Applied duties AVG	MFN Applied duties Duty-free %	Imports Share %	Imports Duty-free %
Animal Products	2.4	31.7	100	2.5	31.0	0.5	26.8
Dairy Products	20.8	0.2	100	23.0	0.3	0.1	15.1
Fruit, vegetables, plants	4.7	23.8	100	5.0	20.1	1.0	23.1
Coffee, tea	3.4	53.3	100	3.8	53.5	0.4	79.2
Cereals and preparations	3.5	19.9	100	3.9	21.0	0.5	34.8
Oilseeds, fats and oils	4.4	29.8	100	4.8	24.3	0.2	33.4
Sugars and confectionery	13.4	2.1	100	16.1	2.9	0.1	8.8
Beverages and Tobacco	16.8	29.0	100	15.5	27.3	1.0	49.4
Cotton	4.7	40.0	100	5.2	38.3	0.0	75.3
Other agricultural products	1.0	66.5	100	1.2	59.7	0.2	68.7
Fish and fish products	1.1	78.1	100	1.0	81.0	0.7	91.8
Minerals and metals	1.7	60.0	100	1.7	60.9	13.8	72.0
Petroleum	1.8	0	50	1.4	20.0	13.9	0
Chemicals	2.9	37.2	100	2.8	40.5	9.2	66.2
Woods, paper	0.4	91.6	100	0.5	89.9	4.2	91.1
Textiles	7.8	17.1	100	8.0	15.1	1.9	12.1
Clothing	11.4	3.4	100	11.7	2.8	4.0	0.7
Leather, footwear	4.6	38.7	100	3.9	38.9	2.2	17.6
Non-electrical machinery	1.2	66.3	100	1.2	65.0	13.7	80.7
Electrical machinery	1.6	49.8	100	1.7	48.4	12.5	64.3
Transport equipment	3.1	54.5	100	3.0	55.7	12.8	13.8
Manufactures, n.e.s	2.2	48.1	100	2.4	44.9	7.0	73.7

Source: WTO (2010).

Table 23.2 Average *ad valorem* rates of protection faced by US exports, past and present

Country	MFN applied tariffs		Actual tariffs		NTBs	
	I	II	III	IV	VII	VIII
	Past tariffs (%)	Present tariffs (%)	Past tariffs (%)	Present tariffs (%)	Past NTB (%)	Present NTB (%)
Australia	15.1	4.3	15.1	1.3	16.9	8.3
Brazil	34.7	13.2	34.7	13.2	33.5	16.4
Canada	9.1	5.9	5.4	1	9.1	4.5
China	38.9	10.4	38.9	10.4	11.5	5.6
EU15	7.3	5.6	7.3	5.6	21.6	10.6
Hong Kong	0	0	0	0	5.8	2.8
India	81.1	23.3	81.1	23.3	29.6	14.5
Indonesia	18.1	6.2	18.1	6.2	9.7	4.7
Japan	4.8	4.5	4.8	4.5	20.5	10
Korea	13.1	10.3	13.1	10.3	20.5	10
Malaysia	12.6	7.4	12.6	7.4	64.1	31.4
Mexico	14.6	13.6	14.6	0	32.7	16
Philippines	22.7	5.5	22.7	5.5	59.3	29
Singapore	0.4	0	0.4	0	5.8	2.8
Taiwan	10.5	7.1	10.5	7.1	64.1	31.4
Thailand	37.7	13.8	37.7	13.8	9	4.4
Venezuela	16.9	12.4	16.9	12.4	19.3	9.5
Weighted average	10.3	7.4	9.4	3.9	20.5	10.3

Note: Due to data constraints, past tariffs refer to the average of three years in the period of 1988–1993, while present tariffs are the average of three years in the period 2002-2005.
Source: Hufbauer and Adler (2010).

Table 23.3   Free trade agreements signed by the United States

Name	Year Ratified
Israel	1985
Canada	1988
NAFTA (Canada, Mexico)	1994
Jordan	2001
Chile	2004
Singapore	2004
CAFTA (Costa Rica, Dominican Republic, El Salvador, Guatemala, Honduras, Nicaragua)	2005
Australia	2005
Bahrain	2006
Morocco	2006
Oman	2009
Peru	2009
Colombia	NA
Korea	NA
Panama	NA
Trans-Pacific Partnership	Under negotiation

Source: USTR (2010).

Pursuit of FTAs successively by the Bush, Clinton and Bush Administrations reflected frustration with the slow pace of multilateral talks and the practical fact that bilateral agreements generally enable faster and deeper liberalization than multilateral rounds, something of interest to US exporters and investors. The United States brings tariffs down to zero on more than 90 per cent of all imports by the fifth year of implementation of its FTAs and some 97 per cent by the tenth year (Estevadeordal, Shearer and Suominen 2009). Bilateral partners are expected to offer reciprocal cuts. Moreover FTAs signed by the United States are usually highly comprehensive, covering such issues as investment, services, intellectual property rights and dispute settlement – subjects covered not at all or only lightly in the GATT and WTO (Estevadeordal, Suominen and Teh 2009). Granted, restrictive rules of origin in sensitive sectors restrict trade in FTAs and there are also reservations to exclude sub-national commitments in services and government procurement (Estevadeordal and Suominen 2009a; Heydon and Woolcock 2009; Suominen 2004). Overall, however, US agreements are still more liberalizing than most FTAs, including those formed by the European Union.

Short Naps in the Post-War Era

Post-war trade policies delivered immense benefits to the US economy. Bradford et al. (2005) contend that the United States has gained no less than $1 trillion *annually* from more intense integration with the global economy in the post-war era and stands to gain another $500 billion per year through a complete embrace of free trade, at home and abroad. Similarly, Aldonas et al. (2007) argue that each American household has gained as much as $15,000 a year due to freer trade.

Benefits notwithstanding, few policy issues are as contentious among Americans as trade. On three occasions since the Second World War, even prior to 2005, the liberalization agenda slowed and slippage occurred (Suominen 2009). In these episodes, the chefs of the protectionist stew were high unemployment, a strong dollar and a ballooning trade deficit (Bergsten 2005; Irwin 2005). Import competing companies and offshoring added seasoning to the broth.

Backtracking in the 1970s

In the 1970s, the US economy was buffeted by oil shocks, unemployment soared to 8.5 per cent and the trade deficit widened. The political response was 'administered protection', along with a dose of currency realignments. Congress loosened the tests for obtaining administrative relief from rising imports (Destler 1995). Following the Trade Act of 1974, petitions for escape clause relief rose from two in 1973 to 13 in 1975, and countervailing duty (CVD) investigations shot up from one in 1973 to 38 in 1975. Between 1975 and 1990, anti-dumping (AD) petitions scored a 48 per cent success rate, up from 13 per cent under the law before 1974. Currency politics mattered as well; the United States agreed to eliminate its across-the-board import surcharge adopted alongside the termination of gold convertibility of the dollar only if Europeans and Japan agreed to launch the multilateral Tokyo Round trade negotiations (1974–9) (Bergsten 1998).

Pause in the 1980s

In the 1980s, the United States embarked on policies aimed at sharpening the edge of American firms in global markets and ensuring reciprocity with US trade partners. The policy mix was heavy both on import relief and export promotion, again with a big helping of currency realignment. These efforts were rooted in unemployment rates above 9 per cent in 1982–3, the strong dollar and the rise of Japan in global trade. Washington helped bring the dollar's value down to competitive levels with the famous Plaza Accord of 1985. By mid-decade, the US government had already granted trade relief for a range of industries, notably autos, textiles, steel and semiconductors. The 1980s were a heyday of AD, CVD and escape clause activity. AD cases filed grew from less than 20 in 1981 to hover between 60 and 70 in 1982 and 1984–6, while CVD cases shot up from the teens to 140 in 1982 and 1984 saw seven escape clause investigations. The 1988 Omnibus Trade Act attacked foreign trade barriers via the so-called Super 301 provision, which enabled the United States Trade Representative (USTR) to impose retaliatory penalties on countries that pursued 'systematically unfair' trade practices.

Lull in the Late 1990s

Once NAFTA was ratified in 1993 and the Uruguay Round in 1995, the Clinton Administration took a rest on new trade initiatives. In the second half of the 1990s, Washington focused on trade barriers in Japan and China, and in both instances huge currency adjustments were essential parts of the policy mix. But with good economic times in the late 1990s, the United States took a less direct approach and addressed trade differences through the WTO system. Cases were brought to the dispute settlement mechanism and the USTR engaged in protracted negotiations to liberalize Chinese trade barriers prior to its WTO accession (finally achieved in 2001, during the Bush Administration).

Another Nap or Long Slumber?

US trade policy after 2005 echoes the tones sounded in past decades. Congress is troubled by foreign competition in import-competing sectors, while the president seeks to promote US export interests. High unemployment, a strong dollar and a huge trade deficit are all feeding protectionist appetites. In addition, three new forces are at play.

Firstly, non-tariff barriers (NTBs), limiting trade in goods but especially services, are systematically deployed as backstops and substitutes for tariff protection around the world. The thorniest ones take the shape of regulations and standards that inadvertently or intentionally discriminate against foreign goods and services. Liberalization requires the reconciliation of different regulations and standards between the United States and its major partners, a process hampered by the turf claims and appeals to sovereign authority.

Secondly, inequality has deepened and incomes have stagnated, feeding deep unease among the United States' vast middle class, a familiar precursor to protectionism. In 2009, the 95th percentile of American wage earners made on average almost nine times more than the bottom quarter of the wage distribution, as opposed to a factor of six in 1970 and seven in 1980, according to US Census Bureau data. The median household income for American families has increased very little since 1987, when it stood at $47,071 (in 2009 dollars) as opposed to US$49,777 in 2009.

Thirdly, the inexorable rise of India and China, while offering major opportunities for US multinationals and export industries and benefiting American consumers, promises to pressure US producers not only of manufactured goods but also of a range of IT-related services. China's export profile is shifting towards the high-tech sector, presaging direct competition with the United States (Bussière and Mehl 2008). Worries about jobs and wages have now spread to service sector workers who are fearful of offshoring in information technology and business services. The blue-collar blues of the 1990s are coupled by white-collar worries in the 2000s.

Growing Trade Angst

Americans' sense of economic stagnation at home and growing competition from abroad translate into a drop in poll numbers supporting free trade. In a 24–26 June 2005 CNN/*USA Today*/Gallup poll, 48 per cent of Americans said trade is a 'threat to the economy', while 44 per cent agreed that trade is an 'opportunity for economic growth' (see Figure 23.1). This was the first time since the hard times of 1992 that a plurality of Americans saw foreign trade as a threat. A 2007 Pew Foundation poll arrived at similar results. While 59 per cent of Americans still supported free trade, the level had dropped markedly from the 78 per cent recorded in 2002. One striking finding was that even 31 per cent of Republicans viewed trade in a negative light – the highest figure in decades.

Similarly, in a March–April 2008 *New York Times*–CBS News poll, 58 per cent of Americans viewed foreign trade as good for the economy, down from 69 per cent in the 1996, while 32 per cent viewed it as bad, up from 17 per cent in 1996. Only 24 per cent agreed that 'free trade must be allowed, even if domestic industries are hurt by foreign competition', down from 36 per cent in 1996. The Great Recession of 2008–9 aggravated these concerns, as millions lost their jobs and unemployment shot up to 30-year highs. By March 2009, almost half of Americans said they feared for their jobs, as opposed to 28 per cent a year prior (CNBC 2009). An October 2010 *Wall Street Journal*/NBC News Poll showed that Americans of all income groups have progressively soured on free trade, with majorities of all segments and both political parties now considering trade agreements to be harmful. In total, 53 per cent of Americas thought free trade agreements had hurt the United States, up from 32 per cent in 1999, while fewer than 20 per cent saw them as having helped, down from more than a third in 1999 (Murray and Belkin 2010).

Falsely Accused of Job Churn

A familiar axiom of trade policy holds that the benefits of liberalization are dispersed, but the pain of liberalization is targeted and sharp (see Chapter 2) – which, in political discourse, means 'lost jobs'. But is the charge justified? Does trade cause job losses and abet inequality? Consider recent research. Of the 16 to 18 million jobs lost annually in the United States, approximately three to four million are displaced workers, who face serious adjustment costs, and of those, about 500,000 workers are displaced by import competition (Rosen 2008). This represents approximately 3 per cent of total job losses, 15 per cent of displaced

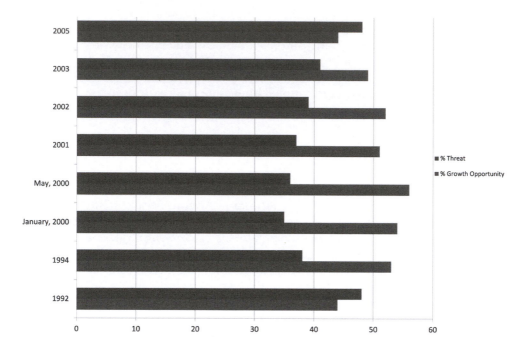

Figure 23.1   Percentage of Americans seeing trade as a 'growth opportunity' or as a 'threat', 1992–2005

Note: The dark line represents '% Threat', the lighter line represents '% Growth Opportunity'.
Source: CNN, *USA Today* and Gallup Organization (2005), www.gallup.com/poll/17605/more–americans–see–threat–opportunity–foreign–trade.aspx.

workers and about one-quarter of workers affected by mass layoffs.[1] Rather than trade, the primary reason for massive job churn is technological change. Among the fastest declining jobs in America from now until 2016 will be such occupations as file clerks, order fillers, photographic processing, sewing machine operators, cashiers, packers and packagers and electrical equipment operators.[2] The roster mirrors innovations ranging from the Internet to digital cameras and automatic packaging machines.

What about offshoring? According to estimates by Jensen and Kletzer (2008), the total number of US jobs that might be outsourced to low-wage countries over the next 20 years is 15–20 million and approximately 40 per cent of these jobs will be in the manufacturing sector. Less well-known is that more jobs are in-shored than

---

[1]   The literature on jobs and trade is vast. See, for example, Amiti and Wei (2005), Becker et al. (2009), Bivens (2007), Falk and Wolfmayr (2005), Kletzer (2001) and OECD (2007).
[2]   See the top-30 list at: www.bls.gov/news.release/ecopro.t08.htm.

are offshored. Slaughter (2007) shows that the number of manufacturing jobs in-sourced to the United States between 1987 and 2002 grew by 82 per cent, while the number of US jobs outsourced overseas grew by only 23 per cent. The United States is a *net exporter* of business services to India, meaning it exports more services to India than India exports to the United States. Moreover, in-sourced jobs usually pay better wages than outsourced jobs.

Does Trade Make the Rich Richer?

Is there a connection between inequality and trade? Lawrence (2008) argues that increased trade probably played a part in causing greater US inequality in the 1980s when imports of manufactured goods from developing countries boomed. By the 1990s, however, many items imported from developing countries were no longer made in the United States. More imports of items no longer made at home cannot possibly undermine wages in the United States. Between 1981 and 2006, without increased trade, blue-collar workers in the United States might have earned 1.4 per cent more than they did, and most of the gain would have come before 2000. Inequality, like job churn, is largely caused by factors other than trade – especially technological change.

Trade Policy in the Obama Administration

Trade angst in the United States has translated into an anti-trade Congress and an Obama Administration that is lukewarm about liberalization. During the 2008 presidential campaign, Obama called for a pause on FTAs, floated an idea to renegotiate NAFTA and hardly mentioned the Doha Round. Rather, the Obama campaign pledged a 'pause' on trade agreements and sturdier trade enforcement. The American Federation of Labour–Congress of Industrial Organizations (AFL-CIO), an influential voice during the campaign, petitioned the incoming administration to suspend bargaining on all new trade and investment pacts and to review all past agreements.[3]

Once elected, President Obama adopted a more moderate tone and recruited a number of senior officials with pro-trade leanings. But the Administration's first two years, 2009 and 2010, saw little movement on trade. FTAs with Colombia, Panama and Korea, along with the Doha Round, were kept in the cooler. To the extent that trade policy was noticed, the Administration focused on enforcing

---

[3]   The AFL-CIO called for 'new administration priorities and benchmarks' for the pending three FTAs and a new template for future trade agreements. The federation also strongly backs the TRADE Act, which would restore congressional primacy in setting the mandates for US trade negotiators, which would order them to write enforceable labour rights into the texts of US trade agreements.

the trade obligations of foreign partners. However, in February 2010, President Obama pledged to double American exports within five years. This goal seems to have served as a wedge for fresh incremental liberalization in the second half of the Obama Administration's term, as the president gave a nod to the pending trade deals, arguing they are about exports, not imports. That the House of Representatives had turned Republican helped grease the president's selling job.

Anti-Trade Congress

From the 1970s up until the implementation of NAFTA in 1994, trade deals usually garnered support from more than three-quarters of Members of Congress in both political parties. Since then, Congressional support, particularly from Democrats, has dwindled (see Figure 23.2). In 2001, Trade Promotion Authority (TPA), which allows for an up-or-down vote in the Congress on trade agreements negotiated by the president, was barely renewed in the House by a vote of 215–214, while the US–Central America Free Trade Agreement (DR–CAFTA) squeaked through by 217–215 in 2005.

Such narrow margins contrast sharply with the 395–7 nod to the Tokyo Round package in 1979, the 288–148 vote on the Uruguay Round in 1994 and even the passage of NAFTA by a 34 vote majority (200–234) in 1993.

Congress has long traced the growing trade deficit of the United States to the undervalued Chinese currency, arguing that Beijing is unfairly driving US companies out of business (Eichengreen and Irwin 2007). In 2003, veteran Senators Charles Schumer of New York and Leslie Graham of North Carolina threatened a blanket 27.5 per cent tariff against Chinese imports unless Beijing revalued the RMB. Similarly, the 109th Congress (2005–7) introduced 27 pieces of anti-China trade legislation (Scheve and Slaughter 2007). In July 2005, China did agree to revaluation and the RMB ended up rising by 21 per cent against the dollar until July 2008, when again it was fixed. However, the currency adjustment did little to alter trade balances or quiet Congress. The 110th Congress (2007–9) put forth some dozen China bills, many of which aimed to force an overhaul of China's exchange rate regime (Roach 2009).

While the Obama Administration sought to deal with the currency issue privately with Beijing as well as multilaterally in the G-20 and the IMF, the 111th Congress (2009–11), seconded by Paul Krugman (2010), revived its calls for steep penalty tariffs against China. On 29 September 2010, the US House of Representatives approved by an overwhelming margin a bill that is interpreted to open the door for an imposition of trade remedies against alleged currency manipulation.[4] As jobless claims kept mounting, the 112th Congress adamantly upheld the law; at the

---

[4]   Specifically, the bill narrows the Commerce Department's discretion to refuse to initiate a countervailing duty investigation on an allegation of export contingency and specifies how the Department must calculate the subsidy benefit.

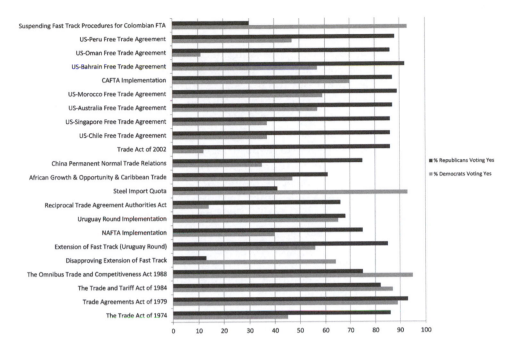

Figure 23.2 Votes on US flagship trade agreements and measures in the House of Representatives, 1973–2009

Source: Brainard (2008).

same time, the White House, entering into campaign mode, took a tougher stance towards Beijing.

Protectionist Responses to the Crisis

At various Summit gatherings, the G-20 announced a standstill on protectionism and reiterated its commitment to conclude the Doha Round. But nearly all G-20 members, including the United States and China, implemented and proposed measures that contravened these commitments. The damage was far less than amid the Great Depression, but the new restrictions are still taking a toll on global supply chains.[5] According to data by the Global Trade Alert, by October 2011, The G20 members alone had implemented as many as 781 protective measures since the first G20 pledge in November 2008 (Evenett 2011). Worse, the protectionist trend continued rather than reversing as the global recovery commenced.

The bulk of new protectionism takes the form of obscure discrimination that has become the hallmark of barriers designed to skirt the GATT/WTO system of tariff

---

[5]   We thank Kenneth Heydon for this notion.

bindings (Hufbauer et al. 2010). The appetite for protectionism grows amid economic downturns, paradoxically just when trade expansion is needed to stimulate the world economy. Consider a few responses to the crisis. Anti-dumping filings grew from 165 to 201 between 2007 and the end of 2009, and proceedings that led to the imposition of duties grew from 108 to 138. US anti-dumping filings, according to the WTO Anti-Dumping database, increased from 12 in 2006 and 8 in 2007 to 28 in 2008 and 20 in 2009, abating to 9 by 2011. Fiscal stimulus packages enacted around the world often contained industrial subsidies that can distort the patterns of global commerce and trigger WTO disputes over 'illegal state aids'. Still another negative was exclusion of foreign suppliers. In February 2009, the US Congress passed and President Obama promptly signed the 'Buy American' provisions in the US economic stimulus plan – designed to make recipients of stimulus money source their inputs solely from US suppliers. Hufbauer and Schott (2009) estimated that retaliation by other nations affecting just 1 per cent of US exports would erase 6,500 American jobs.

Protectionism also spilled over to seemingly non-trade policy areas. The Lieberman–Warner–Boxer bill, among the more ambitious US efforts at climate legislation to reach a Senate vote in 2008, would have required foreign suppliers, based in countries that had not taken 'comparable action' to US control measures, to purchase greenhouse gas allowances before their exports would be allowed into the US market. The bill was defeated mainly due to fierce lobbying by energy-intensive industries. But the idea of border adjustments based on 'comparability' made its way into the Waxman–Markey bill which was narrowly approved by the House in 2009. How climate legislation will fare in future and what trade restrictions will be carried over from previous bills, are matters still to be decided.

Conclusion: Can Policy Avoid a Long Slumber?

US leadership in world affairs has been intimately associated with the long liberal phase in trade policy that began in 1934. If the United States now abdicates leadership on the international economic agenda centred on trade, the damage to US standing across a range of issue areas could be considerable. The extent to which other nations both emulate and react to the United States cannot be underestimated. Conversely, leadership by the United States is imperative for getting world trade and the global economy humming.

Yet today, there are ominous signs pointing to a long slumber in the realm of trade policy. In this concluding section, we outline five policy steps that might awaken trade policy, asleep since 2005, in two or three years, rather than two or three decades.

Conclude the Doha Round

The United States, working foremost with China, must conclude the decade-old Doha Round. Doha would be a great means for injecting vitality in the uncertain global economy and safeguarding the GATT/WTO system the United States has championed in the past six decades. Hufbauer et al. (2010) propose a formula for an ambitious yet balanced deal between the interests of developed and developing countries. Under the agreement, G-20 nations should provide modest increments in market access commitments beyond tariff and subsidy cuts in agriculture and non-agricultural market access (NAMA), slash red tape and cut transactions costs for exporting and importing goods and services. They argue that such measures would lead to a world GDP gain of almost $300 billion per annum.

Conversely, failure to conclude Doha could freeze multilateral trade cooperation for another decade. In the vacuum left by a multilateral failure, various fates can be imagined. Bouët and Laborde (2008) illustrate a scenario where all tariffs revert to bound levels, world trade contracts by $1,770 billion and world income shrinks by $448 billion. This is an extreme scenario, but quantitative studies cannot account for the blow that a Doha collapse could deal to the legitimacy of the multilateral trading system. Core rules and institutions, such as national treatment, MFN treatment and the dispute settlement mechanism, would all be called into question. The political fallout could be severe.

Post-Doha, attention needs to shift to reforming the WTO system (Hufbauer and Suominen 2010). Doha's troubles are amplified by the WTO's cumbersome negotiating principles of a 'single undertaking' and 'consensus'. In a setting where over 150 countries contest a multifaceted agenda, these principles not only water down deals, but create formidable obstacles to any deal at all. Future negotiations must be based on plurilateralism, the negotiating principle effectively in place through the Tokyo Round. Instead of requiring the consent of the entire membership, plurilaterals would enable coalitions of the willing to strike agreements in selected issue areas, like trade in services or civil aircraft or rules on climate change. The benefit of plurilateralism over multilateralism is both depth of agreement and speed of negotiation; those who do not want to accede are left out and do not constrain the talks.

A particular area that needs to be tackled at the multilateral level is the effect of climate change rules on trade. A rise of 'green protectionism' in the United States or other advanced nations would doubtless lead to trade disputes with China, India and other emerging industrial powers, and result in bad economic outcomes. The United States should spearhead efforts to craft a global Climate Code whereby leading emitters of greenhouse gases enumerate permitted and proscribed trade measures (Hufbauer et al. 2009).

Curb Global Imbalances

The record of the past six years shows quite clearly that policy liberalization cannot move forward when current account imbalances are large (over 3 per cent of GDP), growing and persistent for systemically important countries. Some countries (such as China and India) have an insatiable appetite for US, European and Japanese financial assets. But feeding that appetite through large export surpluses seems sure to provoke protective responses in the deficit countries. US fiscal discipline and global currency realignments will both be needed to bring current account imbalances to politically acceptable levels. In addition, aggressive creation of SDRs under the auspices of the International Monetary Fund could quench some of the appetite for financial assets denominated in dollars, euros or yen (Hufbauer and Suominen 2010).

From Bilateralism to FTA Convergence

Multilateralism needs to be complemented by strategic bilateralism and regionalism. The Obama Administration needs to seek a renewal of TPA, which is critical for enticing other countries to negotiate with the United States, as it ensures that Congress will not modify provisions negotiated by the president's team after the agreement is signed. Given the United States' open trade regime, further bilateral and regional agreements would deliver greater export gains and investment opportunities for US industries than for partner nations.

In particular, the United States also needs to revive engagement with the Asia-Pacific region. APEC has failed to meet its trade liberalization goals, but the Trans-Pacific Partnership (TPP) agreement can be a substitute and a strategic counterweight vis-à-vis China, if the nine existing members pursued forceful and comprehensive liberalization and enticed four other important economies to join – Japan, Korea, Mexico and Canada. Washington should also seek to revive the transatlantic economy by pursuing liberalization with Europe of trade in services and deep cooperation on standards, customs procedures and competition rules.

Bilateral and regional agreements must not be pursued as a substitute for, but as a complement to, multilateralism and Washington needs to explore ways to 'multilateralize' core provisions with ad hoc coalitions of the willing in the WTO. Further, the United States needs to seek to knit together its FTAs, for example through common and liberal rules of origin. Convergence efforts are particularly viable in the Western Hemisphere, where the United States already has (or will soon have) FTAs with Canada, Mexico, all Central American nations, Peru, Colombia and Chile (Estevadeordal and Suominen 2009b). Linking the criss-crossing trade deals would enable Washington to move closer to the aspiration of the Free Trade Area of the Americas born two decades ago, only to die in 2003. More far-reaching would be an economic zone that converged the FTAs that the United States and European Union respectively have with such common partners as Mexico, Canada, and Korea (Trans-Atlantic Task Force on Trade 2012). Much like the US bilateral agreements with Korea, Colombia, and Panama, such broad-based regional agreements would advance US foreign policy, emphasizing US resolve to cooperate with its partners and allies.

Safety Nets and Ladders

Whatever the strength of causation (and we think it is slight), the political case for trade liberalization cannot be made if median family incomes in the United States stagnate for another decade. Nor can it be made when job loss stands a high chance of pitching a family into poverty. The sense of precariousness felt by American workers must be reduced and the sense of opportunity increased. The best way to deal with job churn and meagre wage gains is economic growth, including strong export growth. In addition, for dislocated workers, targeted programmes are needed – whether the cause is trade, technology or plain bad luck. The broad goal should be enhanced labour mobility instead of defence of jobs that have become uncompetitive, advance notice requirements and severance pay, unemployment benefits combined with training requirements, lifetime learning programmes for adults and fully portable health insurance (Hufbauer and Suominen 2010).[6] The United States must not become a European social democracy where *not* working can pay better than a nine-to-five job. But the future of the American trade agenda will remain dim if labour policy remains frozen in the model of 1990. Bold and comprehensive measures can also sidestep the catch-22 created by the label of 'trade adjustment assistance'; a term that only cements public perceptions that trade threatens American living standards.

Making the United States a Better Place for Business

Another key non-trade area to address is taxation of multinationals (Hufbauer and Moran 2010). The Obama Administration has repeatedly called for taxes on companies that 'ship US jobs abroad'. The administration fails to acknowledge that outbound firms consistently export more from the United States than do home firms. The plants of US multinationals are the most productive in the United States, most technology-intensive and pay the highest wages. If US tax policy is changed so as to hinder outward investment by US firms, US export performance will be weaker, not stronger. The best policy for American workers is to make the United States an even better place for multinationals to do business. Not only should ideas to tax the foreign income of US-based multinationals be tossed in the trash basket,

---

6   Whether the new healthcare law fosters worker mobility remains to be seen. Programmes with financial incentives for work are to be applauded, such as the US Earned Income Tax Credit, the US wage insurance programme (a component of TAA), or the UK Working Families Tax Credit, or a targeted wage subsidy paid to employers. These programmes are far superior to unemployment benefits with no link to new jobs.

but also the combined federal and state corporate tax rate should be slashed from 39 per cent, the second-highest in the OECD (after Japan), down to 25 per cent, the OECD norm.

References

Aldonas, G.D., Lawrence, R.Z. and Slaughter, M.J. 2007. Succeeding in the Global Economy: A New Policy Agenda for the American Worker. *The Financial Services Forum Policy Research Report*. Washington, DC: The Financial Services Forum.

Amiti, M. and Wei, S.-J. 2005. Service Offshoring, Productivity, and Employment: Evidence from the United States. *IMF Working Papers* 05/238. Washington, DC: The International Monetary Fund.

Becker, S.O., Ekholm, K. and Muendler, M. 2009. Offshoring and the Onshore Composition of Tasks and Skills. *Discussion Paper 7391*. London: Centre for Economic Policy Research.

Bergsten, F. 1998. The International Monetary Scene and the Next WTO Negotiations, in *Launching New Global Trade Talks: An Action Agenda*, edited by J.J. Schott. Washington, DC: Institute for International Economics: 39–46.

Bergsten, F. 2005. Rescuing the Doha Round. *Foreign Affairs* 15, 24. (December – Special Edition).

Bivens, L.J. 2007. Globalization and American Wages: Today and Tomorrow. *Briefing Paper*. Washington, DC: Economic Policy Institute.

Bouët, A. and Laborde, D. 2008. The Potential Cost of a Failed Doha Round. *Issue Brief 56*. International Food Policy Research Institute (IFPRI).

Bradford, S.C., Grieco, P. and Hufbauer, G.C. 2005. The Payoff to America from Global Integration, in *The United States and the World Economy: Foreign Economic Policy for the Next Decade*, edited by F. Bergsten. Washington, DC: Institute for International Economics: 65–109.

Brainard, Lael. 2008. *US Trade Votes, 1974–2008*. [Online] Available at: www.brookings.edu/~/media/Files/rc/articles/2007/1217_trade_brainard/1217_trade_brainard.pdf [accessed: 30 March 2011].

Bussière, M. and Mehl, A. 2008. China's and India's Roles in Global Trade and Finance: Twin Titans for the New Millennium? *European Central Bank Occasional Paper Series*, No.80 (January).

CNBC. 2009. People Fear Losing Job the Most: Poll. 19 February. [Online] Available at: www.cnbc.com/id/29275784 [accessed: 30 March 2011].

CNN, *USA Today* and Gallup Organization. 2005. *More Americans See Threat, Not Opportunity, in Foreign Trade*, 2 August.

Destler, I.M. 1995. *American Trade Politics*. Washington, DC: Peterson Institute for International Economics.

Eichengreen, B. and Douglas A.I. 2007. *The Bush Legacy for America's International Economic Policy*. Paper prepared for the American Foreign Policy after the Bush Doctrine conference, Miller Centre, University of Virginia, 7–8 June 2007.

[Online] Available at: www.econ.berkeley.edu/~eichengr/bush_legacy.pdf [accessed 30 March 2011].

Estevadeordal, A. and Suominen, K. 2009a. *Gatekeepers of Global Commerce: Rules of Origin and International Economic Integration*. Washington, DC: Inter-American Development Bank.

Estevadeordal, A. and Suominen, K. 2009b. *Bridging Trade Agreements in the Americas*. Washington, DC: Inter-American Development Bank.

Estevadeordal, A., Shearer, M. and Suominen, K. 2009. Market Access Provisions in Regional Trade Agreements, in *Regional Rules in the Global Trading System*, edited by A. Estevadeordal, K. Suominen and R. Teh. Cambridge: Cambridge University Press: 96–165.

Estevadeordal, A., Suominen, K. and Teh, R. 2009. *Regional Rules in the Global Trading System*. Cambridge: Cambridge University Press.

Evenett, S.J. 2010. *Trade Tensions Mount: The 10th GTA Report*. London: Centre for Economic Policy Research.

Falk, M. and Wolfmayr, Y. 2005. Employment Effects of Outsourcing to Low Wage Countries: Empirical Evidence for EU Countries. *WIFO Working Papers 262*.

Heydon, K. and Woolcock, S. 2009. *The Rise of Bilateralism: Comparing American, European and Asian Approaches to Preferential Trade Agreements*. Tokyo: United Nations University Press.

Hufbauer, G.C. and Adler, M. 2010. Policy Liberalization and US Integration with the Global Economy: Trade and Investment between 1980 and 2006, in *International Handbook on the Economics of Integration*, Vol. III, edited by M.N. Jovanovic. Cheltenham: Edward Elgar Publishing.

Hufbauer, G.C. and Moran, T.H. 2010. Higher Taxes on US-Based Multinationals Would Hurt US Workers and Exports. *Brief 10-10* (May). Washington, DC: Peterson Institute for International Economic Policy.

Hufbauer, G.C. and Schott, J.J. 2009. Buy American: Bad for Jobs, Worse for Reputation. *Brief 09-2* (February). Washington, DC: Peterson Institute for International Economics.

Hufbauer, G.C. and Suominen, K. 2010. *Globalization at Risk: Challenges to Finance and Trade*. New Haven: Yale University Press.

Hufbauer, G.C., Charnovitz, S. and Kim, J. 2009. *Global Warming and the World Trading System*. Washington, DC: Peterson Institute for International Economics.

Hufbauer, G.C., Kirkegaard, J. and Wong, W.F. 2010. *G-20 Protection in the Wake of the Great Recession*. Report to the International Chamber of Commerce Research Foundation. Washington, DC: Peterson Institute for International Economics.

Hufbauer, G.C., Schott, J.J. and Wong, W.F. 2010. Figuring out the Doha Round. *Policy Analyses in International Economics 91*. Washington, DC: Peterson Institute for International Economics.

Irwin, D. 2005. The Rise of US Antidumping Activity in Historical Perspective. *IMF Working Paper No. 05/31* (February). Washington, DC: International Monetary Fund.

Jackson, J.H., Louis, J.V. and Matsushita, M. 1984. *Implementing the Tokyo Round: National Constitutions and International Economic Rules*. Ann Arbor: University of Michigan Press.

Jensen, J.B. and Kletzer, LG. 2008. Fear and Offshoring: The Scope and Potential Impact of Imports and Exports of Services. *Brief 08-1* (January). Washington, DC: Peterson Institute for International Economics.

Kletzer, L.G. 2001. *Job Loss from Imports: Measuring the Costs*. Washington, DC: Peterson Institute for International Economics.

Krugman, P. 2010. Taking On China. *New York Times*, 14 March.

Lawrence, R.Z. 2008. *Blue-Collar Blues: Is Trade to Blame for Rising US Income Inequality?* Washington, DC: Peterson Institute for International Economics.

Murray, S. and Belkin, D. 2010. Americans Sour on Trade. *Wall Street Journal*, 4 October.

OECD. 2007. *OECD Employment Outlook 2007*. Paris: OECD.

Roach, S. 2009. Are US Protectionist Threats about to Become Reality? *MoneyWeek*, 12 April.

Rosen, H. 2008. Designing a National Strategy for Responding to Economic Dislocation. *Testimony before the Subcommittee on Investigation and Oversight House Science and Technology Committee*. 24 June.

Scheve, K.F. and Slaughter, M.J. 2007. A New Deal for Globalization. *Foreign Affairs* 86, 4 (July/August).

Slaughter, M.J. 2007. *Insourcing Mergers and Acquisitions*. Washington, DC: Organization for International Investment.

Suominen, K. 2004. *Rules of Origin in Global Commerce*. PhD dissertation. San Diego: University of California,

Suominen, K. 2009. *New Era of Protectionism? Post-Crisis Trans-Atlantic Trade Policies*. Brussels Forum Paper for the German Marshall Fund of the United States (March).

Transatlantic Task Force on Trade and Investment. 2012. *A New Era for Transatlantic Trade Leadership*. German Marshall Fund of the United States, Washington, DC (February).

USTR. 2010. *Trade Agreements*. USTR.

WTO. 2010. *International Trade and Tariff Data*. World Trade Organization.

The Functioning of the European Union's Trade Policy

Joakim Reiter

Introduction

The European Union (EU) is the world's biggest exporter, importer and investor. Yet, for many outside observers, the functioning of the union's trade policy remains opaque. Similarly, for many inside the union, there is often a sense that EU trade policy punches below its economic weight.

A key reason for this, it has been suggested, is that EU trade policymaking is constantly undermined by the difficult process of reconciling the conflicting positions of EU Member States. Another suggested reason is that the EU trade policy process remains predominantly technocratic, led by the unelected European Commission. Of course, there are numerous stories of trading partners waiting sometimes literally in the corridors of the WTO building for the EU to return with newly coordinated positions in negotiations. And there are examples when Member States have openly undercut the official EU position.

Nonetheless, such explanations exaggerate the uniqueness of EU trade policymaking. Many countries tend to treat trade policy as a technical matter and find themselves in difficult domestic discussions over trade policy choices. Rather, it is argued here that the sense of perplexity with which some observers view the EU trade policy process derives partly from the continuously evolving nature of EU powers (competence) and policy processes in trade, partly from the distinct institutional features and structure of EU trade policymaking and partly from the different political setting that prevails at the EU level compared to that of Member States or indeed many other countries. In this chapter, each of these aspects will be discussed.

The chapter begins by describing the evolution of EU trade powers and policymaking and then against this backdrop, examines the two key questions regarding the way EU trade policy works. First, 'who does what and why?', which is assessed in light of the recent Lisbon Treaty (or the Treaty of the Functioning of the European Union, TFEU). Second, 'who wants what and why?', where EU trade politics is discussed in terms of the competing interests of protectionism versus liberalism, as well as traditionalism versus modernity and the more recent tensions between trade and other policy areas. Finally, the chapter summarizes some challenges facing EU trade policymaking in the years to come.

The Evolution of EU Trade Policy Process, Powers and Politics

The evolution of EU trade policy can be described in terms of three interlinked trends: the steady path of internal and external economic integration that has created a need for an ever-increasing number of issues to be dealt with at the EU level; the increased powers of the EU, and in particular the Commission, in the formulation of trade policy so as to ensure that this happens; and the growing number of actors involved that has also increased tensions over, and the politicization of, trade policymaking in the EU.

The Expansion of the Scope of EU Trade Policymaking

The expansion of the scope of EU trade policy has tended to mirror both endogenous factors related to the EU's own path of increased integration and exogenous factors related to the evolution in trade negotiations globally.

In terms of the endogenous factors, already with the Treaty of Rome, the creation of a customs union placed tariffs and other commercial policies in the hands of the European Economic Community (EEC). Over time, as EU integration has deepened and widened, more policy matters have followed this pattern. A qualitative leap in the scope of EU trade policymaking came with the Single European Act in 1986. The substantial increase in policy approximation and/or harmonization related to the internal market from the second half of the 1980s onwards, provided the foundation for an equivalent expansion of the scope of EU trade policymaking (Holmes 2006; Jones 2006; Young and Peterson 2006).

Among the exogenous factors influencing the scope of EU trade policy are the evolution in trade negotiations and the development of the GATT and WTO. Until the early 1970s, GATT negotiations were almost exclusively oriented towards reducing (industrial) tariffs. With the Uruguay Round in 1986–94, which also led to the establishment of the WTO, the scope of global trade negotiations expanded further to include *inter alia* services, intellectual property rights and trade-related investment measures.

Post-Uruguay Round, there have been discussions in the WTO on an ever wider range of topics, such as environment, labour standards, competition policy, investments, trade facilitation and e-commerce. Though many of these trade-related issues have subsequently been dropped from the Doha Development

Agenda, WTO discussions influenced and helped crystallize the EU's positions on such matters which are now fully incorporated in the union's negotiating position for bilateral and regional trade agreements (Falke 2005).

The EU's latest trade agreements, for example the free trade agreement (FTA) with Korea, thus consolidate the shift in EU trade policy towards the pursuit of deep integration agreements. As such, they also sharply contrast with the EU's past preference for narrow trade deals mainly preoccupied with industrial tariffs, as illustrated by the EU's first set of trade agreements with its Mediterranean neighbours in the 1990s.

The Expansion of the EU's Trade Policy Powers

The expansion of the scope of EU trade policy prodded the European Commission and Member States into sometimes difficult and protracted debates over the issue of EU powers or competence (Dür and Zimmermann 2007). Competence reflects who has the right to regulate in the EU and hence determines both who negotiates on the Union's behalf and how decisions are adopted internally. In trade, there are two basic options:

- 'exclusive EU competence' in which the Commission negotiates on behalf of the Union and the Council takes its decisions on the basis of qualified majority voting (QMV); or
- shared competence, or indeed Member States retaining competence, in which the Commission may still be authorized to negotiate, including on behalf of Member States, but any Council decisions are taken by unanimity.

The Treaty of Rome established exclusive competence for the EEC in the area of trade policy (or the Common Commercial Policy, CCP). But there were (at least) two problems. The first was political. Member States were uneasy about being overridden by a qualified majority on matters of national interest. Irrespective of the Treaty therefore, from the mid-1960s onwards, decisions by unanimity became established practice. This problem was broadly overcome when, as part of the Single European Act of 1986, the spirit and letter of the original Treaty was not only restored, but the Treaty was also amended to extend qualified majority voting to a large number of issues (Gillingham 2003: 231). At the same time, the modus operandi of the Council's deliberations on trade continued to be – and remains – consensual on more sensitive and political issues.

The second problem was that the Treaty contained no exhaustive definition of the CCP (Woolcock 2002). Without a clear definition of its scope, there was a risk that any new trade-related issues would fall outside exclusive competence – thereby undermining the Commission's role as negotiator and bringing unanimity in through the backdoor.

This is exactly what occurred at the end of the Uruguay Round. Until then, the Commission and Member States had managed to work out pragmatic solutions. But with the inclusion of services and intellectual property rights in the final outcome of the Uruguay Round, the conflicting views on the competence issue came to the fore. The matter was referred to the European Court of Justice in 1994. In its opinion 1/94, the Court ruled against the Commission: while confirming that the Commission had sole competence to conclude international agreements on trade in goods, the Court found that competence was shared with Member States on services (excluding cross-border services) and commercial aspects of intellectual property. Ever since, the Commission has sought, with support of some Member States, to expand the scope of exclusive competence over trade policy in subsequent Treaty revisions.

The Lisbon Treaty, which entered into force on 1 December 2009, has resolved many of these longstanding competence disputes by pushing the boundary of EU competence for CCP well beyond what had been readily accepted in the past. It substantially expands the scope of the CCP by *inter alia*: (1) ending the traditional distinction between trade in goods and trade in services as well as commercial aspects of intellectual property; (2) adding, on an equal footing, foreign direct investment (FDI); (3) limiting unanimity decisions by Member States to only a couple of specific situations; and (4) allowing the EU to negotiate trade agreements even on matters that have not yet been regulated internally, whilst confirming that the EU cannot use external negotiations to force harmonization in areas where the Treaty excludes such harmonization (Dimopoulos 2008).

But the Lisbon Treaty is no panacea for all competence-related disputes, nor does it dispense with the political need for a consensual approach to important trade deals. For the most deep and comprehensive trade agreements, such as the recent Korea FTA, unanimity is still the 'rule'. This is because the expansion of EU competence with the Lisbon Treaty still falls short of the even greater expansion of the scope of trade negotiations.

The Increasing Complexity of EU Trade Policy

In part as a consequence of the expansion of the EU trade policy scope and powers, the actors involved have changed and multiplied, leading to greater complexity in policymaking.

The Commission has evolved from a very slim bureaucracy to an organization with substantially expanded responsibilities, funding and staff. In addition, trade negotiations are not – and have never been – solely a matter for the Trade Commissioner and his service, DG TRADE. As the scope of trade policy has expanded, other commissioners and their services have also become more involved – directly or indirectly – in trade negotiations, or even pursue negotiations of their own which touch upon trade-related aspects, such as fisheries, geographical indications, energy and aviation. In consequence, internal coordination and coherence can, at times, be a challenge.

In the Council there are now 27 Member States and successive enlargements have influenced, to a varying degree, EU trade policy and its formulation. As the constituent Member States have changed and the structure of their economies been transformed, the delicate balance of interests in the Council has altered. It has also become increasingly difficult to have detailed exchanges of views involving all or even most Member States, and individual Member States find it harder to ensure that their specific interests and concerns are taken into account. This change in the character of Council deliberations has in turn forced Member States to develop alternative routes – be they informal contacts, alliance-building or occasionally more politically visible ways – for exerting influence on EU trade policy (Elsig 2008).

The most dramatic and recent change in trade actors, however, concerns the European Parliament. While the Parliament was given substantially extended powers from the 1980s onwards, it was until recently more or less excluded from EU trade policymaking. The Lisbon Treaty has fundamentally changed this situation. Today, the European Parliament needs to give its consent to all EU trade agreements and acts as co-legislature for any regulation implementing the CCP. Given that the Parliament's deliberations are always political in nature, this has changed the character of, and raised the temperatures in, the debates over trade policy.

With growing concerns and intensified debate over globalization, various non-governmental organizations (NGOs) have also become increasingly involved. Traditionally, EU trade policy was mainly influenced by interest groups representing industrial and agricultural producers (Dür 2007, 2008b; Gerlach 2006). Such groups still dominate in many respects the lobbying on trade and, not least within the framework of the EU's trade instruments, tend to have rather privileged access to decision makers (De Bièvre and Eckhardt 2010 and 2011; Evenett and Vermulst 2005; Shaffer 2006).[1] Today, however, apart from broader representation by the private sector (for example, the services sector), NGOs focusing on developmental issues, environment and labour rights are now engaged in lobbying on many trade topics. Although these NGOs' influence has been questioned (Dür and De Bièvre 2007), both the Commission and Member States have responded by increasing transparency, engaging in public discussions and establishing more formalized frameworks for stakeholder dialogues. This has fuelled a more open debate on EU trade policy and, also with the involvement of the Parliament, increased attention to the relationship between trade and non-trade issues, such as in the union's relations with developing countries. Trade policy has become increasingly accessible.

---

[1]   In part, this is due to the exclusive insights and knowledge of trade barriers that the private sector can offer. Such information is needed for the successful negotiation, legal challenges or application of trade measures. But it is also due to the fact that some instruments of the EU specifically build upon the collaboration between the private sector and trade officials, either in the Commission, in Member States or both, such as the Trade Defence Instruments (including anti-dumping), the Market Access Advisory Committees and the Trade Barrier Reports.

The Power Over EU Trade Policy: Decision Making Post-Lisbon Treaty

As discussed above, the Lisbon Treaty has consolidated EU-level decision making in trade policy by expanding the scope of the EU's exclusive competence, restricting the use of unanimity and more fully including the European Parliament on all aspects of trade (Woolcock 2008, 2010a, 2010b). Broadly speaking, the internal division of labour between the Commission, Council and the Parliament is that the Commission is the 'executive' whereas the Council and the Parliament approve all trade agreements and adopt relevant trade legislations. But this does not provide the full picture: both the operation and the distribution of power in the EU's trade policymaking need closer scrutiny.

Internal Procedures Relating to Trade Negotiations and Agreements

The EU decision making process related to trade negotiations and agreements is divided into three stages: (1) the approval of mandates and establishment of negotiating directives; (2) the conduct of the negotiations and the internal consultations on EU positions; and (3) the adoption of trade agreements. During each of these stages, the respective roles and relative powers of the Commission, the Council and the Parliament differ substantially.

The Commission is responsible for proposing a decision to open negotiations and directives on the objectives to be achieved (mandate), for negotiating trade deals usually as sole representative of the EU and for tabling the proposal to adopt the final agreement once negotiations have concluded. But despite its executive role, the Commission has no power to single-handedly decide on the launch of negotiations or to adopt trade deals – no matter how small or limited these may be. Informally, however, the Commission is usually able to exert considerable influence throughout the entire process (Elsig 2007; Meunier 2007). Through its proposal for mandate, the Commission can try to predetermine the form of instructions in subsequent negotiations (Elgström 2009). The fact that the Commission is, on practically all trade matters, conducting the negotiations also gives it a substantial information and knowledge advantage over the Parliament and, albeit to a lesser degree, the Council (see for example Dür 2006; Dür and Zimmermann 2007). This creates necessary room for manoeuvre for the Commission in its negotiating strategy. Considering the competing interests of 27 diverging Member States, this leeway also substantially helps the Commission find outcomes acceptable to the Council and the Parliament. The Commission tends – usually rather successfully – to frame the discussions in the approval process *inter alia* through presenting detailed summaries of the content of the deal negotiated and its benefits.

The Council is solely responsible for authorizing and setting the objectives for the negotiations. For the most part, however, the Council tends to make only limited changes to the Commission's proposed mandates. One reason for this is that the mandate is usually preceded by a lengthy and symbiotic process of reflection between the Commission and the Council, including through feasibility studies and 'scoping exercises' with prospective trading partners. Another reason is that a Commission objection to any amendment to its proposal can only be overridden by a unanimous Council. On the other hand, for mandates covering areas of shared competence, any single Member State can block authorization. In the face of such potential deadlocks between the Commission and the Council, the tendency has been to keep mandates general on the EU's offensive interests in line with the Commission's original proposal, while making certain amendments to cater for specific Member States' defensive concerns.

Equally important is, however, that the Council can effectively supervise the Commission even after the mandate has been adopted. According to the Treaty, the Council shall assist the Commission during trade negotiations. This is done by the so-called Trade Policy Committee (TPC, former 133 or 113 Committee). In principle, any formal positions and proposals of the EU have to be discussed in the TPC before being submitted to negotiating partners. The Committee exists in various formations[2] and meets at least on a weekly basis. In addition, once a month, its meetings involve capital-based Director Generals or Senior Officials. These features ensure not only that the Council's views are properly taken into account by the Commission, but also prevent any undue influence on trade policy of other parts of the Council, such as groups working on foreign policy. Informally, the Council's control in the negotiating phase is further enhanced by the fact that Member States can limit the 'information advantage' of the Commission. Many Member States are members of the international organizations or arrangements where negotiations take place (such as G8, G20, WTO, WIPO and OECD) as well as having their own diplomatic channels with relevant negotiating partners. In addition, the Council and the Commission have agreed on a number of informal arrangements that secure Member States' participation in some restrictive meetings, although these have been called into question with the advent of the Lisbon Treaty (on the role of the Council more generally, and its relation to the Commission, see Damro 2007; De Bièvre and Dür 2005; Kerremans 2006; Meunier 2000, 2005, 2007).

Finally, the Council adopts any final trade agreement. In practice, the Council generally refrains from blocking any final deals at that stage. This is largely due to the Member States' general sense of ownership of the negotiations derived from both their decision on the mandate and their close association with the negotiations through the TPC. Also important is the fact that the Council, due to Member States' own relations with third countries, tends to be wary of the effects of any negative decisions on the EU's international standing and credibility.

---

[2]   The different formations are, on a horizontal level, the Trade Policy Committee (TPC) – Full Members/Titulaires, as well as TPC deputies. In addition, there are three subgroups: TPC–services and investments, TPC–Steel, Textiles and Other Industrial Sectors (STIS) and TPC–Mutual Recognition Agreements. Besides the TPC, there is also a Council working group in charge of trade defence instruments and internal regulations, the so-called Working Party for Trade Questions (WPTQ).

The European Parliament, like the Council, needs to give its consent to all trade deals before they can enter into force. Contrary to the Council, however, it has no formal role in the authorization to launch negotiations. Similarly, the Parliament's role during the negotiating phase is limited to one of information – it has no specific role, as in the case of the TPC, in assisting the Commission – though it can and does debate negotiations in order to send political signals.

Informally, however, the Parliament can exert political influence, especially on the Commission, both with regard to the negotiating directives and in the negotiation phase, by exploiting the fact that its consent is needed for any final deal. Also, the mere fact that the Parliament's statements are public (as opposed to Council negotiating directives) makes it more difficult to disregard them at the negotiating phase. At the same time, however, the Parliament's influence tends to be more occasional and limited to issues which it considers politically significant, given its extensive legislative agenda and its limited expert knowledge on trade matters, which makes it more dependent on the information provided by the Commission.

As for the approval process, the Council and the Parliament are – at first glance – equals. But there are important differences in the Council's and Parliament's respective roles which influence their relative weight. First, the process is sequential. Only if and when the Council has authorized the signature of the agreement will the Parliament be asked to give its consent. Also, whereas the Parliament's consent is provided by simple majority vote, the decision by the Council is taken by QMV only for deals covering matters of EU exclusive competence, while unanimity is required for all other trade deals (even if the elements of shared or Member States' competence constitute a small part of the total deal). And if an agreement goes beyond exclusive competence, each Member State will also have to finalize their domestic ratification process (normally by national parliaments) after the Parliament's consent and before the agreement can enter into full force. Finally, on all matters in a trade deal falling under EU exclusive competence, the Council could decide that these elements are to be provisionally applied even before the Parliament's consent, although the normal route is likely to be that provisional application will follow after the Parliament's views have been heard. Therefore, in the approval process, the Council usually carries more weight. But the Parliament can still block trade deals and, certainly on more politically sensitive issues, its consent may prove more difficult to obtain than that of the Council.

The Legislative Process for Trade Acts

Following the Lisbon Treaty, the process for trade acts is the same as for other internal legislation, the so-called ordinary legislative procedure (OLP). Only the Commission has the power to propose trade legislation, while the Council and the Parliament are co-legislatures.

The procedure has three steps. First, once the Commission has tabled its legislative proposal, the Committee on International Trade (INTA) prepares the

Parliament's position (by simple majority), including possible amendments to the proposal. Second, following discussions in relevant Council groups, the highest ranking preparatory body of the Council, the Permanent Representatives Committee or COREPER approves (by QMV) an agreed position on both the Commission proposal and the Parliament's amendments. Thereafter, negotiations are held between all three institutions where the Commission is represented by the relevant service, the Council by the rotating presidency and the Parliament by the 'rapporteur' (the MEP in charge of preparing the Parliament's position). The procedure is geared towards compromise. But whereas in the past it took a few months to adopt a trade act, OLP may require lengthy negotiations, sometimes extending over one or even a couple of years.

Council and the Parliament are formally equals in the OLP, but experience suggests the Parliament tends to be relatively more influential (Hix 1999: 91–8, although this has been disputed by some theoretical modelling). This is partly because the Parliament is first to present amendments to the draft trade act, but more importantly, because the Parliament is less constrained by the whole-of-government view of Member States and can exploit the collective action problem to secure concessions from both the Council and the Commission. Specifically, the Parliament has tended to have greater impact the longer the legislative process. To date, however, there have been no really lengthy OLPs related to trade acts.

Of course, not all EU trade acts or trade measures are subject to the OLP. This concerns in particular the various implementing acts adopted within the framework of existing trade regulations, such as decisions on anti-dumping duties, countervailing duties, safeguard measures, etc. While such trade decisions were in the past adopted by the Council, following the Lisbon Treaty they are nowadays subject to the general rules of the so-called comitology, whereby the Commission is able to adopt such implementing acts, provided it consults with and secures sufficient support by Member States (or, rather, it does not face overwhelming opposition by Member States). Neither the Council nor the Parliament has any role under this procedure.

Other Factors Influencing EU Trade Policymaking

Beyond the procedural features of EU trade policymaking, the characteristics of each EU institution influence its scope to exercise any formal power in the policymaking process (Dür 2006).

The Commission remains a predominantly technocratic body where its Commissioners lack any direct links to EU constituents. In contrast, the Parliament lacks technical expertise on most trade issues, but carries substantial political weight, especially over the Commission by its control over the Commission's budget. The Council is a hybrid – on the one hand, many Member States tend to have considerable expertise on trade matters and, on the other hand, the elected governments of Member States (especially the larger Member States and the rotating presidency) can – if mobilized – exert considerable political influence at

EU-level. Thereby, both the Parliament and the Council can increase their influence by raising the political stakes on a subject matter. Conversely, the Commission and sometimes Member States can make use of their knowledge advantages, especially compared to the Parliament, in all phases of policymaking. And through its formal detachment from national interests, the Commission can often act as an honest broker between the Council and the Parliament.

Similarly, the degree of internal cohesion or divisions influences the EU institutions' relative power. In the case of the Commission, the sheer number of Commissioners and Commission services involved in trade negotiations increases the risk of divisions. In addition, not least via the Commissioners, Member States can occasionally exert influence directly into internal Commission decision making, especially on politically sensitive issues. When the Commission is faced with such internal divisions and political pressure, its position is weakened (Damro 2007). However, in the case of the Council, Member States rarely see eye to eye on trade policy. On trade matters that do not require unanimity, these divisions usually play into the hands of the Commission (and those Member States allied with the Commission) whereas unanimity – provided there are Member States willing to exploit it – tends to allow the Council to exert relatively more influence (Elgström and Frennhoff Larsén 2010; Meunier and Nicholaïdis 1999). Also, in the Parliament internal divisions are the rule, not the exception. The Parliament is organized into 20 Committees, seven different parliamentary groups and has 736 Members from 27 Member States. The obvious collective action problems arising in such a large legislative body can be used as a tool in negotiations with the Commission and the Council in OLP. But it can equally work to the disadvantage of the Parliament when faced with strong political pressure, especially from Member States. In many instances, the national affiliation of parliamentarians remains stronger than their party affiliation. On important issues, therefore, Member States can substantially influence the positions of their respective parliamentarians and reduce the independent impact of the Parliament over policymaking.

In sum, the nature of the matters at stake, the level of political involvement and the degree of internal divisions in each EU institution – to name but a few factors – can substantially blur the more formal distribution of powers in trade policymaking. Specifically, the more technocratic and narrow a trade decision is the more power the Commission tends to have. In such circumstances, only Member States will have meaningful possibility of controlling and influencing the Commission. Conversely, the Council and the Parliament tend to gain in power the more political and comprehensive a trade decision becomes, even if the Commission can still usefully act as an honest broker. In these cases, relatively speaking, the Council tends to be more influential over trade agreements and the Parliament over trade legislations. In the rare instances when a trade matter is discussed at the highest political level in the G8 or G20, it is the Council and especially large Member States that play a predominant role.

The Politics of the EU Trade Policy: Old and New Tensions

As the scope, power and process of EU trade policy has evolved, so has its politics. Besides the traditional tensions between openness and protectionism, EU trade policy has increasingly been subject to contentious debates over its relationship with the broader objectives of the EU's external relations, as well as other domestic priorities (Baldwin 2006; Young 2007; Young and Peterson 2006).

Liberalism versus Protectionism

The underlying principle of EU trade policy, as set out in the Treaty, is liberal. Compared with many of its trading partners, the EU market is also relatively open for both trade and investment and the EU has, in recent years, increasingly aspired to assume a leadership role in international negotiations (Bretherton and Vogler 2006; Dür 2008a; Ladefoged Mortensen 2009; Van den Hoven 2006).

At the same time, a number of specific elements of the union's trade policy clearly reflect a more protectionist and inward-looking premise. Besides the often-quoted example of agricultural trade, the EU has also traditionally pursued a mainly defensive trade policy in a number of specific sectors, such as fisheries, steel, textiles, clothing and footwear, consumer electronics as well as – albeit perhaps less so – automotives. Naturally, therefore, some of the more difficult trade policy discussions have been in these areas. This remains the case today, as illustrated by the heated discussions on the EU's agricultural offers in the DDA and in the negotiations with MERCOSUR, on the automotive concessions in the Korea FTA, as well as on the EU's use of trade defence instruments (on TDIs, see Davis 2009; Erixon 2007).

Such tensions between liberalism and protectionism arise both between and within each of the different EU institutions. On balance, the Commission tends to be relatively liberal, the Council more middle-ground, and the Parliament more protectionist. These differences can partly be explained by the Commission's and the Council's direct links with trading partners; partly the Commission's relative insulation from constituents; and partly the Parliament's accessibility to lobbying without, as in the case of Member States or the Commission, the balance provided by in-house technical expertise and the necessity to take a whole-of-government view (see Kerremans and Gistelinck 2009, on comparison between Council and US Congress).

Nevertheless, the divisions are, in many instances, more profound within each of the EU institutions than between them. This is not least the case of the Council. Member States are usually divided between the 'Northern Liberals' that seek a more open trade position, and the 'Club Med' that is particularly preoccupied by foreign competition in specific sectors. The former group consists of the United Kingdom, Netherlands, Sweden, Denmark, Estonia and the Czech Republic, as well as – depending on the issue – Germany, Finland, Ireland, Austria, Slovenia and Latvia. The latter group is represented at its core by France, Italy, Greece,

Portugal and, even if it has become more liberally inclined, Spain. Other Member States that tend to have similar, or even coordinated, positions with Club Med are Poland, Lithuania, Romania, Bulgaria and Hungary, whereas Slovakia, Malta, Cyprus, Belgium and Luxembourg usually take the middle ground. The exact composition of the Council alliances will vary with the matter at stake: Ireland, for example, follows the Club Med line on agriculture. But these divisions among Member States are still broadly valid (Evenett and Vermulst 2005).

In the Commission, divisions and alliances can reflect those of the Council, in particular at the level of Commissioners and on more sensitive issues. However, the more common tensions over liberalism versus protectionism within the Commission arise in the relations between the trade and external services and the services in charge of agriculture, fisheries and industry (Damro 2007). In the Parliament, while alliances are normally meant to be built around party lines, divisions are also commonplace following national lines, as in the case of the Council, or following thematic lines (between different Parliamentary Committees), as in the case of the Commission.

In recent years, the tensions between liberalism and protectionism in EU policymaking have also evolved. Particularly with the growth of advanced developing countries, the focus of the debate in the EU has broadly shifted to the issue of reciprocity or a 'level playing field'. Many Member States and their MEPs, especially from the Club Med and some of the recently acceded Member States, are increasingly calling for concrete actions to address the situation, as they see it, that the EU is far more open than key trading partners.

This newer version of the traditional tension – now in the form of openness versus reciprocity – was one of the key aspects that the Commission tried to address, first in the trade strategy 'Global Europe' from 2006 as well as, more recently, in its communication on the future of EU trade policy in November 2010 and its communication on trade, growth and development in January 2012. The underlying political tradeoff presented here is between continued openness at home that is necessary to support EU growth and prosperity, and increased EU assertiveness abroad, especially against emerging economic powers, that is necessary to sustain public acceptance of open trade. This basic tradeoff has so far enjoyed considerable support in the EU. But it is politically unstable. After all, the delivery of the more assertive ambitions takes time and, to the extent it requires negotiations, the EU cannot guarantee equal access to third markets. Faced with what is portrayed as a persistent absence of fair and equitable trade, there is already a growing willingness in certain quarters of all EU institutions to favour a selective reduction in EU openness. The last years' financial and economic crisis has arguably only heightened these tensions.

Traditionalism versus Modernity

The trade policy of the EU today, like that of many other countries, touches upon areas that are at the heart of how states organize themselves and the instruments they have at their disposal for fulfilling different societal needs – nationally as well as globally. In the last two decades therefore, stimulated by the debate over globalization, new political tensions over the EU trade policy have arisen, often linked to social, environmental and developmental policies, as well as the EU's external relations more generally. Among the issues that have received much public attention are the accessibility and affordability of medicines, the temporary access of foreign workers, health and water services, national or indigenous rights in the extraction of natural resources, protection of the environment and biodiversity, the multifunctionality of European agriculture, and matters of personal integrity or internet freedom. In the broadest sense, these tensions are between the traditional core focus of trade policy and a modern or more comprehensive approach to trade.

In the EU, all institutions have adopted this more or less comprehensive outlook on trade policy. For many years already, the Commission and the Council have responded to the need to modernize trade policy by explicitly recognizing that EU trade deals – besides furthering trade openness – can and should also help manage globalization, extend EU values and promote mutually sustainable development (De Bièvre 2006; Falke 2005; Farrell 2007; Grynberg and Qalo 2006; Heydon and Woolcock 2009; Holmes 2006; Jacoby and Meunier 2010; Jones 2006; Meunier 2007; Woolcock 2007). On that basis, for example, the regulatory objectives of the EU are now an integral part of its trade policy, not least in bilateral negotiations. The EU has also granted special and differential treatment to developing countries and included environmental and labour provisions in its agreements. In addition, the EU has pursued association agreements that incorporate trade as well as development cooperation (technical assistance) and political cooperation as, for example, with its neighbouring countries, the ACP countries and Central America (on EU position with ACP, see Elgström 2009). Since the mid-1990s, the EU has also required that all EU preferential trade agreements either include or are linked to political clauses, such as on human rights, democracy and – more recently – weapons of mass destruction, as well as provide for the suspension of trade benefits in the case of noncompliance with these political clauses (Szymanski and Smith 2005 illustrate this in the EU–Mexico FTA).

The Lisbon Treaty also explicitly recognizes that EU trade policy shall be guided by the objectives and principles of the Union's foreign actions. But the Lisbon Treaty remains silent on how this should be achieved. In consequence, there are growing and important differences between and within the EU institutions on what are legitimate societal interests and how best to promote them through trade policy, especially in relation to developing countries.

For the Commission and the Council at large, a modern and comprehensive approach has never equalled the subordination of trade policy to other policy objectives – rather these should be mutually supportive (Zimmermann 2007, 2008). In the Parliament, however, calls have been made for the Lisbon Treaty to require something different and new from the EU's trade policy. There is also much more widespread scepticism of the possibility of a mutually reinforcing relationship between trade liberalization, on the one hand, and the promotion of *inter alia* poverty-reduction, environment or labour standards, on the other hand. Similarly, it has been suggested that trade rules are too intrusive on developing countries' policy space or indeed on the freedom of citizens in Europe. This scepticism is shared by a number of European NGOs, as illustrated not least by the debate over the EU's Economic Partnership Agreements (EPAs) with the African, Caribbean and Pacific (ACP) countries and the Anti-Counterfeiting Trade Agreement (ACTA), as concerns enforcement of intellectual property (on EPAs, see Flint 2008; Koné 2010; Meyn 2006; Oxfam International 2006; Stevens 2008; Thallinger 2007, and for a more positive account, Curran et al. 2008; Farrell 2007; Sauvé and Ward 2009). In addition, many Parliamentarians (and NGOs) tend to be equally sceptical of, or indeed directly opposed to, the conclusion of trade agreements with countries that have poor human rights records or otherwise are considered politically inappropriate.

New tensions surrounding the EU's comprehensive trade policy objectives have also arisen in other – and partly conflicting – ways. Not least some newer Member States and their MEPs have increasingly questioned the continuation of the generous treatment that the EU offers imports from developing countries (Meyn 2008). It has been pointed out that the EU provides preferences to countries that have higher GDP per capita than some EU Member States. Combined with the growing calls for reciprocity, this constitutes a considerable challenge to the future development of the EU's various unilateral preference schemes, but also potentially its position in trade negotiations more generally.

Clear Conscience Protectionism?

A much less noticed development in the politics of trade has occurred entirely outside the realm of EU trade policymakers. This concerns the growing readiness of the EU to use the access to its internal market as a lever to force changes in third countries through the extraterritorial application of domestic regulations and requirements (Falke 2005).

In recent years, the EU has developed a number of internal regulations that ban or restrict what are deemed inappropriate economic activities – irrespective of where these activities occur. In some instances, the driving force has been public morality, like the ban in 2009 on the sale, import and transit of seal products. In other cases, the objective has been to use selected trade obstacles to force companies to avoid certain practices or production methods on a global scale, such as the ban on the sale of illegally logged wood products, sustainability criteria for bioethanol and palm oil, the ban on fish products derived from illegal, unregulated or unregistered fishing, as well as the proposed ban on cloned animals and their offspring.

Of course, there is nothing new about the imposition of domestic regulations which may be considered trade irritants by third countries. However, the novelty lies in fact that regulatory initiatives are increasingly justified by the effects that they should have on economic activities outside the borders of the EU – not by their effects on EU consumers.

One obvious reason for this development is the compelling nature of the matters at hand. After all, the problems of illegal logging or illegal fishing are global challenges that require immediate and decisive actions.

Another reason, however, is the strength of the alliances inside the EU between those caring acutely about the need to address a global challenge or to export European 'values' and those finding the proposed regulations convenient to protect defensive interests. For example, the ban on illegal fish imports was agreed without any additional measures to reform the EU fisheries agreements with developing countries or to curtail the overfishing by the heavily subsidized EU fishing fleet. Similarly, the ban on illegal logging was adopted without either any parallel steps to improve the preservation policies of Member States or any serious upscaling of the EU's support to developing countries' forestry agencies.

The Parliament in particular has been driving this novel development, although alliances with specific Member States in the Council, combined with the lobbying of a few powerful NGOs, have been instrumental in pushing through the regulations. Interestingly, the private sector has been unable to exert any meaningful influence and the developmental NGOs have, to date, stayed clear of the debate despite the impact on developing country exports. Among Member States, paradoxically, some of the main champions of this development can be found among the Northern Liberals, albeit with support from the Club Med countries.

On domestic regulations, there is thus arguably an increasing trend in the EU towards 'clear conscience protectionism'. The irony is that the EU appears to be increasingly replicating the extraterritorial approach of the US Congress – of which the EU has in the past been among the strongest critics.

Future Challenges for EU Trade Policy

While the Lisbon Treaty is likely to have far less effect on the Commission and the Council than is sometimes claimed, the inclusion of the Parliament in all aspects of trade policymaking represents a fundamental departure from past practice. Although it is too early to assess the full implications of this change, there are reasons to expect that its effects will be significant, also for the Union's trading partners.

Regarding the content of EU trade policy, the involvement of the Parliament is likely to pave the way for increased (albeit probably selective) protectionism and reciprocity, especially for traditionally sensitive sectors, as well as for greater emphasis on the relationship between trade and other policy areas, not least social issues, environmental concerns and respect for human rights.

Regarding the formulation of trade policy, the inclusion of the Parliament has increased the accessibility of EU trade policymaking. Trade policy is likely to become more transparent, also providing better opportunity for EU-level public debates and scrutiny of the Union's trade policy actions, although possibly at the expense of national debates and the scrutiny of national parliaments. The other side of this coin is, of course, that trade policymaking is also likely to become more burdensome, complex, politically contentious and, ultimately, inefficient.

From this perspective, EU trade policy is at a critical juncture: efficiency risks being sacrificed at the altar of representational legitimacy.

The key future challenge is what could be done to restore efficiency, also taking into account that the EU still derives much of its public approval from the benefits that citizens derive from its decisions, rather than the method by which the decisions were taken. Merely continuing on the path of expanding EU competence is unlikely to do the trick. Instead, real and effective solutions may require establishing genuine executive powers for the Commission to conclude certain trade deals, as well as formalizing more expedite procedures for the Council's and the Parliament's adoption of trade legislations. But such solutions would be controversial. The question, therefore, is whether the EU needs to go through a period, at least for the coming years, of internal divisions and possible deadlocks before EU trade policy can become more forward-looking, efficient and legitimate.

References

Baldwin, M. 2006. EU trade politics – heaven or hell? *Journal of European Public Policy*, 13(6): 926–42.

Bretherton, C. and Vogler, J. 2006. The EU as an economic power and trade actor, in *The European Union as a Global Actor*. 2nd Edition. London: Routledge: Chapter 3.

Curran, L., Nilsson, L. and Brew, D. 2008. The economic partnership agreements: rationale, misperceptions and non-trade aspects. *Development Policy Review*, 26(5): 529–53.

Damro, C. 2007. EU delegation and agency in international trade negotiations: a cautionary comparison. *Journal of Common Market Studies*, 45(4): 883–903.

Davis, L. 2009. Ten years of antidumping in the EU: economic and political targeting. *ECIPE Working Paper* 2/2009. Brussels: ECIPE.

De Bièvre, D. 2006. The EU regulatory trade agenda and the quest for WTO enforcement. *Journal of European Public Policy*, 13(6): 851–66.

De Bièvre, D. and Dür, A. 2005. Constituency interests and delegation in European and American trade policy. *Comparative Political Studies*, 38(10): 1271–96.

De Bièvre, D. and Eckhardt, J. 2010. The political economy of EU anti-dumping reform. *ECIPE Working Paper* 03/2010. Brussels: ECIPE.

De Bièvre, D. and Eckhardt, J. 2011. Interest groups and the failure of EU anti-dumping reform. *Journal of European Public Policy*, 18(3). [Online] Available at: www.ua.ac.be/main.aspx?c=dirk.debievre [accessed: 24 January 2011].

Dimopoulos, A. 2008. The Common Commercial Policy after Lisbon: establishing parallelism between internal and external economic policy? *Croatian Yearbook of European Law and Policy*, 4: 102–31.

Dür, A. 2006. Assessing the EU's role in international trade negotiations. *European Political Science*, 5: 362–75.

Dür, A. 2007. EU trade policy as protection for exporters: the agreements with Mexico and Chile. *Journal of Common Market Studies*, 45(4): 833–55.

Dür, A. 2008a. Bargaining power and trade liberalization: European external trade policies in the 1960s. *European Journal of International Relations*, 14(4): 645–69.

Dür, A. 2008b. Bringing economic interests back into the study of EU trade policy-making. *British Journal of Politics and International Relations*, 10(1): 27–45.

Dür, A. and De Bièvre, D. 2007. Inclusion without influence? NGOs in European trade policy. *Journal of Public Policy*, 27(1): 79–101.

Dür, A. and Zimmermann, H. (eds). 2007. Introduction: the EU in international trade negotiations. *Journal of Common Market Studies*, 45(4): 771–87.

Elgström, O. 2009. Trade and aid? The negotiated construction of EU policy on economic partnership agreements. *International Politics*, 46(4): 451–68.

Elgström, O. and Frennhoff Larsén, M. 2010 Free to trade? Commission autonomy in the economic partnership agreement negotiations. *Journal of European Public Policy*, 17(2): 205–23.

Elsig, M. 2007. The EU's choice of regulatory venues for trade negotiations: Aa tale of agency power? *Journal of Common Market Studies*, 45(4): 927–48.

Elsig, M. 2008. EU trade policy after enlargement: does the expanded trade power have new clothes? Paper for the APSA Annual Conference, Boston, 28–31 August.

Erixon, F. 2007. Anti-dumping in the European Union, in *Anti-Dumping: Global Abuse of a Trade Policy Instrument*, edited by B. Debroy and D. Chakraborty. New Delhi: Academic Foundation: 119–32.

Evenett, S. and Vermulst, E. 2005. The politicisation of EC anti-dumping policy: Member States, their votes and the European Commission. *The World Economy*, 28(5): 701–17.

Falke, A. 2005. EU–USA trade relations in the Doha Development Round: market access versus a post-modern trade policy agenda. *European Foreign Affairs Review*, 10(3): 339–57.

Farrell, M. 2007. From EU model to external policy? Promoting regional integration in the rest of the world, in *Making History: European Integration and Institutional Change at Fifty*, edited by S. Meunier and K. McNamara. Oxford: Oxford University Press: 299–315.

Flint, A. 2008. *Trade, Poverty and the Environment: The EU, Cotonou and the African–Caribbean–Pacific Bloc*. New York: Palgrave Macmillan.

Gerlach, C. 2006. Does business really run EU trade policy? Observations about EU trade policy lobbying. *Politics*, 26(3): 176–83.

Gillingham, J. 2003. *European Integration 1950–2003: Superstate or New Market Economy?* New York: Cambridge University Press.

Grynberg, R. and Qalo V. 2006. Labour standards in US and EU preferential trading arrangements. *Journal of World Trade*, 40(4): 619–53.

Heydon, K. and Woolcock, S. 2009. Key findings and looking ahead, in *The Rise of Bilateralism: Comparing American, European and Asian Approaches to Preferential Trade Agreements*. Tokyo: United Nations University Press: 231–66.

Hix, S. 1999. *The Political System of the European Union*. London: Macmillian Press.

Holmes, P. 2006. Trade and domestic policies: the European mix. *Journal of European Public Policy*, 13(6): 815–31.

Jacoby, W. and Meunier, S. 2010. Europe and the management of globalization. *Journal of European Public Policy*, 17(3): 299–317.

Jones, E. 2006. Europe's market liberalization is a bad model for a global trade agenda. *Journal of European Public Policy*, 13(6): 943–57.

Kerremans, B. 2006. Proactive policy entrepreneur or risk minimizer? A principal–agent interpretation of the EU's role in the WTO, in *The European Union's Roles in International Politics*, edited by O. Elgström and M. Smith. Oxford: Routledge: 172–88.

Kerremans, B. and Gistelinck, M.M. 2009. Interest aggregation, political parties, labour standards and trade: differences in the US and EU approaches to the inclusion of labour standards in international trade agreements. *European Foreign Affairs Review*, 14: 683–701.

Koné, S. 2010. Economic partnership agreement between West Africa and the European Union in the context of the World Trade Organization (WTO) and the regional integration process. *Journal of Economic Integration*, 25(1): 104–28.

Ladefoged Mortensen, J. 2009. The World Trade Organization and the European Union, in *The European Union and International Organisations*, edited by K.E. Jørgensen. London: Routledge: 156–99.

Meunier, S. 2000. What single voice? European institutions and EU–US trade negotiations. *International Organization*, 54(1): 103–35.

Meunier, S. 2005. *Trading Voices: The European Union in International Commercial Negotiation*. Princeton: Princeton University Press.

Meunier, S. 2007. Managing globalization? The EU in international trade negotiations. *Journal of Common Market Studies*, 45(4): 905–26.

Meunier, S. and Nicholaïdis, K. 1999. Who speaks for Europe? The delegation of trade authority in the EU. *Journal of Common Market Studies*, 37(3): 477–501.

Meyn, M. 2006. *The Impact of EU Free Trade Agreements on Economic Development and Regional Integration in Southern Africa: The Example of EU–SACU Trade Relations*. Bremen: Peter Lang.

Meyn, M. 2008. EPAs: A 'historic step' towards a 'partnership for equals'? *Development Policy Review*, 26(5): 515–28.

Oxfam International. 2006. Slamming the door on development: analysis of the EU's response to the Pacific's EPA negotiating proposals. *Oxfam Background Paper*, December 2006.

Sauvé, P. and Ward, N. 2009. The EC–CARIFORUM economic partnership agreement: assessing the outcome on services and investment. *ECIPE Paper*, January 2009. Brussels: ECIPE.

Shaffer, G. 2006. What's new in EU trade dispute settlement? Judicialization, public–private networks and the WTO legal order. *Journal of European Public Policy*, 13(6): 832–50.

Stevens, C. 2008. Economic partnership agreements: what can we learn? *New Political Economy*, 13(2): 211–23.

Szymanski, M. and Smith, M.E. 2005. Coherence and conditionality in European foreign policy: negotiating the EU–Mexico global agreement. *Journal of Common Market Studies*, 43(1): 171–92.

Thallinger, G. 2007. From apology to utopia: EU–ACP economic partnership agreements oscillating between WTO conformity and sustainability. *European Foreign Affairs Review*, 12(4): 499–516.

Van den Hoven, A. 2006. European Union regulatory capitalism and multilateral trade negotiations, in *Values and Principles in European Union Foreign Policy*, edited by S. Lucarelli and I. Manners. London: Routledge: 185–200.

Woolcock, S. 2002. Utvecklingen av EU's handelspolitik, in *Handelspolitik i förändring: Organisation och förhandling i Sverige, EU och WTO*, edited by J. Reiter and C. Jönsson, Stockholm: SNS Förlag: 73–92.

Woolcock, S. 2007. European Union policy towards free trade agreements. *ECIPE Working Paper No. 03/2007*. Brussels: ECIPE

Woolcock, S. 2008. The potential impact of the Lisbon Treaty on European Union external trade policy. *SIEPS 2008:8epa*. Stockholm: Swedish Institute for European Policy Studies.

Woolcock, S. 2010a. The Treaty of Lisbon and the European Union as an actor in international trade. *ECIPE Working Paper No. 1/2010*. Brussels: ECIPE.

Woolcock, S. 2010b. Trade policy: a further shift towards Brussels, in *Policy Making in the European Union*, 6th Edition, edited by M. Pollack, A.R. Young and H. Wallace. Oxford: Oxford University Press: 381–99.

Young, A.R. 2007. Trade politics ain't what it used to be: the European Union in the Doha Round. *Journal of Common Market Studies*, 45(4): 789–811.

Young, A.R. and Peterson, J. 2006. The EU and the new trade politics. *Journal of European Public Policy*, 13(6): 795–814.

Zimmermann, H. 2007. Realist power Europe? The EU in the negotiations about China's and Russia's WTO accession. *Journal of Common Market Studies*, 45(4): 813–32.

Zimmermann, H. 2008. How the EU negotiates trade and democracy: the cases of China's accession to the WTO and the Doha Round. *European Foreign Affairs Review*, 13(2): 255–80.

Trade Policymaking
in Latin America

Alejandro Jara and Sebastian Herreros[1]

Introduction

This chapter focuses on the evolution of trade policy in Latin America in the last two decades. The first section briefly describes the region's trade policies since the early twentieth century. The second section examines some recent trends in the region's trade. The third section discusses Latin America's economic integration efforts, including through negotiations with extra-regional partners. The fourth section looks at Latin American countries' participation in the multilateral trading system and the fifth section concludes.

Historical Overview

At the turn of the twentieth century, and up to the Great Depression, Latin America was highly integrated into the world economy. The region's economies were relatively open and derived most of their export income from primary products (such as wheat, meat, nitrate, rubber, sugar and coffee), while the industrial sector was little developed. The devastating effects of the Great Depression, compounded by the disruption of supplies during the Second World War, encouraged industrialization policies across the region. These included high tariff and non-tariff barriers to imports and the provision of credit by the state to selected industries. This strategy of import-substitution industrialization (ISI) prevailed in most of the region until the 1980s.

---

[1]   The opinions are the personal responsibility of the authors and do not represent the views or positions of the United Nations Economic Commission for Latin America and the Caribbean (ECLAC) and the World Trade Organization (WTO), respectively.

As Latin American countries were transitioning from predominantly agrarian to mostly urban societies, the emerging working and middle classes – made up largely of industrial workers and state employees – supported the new ISI strategy and prevailed over the interests of the region's traditional exporting sectors, agriculture and mining. ISI was also underpinned by proposals from the United Nations (UN) Economic Commission for Latin America and the Caribbean (ECLAC), created in 1948.

The ISI strategy was instrumental in the creation of several basic industries such as steel and cement, as well as in absorbing the workforce that left the farms for the cities. However, it hampered the absorption of new technologies and knowledge embodied in imports, thus impacting negatively on overall efficiency and productivity levels. It also led to the development of numerous uncompetitive industries across the region, which could nevertheless survive in the absence of international competition. Overvalued exchange rates were common and resulted in a severe anti-export bias, which was compounded by policies selectively channelling credit to industry to the detriment of agriculture and mining. As will be seen in the third section of this chapter, some attempts were made at overcoming these limitations through economic integration.

By the mid-1970s, most Latin American economies had restrictive trade policies, characterized by high average tariffs, a large variance in tariff levels and numerous non-tariff barriers, complemented by price controls and multiple exchange rate regimes. Partly as a result of the inefficiencies created by ISI, Latin America failed to achieve sustained growth and significantly reduce income inequality and poverty (Corbo 2008).

The debt crisis that hit the region in 1982 prompted the abandonment of ISI.[2] Faced with a severe reversal of capital inflows and the loss of access to international private capital markets, many Latin American countries underwent dramatic falls in gross domestic product (GDP), coupled with currency and financial crises. For some, international financial institutions like the International Monetary Fund (IMF) and the World Bank became the main sources of capital. These institutions thus acquired increased leverage to promote market-led policy reforms that went beyond restoring macroeconomic stability.

Along with the privatization of state-owned enterprises and a deregulation of economic activity, the reduction of trade barriers was a key component of the reforms of the 1980s. The reduction of the anti-export bias of ISI was made more pressing by the need to increase export income to service the region's high foreign debt. Table 25.1 illustrates, for the seven largest Latin American economies, the deep reduction of import tariffs that has taken place since the mid-1980s across the region.

---

[2]   The exception is Chile, which abandoned ISI in the mid-1970s, under the military dictatorship that took power in 1973 (Herreros 2009).

Table 25.1   Simple average most-favoured-nation applied tariffs in selected LAC countries (in percentages)

	1985–1989	1990–1994	1995–1999	2000–2004	2005–2008
Argentina	27.5	13.9	14.7	14.0	10.7
Brazil	45.8	21.0	15.1	14.7	12.5
Chile	18.0	11.8	10.7	7.0	6.0
Colombia	29.4	16.6	12.7	12.2	11.2
Mexico	16.7	12.8	14.1	16.1	7.9
Peru	45.8	17.2	13.9	11.0	7.5
Venezuela, BR	31.1	15.8	13.0	13.0	12.3

Source: Data on Trade and Import Barriers, World Bank.

As a result of these reforms, including those aimed at attracting foreign direct investment (FDI), Latin American economies generally became more open. This is especially the case in Chile, Peru and Mexico that have gone furthest in trade liberalization (see Table 25.2).

Table 25.2   Merchandise trade (exports plus imports) as a percentage of GDP in selected LAC countries

	1980	1985	1990	1995	2000	2005	2008
Argentina	24	14	12	16	18	38	39
Brazil	19	18	12	13	18	22	24
Chile	38	42	51	45	50	63	77
Colombia	26	22	31	26	26	29	32
Mexico	21	25	32	54	60	53	57
Peru	31	25	22	25	27	38	48
Venezuela, BR	46	39	53	42	42	55	46

Source: World Development Indicators, World Bank.

The bulk of trade liberalization in Latin America has been unilateral. Reciprocal trade agreements have become an important factor since the 1990s, first with a renewed momentum in regional integration along with the results of the Uruguay Round of multilateral trade negotiations and later as several countries engaged in preferential trade agreements (PTAs) with extra-regional partners.[3]

---

[3]   PTAs form a very broad category in terms of their product, sectoral and thematic coverage as well as the depth of the commitments undertaken by their members. They include Free Trade Agreements (FTAs) as well as more limited agreements. Henceforth the FTA acronym will be used to refer only to agreements specifically described as such by their signatories.

During the past decade, there has been an erosion of support for trade liberalization in some Latin American countries. Most notably, in 2004 Cuba and Venezuela formed the Bolivarian Alliance for the Peoples of Our America (ALBA), adopting an openly critical stance towards capitalism in general, including free trade. Subsequently, other countries joined ALBA: Bolivia in 2006; Nicaragua in 2007; Dominica in 2008; Antigua and Barbuda in 2009; Ecuador in 2009; and St. Vincent and the Grenadines in 2009. ALBA is not a 'classic' trade agreement as it is largely based on voluntary cooperative undertakings by its members, such as barter of oil for agricultural products or even medical services.

Disenchantment with trade liberalization seems to be part of a broader erosion of support for market-based reforms. This has happened despite the fact that between 2003 and 2008 the region's GDP grew at an average 5 per cent a year, its strongest performance since the 1970s, along with a reduction in poverty (from 44 per cent to 33 per cent) and unemployment (from 11 per cent to 7.4 per cent) (Barcena 2010). It has been argued that an important reason for this is that large segments of the region's population did not feel included in the benefits from growth (Rojas-Suarez 2010). In fact, despite its recent good performance, Latin America continues to be one of the world's most unequal regions (Barcena 2010). In contrast, successful reform in other countries has translated into political support allowing for further liberalization, whether unilateral or based on reciprocal arrangements, as shown by Mexico, the Central American countries, Colombia, Peru and Chile.

Latin America's Trade at a Glance

The past decade has seen the share of Latin America and the Caribbean (LAC) in world merchandise trade register a small decrease, whereas its share in world trade in commercial services fell more sharply. This stands in contrast with the significant gains made by developing countries as a whole and especially by developing Asia during the same period. In the case of merchandise trade, Latin America's weak performance is explained almost exclusively by the substantial drop in the share in world trade of Mexico, the region's largest exporter. This loss was compensated by the gains made by Brazil and all other major economies in the region. In the case of trade in commercial services, Mexico's share also fell, but so did those of other major Latin American economies (although not Brazil's) (see Table 25.3).

The stagnation of Latin America's share in world merchandise exports mirrors the loss of dynamism of the region's exports during the past decade when compared to the previous one. Consistent with the results in Table 25.3, this trend is reversed – and the region's export performance shows an improvement – if Mexico is excluded (see Figure 25.1)

While LAC exports of primary products (measured by value) grew much faster in the past decade as compared to the 1990s, the opposite happened with the region's exports of manufactures. This result is heavily influenced by both the high prices registered by several commodities during most of the past decade and the

Table 25.3 **Shares of developing economies, regions and selected countries in world trade, 2000 and 2008 (in percentages)**

	Share in world merchandise trade				Share in world commercial services trade			
	Exports		Imports		Exports		Imports	
	2000	2008	2000	2008	2000	2008	2000	2008
Developing economies	30.6	38.1	27.8	34.1	24.5	27.3	27.6	31.6
LAC	5.8	5.7	5.9	5.7	4.1	3.4	4.9	4.1
Brazil	0.9	1.3	0.9	1.1	0.6	0.8	1.1	1.3
Mexico	2.7	1.9	2.8	2.0	0.9	0.5	1.2	0.7
Developing Europe	0.6	1.1	1.1	1.8	1.7	1.6	0.7	0.8
Africa	2.4	3.5	2.0	2.9	2.1	2.3	2.6	3.5
Middle East	4.3	6.5	2.5	3.6	2.3	2.6	3.4	4.8
Developing Asia[a]	17.6	21.3	16.3	20.2	14.3	17.4	16.0	18.4

Note: [a] Excluding re-exports and imports for re-export by Hong Kong, China.
Source: WTO (2010).

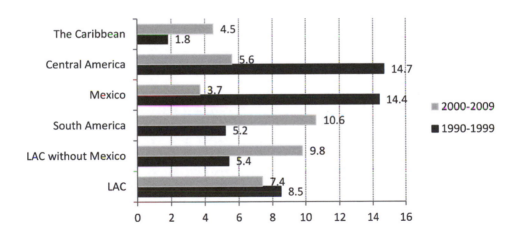

Figure 25.1 **Evolution of total LAC merchandise exports by value, 1990–1999 and 2000–2009 (average annual growth rates)**
Source: ECLAC (2010).

dramatic fall (of almost 90 per cent) in the average rate of expansion of Mexican manufacturing exports, a phenomenon that also affected Central America (see Table 25.4).

Table 25.4   LAC: Evolution of exports of primary products and manufactures by value, 1990–1999 and 2000–2009 (average annual growth rates)

	Primary products		Manufactures	
	1990–1999	2000–2009	1990–1999	2000–2009
LAC	2.6	11.4	14.7	5.3
South America	2.7	13.0	6.4	8.3
Mexico	1.8	6.3	27.3	2.9
Central America	6.4	4.9	19.8	7.8
The Caribbean	-1.4	12.2	4.8	2.9

Source: ECLAC (2010).

As a result of the divergent paths followed by LAC exports of primary products and manufactures, the share of the former category in the region's total exports by value increased by more than ten percentage points during the last decade, reaching nearly 40 per cent. If resource-based manufactures are added, their combined share in total LAC exports approaches 60 per cent (see Table 25.5).

Table 25.5   LAC: Breakdown of exports by value according to technological intensity, 1981–1982 to 2008–2009 (in percentages of total exports)

	1981–1982	1985–1986	1991–1992	1995–1996	1998–1999	2001–2002	2005–2006	2008–2009
Primary products	51.5	48.4	39.5	32.5	26.7	27.6	35.1	38.8
Resource-based manufactures	25.5	25.0	23.5	21.7	18.4	16.6	19.3	20.2
Low-technology manufactures	8.2	9.2	11.5	12.0	12.9	12.2	9.3	7.6
Medium-technology manufactures	11.6	13.6	20.1	24.4	26.7	26.8	23.9	21.5
High-technology manufactures	3.2	3.8	5.4	9.4	15.3	16.8	12.4	11.9

Note: Based on Sanjaya Lall's classification and 3-digit Standard International Trade Classification (SITC) categories.
Source: ECLAC (2010).

The clear shift in LAC exports towards primary products is consistent with the more dynamic performance of South America as compared with Mexico and Central America. Both elements are in turn directly related with a third major shift in LAC's trade: the emergence of Asia – and China in particular – as a key trade partner. As Table 25.6 shows, during the last decade, Asia's share in LAC exports tripled from 5 per cent to 15 per cent, whereas its share in the region's imports more than doubled from 11 per cent to 25 per cent. These gains have been mostly at the expense of the United States, which nevertheless continues to be the region's main individual trade partner.[4]

Asia's economic dynamism has resulted in sustained demand and high prices for commodities such as copper, iron ore, crude oil, wheat and soybeans, which are mostly exported by South American countries. On the other hand, the loss of dynamism of Mexican and Central American exports of manufactures is largely explained by increased competition from Asia (especially from China) in those countries' main market, the United States. The erosion of Mexico's and Central America's competitive position in the United States has occurred despite the trade preferences that both enjoy in that market as a result of FTAs.

Table 25.6   Share of main partners in LAC's trade, 2000 and 2006–2009 (in percentages)

Share of partners in LAC exports					
	2000	2006	2007	2008	2009
LAC	19.0	16.4	17.2	18.4	17.2
Asia	5.0	9.7	11.3	11.8	14.5
China	1.1	3.4	4.6	5.0	6.9
US	61.0	47.6	44.0	41.4	39.8
European Union	11.8	12.8	13.8	13.7	12.8
Share of partners in LAC imports					
	2000	2006	2007	2008	2009
LAC	15.1	18.9	19.1	18.9	18.8
Asia	10.9	22.2	23.0	23.5	24.9
China	1.8	8.4	9.6	10.4	11.8
US	55.0	32.4	30.3	29.0	29.2
European Union	12.1	12.8	13.3	13.5	13.8

Source: ECLAC (2010).

While Latin America's trade with regions such as Asia and Europe is mostly inter-industrial (that is, the region exports natural resources and imports manufactures), its intra-regional trade has a much larger intra-industry component, as the region's countries export manufactures to each other. However, intra-regional trade accounts for just 18 per cent of total Latin American trade, a much smaller share

---

4   This trend was reinforced by the recent global financial crisis, as LAC exports to the United States and the European Union fell much more dramatically in 2009 than those to Asia.

than in Asia and Europe, thus limiting its potential to upgrade the technological content and otherwise increase the value-added of the region's exports.[5]

Latin America's Main Trade Integration Efforts

The Latin American Free Trade Association

Latin American integration has, since independence, been an aspiration that has taken many shapes and forms. Besides the political rhetoric, since the 1960s the shortcomings of ISI provided the rationale to seek enlarged – yet still protected – markets through regional integration. At the time it was thought that freer trade within the region, coupled with high tariffs vis-à-vis third parties, would facilitate the achievement of economies of scale, thus overcoming the restriction imposed by the small size of most LAC economies.

In 1960, seven Latin American countries signed the Treaty of Montevideo establishing the Latin American Free Trade Association (LAFTA) with the long-term aim of becoming a common market.[6] Initially, a free trade area was to be established over 12 years through annual tariff cuts. This plan never went beyond the first instalment because of the resistance of sensitive sectors to external competition and the wide disparities in development levels among LAFTA members. However, LAFTA allowed some increase in the amount of intra-regional trade covered by preferences, while providing a temporary legal cover under the General Agreement on Tariffs and Trade (GATT).[7]

In 1980 LAFTA was replaced by the Latin American Integration Association (LAIA).[8] LAIA is essentially an umbrella agreement that provides a GATT cover to bilateral or plurilateral agreements among its members.[9] It also provides for limited regional preferences for some goods which have been largely superseded

---

[5]   Even among Central American countries, which are the most commercially integrated, the intra-regional trade ratio does not exceed 25 per cent.

[6]   LAFTA members were Argentina, Brazil, Chile, Mexico, Paraguay, Peru and Uruguay. By 1970, Bolivia, Ecuador, Colombia and Venezuela had also joined.

[7]   As an increasing number of Latin American countries acceded to the GATT, it became more necessary to justify their departures from the most-favoured-nation (MFN) obligation enshrined in GATT's Article I. LAFTA provided such justification by way of the exception to MFN granted to free trade areas and customs unions in GATT's Article XXIV.

[8]   The legal instrument establishing LAIA is the Treaty of Montevideo 1980. LAIA is better known by its Spanish acronym ALADI.

[9]   In 1979 the GATT contracting parties approved a decision, the 'Enabling Clause' (a Brazilian initiative), whereby developing countries may conclude preferential agreements that do not meet the requirements of Article XXIV.

by bilateral agreements. It has therefore not played a significant role in LAC efforts towards the liberalization of intra-regional trade over the last two decades.

The Andean Community (AC)

By the end of the 1960s the LAFTA was all but abandoned, as reflected by the creation in 1969 of the AC. Its founding members were Bolivia, Chile, Colombia and Ecuador, while Venezuela joined in 1973. Originally the AC was intended to become an economic union beyond the confines of trade policy. For example, it included sectoral industrial policies allocating specific lines of production to member states, as well as a common – but restrictive – foreign investment and intellectual property regime. Chile withdrew from the AC in 1976, following the military coup that resulted in a shift in its economic policies towards a market-driven approach (Herreros 2009).

The AC languished during the remainder of the 1970s and through the 1980s, while its member states experienced the severe effects of Latin America's 'lost decade' following the outbreak of the debt crisis in 1982. In the early 1990s, the AC was revamped, against the backdrop of the market-led reforms they had started implementing since the late 1980s. A free trade area for goods was established in 1993 and a common external tariff (CET) in 1995.[10] In 2006 a free trade area in services was attained, providing for national treatment and market access in most sectors.

The trade policy stances of AC members have diverged in recent years. While Colombia and Peru have maintained open trade policies and individually or jointly pursued FTAs with extra-regional partners, Bolivia and Ecuador have joined ALBA. Both countries have also enacted new constitutions that restrict their ability to include issues such as trade in services, investment, intellectual property and government procurement in trade negotiations.[11] Following Colombia and Peru's decisions to negotiate FTAs with the United States, Venezuela withdrew from the AC in 2006 and applied to join the Common Market of the South (MERCOSUR).[12] Against this background, AC members have focused their cooperation efforts on issues other than trade liberalization, thus straying from the goal of forming a customs union with a common trade policy.

---

[10]   Peru did not participate in the CET, while the other members enjoyed some exceptions. The CET did not prevent individual governments from concluding their own bilateral agreements with other Latin American countries.

[11]   In December 2009 Bolivia denounced its FTA with Mexico, which had been in force since 1995, due to the incompatibility between its new constitution and the agreement's chapters on services, investment, intellectual property and government procurement. The FTA was replaced by a new agreement covering only trade in goods.

[12]   At the time of writing, Venezuela's accession to MERCOSUR still had to be approved by Paraguay's Congress.

The Common Market of the South (MERCOSUR)

MERCOSUR was established in 1991 by Argentina, Brazil, Paraguay and Uruguay. Among its goals is the free circulation of goods, services and factors of production, along with the establishment of a CET and a common trade policy. By 1995 both duty-free trade among MERCOSUR members and the CET were achieved. However, tariffs remain for intra-MERCOSUR trade in the automotive sector and sugar. Moreover, trade remedies and non-tariff barriers such as non-automatic import licenses continue to be used, especially between Argentina and Brazil. As to the CET and common trade policy, they are somewhat undermined by national exceptions and the conclusion by individual MERCOSUR members of bilateral FTAs with other Latin American countries (for example the Uruguay–Mexico FTA). Some progress has been made towards liberalization of trade in services, a process foreseen to be completed in 2014. On government procurement, a protocol was agreed in 2004 providing for most-favoured-nation (MFN) and national treatment. However, as of March 2012 it is not yet in force. Trade disputes within MERCOSUR are often subject to diplomatic negotiations (with outcomes not necessarily based on the legal obligations binding the parties) rather than being settled through MERCOSUR's dispute settlement mechanisms.

MERCOSUR has concluded PTAs with all other South American countries. However, it has mostly refrained from seeking negotiations with its main extra-regional partners, except the European Union (EU).[13] This has largely been influenced by the strong defensive sensitivities of Argentina and – to a lesser extent – Brazil in the industrial sector. MERCOSUR has privileged trade agreements with developing partners such as India, Egypt and the South African Customs Union, or small economies like Israel. However, some of those agreements are limited in so far as tariffs are reduced – not eliminated – for a limited number of products and issues such as services and government procurement are not covered. It is often argued that these agreements have little commercial interest and respond mostly to foreign policy considerations (Marconini 2009).

The Central American Common Market (CACM)

Founded in 1960 by Costa Rica, El Salvador, Guatemala, Honduras and Nicaragua, the CACM has been successful in achieving free trade among its members and eliminating other barriers to trade. Most notably, Central American countries plus the Dominican Republic were able to negotiate a comprehensive FTA with the United States in 2005, the DR-CAFTA, covering trade in goods, services,

---

[13]   Negotiations towards an Association Agreement between MERCOSUR and the EU (including an FTA) were launched in 1999 and suspended in 2004, mostly due to the EU's agricultural sensitivities and those of MERCOSUR in industry. Negotiations resumed in June 2010 and are still ongoing.

investment and several other areas.[14] This agreement also applies between the Central American countries, thus superseding the corresponding provisions of the CACM.

In 2010 the CACM, this time along with Panama, also completed successfully negotiations towards an association agreement with the EU, which includes a comprehensive FTA. CACM members have equally been able to negotiate individually FTAs with other countries such as Canada, Chile, China, Mexico and Singapore.

Regionwide Initiatives

The early 1990s mark a turning point in trade policy and integration in Latin America. Democratic regimes coincided with the adoption of market-led economic policies across the region. This alignment of politics and economic policies resulted in a renewed interest in strengthening trade links between Latin American countries. It is within this context that MERCOSUR was created in 1991 and a free trade area established within the AC in 1993.

In 1991 Mexico and Chile concluded a free trade agreement (FTA), with very few products excluded. This was the first real FTA in the region, and it set a model for future negotiations by these and other Latin American countries. More importantly, it quickly led to agreements with and among other countries in the region. Exporters of countries not party to any such agreements pushed their governments to also conclude bilateral or plurilateral accords and thus avoid losing markets.

As a result of the dynamics set in motion in the early 1990s, today trade among Latin American countries is conducted mainly through a vast web of bilateral and plurilateral agreements (Table 25.7). While these pacts reflect an interest in freeing up intra-regional trade, the absence of a unified single market imposes significant transaction costs, including those derived from different regulatory regimes and rules of origin. Several initiatives to achieve convergence among these different agreements and integration schemes have been tried, with little success so far

The most ambitious economic integration project so far in the Americas was the US initiative to establish the Free Trade Area of the Americas (FTAA), encompassing North, Central and South America as well as the Caribbean.[15] The preparatory process that began in 1993 and concluded with the launching of negotiations in 1998 suggested a consensus on the FTAA's scope and objectives. However, this consensus unravelled when new governments in some countries (Brazil, Venezuela and Argentina, among others) challenged the inclusion of issues such as investment, services and intellectual property. In addition, the United

---

[14]   CAFTA entered into force for its members between 2006 and 2009 depending on the completion of their domestic approval procedures.

[15]   There were 34 participating countries in total. Within the western hemisphere, only Cuba was excluded (on political grounds).

Table 25.7   PTAs in force, under negotiation or announced among Latin American countries (as of November 2010)

	Andean Community	MERCOSUR	CACM	Chile	Mexico	Panama
Andean Community		MERCOSUR–Bolivia PTA MERCOSUR–Peru PTA MERCOSUR–Colombia–Ecuador–Venezuela PTA	Colombia–Northern Triangle PTA[a] Peru–Central America–Panama FTA (currently in negotiations)	Chile–Bolivia PTA Chile–Ecuador PTA Chile–Colombia FTA Chile–Peru FTA	Bolivia–Mexico PTA Colombia–Mexico FTA Peru–Mexico FTA (currently in negotiations)	Colombia–Panama FTA (currently in negotiations)
MERCOSUR				MERCOSUR–Chile PTA Venezuela–Chile PTA	MERCOSUR–Mexico Framework Agreement MERCOSUR–Mexico automotive agreement Uruguay–Mexico FTA Brazil–Mexico economic integration agreement (negotiations announced)	
CACM				Central America–Chile FTA	Costa Rica–Mexico FTA Nicaragua–Mexico FTA Northern Triangle–Mexico FTA	Central America–Panama FTA
Chile					Chile–Mexico FTA	Chile–Panama FTA
Mexico						

Note: [a] The term Northern Triangle refers to El Salvador, Guatemala and Honduras.

Source: Authors, based on Organization of American States, Foreign Trade Information System. Available at: www.sice.oas.org.

States was unwilling to negotiate away agricultural subsidies – except in the WTO – or anti–dumping measures, posing additional difficulties to reach an agreement. The negotiations were eventually terminated in 2005, after which the United States began a strategy of bilateral negotiations with individual Latin American countries.

Following the failure of the FTAA, the project to create a South American Free Trade Area comprising the AC, MERCOSUR and Chile was launched in 2005 within the context of the recently created South American Community of Nations. However, it was subsequently abandoned, and today it is not in the agenda of the Community's successor, the Union of South American Nations (UNASUR). This reflects the wide divergences that exist among the region's governments in terms of their approaches to development, including the role of trade liberalization.

Notwithstanding the above, there has been some progress on convergence at the subregional level. For example, since 2009 Mexico and the CACM have been working towards unifying the three FTAs currently linking them (Table 25.7). This offers a good potential to further integrate these six economies, reducing transaction costs and fostering the formation of value chains spanning several countries. Work has also been undertaken since 2008 towards convergence of the FTAs that link Mexico, Central America, Panama, Colombia, Ecuador, Peru and Chile, within the so-called Latin American Pacific Basin Initiative (LAPBI). This effort aims, among others, at harmonizing rules of origin and verification procedures, and at allowing cumulation of origin among the 11 LAPBI members.

In November 2010 the governments of Brazil and Mexico announced their decision to start negotiations towards a comprehensive 'economic integration strategic agreement', covering not only tariffs but also services, government procurement, investment and intellectual property, among other topics. This negotiation may have substantial implications for the whole Latin American integration process, as it involves the region's two largest economies and its two largest exporters of goods and services. Moreover, if successful it could lead to a Mexico–MERCOSUR FTA, which in turn could pave the way for the gradual creation of a Latin American free trade area.

The Negotiations with Extra-regional Partners

Mexico pioneered Latin America's efforts to develop preferential trade ties with extra-regional partners when it proposed to the United States to begin negotiations for what would become the NAFTA. Chile followed suit in 1997 with its FTA with Canada.[16]

During the past decade the majority of Latin American countries have followed Chile's and Mexico's steps and engaged in FTA negotiations with extra-regional

---

[16]   Chile was invited to join NAFTA in 1994, but negotiations failed when the Clinton Administration was unable to obtain Fast Track Authority from Congress. Instead, Canada and Chile negotiated a bilateral FTA which, at the time, was viewed as an interim arrangement until Chile became a NAFTA partner.

partners. Most of them have been conducted with the United States and the EU, Latin America's most traditional foreign markets. However, in recent years, some countries have also entered FTA negotiations with Asia–Pacific partners such as Japan, China, India and Korea. The countries that have been most active in this effort are Chile, Peru, Mexico, Colombia and Costa Rica (see Table 25.8).

Table 25.8   FTAs between LAC and integration schemes and selected extra-regional partners (as of September 2010)

	USA	EU	Japan	China	Korea	India
MERCOSUR[a]	...	Currently in negotiations	...	...	...	Partial scope agreement[b]
Central American Common Market	FTA (CAFTA-DR)	FTA negotiations concluded	...	...	...	...
Costa Rica			...	FTA signed	...	...
Colombia	FTA signed in 2006, not yet in force	FTA negotiations concluded	...	...	Currently in negotiations	...
Peru[c]	FTA	FTA negotiations concluded	FTA negotiations concluded	FTA	FTA negotiations concluded	...
Chile[d]	FTA	FTA	FTA	FTA	FTA	Partial scope agreement[b]
Mexico[e]	FTA (NAFTA)	FTA	FTA	...	FTA negotiations suspended in 2008	...

Note: [a] It also has an FTA in force with Israel and one signed with Egypt; [b] A partial scope agreement is one that covers trade in goods only, with a limited product coverage and in which tariffs are reduced rather than eliminated (see Chapter 22); [c] It also has FTAs in force with Canada and Singapore, and one signed with the European Free Trade Association (EFTA); [d] It also has FTAs in force with Australia, Canada, EFTA and Brunei Darussalam, New Zealand and Singapore (the latter three in the context of the Trans-Pacific Strategic Economic Partnership Agreement), plus FTAs signed with Turkey and Malaysia and ongoing FTA negotiations with Vietnam; [e] It also has FTAs in force with Canada (NAFTA), EFTA and Israel.
Source: Authors, based on Organization of American States, Foreign Trade Information System. Available at: www.sice.oas.org.

Latin America in the GATT/WTO

Until the Uruguay Round (1986–1994) participation in the GATT had not resulted in much liberalization on the part of Latin American countries, having been rather passive participants in tariff negotiations.[17] As the region's economies opened up unilaterally, the multilateral trading system became more important to both lock-in trade policy reform and pursue offensive interests such as disciplines and liberalization of agricultural trade.

In the Uruguay Round most participating Latin American countries bound all their tariffs but usually at levels substantially higher than the actual applied rates (Table 25.9).[18] The commitments negotiated by Latin American countries under the General Agreement on Trade in Services (GATS) were few and limited to binding totally or partially the status quo, very much in line with what other countries did.

There has been no unified Latin American stance in the ongoing Doha Round negotiations. Indeed, not even the region's main integration schemes have articulated common positions. On the contrary, differences between members of the same integration scheme have not been infrequent. This has been the case, for example, with differences between Costa Rica and the other Central American countries on agricultural market access (with the former adopting a much more offensive position than the latter) or among Andean Community members (replicating the same split which has become evident in preferential negotiations). In sum, negotiating positions in the WTO tend to be largely national and replicate Latin American countries' overall trade policy stances.

Despite being all developing economies, LAC countries pursue widely different objectives in terms of special and differential treatment, with some attaching much more importance to this concept than others. The one interest common to the entire region is reducing as much as possible the trade-distorting agricultural subsidies provided by developed countries.

As to coalitional activity, it is mostly issue-specific and based on common interest, rather than along regional lines. Thus Latin American countries participate with developed countries and with developing countries from other regions in issue-specific groups such as the Cairns Group, G20, G33, Friends of Fish, Friends of Anti-dumping Negotiations, etc.

Brazil is by far the most influential Latin American country in the Doha Round, being part – together with the United States, EU, China and India – of the core group of members in the negotiations, the so-called G5. This leading role reflects the vast size and strong dynamism of the Brazilian market, but has also been underpinned, among other factors, by the proven technical expertise of its negotiators and by the

---

[17] This is a reflection not only of the ISI strategy but also of the fact that until the Uruguay Round tariff negotiations were carried out on the basis of request and offer, and thus only the main suppliers of a product got involved, reducing Latin American participation to very few tariff lines.

[18] Chile had been the first GATT signatory to bind 100 per cent of tariffs (at 35 per cent) in the Tokyo Round (1973–1979) even though its applied rate at the time was 10 per cent.

Table 25.9 Latin American countries: tariff profiles (2009)

Country	Average bound rate (%) (1)	Average applied rate (%) (2)	Binding overhang (%) (1)–(2)	Binding coverage (%)
Argentina	31.9	12.6	19.3	100.0
Bolivia, Plurinational State	40.0	10.3	29.7	100.0
Brazil	31.4	13.6	17.8	100.0
Chile	25.1	6.0	19.1	100.0
Colombia	42.8	12.5	30.3	100.0
Costa Rica	42.9	5.4	37.5	100.0
Cuba	21.3	10.7	10.6	30.9
Dominican Republic[a]	34.0	7.1	26.9	100.0
Ecuador	21.8	11.2	10.6	100.0
El Salvador	36.6	5.9	30.7	100.0
Guatemala	41.2	5.6	35.6	100.0
Honduras	31.8	5.6	26.2	100.0
Mexico[b]	36.1	11.5	24.6	100.0
Nicaragua	40.7	5.6	35.1	100.0
Panama	23.5	7.1	16.4	100.0
Paraguay	33.5	10.3	23.2	100.0
Peru	29.3	5.5	23.8	100.0
Uruguay	31.6	10.5	21.1	100.0
Venezuela, Bolivarian Rep.	36.5	12.5	24.0	100.0

Note: [a] Corresponds to 2008; [b] In January 2009 Mexico started a programme of unilateral tariff reduction, to be implemented over five years. Tariffs will be lowered for practically all non-agricultural items whose applied MFN tariff is not already zero.
Source: World Trade Organization, World Tariff Profiles 2010.

clear political commitment Brazil has made to the Doha Round as its main concern in terms of trade negotiations. Proof of this is Brazil's leading role – along with India – in the creation of the G20 agricultural coalition of developing countries.

Several Latin American countries have made extensive use of the dispute settlement system of the WTO, scoring important victories in landmark cases. Among these are the complaint by Central American countries, plus Ecuador and Colombia, against the EU's import regime for bananas; and Brazil's victories on cotton subsidies versus the United States and on sugar against the EU.

Conclusion

Today Latin American countries are much more open and integrated into the world economy than they were 30 or even 20 years ago. However, this general assessment overlooks important differences. At the risk of oversimplifying a regional landscape that is full of nuances, today there appear to be three main approaches to trade within Latin America. Those countries with coasts on the Pacific Ocean (with the exception of Ecuador) tend to show the most open trade policies and actively seek to improve their links with the global economy, including through the negotiation of PTAs with their main partners within and outside the region. At the other end of the spectrum are those countries within ALBA. MERCOSUR members fall somewhere in between, although with important variations among themselves.

The erosion of support for trade liberalization in some countries has not resulted in massive tariff increases, even in the face of the recent world economic crisis. By and large, Latin American countries have not used the large space to raise tariffs allowed by their ceiling bindings at the WTO. Indeed, most countries in the region have not increased trade barriers at all, regardless of their public discourse on trade. Nevertheless, in recent years some countries have made use of non-tariff barriers such as non-automatic import licenses, minimum custom values, exchange controls, dual exchange rate regimes for foreign trade, an increased use of managed trade and outright import bans.

In the coming years, the role of trade policy in Latin American countries' overall development strategies will surely differ from the one it had at the start of trade reforms in the 1980s. Despite some backtracking in recent years, Latin America has achieved trade opening levels roughly equivalent to those of East and South East Asia. Although further reduction of trade barriers could have a positive impact on the region's overall competitiveness, the gains are likely to be smaller than those reaped as a result of the reforms of the 1980s and 1990s.

Trade agreements, particularly those concluded within the region and with other developing countries, will need to be reinforced in several aspects. First and foremost is the need to abide by the obligations established in these international treaties. There is often, among countries in the region, too much tolerance when a party disregards or does not properly enforce the commitments entered into in trade agreements. This creates problems for governments when resisting domestic protectionist pressures. Moreover, legal security and predictability are key elements of good governance. Second, trade agreements need to provide better disciplines and transparency for trade in services, investment and government procurement. A third issue that needs to be tackled at both national and regional levels is competition policy, so as to prevent uncompetitive behaviour by private firms in an environment characterized by fewer barriers to trade and foreign investment.

A recurrent concern is how to improve Latin America's export performance. South American countries are still largely dependent on exports of natural resources. Although they have benefitted in recent years from a strong Asian demand for commodities, this export structure has generally resulted in insufficient value addition, weak links with the rest of the economy and vulnerability to sudden declines in commodity prices. Moreover, several of the extractive industries in which South America has become specialized (for example mining) are capital-intensive, with little employment creation, and also pose important environmental challenges. An additional problem is that the large foreign currency inflows associated with high commodity prices push towards real appreciation of local currencies, hurting the international competitiveness of other export and import-competing sectors and thus reinforcing commodity dependence.

For their part, the Central American countries and Mexico, which show a larger component of industrial products in their export basket, face a different problem: the loss of share in the US market due to Asian competition in low and medium-technology manufactures. In the Mexican case, this is compounded by its excessive export dependence on the US market.

Brazil appears as a relative exception to the region's trade predicament. Besides being one of the world's main commodity exporters, it has displaced Mexico as the region's main exporter of commercial services. It is also a successful exporter of manufactures in some medium and high-technology segments, most notably aircraft. This is the result of a number of factors, including a higher spending on research and development (as a percentage of GDP) than the Latin American average, an abundant provision of credit from the powerful state-owned national development bank (BNDES) and large FDI inflows. The sheer size of the Brazilian market (with almost double the population of Mexico) has most likely also played a part, by enabling Brazilian companies to develop scale and learning economies that can later be exploited in international markets. However, because of the particularities of the Brazilian case, it is unclear that other LAC countries could upgrade their productive capacities simply by following its example.

Against this background, it seems that Latin America's main challenges lie in areas other than trade policy understood in a narrow sense. The region does not sufficiently participate in the global value chains that today dominate international trade, and where it does is generally in their least sophisticated segments. Addressing this requires increasing the value and knowledge content of the region's exports, including those of natural resources (or based on them). Over the coming years it will also be important to reduce the vulnerability of LAC exports to climate change-related trade measures in third markets, by reducing their 'carbon footprint'. Addressing these challenges will require changes in a wide range of policies such as those dealing with innovation, science and technology, education and training, environmental management and the attraction of FDI. The nature of those adjustments lies beyond the scope of this chapter.

Notwithstanding the above, there is at least one area where trade policy should play a very important role in increasing the region's international competitiveness: the promotion of intra-regional trade. Progress towards the establishment of a unified economic space along the lines of the EU's Single Market would greatly contribute to raising Latin America's low levels of intra-regional trade, in turn fostering the development of intra-regional value chains and increasing the value content of the region's exports. While such an ambitious goal does not appear feasible in the short term due to political differences, especially in South America, it should nonetheless remain as a top priority for the region's governments in the coming years.

Looking in perspective at the last two decades, what Latin America has achieved in terms of increased openness to trade and investment represents a good basis to continue building a trade architecture that underpins better and deeper integration across the region. Incremental progress towards that end looks much more promising than the very ambitious – yet ultimately unsuccessful – integration initiatives the region has often embarked upon in the past.

References

Barcena, A. 2010. Structural constraints on development in Latin America and the Caribbean: a post-crisis reflection. *CEPAL Review*, 100: 7–27.

Corbo, V. 2008. *Latin America in the Global Economy: Challenges and Opportunities*. Richard Snape Lecture: Productivity Commission, Melbourne, 18 November.

Economic Commission for Latin America and the Caribbean (ECLAC). 2010. *Latin America and the Caribbean in the World Economy 2009–2010. A Crisis Generated in the Centre and a Recovery Driven by the Emerging Economies*. Santiago de Chile: Chile.

Herreros, S. 2009. Chile, in *The Political Economy of Trade Reform in Emerging Markets: Crisis or Opportunity?*, edited by P. Draper, P. Alves and R. Sally. Cheltenham: Edward Elgar: Chapter 3.

Marconini, M. 2009. Brazil, in *The Political Economy of Trade Reform in Emerging Markets. Crisis or Opportunity?*, edited by P. Draper, P. Alves and R. Sally. Cheltenham: Edward Elgar: Chapter 6.

Rojas-Suarez, L. 2010. The international financial crisis: eight lessons for and from Latin America. *CGD Working Paper*, No. 202. Washington, DC: Center for Global Development.

WTO. 2010. Participation of Developing Economies in the Global Trading System – Note by the Secretariat. Geneva: WTO.

Trade Policy-Making
in East Africa

Peter Kiuluku and Caiphas Chekwoti

Introduction

This chapter explores the trade policy-making process in four East African countries: Kenya, Uganda, Tanzania and Rwanda. The focus is mainly on the institutional framework, agenda setting and consultative processes. The choice of the four out of five countries making up the East African Community (EAC) is informed by the accessibility of basic information regarding the trade policy process. Information for Burundi, the other East African country left out, was found to be too scanty to furnish useful insights. In each of the four countries, information on the trade policy process was gleaned from country reports based on interviews with key actors in each of the countries. This was complemented by earlier works related to the trade policy-making process in some of the countries in the sample.

Trade policy-making in East Africa is a relatively recent phenomenon. Indeed the birth of the World Trade Organization (WTO) in 1995 gave new impetus to trade policy-making. Tanzania led the way in introducing a new trade policy framework, before Uganda, Rwanda and Kenya unveiled their blueprints. The trade policy reviews of the WTO have also helped to motivate and energize the countries to move towards a more open trade policy regime in line with their multilateral commitments. The economic and development gains promised by the Doha Development Agenda increased the momentum of the East African countries to position themselves to gain from globalization. In recent years East African countries have benefitted from two related issues: the protracted negotiations of the Economic Partnership Agreements (EPA) and the Doha Round. The level of consciousness has been increased by both events and all stakeholders are better informed regarding the benefits of an international developmental trade regime and the dangers of failure to actively participate and make contributions. The role and influence of international actors has also helped push for a favourable conclusion or movement to an early return to the negotiating table. The EPA negotiations have been the most illuminating towards this end. The African stakeholders believe that the negotiations have stalled and that the European Union needs to close the gap by moving closer to the position of the East African Community (EAC). On the other hand the official European Union position has been that many of the important issues have been agreed upon and that it remains only a matter of time before closure. The major drivers exerting pressure on government have been a vibrant civil society, the East African Legislative Assembly and a media which has been highlighting opinions on both sides of the divide.

In this chapter we show that there is a more robust trade policy-making process in motion and, most importantly, being institutionalized in the EAC. This does not, however, necessarily mean effectiveness in terms of strategy and execution. It will take more time and capacity development to increase the effectiveness of the trade policy process and more so the implementation. There is more documentation of trade policy than in the past and wider consultation, although this does not necessarily mean effective participation of all stakeholders. Government and the private sector still have an uneasy relationship as regards trade policy formulation, implementation and negotiations. Civil society has increased its role in providing an alternative voice, especially in regard to multilateral trade negotiations.

Trade Performance: Stylized Facts

In the sample countries, the trade policy framework has been shaped by the evolution of the historical, political and economic processes. The 1970s were characterized by closed, import substitution policies with a dominant public sector. This evolved into more export-orientation in the 1980s, with liberal trade policies generally becoming dominant in the 1990s (Bonger 2004; Ikiara et al. 2004; Kweka 2004; Takahashi et al. 2007). Subsequent privatization and deregulation translated into greater visibility for the private sector and a shrinking of the public sector.

The countries in the sample have all undertaken a series of trade reforms, principally as part of the structural adjustment programmes of the 1990s and more recently due to the deeper integration initiatives within the EAC common market. This was expected to have translated into dramatically reduced customs duty rates. However, judging from the MFN restrictiveness index (World Bank, www.worldbank.org/wti) two of the EAC countries still exhibit relatively restrictive trade regimes with Rwanda at 16.2 and Uganda at 14.6 respectively (see Table 26.1). This is well above the EAC average of 11.8. Kenya and Tanzania, on the other hand, appear to have less restrictive trade regimes in relative terms with indices at 8.2 and 7.7 respectively. It is expected though that with the adoption of the EAC common external tariff (CET), a significant reduction in the duty rates will be realized.

The trade in services sector across the EAC countries is still highly restricted, especially in modes 1, 3 and 4 (Dihel et al. 2010). Negotiations towards reforms and harmonization of the regulatory framework within the common market have yet to be effected. This is reflected by the high GATS restrictiveness index figures.

In the mirror perspective, three of the sample EAC countries: Rwanda, Uganda and Tanzania, face a relatively unfavourable trading environment in their global markets. The market access indicator, Market Access-Trade Tariff Restrictiveness Index (MA-TTRI)[1] shows Rwanda's exports facing a more restrictive trading environment than the rest of the EAC countries. During the period 2006–2009, Rwanda's market access impediment was 8.3 per cent, a much higher rate than the EAC average of 5.6 per cent. In the group, Kenya's exports face a relatively favourable trading environment with a market access impediment of 3.9 per cent.

The EAC countries signed an interim Economic Partnership Agreement (EPA) with the EU in 2007 and negotiations are still to be concluded on the comprehensive EPA. Except for Tanzania, a member of the Southern African Development Community (SADC), the other three EAC countries are members of the Common Market of Eastern and Southern Africa (COMESA). In addition, Kenya and Uganda belong to the Intergovernmental Authority on Development (IGAD). Overlapping membership in regional economic groupings still presents policy heterogeneity issues which escalate the barriers to intra-member cross-border trade. Harmonizing membership and thus the regulatory framework appears to be a more desirable way forward. As an effort in this direction, the four EAC countries are part of the ongoing COMESA-EAC-SADC tripartite initiatives towards a wider Free Trade Area (FTA). At the multilateral level, all four EAC countries are members of the WTO.

The four countries, as members of the EAC, signed a Trade and Investment Framework Agreement with the United States in July 2008 aimed at fostering trade and investment relations with the United States. The countries remain eligible for duty and quota free access to the US market under the African Growth and Opportunity Act (AGOA) for certain goods.

The export composition of the four countries is quite narrow with some two or three commodities contributing at least 60 per cent of total exports. The export basket across the four countries is dominated by agricultural products, accounting for at least 40 per cent of the total exports. Rwanda has the highest export concentration with exports dominated by metal ore, tea and coffee, constituting about 89 per cent of total exports. There has, however, been a general improvement towards diversification of exports into non-traditional products across the four countries. Kenya and Uganda have diversified into high value export commodities with Kenya having been successful in aligning its horticultural potential with strict European standards. Similarly, Uganda has made significant efforts in diversifying into fish and fish products. The export markets are relatively diversified. Kenya, Uganda and Rwanda are big players in the intra COMESA and EAC trade with significant trade (exports and imports) taking place in comparison with other export markets.

In terms of intra-member trade performance, it is evident from Figure 26.1 that Kenya has been the dominant player. Goods from Kenya have flowed to the other partner states even before the customs union entered into force. What is

---

[1]   Source: www.worldbank.org/wti. MA-TTRI calculates the equivalent uniform tariff of trading partners that would keep their level of imports constant and it is weighted by import values and import demand elasticities of trading partners.

Table 26.1 Trade performance of the case study countries

	2006–2009	2006–2009	2006–2009	2006–2009	2006–2009
	Rwanda	Uganda	Kenya	Tanzania	EAC average
TTRI (MFN applied tariff) – All Goods	16.18	14.63	8.21	7.76	11.84
MA-TTRI (applied tariff incl. prefs.) – All Goods	8.31	6.28	3.89	5.24	5.58
Ease of Doing Business – Rank	67	112	95	131	116.2
Real growth in total trade (g+s,%)	-1.1	2.9	2.1	-2.6	1.3
GATS commitments restrictiveness index – all service sectors	5.61	3.16	3.21	0.98	3.17
Agricultural exports share of goods exports (%)	59.31	58.35	48.42	41.83	49.63
Trade integration (% of GDP)	33.12	60.29	60.37	57.6	54.5
Real GDP growth (%)	5.1	5	2.6	4.8	4.02
Export product concentration index	44.19	35.27	28.77	21.45	38.07
Export market destination concentration index	9.16	12.82	16.06	18.47	15.9
FDI inflows (% of GDP)	1.97	3.85	5.42	0.28	2.37
Share of trade with FTA/CU partners – exports (%)	16.97	14.95	32.22	1.13	15.6

Source: World Bank, World Trade Indicators database.

interesting, however, is the emergence and significant increase of exports to Kenya from Uganda and Tanzania. This coincides with the EAC Customs Union protocol coming into force and the increased intra-member trade may thus be attributed to the reforms arising from the EAC customs union.

An examination of the trend in merchandise trade over the last 20 years shows significant growth in the last decade (see Figure 26.2). This is attributed mainly to various reforms undertaken by the countries concerned towards easing the tariff rates or total elimination of tariffs such as within the EAC Customs Union and now the Common Market. The spike of merchandise trade during the mid-1990s, however, can be explained by the coffee boom, coinciding with a severe frost in Brazil. Coffee is a significant export product in all four countries.

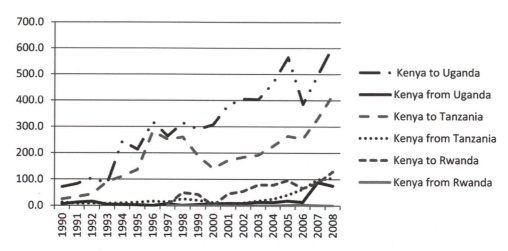

Figure 26.1 EAC intra-partner trade trends (USD millions)
Source: EAC Secretariat.

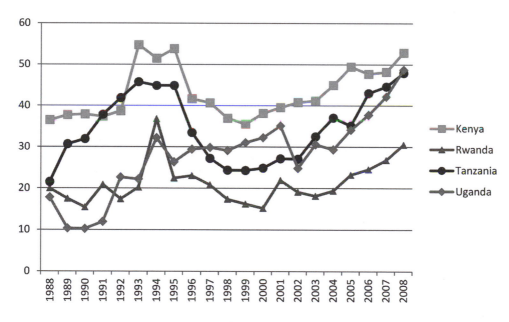

Figure 26.2 Merchandise trade as a percentage of GDP
Source: World Bank.

The Trade Policy-Making Process

The Institutional Framework

Effective trade policy direction, formulation and implementation are highly dependent on the quality of the institutional framework, given the direct effect on policy coherence and indirect effect on policy outcomes. The trade policy process and institutional structure within the four EAC countries is shaped importantly by their membership of regional and multilateral trade organizations. Membership obligations motivate the countries to undertake domestic economic and sectoral reforms.

The requirements inscribed in the WTO agreements have influenced the direction of the trade policies in these countries as well as the trade policy reviews (TPR) conducted by the governments and the WTO Secretariat. For example, the Ugandan government undertook commercial law reform to bring its trade-related laws, regulations and procedures into conformity with the WTO requirements. This has also shaped the commercial reforms in Tanzania with the establishment of Tanzania Trade to provide strategic direction to the country's export markets. The trade regime in Kenya has equally undergone reform leading to the publication of a strategic plan and a new trade policy in 2009.

At the regional level, an EAC negotiating mandate provides the institutional framework for the trade negotiations involving EAC partner states. This framework was decided by the summit on the ongoing COMESA-EAC-SADC tripartite negotiations. Among the key requirements is that the EAC will negotiate as a bloc. It should be noted that the EAC partner states have experience negotiating as a bloc in the WTO's Joint Trade Policy Review (2006), the Framework for EPAs (2007), the Trade and Investment Framework Agreement (2008) and full EPA negotiations (East African Community Secretariat 2010). The negotiating mandate delineates, between the EAC Secretariat and the partner states, the roles and negotiating structures both with the other parties and/or any third party. It is observed, however, that the EAC partner states have a tighter control on what gets negotiated and thus handle the negotiations directly. The role of the Secretariat is limited to acting as a backstop – facilitating and managing the negotiations for the partner states.

By virtue of the treaty establishing the EAC, the number of stages in the trade policy process in the four countries has increased relative to the previous national policy process. In the same context, the recent addition of a ministry in charge of EAC affairs, which is central to EAC trade policy, adds another institutional structure in policy formulation. Under the current EAC rules of procedure, the formation of national positions in the current EAC regional mandate is facilitated by the Secretariat through a notice to partner states for a meeting with requisite documentation on national positions. This triggers the process of forming national positions through the constitution of an inter-ministerial committee consisting of experts from the key ministries, parastatals and private sector representatives

(Omiti et al. 2007). In the next link in the chain, the coordination committee, consisting of permanent secretaries from key ministries in each member state, considers reports from the sectoral committees and submits a proposal to the Council, consisting of ministers from EAC affairs, trade and finance and including heads of the central banks, revenue authorities and the attorneys-general. Once consensus is reached, the Council tables Bills before the East African Legislative Assembly (EALA) for discussion. The discussed Bills are finally forwarded to the Heads of State summit for assent. Admittedly, there are still weak links in this apparently strong institutional framework. However, as trade becomes the engine of growth in EAC countries, capacities will develop and lessen the weaknesses.

EAC members have equal rights but at times particular members are more influential depending on personalities and issues on the table. For example, during the tenure of Dr Mukhisa Kituyi as minister for trade, Kenya was very influential in the EAC, COMESA and even the Africa Group. Uganda currently seems keener to fast-track the political federation of the EAC. On this issue, Uganda is providing the leadership. Burundi is a more ambivalent member, Rwanda is increasingly assertive and at times has shown leadership (it waived visa requirements long before the common market). Tanzania is a cautious member depending on issues on the table and moves at a slow pace in terms of common market matters, especially on land and free movement of people. Kenya's stance on issues tends to influence the tone if not the speed of the negotiations.

At the national level, across the sample countries there is a similar institutional structure that defines the trade policy-making process. The role for the public institutions is structured on three key trade policy areas: policy direction, formulation and implementation. This national phase of the policy process includes the president's office in all four countries, together with key officials from the ministry of finance and planning. Across the four countries, trade policy direction is driven by the president's office. This is to be expected given the political ownership implications of the policy process, as the political performance of the ruling party is to some extent gauged by the policy frameworks initiated and pursued.

Notable within policy direction and guidance at the national level is the existence of an economic forum that incorporates key officials from the public and private sector. Policy formulation is driven by inputs from key ministries that include trade and industry, foreign affairs, agriculture, finance and EAC affairs. At the policy implementation level, key bodies dealing with revenue, standards and line ministries play a significant role. From the table in Appendix 26.1, it is evident that some of the ministries execute the three aspects of the policy process generating potential conflict of interest and biases in the policy process especially if influential lobbyists exist in the country.

The ministry of trade and industry and its departmental variations within the EAC countries has a major coordination role and takes the lead in both the policy formulation and implementation levels. In this respect, specific departments exist within the ministry that cater for bilateral, regional and multilateral trade policy issues. The exception being that all EAC related issues are specifically coordinated by the ministry of EAC affairs in each of the countries under study. In addition to the ministry of trade and industry, one of the most important actors in the trade policy process is the ministry responsible for agriculture. This is attributed to the central role of agriculture in the export sector of these countries. Other ministries critical in the policy formulation level include ministries of finance and planning and foreign affairs. This representation is similar across the four countries.

Visible at the policy implementation level across the four countries are the key parastatals and departments dealing with revenue collection, standards and immigration issues.

Within the EAC, the private sector's role is becoming more apparent. For example, the East Africa Business Council (EABC), an umbrella organization for the business community in the EAC, has observer status during the EAC Secretariat activities. In reality however, the EABC does not have the gravitas and capacity as an effective interlocutor for regional business. This perception has limited its membership and participation in trade policy-making. The private sector comprises both multi-sector and sector umbrella organizations. However, the views represented are biased towards the interests of the manufacturers who appear to have more lobbying power. Common across the four countries are private sector institutional establishments with a coordinating role. These comprise the chambers of commerce and the private sector foundations. Effective influence of the private sector in trade policy-making, however, is mainly limited to the individual private sector vested interests close to the president.

The civil society organizations' (CSOs) role in trade policy has been mainly from an advocacy perspective concentrating on the ramifications of trade policy initiatives. In each of the countries, there is an established policy research institution that plays a crucial role in this aspect. In Kenya, the Kenya Institute for Public Policy Research and Analysis (KIPPRA) and Institute of Economic Affairs (IEA) play this role corresponding to that of Institute of Policy Analysis and Research (IPAR) in Rwanda, Economic Social Research Foundation (ESRF) in Tanzania and Economic Policy Research Centre (EPRC) in Uganda. The African Economic Research Consortium (AERC), an economics training and research coordinating centre based in Nairobi, complements the national research institutions on trade policy research and training. In addition, this is also complemented by specific and tailored trade policy capacity building activities executed by the Trade Policy Training Centre in Africa (trapca) for which the study countries are target stakeholders. Civil society has become more assertive, although capacity constraints make it intellectually less effective in trade policy matters. To bridge this gap, there is a reliance on research based civil society from the developed countries. The flow chart in Figure 26.3 presents a summary of the trade policy decision-making process.

Agenda Setting

The agenda-setting process is in a state of dynamism with many layers involved, as shown in Figure 26.4. But the multilateral trading system shapes and tends to influence the process, followed by regional economic communities. All the EAC

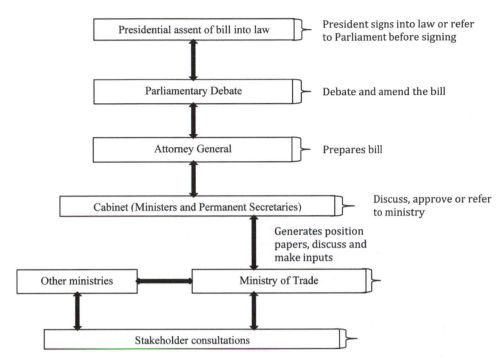

Figure 26.3 Trade policy decision-making flow chart
Source: Authors' construction.

countries are World Trade Organization members and therefore bound by the WTO Law. In addition, the trade policy reviews of the WTO have encouraged the countries to reform and realign their domestic policies and laws. As a result of the reviews, the countries now have consolidated trade policy documents.

The pressure of both the global and regional trade discourse is directed at government as the first interlocutor. On the other hand, government reaches out to various stakeholders to sense issues that could inform the national trade policy-making process. This interaction places government at pole position in trade policy-making. The public sector is therefore the driver of the agenda-setting process, though consultations at various layers of the process have a strong influence on the outcome.

Civil society in all four countries has played a significant role in the recent past, advocating more inclusive and pro-poor trade policies. As noted, however, many of these organizations have serious capacity constraints to fully articulate informed positions in trade policy during negotiations.

The private sector tends to have weak national associations whose capacity to set the agenda for trade policy-making appears compromised by two factors. First, big businesses tend to shun national private sector associations and instead opt to belong to sectoral associations, or to use their capacity to engage at the highest levels of government, as mentioned above. The second factor, which is linked to the first, is the perceived lack of capacity at the institutional level of the private sector associations to effectively prosecute issues that affect private business. The political class has been very reactive in the trade policy formulation discourse. In many cases they marginally participate at the tail end, opting to wait for debates in the chamber or the appropriate portfolio committee, and therefore shape the final outcomes of legislation.

In general, public policy agenda setting is strongly influenced by the media in Kenya, Uganda and Tanzania. The media are still not very influential in Rwanda. Rwanda's agenda setting and consultation process is lean as the private and civil society organizations are few compared to the other countries.

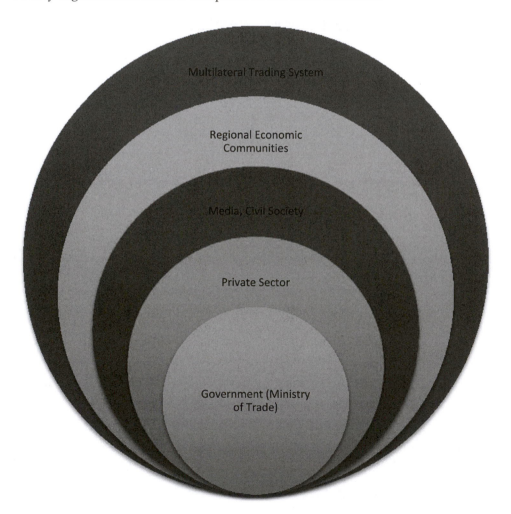

Figure 26.4 Layers of agenda-setting environment
Source: Authors.

Groups Involved in the Consultation Process

Although the groups in the consultation process appear to be well structured, in some cases they are only consulted as a formality or in some cases are expected to rubberstamp the government position. This tends to reduce the efficacy of their contributions. In each of the four countries, issue-based consultation, for example during the negotiation of EPAs, tends to dominate the policy discourse and the intensity of consultation generally loses steam as negotiations drag on. In this case inclusiveness is not directly correlated with effectiveness. A recent study by the Consumer Unity and Trust Society (CUTS) (2009b) used qualitative data to calculate the Inclusive Trade Policy Making Index (ITPM) of several African countries. The results showed above average participation and inclusiveness in Kenya, Tanzania and Uganda, and all four countries have become active in trade policy-making in the last five years. This may be attributed to the new consciousness brought about by participation in various trade policy negotiations.

The Consultation Procedures and Mechanisms

A common thread runs through the consultative process across the countries in the sample as inferred from the interviews and government documents. Consultations on trade policy issues are executed through committees involving government actors and private sector and civil society organizations. Governments have inter-ministerial committees established to advise them on all matters pertaining to trade and the WTO. The ministries act as focal points for sub-committees handling relevant trade-related issues. The ministry of trade and industry coordinates the committees and plays a critical role in identifying those to be invited. The inter-ministerial committee then meets, discusses and forms a position on each of the areas to be negotiated. Once a position document is agreed, that includes a fallback position by the technical officials, it is taken through the approval process by permanent secretaries, ministers and the president before it becomes a national position. There is, however, a pessimistic view from non-state actors about the level of representation in the official delegation to ministerial conferences and negotiating teams. Non-state actors talked to by the authors argue that their main input is more of a draft policy validation exercise since their input is sought after the draft document is ready. There is a feeling of inclusion without effective involvement.

The effectiveness of the committees is, however, very much dependent on the availability of resources for organizing the meetings and the coordinating efficiency of the ministry of trade. Across the sample countries, despite the potentially critical role played by the committees, they do not have a legal mandate and thus no budget line. Moreover, the government does not have any binding obligation to adopt their recommendations. This has an immediate implication for the frequency of the meetings, the nature of representation and the productivity of the discussions. Evidence gleaned from the country documents and interviews indicates that meetings are irregular, with uneven attendance and limited enthusiasm in the discussions.

It is observed that the effectiveness of the private sector in influencing trade policy is dependent on the negotiation and lobbying strength at the highest level. This is evidenced by the presence of a presidential forum comprising key stakeholders from the private sector. In all the countries there are high-level meetings between the president and private sector. In the case of Kenya, this comes in the form of the Prime Minister's Round Table that senior government officials attend and the captains of industry. One of the key weaknesses of the umbrella representation is the variety of the interests of the member organizations and the lack of a common position. In this respect, middle to large private sector firms have had the opportunity to exert significant influence relative to the polarized and financially constrained small and medium scale players (Onyango 2008). This is exacerbated by the observed weak understanding of the rather complex trade issues by the majority of the private sector constituents. The most active and vocal private sector representatives in EAC processes are those who are involved in manufactures.

Country Cases: Comparative Analysis

It is evident from both the country documents reviewed and the preceding discussion that there is a lot of similarity in the trade policy process across the EAC countries in the sample. The ministry responsible for international trade issues has an overall responsibility for both initiating and coordinating the various actors during the trade policy-making process. In the case of EAC common market, the Ministry of EAC Affairs coordinates its position with the Ministry of Trade.

On the basis of government documents and of interviews we have conducted, we conclude that trade policy in Uganda is driven by a variety of inputs ranging from lobbyists to directives from the president, but that the top-down element is very important. The influence of multilateral, bilateral and regional agreements to which Uganda is a signatory is significant in the sense that most are adopted as part of the national trade policy. Uganda's trade policy is also, in a holistic way, aligned to national development policies such as Vision 2025, the Medium Term Competiveness Strategy and the plan for the modernization of agriculture. Stakeholder participation in trade policy-making is limited, with the private sector playing a minor role in the process. However, views and concerns from the private sector are channelled through a high-level business advisory council, the Presidential Investors Roundtable (Republic of Uganda 2009).

It is the mandate of the Ministry of Trade, Tourism and Industry (MTTI) to initiate policy ideas and vet them through a multi-stakeholder arrangement – the Inter-Institutional Trade Council (IITC). Coordination is executed by the MTTI, and the IITC prepares draft policy white papers that are presented to the cabinet and parliament for vetting and approval. The policy acquires the necessary legal instruments after the president gives his assent.

In Tanzania, trade policy formulation and review rests with the Ministry of Trade, Industry and Marketing (MTIM) as a key coordination body. The departments and divisions within the line ministries responsible for trade policy issues collaborate with the MTIM. There are five stages in the policy formation process: initiation by the MTIM; scrutiny by the Cabinet Secretariat; review by the Inter-Ministerial Technical Committee (IMTC); review and decision by the Cabinet; and finally, implementation and monitoring (United Republic of Tanzania 2003).

In Kenya, the Ministry of Trade (MOT) is the key institution in trade policy formulation, adoption and implementation, with support from relevant government agencies engaged in trade-related activities. The ministry is the lead agency on bilateral, regional and multilateral negotiations presenting somewhat top-down policy-making at the ministry level (Ministry of Trade, Kenya 2007).

In Rwanda, as in the other three sample countries, the Ministry of Trade and Industry (MTI), plays a critical role in the identification of the trade policy needs of the country. It is also the lead agency responsible for the key aspects of the trade policy-making process with inputs from partner institutions representing finance, foreign affairs, agriculture, East African Community and the private sector. The private sector however, features more as a consultation and validation body rather than being involved in the entire process (UNCTAD 2010). This is a similar scenario across the other three countries in the sample.

It worth noting that in each of the five EAC countries, the Ministry of East African Community Affairs is mandated to be the lead agency handling EAC issues. Potential coordination challenges arise given the cross-cutting nature of the trade issues dealt with by this agency and by the principal trade ministry, leading to increased bureaucracy and poor coordination in trade policy-making. It has been observed too that overlaps in the negotiations do exist between the specific units dealing with bilateral and multilateral trade issues within the trade ministry.

Conclusion

In conclusion, we can infer that the legislative bodies tend to be rather weak in African countries, including in East Africa (and so have relatively limited impact on trade policy). Presidential authority, however, looms large in African trade policy-making and there is therefore an important top-down element in the trade policy process. For this reason, private sector influence is likely to come via high-level connections rather than from the role of umbrella bodies. In fact multinationals mostly participate in sectoral lobby groups, which seem to have high-level connections in government. When local efforts do not bear fruit, a visit from the top honchos of transnational corporations' headquarters tends to rewrite government policy. A visit to the state house is arranged and any political decision made takes precedence.

In trade policy-making, the regional dimension (EAC) both helps, by fostering market opening, and hinders, by adding complexity to the institutional framework.

But on balance, it is a good thing given the increasing move towards harmonization of regulatory frameworks in line with the regional norm. It is clear too that the partner states within the EAC have significant influence on the direction and outcome of any trade policy decisions even within the common market, with the role of the Secretariat limited to facilitation at most.

Compared with the advanced industrialized countries, developing countries, including those in East Africa, are subject to greater external influence over trade policy-making (IMF, World Bank, WTO, bilateral aid donors, and bilateral trade partners, etc.) through the financing channel. And in terms of external influence on East Africa, though WTO disciplines and monitoring are important, bilateral influences with key trading partners, such as via the EPAs, are becoming increasingly important.

This said, the domestic environment for reform is still the crucial element. On this score there are grounds for optimism, given the irreversible shift from import-substitution and the growing recognition within each of the sample countries of the potential gains from trade and market opening. But these trade gains will only be fully realized if broad supporting policies and implementation frameworks are in place such as infrastructure development, training, institution-building and macroeconomic stability.

Do the observations on trade policy process from the sample countries feature in other parts of Africa? In our view, they do. A brief survey of literature affirms that a similarity exists in Malawi, Zambia and South Africa (CUTS 2009; FANRPAN 2001). The Eastern and Southern African countries exhibit a similar process in trade policy formulation.

References

Bonger, T. 2004. Uganda: strategic trade and industrial policy-making in Africa, in *The Politics of Trade and Industrial Policy in Africa: Forced Consensus?*, edited by Charles Soludo, Osita Ogbu and Ha-Joon Chang. Trenton, NJ and Asmara, Eritrea: Africa World Press: 253–70.

CUTS International. 2009a. Improving ownership through inclusive trade policy making processes: *Lessons from Africa*. Geneva: CUTS.

CUTS International. 2009b. Towards more inclusive trade policy making: process and role of stakeholders in selected African countries. Geneva: CUTS.

Dihel, N., Fernandes, A.M., Mattoo A. and Strychacz N. 2010. Reform and regional integration of professional services in East Africa. *Note No. 5 Africa Trade Policy Notes*. Washington, DC: World Bank.

East African Community Secretariat (EAC). 2010. Draft COMESA_EAC_SADC Tripartite Free Trade Area Negotiating Mandate. Arusha, Tanzania: EAC.

FANRPAN. 2001. Agricultural policy making in Southern Africa: issues and challenges, *Report of the Second Regional Stakeholder Meeting* held on 6–9 May,

2001 – the Holiday Inn, Harare, Zimbabwe. The Food, Agricultural and Natural Resources Policy Analysis Network of Southern Africa (FANRPAN).

Ikiara, G.K., Olewe-Nyunya, J. and Odhiambo, W. 2004. Kenya: formulation and implementation of strategic trade and industrial policies, in *The Politics of Trade and Industrial Policy in Africa: Forced Consensus?*, edited by Charles Soludo, Osita Ogbu and Ha-Joon Chang. Trenton, NJ and Asmara, Eritrea: Africa World Press.

Kweka, Josephat. 2004. Trade policy and transport costs in Tanzania. *CREDIT Research Paper 06/10*, University of Nottingham.

Ministry of Trade, Kenya. August 2007. *Interim Draft Report: National Trade Policy* [mimeo].

Omiti, J., Waiyaki, N. and Verena, F. 2007. Trade policy-making process in Kenya: the Institutional arrangements and interaction of actors. Unpublished report by KIPPRA and ODI.

Onyango, Christopher. 2008. *Role and Influence of Main Interest Groups in the Trade Policy Making Process.* Paper for CUTS Geneva Resource Centre FEATS, National Inception Meeting in Nairobi, Kenya, 14 October.

Republic of Uganda, PIRT. 15 October 2009, Report on the Inaugural Presidential Investors Round Table Meeting, Phase Three (2009–2011) (Courtesy of Uganda Investment Authority), Kampala.

Takahashi, Y., Ohno, A. and Matsuoka, S. 2007. Alternative export-oriented industrial strategy for Africa: extension from 'spatial economic advantage' in the case of Kenya. *Discussion Paper Series vol. 2006-7*. Hiroshima: Graduate School of International Development and Cooperation, Hiroshima University.

United Nations Conference on Trade and Development. 2010. Rwanda's Development-driven Trade Policy Framework. Geneva and New York: United Nations.

The United Republic of Tanzania, Ministry of Industry and Trade. February 2003. National Trade Policy: *Trade Policy for a Competitive Economy and Export-Led Growth*, Dar es Salaam.

Appendix Table 26.1 Matrix of trade policy process actors

		Kenya	Rwanda
State	Policy direction	• President's office • National Economic and Social Council • Office of the Prime Minister, • Ministries of Planning, National Development and of Finance	• President's office (Strategic Unit) • National Trade Policy Forum • Rwanda Economic and Social Council • Ministry of Finance
	Policy formulation	• Ministries of Trade, East African Community, Industrialization, Foreign Affairs and of Agriculture	• The Rwanda Development Board (RDB), the Ministries of Finance and Economic Planning, Foreign Affairs, Agriculture and Animal Resources and East African Affairs
	Policy implementation	• Ministries of Trade and of East African Community • Kenya Revenue Authority • Kenya Bureau of Standards • Other Line Ministries and Agencies	• The Ministries of Finance and Economic Planning, • Foreign Affairs, • Agriculture and Animal Resources • and East African Affairs • Revenue Authority • Bureau of Standards • Immigration
Private sector		Multi-sector Umbrella Organizations • Kenya National Chamber of Commerce and Industry • Kenya Private Sector Alliance • Federation of Kenya Employers Sectoral Umbrella Organizations • Kenya Association of Manufacturers • Kenya Flower Council • Fresh Produce Exporters Association of Kenya	• Rwandan Private Sector Federation • The Flower council
Civil Society		Local NGOs • Kenya Human Rights Commission • EcoNews Africa • Consumer Information Network Regional/International NGOs • Oxfam, CUTS International • SEATINI • ActionAid Kenya Research CSOs • Institute for Economic Affairs • African Economic Research Consortium • KIPPRA CSOs Networks • The Kenya Civil Society Alliance	• Institute of Policy Analysis and Research

Source: Adopted from CUTS report (2009b) and modified with country reports.

Tanzania	Uganda
• President's Office – Planning Commission • Ministries of Industry, Trade and Marketing • and of Finance	• President office • Cabinet • Presidential Economic Policy Forum • Ministry of Finance, Planning and Economic Development
• Ministries of Industry, Trade and Marketing, Foreign Affairs and International Cooperation, Finance, Agriculture and Cooperatives and of East African Affairs	• Ministries of Tourism, Trade and Industry, Agriculture, Animal Industry and Fisheries, Foreign Affairs and of East African Affairs
• Ministry of Industry, Trade and Marketing • Tanzania Review Authority • Board of External Trade • Other Specialised Government Agencies • Other Line Ministries and Agencies	• Ministries of Tourism, Trade and Industry, Justice and Constitutional Affairs, and Local Government • Uganda Export Promotion Board • Uganda Revenue Authority • Other Line Ministries and Agencies
Multi-sector Organizations • Private Sector Foundation • Tanzania Chamber of Commerce, Industry and Agriculture Sectoral Umbrella Organizations • Confederation of Tanzania Industry • Tanzania Exporters Association	Multi-sector organizations • Private Sector Foundation • Uganda National Chamber of Commerce Umbrella sectoral organizations • Uganda Manufaturers Association • Uganda General Importers and Exporters Association • Uganda Small Scale Industries Association
Local NGOs • Faith-Based Organizations • Tanzania Networking Gender Programme • Media Council and MISA Economic and Social Research networks	Local NGOs • National Farmers Federation Research CSOs • Economic Policy Research Centre • Centre for Development Initiatives Regional and International NGOs • CSOs network

Appendix Table 26.2 Consultation mechanisms

Country	Consultation mechanisms	Composition	Role
Tanzania	National Business Council (NBC)	Various government agencies and the private sector. Private Sector Foundation coordinates the private sector representation in the NBC	A wide ranging forum for public sector institutions and the private sector on general policy issues including trade
	Inter-Ministerial Technical Committee(IMTC)	All government ministries	A forum for harmonization and coordination among all government ministries on all relevant issues including trade.
	National EPA Technical Team (NETT)	Related government ministries and departments, the civil society, research institutions and academics, and the private sector	A forum to discuss and coordinate Tanzanian interests and position in EPA negotiations with the EU
Uganda	President's Economic Council (PEC)/The National Forum	Headed by the President, PEC included ministers and high level government technocrats dealing with economic policy issues, and the representative of private sector	These have broad mandate and high level consultations on trade policy issues
	The National Trade Negotiations Team (NTNT)	Led by the Minister responsible for Trade. The Permanent Secretary in MoT to determine composition of Team. But to take consideration of private sector and Inter-Institutional Trade Committee (IITC)	Harmonize stakeholder views and take a lead in trade negotiations
	Trade, Debt and Finance Committee (TDFC)	Composed of political leaders trade, finance and economy, and technocrats: National Planning Authority and Bureau of Statistics	Enhance Uganda's competitiveness of exports and as an investment destination, among other issues
	Inter-Institutional Trade Committee (IITC)	Relevant government ministries, private sector and CSOs. The staff of the MTTI Trade department is ex officio member of the IITC	The IITC mandate covers both the functions of inter-ministerial coordination, and consultation with the private sector
	Uganda National Development and Trade Policy Forum (NDTPF)	Relevant governmental negotiators, the private sector, and the CSOs	Coordinates Ugandan participation in the negotiations for EPA with the EU
Kenya	National Committee on the WTO (NCWTO)	• All stakeholders from the public sector, private sector, and the civil society • MoT convenes and chairs the meetings	Mandated to develop national positions on WTO issues

Country	Consultation mechanisms	Composition	Role
	Joint Industrial and Commercial Consultative Committee (JICCC)	• Public and private sector representatives • The MoT convenes and chairs the meetings	To be a consultative forum on trade and industrial issues
	Kenya-European Union Post-Lome Trade Negotiations (KEPLOTRADE) Support Programme/ National Development and Trade Policy Forum (NDTPF)	• Public sector, private sector, and civil society representatives • The MoT coordinates and is also secretariat	To facilitate Kenyan preparations for the EPA negotiations with the EU and disseminate the EPA-related information
	Cabinet's Sub-Committee on Trade	Ministers responsible for relevant government ministries	Ministerial level consultations and coordination on trade-related issues
	Inter-Ministerial Committees (IMCs)	Government ministries	Inter-ministerial coordination including on trade
Rwanda	Ministry of Trade and Industry	Ministries of Finance and Economic Planning, Agriculture, Infrastructure, Lands, Environment, Forestry, Water and Mines, and RRA, the Investment Promotion Agency and National Bank of Rwanda	Trade policy formulation, implementation and negotiations. Coordinates with other ministries and government agencies
	The government–private sector institutional dialogue	Private sector lobby groups and government ministries and agencies	Responsible for lobbying government for incentives to private sector and protecting their interests
	Other non-state actors	Civil society	Engages the state to articulate concerns on negative impacts of trade agreements

Source: Authors and Table 1.7, CUTS International, 2009b.

China's Trade Policymaking: Domestic Interests and Post-WTO Contestations

Yang Jiang

Introduction

With its huge domestic market, robust outflow of exports and an authoritarian government, China seems a natural candidate as a proponent of global free trade. In fact, tensions already abound as China is criticized for manipulating its exchange rate to promote exports while protecting domestic companies from foreign competition, an accusation that labels China as mercantilist. China, however, has rejected the criticism, instead demonstrating that it has a 'great power style' (*daguo fengfan*) in bilateral free trade agreements (FTA) and in buying foreign products during the 2008–9 global financial crisis. With its economic size surpassing Japan in 2010 to become the world's second largest economy, China appears to be on its way to becoming the third hegemony in the international system after the *Pax Britannica* and the *Pax Americana*.

However, conventional views tend to overestimate both the potential of China's domestic market and Beijing's autonomy in trade policymaking. Studies of China's economic policymaking during the reform era record much political struggle (Harris 2002; Kennedy 2005; Lampton 2001; Lardy 1998; Nolan 2004; Pearson 2001; Reardon 2002; Shirk 1994; Zweig 2002). 'Fragmented authoritarianism' is a widely accepted model to describe the Chinese policymaking structure (Lieberthal and Lampton 1992). In particular, existing studies have depicted how liberalizing forces have won over vested interests over the years to push reform forward. Liberalizing forces include determined leadership, for example, from Deng Xiaoping and Zhu Rongji, local governments that seek foreign connections, bureaucrats who believe in reform, for example Long Yongtu, and companies that pursue market opportunities.

To date, there are not many studies of the domestic politics of China's trade policy in general (Zeng 2007). Although China's policymaking with a view to its accession to membership of the World Trade Organization (WTO) is well documented (Breslin 2003; Feng 2006; Fewsmith 1999; Fung et al. 2006; Holbig and Ash 2002; Lardy 2002; Pearson 2001; Sheng 2002; Y. Wang 2000), little research has been undertaken on the domestic politics of China's trade policy post-WTO accession, with the exception of Zeng (2007) who focuses on trade disputes. The distribution of power between liberals and protectionists in Chinese post-WTO trade politics is far from clear. This chapter seeks to explore China's trade policymaking in the context of diverging domestic interests and complex international environments, with a focus on post-WTO dynamics. It argues that, contrary to the conventional view, Chinese trade policymakers have met formidable domestic obstacles in pushing forward liberalization beyond the commitments made upon WTO accession. Even in economic diplomacy, where China appears to have been extremely proactive in the past decade, the Chinese state has had limited autonomy in trade negotiations.

After a brief review of the history of China's trade policy in the context of China's reforms up until WTO accession, this chapter analyses the question of whether China is turning away from multilateral free trade towards bilateralism and protectionism. It underlines the roles of agriculture, services, state-owned enterprises and relevant government agencies in Chinese domestic political economy.

Self-Sufficiency, Import-Substitution, Processing Trade and Free Trade?

China has adopted several models of development and, accordingly, trade policy strategy. 'Feeling the stones to cross the river' may best describe the modus operandi, but in the past each policy change was the result of intensive ideological debate, domestic interest bargaining and external pressure. In particular, domestic interests have become increasingly vocal.

The founders of the newly established People's Republic of China (PRC) debated whether China should be self-sufficient or accept international interdependence. As the PRC was not recognized by most of the international community and much of the Chinese elite questioned whether the concept of comparative advantage was consistent with Marxism (Harris 2002), Chinese elites made a conscious decision to limit foreign economic interactions in the early 1950s. The inwardly oriented development strategies were, until 1979, primarily determined by domestic debates over the best path to self-reliance (Perkins 2001: 488–90; Reardon 2002: 4–5). Overall, trade was highly restricted except for small amounts of food aid and exports of raw materials for necessary foreign exchange. China adopted an import substitution strategy for industrialization, following the example of the Soviet Union. But unlike the developing paths of other Asian and Latin American countries, China imported capital-intensive goods and equipment as it believed that heavy industry represented national competitiveness and should be at the core of a socialist economy.

Despite the strategy of self-reliance, China's economic interactions with the outside world expanded as elites gradually learned from their policy successes and failures. The souring of its relationship with the Soviet Union and the economic damage resulting from ten years of Cultural Revolution convinced Beijing that self-sufficiency was no longer a feasible option. It also hurt Beijing's pride to see that the small neighbouring countries were developing faster. Finally, in December 1978 Deng won the battle with his motif 'practice is the only standard to judge truth' (*shijian shi jianyan zhenli de weiyi biaozhun*). The 'reform and opening up' plan was launched.

The debate about market economies and planned economies, as well as around self-sufficiency and interdependence continued after 1978. Opponents to the open-door policy were afraid of being exploited, having China's sovereignty undermined, or suffering an insult to the nation (Zhao 2009: 107). However, Chinese policymakers and producers gradually learned 'the magic of free trade' — enhanced productivity, the leapfrogging of primitive industrial processes and better utilization of China's advantages (Zhao 2009: 136). Moreover, overseas trained intellectuals, foreign experts and institutions brought in new ideas and knowledge about economic development and globalization. When Stuart Harris, Head of the Australian Department of Foreign Affairs and Trade (DFAT), visited China in 1984, a Chinese Vice Premier asked him to explain Ricardo's theory of comparative advantage (Interview with Stuart Harris, Canberra, February 2008). The initial socialization process between China and international organizations brought a convergence of ideas on the two sides concerning the measures needed for growth (Jacobson and Oksenberg 1990). Likewise, China's experience in the second-track Pacific Economic Cooperation Council (PECC) and Pacific Trade and Development Forum (PAFTAD) prepared China for the Asia-Pacific Economic Cooperation (APEC). Such inputs played a prominent role in drawing up reform blueprints for the Chinese leadership. Special Economic Zones were established, which offered preferential policies to foreign investment that engaged in processing trade. Labour-intensive manufacturing thus gained rapid growth and by the mid-1980s import substitution had largely been replaced by the promotion of processing trade.

Increased trade brought economic as well as political benefits to the companies that had trading rights and to the localities that were designated for processing trade. Domestic actors competed to obtain such preferential policies. Even when the weaknesses of reform — corruption, smuggling and inequality — became contentious, as demonstrated in 1989, Deng Xiaoping was able to gather enough support for the market economy during his Southern Tour in 1992. Pragmatism instead of ideology was established in Deng's famous 'black-cat white-cat' thesis: whether black or white, as long as it catches mice, it is a good cat. Similarly, whether a market economy or a planned economy, as long as it is good for China's development and modernization, it should be adopted. The third-generation leadership of Jiang Zemin and Zhu Rongji (the first two being Mao Zedong and

Deng Xiaoping respectively) inherited the baton of liberalization. Zhu Rongji in particular used an iron fist to push forward market economy reform. A major goal of his premiership was China's WTO membership, which served both as an objective of and a means to trade liberalization.

WTO Accession

China was fully aware of the importance of global trade and multilateral institutions. A major force behind China's determination to join the WTO was to end the uncertainty in receiving most-favoured-nation (MFN) treatment from other countries, which not only limited China's exports but also hurt national pride when the granting of MFN treatment was associated with human rights. WTO membership was also regarded by Beijing as bringing access to international rules making, whereby China could defend its own interests and engage in trade diplomacy. Moreover, WTO accession was imperative to the Chinese leadership, despite costly domestic reforms, because in domestic discourse it was closely linked with China's national pride as a great power that deserved the same trading rights as enjoyed by most other countries. WTO membership also meant international recognition of both China's reform efforts and the government's competency in international negotiations. In the end, domestic reform reached such a stage of extreme difficulty that reform-minded leaders like Zhu Rongji needed external pressure to impose domestic change.

Before China's accession to the WTO, there was staunch domestic resistance to liberalization. In the late 1990s, agriculture, manufacturing industries such as steel, automobile and petro-chemicals, as well as services including banking, telecommunications and transportation put huge pressure on Chinese trade policymakers against increasing foreign competition. The Chinese elite were torn between neo-leftists and liberals (Chen 1999; Mishra 2006). They differed on both the pace and depth of China's continued economic liberalization. The final decision to pursue GATT membership had to be made in a relatively centralized fashion through creating a Central Leading Group for WTO Affairs headed by Vice Premier Wu Yi and through the top leadership's direct participation in negotiations (Feng 2006; Fewsmith 1999; Pearson 2001; Y. Wang 2000).

Post-WTO Turn?

Since its WTO entry in December 2001, China's proactivity at forging FTAs, in contrast to its low profile at the WTO, as well as its industrial policy of cultivating national industries and global champions invites the question of whether China's post-WTO accession trade policy has turned to bilateralism and protectionism.

Although WTO accession was celebrated as a national victory, domestic debate continued over whether the commitments under the WTO had been a sell-out of China's national interest. It is true that WTO membership has brought China huge benefits in terms of surging export volumes and cheaper consumer goods. Moreover, the impact of the WTO on some domestic producers has turned out to be better than expected. In particular, the automotive industry is often used by Chinese policymakers as an example of the wonders of the invisible hand.

However, as discussed later, a number of sectors faced a severe adjustment challenge as a result of increased foreign competition. Moreover, despite burgeoning exports, WTO accession did not bring about the *expected* growth rate of exports because of non-tariff barriers and trade disputes. China's over-dependence on a few markets – the United States, Japan and Europe – has ignited resentment in those countries about trade deficits with China. Many countries, including developing ones, have taken restrictive measures and have pressured the Chinese government to appreciate their currency, the Renminbi (RMB). China has received by far the largest number of anti-dumping lawsuits at the WTO (www.wto.org/english/tratop_e/adp_e/adp_e.htm). China has also been pessimistic about progress in the Doha Round of negotiations. It criticized major Western countries such as the United States, the European Union and Japan for failing to reduce agricultural tariffs or subsidies, while China itself had difficulty in committing to further concessions, in particular on agriculture, services and intellectual property rights (IPRs). China has successfully created a category of 'recently-acceded members' at the WTO to avoid further major concessions in the near future. However, China does not wish to be labelled as the leader of developing countries because 'the distribution of interests at the WTO is very complex and changeable' (author's interview with Ministry of Commerce (MOFCOM) officials, Beijing, May 2006, July 2009). Some developing countries, for example, Brazil, strive for more agricultural liberalization, while China cannot make substantial concessions on agriculture under current domestic conditions, as will be discussed later. Chinese policymakers thus have become determined that China look for alternative, short-term strategies to expand trade.

Bilateralism

Compared with its low profile in multilateral trade diplomacy, China has been much more active in bilateral FTA talks, noting that negotiations among a small group are easier to manage. In response to criticism that bilateralism is discriminatory and destructive to global free trade, Chinese trade policymakers are aware that FTAs are exceptions to the MFN treatment (MOFCOM 2006), but they argue that FTAs are legal under the WTO. Chinese trade policymakers point out that bilateral FTAs have become a common practice of other countries, that many of the agreements do not cover 'substantially all trade' and that China does not want to lose out in this game (MOFCOM 2007).

In practice, China prefers a selective, gradual approach to trade liberalization under its FTAs rather than a comprehensive 'single undertaking'. The FTAs with the Association of Southeast Asian Nations, or ASEAN, (CAFTA) and with New Zealand cover trade in goods, services and investment, but a wide range of sensitive goods and sectors in services and investment are exempt. China is also reluctant to include 'behind-the-border issues' in FTAs. Beijing argues that problems in intellectual property rights and transparency cannot be solved overnight in China. Nor does China seek to forge its bilateral FTAs into multilateral arrangements. Beijing is suspicious of the plausibility of a Northeast Asia FTA or an East Asia FTA, blaming obstacles on Japan's position on historical issues and its protection of agriculture. An FTA in Asia-Pacific is regarded as being as difficult as the WTO negotiations. Moreover, China's FTAs take various forms in terms of tariff levels, non-tariff barriers and Rules of Origin (RoO), which could contribute to the 'spaghetti bowl' or 'noodle bowl' effect on international trade (Bhagwati 1993). Just as United States bilateralism in the 1990s launched a second wave of FTAs across the world, Chinese activism seems to have tumbled another domino.

Multilateralism and bilateralism serve different objectives in China's international strategy. Multilateralism is used to pursue China's global economic interests, gain access to global rule-making and build China's international image as a responsible power. Bilateralism is used for China's pragmatic and strategic objectives. China's first FTA proposal, to ASEAN, was to allay ASEAN's worry about China's economic threat upon its accession into the WTO and to ensure a safe strategic neighbourhood. China also hopes to establish rules in bilateral relations and to gain power in global arenas through a regional voice. Chinese scholars think that 'if the most important thing in China's entry into the WTO is to obey the rules of the game, the negotiations of CAFTA will be the start of China in making the rules of the game' (Xu *et al.* 2003: 163). Apart from helping China expand exports and diversify export markets, FTAs are used to ensure a 'stable supply' of resources – meaning long-term and stably priced – from partners such as Australia, the Gulf Cooperation Council (GCC), Chile, ASEAN, Peru and the South African Customs Union (SACU). China also demands Market Economy Status as a precondition to start formal FTA negotiations with its FTA partners (except the GCC). In anti-dumping investigations at the WTO, Chinese policymakers and businesses feel greatly disadvantaged by the Economy in Transition Status that China has within the WTO for 15 years and which they believe leads to an unduly arbitrary determination of dumping.

An important goal of trade bilateralism for China is to demonstrate its 'great power style', in contrast, it is claimed, to predatory big powers that exploit the power asymmetry in trade negotiations. Beijing claims to take less from and give more to smaller countries (*houwang bolai*), as exemplified in the Early Harvest Programmes (EHP) with ASEAN and with Pakistan. However, such arrangements cannot completely convince smaller countries of China's benign intentions. While the EHP boosted ASEAN's exports of tropical produce to China, the increased Chinese exports of temperate produce and manufactured goods to ASEAN countries stirred up fears of Chinese domination again (Narintarakul 2004; Wattanapruttipaisan 2003).

China has also unilaterally reduced tariffs for some goods from least developed countries (LDCs). As of 1 July 2010, 60 per cent of the goods from 26 African countries enjoy zero tariffs when exporting into China, and the list will expand to 95 per cent of goods from all the 30 African LDCs with which China has diplomatic relations. Beijing emphasizes that such measures are 'unitary, voluntary and giving out benefits' (Xinhua News Agency 2010). However, reports abound of cheap Chinese goods flooding the African market, causing some African producers and politicians to call China a new imperialist or colonialist.

The limited success of China in demonstrating 'great power style' in trade diplomacy may stem from a lack of coordination among its foreign policy and trade policy agencies, led by the Ministry of Foreign Affairs (MFA) and MOFCOM respectively. Although the MFA still plays a significant role in initiating bilateral cooperation, it only acts as the reviewer of the 'political qualifications' of a potential partner. In other words, it prioritizes countries that the Chinese government has political trust in and penalizes countries that have violated China's political taboos, in halting trade talks, for example, with Singapore and with Norway. However, specific terms of the FTAs are negotiated by MOFCOM and MOFCOM is easily lobbied by industrial agents. Compared with its power before WTO accession, MOFCOM now enjoys less autonomy in trade negotiations.

A fundamental reason for MOFCOM's limited autonomy lies in China's domestic political economy. The Chinese economy depends heavily on exports and needs multiple markets, even those of smaller or developing countries. The decision to halt the appreciation of RMB in mid-2008 during the global financial crisis demonstrated China's reliance on exports once more. China also resumed tax rebates for the export of labour-intensive products that China has traditional comparative advantage in and had been trying to gradually move away from, which caused more direct competition with products from developing countries. For China, reduced exports meant that large numbers of workers were laid off from plants in coastal areas and were forced to return to their farmland, some of which no longer existed because of private land development and local government appropriation. The risk of social unrest looks very real to policymakers in Beijing. Even at bilateral FTA talks, China has been defensive of the interest of several domestic sectors. As will be discussed in the next section, protectionist industries and agencies have gained power in Chinese domestic politics.

Protectionism?

The Chinese government repeatedly warned against protectionism during the financial crisis, due to increased foreign restrictions against Chinese exports and outward investments. At the same time, foreign companies became vocal about the difficulty of doing business in China (Beattie and Anderlini 2010). Is it possible that China has turned into a typical mercantilist country — supporting exports while protecting domestic industries from foreign competition? It may be too early to draw a conclusion but indicators can be found in China's trade politics. Firstly, the impact of the WTO on the Chinese economy and society is not all positive (S.G. Wang 2000). Economic liberalization has caused social and regional disparities in China, reflected in the rising incidence of protests by peasants and laid-off workers, and of ethnic unrest, as well as widespread resentment in the citizenry of poor social welfare, corruption and the increasing stratification of society. Social unrest is seen as the biggest threat to the regime's legitimacy (Moneyhon 2004; Xue and Lu 2001), and the fourth-generation leadership of Hu Jintao and Wen Jiabao has made the idea of a 'harmonious society' a paramount goal in domestic politics and 'scientific development', instead of simply choosing the economic goal of economic growth. Secondly, domestic interests that have benefited from partial reform, such as telecommunications, transportation and financial services, resist further reform for fear of losing their existing privileges. Thirdly, state-owned enterprises (SOEs), most of which are in heavy industry, have become politically powerful because of the government's grand strategy of developing 'national industry'. Their close political ties with the Communist Party and their huge numbers of employees make them indispensable in Chinese politics.

Agriculture

Agriculture in China was a staunch opponent of liberalization under the WTO and has been forced to accept tariff reductions. Trade negotiators reasoned that foreign competition would enhance the productivity of Chinese agriculture. During the negotiations of the China–ASEAN FTA, even though the Ministry of Agriculture (MOA) and some local governments had concerns over the potential costs, they kept silent as a result of political pressure. Importantly, the State Council granted the Ministry of Foreign Trade and Cooperation (MOFTEC) a lot of power to coordinate domestic interests (interviews with MOFCOM officials and scholars involved in the policymaking process, Beijing, March to May 2006). However, the experience with the WTO and FTAs provided protectionists with arguments against further substantial agricultural liberalization. MOA holds that all domestic wool production has been wiped out by foreign competition. The slow progress of China's FTA negotiations with Australia is one result of such domestic concern.

The interests of farmers are represented by the MOA because there is no farmers' union in China, and the Ministry, as in most other countries, is protectionist for its own reasons — career prospects for officials and profits from existing rents for the bureaucracy in the form of cronyism, monopoly profits and corruption. Whether or not the reduction of tariffs would make a real difference to the life of farmers, agricultural issues remain sensitive in China and peasant protests have been on the rise in recent years. In response the government put solving 'three agricultural' problems — peasants, rural areas and agricultural production — on the top of its policies at the 16th National Congress of the Communist Party of China in 2003.

There has also been some change in the thinking of trade policymakers regarding agriculture. MOFCOM officials are in general proponents of liberalization, but they have taken a cautious position on agricultural trade after negotiating the FTAs with ASEAN and with Pakistan. Their experience at the WTO negotiations has led to the conclusion that agriculture, for political and historical reasons, is a special and sensitive sector for every country and that China needs to consider whether it should follow the path of many developed countries — to significantly shrink the agricultural sector and protect what remains (interviews with Chinese negotiators from MOFCOM, Beijing, April 2006 and May 2007).

Recent fluctuation in food prices in China has attracted domestic attention towards food security. Chinese media report that large numbers of domestic food companies have gone bankrupt and that the trade and distribution of several important food stocks such as soya beans and vegetable oil have become dominated by foreign companies (http://finance.sina.com.cn/g/20080908/06335281167. shtml). Considering that the Chinese government has a food self-sufficiency policy that seeks to ensure 95 per cent of the supply of grains from domestic sources, China's food security is seen as being under great threat. There are signs of new thinking about 'outsourcing food security' [author's words], that is, to establish stable strategic partnerships with food exporting countries such as Australia and Thailand, which have been mentioned in the FTA negotiations between China and the two countries. However, Australia's initial rejection of the bid of Chinalco for Rio Tinto and domestic political ruptures in Thailand are not conducive to the new thinking's realization into policy.

Services

In recent years China has realized the importance of developing the services sector for industrialization and employment. It also noticed that services trade has become an important part of multilateral and regional trade talks. However, compared with its commitments under WTO accession, Beijing is now taking a more conservative approach to reform in this area.

One reason is that security and stability have become the priority in China's current economic policy. The government thinks that it has already made substantial concessions on services upon WTO accession and has carried them out faithfully, and that the full consequences of the accession must be experienced before any commitment to further liberalization is made. In particular, the regulators of the banking sector believe that Chinese banks are still vulnerable to foreign competition.

For telecommunication and cultural industries, China has sought protection on grounds of national security. A more important reason is that a huge amount of profit is generated from monopolies in partially reformed sectors. For example, as a result of the strong influence of major state-owned telecom companies in the Ministry of Industry and Information Technology (MIIT), the latter retains a conservative position in trade negotiations (Interview with a MOFCOM official and a MIIT official, April 2007, Beijing). Similar examples exist in the transportation sector, where despite inefficiency and corruption, reform has been very difficult to push forward, regardless of using trade to break monopoly power. An important reason is the dominance of SOEs.

State-Owned Enterprises

The monopoly in many of the above-mentioned sectors is held by SOEs, which have become increasingly independent and powerful in domestic politics. Because of reform, SOEs have gained economic benefits from a reduction in their burden of providing social welfare and from greater autonomy to make market-based business decisions. Meanwhile, because reform is only partial, they have retained rents previously created by the monopolized system and have become even more powerful in politics since the government relies heavily on them for revenue and employment. The managers of major SOEs are often members of important political bodies of the state and the rotation system means that they are not only businessmen but also politicians. Therefore, the sectors that benefited from partial reform have become a significant source of resistance to further reform as their profits and rents under the current system are likely to be lost under external competition and scrutiny.

The Chinese government's strategy to develop 'national industry' and to cultivate national champions provides a crucial condition for the growth of monopoly SOEs. Chinese leaders consider the ownership of global brands as an indicator of national competitiveness and, since 2004, the Chinese government has encouraged the internationalization of Chinese enterprises by providing soft loans and credit insurance. This support has, paradoxically, been the reason cited by foreign governments for putting special scrutiny on or directly rejecting the attempts of Chinese companies to acquire local companies based on 'national security' or 'national interest' considerations.

China's support for domestic champions is not only applied to their international expansion but also to the domestic market. SOEs were the major beneficiaries of the stimulus packages during the financial crisis. The stimulus plans for ten industries (automotive, steel, nonferrous metals, textile, equipment and machinery manufacturing, ship manufacturing, information technology (IT), light manufacturing, petro-chemical and logistics) have a clear bias towards heavy industries which are dominated by SOEs. Each of the industrial stimulus plans was drafted by the National Development and Reform Commission (NDRC), supported by the MIIT, national business associations and representatives of big enterprises in the industry. In several of them (automotive, shipbuilding, electronics, IT), expansion of SOEs through mergers or alliances is encouraged. Instead of furthering market reforms, the regulator of SOEs — the State–owned Assets Supervision and Administration Commission — was authorized by the State Council to bail out loss-making SOEs. Likewise, the Enterprise State Asset Law that came into force on 1 May 2009 leaves room for several industries to keep their state monopoly.

As the preferential policies for foreign investors in the Special Economic Zones were gradually phased out in accordance with WTO guidelines, foreign businesses have complained about the difficulty of doing business in China, in particular because of state support for SOEs and lack of transparency (Anderlini 2010; Li 2009). Studies have concurred that China's level of compliance with WTO commitments on behind-the-border issues is not satisfactory, for example on IPRs, transparency, industrial standards and market access for foreign investment (Chan 2004; Pearson 2003; Stewart 2004). Upon its WTO accession China promised to start Government Procurement Agreement (GPA) talks, but it only provided the first offer to the GPA in 2007 and the second in 2010. In response to criticism that government procurement in China's four-trillion-Yuan stimulus package excluded foreign bidders, the NDRC claimed that in fact domestic suppliers had been excluded by local governments and stressed that China had already sent delegations on 'shopping tours' to the United States and Europe (http://business. sohu.com/20090602/n264288508.shtml). Although China is not yet a member of the GPA whereas the United States is, the initiative of both countries to encourage the purchase of domestic products during the global financial crisis suggest that nationalism speaks louder than internationalism.

Government Agencies

As can be seen from the previous discussions, Chinese trade policymaking is fragmented amongst the foreign trade ministry, the foreign ministry, industry-line ministries and national economic commissions, and faithful implementation of policies largely depends on the determination of these ministries and local governments. Reform has only been partial in some industries and the government agencies in charge of these sectors have retained significant regulatory power; any further reform needs their consent. These agencies would like to retain their power over the national economy and some would like to retain the rents for the bureaucracy generated from such power such as favouritism in government procurement, corruption in issuing licenses and the huge profits for the sector from administrative monopoly.

Among other economic policy agencies, the NDRC has inherited a conservative position on reform and opening up from its former incarnation as the State Planning Commission. Despite Premier Zhu Rongji's attempt to weaken this agency during government restructuring in 1998 and 2003, the NDRC has enjoyed increased power in domestic politics under the Hu-Wen leadership, particularly in industrial policies and investment policies. So far, the position of the NDRC has constrained Chinese trade negotiators' autonomy to liberalize some sectors that it regards as important to the Chinese national economy, including large staple agricultural products (such as wheat, barley, cotton, rice and sugar) and major services industries.

The National People's Congress (NPC) has evolved from merely a 'rubber stamp' to a stronger power centre in China's domestic politics. Traditionally only a venue to discuss domestic issues, the NPC has submitted formal bills to investigate the problems within sectors or localities caused by foreign economic policies, requiring MOFCOM to respond and explain such issues to the NPC at special hearings (interviews with MOFCOM officials, Beijing, May 2007).

Although MOFCOM is formally the lead trade policy agency and usually represents China in trade negotiations, it only has the authority of a negotiator on behalf of industries but not that of a coordinator. In other words, MOFCOM needs the endorsement of relevant industrial ministries or national commissions for its trade policy agenda. As a result, consensus is often difficult to achieve unless the political leadership directly intervenes in the policymaking process.

Compared with the previous generations of leadership, the Hu-Wen leadership, at the time of writing, is under greater domestic pressure to care about social welfare and distributive justice. Factional politics within the Chinese elite, in particular over the pace of reform, continues to be a crucial factor in shaping Chinese domestic politics after its WTO accession (Bo 2007; Dittmer and Liu 2006; Hook 2007). More importantly, social tensions in China have escalated and become more widespread. Political coalitions have traditionally organized themselves along the lines of export-promoting and import-competing industries, but recently they have shown potential to form along the lines of ethnicity or even class. Although the existence of classes is denied by the Communist government, recent incidents demonstrate that strikes by workers and farmers can spread to different industries and locations and that Chinese labourers may organize their own workers' unions because of the weak role of the All China Federation of Trade Unions in protecting their interests. In the current political environment that emphasizes 'harmonious society' and 'scientific development' instead of purely economic growth, the Chinese state has to pay more attention to potential losers from the reform process.

Conclusion

Without doubt, the PRC has adopted phenomenal changes in trade policy. Since it overcame the bias of socialist ideology over the market, reform-minded leadership has brought China through drastic unilateral and multilateral trade liberalization. However, China's trade policymaking has never been without contention and it has become more difficult since China gained WTO membership. Gradual reform may have shielded the Chinese economy from some external shocks, but it has strengthened the political power of protectionist forces vis-à-vis liberalizing ones. Vested interests and the resultant inequality, corruption and non-market practices are now extremely difficult to break. At the same time, domestic social instability has become the highest concern for the Chinese government, which means that it often has to prioritize employment over economic efficiency. In other words, a 'harmonious society' precedes a 'harmonious world'. Domestic political economy constrains China's effort to break away from the long-standing reliance on labour-intensive exports, not only exacerbating tensions with the United States, European Union and Japan but also prolonging the 'Chinese threat' fear amongst developing countries. In the past decade China's industrial policy of promoting national champions has demonstrated a bias towards state-owned enterprises, which has prompted not only charges of protectionism but also suspicions of China's hidden strategic agenda in other countries.

If the Asian financial crisis ended 'the East Asian miracle' (Stubbs 2005; World Bank 1993), China's economic rise may signal the revival of the developmental state or even the challenge of a Beijing Consensus to the Washington Consensus, thereby demonstrating that the neoliberal economic ideology fell into crisis together with the global economy in 2008. However, time will tell how far China can proceed in economic terms through current trade policy, how sustainable it is for domestic economic and political progress and indeed whether China's fragmented authoritarianism will actually be able to generate a consensus.

References

Anderlini, J. 2010. China's partners set to reject trade plan. *Financial Times*, 19 July.

Beattie, A. and Anderlini, J. 2010. 'Friends' of China question relationship. *Financial Times*, 19 July.

Bhagwati, J.N. 1993. Regionalism and multilateralism: an overview, in *New Dimensions in Regional Integration*, edited by J. de Melo and A. Panagariya. New York: Cambridge University Press: 22–51.

Bo, Z.Y. 2007. *China's Elite Politics: Political Transition and Power Balancing*. Singapore: World Scientific.

Breslin, S. 2003. Reforming China's embedded socialist compromise: China and the WTO. *Global Change, Peace and Security*, 15(3): 213–29.

Chan, G. 2004. China and the WTO: theory and practice of compliance. *International Relations of the Asia-Pacific*, 4(1): 47–72.

Chen, F. 1999. The unfinished battle in China: the leftist criticism of the reform and the third thought emancipation. *The China Quarterly*, 158: 447–67.

Dittmer, L. and Liu, G.L. 2006. *China's Deep Reform: Domestic Politics in Transition*. Lanham: Rowman & Littlefield.

Feng, H. 2006. *The Politics of China's Accession to the World Trade Organisation: The Dragon Goes Global*. London and New York: Routledge.

Fewsmith, J. 1999. China and the WTO: politics behind the agreement. *NBR Analysis*, 10(5): 23–39.

Fung, H.G., Pei, C. and Zhang, K.H. (eds). 2006. *China and the Challenge of Economic Globalization: The Impact of WTO Membership*. Armonk: M.E. Sharpe.

Harris, S. 2002. Globalization and China's diplomacy: structure and process. *Department of International Relations Working Paper*. Canberra: Australian National University.

Holbig, H. and Ash, R. (eds). 2002. *China's Accession to the World Trade Organization: National and International Perspectives*. New York: RoutledgeCurzon.

Hook, L. 2007. The rise of China's new left. *Far Eastern Economic Review* (April): 8–14.

Jacobson, H.K. and Oksenberg, M. 1990. *China's Participation in the IMF, the World Bank, and GATT: Toward a Global Economic Order*. Ann Arbor: The University of Michigan Press.

Kennedy, S. 2005. *The Business of Lobbying in China*. Cambridge, MA: Harvard University Press.

Lampton, D.M. (ed.). 2001. *The Making of Chinese Foreign and Security Policy in the Era of Reform, 1978–2000*. Stanford: Stanford University Press.

Lardy, N.R. 1998. *China's Unfinished Economic Revolution*. Washington, DC: Brookings Institution Press.

Lardy, N.R. 2002. *Integrating China into the Global Economy*. Washington, DC: Brookings Institution Press.

Li, Q. 2009. fagaiweihuiying 4 wanyicaigoupaiwaizhize: chengguohuozaoqishi [NDRC responds to 4 trillion procurement excludes foreign products: saying domestic products are discriminated against], *Xinwen Chenbao* [News Morning], 2 June.

Lieberthal, K. and Lampton, D.M. 1992. *Bureaucracy, Politics, and Decision Making in Post-Mao China*. Berkeley: University of California Press.

Mishra, P. 2006. China's new leftist. *New York Times*, 15 October.

MOFCOM. 2006. Director of the International Economic and Trade Relations Department Yu Jianhua Talks about Free Trade Areas and Regional Economic Cooperation, 29 December. [Online] Available at: www.mofcom.gov.cn/ fangtan/061229.shtml [accessed: 4 October 2010].

MOFCOM. 2007. Vice Minister Yi Xiaozhun Talks about China's Choices and Achievements in Regional Economic Cooperation, 29th May. [Online] Available at: http://yixiaozhun.mofcom.gov.cn/aarticle/speeches/200705/20070504725234. html [accessed: 4 October 2010].

Moneyhon, M.D. 2004. Taming China's 'Wild West': ethnic conflict in Xinjiang. *Peace, Conflict, and Development: An Interdisciplinary Journal*, 5(5): 2–23.

Narintarakul, K. 2004. Thai-China Free Trade Agreement for whose benefit? Asia Pacific Network on Food Sovereignty Regional Workshop Papers, 6 –9 November.

Nolan, P. 2004. *Transforming China: Globalization, Transition and Development*. London and New York: Anthem Press.

Pearson, M.M. 2001. The case of China's accession to GATT/WTO, in *The Making of Chinese Foreign and Security Policy in the Era of Reform, 1978–2000*, edited by D.M. Lampton. Stanford: Stanford University Press: 337–70.

Pearson, M.M. 2003. Is China Playing by the Rules? Free Trade, Fair Trade and WTO Compliance, Statement at the Congressional-Executive Commission on China, 24 September.

Perkins, D.H. 2001. China's economic policy and performance, *in Cambridge History of China*, edited by R. MacFarquhar and J.K. Fairbank. Cambridge: Cambridge University Press: 488–90.

Reardon, L. 2002. *The Reluctant Dragon: Crisis Cycles in Chinese Foreign Economic Policy*. Seattle and London: University of Washington Press.

Sheng, B. 2002. *ZhongguoDuiwaiMaoyiZhengce De ZhengzhiJingjiFenxi* [The Political Economy of China's Foreign Trade Policies]. Shanghai: Shanghai Sanlian.

Shirk, S.L. 1994. *How China Opened Its Door: The Political Success of the PRC's Foreign Trade and Investment Reforms*. Washington, DC: Brookings Institution.

Stewart, T.P. 2004. China's Compliance with World Trade Organization Obligations: A Review of China's 1st Two Years of Membership. U.S.-China Security and Economic Review Commission.

Stubbs, R. 2005. *Rethinking Asia's Economic Miracle*. Basingstoke: Palgrave.

Wang, S.G. 2000. The social and political implications of China's WTO membership. *Journal of Contemporary China*, 9(25): 373–405.

Wang, Y. 2000. China's domestic WTO debate. *The China Business Review*, 27(1): 54–8.

Wattanapruttipaisan, T. 2003. ASEAN-China Free Trade Area: advantages, challenges, and implications for the newer ASEAN member countries. *ASEAN Economic Bulletin*, 20: 31–48.

World Bank. 1993. The East Asian miracle: economic growth and public policy, *World Bank Policy Research Reports*. New York: Oxford University Press.

Xinhua News Agency. 2010. 60% of exports from 26 least developed African countries enjoy zero tariff to China, 1 July. [Online] Available at: www.gov.cn/jrsg/2010-07/01/content_1643086.htm [accessed: 4 October 2010].

Xu, C. W., Li, G.H. and Li, W. 2003. *ZhongguoLingpaoDongyaJingjiHezuo* [China Leading the Race of East Asian Economic Cooperation]. Beijing: China Customs Press.

Xue, F.X. and Lu D.D. (eds). 2001. *China's Regional Disparities: Issues and Policies*. Huntington: Nova Institute Press.

Zeng, K. 2007. *China's Foreign Trade Policy: The New Constituencies*. London and New York: Routledge.

Zhao, Z.Y. 2009. *Prisoner of the State*. London: Simon & Schuster.

Zweig, D. 2002. *Internationalizing China: Domestic Interests and Global Linkages*. Ithaca: Cornell University Press.

PART VIII
Conclusions

Trends in Trade Policy and Challenges Ahead

Kenneth Heydon and Stephen Woolcock

The initial chapters of this volume identified a number of key questions concerning international trade policy that also constitute the main challenges facing the international trading system. This chapter first revisits these key questions and then summarizes how the preceding chapters have answered them.

Key Questions

The first key question is the *ideological or ideational basis for trade policy*. Chapter 1 discussed the historical debate on free trade versus protection or more interventionist policies. This showed how the issue has been debated over centuries. At various times over the decades there have been periods in which one could argue there was a broad consensus on trade, whether this was the 'embedded liberalism' of the early GATT years, or more recently the general shift to a liberal paradigm during the 1980s and 1990s. But the ideological debate on free trade versus more interventionist or mercantilist policies has not been settled. There are still actors who believe that a positive balance of trade is an essential national aim. Despite evidence – including in this book – that trade openness favours development, there remains a persistent view that infant industry protection and state intervention are essential if developing countries are to be able to share ultimately in the benefits of the global economy.

The second question, introduced in Chapter 2, concerns the *political economy* of trade policy and why pressures for protection and intervention persist given the evidence and the strength of the economic argument for open markets. This question goes to the heart of the functioning of the trading system and it is essential that any discussion of trade policy takes proper account of it. An analysis of the political economy of trade enables an assessment to be made of the benefits and costs of trade opening, and thus the likely distribution of interests in any debate on trade policy. Chapter 2 also stressed that trade policy must be seen in the context of other policies. Viewing trade policy in isolation can lead to unrealistic expectations that trade policy can address non-trade goals. Equally, trade policy could be said to be effective in promoting sustainable economic development only when it is supported by a range of other policies.

The third question, raised in Chapter 3, concerns the *balance between multilateral and preferential approaches to trade policy*. There is a need to be clear that there have always been elements of preferential approaches or bilateralism in trade policy, even during the period of a US-led GATT that is generally characterized as multilateralist. But the trend since around the mid-1990s has clearly been towards a greater emphasis on preferential approaches to trade policy. The alarmist view of this trend is that the open liberal system is under threat, but even the more sanguine views on the growth of bilateral trade agreements must recognize that a continued growth of bilateral agreements and no progress multilaterally could ultimately undermine the credibility of the multilateral system of the WTO.

The fourth question is closely linked to that of preferential versus multilateral trade policy and concerns *the scope of the multilateral regime*. Should this be narrowly defined to primarily cover measures at the border, or should it extend to include topics such as investment and competition policy, that are clearly central to a global economy? This question is linked to that of the balance between preferential and multilateral trade policy in the sense that more comprehensive multilateral trade policy, meaning that more and more trade-related issues are covered, is often seen as becoming increasingly difficult to manage. Preferential approaches may then come to be seen as a means of dealing with such issues.

The final question of course is *how to proceed in trade policy*? What policy implications can be drawn from the chapters of this book?

The Ideological Basis for Trade Policy

Chapter 1 set out a strong intellectual case for free trade. It illustrated how the arguments were synthesized in eighteenth-century Britain by Adam Smith and David Hume who placed open markets in a classical-liberal trinity of freedom, prosperity and security. Smith and Hume developed a dynamic analysis based, for Hume, on 'emulation as the source of every excellence' in which they anticipated later arguments about technology transfer, rent-seeking and government failure. In doing so, Smith and Hume effectively rebutted earlier zero-sum assumptions embodied in mercantilist thinking. This is not to say, however, that free trade advocacy has gone unchallenged. Even in the golden age of free trade in Britain in the second half of the nineteenth century, protection was the norm elsewhere, including in the United States where Alexander Hamilton developed the infant industry protection argument.

The infant industry argument, and support for government intervention, has proved remarkably resilient and remains so today especially in developing countries. Despite empirical support for outward orientation, there remain proponents of infant industry protection from developing countries that would otherwise, it is argued, have little to offer in terms of exports or would remain dependent on raw materials. The case for infant industry protection has invoked support from the growth of the Newly Industrializing Countries that are said to have industrialized thanks to government support for industry and trade protection in the early phases of development. But as Chapter 17 in this volume argues there is a case based on the experience of Taiwan that success depends on governments following the lead of the private sector, reinforcing what the market equilibrium under neutral trade policies would have produced in the first place and that Taiwan's experience supports rather than challenges neoclassical precepts.

Individual chapters bring particular insights to the case for open markets. The discussion of tariffs in Chapter 4 observes that the tariff prevents trading nations from capturing the gains associated with their comparative advantage and that a tax on imports is also tax on exports. This explains the estimates of large potential gains from unilateral liberalization not least for developing countries whose tariff and other barriers tend to be higher than those of the industrialized countries. Chapter 11, which deals with the complementary links between trade and investment, argues that, in the context of global supply chains, the case for tariffs is further weakened because they increase the costs of inputs for domestic producers within such chains. The global supply chain thus serves to lower the 'optimal tariff' of countries. It follows that opening markets to foreign investors from a partner country should also reduce tariff barriers faced by the domestic firms exporting to that country because the 'optimal tariff' of the partner country becomes lower. In the discussion of commercial instruments in Chapter 6 it is seen that antidumping action, by far the most popular trade remedy, is likely to raise domestic prices and reduce welfare, while also leading to collusive behaviour. At the same time Chapter 7 points out that tariffs are only part of the picture and that practical measures to reduce the costs of trade in the form of trade facilitation, a topic in the current Doha Development Agenda (DDA), can also have considerable economic benefits.

Each of the chapters on the different sectors of production highlight further aspects of the economics underlying the case for free trade. In agriculture, we see in Chapter 8 that because of the low income elasticity of demand for food – expenditure on food lags behind overall economic growth – protection is powerless in seeking to negate the secular adjustment process going on in the farm sector. At the same time however, agricultural protection is highly damaging to the interests of developing country farmers and inimical to the pursuit of food security. In manufacturing, as discussed in Chapter 10, while the forces of competition have virtually eliminated Japanese manufacturers from the production of finished electronics products, they have helped foster Japan's underlying comparative advantage enabling it to become an overwhelming presence in the production of skill-intensive raw materials such as the lead frames and silicon wafers on which chips are built or the chemical surface coating for flat-panel TVs. Chapter 9 on services points out that services constitute such an important element in manufacturing that retaining closed services markets is likely to undermine the ability to compete in manufactures.

More generally, opening service markets helps countries – both developed and developing – to realize more effectively their underlying competitive strengths, to create jobs, to help downstream users and to benefit more from the lower demand cyclicality and greater resilience of services, compared with manufactures, to economic downturns.

In short, the preceding chapters support the argument that trade has a key place in the continuum trade–innovation–growth. Trade openness makes markets more competitive, reducing prices and raising incentives to innovate, while also boosting productivity.

The General Trend Towards Open Markets

There is ample evidence of past moves towards trade liberalization, often on a unilateral basis, in each of the regions examined in this book. This is evidenced by the fact that global trade grew three times faster than GDP in the five decades after 1945. In Asia, South Korea and Taiwan began to liberalize trade policy in the 1960s, and China, India and Vietnam in the 1980s and 1990s. In Africa, trade policy became more export-oriented in the 1980s and liberal trade policies generally became dominant in the 1990s. And in Latin America, Chile led the way, by abandoning import-substitution industrialization (ISI) in the mid-1970s, followed by a more general shift triggered by the crisis of 1982 when the reduction of the anti-export bias of ISI was made more pressing by the need to increase export income to service the region's high foreign debt.

In the United States, we have seen that from 1934 until the 2000s, a span of some 70 years, trade policy sought and delivered reciprocal market opening at home and abroad. As a result of unilateral, bilateral and multilateral commitments, the US tariff level was reduced from 20 per cent in 1930 to 3.5 per cent in 2008. At the same time, there was a marked shift towards intra-industry trade and trade in services. And in the European Union, though common external trade policy was defensive in the early years of European integration, the underlying principle of trade policy, as set out in the Treaty, is liberal. As European integration has advanced so has EU support for a multilateral, rules-based system, with the EU aspiring to a leadership role in the run up to the DDA.

We thus see from a broader perspective, strong evidence of past liberalization. A series of multilateral negotiations under the GATT reduced industrialized countries' average tariff on manufactures from close to 40 per cent in 1947 to less than 5 per cent at the close of the Uruguay Round in 1994. In agriculture, trends in the OECD countries in both decoupling (breaking the link between support and producer decisions) and support-reduction have been moving in the right direction. The DDA holds the promise of market opening in manufactures and agriculture. In trade facilitation, concerns to promote supply chain security have boosted efforts to make cross-border goods movements more effective and transparent. And while progress in services liberalization in general has been disappointingly slow, a successful WTO Agreement on Basic Telecommunications and a sector agreement in financial services have been completed and a framework for broader liberalization agreed upon.

This progress has been mirrored by changes in the international trading system itself as it has evolved from a US-led system to one shaped by an OECD club into, now, a more inclusive, heterogeneous arrangement. This heterogeneous structure in trade relations has been emerging for some time and has preceded similar developments in financial and summit diplomacy such as in the emergence of the G20 at summit level in response to the 2007–8 financial crisis. In trade the US-led system gave way to a club model already in the 1970s and became more inclusive around the time of the conclusion of the Uruguay Round in the mid-1990s thus ending the Atlantic-dominated system that prevailed until then. As Chapters 3 and 21 discuss, the system of trade governance has been arguably more flexible and able to accommodate shifts in the balance of economic power than that of financial governance, but this does not make the pressures any less real.

In the process of evolution, the international trading system has also adapted to a much broader notion of market access as behind-the-border issues of domestic regulation have increasingly come under scrutiny. As described in Chapter 3 the scope of agreements has expanded in line with the contemporary preferences of major players concerning what constitutes trade, rather than on the basis of any objective criteria. The evolution of the international trading system has also seen a shift towards a more rules-based approach, not least with the strengthening of the dispute settlement mechanism of the WTO.

Signs of Backsliding

Notwithstanding these moves towards greater liberalization and institutional adaptability – or perhaps in some cases because of them – there are now, as Chapter 1 and the country chapters show, clear signs that support for liberalization has been draining away, which has resulted in a halt to trade opening at the multilateral level and some signs of general backtracking.

In the United States, since 2005 the political system has balked at fresh liberalization. As discussed in Chapter 23, both the Congress and the president are responsive to a trade angst fuelled by high unemployment, a huge trade deficit, the seemingly inexorable rise of China and India and, as inequality has grown, a deep unease among America's vast middle-class, a familiar precursor to protectionism. US trade policy has emphasized a degree of reciprocity in market opening that is seen as excessive by the major emerging markets, a situation that has contributed to the stalemate in the DDA. The US response to the global financial crisis saw increased resort to antidumping measures and robust Buy-American provisions as part of the stimulus package. These responses may moderate. More worrying is the provision for border adjustments on imports from countries judged not to have taken comparable action to the United States in climate legislation which made its way into the Waxman–Markey bill approved by the House in 2009. In the European Union, it has been argued in Chapter 24 that the involvement of the European

Parliament – strengthened by the 2009 Lisbon Treaty – could fuel protectionism, especially in traditionally sensitive sectors, as well as prompting greater emphasis on the relationship between trade and other policy areas, particularly social issues, environmental concerns and respect for human rights. For example, it is suggested in Chapter 24 that it was the influence of the Parliament, together with alliances with specific Member States in the Council and lobbying by a few powerful NGOs that saw a ban on fish imports without any measures to curtail overfishing by the heavily subsidized EU fishing fleet.

In China, we have seen that following WTO accession in 2001, during which China believes it made considerable concessions, there is resistance to further liberalization on the grounds that China is a Recently Acceded Member (RAM) in the WTO. As explained in Chapter 27, in agriculture, farm interests are forming alliances with protectionist elements in the Ministry of Agriculture, as officials seek to reap personal benefit from the rents of protection. And in services – particularly in telecommunications and cultural activities – protection is being sought on national security grounds. And, again, vested interests are anxious to retain their share of the huge monopoly profits being generated by these partially reformed industries. These tendencies are compounded by the Chinese government's promotion of national champions – a move that is conducive to the growth of monopoly state-owned enterprises – the principal beneficiaries of the stimulus package during the global financial crisis.

Parts of Latin America too have seen disenchantment with trade liberalization over the past decade, as discussed in Chapter 25. Though this is not the case in Mexico, Chile, Peru or Central America, in other countries there is resentment that large segments of the population have failed to benefit from the gains from trade. The erosion of support for trade liberalization has not led to tariff increases allowed by high ceiling bindings, but rather has seen increased resort to non-tariff barriers such as non-automatic import licenses and increased use of managed trade.

In East Africa, discussed in Chapter 26, it may be too early to talk of backtracking though it has been observed that the dual nature of trade policymaking – national and regional, via the Ministry of East African Community Affairs – is leading to poor coordination in policymaking. And the Economic Partnership Agreements being signed with the EU bring an inevitable risk of trade diversion at the expense of third parties.

The Political Economy of Trade

The widespread signs of weakening support for or backtracking from liberal trade are occurring in institutional frameworks that differ fundamentally from one country to another, such as in the complex interplay between the Congress and the administration in the United States, the evolving relations between the institutions of the EU or the tensions and fears underlying China's fragmented authoritarianism. But the checks on further liberalization share two things in common.

First they are occurring in an international institutional environment that still reflects the post-1945 GATT–Bretton Woods system of 'liberalization from above' based on reciprocal market opening, with admitted safety valves and an effective decoupling of free trade from laissez-faire in domestic politics.

Second, the checks on further liberalization or backtracking are all shaped by the political economy of trade – in other words, as discussed in Chapter 2, the fact that trade liberalization involves both winners and losers and that while overall gains can be expected to exceed losses, the costs of liberalization tend to be concentrated and easy to measure while the benefits are often highly dispersed and hard to measure. The concentrated costs of market opening thus means that political influence tends to be greater for those seeking continued government assistance or protection because those who stand to lose from liberalization have more at stake than those who stand to gain.

It is this characteristic of costs and benefits that fuels the drop in US poll numbers supporting free trade, the concerns of Europe's 'Club Med' countries about foreign competition in specific sectors and the growing view in China that domestic food companies need protection. The political economy of trade also helps explain the protracted process of the Doha Development Agenda and the steady scaling down of reform ambition to the point where the game is seen to be hardly worth the candle.

The conclusion that might therefore be drawn is that it is an inability or unwillingness to address the political economy of trade that is weakening support for trade liberalization. This point is addressed below in terms of the way ahead: making a more persuasive case for liberal trade while acting directly through complementary measures to ease the cost of adjustment for those that feel the strains of open markets.

The Balance Between Preferential and Multilateral Trade Policy

The political economy of trade can also help explain the growth of reciprocal preferential trade agreements – whether Free Trade Agreements (FTAs) or Customs Unions – insofar as these arrangements enable countries to focus on a narrow range of partners making it easier to exclude politically sensitive sectors, to avoid MFN commitments that open them to major competitors and to secure reciprocity from other signatories.

In the space of the past 20 years the number of preferential trade agreements (PTAs) notified to the WTO has grown from a mere 30 to over 200, with an additional 100 agreements signed by non-members.

As discussed in Chapter 22, horizontal intra-industry trade, which has also been growing strongly, may be particularly conducive to preferential rather than non-discriminatory liberalization in that governments can reduce adjustment costs by trading off bilaterally opportunities to specialize within an industry. The way in which PTAs have become a springboard for Asia-wide value chains in the automotive industry is an illustration of this point.

We have also seen that the motivations for signing PTAs differ from country to country and often have an important foreign policy dimension: for China in demonstrating its great power style; for the United States in asserting its presence in areas of strategic importance; and for the EU in consolidating its relations with prospective growth markets. Developing countries themselves have used PTAs as a way of fostering regional cooperation and strategic goals while also underpinning domestic reform, often linked to the shift from policies of import substitution.

And so today, PTAs are seen – by business – as a way of obtaining improved market access more quickly than through multilateral negotiation, whether by addressing issues such as investment that have been excluded from the multilateral agenda but are increasingly seen as a complement to trade, by pushing for more ambitious market opening such as the 'negative list' approach to services liberalization or by including more ambitious rules on non-tariff measures that assume greater importance when tariffs are eliminated.

At a time when there is no progress at the multilateral level in the DDA, negotiation of preferential market opening can be seen as offering a second-best alternative. As explained in Chapter 22, even without net trade diversion, any preferential tariff agreement that influences trade must have a negative effect on some exporters outside the agreement, and thus be second-best to multilateral liberalization. Moreover, while PTAs do have some building-block attributes, such as by promoting transparency or regulatory best practice so that their distorting effects should not be exaggerated, there is little doubt that, on balance, they weaken rather than strengthen the incentive to engage in multilateral trade negotiation. As we have seen, as PTAs move ahead with tariff reductions and beyond WTO commitments in services and investment, the multilateral trade regime is saddled with the apparently intractable problem of liberalizing agricultural trade, but left with nothing that market opening in protectionist countries could be traded off against. WTO-plus does not necessarily mean 'better', as seen by the TRIPS-plus provisions in many US and EU-centred agreements. And the fact remains that PTAs are not the optimal way of liberalizing trade. The dynamics of the interaction between multilateral and preferential go beyond the scope of this volume, but as Chapter 22 implies, what is required is a division of labour between the WTO and preferential agreements that does not undermine the WTO (see Heydon and Woolcock 2009).

The Scope of the WTO

Lack of Consensus on the Trade Agenda

As Chapter 3 argued the scope of the multilateral trade regime has evolved over time and the agenda has been largely shaped by the interests of the predominant trading nations at any point of time. The debate on trade during the twenty-first century has to date shown a clear difference between the views of the advanced developed economies, and in particular the European Union, on the one hand, and the now powerful emerging markets on the other. The developed economies tend to favour a comprehensive agenda that addresses their interests in dealing with global externalities, such as those related to the environment or public health. The emerging markets tend to favour a more limited agenda that reflects their interests, which are geared to development and growth through improved market access rather than addressing issues of global externalities.

There is also the unresolved issue of 'fair trade'. This very slippery concept has numerous, conflicting, interpretations. It can be seen as a way for developed countries to impose their standards (whether environmental, labour, or health and safety) on developing countries in order to negate the latter's comparative advantage. It is used as an argument for a form of reciprocity in which liberal countries expect exporting nations that have benefited from access to their markets to assume equivalent liberal policies as they develop. It is invoked as a way of increasing the returns to developing country raw material exporters, such as coffee producers. And it is drawn on to justify greater discipline on the use of government intervention or national industrial policies.

With no consensus on a trade agenda, protectionist policies in the advanced economies are likely to be rationalized on the basis that trade partners are, allegedly, gaining an unfair competitive advantage through noncompliance with international standards dealing with the environment (see Chapters 13 and 14), public health (Chapter 14), social conditions (Chapter 15), or respect for intellectual property rights (Chapter 16).

As noted in earlier chapters, it is becoming increasingly clear that trade measures will be part of the international effort to combat global warming, whether by border tax adjustment, preferential treatment of climate-friendly goods and services, renewable energy subsidies or product labels indicating carbon content. The challenge will be to prevent such policies sliding into green protectionism – or more broadly, 'clear conscience protectionism' (Chapter 24) – as countries seek to enforce the extraterritorial application of domestic regulations through restrictive trade measures.

The challenge is likely to be particularly acute as it bears on global supply chains. Fragmented global production is a recurring theme in many chapters of this book and is seen to be major source of growth in world trade and investment and a disincentive to protection, including via resort to trade remedies. But the future of the global supply chain is not assured. As discussed in Chapter 11, as coordination costs increase along the supply chain an optimal level of fragmentation is ultimately achieved. The risk is that protective trade policies linked to environmental concerns about trade and offshoring will cause this optimal level to be reached earlier than might otherwise be the case.

Compounding these dangers will be the risk that developing countries will seek to avoid or delay market opening whether by forgoing *absolute* gains from their own liberalization in the pursuit of a greater *share* of the gains on offer or by invoking the need for policy space, such actions risk being to the detriment of other developing countries. There is thus evidence, seen in Chapter 6, that antidumping and other commercial instruments are increasingly a South–South phenomenon.

The risk of protective trade policy in the absence of an agreed agenda is all the more real because numerous instruments exist to make protection possible. One such instrument comes from the tariff overhang and the ample scope that exists for many countries to raise their applied tariffs up to the higher level of their tariff bindings. Another comes from the plethora of non-tariff instruments, as discussed in Chapter 5, and the potential for substitution among them depending on their relative capacity to provide protection and the respective costs in doing so.

And the protective danger is likely to be augmented as WTO jurisprudence becomes more attuned to environmental objectives and as differences persist about the definition and use of precaution and the appropriate balance between a sound-science criterion for policymaking against a broader interpretation of the evidence basis for risk assessment.

Trends in WTO Jurisprudence

The relative slowing of the WTO's negotiating, or legislative, function has been matched by a corresponding increase in the relative importance of the organization's litigation function embodied in the dispute settlement system – a system that was greatly strengthened as a result of the Uruguay Round. This shift is all the more important because of the change that has been taking place in WTO jurisprudence that begins to reach beyond GATT or WTO law to include other elements of international economic law. As a consequence of three particular cases of WTO dispute settlement, *US Gasoline*, *Shrimp Turtle* and *Brazil Retreaded Tyres*, the WTO has come to accept that while trade-restricting measures should not constitute an arbitrary or unjustifiable discrimination, they can be justified on the grounds of environmental protection. Underpinning this shift, as discussed in Chapter 21, is the view of the Appellate Body, as expressed in *Shrimp Turtle*, that not balancing any non-trade policies could ultimately lead to the inability of the organization to maintain a degree of legitimacy that would enable it to carry out its broader objectives relating to trade liberalization.

There is a danger that the predominance of the WTO's litigation function will increase the tension between, on the one hand, the claims of authority by individual nation-states and, on the other hand, the assertions of the WTO as an international legitimate authority requiring control of certain issues in order to carry out its responsibilities. The risk of disenchantment with the dispute settlement system is likely to increase if countries feel that the collective legislation of new rules and disciplines is not keeping pace with the legal process. The ruling of the WTO Appellate Body in March 2011 that the United States could not simultaneously impose both countervailing duties and antidumping duties against imports of Chinese steel pipes and off-road tyres stood in sharp contrast to the failure to address rules issues in the Doha Round.

How to Proceed: Some Policy Implications

This final section addresses some of the policy implications arising from the themes and challenges identified in this book, before returning briefly to the conundrums of trade identified in the introduction.

For the foreseeable future, trade policy will be conducted under global conditions particularly challenging to growth and stability, as countries face a complex set of problems: the fiscal consolidation needed in the aftermath of the global financial crisis; the adjustment occasioned by policies to counter climate warming; the budgetary burden imposed by ageing populations; and the uncertainties inherent in persisting global imbalances. The last problem is especially challenging. It should not be forgotten that current account imbalances that had built up during the preceding decade were a key factor in the global financial crisis of 2008–9 as major outflows from surplus countries helped fuel the rapid credit expansion in deficit countries, allowing them to postpone hard policy choices (Obstfeld and Rogoff 2009). Looking ahead, as the chapter on US trade policy has put it, feeding the appetite of countries such as China and India for US, EU and Japanese financial assets through large export surpluses seems sure to provoke protective responses in deficit countries. Trade liberalization cannot move forward when current account imbalances are large and growing.

Opening Markets in Support of Innovation and Growth

In coming years there will thus remain a compelling case for open markets as a stimulus to the innovation and growth that will be needed to cope with fiscal consolidation, demographic change and the challenge arising from policies to address climate warming. Given the scale of potential gains on offer, the liberalization of trade in services deserves particular attention.

Care will be needed to ensure that market opening in pursuit of innovation and productivity growth is not frustrated by unnecessary restrictions in areas of trade that directly embody innovation and technological improvement. A case in point here, discussed in Chapter 14, is that of SPS measures taken to restrict trade in genetically modified seeds and crops, notwithstanding the need for technology that can increase crop yields and food production. At the same time democratic states must respond to consumer demands. With new techniques such as nanotechnology coming up, how can the benefits of trade be achieved whilst retaining the right to regulate? What are needed are effective multilateral rules defining what is a legitimate or necessary regulation. Another example concerns the risk that the exclusion from liberalization of 'services supplied in the exercise of government authority' will inhibit skills transfer in areas such as health and education.

Trade liberalization will be particularly important in helping to counter the constraints facing global supply chains. It can do so by: promoting harmonization around international technical standards to which firms in fragmented markets can conform; addressing the danger that restrictive rules of origin will disadvantage low-cost suppliers; encouraging trade facilitation, enabling suppliers to respond quickly to developments further down the chain; and by fostering the liberalization of environmental goods and services and so, perhaps, helping to allay environmental concerns linked to trade.

Demonstrating Gains and Dealing with Losses

Actually opening markets may not be sufficient in winning public support without complementary efforts to better evaluate and demonstrate the gains from trade and to support those who lose from market opening.

Four related aspects of demonstrating-the-gains are of particular importance – all associated with common misperceptions. First, where protection is being sought it should be assessed in terms of the overall national interest, as a way of dealing with the political economy issues discussed above. An example is the mandatory public interest clause that some policymakers are seeking in antidumping investigations to prevent regulatory capture, to increase transparency and to demonstrate the costs and benefits of protection. Second, the case for liberalizing one's own barriers needs to be more clearly articulated, recalling that some 80 per cent of the developing country gains from worldwide agricultural liberalization would come from opening up developing countries' own highly protected markets and that gains in manufacturing and services increase with countries' commitment to their own liberalization. Third, it needs to be stressed that infant-industry protection has a questionable track record and that the information demands of government in pursuing such policies are, with the advent of the global supply chain, more complex than ever. And fourth, it needs to be more effectively articulated that it is technological change and not trade that is leading to widening income inequality within countries.

But there will be losers from market opening and they will need help. Where it is considered necessary to target assistance to particular sections of the workforce, support should be forthcoming. Such support should be time-bound, with a clear exit strategy; decoupled from production, with incentives to adjust and innovate; aimed at re-employing displaced workers; compatible with general safety net arrangements; and transparent and accountable.

Fostering International Cooperation through the WTO

The key forum for efforts to foster international cooperation should be the WTO. Several chapters of this book have stressed the importance of realizing the promise of the Doha Development Agenda: to bolster the legitimacy, stability and predictability of the system of pooled sovereignty; to reap the gains of liberalization and the opportunities it brings for growth, development and poverty reduction; and to reduce the risk of backsliding. Attention also needs to be devoted to the post-Doha agenda, including what to do about issues such as investment, competition and government procurement and how to strengthen the multilateral rules in a manner that facilitates and promotes complementarity between PTAs and the multilateral trading system. More progress also needs to be made in services where there are large potential benefits from market opening that far exceed those in agriculture and manufacturing combined.

It has also been recognized (Chapter 21) that while the protracted nature of the DDA shows a dysfunction in the WTO's legislative branch, it is important not to assume that the exclusive legislative output of the WTO is completed trade rounds based on a Single Undertaking. Apart from the crucial role of dispute settlement, other important ongoing activities include accession, the administration of all the existing WTO agreements and the review of national trade policies.

In addition to trade and the environment, which we have already touched on, this volume has covered some of the key trade related issues. Chapter 11 suggests that while there is a compelling case for discussing investment issues in the WTO, the success or failure of any such negotiations depends, *inter alia*, on the tradeoffs and cross-issue linkages between investment and other policy areas. Chapter 12 suggests that the WTO is unlikely ever to be the venue for a multilateral agreement on competition policy given EU unwillingness to see disciplines imposed on the behaviour of its own firms in the rest of the world, US satisfaction with the extraterritorial reach of its own laws and developing country suspicion of a hidden market-access agenda. But the WTO could be the focus for a codification of best practice as it emerges from bilateral accords, which, paradoxically, developing countries seem prepared to sign. Such a codification could bring particular benefits to developing countries, given their relative lack of competition culture and low market contestability, and their exposure to the import of cartelized products.

Another important ongoing dimension of international cooperation involves the links between the WTO and other bodies such as the ILO, with respect to core labour standards that are discussed in Chapter 15. Concerns about protectionist capture and the fact that there is no general economic justification for the sanction-driven promotion of labour standards, suggests that this issue is unlikely to become core business of the WTO.

The links between trade and development are covered in a number of chapters, such as that on special and differential treatment (SDT) for developing countries. As discussed in Chapter 18, the provision of special and differential treatment of developing countries, including the principle of less than fully reciprocal market opening, has been a key element of the GATT/WTO for over 50 years. It is also firmly enshrined in the Doha Development Agenda, driven in part by a widespread view among developing countries that the results of the Uruguay Round were biased against them. Nevertheless, as we have seen, in the evolution of SDT, the Uruguay Round represented a watershed in that, under the Single Undertaking, developing countries became more engaged in multilateral negotiation. They did so in recognition that earlier limited engagement had led to a two-tier trading system (with higher barriers on exports of interest to them) in which developing countries failed to gain the full benefits of their own liberalization.

But many of the underlying concerns of developing countries persist – the fragility of domestic industry, the costs of implementing institutional reform and the reliance on tariffs for revenue. If the increased engagement of developing countries is to be maintained a number of measures will be called for. Continuing aid for trade will be needed to address supply-side deficiencies and to help in reducing the recourse of poor countries to defensive policies. SDT will need to be better targeted to those in genuine need, including through the graduation of the more advanced countries and perhaps by issue-specific approaches that automatically identify the beneficiary. And there may also be scope for some variable geometry whereby plurilateral agreements are negotiated among the more advanced developing countries.

The granting of non-reciprocal preferences to developing countries will continue to be part of the development agenda. As different chapters have shown, however, this is a complex area with mixed blessings. Perhaps most importantly, for the majority of developing countries, MFN liberalization by preference-giving countries, by opening up new opportunities for trade, brings positive welfare gains, notwithstanding the effects of preference erosion. Consistent with this finding is the observation in Chapter 19 that over the past two decades, the EU has managed its market opening in a way that, at least initially, maintains greater restrictions on more competitive countries. Preference schemes also complicate the trading environment and raise transaction costs; collectively, the United States, EU, Japan and Canada have no less than 23 different preference agreements with Africa. And as countries' preference status changes, within schemes, there is a bewildering combination of discriminatory effects on other trading nations.

We have seen that the construction of the international trading system has been an iterative process. The system has progressively adapted to wider membership and to shifts in economic power – it will need to continue doing so in future.

Encouraging Regional and South–South Cooperation

Regional cooperation, particularly between developing countries, can be a useful stepping stone to international cooperation. We have seen that in the context of services development in East Africa in Chapter 20, deeper regional integration through regulatory cooperation with neighbouring partners who have similar regulatory preferences can usefully complement non-preferential liberalization. Regional integration can also enhance competition among service providers, enable those providers to exploit economies of scale and produce a wider variety of services. Regional integration brings further benefits in that a larger market is able to attract greater domestic and foreign investment.

In Latin America, it has been observed in Chapter 25 that agreements within the region and with other developing countries need to enforce stricter compliance with the obligations established, in order to create more legal security and predictability. In particular, the lack of effective regional competition remedies has contributed to the degrading of the free trade schedules of the MERCOSUR agreement.

South–South goods trade, more generally, has been growing strongly in recent years, at an annual rate of some 12 per cent, compared with 7 per cent for North–North trade (OECD 2006). However, trade in manufactures between developing countries still represents only 6 per cent of world trade. While encouragement can be taken from the fact that South–South tariff barriers are now lower than tariffs imposed by developing countries on goods from high income countries, the emergence of trade remedies as an increasingly South–South phenomenon is less encouraging.

Putting Trade Policy in an Economy-wide Setting

While cooperation at the international and regional level is important, the key to successful trade policy is to place it holistically in a framework of sound domestic economic management so that in the course of trade-related structural adjustment labour and capital can move from declining to expanding areas of activity. The Taiwan case study of outward orientation, while stressing the need for tailored, country-by-country policy application, vividly demonstrates the policies that need to accompany trade liberalization: a flexible labour market; a stable macroeconomic environment; expanding infrastructure; vocational education support for an adaptable workforce; and liberal rules governing foreign direct investment. The message is underscored in the study of education services in East Africa, showing that the reduction of trade barriers needs to be accompanied by reforms to the education system and the regulatory framework. In the study of Latin America, it is recognized that participating more fully in global value chains will involve meeting challenges beyond trade policy narrowly defined, requiring changes in a wide range of policies dealing with innovation, science and technology, education and training, environmental management and the attraction of FDI. The discussion of trade and competition policy in Chapter 12 makes clear that trade liberalization is necessary but not sufficient. The reduction of trade barriers needs to be accompanied by a strengthening of competition laws, and competition culture, to help ensure that markets are genuinely contestable and that there are no barriers to the entry of new suppliers when market prices, and therefore profits, rise above normal levels.

Put differently, trade cannot do it all. Arguably the biggest challenge facing the international trading system, the persistence of global macroeconomic imbalances and attendant protectionist threats, can only be met by domestic action quite distinct from trade policy. Global imbalances stem from a discrepancy between domestic savings and investment. Rebalancing will therefore require a closer alignment between savings and investment in the big surplus as well as the big deficit countries. Exchange rate realignment may be part of the adjustment process but exchange rate changes alone would do little to reduce current account surpluses in, for example, China as long as household savings are motivated by weak and shallow financial markets and inadequate social security nets.

Similarly, the risk of green protectionism will be best addressed by tackling environmental problems directly at their source, that is, by dedicated environmental policies not by the threat of trade sanctions that serve only to distort resource allocation and prompt retaliation. This is the same underlying logic that we saw in Chapter 8 in relation to the reform of agriculture in the advanced developed economies. Positive contributions of farmers to improving the environment and biodiversity are better encouraged through specific payments based on the service desired rather than by support of farm output that may or may not provide the required service as a by-product.

In short, we are reminded of the Tinbergen (1956) principle that in order for a policy regime to be effective there must be as many independent policy instruments as there are targets to be pursued.

A number of chapters have referred to the global financial and economic crisis of 2008–2009. While care has been taken throughout the book not to dwell on transient issues, whether phases of the negotiation cycle or shifts in the economic cycle, the global financial crisis of 2008–2009, and its aftermath, serve as a stark illustration of the importance of seeing trade policy in its wider setting. The linkage works in both directions: external shocks impact on the domestic economy but domestic imbalances, and domestic political imperatives, permeate the international economy. The crisis also serves to highlight the critical importance of the service economy, as being less cyclically vulnerable than manufacturing but acutely sensitive to the regulatory environment – domestic and international. Finally, the crisis has illustrated the complex link between trade reform and international economic conditions. Slower growth increases the need for the competitive boost of open markets, but also makes the trade-related adjustment process more difficult. In the words of a former WTO Director-General, Mike Moore, the roof is more likely to get fixed when it is raining, but it is easier to do when the sun is shining.

Coming back to the conundrums outlined in the introduction to this book, we find that all of them are better understood, if not totally resolved, when trade liberalization is viewed as an exercise in enlightened self-interest – liberalization from below – within the framework of multiple, mutually supportive domestic economic policies. A holistic approach to trade policy will thus help in a number of ways:

- promoting both *accountability* and *efficiency* in trade policy by addressing directly the social, public health and environmental concerns of non-governmental organizations, in a way that is distinct from but complementary to trade liberalization, so that the pursuit of increased efficiency in the WTO is not compromised by giving non-state actors a role in the WTO that would be inconsistent with the organization's responsibilities as an inter-governmental body;
- facilitating both the *entry* and *exit* of firms and workers as part of trade-related structural adjustment through complementary policies that facilitate the movement of factors of production from declining to expanding areas of activity;

- matching *ends* and *means* such as when tariff reductions bring budgetary strains so that rather than forgo the benefits of liberalization action is taken to tackle the budget problem directly through reform of the tax system;
- resolving tensions between *present* and *future* benefits. For example, the paradox of patents – restricting access to knowledge now in order to have more in the future – may never be totally resolved, but it becomes less of a puzzle, or less of a constraint, in a broad policy environment, including open markets, that is conducive to innovation;
- promoting *complementarities* such as by liberalizing both trade and investment in a mutually reinforcing way, by bringing some of the spirit of unilateral liberalization, as an element of sound domestic management, to multilateral market opening, or by multilateralizing certain elements of preferential trade agreements;
- fostering both *cooperation* and national *sovereignty* by recognizing that international cooperation in the pursuit of trade liberalization does not mean abandoning the sovereign right to regulate. Indeed as the global financial crisis has shown, the liberalization of trade in financial services may call for more – or certainly better – rather than less domestic regulation; and
- tackling *market failures* such as environmental externalities directly at source – via environment policies – in a way that complements the pursuit of market opening and reduces the risk of protectionist capture inherent in sanctions-driven promotion of non-trade goals.

References

Heydon, K. and Woolcock, S. 2009. *The Rise of Bilateralism: Comparing American, European and Asian Approaches to Preferential Trade Agreements*. Tokyo: United Nations University Press.

Obstfeld, M. and Rogoff, K. 2009. *Global Imbalances and the Financial Crisis: Products of Common Causes*. Paper presented at the Federal Reserve Bank of San Francisco Asia Economic Policy Conference, Santa Barbara, 18–20 October.

OECD. 2006. *Trading Up: Economic Perspectives on Development Issues in the Multilateral Trading System*. Paris: OECD.

Tinbergen, J. 1956. *Economic Policy: Principles and Design*. Amsterdam: North Holland.

Index